Quick Guide

SO-BXY-213

Written and Compiled by

**Dave Kemper, Patrick Sebranek,
and Verne Meyer**

Illustrated by

Chris Krenzke

WRITE SOURCE®

GREAT SOURCE EDUCATION GROUP

a division of Houghton Mifflin Company
Wilmington, Massachusetts

Reviewers

Randolph C. Bernard
Lafayette Parish School System
Lafayette, LA

Susan Dinges
Mt. Olive Public School District
Budd Lake, NJ

Shara W. Holt
St. Johns County School District
St. Augustine, FL

Guy M. Kinney
Orange County Public Schools
Orlando, FL

Raymond Klejmont
Desoto County
Arcadia, FL

Connie McGee
Miami-Dade County Public
Schools
Miami, FL

Harriet Maher
Lafayette Parish School System
Lafayette, LA

Jenny R. May
Mason City Schools
Mason, OH

Pamela Miltenberger
J. C. Harmon High School
Kansas City, KS

Christine Neuner
Iberia Parish School System
New Iberia, LA

Marie T. Raduazzo
Arlington High School
Arlington, MA

Marianne Raver
William R. Boone High School
Orlando, FL

Elizabeth Rehberger
Huntington Beach High School
Huntington Beach, CA

Stephanie Sahikov-Izabal
Huntington Beach Union High
School District
Huntington Beach, CA

Ann Marie Seely
Henrico County Public Schools
Richmond, VA

Technology Connections for *Write Source*

This series is supported by two Web sites:

The **Great Source iwrite** site is a writing resource that supports students, teachers, and parents. You'll find tutorials about the forms and traits of writing, as well as the latest articles, features, tips, and contests. Go to **www.greatsource.com/iwrite**.

The **Write Source** site features all the materials available from Write Source, as well as handy writing topics, student models, and help with research. You can even read about the history of Write Source. Go to **www.thewritesource.com**.

Trademarks and trade names are shown in this book strictly for illustrative purposes and are the property of their respective owners. The authors' references herein should not be regarded as affecting their validity.

Copyright © 2009 by Great Source Education Group, a division of Houghton Mifflin Company. All rights reserved.

No part of this work may be reproduced or transmitted in any form or by any means, electronic or mechanical, including photocopying and recording, or by any information storage or retrieval system without the prior written permission of Great Source Education Group unless such copying is expressly permitted by federal copyright law. Address inquiries to Permissions, Great Source Education Group, 181 Ballardvale Street, Wilmington, MA 01887.

Great Source and **Write Source** are registered trademarks of Houghton Mifflin Company.

Printed in the United States of America

International Standard Book Number: 978-0-669-00648-3 (hardcover)

2 3 4 5 6 7 8 9 10 -DOC- 15 14 13 12 11 10 09

International Standard Book Number: 978-0-669-00908-8 (softcover)

2 3 4 5 6 7 8 9 10 -DOC- 15 14 13 12 11 10 09

Using *Write Source*

Your **Write Source** book is loaded with information to help you learn about writing. One section that will be especially helpful is the "Proofreader's Guide" at the back of the book. This section covers the rules for language and grammar.

The book also includes four main units covering the types of writing that you may have to complete on district or state writing tests. In addition, a special section provides samples and tips for writing in science, social studies, math, the applied sciences, and the arts.

Write Source will help you with other learning skills, too—test taking, note taking, and making oral presentations. This makes *Write Source* a valuable writing and learning guide in all of your classes. (The **Quick Tour** on the next two pages highlights many of the key features in the book.)

Your *Write Source* guide . . .

With practice, you will be able to find information in this book quickly using the guides explained below.

- The **Table of Contents** (starting on page **vi**) lists the five major sections in the book and the chapters found in each section.
- The **Index** (starting on page **765**) lists the topics covered in the book in alphabetical order. Use the index when you are interested in a specific topic.
- The **Color Coding** used for the "Proofreader's Guide" (yellow) makes this important section easy to find. Colorful side tabs also provide a handy reference.
- **Page References** in the book tell you where to turn for additional information about a specific topic. *Example:* (See page **26**.)

> If, at first, you're not sure how to find something in *Write Source,* ask your teacher for help. With a little practice, you will find everything quickly and easily.

A Quick Tour of *Write Source*

Write Source contains many key features that will help you improve your writing and language skills. Once you become familiar with this book, you will begin to understand how helpful these features can be.

Writing guidelines help you, step-by-step, to complete different forms of writing.

Checklists serve as effective revising and editing guides within the writing units.

Rubrics help you evaluate your finished pieces of writing. They also help to keep you on track during your writing.

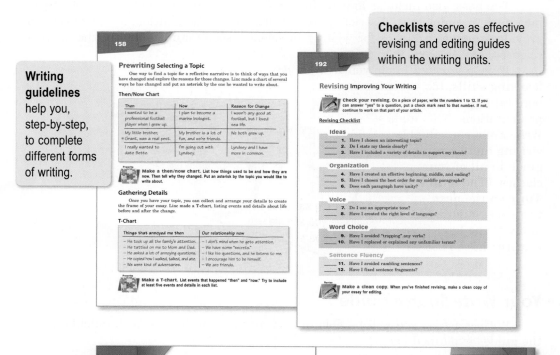

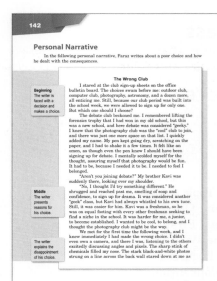

The **writing samples** will stimulate you to write your own effective essays.

Graphic organizers show you how to organize your ideas for writing.

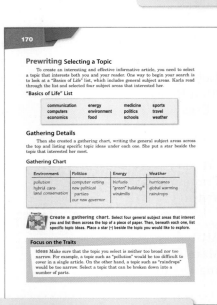

Links to the traits help you appreciate the importance of different traits at different points in the writing process.

The Writing Process

contents

The Forms of Writing

NARRATIVE WRITING

EXPOSITORY WRITING

contents

PERSUASIVE WRITING

RESPONSE TO LITERATURE

RESEARCH WRITING

contents

WRITING ACROSS THE CURRICULUM

The Tools of Learning

Basic Elements of Writing

Proofreader's Guide

Test Prep!

A review test in standardized-test format follows each of the six sections in the Proofreader's Guide.

Why Write?

The very best answer to that question is this: Write to know yourself. Aside, perhaps, from professional analysis, no other activity allows you to explore your thoughts and feelings and then express them as a unique part of you. This personal exploration occurs every time you write something, whether it's a journal entry, a poem, or a personal essay.

Write every day, preferably at a set time. Some writers do their personal writing early in the morning when they are fresh and alert. Others record their thoughts at the end of the day. Write when and where it feels comfortable for you—during your study hall, on the bus, at a coffee shop, while taking a bath.

Meaning will come if you make the effort and stick to it. You'll enter the world of your inner thoughts and soon feel a little sharper, as if your senses had been fine-tuned. Your writing will give you the special opportunity to "taste life twice," as writer Anaïs Nin has so aptly stated.

- **Using a Writer's Notebook**
- **Sample Notebook Entries**

"We are cups, constantly and quietly being filled. The trick is knowing how to tip ourselves over and let the beautiful stuff out."

—Ray Bradbury

Using a Writer's Notebook

Your most powerful writing tool can be a notebook reserved exclusively for daily writing. A writer's notebook (also called a journal) is a place to record your thoughts on any topic. As you do so, you will make countless discoveries about your world. You may also find yourself inspired to create more polished forms of writing—poems, stories, and narratives.

In her book of autobiographical essays, *Something to Declare,* Julia Alvarez writes: "The writing life is a life with all the windows and doors opened." That's exactly what a writer's notebook does! It opens all the windows and doors to your world.

Ensuring Success

To make sure that your writer's notebook is a success, consider the quantity, quality, and variety of your entries.

- **Quantity:** Approach each entry with a high level of enthusiasm. Write about things that matter to you, and develop your ideas fully.
- **Quality:** Focus on exploring and developing your ideas, not on producing perfect copy. Some of your entries are bound to be messy. Your notebook is your place to experiment, take risks, and make mistakes.
- **Variety:** Write some of your entries from different points of view. For example, after a disagreement with a family member, write about the experience from the other person's point of view, or from the perspective of someone who overheard the discussion.

Suggestions for Notebook Writing

1. Date each entry. The date on an entry helps you find it later and places it in a context with other entries and experiences.

2. Write freely. Push to keep your pen moving or your fingers keyboarding. Continuous writing helps you make new discoveries.

3. Write regularly. Develop the habit of writing daily. Then reread your entries to consider what you've discovered. Those ideas may prompt additional writing.

"You write down a few sentences in your journal and sigh. This exhalation is not exhaustion but anticipation at the prospect of a wonderful tale exposing a notion that you still only partly understand."

—Walter Mosley

Writing About Anything—and Everything

There are no limits to what you can write about—just as long as each of your entries connects with you personally. Write about people, places, and things; delve into your hopes, dreams, and memories; explore snippets of conversations that you overhear. Your notebook is the perfect place to explore these topics and form new understandings in the process.

When you can't think of something to write about, refer to the following questions for ideas.

- **Observations:** What is happening around you right now? What are your thoughts about what's happening?

- **Memories:** What was the best moment of your day? The week? The year? What was the worst moment?

- **Hopes and dreams:** What do you want in life? What do you hope for in the future?

- **People:** What person means the most to you? What person do you most admire? What sort of person do you think you are or wish you were?

- **Places:** Where are you right now? Where do you wish you were? Where do you never want to be again?

- **Things:** What is your favorite possession? Your least favorite? What one thing most closely links you to your past?

- **Thoughts:** What is the most peculiar thing you've learned recently? What is the best piece of advice you've given or received?

Find inspiration. Write freely for 8 to 10 minutes. The topic is *you.* Begin with *I am . . .* and see where your writing takes you. Afterward, underline at least two discoveries that you made in this writing.

Taking It Personally

Here is a page from a student writer's notebook. This entry focuses on an old photo album and does several important things. It . . .

- captures a time in the writer's life,
- describes something that is important to the writer,
- starts with a "seed idea" (an old photo album), and
- reflects on the writer's insight, thoughts, and feelings.

Sample Notebook Entry

February 28, 2009

Last Saturday, I found a treasure. It wasn't gold or precious stones, nor was it a bundle of bills or a sack of coins. The treasure was an old photo album. Glued to the yellowing pages were pictures of my ancestors: grandparents, great–aunts and –uncles, and distant cousins. I found the album as I helped my mom clean out Abuelita's attic. I knew that in my hands I held branches from our family tree.

I sat on a rickety chair and opened the dusty, brittle cover. The face of a stranger stared back at me. She looked somewhat familiar. As I gazed into her eyes, I saw my mother's eyes, and then my eyes. The words under the photo read, "Gloriosa Rey Acevedo." She was my great-great-grandmother.

Slowly, I turned the pages, looking carefully at every photograph. In each of my ancestors, I saw a part of myself. There was my smile, my naturally curly hair, my short (and, in my opinion, too round) body. I caught glimpses of my personality in the faces of the people—a pout, a mischievous twinkle in the eyes, a look of loneliness (perhaps a need to feel wanted and loved).

After closing the album's cover, I felt different. The loneliness that has been with me for a while now is gone. I know that I belong, not only to my immediate family, but also to all the generations that came before me.

Note: Keeping a writer's notebook lets you look at ordinary things in a new way, talk about your feelings, use descriptive language, and simply practice writing until you feel confident.

Try It!

Write a quick reflection. Write freely for 8 to 10 minutes about some aspect of your immediate or extended family. What did you learn?

Sample Notebook Entries

A journal can be a useful tool for sorting out your thoughts. Below are samples that show how three different students use their journals.

Working Out a Problem

This student uses her journal to explore and sort out her feelings.

I just don't know if I should keep seeing Michael. I mean, I really like having someone who's always there. But that's just it. He's always there. Like today, I really wanted to get to know the new exchange student. So we were talking, and I guess I was flirting. Anyway, Michael came right up and totally wrecked the moment. I just wanted to get to know Georg, without Michael hanging around. I like Ben in my physics class, too. Maybe I do want to go out with other people. . . .

Reliving an Experience

Here the student shows how an informal style is appropriate in a journal.

Awesome concert! Music pulsing, crowd cheering. Man, the band was flying! Light sticks, stripes of green and purple neon, streaks against the night. There were strangers around me, but we felt like one. We linked elbows and swayed together. We all sang. The lights, the sound! I could feel the music like it went through me. It filled me and I thought I would burst. I was connected with everyone there. We were like one giant family. I just want to remember that feeling forever.

Questioning/Solidifying a Belief

This student explores her disappointment in an effort to understand herself better.

I saw Ms. Harris outside the school building smoking! I mean, I thought she was the smartest teacher ever, and there she was, doing something so stupid. Why should I feel so betrayed? I mean, it's not like she's an ax murderer or something. I guess I idealize people, and then I feel disappointed when they turn out to be human. Why can't I just accept people for who they are? Why do I always put them on a pedestal? I have to stop trying to make everyone perfect. . . .

Using the Writing Process

Understanding Writing

A process is a series of actions resulting in a desired end product. Think of the process of baking bread, changing a tire, or painting a model aircraft. One action or step follows another until the bread is cooling, the tire is replaced, or the model is drying. To write an essay, however, you may not always move in such a linear fashion. As you reach one step in the process *(writing the first draft),* you may see the need to return to the previous step *(prewriting)*. This interplay between the steps often continues until the essay is complete.

There is nothing "instant" about effective writing. Working with a computer does, of course, speed up the process; but when it comes to writing, speed doesn't count for much. What really counts is your ability to stay with a piece of writing until it says exactly what you want it to say. Each time you start a new writing project, keep this thought by Dr. Samuel Johnson in mind: "What is written without effort is in general read without pleasure."

- ■ **Writing Is Discovering**
- ■ **Understanding the Writing Process**
- ■ **The Process in Action**
- ■ **A Closer Look at the Process**

"My method is one of continuous revision. While writing a long novel, every day I loop back to earlier sections to rewrite, in order to maintain a consistent, fluid voice."

—Joyce Carol Oates

Writing Is Discovering

Writing is not trying to figure out everything you want to say *before* you put pen to paper or fingers to the keyboard. Overplanning in this way will almost certainly result in writer's block. (Ever heard of it?) Writing will spring from the discoveries you make *during* the writing process.

Setting the Stage

Before you use the writing process, it's important that you understand these points about writing:

- **Experience shapes writing.** Each of your experiences becomes part of what you know, what you think, and what you have to say. Writing is the process of capturing the essence of your experience in words.
- **Writing seldom follows a straight path.** Writing is a backward as well as a forward activity, so don't expect to move neatly through the steps in the process. By its very nature, writing includes detours, wrong turns, and repeat visits.
- **Each assignment presents special challenges.** For one assignment, you may search high and low for a topic. For another, you may do a lot of prewriting and planning. For still another, you might be ready to write your first draft almost immediately.
- **Each writer works differently.** Some writers work more in their heads, while others work more on paper. Some writers need to talk about their writing early on, while others would rather keep their ideas to themselves. As you continue to use the writing process, your unique writing personality will develop.

Tip

You are sure to improve your writing ability if you (1) become a regular reader, (2) write every day, (3) write about topics that truly interest you, and (4) experiment with different forms of writing. Remember: Writing is like any other skill. It takes a lot of practice and patience to become good at it.

Try It!

Write a brief paragraph, answering the following questions about a recent writing assignment that challenged you: *Why was it so challenging? What did you do to complete the assignment? Were you satisfied with the finished product? Why or why not?*

Understanding the Writing Process

Before you share a piece of writing, you should take it through a series of steps called the *writing process.* This page briefly describes these steps.

The Steps in the Writing Process

Prewriting

The first step in the writing process involves selecting a specific topic, gathering details about it, and organizing those details into a writing plan.

Writing

During this step, the writer completes the first draft, using the prewriting plan as a guide. This draft is a writer's *first* chance to get everything on paper.

Revising

During revising, the writer reviews the draft for five key traits: **ideas, organization, voice, word choice,** and **sentence fluency.** After deciding what changes to make, the writer deletes, moves, adds to, and rewrites parts of the text.

Editing

Then the writer edits the revised draft for the **conventions** of punctuation, capitalization, spelling, and grammar and proofreads the final copy before sharing it.

Publishing

Finally, the writer publishes the work by preparing a final copy and sharing it with others.

Analyze your own process. Which steps in the process explained above do you use regularly? Which ones should you use more often?

The Process in Action

The next two pages give a detailed description of each step in the writing process. The graphic below reminds you that, at any time, you can move back and forth between the steps in the process. Also remember that carefully attending to the first steps in the writing process will make the final steps much easier.

Prewriting Selecting a Topic

- Search for topics that meet the requirements of the assignment.
- Select a specific topic that appeals to you.

Gathering and Organizing Details

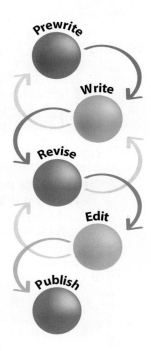

- Gather as many ideas and details as you can about the topic.
- With the purpose of the assignment in mind, find one point to emphasize about the topic—either an interesting part or your personal feeling about it. This will be the focus, or thesis, of your writing.
- Decide which details to include.
- Organize your details into a writing plan, using an outline, a chart, or some other method.

Writing Developing the First Draft

- When writing the first draft, concentrate on getting your ideas on paper. Don't try to produce a perfect piece of writing.
- Use your prewriting plan as a guide and include the details you collected, but feel free to add new ideas that occur to you as you go along.
- Be sure your writing has a beginning, a middle, and an ending.

Tip

Write on every other line and on only one side of the paper when using pen or pencil and paper. Double-space on a computer. This will give you room for revising, the next step in the process.

Revising **Improving Your Writing**

- Set aside your first draft for a while so you can return to it with a fresh perspective.
- Read your first draft slowly and critically.
- Use these questions as a revising guide:
  - Is my topic interesting for the reader?
  - Does the beginning catch the reader's attention?
  - Are the ideas in order and easy to understand?
  - Have I included enough details to support my central idea?
  - Does the ending leave the reader with something to think about?
  - Do I sound interested in and knowledgeable about the topic?
  - Are the nouns specific and the verbs active?
  - Are the modifiers (adjectives and adverbs) clear and descriptive?
  - Does the whole piece read smoothly?

- Ask at least one person to review your writing and offer suggestions.
- Make as many changes as necessary to improve your writing.

Editing **Checking for Conventions**

- Check for errors in punctuation, capitalization, spelling, and grammar.
- Have another person check your writing for errors.
- Prepare a neat final copy.
- Proofread the final copy before publishing it.

Publishing **Sharing Your Writing**

- Share your writing with friends, classmates, and family.
- Consider submitting your writing to a newspaper or other publication.
- Include the writing in your portfolio.

Tip

For assignments, save all your work. Refer to the earlier drafts and to the teacher's comments on each graded piece for ideas and inspiration for future writing projects.

Consider the process. Study the graphic on page 10. Then, in a brief paragraph, explain what it says about the writing process. Include at least five or six sentences in your explanation.

A Closer Look at the Process

Although writing is a complex process, there are ways to have a meaningful experience whenever you write.

Keep time on your side. Effective writing requires a lot of searching, planning, reflecting, and revising, so give yourself plenty of time. Follow the timetable your teacher provides, or create your own. And always reserve enough time for revising. As you probably know, waiting until the last minute takes all the fun out of writing.

Remember: **Good writing takes time.**

Limit your topic. It would be almost impossible to write an effective essay or report about a general subject like photography. You wouldn't know where to begin . . . or end. But if you narrowed this subject to the use of photography by investigative reporters, for instance, you would find it much easier to manage your writing.

Remember: **Good writing has a focus.**

Work from a position of authority. The more you know about your topic, the easier it is to write about it. So collect plenty of information by tapping into your own knowledge and thoughts, asking others about the topic, consulting print material, surfing the Net, and so on.

Remember: **Good writing requires good information.**

Pace yourself when you revise. Many professional writers believe that the real writing happens when they add, cut, rearrange, and rewrite different parts of their first drafts. They do not rush these changes or make them all at once. Instead, they pace themselves, patiently and methodically revising until the entire piece is clear and complete.

Remember: **Good writing usually requires numerous changes.**

Take some risks. Don't be afraid to experiment. Share a personal anecdote in an essay or develop an interview report in a question-and-answer format, much as you would find in many magazine articles. Rearrange the events of a narrative to add suspense. If one experiment doesn't work out, try another.

Remember: **Good writing is a process of discovery.**

 ## Try It!

Find an article in a magazine or newspaper that seems out of the ordinary. Discuss the article with your class, pointing out features that demonstrate what makes it outstanding.

One Writer's Process

As you know, computer applications for writing are called word-processing programs. These programs make the whole process of writing easier and more enjoyable. More importantly, they allow you to stay with a piece of writing longer until it says exactly what you want it to say.

This chapter shows how one student, Lakendra Harris, used the writing process to develop an expository essay in her history class. She first previewed the goals for the assignment. Then she selected an appropriate topic—the Cuban Missile Crisis—to write about. After gathering information about her topic, Lakendra wrote her first draft. She then made a series of changes in her writing until she felt it was ready to share.

- **Previewing the Goals**
- **Prewriting**
- **Writing**
- **Revising**
- **Editing**
- **Publishing**
- **Assessing the Final Copy**
- **Reflecting on Your Writing**

"Writing is an exploration. You start from nothing and learn as you go."

—E. L. Doctorow

Previewing the Goals

Before Lakendra began writing her essay, she previewed the goals for expository writing, which are shown below. She also looked over the expository rubric on pages **198–199**. Both of these activities helped her get started.

Traits of Expository Writing

- **Ideas**

  Select a specific topic that captures your interest. Create and support a thesis statement that explores an important part of the topic.

- **Organization**

  Organize your essay's ideas into three main parts—beginning, middle, and ending—and connect them smoothly.

- **Voice**

  Use a level of language that fits the audience and the purpose of your writing. Also sound knowledgeable about the topic.

- **Word Choice**

  Choose precise words that clearly explain your topic. Explain any specialized or unfamiliar terms.

- **Sentence Fluency**

  Use a variety of sentences that connect your ideas smoothly.

- **Conventions**

  Use correct punctuation, capitalization, spelling, and grammar.

Review the traits. What kind of voice would you use in an essay for a U.S. history class? What type of organization would best suit such an essay?

Prewriting Selecting a Topic

Lakendra's history teacher asked the students to write an essay explaining a major event in twentieth-century United States history. Lakendra listed several possible topics. Then she underlined the idea that she was most interested in.

Topics List

the use of the atom bomb	Prohibition
Cuban Missile Crisis	Watergate

Gathering Your Thoughts

Lakendra knew that listing the 5 W's and H—*who? what? where? when? why?* and *how?*—about her topic would help her gather her initial thoughts.

5 W's and H Chart

Who?   John F. Kennedy and Nikita Khrushchev

What?   a nuclear missile confrontation

Where?   in Cuba

When?   October 1962

Why?   the two countries were involved in an arms race

How?   Soviets built a nuclear missile base near the U.S.

Lakendra then did some freewriting about the event to gather more of her initial thoughts. Here is a part of her freewriting.

Freewriting

I know about the Soviet base in Cuba. Did the U.S. have any bases close to the Soviet Union? It's hard to believe that almost half a century ago, countries were involved in an arms race. I think it even continues today, unfortunately. Even though the Cuban Missile Crisis ended peacefully, it resulted only in an agreement to ban nuclear testing—not on the nukes . . .

Prewriting Gathering Details

Lakendra next went to the library to find resources about the Cuban Missile Crisis; she also looked on the Internet for reliable Web sites.

Sources of Information

She recorded her source information on note cards.

Stern, Sheldon M. *The Week the World Stood Still: Inside the Secret Cuban Missile Crisis.* Stanford University Press: Palo Alto, 2005.

Kennedy, Bruce. "The Birth of the Hotline." *CNN.* April 6, 2006. <http://www.cnn.com/SPECIALS/cold.war/episodes/10/spotlight/>.

Quotations and Paraphrases

Lakendra also used note cards to record quotations and paraphrases. The source of the information is listed at the bottom of each card.

Quotation

"Sensing an opportunity to gain a strategic foothold in America's backyard, Khrushchev eagerly extended an offer of assistance to the desperate Cuban general."

Source: Goldman and Stein

Paraphrase

Today electronic transmissions are achieved via two satellite systems, but they are still written rather than verbal to reduce the chance of an incorrect translation.

Source: Kennedy

Try It!

Find at least one book or magazine and one Web site containing information about the Cuban Missile Crisis. Write down one quotation and one paraphrase from either source of information.

Forming a Thesis Statement

Once Lakendra had enough information, she was ready to write a *thesis statement* for her essay. (A thesis statement identifies the focus of the writing.) An effective thesis statement consists of two parts: a specific topic plus a particular feeling or opinion about it. Lakendra wrote this thesis statement:

Lakendra's Thesis Statement

The Cuban Missile Crisis of October, 1962 (specific topic), **was the closest the United States and the Soviet Union ever came to a nuclear war** (particular feeling).

Organizing the Essay

Next, Lakendra created an organized list, arranging the main points and details that support her thesis statement. (An organized list is a modified form of outlining.)

Lakendra's Organized List

Thesis statement: The Cuban Missile Crisis of October, 1962, was the closest the United States and the Soviet Union ever came to a nuclear war.

+ Background
 – The Soviets were losing the arms race.
 – The Cubans were fearful of a U.S. invasion.
 – The Soviets constructed a missile base in Cuba.

+ The Impending Crisis
 – Kennedy discovered the secret base.
 – He ordered a blockade and a dismantling of the base.
 – Khrushchev authorized use of force.

+ Crisis Averted
 – Khrushchev proposed an exchange.
 – Kennedy agreed to the first part of the proposal.
 – Khrushchev announced plans to dismantle the base.

+ Outcomes
 – Reliable communication was established.
 – Both sides signed a nuclear test ban agreement.

Writing Developing Your First Draft

Lakendra referred to her organized list as she wrote her first draft. At this point, she just needed to get all her ideas on paper. She also rephrased her thesis statement to fit the flow of her ideas.

Lakendra's First Draft

Beginning
The first paragraph ends with the thesis statement.

Middle
The middle paragraphs describe the crisis.

The Cuban Missile Crisis

Both the United States and the Soviet Union have had nuclear capability since the early 1940s. The closest the cold war ever came to a nuclear war was the Cuban Missile Crisis of October, 1962.

The Soviet Union was losing the arms race big-time. They knew that the U.S. had more missiles than they did. And they knew that some of these missiles were based in Turkey, only 150 mi. from the Soviet border.

In an effort to even things out, the Soviets wanted to be friends with Cuba in order to "gain a strategic foothold in America's backyard" (Goldman and Stein). Cubas leader, Fidel Castro, believed Cuba would be attacked again by the U.S. He jumped on an offer from Nikita Khrushchev, leader of the Soviet Union, to protect Cuba from the U.S.

By October of 1962, the construction of a missile base was well under way. The U.S., which was under the leadership of John F. Kennedy at the time, discovered the secret while checking out some reconaissance photos. Kennedy demanded that the Soviets dismantle the base and ordered a navel blockade of Cuba. Khrushchev, in turn, authorized payback if U.S. forces invaded.

For 5 days, neither side backed down. Then Khrushchev made a written proposal. Soviet missiles would be removed from Cuba in exchange for a guarantee that the U.S. would not invade Cuba. A day later, he put his foot down and demanded removal of U.S. missiles from Turkey. Kennedy ignored this second proposal but agreed to the first, Khrushchev backed down and announced plans to dismantle the base.

The crisis had another result, too. The lack of a reliable form of communication meant a delay of several hours between the two world powers when sending messages. So a set of teletype machines linked the Kremlin and the White House, allowing the leaders to communicate directly. Today the electronic transmissions are achieved via two satellite systems, but they are still written rather than verbal to reduce the chance of an incorrect translation (Kennedy).

A paraphrase explains an important concept.

Nine months later, Kennedy and Khrushchev signed an agreement to ban nuclear testing in the atmosphere. The world's relief was clear at having avoided this war. Many praised Kennedy's calm in the matter, for if he had authorized an invasion, the Soviets may well have evened the score with their nuclear weapons. And the U.S., of course, would follow with their own ("Cuban"). The willingness of the two world leaders to compromise, avoiding such a boondoggle, was a welcome sign. That they knew the prevention of nuclear war was not only possible but necessary. Kennedy and Khrushchev agreed on that—and their pact was the most obvious outcome of the crisis.

Sources of information are given in parentheses.

Ending
The ending paragraph sums up the topic and provides a final thought.

Tensions between world leaders will probably always prevent world peace. However, the actions of two opposing forces in October 1962 showed the world that cool heads beat hot heads. They gave the world hope.

Try It!

Look through Lakendra's planning list and first draft. Does her first draft contain all the details from her organized list (page **17**)? Does she add any new details? If so, what are they?

Revising Improving the Writing

Lakendra set her first draft aside for a day. Then she rechecked the goals on page 14 before reviewing her first draft. Lakendra's thoughts below reveal the changes she planned to make.

Ideas

"I need to add more background details to lead up to my thesis statement. I could also explain some parts better."

Organization

"I should change the order of the fifth and sixth middle paragraphs for smoother organization."

Voice

"I need a more formal voice."

Lakendra's First Revision

Here are the revisions that Lakendra made in the first part of her essay.

More background information is added in the first paragraph.

> The U.S. was a pal of the Soviet Union during World War II, but tensions between the two countries began to mount following the war. These tensions led to a period of time known as the cold war.
>
> ∧ ~~Both the United States and the Soviet Union have~~
>
> ~~had nuclear capability since the early 1940s.~~ The closest
>
> conflict
> the ∧ ~~cold war~~ ever came to a nuclear war was the Cuban
>
> Missile Crisis of October, 1962.

Organization is improved by combining two paragraphs.

>   at the time
> The Soviet Union ∧ was losing the arms race ~~big-time~~.
>
> They knew that the U.S. had more missiles than they did.
>
> And they knew that some of these missiles were based in
>
> Turkey, only 150 mi. from the Soviet border.
>
>   In an effort to even things out, the Soviets wanted
>
> to be friends with Cuba in order to "gain a strategic

foothold in America's backyard" (Goldman and Stein).

Cubas leader, Fidel Castro, believed Cuba would be attacked

again by the U.S. He ~~jumped on~~ *eagerly accepted* an offer from Nikita

Khrushchev, leader of the Soviet Union, to protect Cuba

from the U.S.

By October of 1962, the construction of a missile base

was well under way. The U.S., which was under the leadership

of John F. Kennedy at the time, discovered the secret *through careful analysis of*

~~while checking out some~~ reconaissance photos. Kennedy

demanded that the Soviets dismantle the base and ordered

a navel blockade of Cuba. Khrushchev, in turn, authorized

retaliation in the event that ~~payback if~~ U.S. forces invaded.

For 5 days, neither side backed down. Then

Khrushchev made a written proposal. Soviet missiles would

be removed from Cuba in exchange for a guarantee that the

U.S. would not invade Cuba. A day later, he *also* ~~put his foot~~

~~down and~~ demanded removal of U.S. missiles from Turkey.

Kennedy ignored this second proposal but agreed to the

first, Khrushchev backed down and announced plans to

dismantle the base.

The crisis had another result, too. The lack of a

reliable form of communication meant a delay of several

hours between the two world powers when sending

messages. *To improve the situation* ~~So~~ a set of teletype machines linked the

Kremlin and the White House, allowing the leaders . . .

The voice is made more formal throughout.

Details that provide a better explanation are added.

Unnecessary details are deleted.

The order of the paragraphs is revised.

Revising Using a Peer Response Sheet

Ashley evaluated Lakendra's essay using a rubric like the one on pages **198–199**. Her suggestions on the response sheet below showed Lakendra where she could make additional improvements.

Peer Response Sheet

Writer: <u>Lakendra Harris</u>   Responder: <u>Ashley Wright</u>

Title: <u>The Cuban Missile Crisis</u>

What I liked about your writing:

> You chose an interesting topic, and you cover it well—from
>
> background info to the outcome of the crisis.

Changes I would suggest:

> Could you add more details about the following?
>
> • the cold war
>
> • why Cuba needed protection
>
> • the purpose for the blockade
>
> Also, could you check the ending? It seems to end too suddenly.

Try It!

Review Ashley's suggestions for improvements above. Which suggestion seems to be the most important? Explain why. Add at least one new suggestion to improve Lakendra's writing. Look at the explanations of ideas, organization, and voice on page **14** to help you make your suggestions.

Lakendra's Revision Using a Peer Response

Using Ashley's comments, Lakendra revised her essay again. Some of the changes that she made are shown here.

> **More details about the cold war are added.**

The U.S. was a pal of the Soviet Union during World War II, but tensions between the two countries began to mount following the war. These tensions led to a period of time beginning in the late 1940s ∧ known as the cold war. Each country perceived the other as hostile. ∧ The closest the conflict ever came to a nuclear war was the Cuban Missile Crisis of October, 1962.

> **New details explain why Cuba needed protection.**

The Soviet Union at the time was losing the arms race. They knew that the U.S. had more missiles than they did. And they knew that some of these missiles were based in Turkey, only 150 mi. from the Soviet border. In an effort to even things out, the Soviets wanted to be friends with Cuba in order to "gain a strategic foothold in America's backyard" (Goldman and Stein). Cubas leader, Fidel Castro, believed Cuba would be attacked again by the U.S. following the 1961 Bay of Pigs invasion ("Cuban"). ∧ He eagerly accepted an offer from Nikita Khrushchev, leader of the Soviet Union, to protect Cuba from the U.S.

> **More details about the purpose of the blockade are added.**

By October of 1962, the construction of a missile base was well under way. The U.S., which was under the leadership of John F. Kennedy at the time, discovered the secret through careful analysis of reconaissance photos. Kennedy demanded that the Soviets dismantle the base and ordered a navel blockade of Cuba. to prevent any more supply deliveries ∧ Khrushchev, in turn, authorized retaliation in the event that U.S. forces invaded.

Revising Focusing on Style

Lakendra next reviewed her writing for its flow and style. Her thoughts below tell what changes she planned to make.

Word Choice

"I can improve my choice of verbs in some spots. There are still some places where I need to use different words to reflect a more serious tone."

Sentence Fluency

"I could combine related sentences to improve the flow. And some sentences could be rearranged to make them clearer."

Lakendra's Improvements in Style

After reviewing the style and sound of her writing, Lakendra focused on improving her word choice and sentence structure.

> Combining sentences improves sentence fluency.

> Verb choice is improved, and more formal wording is used.

The Soviet Union at the time was losing the arms race. They knew ∧ not only that the U.S. had more missiles than they did ∧ but also And they knew that some of these missiles were based in Turkey, only 150 mi. from the Soviet border. In an effort to even things out, the Soviets ∧ actively sought an alliance ~~wanted to be friends~~ with Cuba in order to "gain a strategic foothold in America's backyard" (Goldman and Stein). Cubas leader, Fidel Castro, believed Cuba would be attacked again by the U.S. following the 1961 Bay of Pigs invasion ("Cuban"). He eagerly accepted an offer from Nikita Khrushchev, leader of the Soviet Union, to protect Cuba from the U.S.

By October of 1962, the construction of a missile base was well under way. The U.S., ~~which was~~ under the leadership of John F. Kennedy ~~at the time,~~ discovered the secret through careful analysis of reconaissance photos. Kennedy demanded that the Soviets dismantle the base and ordered a navel blockade of Cuba to prevent any more supply deliveries. Khrushchev, in turn, authorized retaliation in the event that U.S. forces invaded.

Unnecessary words are deleted.

For 5 days, neither side backed down. Then Khrushchev made a written proposal: Soviet missiles would be removed from Cuba in exchange for a guarantee that the U.S. would not invade Cuba. A day later, he also demanded removal of U.S. missiles from Turkey. Kennedy ignored this second proposal but agreed to the first, Khrushchev backed down and announced plans to dismantle the base.

A colon is used to introduce an important point.

The world's relief was clear at having avoided this war. Many praised Kennedy's calm in the matter, for if he had authorized an invasion, the Soviets may well have retaliated with their nuclear weapons. And the U.S., of course, would follow with their own ("Cuban"). The willingness of the two world leaders to compromise, avoiding such a ~~boondoggle~~ catastrophe, was a welcome sign, that they knew the prevention of nuclear war was not only possible but necessary. Kennedy and Khrushchev agreed on that—and 9 months later, they signed an agreement to ban nuclear testing in the atmosphere (although underground testing continued). This pact was the most obvious outcome of the crisis.

A phrase is moved for clarity.

Word choice is improved, and a fragment is fixed.

Editing Checking for Conventions

Lakendra's last step in the process was to check for punctuation, capitalization, spelling, and grammar errors. She used the "Proofreader's Guide" in the back of her *Write Source* textbook and the checklist below.

Conventions

"I'll look carefully at my essay for punctuation, capitalization, spelling, and grammar errors."

PUNCTUATION

_____ **1.** Do I use end punctuation correctly?

_____ **2.** Do I use commas correctly?

_____ **3.** Do I correctly italicize or use quotation marks for titles?

_____ **4.** Do I use apostrophes correctly?

MECHANICS (CAPITALIZATION AND SPELLING)

_____ **5.** Have I capitalized all the proper nouns and adjectives?

_____ **6.** Have I spelled words correctly?

_____ **7.** Have I used the spell-checker on my computer?

_____ **8.** Have I used abbreviations correctly?

GRAMMAR

_____ **9.** Do I use the proper tense and voice for my verbs?

_____ **10.** Do my subjects and verbs agree in number?

_____ **11.** Do my pronouns clearly agree with their antecedents?

DOCUMENTATION

_____ **12.** Are sources properly presented and documented?

Try It!

Find three or four errors in Lakendra's revised draft on pages 24–25. Did you find the same errors as she found (on page 27)?

Lakendra's Editing

Here is a sample of Lakendra's editing. (See the inside back cover of this textbook for common editing and proofreading marks.)

> **The first instance of an abbreviated term is spelled out.**
>
> United States
> The U.S. was an ally of the Soviet Union during World War II, but tensions between the two countries began to mount following the war. These tensions led to a period of time beginning in the late 1940s known as the cold war. Each country perceived the other as hostile. However, the closest the conflict ever came to a nuclear war was the Cuban Missile Crisis of October, 1962.
>
> **An incorrectly placed comma is deleted, and an abbreviation is replaced.**
>
> The Soviet Union at the time was losing the arms race. They knew not only that the U.S. had more missiles than they did, but also that some of these missiles were based
> miles
> in Turkey, only 150 mi. from the Soviet border. In an effort to even things out, the Soviets actively sought an alliance with Cuba in order to "gain a strategic foothold in America's
> **An apostrophe is added to indicate possession.**
> backyard" (Goldman and Stein). Cubas leader, Fidel Castro, believed Cuba would be attacked again by the U.S. following the 1961 Bay of Pigs invasion ("Cuban"). He eagerly accepted an offer from Nikita Khrushchev, leader of the Soviet Union, to protect Cuba from the U.S.
>
> By October of 1962, the construction of a missile base was well under way. The U.S., under the leadership of John F. Kennedy, discovered the secret through careful analysis of
> **A spelling error is corrected.**
> reconnaissance
> reconaissance photos. Kennedy demanded that the Soviets . . .

Publishing Sharing Your Writing

Lakendra used the information below to produce a clean and effective copy of her final essay. She then showed her essay to her classmates.

Tips for Handwritten Copies

- Use blue or black ink and write clearly.
- Write your name according to your teacher's instructions.
- Skip a line and center your title on the first page; skip another line and begin your essay.
- Indent each paragraph and leave a one-inch margin on all four sides.

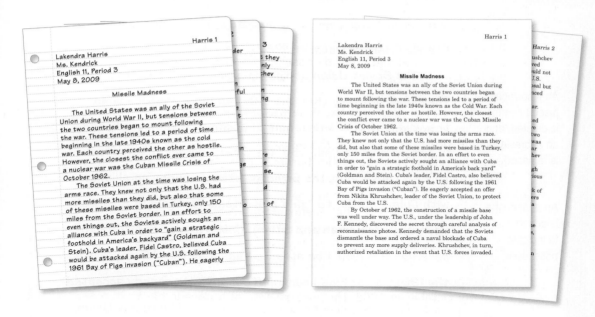

Tips for Computer Copies

- Use an easy-to-read font set at a 12-point type size.
- Double-space the text and set your margins so that you have a one-inch space around the outside of each page.
- For more tips on using a computer, see pages **91–95**.

Lakendra's Final Copy

Lakendra submitted her final essay with confidence. She felt that her writing met her goals and satisfied the terms of the assignment.

Harris 1

Lakendra Harris
Ms. Kendrick
English 11, Period 3
May 8, 2009

Missile Madness

The United States was an ally of the Soviet Union during World War II, but tensions between the two countries began to mount following the war. These tensions led to a period of time beginning in the late 1940s known as the Cold War. Each country perceived the other as hostile. However, the closest the conflict ever came to a nuclear war was the Cuban Missile Crisis of October 1962.

The Soviet Union at the time was losing the arms race. They knew not only that the U.S. had more missiles than they did, but also that some of these missiles were based in Turkey, only 150 miles from the Soviet border. In an effort to even things out, the Soviets actively sought an alliance with Cuba in order to "gain a strategic foothold in America's back yard" (Goldman and Stein). Cuba's leader, Fidel Castro, also believed Cuba would be attacked again by the U.S. following the 1961 Bay of Pigs invasion ("Cuban"). He eagerly accepted an offer from Nikita Khrushchev, leader of the Soviet Union, to protect Cuba from the U.S.

By October of 1962, the construction of a missile base was well under way. The U.S., under the leadership of John F. Kennedy, discovered the secret through careful analysis of reconnaissance photos. Kennedy demanded that the Soviets dismantle the base and ordered a naval blockade of Cuba to prevent any more supply deliveries. Khrushchev, in turn, authorized retaliation in the event that U.S. forces invaded.

For five days, neither side backed down. Then Khrushchev made a written proposal: Soviet missiles would be removed from Cuba in exchange for a guarantee that the U.S. would not invade Cuba. A day later, he also demanded removal of U.S. missiles from Turkey. Kennedy ignored this second proposal but agreed to the first. Khrushchev backed down and announced plans to dismantle the base.

The world's relief at having avoided this war was clear. Many praised Kennedy's calm in the matter, for if he had authorized an invasion, the Soviets may well have retaliated with their nuclear weapons. The U.S., of course, would have followed with their own ("Cuban"). The willingness of the two world leaders to compromise, avoiding such a catastrophe, was a welcome sign that they knew the prevention of nuclear war was not only possible but necessary. Kennedy and Khrushchev agreed on that—and nine months later, they signed an agreement to ban nuclear testing in the atmosphere (although underground testing continued). This pact was the most obvious outcome of the crisis.

The confrontation, however, had another result. The lack of a reliable form of communication between the two world powers meant a delay of several hours when sending messages—not a good thing when tensions are high. To improve the situation, a set of teletype machines linked the Kremlin and the White House, allowing the leaders to communicate directly. Today the electronic transmissions are achieved via two satellite systems, but they are still written rather than verbal to reduce the chance of an incorrect translation (Kennedy).

Tensions between world leaders will probably always be an obstacle to world peace. However, the actions of two opposing forces in October 1962 showed the world that diplomacy and compromise can work. The government leaders involved in the Cuban Missile Crisis weighed their options carefully and, in the end, made hard choices. Fortunately, their decisions under duress ultimately led to increased cooperation of governments the world over.

Assessing the Final Copy

Lakendra's teacher used a rubric like the one found on pages **198–199** to assess her final copy. A 6 is the very best score that a writer can receive for each trait. The teacher also included comments under each trait.

Rubric Checklist

Title: Missile Madness

Writer: Lakendra Harris

5 **Ideas**
You chose a very interesting topic, researched it, and provided solid information. However, I wish you had included a few more quotations.

5 **Organization**
You wrote a solid beginning, middle, and ending, and each paragraph is well developed.

4 **Voice**
The voice is much improved from the first draft. It's more formal and knowledgeable.

5 **Word Choice**
Your essay contains many topic-specific words and defines them either directly or in context. Well done.

5 **Sentence Fluency**
Your sentences read smoothly and show good variety.

6 **Conventions**
Your writing is free of careless errors.

Review the assessment. Do you agree with the scores and comments made by Lakendra's teacher? Why or why not? In a brief paragraph, discuss your own reaction to Lakendra's essay and how you would grade it.

Reflecting on Your Writing

After the whole process was finished, Lakendra filled out a reflection sheet. This helped her think about the assignment and plan for future writing. (Complete a reflection sheet like this right after you finish your writing.)

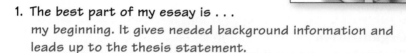

Lakendra Harris
Ms. Kendrick
English 11, Period 3
May 8, 2009

Expository Essay: Missile Madness

1. **The best part of my essay is . . .**
   my beginning. It gives needed background information and leads up to the thesis statement.

2. **The part that still needs work is . . .**
   my use of sources. Maybe I should have used more quotations to support the main idea of each paragraph.

3. **The most important part of my prewriting and planning was . . .**
   listing the 5 W's and H and using freewriting to gather my thoughts.

4. **During revising, I spent a lot of time dealing with . . .**
   adding more details to support my main points.

5. **What I've learned about this type of essay is . . .**
   that it's important to start with plenty of information. I also learned that using a formal voice for my essay makes it seem more authoritative.

6. **Here is one question I still have . . .**
   What are some good transitions to use to connect paragraphs smoothly?

Using a Rubric

Imagine a high jumper studying the crossbar he must leap over. Think of a long jumper pacing along the sand pit where she will land. Envision a weight lifter examining the bar that holds a gold medal winning weight. From start to finish, each of these athletes is focused on a specific, measurable mark for excellence.

When you write, you do the same thing. A writing rubric tells you how high you must jump, how far you must fly, how much you must lift. It measures the excellence of your ideas, organization, and voice—and the precision of your words and sentences and every last punctuation mark.

This chapter will show you how to use a rubric throughout the writing process to ensure your best possible score at the end. Like a great athlete, you'll learn to focus on the rubric not just when your work is assessed but from start to finish.

- **Understanding Rubrics**
- **Reading a Rubric**
- **Getting Started with a Rubric**
- **Revising and Editing with a Rubric**
- **Assessing with a Rubric**
- **Assessing in Action**
- **Assessing an Expository Essay**

"Either write something worth reading or do something worth writing."

—Benjamin Franklin

Understanding Rubrics

A **rubric** is simply a rating scale. Have you ever rated the popularity of something on a scale of 1 (terrible) to 10 (fantastic)? With rubrics, you can rate your writing—in this case on a scale of 6 (amazing) to 1 (incomplete).

6	5	4	3	2	1
Amazing	Strong	Good	Okay	Poor	Incomplete

The quality of any piece of writing can be rated on the basis of six traits: *ideas, organization, voice, word choice, sentence fluency,* and *conventions.* (For an introduction to these traits, see pages **47–90**.) A single essay might be well organized (score of 5) but have repetitive, general word choice (score of 3).

Rating Guide

Here's a brief description of the rating scale.

A **6** means that the writing is **amazing**.
It far exceeds expectations for a certain trait.

A **5** means that the writing is very **strong**.
It clearly meets the requirements for a trait.

A **4** means that the writing is **good**.
It meets most of the requirements for a trait.

A **3** means that the writing is **okay**.
It needs work to meet the main requirements for a trait.

A **2** means that the writing is **poor**.
It needs a lot of work to meet the requirements of a trait.

A **1** means that the writing is **incomplete**.
The writing is not yet ready to be assessed for a trait.

Reading a Rubric

Rubrics in this book are color coded according to the trait. *Ideas* appear in a green strip, *organization* in a pink strip, and so forth. There is a description for each rating to help you assess your writing for a particular trait.

Rubric for Expository Writing

6 Ideas	**5**	**4**
The ideas in the essay are compelling from start to finish.	The essay shows a clear relationship between thesis and supporting evidence.	The essay presents a clear topic and thesis. More support is needed.
Organization		
The essay shows thoughtful use of an organizational pattern. Transitions are strong.	The essay uses an effective organizational pattern. Transitions are appropriate.	The essay follows an organizational pattern. Transitions could be stronger.
Voice		
The writing voice is lively, engaging, and memorable.	Voice is appropriate for the topic, purpose, and audience and sounds knowledgeable.	Voice fits the audience and sounds knowledgeable in most places.

Guiding Your Writing

A rubric helps you . . .

- **plan your work**—knowing what is expected,
- **create a strong first draft**—focusing on *ideas, organization,* and *voice,*
- **revise and edit your work**—considering each trait, and
- **assess your final draft**—rating the traits throughout the whole piece of writing.

Think about the rubric. Read the level-5 descriptions above and consider what they have to say about ideas, organization, and voice. What should the essay include in addition to the thesis statement? What needs to be used to help with organization? How should the writer sound?

Getting Started with a Rubric

Each of the writing units in this book includes a page like the one below. This page, which is arranged according to the traits of writing, explains the main requirements for developing the essay in the unit. Studying the "goals" page will help you get started with your planning.

166

Understanding Your Goal

Your goal in this chapter is to write a well-organized informative article that engages and informs the reader. The traits listed in the chart below will help you plan and write your article.

Traits of Expository Writing

- **Ideas**
  Choose a topic that will interest the reader, write a clear focus statement, and include details that support the focus.

- **Organization**
  Start with a hook that captures the reader's attention. Expand the main focus in the middle paragraphs. Sum up the topic in the closing paragraph.

- **Voice**
  Use an engaging voice that shows your knowledge of the topic.

- **Word Choice**
  Choose words that explain your topic clearly. Use technical terms accurately.

- **Sentence Fluency**
  Write clear sentences with varied beginnings and lengths.

- **Conventions**
  Be sure that your punctuation, capitalization, spelling, and grammar are correct.

 Get the big picture. Look at the rubric on pages 198–199 before you begin to write. You can use the rubric as a guide to develop your essay and as a tool to assess your completed writing.

"There are a thousand ways to write, and each is as good as the other if it fits you."
—Lillian Hellman

Writing

A Closer Look at Understanding Your Goal

The following steps will help you get an overview of the assignment in each writing unit.

1. **Read** through the traits chart to familiarize yourself with the unit's goals.

2. **Focus** on *ideas, organization,* and *voice* at the start of the project, when you are prewriting and writing. These traits form the foundation of good writing.

3. **Identify** specific requirements for each trait (such as using "a point-by-point organizational pattern" and "a knowledgeable-sounding voice").

4. **Ask** questions if you aren't sure about any part of the assignment.

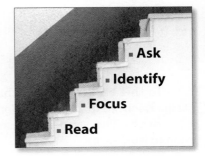

A Special Note About the Traits

Different traits are important at different stages of the writing process. The following chart shows when the specific traits are important.

During **prewriting** and **writing**, focus on the *ideas, organization,* and *voice* in your work.

During **revising**, focus on *ideas, organization, voice, word choice,* and *sentence fluency.* (For some assignments, your teacher may ask you to pay particular attention to one or two of these traits.)

During **editing** and proofreading, concentrate on *conventions—* spelling, punctuation, capitalization, and grammar.

During **publishing**, concentrate on *presentation.* Presentation is the "plus-one" trait in the "six plus one" traits of writing. Presentation simply means how your work looks on the page. (See pages **91–95** for more on presentation.)

When you are **assessing** your final copy, consider all six traits. (For some assignments, your teacher may ask you to assess the writing for just a few of the traits.)

Exercise

Review the goals on page **36**. Then write an expository paragraph comparing two people. Keep the traits in mind as you write.

Revising and Editing with a Rubric

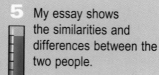 **6** My essay shows strong similarities between the two people and is full of surprising contrasts.

5 My essay shows the similarities and differences between the two people.

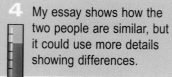 **4** My essay shows how the two people are similar, but it could use more details showing differences.

In this book, the pages that deal with revising and editing begin with a rubric strip. Each strip focuses on one trait of writing and will help you improve your first draft. The strip on these two pages focuses on the *ideas* for an expository comparison essay.

How can rubric strips help me assess my writing?

A rubric strip can help you look objectively at your writing. Follow these steps as you use the rubric strip to consider each trait:

1. Begin by reading over the number 5 description (a rating of strong).

2. Decide if your writing rates a 5 for that trait.

3. If not, check the 6 or 4 descriptions.

4. Continue until you find the rating that most closely matches your writing.

5. Notice how levels 4, 3, 2, and 1 offer suggestions on how you can improve your writing.

 Try It!

Review the expository paragraph below. Then rate it for ideas using the strip at the top of these two pages as a guide. Give reasons for the rating you provide.

> Pop music artists Shakira and Jennifer Lopez have some things in common besides their Latin heritage. Although Shakira was born in Columbia and Lopez in the United States, both have become known around the world. Each singer's music has dance and Latin pop influences and has won music-industry awards. Both women began their careers in music but switched to acting before returning to music. Despite a few differences, they are more alike than not.

3 I need more details that show the similarities and differences between the two people.

 2 I need to address the similarities and differences between the two people.

 1 I need to understand how to compare and contrast two people.

How can rubric strips help me revise and edit?

Once you have rated your writing for a given trait, you will see ways to improve your score. The writer of the paragraph on page **38** gave her ideas a score of 4, meaning that the writing meets *most* of the requirements for the trait. The score description told her just what she needed to do to improve her work: include "more details showing differences." (Scores of 4 or lower offer suggestions for improving your writing.)

In the main writing units, each rubric strip is followed by brief lessons that will help you revise or edit your writing to improve that trait. There are separate rubric strips and lessons for each trait—ideas, organization, voice, word choice, sentence fluency, and conventions.

Making Changes

The writer decided to add another detail that shows how the artists are different. She made the following changes.

Additional details help make the contrast clearer.

The revision to the closing sentence strengthens the paragraph.

. . . Both women began their careers in music but switched
                    Only Jennifer Lopez has continued to act.
to acting before returning to music. Despite a few
Jennifer Lopez and Shakira are both popularizing Latin-inspired
differences, ~~they are more alike than not.~~
music for an international audience.

 Revise your paragraph for ideas. Revise the paragraph you wrote on page 37, using the strip on these two pages as a guide.

Assessing with a Rubric

Follow these four steps when you use a rubric (see pages **42–43**) to assess a piece of writing.

1. Create an assessment sheet. On your own paper, write each of the key traits from the rubric, preceded by a short line. Under each trait, leave two or three lines to allow for comments.

2. Read the final copy. First, get an overall feeling for the writing. Then read more carefully, paying attention to each trait.

3. Assess the writing. Use the rubric to rate each trait. First, check the level-5 rubric description and then go up or down the scale until you find the correct rating. Write the score next to the trait on your assessment sheet.

Assessment Sheet   Title: _____

_____ Ideas

_____ Organization

_____ Voice

_____ Word Choice

_____ Sentence Fluency

_____ Conventions

Evaluator: _____

4. Provide comments. Under each trait, make whatever comments would be helpful for improving the writing.

Exercise

Assess your expository paragraph. Make an assessment sheet like the one above. Evaluate your paragraph using the rubric on pages **198–199**. For each trait, write a comment about something you did well and something you'd like to improve. (See the sample on page **43**.)

Writing

198

Rubric for Expository Writing

Use the following rubric to guide and assess your expository writing. Refer to it whenever you want to improve your writing using the six traits.

Each rubric addresses all six traits of writing.

	6	5	4			1
Ideas	The ideas in the essay are compelling from start to finish.	The essay shows a clear relationship between thesis and supporting evidence.	The essay presents a clear topic and thesis. More support is needed.			The topic should be reworked and a new thesis formed.
Organization	The essay shows thoughtful use of an organizational pattern. Transitions are strong.	The essay uses an effective organizational pattern. Transitions are appropriate.	The essay follows an organizational pattern. Transitions could be stronger.			The essay must be rewritten using an organizational plan.
Voice	The writing voice is lively, engaging, and memorable.	Voice is appropriate for the topic, purpose, and audience and sounds knowledgeable.	Voice fits the audience and sounds knowledgeable in most places.			Voice does not show confidence.
Word Choice	Word choice is vivid and precise. Special terms are defined or explained.	Word choice is effective. Words are not repeated and special terms are defined.	Word choice is adequate. Some overused words could be replaced.	Word choice needs to be more precise, and overused words need to be replaced.	A thesaurus is needed to find more-expressive words in many places.	The writer needs help choosing stronger words throughout.
Sentence Fluency	Sentences are carefully crafted. Sentences flow naturally and vary in type and length.	Sentences flow well and are varied in type and length.	Sentences could use more variety in type and length.	Sentences are basic. More variety is needed in sentence type and length.	Too many sentences are simple and begin the same way.	Most sentences need to be rewritten.
Conventions	Editing shows mastery of conventions. Essay is error free.	Editing is effective, but a few errors in grammar, spelling, or punctuation remain.	A few too many errors remain.	Control of conventions is basic. Errors sometimes get in the way of understanding.	Many corrections are needed to make the essay less confusing.	The writer needs help in understanding editing conventions.

Informative Article   199

Expository

The rubrics provide a scale in which 6 is the highest rating. A 1 is the lowest.

Assessing in Action

In the following expository essay, the writer shares information about a scientific journey of discovery. Read the essay, paying attention to its strengths and weaknesses. Then read the student self-assessment on the following page. (**The essay contains some errors.**)

Icy Surprises

The ten-year Census of Marine Life—a global effort funded by both public and private entities—began in 2000. Some scientists working on the Census, from Russia, China, Canada, and the United States, recently returned from a 30-day investigation of the Arctic Ocean. What they found was surprising: these dark, icy waters are full of life!

It was unexpected that there would be so much life and that species of jellyfish and worms previously unknown live in the depths of this ocean. Also surprising to see in such a cold environment were squid and octopuses, known to thrive in warmer waters.

Why were the researchers surprised? Because this ocean has a year-round ice cover and limited light during long periods. They thought the plant life would not be adequate to support the seafloor animals. They thought that a limited food supply in the Arctic Ocean would restrain the survival of sea life. The creatures, however, seem to have adopted to the extreme conditions.

The scientists, too, had to adjust to the harsh environment. Their living quarters were in an American icebreaker, the *Healy*. They were able to probe the unfriendly waters with the help of robot submarines, which were developed to withstand both the cold and crushing pressure of the deep ocean. Sonar was also used to determine the water depth and to find objects.

Once perceived as a barren sea, the Arctic Ocean apparently has a few things to teach us. That researchers are learning so much about it is amazing and encouraging. The knowledge they gain will benefit all of society as we deal with humanity's effects on every environment.

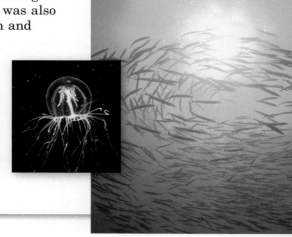

Sample Self-Assessment

The student who wrote "Icy Surprises" created the following assessment sheet to evaluate her essay. She used the expository rubric on pages **198–199** as her assessment guide. Under each trait, she wrote comments about the strengths and weaknesses of her writing.

Assessment Sheet   **Title:** Icy Surprises

5   Ideas
The topic seems interesting.
The essay could use a few more details.

4   Organization
My essay follows my plan.
Transitions between paragraphs need work.

4   Voice
I sound interested.
I'm not sure if the voice fits the audience.

4   Word Choice
My words are accurate.
I could have used more specific verbs.

4   Sentence Fluency
I used different sentence structures.
Some of my sentences are too long, and there
is one fragment.

5   Conventions
I caught many errors.
I used "adopt" instead of "adapt" in one sentence.

Evaluator: Rose

Exercise

Review the assessment. On your own paper, explain why you agree with the responses above (or why you don't). Consider each trait carefully.

Assessing an Expository Essay

Read the essay below, focusing on its strengths and weaknesses. Then follow the directions at the bottom of the page. **(The essay contains errors.)**

Jim Hamar
Mr. Fremont
Comp I
November 17, 2009

Ebola: The Scourge of Africa

In 1976, 318 people in one area of the Democratic Republic of the Congo were stricken with a horrific illness; it progressed so rapidly that it had killed 280 of the victims within a few weeks. Scientists named the virus causing the disease after the Ebola River, near where the outbreak occurred. Today, Ebola is known as a deadly viral illness that has no known source and no known cure.

Once a person becomes infected with the virus, there is nothing doctors can do except offer pain relief and life support. In addition, family members caring for the sick person are likely to become ill, too. Direct contact with virus-infected blood or other body fluid leads to contraction of the disease. Unless caretakers take strict precautions, such contact may be hard to avoid; vomiting, diarrhea, and internal and external bleeding are common secondary symptoms. Death is usually 7 to 10 days after

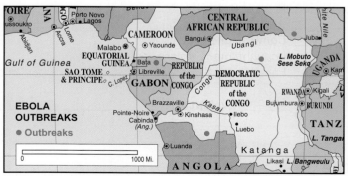

Source: Jenkins, David. "Tracking a Killer." Immunological Quarterly Review 63, 4: 184.

Hamar 2

symptoms begin: In more than 80 percent of confirmed Ebola cases, the sufferers have died ("Ebola"). Four countries in Central Africa have had outbreaks of Ebola (affecting not only human populations but gorilla and chimpanzee populations, as well.) Local health practitioners have had to learn to control the epidemics through the use of basic hygiene practices including masks, goggles, and gloves. Sterilization of needles is, of course, paramount to preventing the spread of the disease. Patients are kept in isolation, and precautions are continued as a corpse is readied for burial.

Although the origin of the virus is indefinite, researchers believe that its natural host is an animal native to Africa. How it gets from animal to human is still a mystery, but one hypothesis is that the initial transmission occurs via ingestion—that is, the virus is present in an animal that the victim eats. Some people in central Africa regularly eat fruit bats, and scientists have recently discovered that three species of fruit bats in the region carry the Ebola virus despite showing no symptoms (Lovgren). This research is the latest step in our understanding of this lethal disease.

Other viral diseases are fatal, too; but what makes Ebola so remarkable is its speed of destruction. It seems to come from nowhere and then just annihilates some small population. The only hope to avoid more suffering is that science can develop a vaccine or determine the source—and the cure.

Exercise

Assess this expository essay, using the rubric on pages **198–199** as your guide. To get started, create an assessment sheet like the one on page **40**. *Remember:* After each trait, try to write one comment about a strength and one about a weakness.

Understanding the Traits

Understanding the Traits of Writing

What makes a great piece of pizza? First of all, it needs to look good, with a golden crust, bubbly cheese, and colorful toppings. Then it needs to smell wonderful: yeasty crust, Italian spices, fragrant cheese . . . Of course, the pizza should be hot and baked to perfection. And last, but certainly not least, it should taste delicious! A great piece of pizza has many traits, but it takes just one bite to discern the quality.

Writing works the same way. A great piece of writing exhibits many essential traits, which a careful reader can recognize after a few paragraphs. These traits include powerful ideas, logical organization, engaging voice, precise word choice, smooth-reading sentences, and clear, correct copy. Skillful writers pay attention to all these traits, just as skillful chefs worry about the look, smell, and taste of their creations.

In this chapter, you'll get a quick overview of the traits of writing, and you'll see how these traits fit into the writing process.

- **Understanding the Six Traits**
- **Using the Traits**
- **Checklist for Effective Writing**

"I have an 'ideas' file full of newspaper clippings of scientific facts and human interest stories."

—Monica Hughes

Understanding the Six Traits

Throughout this book, you'll use the six traits to make your writing the best it can be. Here is a brief description of each trait.

Ideas

The **ideas** in your writing include the topic, the focus (thesis), and the main supporting points and details. Ideas are the heart of writing—the message you want to communicate to your reader.

Organization

Organization refers to the way your writing begins, the order of the ideas in the middle, and the way your writing ends. By using logic and transitions, you can lead your reader step by step through your ideas.

Voice

Your writing **voice** reflects your personality, your feelings about the topic, your purpose in writing, and your relationship with the reader. Voice can be bubbly or angry, hopeful or sarcastic, formal or casual.

Word Choice

Word choice considers the quality of the nouns, verbs, and modifiers in your writing. Writers work with words the way jewelers work with gems.

Sentence Fluency

Sentence fluency refers to the flow of sentences and the rhythm of phrases and clauses. Some sentences meander like a melody. Others crack like a rim shot. Fluid sentences can make your writing memorable.

Conventions

Conventions are the rules of punctuation, capitalization, spelling, and grammar. Once upon a time, the rules of writing were taught as writing itself. Now, the rules are a separate consideration, especially important near the end of the writing process.

Try It!

Reflect on the traits by answering the following questions:

1. Which trait is strongest in my writing? Explain.
2. Which trait is weakest in my writing? Explain.

Using the Traits

Since no one can focus on all six traits at once, different traits are important at different stages in the writing process.

Traits

Prewriting	
Ideas	Select a topic, gather details, choose your focus (thesis), and decide on main points.
Organization	Write your thesis statement and topic sentences, decide on a method of organization, and create a list or an outline.

Writing	
Ideas	Connect all your ideas and details.
Organization	Write a beginning, a middle, and an ending, using the plan you have made.
Voice	Use a voice appropriate to your personality, topic, purpose, and reader.

Revising	
Ideas	Revise your focus, main points, and details.
Organization	Check the order and unity of your paragraphs.
Voice	Adjust your voice as needed.
Word Choice	Make sure you use precise nouns, active verbs, and appropriate modifiers.
Sentence Fluency	Check your sentences for varied beginnings and lengths.

Editing, Proofreading, and Publishing	
Conventions	Edit your work for punctuation, capitalization, spelling, grammar, and format.

Try It!

Answer the following questions:

1. Which traits get the most attention early in the process? Why?

2. Which traits get the most attention later in the process? Why?

Checklist for Effective Writing

If a piece of writing meets the following standards, it exhibits the traits of effective writing. Check your work using these standards.

Traits Checklist

Ideas

_____ **1.** Is the topic interesting?

_____ **2.** Is there a specific focus and purpose?

_____ **3.** Do a variety of details support the focus?

Organization

_____ **4.** Is there a clear beginning, middle, and ending?

_____ **5.** Are the details arranged in the best order to support the focus?

_____ **6.** Do transitions and key words connect the ideas?

Voice

_____ **7.** Does the writing sound natural?

_____ **8.** Does the voice fit the topic and the purpose?

_____ **9.** Is the voice appropriate for the audience?

Word Choice

_____ **10.** Are the nouns specific and the verbs active?

_____ **11.** Are the modifiers colorful and necessary?

Sentence Fluency

_____ **12.** Do the sentences have rhythm and flow?

_____ **13.** Do the sentence beginnings and lengths vary?

Conventions

_____ **14.** Does the work follow the rules of punctuation, capitalization, spelling, and grammar?

_____ **15.** Is the work presented in a clear, correct format?

Ideas

In his book *Breathing In, Breathing Out,* Ralph Fletcher talks about the "food chain" of writing ideas. High on the food chain are the main ideas (the meat or protein) that prompt you to write. Lower on this chain are the details (the fruits and vegetables, the fiber) that you include in your writing to support or explain the main idea. You only need one main idea (topic) to get started on an essay or an article, but you need many details to develop the idea.

Of course, the key to effective writing is identifying a writing idea that truly interests you. If you have strong feelings about a topic, you will naturally put more effort into your writing right from the start. As writer and philosopher Lancelot Law Whyte once said, "There are few experiences quite so satisfactory as getting a good idea. . . . You're pleased with it, and feel good [about getting started]." The information in this chapter will help you focus on the best main ideas and details for your writing. You will also learn about developing the proper attitude for writing.

- **Developing the "Write" Attitude**
- **Starting with a Strong Main Idea**
- **Reviewing Possible Starting Points**
- **Using Effective Supporting Details**
- **Including Surprising Realities**

"Life-transforming ideas have always come to me through books."

—Bell Hooks

> "If I want to write movingly, I must first pay attention to what moves me."
>
> —Ralph Fletcher

Developing the "Write" Attitude

Professional writers are frequently asked where they find their ideas. Most pros would respond that the best ideas often *find them* quite unexpectedly, more by chance than by any systematic process. As novelist Stephen King says, "Let's get one thing clear. . . . There is no Idea Dump, no Story Central, no Island of the Buried Bestseller." For King, the point is not to track down ideas, but more to recognize them when they "show up." The following guidelines will help you become more receptive to effective writing ideas.

Take inventory of your life. Keep lists of people, places, and things that matter to you. Consider the following categories for your personal inventory:

- favorite books, movies, etc.
- things to change
- goals and desires
- areas of expertise
- unforgettable people
- memorable places

Write regularly. Experienced writers often write daily in a notebook or journal. Daily writing deepens your thinking, gives you new writing ideas, and helps you become fluent.

FYI

Once you get into personal writing, you'll soon realize that your experiences and thoughts are no more than points of departure. As you write, you will bend, stretch, and turn these initial ideas inside out. You'll see them in new ways.

Be on sensory alert. Writing ideas may unexpectedly show up as you drive to school, hang out with friends, overhear a conversation, and so on. Here's an example: While walking down a street, you and a friend come across a well-cared-for, healthy plant growing in front of a neglected, ramshackle house. Such a "flower in the rough" scene could elicit several writing ideas.

Try It!

Take inventory of your life right now, following the guidelines above. Keep adding to these lists throughout the school year. Use the ideas in your personal writing and for writing assignments.

Traits

Get involved. Experience different aspects of your community. Volunteer your services, learn about various businesses, visit different neighborhoods, attend community meetings, tour museums, and so on. Your involvement will naturally expand your inventory of writing ideas.

Read like a writer. Reserve part of a notebook for intriguing ideas that occur to you as you read—interesting names, revealing character traits, eye-opening statistics, alarming predictions, fluent sentences, surprising turns in a story, and so forth. Again, these notes will serve as a valuable writing resource.

Map out your experiences. Writing teachers Dan Kirby and Tom Liner suggest that you create a life map of important experiences. This is not a typical map, but a map with only one road representing your life, a map of time. From birth to the present, you illustrate the important events, stories, and experiences of your life.

Life Map

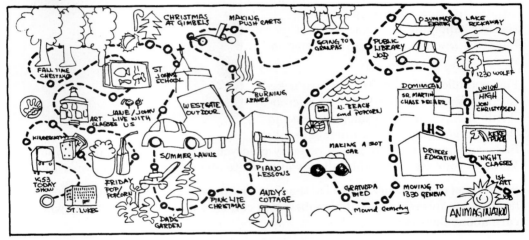

Try It!

Create a life map. Design a life map using the information and sample above as a guide.

> "A strange thing happens when you write: you discover what you truly think; you find out what your heart means."
>
> —Shirley Rousseau Murphy

Starting with a Strong Main Idea

Writing is hard work, but trying to write about something that doesn't really interest you can be pure torture. That is why it is important to select writing ideas carefully. The following tips will help you connect with effective topics.

Be receptive. The previous two pages point out that interesting writing ideas will find you if you think and act like a writer—keeping a writer's notebook, being on sensory alert, and so on.

Test an idea. Whenever you feel like writing, don't hesitate. Put pen to paper or fingers to the keyboard and see what develops. Even if this writing doesn't pan out, it may give you other ideas.

Make an assignment your own. Some writing assignments are open-ended, allowing you to choose your own topic. Others are very specific, with your teacher supplying the topic. When this happens, try to "customize" the topic so it becomes your own.

For example, let's say that you are asked to classify the different types of microbes. While the overall assignment may seem "blah" to you, one type of microbe, a nasty little cold or flu virus that has recently paid you a visit, may "fascinate" you. Perhaps your teacher would allow you to write about how this virus operates.

Show restraint. Don't settle for the first or even the second writing idea if neither one interests you. Remember: You can only do your best writing when you care about the topic.

Use selecting strategies. When you need help to come up with a writing idea, try a selecting strategy such as clustering or brainstorming. (See page **98**.)

Try It!

Recall your best writing idea this year. Discuss this idea in a brief paragraph, considering these questions: *What was the assignment? How did you come across this topic? Why was it enjoyable? How did the finished piece turn out?*

Reviewing Possible Starting Points

You come across many people, places, experiences, concepts, trends, and beliefs during the school year, all of which may lead to interesting writing ideas. Listed below are a number of starting points for the basic modes of writing. Considering subjects you are studying currently, recent experiences, and so on, you can translate the ideas below into writing topics of your own.

Expository

- Discuss the impact of the Magna Carta on modern government.
- Select one character (including Willy) in the play *Death of a Salesman* and analyze that character's role in Willy Loman's downfall and death.
- What one thing would you change in the world?
- Explore the evolution of the modern-day trumpet.
- Explain why the F-11 is virtually invisible to radar.

Persuasive

- Persuade the school board to add a class you would like to take.
- Convince your best friend to quit smoking.
- Identify America's greatest poet and defend your choice.
- Pretend you are the lawyer for Dred Scott. Defend him in his case before the Supreme Court.
- Convince your school board to include vegetarian meals in the cafeteria.

Narrative

- Tell about a time you were frightened by something or someone.
- Write about the love story of Elizabeth Barrett and Robert Browning.
- Tell the story of the Donner party.
- Tell the story behind your favorite toy as a child.
- Write about meeting your first girlfriend/boyfriend.
- Write about the moment you knew life wasn't always fair.

Descriptive

- Describe the most beautiful/unusual sight you have ever seen.
- Describe the school building a half hour after school ends.
- Describe your best friend's hands.
- Describe your favorite store on a Saturday afternoon.
- Describe the Mars landscape.

Try It!

Identify three writing ideas that truly interest you by reviewing your writer's notebook (if you keep one), your class notes, your textbooks, and the Internet.

Traits

Using Effective Supporting Details

There are many types of details you can include in your writing. Your main idea or topic, plus the purpose of your writing, determines which details you should use. The key types are explained below and on the following page.

Facts are *details* that can be proven.

> The construction of the Panama Canal greatly decreased the number of cargo ships that traveled around Cape Horn.
>
> *The Jazz Singer,* which opened on October 6, 1927, in New York, was the first motion picture to use dialogue as part of the movie's action.

Statistics present *numerical information* about a specific topic.

> According to the American Academy of Allergy, Asthma, and Immunology (AAAAI), 12.8 million school days are missed annually due to asthma.
>
> Russ McCurdy, the coach with the most wins in NCAA Women's Ice Hockey, holds a record of 264 wins, 36 losses, and 10 ties in 15 years of coaching for New Hampshire.

Examples are *statements that illustrate a main point.*

> Different breeds of horses exhibit distinct characteristics, developed either purposefully or randomly through generations (main point). For example, Morgan horses are known for their power and stamina in either working or racing, and Arabians are prized for their graceful, arched necks and delicately shaped heads. While these characteristics were carefully cultivated in the breeds, no one really knows where the Bashkir Curly got its distinctive curly coat.

Anecdotes are *brief stories* that help to make a point about a topic. Because they are usually very engaging, they are much more effective than a matter-of-fact list of details.

> It's difficult to pigeonhole gender roles in today's world, and even more so when both partners have powerhouse careers. Bob Dole was an important and powerful senator from Kansas when, in 1985, his wife, Elizabeth, was appointed secretary of transportation in President Reagan's cabinet. Magazines had a field day following the pair, and one ran a photo of them working together to make their bed at home. Afterward, the senator received a humorous letter from a man complaining that he should stop doing work around the house, as he was creating some problems for men around the country.
>
> "You don't know the half of it," Senator Dole wrote back. "The only reason she was helping was because they were taking pictures."

Quotations are *people's statements* repeated word for word. Quotations can provide powerful supporting evidence.

> Sometimes a funny statement can also be a chilling wake-up call. For example, comedian Robert Orben once observed, "There's so much pollution in the air now that if it weren't for our lungs there'd be no place to put it all." We laugh at this idea, but when we actually think about it, the statement is downright frightening.

Definitions give the *meaning* of unfamiliar terms. Definitions of technical terms are especially important for the reader. Defining such terms makes your writing clear.

> Casein paint, a milk-based artist's medium, was used by early Egyptians and was even found in 9,000-year-old cave drawings.

Reasons answer *why* and can explain or justify ideas.

> We need to preserve the South American rain forest. The rain forest is home to many unusual species of animals, birds, and insects that could become extinct if the forest is destroyed. In addition, the rain forest prevents the land from eroding away and also plays a vital role in human health. Many medicines are continually being discovered or developed from the forest's plants and animals. Most importantly, the rain forest plays an important role in maintaining the delicate ecological balance of the world. Without the oxygen and water produced by the rain forest, weather patterns will probably change, wreaking havoc around the globe.

Comparisons address the *similarities* or *differences* between two things. It is especially helpful to compare something new or unknown to something your reader understands.

> Not all vegetarians are equal. While ovo-lacto vegetarians and vegans may seem the same, they have some differences. Those who follow an ovo-lacto diet avoid eating meat or meat products, although they do include dairy products and eggs in their diets. Vegans not only skip the meat, they also avoid dairy products and eggs. While ovo-lacto vegetarians will use animal products such as leather, vegans avoid anything made from or by an animal, including leather, silk, or even honey. Both groups maintain the philosophy of animal dignity, but the level of their commitment varies.

Try It!

Find examples of writing in this book that show four of the detail types explained on the previous two pages. On your own paper, write the examples and the pages on which you found them.

"Surprising realities [run through] good essays and articles as they do good stories."

—Ken Macrorie

Including Surprising Realities

According to writer Ken Macrorie, the most memorable informational writing (essays and articles) continually engages the reader with "surprising realities"—eye-opening facts, anecdotes, and examples that pack a punch.

Here is an example of a surprising reality in *People of the Abyss,* a book about London, England, written by Jack London in 1902. In this revealing passage, the author expresses a disturbing irony about the great city.

> **From the slimy spittle-drenched sidewalk, they were picking up bits of orange peel, apple skin, and grape stems, and they were eating them. The pits of green gage plums they cracked between their teeth for the kernels inside. They picked up stray crumbs of bread the size of peas, apple cores so black and dirty one would not take them to be apple cores, and these things these two men took into their mouths, and chewed them, and swallowed them; and this, between six and seven o'clock in the evening of August 20, year of our Lord 1902, in the heart of the greatest, wealthiest, and most powerful empire the world has ever seen.**

Staying Alert

You'll find surprising realities all around if you keep your eyes open. Here's an example: While driving to school, you see the sign "MEN WORKING," and around the sign sit three workers drinking coffee and talking. Surprising realities are everywhere—even in the research you do.

Tip

To surprise the reader, the writer must include the unexpected twist, turn, or irony in an otherwise straightforward piece of information.

Try It!

Look for surprising realities in your world. Write down at least three of them. Afterward, share your examples with your classmates.

Special Challenge: Try to use two or more surprising realities in your next essay.

Organization

Organization becomes important when, and only when, you have an intriguing idea that prompts you to write. Writers and teachers Dan Kirby and Tom Liner state, "A subject often seeks its own form," meaning that once you have a writing idea in mind, a method of organization often becomes clear early in the writing process.

For example, when you have a personal story to tell, you will naturally recall the key details chronologically. Or when a short story idea pops into your head, you will almost automatically envision the main character and establish his or her conflict. This is the way writing should work: You start out, knowing you will find an appropriate structure or shape for your ideas.

On the other hand, you don't want to become trapped by a basic structure or pattern of organization. According to Kirby and Liner, that makes writing a "cookie cutter operation." Formulas and patterns are indispensable for mathematicians; not so for writers. Writing is often more engaging or compelling when it blazes an unpredictable path.

This chapter provides background information about the basic methods of organization. Use this information as a helpful starting point when you develop different types of writing.

- **Understanding the Big Picture**
- **Knowing the Patterns of Organization**
- **Using Graphic Organizers**
- **Understanding Coherence**
- **Fine-Tuning Organization**

"Good writing cannot be a cookie cutter operation."

—Dan Kirby and Tom Liner

Understanding the Big Picture

The basic structure of informational writing is quite simple. Essays, articles, and reports contain three main parts: the *beginning,* the *middle,* and the *ending.* Each part plays an important role in an effective piece of writing.

Beginning The opening paragraph should capture the reader's attention and state your thesis. Here are some ways to capture your reader's attention.

- Tell a dramatic or exciting story (anecdote) about the topic.
- Ask an intriguing question or two.
- Provide a few surprising facts or statistics.
- Introduce an interesting quotation.
- Explain your personal experience or involvement with the topic.

> **Beginning**
> Middle
> Ending

Middle The middle paragraphs should support your thesis statement. For example, in an essay about improved safety in Grand Prix racing, each middle paragraph would focus on one main aspect of improved safety. (An outline will help you write this section. See pages **174, 230,** and **591.**)

> Beginning
> **Middle**
> Ending

Ending The closing paragraph should summarize your thesis and leave the reader with something to think about. Here are some strategies for creating a strong closing.

- Review your main points.
- Emphasize the special importance of one main point.
- Answer any questions the reader may still have.
- Draw a conclusion and put the information in perspective.
- Provide a final significant thought for the reader.

> Beginning
> Middle
> **Ending**

Try It!

As a class or in a small group, discuss one of the essays in this book. Focus your remarks on the development of the three main parts.

Knowing the Patterns of Organization

Almost all essays follow a basic pattern of organization. As you will see in the chart below, some of these patterns are specific and others are more general. Knowing how these patterns work will help you plan and organize your essays.

Using Organizing Patterns

Essay Types	Organizing Patterns
Process How something works	Chronological order
Narrative How something happened	Chronological order
Description How something/someone appears	Spatial order
Comparison How two things are alike/different	Whole vs. whole/point by point
Cause-effect How one thing affects something else	Identify cause/explore effects Identify effect/explore causes
Problem-solution How a problem can be solved	Study the problem/solutions
Classification How something can be categorized	Name categories/examine each one
Argumentation How a position or an opinion can be asserted and supported	State an opinion/support it/ consider the opposing point of view/restate the opinion

Try It!

For each assignment listed below, identify the organizing pattern that you would use to develop your writing.

1. A history paper pointing out the results of the Missouri Compromise
2. An economics paper arguing for or against a flat tax
3. An art paper describing a Van Gogh painting
4. A health paper identifying the different types of weight lifters
5. A social studies paper exploring the issue of your city's deteriorating downtown
6. An English paper detailing a life-changing experience
7. A science paper explaining how a tsunami develops

Using Graphic Organizers

Graphic organizers can help you gather and organize your details for writing. Clustering is one method (see page 98); the next two pages list other useful organizers. (Re-create the organizer on your own paper to gather details for an essay.)

Cause-Effect Organizer

Use to collect and organize details for cause/effect essays.

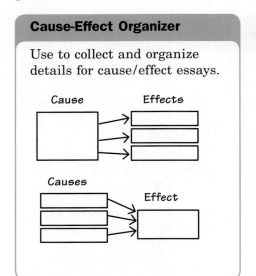

Problem-Solution Web

Use to map out problem/solution essays.

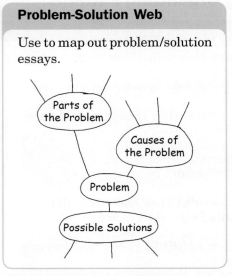

Time Line

Use for personal narratives to list actions or events in the order they occurred.

Subject: _____

(Chronological Order)

① _____
② _____
③ _____
④ _____
⑤ _____

Evaluation Collection Grid

Use to collect supporting details for essays of evaluation.

Subject: _____

Points to Evaluate	Supporting Details
1.	
2.	
3.	
4.	

Venn Diagram

Use to collect details to compare and contrast two topics.

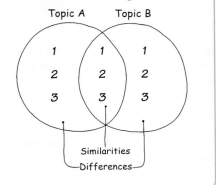

Line Diagram

Use to collect and organize details for academic essays.

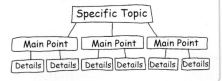

Process (Cycle) Diagram

Use to collect details for science-related writing, such as how a process or cycle works.

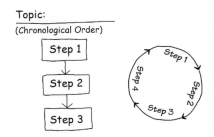

5 W's Chart

Use to collect the *Who? What? When? Where?* and *Why?* details for personal narratives and news stories.

Subject: _____

Who?	What?	When?	Where?	Why?

Definition Diagram

Use to gather information for extended-definition essays.

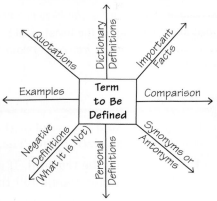

Sensory Chart

Use to collect details for descriptive essays and observation reports.

Subject: _____

Sights	Sounds	Smells	Tastes	Textures

Understanding Coherence

Writing that is coherent allows a reader to move smoothly through an essay. (*Coherence*, by definition, is the logical arrangement of ideas.)

Achieving Sentence Coherence

Most often, the sentences within your paragraphs will naturally move logically from one to the next. However, if some of your sentences lack coherence (a smooth logical flow), try one of the following techniques:

Repeating a Key Word

Two to five percent of the donor's bone marrow is extracted from the back of the pelvis. The extraction is fairly simple—only a few tiny incisions are made.
(The **boldfaced** key words connect the two sentences.)

Using Transitional Words or Phrases

Jack's cause in *The Lord of the Flies* is a noble one: purify the world of evil. However, he goes about looking for the beast in all the wrong places.
(The transitional word *however* provides a logical link between the two sentences.)

Try It!

List the repeated key word or the transitional word or phrase that links each set of sentences below. The first one has been done for you.

1. Doctors must be truthful. If a patient is diagnosed with a serious illness, a doctor should tell the truth—tactfully.

    The key words *truthful* and *truth* link the two sentences.

2. New technologies make it possible to recycle high-quality paper. For example, equipment is currently under development to remove ink from glossy magazines.

3. One form of malnutrition is marasmus and occurs when children are weaned too soon. Children with marasmus are extremely underweight, lacking any body fat or defined muscles.

4. Coaches and parents should keep teens away from supplements like creatine. Instead, student athletes should rely on their natural talents and strengths.

5. What is authentic assessment, and how can exit exams be changed to include it? Authentic assessment requires students to demonstrate knowledge by doing something "real."

Achieving Paragraph Coherence

The same techniques that help you achieve sentence coherence can also help you achieve paragraph coherence.

Repeating a Key Word

You can repeat a key word from the end of one paragraph in the beginning of the next.

> . . . Most farmers in the market for new irrigation equipment are buying efficient, environmentally friendly systems.

> These systems have done much to reduce the amount of water used by wheat farmers.

(The **boldfaced** words connect the paragraphs.)

Using Transitional Words and Phrases

You can also use transitional words or phrases to connect paragraphs. (See pages **179, 234,** and **595–596.**)

> Early in the summer, the first sign of the oil crisis appeared. It showed up in the front windows of gasoline stations across the land: "Closed." And they were . . .

> Later in the year, the reality of the crisis really hit home. A mandatory fuel allocation program was announced to take effect within 30 days. It called for . . .

> By the end of 1973, even a six-gallon ration was too much to expect. It was in November that Arab oil-producing nations cut off oil . . .

Try It!

Review the following sets of related transitions. Identify which set of transitions you would use to develop each of the essays listed below.

a. First   Then   Next   In the end
b. In the same way   Also   Similarly
c. Above   Below   To the left   To the right
d. First of all   Additionally   Most importantly

_____ **1.** Comparing two unique politicians
_____ **2.** Sharing a life-changing experience
_____ **3.** Arguing for a remodeled school theater
_____ **4.** Describing a striking new monument

Traits

Fine-Tuning Organization

Writer Donald Murray recommends the 2-3-1 principle for arranging supporting ideas in persuasive essays. According to this principle, you should present the *second most important* idea first, the *least important* idea next, and the *most important* idea last. He believes the reader will naturally pay close attention to the first supporting point that you present, and even closer attention to the last one.

Using the 2-3-1 Principle

In a persuasive essay about students and television, the writer used the 2-3-1 principle to arrange support for this thesis (opinion) statement.

Thesis Statement

Students should pull the plug on their most valued life-support system, their television sets.

Main Supporting Points

2   Television viewing takes away from time students could spend on schoolwork. (*second most important*)

3   Many students are held hostage, hour after hour, by mindless shows. (*least important*)

(1)   Watching television is a reactive pastime, taking absolutely no skill or thinking on the part of the participant. (*most important*)

Try It!

Organize each set of supporting points below according to the 2-3-1 principle. Be able to justify your arrangement.

Opinion: Metal detectors are not needed in our school.
Supporting points: –send wrong message
                          –not foolproof
                          –management nightmare

Opinion: Overcrowded classrooms are a real turnoff.
Supporting points: –limit opportunities to learn
                          –cause tension
                          –lead to more students dropping out

Opinion: Art classes help all students.
Supporting points: –improve visual learning
                          –improve entrance and exit test scores
                          –prepare students for the business world

Voice

Writer and teacher Dan Kirby says, "Voice is the aspect of writing closest to the writer." Voice tags you like a thumbprint, establishing your special place among all other writers. As the quotation below states, however, finding your natural voice may take time. That is, you may not automatically write with a lot of voice. Reading, regular journal writing, tuning in to the language—these are the practices that will help you develop your natural writing voice.

How do you know if your writing has voice? First of all, it should communicate to the reader something about you as an individual. Secondly, it should engage the reader, making him or her feel that you sincerely care about what you say—and how you say it. Lastly, it should move the reader to feel that reading your work has been a pleasurable and worthwhile experience. The purpose of this chapter is to help you better understand voice, one of the most important, yet least understood, traits of writing.

- **Developing Voice**
- **Knowing Your Purpose**
- **Identifying Your Audience**
- **Understanding Diction**
- **Experimenting with Voice**

"All of us who write need a certain amount of time, often quite a lot of time, to relax and find our natural voice."

—William Zinsser

Developing Voice

Your natural voice will begin to develop once you reach a certain comfort level with writing. Writing regularly in a notebook or journal will help you reach that level. (See pages **1–5.**)

Read the following notebook entry. It shows a regular writer in action. This entry reflects the writer's personality.

Sample Notebook Entry

March 3

    It happened again today. At the mall someone yelled, "Katie!" to me, or actually to my identical twin sister. For some reason, people think of us as "the twins," almost as if we are not separate beings. I love my sister and all, but I get so mad when people call me Katie. Listen everyone! I'm Cali: I play center field on Park's softball team. Katie plays third base. I'm good at running down fly balls; she's good at keeping ground balls in the infield. I'm fast on the base paths; she's a big bopper, with three home runs this year.

Exercise

Decide whether or not each of the following passages exhibits voice. Be able to explain your answers.

1. It was the movie Hollywood was born to make, and was born making. It has buried treasures and Nazi villains, poison darts and mystical phantoms, damsels in distress and Arabian swordsmen.

2. When I was little, I had a great interest in drawing. As I grew older, I stopped drawing. Then I found some of my old drawings. They helped me remember what I liked about drawing.

3. In today's society there is a lot of advertising. You can find interesting ads in magazines, and there are many commercials on TV. A lot of people think the ads are better than the regular programming.

4. Yazoo City was a lazy town, stretched over its hills and its flat streets in the summer sun; it was a dreamy place, always green and lush except for the four cold months at the beginning and end of each year.
   —Willie Morris, *Good Old Boy*

Knowing Your Purpose

Once your natural voice has had a chance to develop, you'll be ready and able to adjust it depending on the purpose of your writing. (The purpose is your specific reason for writing.)

Identifying Reasons for Writing

Purpose: To share an experience
Voice: Engaging and personal

> I had to get back to class as fast as I could. First graders follow rules in a serious way, and the first rule of order is to be on time, always. Once I got into class, I rubbed my chin and noticed blood on my hand. Mrs. Gehring said my chin just looked skinned. I personally thought it was more serious than that, but I didn't say anything. The second rule of order in first grade is to listen to your teacher.

Purpose: To express an opinion
Voice: Convincing and informed

> The school board should realize just how necessary art really is for student success. First of all, art improves visual literacy. According to the International Visual Literacy Association, visual literacy is fundamental to normal human learning.

Purpose: To share information
Voice: Interesting and knowledgeable

> Safety wasn't always a primary concern on the Formula One racing circuit. When the Grand Prix began in 1906, the race ran on city streets and country roads, and accidents involving drivers and spectators were common.

Exercise

Identify the purpose and appropriate voice for the passages below. Use the information above as a guide.

1. Unlike the typical ocean waves caused by storms, a tsunami begins with a fault line in the seabed. Faults occur when two or more of the earth's tectonic plates meet and rub against each other.

2. The rain hit my helmet lightly, like a soft tapping on a door. I pulled my chin strap across my chin and snapped it on the other side. Forty-three teammates standing beside me started to jog, workhorses on the move.

3. Upper-level students in McKinley High School need access to work-study programs. Studies have shown that students retain new information more effectively if they experience it.

Identifying Your Audience

Your writing voice will change depending on whom you are addressing. The three passages below demonstrate this principle.

Possible Audiences
- Classmates
- School board members
- Grade school students
- Grandparents
- Community members

Audience: school board members

The problem of disruptive behavior on our school buses is everyone's concern. During the last few weeks there have been reports of bullying, fights, and vandalism. Unless we deal with this problem now, someone may get seriously hurt. Students, administrators, school board members, and bus drivers need to get together and establish a workable safety plan for the buses.

Audience: grade school students

It's really important that you follow the rules on the bus. If you get out of your seat or act rowdy, someone might get hurt. Also, if someone is bothering you, make sure to report this person to the bus driver. Everyone must work together to keep our buses safe.

Audience: classmates

We need to set a better example on the school buses. Grade school kids look up to us, and they try to copy our behavior. If we act like jerks on the bus, the younger students are going to do the same thing. Someone is going to get hurt if things don't change. We are the young adults. Let's act like it.

Try It!

Rewrite a paragraph in one of your essays so that it speaks to a different audience. Discuss your rewrite with your classmates.

Understanding Diction

Diction is the level of language that you use based on the purpose and intended audience for a piece of writing. Here are the two basic levels of diction that you will use for most of your assigned writing.

Formal English

Your essays, research papers, and business letters should meet the standards of formal English. This level of language pays careful attention to word choice, follows the conventions for grammar and usage, and maintains a serious, objective (factual) tone throughout.

> Shakespeare lived in a rough-and-tumble world. He began his career as a poor actor in a traveling troupe, much like one of the "Rustics" in *A Midsummer Night's Dream*. Once in London, Shakespeare became a poor playwright, struggling to win audiences away from "bear baiting"—staged fights between bears and dogs.

Tip

Generally, avoid using *I, we,* and *you* in academic writing. Instead, focus on the topic itself and let your attitude be revealed indirectly.

Informal English

For many other pieces, such as personal narratives and feature articles, you may use a more informal level of language. Informal English usually includes some personal references, a few popular expressions, and shorter sentences.

> On Friday, I took my girlfriend Tasha to see *The Complete Works of William Shakespeare (Abridged)*. She loves Shakespeare, but I thought I'd just thrown away my Saturday night. The curtain opened, and out came three actors who said they were going to do all of Shakespeare's plays in an hour and a half. They started with *Romeo and Juliet*, with one of the guys in a dress.

Other Forms of Diction

- **Colloquial language** refers to expressions that are accepted in informal situations: I'll just hang out since I've got nothing better to do.
- **Slang** is language used by a particular group of people among themselves: Arissa drove to the hoop, got huge air, and slammed it for two.
- **Jargon** (technical diction) is the specialized language used by a specific group, such as those who use computers: The initialism PCMCIA means Peripheral Component Micro-Channel Interconnect Architecture.

Experimenting with Voice

Once you feel ready to experiment with your writing voice, consider the following activities.

Voice Activities

Change a piece of writing from one form to another: an essay to a short story or a poem. In your rewrite you will naturally change your voice.

Rework a piece of writing that you are still not happy with, even after you have turned it in. Try adding more personality to the piece.

Rewrite a piece by making something serious sound humorous, something light seem heavy.

Make a longer piece shorter and a shorter piece longer.

Experiment with different beginnings for your finished pieces.

Predict the questions a specific audience might ask about a piece of writing, perhaps a group of youngsters or a group of retirees, and then rewrite it.

Rewrite the best parts of your writing. See how many variations you can come up with.

Rework a piece of writing by cutting the first half and starting right in the middle.

Decide where you could digress in a piece of writing and do so. Digressions are little stories that are interesting but not directly essential to the writing.

Draw a shape and limit your writing within that shape.

Write an essay or a story in the voice of a favorite author.

Break some rules in your writing. Include some sentence fragments, sentences that never seem to end, sentences with no connecting words, and so on.

 ## Try It!

Try at least two or three of the activities listed above. After each activity, consider what you have learned about writing and voice.

Word Choice

Your writing style says something about you, but not in the same way as your clothes and hairstyle do. Your writing style reflects you on the inside—your thoughts, your feelings, your enthusiasm. And you should be glad to know that you don't have to be overly concerned about style, at least not for now. Style will develop naturally as you continue to read and write.

When you write, you should simply be yourself. Also, write about ideas and issues that are important to you; then revise your writing until you are satisfied with it. If you feel good about your writing, it probably reflects the "real" you. This chapter deals with one important aspect of style—the words you use. The best words are the ones that effectively add meaning, feeling, and sound to your writing.

- **Selecting Specific Nouns**
- **Choosing Vivid Verbs**
- **Using Effective Modifiers**
- **Including Sensory Details**
- **Understanding Word Connotation**
- **Identifying Problems with Word Choice**
- **Adding Style to Your Writing**

"Remember that the basic rule of vocabulary is use the first word that comes to mind, if it is appropriate and colorful."

—Stephen King

Selecting Specific Nouns

Nouns are an indispensable part of writing. Without them, you won't have much to say. Remember that some nouns *(boots, movement, fruit)* are general and give the reader a vague, uninteresting picture. Other nouns are specific *(cowboy boots, civil rights, mango)* and give the reader a clearer picture. Be sure to use appropriate specific nouns in your writing.

In the chart that follows, the first noun in each category is general. The second and third nouns are more specific, and those at the bottom of the chart are the most specific, the type of nouns that can make your writing clear.

General to Specific Nouns			
person	*place*	*thing*	*idea*
woman	school	book	pain
government official	university	novel	headache
Condoleezza Rice	Notre Dame	*The Great Gatsby*	migraine

Try It!

Create you own chart showing four sets of nouns *(person, place, thing,* and *idea)* that become progressively more specific. Use the chart above as a guide.

Revising for Specific Nouns

You've had enough experience as a writer to naturally use specific nouns in your stories and essays—most of the time. When you revise, just make sure that you haven't missed any opportunities to use specific nouns.

First draft sentence: Our teacher warned us about the test, saying our futures depend on it.

Revised version: Mr. Gardner warned us about the exit exam, saying our futures depend on it. (Two nouns are made more specific.)

Try It!

Write freely for 5 to 10 minutes about your favorite class. Afterward, circle any nouns that are too general. Substitute a more specific noun for each word that you have circled.

Choosing Vivid Verbs

Like nouns, verbs can be too general to create a clear word picture. For example, the verb *looked* does not say the same thing as *stared, glared, glanced, peeked,* or *inspected.* The statement "Officer Shaw *inspected* the crime scene" is much clearer than "Officer Shaw *looked* at the crime scene." The tips that follow will help you choose the best verbs for your writing.

- Whenever possible, use a verb that is strong enough to stand alone without the help of an adverb.

  Verb and adverb: Mr. Walters fell down in the hospital.

  Vivid verb: Mr. Walters collapsed in the hospital.

- Don't overuse the "be" verbs *(is, are, was, were, . . .).* Also avoid overusing *would, could,* or *should.* Often a better verb can be made from another word in the same sentence.

  A "be" verb: Yolanda is someone who plans for the future.

  A stronger verb: Yolanda plans for the future.

- Include active rather than passive verbs as much as possible.

  Passive verb: Another deep pass was launched by Geraldo.

  Active verb: Geraldo launched another deep pass.

- Work with verbs that show rather than tell.

  A verb that tells: Greta is very tall.

  A verb that shows: Greta towers over her teammates.

Revising for Vivid Verbs

When you revise a first draft for verbs, use the information above as a basic guide. Also remember that making every verb vivid and colorful may result in a forced, unnatural style. Instead, just change those verbs that you know will improve your writing.

First draft sentence: Mr. Gardner talked to us about the exit exam, saying our futures depend on it.

Revised version: Mr. Gardner warned us about the exit exam, saying our futures depend on it.

Try It!

Review the freewriting you did on the previous page. Change at least four or five verbs that are too general.

Using Effective Modifiers

The two main types of modifiers, adjectives and adverbs, can create clear and colorful word pictures for the reader. Just as fresh seasonings and sauces are essential to delicious entrées, specific modifiers are essential to clear writing.

Selecting Specific Adjectives

Follow these guidelines to choose strong adjectives that will clarify the nouns in your writing.

- Use adjective to create a clear picture for your reader.

      Unclear: My neighbor drove up in his convertible.

      Clear: My neighbor drove up in his *sleek, red* convertible.

- Avoid using adjectives that carry little meaning: *neat, big, pretty, small, cute, fun, bad, nice, good, great, funny,* and so on.

      Overused adjective: His old roadster is in storage.

      Specific adjective: His classic roadster is in storage.

- Use adjectives selectively so they don't lose their effectiveness.

      Too many adjectives: A tall, narrow column of thick, yellow smoke marked the exact spot where the unexpected explosion occurred.

      Selective use: A column of thick, yellow smoke marked the spot where the explosion occurred.

Choosing Specific Adverbs

Sometimes adverbs are needed to describe the action in a sentence.

      Okay: Mayor Meyer agreed to meet the protesters.

      Better: Mayor Meyer reluctantly agreed to meet the protesters.

 ## Try It!

Revise the following passage. You may substitute specific adjectives for overused ones, delete adjectives when too many are used, and add an adverb to describe the action.

It was three o'clock when my mother rushed down the hall waking us up. She told us to grab the dog and to get out of the house. The temperature began to rise as I ran down the steep, dark, winding stairs, and I was hit with a blast of hot air and the sound of breaking glass when I opened the wooden, paneled, decorative side door. The first thing I saw was my neighbor's nice red motorcycle explode with pieces flying in all directions, and I saw a bright blaze engulf a neat Honda.

Traits

Including Sensory Details

Sensory details are details that are experienced through the senses. They help a reader to see, feel, smell, taste, and hear what is being described. Here is a passage from a descriptive essay that contains sensory details:

> I stood backstage, surrounded by giggles and rustling gowns. The smell of talcum powder, hair spray, and rosin rolled in from the stage, and a familiar bitter taste filled my mouth. The music rose, and the dancers swept onto the stage in a frothy swirl of pink and blue.

Charting Your Senses

You can use a graphic organizer to collect sensory details for your writing. The chart below includes some of the sensory details one writer used in a personal narrative about his last football game. (Whether or not a writer covers all of the senses depends on the chosen topic.)

Sensory Chart

sights	sounds	smells	tastes	textures
the packed bleachers, bursting onto the field	rain tapping on my helmet, clip-clopping of our spikes	fresh popcorn, wet cut grass	plastic mouthpiece	chin strap tight across chin, spikes sinking in the muddy field

FYI

Keep in mind that different senses have different effects on the reader. For example, smells may be positive or negative. The smell of fresh popcorn suggests something good to the reader, while the stink of burning tires suggests something bad.

Try It!

Evaluate one of your personal narratives by filling in a chart like the one above with the sensory details you used. Then answer these questions: *Did you include enough sensory details? Which senses did you cover? Where could you use more sensory details?*

Understanding Word Connotation

The words in your writing should be specific and colorful, and they should also have the right connotation. The *connotation* of a word is the feeling it suggests beyond its dictionary definition. (The *denotation* of a word is its direct dictionary definition.) Note how the underlined words in the passage below suggest negative, almost depressing feelings about the subject, an abandoned building.

> The small factory had been <u>abandoned</u> long ago, each year <u>losing strength</u> until the roof <u>sagged</u> and the walls bowed with <u>fatigue</u>. Years had darkened the bricks to the color of <u>dried blood</u>, as though the life of the building had <u>seeped</u> out through its walls. The windows were <u>cracked</u> or <u>broken</u>, and a <u>weathered</u> piece of plywood <u>barred</u> the door. On that whole building, only one thing was new: a sign that read, "<u>Condemned</u>."

Charting Your Feelings

The following web includes some of the words that a writer gathered to suggest the excitement associated with going to the state championship as a basketball player.

Connotation Web

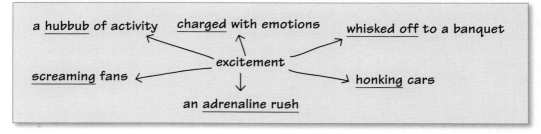

Try It!

First copy the following passage on your own paper. Then identify the main feeling suggested in the writing. Lastly, underline the words or phrases that suggest this feeling.

> The cool breeze whispered through the pine boughs. Branches rocked back and forth, sending bursts of pollen to pirouette on the wind before settling to the ground. Every tree in the grove danced in turn to the rhythm of the breeze. Watching and listening, Sarah breathed in the pine fragrance and swayed with the tree limbs.

Identifying Problems with Word Choice

The best words add to the meaning, tone, and sound of your writing. When you revise for word choice, check your work one passage at a time to discover what ought to be changed.

Checking For Problems

Listed below are common problems related to word choice. Your teacher may suggest other problems to address.

- **Redundancy** occurs when words or phrases are used together but mean the same thing.

  Original version: **I helped Carlos paint his car cherry red in color.**
  Revised version: **I helped Carlos paint his car cherry red.**

- **Repetition** occurs when words or phrases are unnecessarily repeated.

  Original version: **I knew that Carlos liked his car because he was always polishing the chrome on his car.**
  Revised version: **I knew that Carlos liked his car because he was always polishing the chrome.**

- **Jargon** refers to specialized words that are not adequately explained.

  Original version: **The spoiler improved the car's stability.**
  Revised version: **The spoiler—an air deflector on the trunk—improved the car's stability.**

- **Cliches** are overused phrases that give the reader nothing new.

  Original version: **Carlos's car is the apple of his eye.**
  Revised version: **Carlos treated his car like a beloved family member.**

Try It!

Identify and correct the word problem in each of the following sentences. (Corrections may vary.)

1. Everyone on the work detail wants to be teamed with Dorian because he is a jack-of-all-trades.
2. The book was interesting, but Josie was too tired to read the book.
3. After driving through a particularly rocky field, James checked the skid plate of his truck.
4. The sailboat is drifting helplessly, rising on the waves and falling on the waves.
5. Our principal's obstinate little boy stubbornly refuses to eat.

Adding Style to Your Writing

Metaphors can add style to your writing by comparing an idea to something new, creating a powerful image for the reader. (A metaphor compares two ideas without using *like* or *as*.)

Writing Metaphorically

Including effective metaphors can make your writing come alive. In the following examples, notice how the basic ideas are enhanced when stated metaphorically. (Be careful not to overuse this technique.)

Basic idea: **The loose papers in the wind float and dip above us.**

Metaphor: **The loose papers are silent seagulls soaring above us.**

Basic idea: **The sunset changes the color of the lake.**

Metaphor: **The sunset is a cauldron of molten metal poured over the lake.**

Points to Consider

- **Create original comparisons:** The student who wrote "Julia Roberts' last movie sent me to the moon" has spent too much time gazing into space and not enough time creating fresh comparisons.

- **Be clear in your thinking:** The student who wrote "Homelessness is a thorn in the city's image" has created a confusing figure of speech. Homelessness may be a thorn in the city's side, but not in its image.

- **Be consistent:** The reporter who wrote "In the final debate, Senator Jones dodged each of his opponent's accusations and eventually scored the winning shot" has created a mixed metaphor. He shifts from one comparison (boxing) to another (basketball).

FYI

Sometimes a metaphor can serve as the unifying element throughout a series of sentences. Extending a metaphor in this way clarifies an idea in your writing.

Try It!

Review one of your narratives or essays for two or three ideas that you can turn into metaphors. Afterward, share the results with a partner. *Does each metaphor create an effective image? Is the comparison original and clear?*

Sentence Fluency

You may be surprised if you study the writing style of accomplished authors. You are likely to find some sentences that flow on forever, some that are so short they sneak up on you, and some that are not, by definition, sentences at all. Writers do break the rules occasionally.

For the most part, writers work unscientifically. They don't say, "Gee, a compound sentence sure would work well here" or "It's time that I use a complex sentence." Instead, they go with what feels right at the moment. Then, when they revise, they pay attention to the sentences that don't work for them—often rewriting them many times until they have the right sound, balance, and substance.

This chapter identifies key features of effective sentence writing as well as certain sentence problems to avoid. Use this information as a guide to help you develop your own sense of sentence style.

- **Varying Your Sentences**
- **Sentence Combining**
- **Sentence Expanding**
- **Using Repetition for Effect**
- **Checking for Sentence Problems**
- **Checking for Additional Problems**

"Don't worry about writing the perfect sentence or you'll never get past the first line."

—Jan Greenberg

Varying Your Sentences

According to author William Zinsser, writing in which "all the sentences move at the same plodding gait" is deadly. Such writing lacks sentence variety.

Varying Sentence Beginnings

If all of your sentences begin in the same way, they will sound stilted and robotic. To avoid this problem, vary your beginnings.

Starting with the Main Subject

Original version: The U.S.S. *Constitution,* known as Old Ironsides, is a famous United States sailing ship that workers began building in 1794. Old Ironsides was one of six ships approved by Congress to fight piracy. This ship helped defeat the Barbary pirates during its years of service.

Varied Beginnings

Revised version: In 1794 workers began to build the famous U.S.S. *Constitution* sailing ship known as Old Ironsides. This ship was one of six approved by Congress to fight piracy. During its years of service, Old Ironsides helped defeat the Barbary pirates.

Varying Sentence Lengths

A series of sentences that are similar in length may also sound robotic. To avoid this problem, write sentences of different lengths.

Similar Lengths

Original version: Amateur photographers once relied on film for taking pictures. In recent years, however, that has all changed. Today's amateurs are replacing film cameras with digital ones. Consumers are gleefully embracing changes in this industry.

Varied Lengths

Revised version: Amateur photographers once relied on film for taking pictures. That has all changed. Today's amateurs, gleefully embracing changes in the industry, are replacing film cameras with digital ones.

Try It!

Find a passage in something you have written in which all (or most) of the sentences begin with the main subject. Rewrite this passage, varying the sentence beginnings. Then do the same for a passage in which all (or most) of the sentences are similar in length.

"Have something to say and say it as clearly as you can. That is the only secret of style."
—Matthew Arnold

Sentence Combining

Sentence combining, which can be done in a variety of ways, can help you improve fluency. By combining a series of short, choppy sentences, you create a smooth-reading, longer sentence.

Combining Shorter Ideas

Suppose you were writing about a tornado that struck a small town without warning, causing extensive damage, a number of serious injuries, and several deaths. You wouldn't put each idea into a separate sentence. Instead, you would combine the ideas in a variety of ways.

- Use a **series** to combine three or more similar ideas.
  The tornado struck the small town, causing extensive damage, numerous injuries, **and** several deaths.

- Use a **relative pronoun** *(who, whose, that, which)* to link two related ideas.
  The tornado, which was completely unexpected, **swept through the small town.**

- Use an **introductory phrase** or **clause** to link two related ideas.
  Because the tornado was unexpected, **it caused extensive damage, numerous injuries, and several deaths.**

- Use a **participial phrase** *(-ing, -ed)* to begin or end a sentence.
  The tornado swept through the town, leaving a trail of death and destruction.

- Use an **appositive** to emphasize a key point.
  A single incident, a tornado that came without warning, **changed the face of a small town forever.**

- Repeat a **key word** or phrase to emphasize an idea.
  The unexpected tornado left a permanent scar **on the small town, a** scar **of destruction, injury, and death.**

Try It!

Consider these ideas: A group of students have volunteered for a six-month period to clean and paint homes owned by older people in your neighborhood. Compose at least four sentences, combining these ideas in different ways.

Sentence Expanding

Experienced writers often expand a basic idea by adding engaging details. A sentence that expands an idea in this way is called a *cumulative sentence*. The main idea is modified by words, phrases, or clauses. In the following sentence, the main clause (in blue) precedes the modifying phrases.

> **Maly was studying at the kitchen table,** memorizing a list of vocabulary words, completely focused, intent on acing tomorrow's Spanish quiz.

In the cumulative sentence that follows, modifiers are placed before and after the main clause (in blue):

> **Before every practice,** Kesha Sims and Tonya Harper work on free throws, **taking 50 shots each.**

FYI

There are five basic ways to expand upon a main clause:

Individual words: Jose prepared his breakfast *quickly.*

Prepositional phrases: Jose ate *with his cat on his lap.*

Participial (-*ing* or –*ed*) phrases: *Looking at the clock,* Jose gobbled his first piece of toast.

Subordinating clauses: Jose was still eating *when his mother left for work.*

Relative clauses: The cat, *who loves leftovers,* purred for a treat.

Try It!

Expand each of these main clauses by adding at least two modifying words, phrases, or clauses.

1. Toshi entered the store.
2. Alberto and Benito ran onto the field.
3. Mr. Gardner talked to the student.
4. The car squealed around the corner.
5. Our dog Max watches us eat.

Using Repetition for Effect

You can use repetition to add rhythm, emphasis, and unity to your sentences. The repeated words or ideas must be parallel, or stated in the same way. (The examples below are all parallel in structure.) As with any stylistic technique, repetition is effective only when used selectively.

For Rhythm and Balance: Notice how each series of words or phrases creates a smooth rhythm in the following sentences.

> **At one time or another,** the Austrians, the Russians, **and** the British **fought against Napoleon's army.**

> **That scrumptious sandwich contains** tender ham, crisp lettuce, **and** juicy tomatoes.

> **Jumal wants to** graduate from college, become a volunteer medic, **and** work in the African sub-Sahara.

For Emphasis and Effect: Repeating a basic sentence structure intensifies the feeling in these passages.

> **Mom and Dad danced in the rain.** They waltzed cheek to cheek; they schottisched side by side; they do-si-doed arm in arm. **Because the drought had broken, the wheat would grow.**
> —Mary Anne Hoff

> We shall fight on the beaches, we shall fight on the landing grounds, we shall fight in the fields and in the streets, we shall fight in the hills: we shall never surrender.
> —Winston Churchill

For Unity and Organization: The repeated idea beginning each series of thoughts unifies this passage.

> I see Grandfather Aurelio in the **wrinkled black-and-white photo, his eyes young and sharp as he looked beyond the hills of Sicily to America.** I see Grandfather Aurelio in the **folded napkins that bear his name, in the checkered tablecloths and the wooden chairs of his Brooklyn restaurant.** I see Grandfather Aurelio in my **father's face, the keen eyes and granite jaw, the care lines carved by 50 years of clanking dishes and hot ovens.**

Try It!

Find two or three examples of effective repetition in books, magazines, and newspapers. Share the examples with your classmates. Then experiment with repetition in your own writing.

Checking for Sentence Problems

Complete, correct sentences can contain several ideas. The trick is getting those ideas to work together and make sense. Incorrect sentences can disrupt the flow of your writing and leave the reader with nothing but questions. The most common errors are fragments, comma splices, run-ons, and rambling sentences.

Watching for Fragments

A sentence fragment lacks a subject, a verb, or some other essential part. Because of the missing part, the thought is incomplete.

Fragment: **Spaghetti all over the table.** (This fragment lacks a verb.)

Corrected: **Spaghetti slipped all over the table.**

Fragment: **When Aneko opened the box.** (This fragment does not express a complete thought. We need to know what happened "when Aneko opened the box.")

Corrected: **When Aneko opened the box, spaghetti slipped all over the table.**

Fragment: **Laughing and scooping up a pile of spaghetti. Kate remarked, "Now, that's what I call a spaghetti mess!"** (The fragment, a participial phrase, is followed by a complete sentence. It can be combined with the sentence that follows it.)

Corrected: **Laughing and scooping up a pile of spaghetti, Kate remarked, "Now, that's what I call a spaghetti mess!"**

FYI

You can use fragments if you have a good reason. For example, dialogue often contains fragments. You can also use single words or phrases for dramatic effect. In one of her articles, writer Anna Quindlan uses the following three fragments to emphasize the problems facing urban youths:

"Teenage mothers. Child abuse. Crowded schools."

Try It!

Rewrite the following passage, correcting any fragments that you find.

When I tripped and fell. I must have tried to brace myself. Looking over my shoulder, I spotted the problem. A root the color of the ground. Spikes of pain up my left arm as I tried to stand. Feeling woozy, I sat back down. After resting a bit, again to get back on my feet.

Checking for Comma Splices

A comma splice results when two independent clauses are connected with only a comma. A period, semicolon, or conjunction is needed to correct this error.

Comma splice: **The concertgoers had been waiting for two hours, many of them were becoming impatient.**

Corrected: **The concertgoers had been waiting for two hours, and many of them were becoming impatient. (A coordinating conjunction has been added.)**

Corrected: **The concertgoers had been waiting for two hours; many of them were becoming impatient. (A semicolon replaces the comma.)**

Revising Run-On Sentences

A run-on is two (or more) sentences joined without adequate punctuation or a connecting word. To correct this error, turn the run-on into two sentences or into a compound sentence.

Run-On: **I thought the ride would never end my eyes were crossed, and my fingers were numb.**

Corrected: **I thought the ride would never end. My eyes were crossed, and my fingers were numb.**

Try It!

Rewrite the following passage, correcting the comma splices and run-ons.

Technicians have installed a new computerized telescope in Arizona. This special telescope uses two mirrors they act like a pair of binoculars to make distant objects easier to observe. The telescope can also neutralize the refraction problem caused by the atmosphere, this capability makes very clear pictures of celestial bodies possible. Astronomers hope to uncover secrets of the universe using this device.

Avoiding Rambling Sentences

A rambling sentence seems to go on and on (often because it includes too many *and*'s). To correct this error, remove some of the *and*'s and recast as necessary.

Rambling: **The intruder entered through the window and tiptoed down the hall and stood under the stairwell and waited in the shadows.**

Corrected: **The intruder entered through the window. He tiptoed down the hall and stood under the stairwell, waiting in the shadows.**

Checking for Additional Problems

The following errors can confuse a reader. Avoiding them will make your sentences clear and readable.

Checking for Misplaced Modifiers

Misplaced modifiers are modifiers that have been placed incorrectly, muddying the meaning of the sentence.

> **Misplaced:** **We have an assortment of combs for physically active people with unbreakable teeth.** (People with unbreakable teeth?)

> **Corrected:** **For physically active people, we have an assortment of combs with unbreakable teeth.**

Looking for Dangling Modifiers

Dangling modifiers are modifiers that appear to modify the wrong word or a word that isn't in the sentence.

> **Dangling:** **After standing in line for five hours, the manager announced that all the tickets had been sold.** (The manager stood in line?)

> **Corrected:** **After I stood in line for five hours, the manager announced that all the tickets had been sold.**

Correcting any Double Negatives

A double negative is the improper use of two negative words to perform the same function in a sentence. (Using *hardly, barely,* or *scarcely* with *no* or *not* also results in a double negative.)

> **Double negative:** **I don't have no money.**

> **Corrected:** **I don't have any money.** (or) **I have no money.**

Try It!

Rewrite each of the following sentences, correcting the misplaced modifier, the dangling modifier, or the double negative.

1. Hanna hardly had no money left to buy lunch.
2. After passing the written test, my driving instructor told me I was ready for behind-the-wheel practice.
3. Dale bought the classic DVD's for his father in the glass display case.
4. I found an old suitcase under my father's workbench made of leather.
5. Meeka couldn't find no rock sample in the box.

Conventions

Effective writing is edited with care to ensure that the work is clear and correct. It follows the conventions of our language, the accepted standards of punctuation, mechanics, spelling, and grammar. To check your own writing for conventions, it's important to have the proper editing tools on hand—including the "Proofreader's Guide" in this book (pages **604–763**), a dictionary, a thesaurus, a computer spell-checker, and so on.

Like other aspects of writing, the best way to learn about the conventions is to pay attention to them—in conversations, in reading, and in writing. As writer Stephen King says, "One either absorbs the grammatical principles of one's native language . . . or one does not." The grammar work that you do in your English classes adds to your understanding of the language in two basic ways. It helps you (1) to recognize and name the different parts of the language and (2) to know what to look for when you edit your writing. The next page serves as a helpful guide for checking the conventions in your writing.

- **A Quick Guide to Conventions**

"I really never knew what editing was until I started reading my own stuff and thinking about it and listening to it."

—Sandra Belton

"The best writers may not follow every rule every time, but they follow most of them most of the time."
—Patricia T. O'Conner

A Quick Guide to Conventions

Checking for conventions becomes especially important near the end of a writing project to be sure that your work is free of errors.

Starting Point: You're ready to check for conventions once you . . .

- complete your major revisions—adding, cutting, rewriting, or rearranging the ideas in your writing;
- make a clean copy of your revised writing; and
- set your writing aside for a day or two (if time permits).

When you check for conventions, try to focus on one type of error at a time. This will help you edit more carefully and thoroughly. (See page **128** for a checklist.)

Tip

Have someone else check your work as well. You're too close to your writing to spot everything that needs to be changed.

Form: If you're working with pen and paper, do your editing with a different color of ink on a neat copy of your revised writing. Then complete a final copy of your work.

If you're working on a computer, do your editing on a printed copy of your writing and key in the changes. Save the edited copy so you have a record of your changes.

The Big Picture: When you check for conventions, remember that you are looking for punctuation, mechanics, spelling, or grammar errors.

- **Punctuation:** Review your work for all forms of punctuation; however, the most common errors involve commas and apostrophes. (See pages **130–131**, **608–617**, and **628–631**.)
- **Mechanics and spelling:** Check your writing for capitalization, the use of numbers, and spelling. (See pages **648–653** and **656–665**.)
- **Grammar:** Review your work for grammar errors. Pay special attention to subject-verb agreement, pronoun-antecedent agreement, and usage errors. (See pages **130–131** and **604–763**.)

Presentation

Writer Peter Stillman says, "No piece of writing, regardless of how much you polish and fuss with it, comes out exactly as you want it to." That may be true, but you can come close, especially if you put forth your best effort—prewriting through publishing (or presentation). If you truly care about your writing and stick with it, there's a good chance that you will produce a quality finished product, one that you really can feel good about.

Presenting the reader with a neat final copy puts the stamp of approval on your writing. Of course, working with a computer makes it easy to produce clean, easy-to-read copy. If you understand the design features on your word-processing program, you can do much more, such as incorporating graphics and charts into your text. This chapter will help you make the best design choices for your academic essays and articles.

- **Designing Your Writing**
- **Effective Design in Action**
- **Adding Graphics**

"Form follows function—that has been misunderstood. Form and function should be one, joined in a spiritual union."

—Frank Lloyd Wright

Designing Your Writing

The test of a good page design is that your writing is clear and easy to follow. Consider these guidelines for creating clean, attractive essays and articles.

Selecting an Appropriate Font

- **Choose an easy-to-read font for the main text.** In most cases, a serif typestyle is best for the text, and a sans serif style works for any headings. For most forms of writing, use a 12-point type size. Use **boldface** for headings if they seem to get lost on the paper.

  The letters of serif fonts have "tails"—as in this sentence.

  The letters of sans serif fonts are plain, without tails—as in this sentence.

- **Make titles and headings short and to the point.** Headings of equal importance should be stated in the same way. Follow the basic rules for capitalizing titles and headings. (See page **650**.)

Using Consistent Spacing and Margins

- **Set clear margins.** Use a one-inch margin around each page (top, bottom, left, and right).
- **Hit the tab key to indent the first line of each paragraph.** This key should be set at five spaces.
- **Leave one space after every period.** This will improve the readability of your paper.
- **Avoid placing headings, hyphenated words, and first lines of new paragraphs at the bottom of a page.** Also avoid single-word lines at either the bottom or the top of a page.

Including Graphic Elements

- **Use lists if appropriate.** Use numbered lists if your points have a clear number order. Otherwise, use bulleted lists (like the ones on this page).
- **Include graphics.** Use tables, charts, or illustrations to help make a point. Keep graphics small within the text. If a graphic is complex and needs to be large, display it on its own page. (See page **95**.)

Try It!

Compare an article from an entertainment, hobby, or special interest newsmagazine with an article in a newsmagazine like *Time* or *Newsweek*. *Which design elements are the same? Which are different? Explain how the design of each article fits the intended audience.*

Effective Design in Action

The following two pages from a student essay show effective design elements.

McGinn 1

Kendall McGinn
Mr. Gilding
Social Studies
March 25, 2010

> The title is 18-point sans serif type.

The Return of the Buffalo

At one point in the early twentieth century, it seemed that the American buffalo would continue to exist only in pictures or on the buffalo nickel. Its population of 100 million in 1700 had been reduced to 1,000 by 1889. In recent years, that number has increased to nearly 400,000 (Hodgson 71). The buffalo, once endangered, has returned.

> The main text is 12-point serif type.

Before the Europeans came to North America, the native people of the North American plains and the buffalo were one *Pte Oyate,* or Buffalo Nation. The big bull *tatanka* was life itself. These Native Americans followed the herds and used the buffalo for food, clothing, shelter, religious ceremonies, and medicine. A Lakota leader summed up this unity between human and animal: "When the Creator made the buffalo, he put power in them. When you eat the meat, that power goes into you, heals the body and spirit" (qtd. in Hodgson 69).

> The heading is 14-point sans serif type.

Open Season on Buffalo

During the westward expansion of the United States, European settlers did not consider buffalo to be sacred and slaughtered many for sport. As trains thundered west, Europeans often shot into buffalo herds, killing hundreds of creatures and leaving their carcasses to rot by the rails. Though 30 million buffalo roamed the plains in 1800, after a century of westward expansion, only 1,000 of the creatures remained ("Near-Extinct").

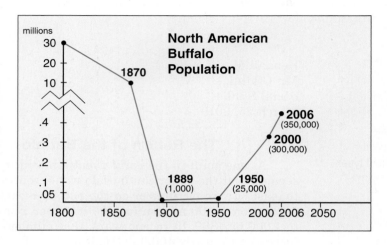

North American Buffalo Population

A graphic provides information in a visual way.

Buffalo as Livestock

Buffalo ranchers are, in fact, learning that raising buffalo has many benefits. Raising buffalo is more cost-effective and more environmentally safe than raising cattle. Here are four main benefits:

A bulleted list is easy to read.

- Buffalo don't overeat.
- Their sharp hooves loosen hard soil.
- Buffalo improve grass crops.
- They adapt to any climate.

Buffalo living in Florida seem just as happy as those living in Alaska. In Hawaii, they even survived a hurricane. Hawaiian rancher Bill Mowry recalls how the buffalo "loved every minute of it" (qtd. in Allen 105).

Try It!

Redesign all or part of one of your essays using the information on pages 92–95 as a guide. Share the new version with your classmates.

Adding Graphics

When adding graphics to your writing, make sure you aren't simply "dressing up" the words. Instead, include graphics to add information or enhance the reader's understanding. Follow these guidelines:

Use tables to provide statistics in a compact form. Clearly label rows and columns so that the reader can quickly grasp the information.

COMPARING COUNTRIES			
	Canada	Mexico	United States
Size (Sq. Miles)	3.85 million	759,000	3.8 million
Type of Government	Parliamentary	Republic	Republic
Voting Age	18	18	18
Literacy	99%	87%	98%

Use graphs to show statistics visually. Line graphs show how quantities change over time. Bar graphs compare and contrast amounts. Pie graphs show the parts of a whole. Be sure to provide a clear title, labels, and a legend (if needed).

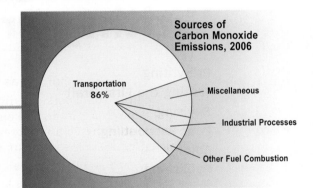

Sources of Carbon Monoxide Emissions, 2006

Transportation 86%

Miscellaneous

Industrial Processes

Other Fuel Combustion

Use diagrams to show the parts of something. Include labels or arrows to inform the reader about the parts being shown.

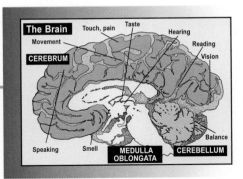

The Brain

Touch, pain — Taste — Hearing
Movement — Reading
CEREBRUM — Vision
Speaking — Smell — MEDULLA OBLONGATA — CEREBELLUM — Balance

Try It!

Review essays you have written and select one that could include a table, chart, or diagram. Create a graphic that demonstrates important ideas or statistics in the essay.

Exploring the Writing Process

Prewriting

Writer and teacher James Burke says, "Good writing is built, not born. It requires time." Approaching writing as a process allows for effective "building" to take place. As you know, prewriting is the first step in the writing process. During prewriting, you (1) select a specific topic, (2) gather information about it, (3) establish a focus (thesis) to guide your writing, and (4) organize the details that support your focus. Prewriting also refers to any additional research and planning that you may do after you've begun to write.

The amount of prewriting you do depends on the writing project. If you are writing about a personal experience, you may do very little planning. On the other hand, if you are developing a complex persuasive essay, you may do a great deal of research and planning. Whatever the case, giving prewriting the proper attention will lay a solid foundation for all the other steps in the writing process.

- **Selecting a Topic**
- **Gathering Details**
- **Finding Additional Information**
- **A Closer Look at Prewriting**
- **Forming Your Thesis Statement**
- **Organizing Your Details**

"Writing is a long process of self-understanding."
—Edwidge Danticat

Selecting a Topic

Your teacher may provide you with a general subject and ask that you narrow it to a specific topic

General Subject: Abolitionist movement
Specific Topic: Siege of fort at Harper's Ferry

Depending on the assignment, use one of the following strategies to select an effective, specific writing topic.

Keeping a Writer's Notebook

Write on a regular basis in a personal notebook (journal), exploring your experiences and thoughts. Review your entries on occasion and underline ideas that you could explore in writing assignments. (See pages **1–5** for more information.)

Developing a Cluster

Begin a cluster with a nucleus word, usually a general term or idea related to your writing assignment. Then cluster related words around it.

Sample Cluster

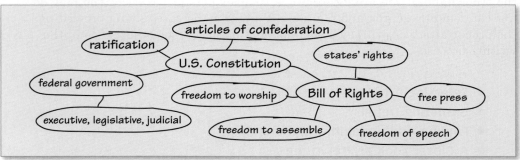

Note: After 3 or 4 minutes, scan your cluster for a word or an idea that interests you. Write nonstop about that idea for 5 to 8 minutes. A few writing topics should begin to occur to you.

Making a List

Begin with a thought or a key word related to your assignment and simply start listing words and ideas. Listing ideas with a group of classmates (brainstorming) is also an effective way to search for writing topics.

Trying Freewriting

Begin writing with a particular focus in mind—one that is related to your assignment. Write nonstop for 5 to 10 minutes to discover possible writing topics.

- Don't stop to judge, edit, or correct your writing.
- Keep writing even when you seem to be drawing a blank. If necessary, write "I'm drawing a blank" until a new idea comes to mind.
- Review your writing and underline ideas you like.
- Continue freewriting about ideas you want to explore further.

Sample Freewriting

> Unlike the citizens of a lot of other countries, we have the freedom of assembly. Our Constitution guarantees that. That means students or teachers or any group can get together to talk about our country. We can debate the work of the government and ask questions. We don't have to worry about being arrested. Our first political thinkers, who helped . . .

Considering the "Basics of Life" List

Below you will find a list of the essential elements in our lives. The list provides an endless variety of topic possibilities. For example, the category *education* led to the following writing ideas:

- internships for high school students
- community service requirements
- open campus vs. closed campus

Basics of Life

clothing	education	love	entertainment
communication	machines	rules/laws	health/medicine
exercise/training	faith/religion	science/technology	recreation
housing	family	energy	literature/books
community	trade/money	land/property	tools/utensils
food	agriculture	work/occupation	freedom/rights
arts/music	heat/fuel		

Try It!

List four or five possible writing ideas for any two categories in the "Basics of Life" list. (For your next writing assignment, use one of the strategies above to identify possible topics.)

Gathering Details

Once you've selected a specific topic, you need to gather details for writing. In most cases, it's a good idea to first collect your initial thoughts about the topic, including personal experience and past knowledge. Then, if necessary, do research to find more information.

Gathering Your Thoughts

The following strategies will help you to recall what you already know and establish how you feel about your topic.

- **Freewriting:** At this point, you can approach freewriting in two ways. (1) You can do a focused freewriting, exploring your topic from a number of different angles. (2) You can approach your freewriting as if it were a quick version of the actual paper.
- **5 W's:** Answer the 5 W questions—*who? what? when? where?* and *why?*—to identify basic information about your topic. Add *how?* to the list for even better coverage.
- **Audience appeal:** Address a specific audience as you write about your topic. Consider a group of parents, a live television audience, or the readers of a popular teen magazine.
- **Directed writing:** Write whatever comes to mind about your topic, using the questions listed below.

Describe it.	What do you see, hear, feel, smell, or taste?
Compare it.	What is it similar to? What is it different from?
Apply it.	What can you do with it? How can you use it?
Associate it.	What connections between this and something else come to mind?
Analyze it.	What parts does it have? How do they work together?
Argue for or against it.	What do you like about it? What don't you like about it? What are its strengths and its weaknesses?

- **Directed dialoguing:** Create a dialogue between two people in which your specific topic is the focus of the conversation. This writing will help you explore differing opinions about the topic.

Try It!

Gather your initial thoughts. Use one of these strategies when you are ready to collect your own thoughts about a writing topic.

Finding Additional Information

For most writing assignments, it won't suffice to simply gather your own thoughts about a topic. Expository and persuasive essays, for example, will almost always require that you consult other sources for information. These sources can be divided into two categories—*primary* and *secondary*.

Exploring a Variety of Sources

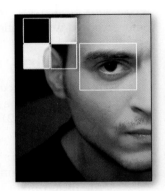

- **Primary sources** include interviews, personal observations, firsthand experiences, surveys, experiments, and so on. A primary source informs you directly, not through another person's explanation or interpretation.
- **Secondary sources** include periodicals, books, references, Web sites, and so on. A secondary source is one that contains information other people have gathered and interpreted. It is at least once removed from the original.

Tips for Researching

Follow these guidelines when gathering information:

- Whenever possible, use both primary and secondary sources to get a thorough understanding of your topic.
- Read secondary sources with a critical eye, always evaluating the quality and the purpose of the information. (See page **373**.)
- Take careful notes, writing down important facts, opinions, and quotations. Record any source information you will need to cite. (See page **399**.)
- Consider using a graphic organizer such as a gathering grid (page **396**) to keep track of the facts and details your research uncovers.
- Consult librarians and teachers if you have trouble finding useful sources of information.

Try It!

Identify the best resources. List at least one or two primary sources and one or two secondary sources that you could use to gather information for each of the following writing assignments:

- an article about a high school basketball game
- an editorial about cutting park jobs for students
- an essay about the quality of medical care during the Civil War
- a research paper exploring some aspect of U.S. immigration policy

Process

"The discipline of the writer is to learn to be still and listen to what his subject has to tell him."
—Rachel Carson

A Closer Look at Prewriting

After you've selected a topic and gathered details about it, you can plan and write your first draft, or you can consider how well you match up with your topic before you go any further.

Taking Inventory of Your Thoughts

After carefully considering the questions that follow, you will be ready to (1) move ahead with your writing or (2) change your topic.

Purpose

- Does my topic meet the requirements of the assignment?
- Am I writing to explain, persuade, describe, entertain, or retell?

Self

- How do I feel about the topic? Have I made a personal connection with it?
- Do I have enough time to develop it?

Topic

- How much more do I need to know about this topic?
- Has my research changed my thinking about the topic?
- What part of the topic will I focus on?

Audience

- Who are my readers?
- How much do they already know about my topic?
- How can I keep them interested in my ideas?

Form

- How should I present my ideas—in a story, an essay, a report, a multimedia presentation?
- What form of writing should I use—narrative, descriptive, persuasive, expository?

Forming Your Thesis Statement

After you have explored the topic and collected information, you should begin to develop a more focused interest in your topic. If all goes well, this interest will become the thesis of your writing. **A thesis statement identifies the focus of an academic essay.** It usually highlights a particular condition, feature, or feeling about the topic or takes a stand.

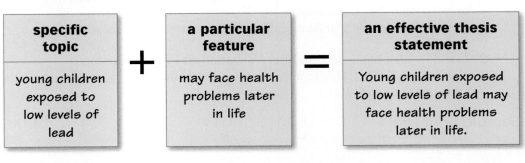

specific topic	**+**	**a particular feature**	**=**	**an effective thesis statement**
young children exposed to low levels of lead		may face health problems later in life		Young children exposed to low levels of lead may face health problems later in life.

Sample Thesis Statements

Writing Assignment: Essay about opportunities in education
Specific Subject: High school internships
Thesis Statement: Internship programs **(specific topic)** give students real-world experiences **(particular feature)**.

Writing Assignment: Essay on the Civil War
Specific Subject: General George McClellan
Thesis Statement: General George McClellan's overcautious tactics **(specific topic)** prolonged the war **(particular feeling)**.

Try It!

Rewrite each of the following thesis statements on your own paper. Circle the specific topic. Then underline the part of the statement that identifies the feature, feeling, or stand that will be developed.

1. The new graduated licensing laws have had a positive effect on young drivers.
2. Tighter immigration policies will negatively impact the American way of life.
3. Bilingual education benefits English learners and mainstream students.
4. The pressures of being the best can overload some students.
5. Practicing conflict resolution reduces violence in schools.

Organizing Your Details

After forming a thesis statement, you may need to design a writing plan before you start your first draft. Your plan can be anything from a brief list of ideas to a detailed sentence outline. Use the guidelines that follow to help organize your details for writing.

1. Study your thesis statement. It may suggest a logical method of organization for your essay.

2. Review the details you have gathered. Be sure all of them support your thesis.

3. Decide which basic pattern of organization fits your essay topic—chronological, spatial, compare-contrast, problem-solution, and so on. (See pages **584–588**.)

Sample Brief List

Topic: Freedom of Assembly
- Opposition to citizen assemblies
- Opportunities for debate
- Concerns about society and government
- Suggestions for change

Sample Sentence Outline

Topic: Freedom of Assembly

I. Tyrants or dictators oppose citizen assemblies.
   A. Dictators know it is easier to control people who are uninformed.
   B. People might learn that many oppose certain policies.
   C. Such meetings might lead to the overthrow of the dictator.
II. Citizens have the right to assemble for any number of purposes.
   A. Government cannot restrict who may or may not assemble.
   B. United States citizens have a right to decide . . .

Writing the First Draft

Once you have collected and organized your details, you're ready to write your first draft. Note the word "first." This is your first chance to develop your prewriting into a complete, cohesive unit of writing.

There can be a great satisfaction in writing a first draft, an excitement at seeing your initial thinking about a topic take shape. Write your first draft freely without being overly concerned about correctness. Your goal is to get all your ideas on paper in a form that is easy to follow. Use the planning you've done (outline) as a basic guide, but be open to new ideas that come to mind as you write.

If you are writing an essay or a research paper, develop each main point in a separate paragraph. Also connect the paragraphs with linking words or transitions. The information in this chapter provides many additional drafting tips and strategies.

- **Considering the Big Picture**
- **Writing the Beginning**
- **Developing the Middle**
- **Writing the Ending**

"If you want to write, you must begin by beginning, continue by continuing, finish by finishing. This is the great secret."

—Jack Heffron

Considering the Big Picture

As you prepare to write a first draft, keep in mind these three traits of good writing: *ideas, organization,* and *voice.*

Ideas Develop the main points you formed during your prewriting. Write freely, and don't be afraid to add new ideas as they come to you.

Organization Using your planning as a guide, get all of your thoughts on paper. Remember to include a beginning, a middle, and an ending. (See below.)

Voice Let your words flow naturally and freely, almost as if you were in a conversation with the reader.

Drafting Hints

- *Review your prewriting materials before you begin.*
- *If you are writing by hand, write on every other line; if you are writing on a computer, double-space your work so you will have room to revise.*
- *Don't be overly concerned about being neat and avoiding errors. You can make corrections later on.*

Remembering the Parts of Writing

As you write, keep in mind the three parts of any writing: the beginning, the middle, and the ending.

The Beginning

- gets the reader's attention
- identifies the thesis or purpose of your writing

The Middle

- presents the main points that support the thesis
- includes details that develop the main points

The Ending

- restates the thesis
- wraps up the paper

Try It!

Be sure to review this page before you write your next first draft. Afterward, assess your results. *Did you write naturally and freely? Did you get all of your ideas on paper? Did you include all three parts— beginning, middle, and ending?*

Writing the Beginning

Your opening paragraph should "hook" the reader with its interesting information. Here are some ways to attract the reader's interest.

Grabbing Your Reader's Attention

- Give a surprising fact or statement.
  The Bushmen of Kalahari face extinction; yet, ironically, it is modern tourism that might save them.

- Ask a question.
  With the world rapidly changing, how is it that one group of people has survived without modern conveniences?

- Use a relevant quotation.
  "If the government has its way, my people will be gone," says a member of the once proud Bushmen tribe.

- Present an interesting detail about the topic.
  In the wild, inhospitable Kalahari Basin, a hardy people live much as their ancestors did 30,000 years ago.

Shaping Your Beginning Paragraph

The first part of your opening paragraph should identify your topic and hook the reader. Follow with any necessary background information. End with your thesis statement, identifying the specific part of the topic you plan to emphasize.

Sample Beginning Paragraph

Attention-getting opening	*"If the government has its way, my people will be gone," says a member of the once proud Bushmen tribe.* **Although the tribe has lived in the African Kalahari Basin for more than 30,000 years, its members are now being relocated and modernized by the government. Soon the remaining members of the tribe will have either died out or become assimilated. Because of modernization and greed, the lifestyle of the Kalahari Bushmen is in jeopardy.**
Background information	
Thesis statement	

Try It!

Analyze the opening paragraph of one of the essays in this book. Using the information above as a guide, tell how the opening accomplishes its purpose.

Developing the Middle

Your middle paragraphs should contain the details that support your thesis. Here are some ways to support your thesis:

Explain: Provide important facts, details, and examples.

Narrate: Share a brief story (anecdote) to illustrate or clarify an idea.

Describe: Tell how someone appears or how something works.

Summarize: Present only the most important ideas.

Define: Identify or clarify the meaning of a specific term or idea.

Argue: Use logic and evidence to prove something is true.

Compare: Show how two things are alike or different.

Analyze: Examine the parts of something to better understand the whole.

Reflect: Express your thoughts or feelings about something.

FYI

Most essays, articles, and research papers require a number of these methods to thoroughly develop their theses. For example, an essay of definition may contain two or more definitions, a comparison, a brief story, and so on.

Using Various Types of Support

Below and on the next page are some examples of how one student used various types of support in his paper about the Bushmen of the Kalahari.

Define: Identify or clarify the meaning of a specific term or idea.

> The people of the Kalahari go by several names, depending on the regional language. Some call the natives "San," a Khoi word that means "outsider," or "Basarwa," a Herero word meaning "person who has nothing." Understandably, the Kalahari people themselves prefer to be called, simply, "Bushmen."

Explain: Provide important facts, details, and examples.

> The drive to relocate the Bushmen is just one more—perhaps the last—chapter in a story of cultural annihilation. For more than 30,000 years, the Bushmen lived as peaceful hunter-gatherers until they were made slaves by Afrikaner farmers to the south and the Tswana tribes to the north. In the 1960s, the Central Kalahari Game Reserve was established to preserve their way of life, but in the 1980s, the Botswana government, embarrassed by the backward image projected by the Bushmen, decided to bring them into the present. The natives were forcibly resettled in the city, into a life of squalor and humiliation.

Compare: Show how two things are alike or different.

> Botswana's treatment of this indigenous people can be compared with the United States' treatment of Native Americans. In 2002, the Botswana government began relocating the native Bushmen to "settlements" in much the same way that Native Americans were placed on reservations by the United States government. Both groups have suffered a loss of their culture through the insensitivity of the ruling government. Unfortunately, the transplanted Bushmen battle alcoholism and poverty in much the same way as Native Americans have done in this country. The Bushmen, like Native Americans, are also beginning to use the courts to reclaim their land. In both cases, the government has insisted that relocation is actually good for the people.

Analyze: Examine the parts of something to better understand the whole.

> The reasons given for the relocation are suspect when examined closely. The government cites environmental reasons, stating that the growth of farming in the area has lowered the water table. This provides the financial reason for resettlement: the expense of bringing in water for the Bushmen's use. Finally, the government alleges that the change is for the people's own good, that their archaic culture must adapt to a changing society so they can live better lives. Despite all this rhetoric, it is interesting to note that the Bushmen's territory is a valuable diamond area. Moving the natives opens the way for extensive—and lucrative—mining.

Summarize: Present only the most important details.

> The encroaching modern world threatens the entire Kalahari as ever-expanding diamond mines threaten the environment, bit by bit devouring the land in the quest for riches. Even as it enriches the country, the greed of industry destroys a way of life. Today, in the shadow of the modern city of Gaborone, the proud Bushmen, dressed in secondhand clothing rather than their traditional breechcloths, dance their ancient dances. They cling to the thread of their ancestry even as the door to the past slams shut in their faces.

Process

Try It!

Analyze the middle paragraphs in one of the essays in this book. Tell which method of support is used to develop each main point (explaining, comparing, analyzing, and so on).

Developing the Middle Using Different Levels of Detail

In most cases each main point is developed in a separate paragraph. Remember that specific details add meaning to your writing and make it worth reading, while writing that lacks effective detail leaves the reader with an incomplete picture and questions about the topic. A well-written paragraph often contains three levels of detail.

Level 1: A controlling sentence names the topic.

"If the government has its way, my people will be gone," says a member of the once proud Bushmen tribe.

Level 2: A clarifying sentence provides supporting points.

Although the tribe has lived in the African Kalahari Basin for more than 30,000 years, its members are now being relocated and modernized by the government.

Level 3: A completing sentence adds details to conclude the idea.

Soon, the remaining members of the tribe will have either died out or become assimilated.

Try It!

Identify one set of sentences that show the three levels of detail in the paragraph below. Label each sentence after writing it down. (The topic sentence is the one controlling sentence in the paragraph.)

The struggle between the Bushmen and the government is rooted in modern changes in the area. The Botswana government claims that the Bushmen do not necessarily stick to the ancient practices. Instead of maintaining their isolated, nomadic existence, the tribes are creating settlements and using guns and trucks. For this reason, the government has sought to move the Bushmen. The government feels that moving the tribe will help preserve the delicate ecological balance in the Kalahari area. Backed by Survival International, the Bushmen are taking their case to the courts. They have, as of yet, nothing to show for their legal efforts. The struggle continues in earnest, with the government attempting to relocate those Bushmen still remaining in the Kalahari.

Integrating Quotations

Always choose quotations that are appropriate for your writing. Quotations should support your ideas, not replace them.

Strategies for Using Quotations

Use the strategies below to make the most effective use of quoted material in your writing.

- **Use quotations to support your main points.**
  Effective quotations can back up your key ideas or support your arguments.

  > For many, the destruction of the environment in remote regions is far removed from daily life. Yet, as John C. Sawhill, president of the Nature Conservancy, once said, "In the end, our society will be defined not only by what we create, but by what we refuse to destroy." In other words, man's legacy is tied directly to the management or mismanagement of the land.

- **Use quotations to lend authority to your writing.**
  Quoting an expert shows that you have researched your topic and understand its significance.

  > The nations of the world must band together to make sure that we never reach the point of using nuclear weapons in war. Perhaps it was put best by General Omar Bradley, first chairman of the Joint Chiefs of Staff, when he said, "The way to win an atomic war is to make certain it never starts." With this type of "victory," everyone wins.

- **Use quotations that are succinct and powerful.**
  Distinctive quotations add value to your writing.

  > Pianist Benny Green defines a jazz musician as "a juggler who uses harmonies instead of oranges." The test of jazz is how these harmonies, tossed about seemingly at random, actually hold together in a smooth, if loosely defined, pattern.

Common Quotation Problems to Avoid

Avoid these problems as you choose quotations.

- **Plagiarism**
  Cite sources for all quotations (and paraphrases).
- **Long quotations**
  Keep quotations brief and to the point.
- **Overused quotations**
  Use a quotation only when you cannot share its message as powerfully or effectively in another way.

Process

Writing the Ending

Your ending paragraph allows you to tie up all the ideas in your essay. It should do at least two of the following things.

- Restate the thesis of your paper.
- Review the main points.
- Leave the reader with something to think about.

Sample Closing Paragraph

Restatement of the thesis	**The Bushmen of the Kalahari are in danger of extinction as a separate cultural entity.** The government of Botswana has moved them from their tribal lands. It has taken away their means of self-support as it tries to include them in a society for which they are neither eager nor equipped. Whether the Bushmen can survive as a people in such a world is yet to be seen. Perhaps the government's relocation plan is a positive, inevitable move, or perhaps it is simply a form of legalized elimination.
Review of a main point	
A final thought	

Forming a Final Thought

Here are three different ways to form a final thought.

A call to action often directs the reader to do something.

> If you see litter on the street, don't just shake your head in disgust. Pick it up and toss it away. If everyone acted in this way, we would have a cleaner town.

A lingering question encourages the reader to further examine the subject.

> People may be threatened by the very water they drink. Can they live with that?

A good or bad conclusion suggests that your topic poses a possible benefit or threat the reader should be aware of.

> Using aromatherapy to manage stress, heal tired bodies, and simply feel good is cheap, safe, and enjoyable.

Try It!

Analyze the ending paragraph of one of the essays in this book. Using the information above, tell what the paragraph has accomplished.

Revising

Experienced writers have an extensive working knowledge of the revising process. More specifically, with a first draft in hand, they know just how much work is ahead of them. They will continue to work with a piece of writing until it says what they want it to say from start to finish. They also know the importance of setting aside the first draft for a reasonable length of time—before they begin making changes. As writer Kenneth Atchity says, "It would be crazy to begin revising immediately after finishing the first draft, and counter to the way the mind likes to create."

This chapter will help you gain a better understanding of the revising process. It covers everything from a review of basic revising guidelines to an explanation of a valuable revising strategy. As you go through this material, remember that revising may be the most important step in the writing process, because when you revise, you improve the thoughts and details that carry your message.

- **Understanding the Basics**
- **Using a Strategy That Works**
- **A Closer Look at Revising**
- **Revising Checklist**
- **Revising in Action**
- **Checking for Snapshots**

"The first draft reveals the art; revision reveals the artist."

—Michael Less

Understanding the Basics

No writer gets it right the first time. Few writers even get it right the second time. In fact, professional writers almost always carry out many revisions before they are satisfied with their work. As writer Virginia Hamilton says, "The real work comes in the rewriting stage." The following guidelines will help you make the best revising moves.

- **Set your writing aside.** Get away from it for a day or two. This will help you see your first draft more clearly when you are ready to revise.
- **Carefully review your draft.** Read it at least two times: once silently and once aloud. Also ask another person to react to your writing—someone whose opinion you trust.
- **Consider the big picture.** Decide if you've effectively developed your thesis.
- **Look at the specific parts.** Rewrite any parts that aren't clear or effective. Cut information that doesn't support your thesis, and add ideas if you think your reader needs more information.
- **Assess your opening and closing paragraphs.** Be sure that they effectively introduce and wrap up your writing.

Revising a Timed Writing

When you have little time to make changes, writer Peter Elbow recommends "cut and paste revising." For example, if you are responding to a writing prompt on a test or for an in-class assignment, you may have just 10 to 15 minutes to revise your writing. The steps that follow describe this quick revising strategy.

1. Don't add any new information.
2. Cut unnecessary details.
3. Check for basic organization.
4. Do whatever rewriting is necessary.

Try It!

Take 30 minutes to respond to the prompt below. Then spend 10 to 15 minutes revising your writing with the cut-and-paste strategy.

Write about a time in which you either gained someone's respect or came to respect someone else.

Process

Using a Strategy That Works

The strategy below covers everything from reading the first draft to improving specific ideas. Use this strategy when you have time for in-depth revising.

Read: Sometimes it's hard to keep an open mind when you read your first draft. It's good to put some distance between yourself and your writing.

- Whenever possible, put your writing aside for a day or two.
- When you return to it, read your first draft aloud.
- Ask others (peers, family members) to read it aloud to you.
- Listen to your writing: What does it say? How does it sound?

React: Use these questions to help you react to your writing:

- What parts of my writing work for me?
- Do all of these parts work together?
- Have I arranged the parts in the best possible order?
- What other revising should I do?

Rework: Make changes until all parts of your writing work equally well. There is usually plenty of reworking to do in the early stages of revising, when you are still trying to bring a clear focus to a topic and share it effectively.

Reflect: Write comments in the margins of your paper (or in a notebook) as you revise. Here are some guidelines for reflecting:

- Explore your reactions freely. Be honest about your writing.
- Note what you plan to cut, move, explain further, and so on.
- Reflect on the changes you make. (How do they work?)
- If you are unsure of what to do, write down a question to answer later.

Refine: Refining is checking specific ideas for logic, readability, and balance. Use these questions to help you refine your ideas:

- Will the reader be able to follow my train of thought from idea to idea?
- Do I use transitional words or phrases to link ideas?
- Have I overdeveloped or underdeveloped certain points?

Tip

Remember that revising is the process of improving the ideas and the details that carry the message in your writing. Don't pay undue attention to conventions too early in the process; just concentrate on improving your message.

A Closer Look at Revising

The later stage of revising allows you to deal with those aspects of your writing that may make it seem boring. Use the questions that follow to check for any uninspired "badlands" in your writing.

- **Is your topic worn out?** An essay entitled "Lead Poisoning" sounds uninteresting. With a new twist, you can enliven it: "Get the Lead Out!"

- **Is your approach stale?** If you are writing primarily to please your teacher, start again. Try writing to learn something or to trigger a particular emotion within the reader.

- **Do you sound uninterested or unnatural?** If you do ("A good time was had by all"), try another approach. This time, be honest. Be real.

- **Do parts of your writing seem boring?** Maybe those parts are boring because they don't say enough, or they say too much. To rework these parts, think of them as a series of snapshots. Each picture needs the proper balance between its idea and the supporting details.

- **Is your writing choked by an overly tight organization?** The structure of an essay provides you with a frame to build on. However, if the frame is followed too closely, your writing may become predictable. If the "formula" is obvious when you read your draft, change the structure in order to more freely present your ideas.

Try It!

As a class (or in a small group) evaluate this paragraph using the questions above as a guide.

McCarthyism

MaCarthyism is associated with Joseph McCarthy, a Wisconsin resident who served from 1947–1957 as a United States senator. On February 20, 1950, McCarthy spoke for six hours on the senate floor, arguing that there was a large foreign espionage ring operating within the United States government. He accused the Truman administration of dismissing the entire issue. This criticism came at a time of strong anticommunist sentiments in the United States. There was anxiety that communists were quietly penetrating the government and the culture. People from all walks of life were accused of being communists—often without evidence. This anticommunist movement was called McCarthyism. Some writers used their craft to protest McCarthy. Arthur Miller, for example, wrote *The Crucible* in which the Salem witch trials serve as a metaphor for McCarthyism.

"I rush through a first draft, and then I go back and rewrite because I can usually see what the problems are going to be. Rewriting is more fun to me than the writing is."

—Walter Dean Myers

Revising Checklist

Use this checklist as a guide when you revise your writing. Remember: When you revise, you improve the thoughts and details that carry your message.

Ideas

_____ **1.** Is my topic important and relevant?
_____ **2.** Have I developed a specific focus or thesis statement?
_____ **3.** Does each paragraph support my thesis?
_____ **4.** Have I included enough details to make my ideas clear?

Organization

_____ **5.** Does my writing follow a clear pattern of organization?
_____ **6.** Have I developed effective beginning, middle, and ending parts?
_____ **7.** Do I need to reorder any parts?

Voice

_____ **8.** Does my voice fit the purpose of my writing?
_____ **9.** Do I sound interested in and knowledgeable about my topic?

Word Choice

_____ **10.** Have I used an appropriate level of formality?
_____ **11.** Do I use specific nouns and vivid verbs?
_____ **12.** Do I avoid repetition and redundancy ?

Sentence Fluency

_____ **13.** Are my sentences complete and clearly written?
_____ **14.** Do my sentences flow smoothly?
_____ **15.** Have I varied my sentence beginnings and lengths?

Revising in Action

When you revise a first draft, focus on improving the writing overall. You can improve a piece by adding, deleting, moving, or reworking information. (See the next page for examples.)

Adding Information

Add new information to your writing if you feel you need to . . .

- share more details to make a point,
- clarify or complete an interesting idea, or
- link sentences or paragraphs to improve clarity and flow.

Deleting Information

Delete material from your draft if the ideas . . .

- do not support your focus or
- are redundant or repetitious.

Moving Material

Move material in your writing in order to . . .

- create a clear flow of ideas,
- present points in order, or
- make a dramatic impact.

Reworking Material

Rework material in your writing if it . . .

- is confusing or unclear,
- does not maintain the proper voice, or
- needs to be simplified.

Being Your Own Critic

When revising, try to anticipate your reader's concerns. Doing so will help you determine what changes to make. Here are some questions and concerns a reader may have:

- What is the main point of this essay?
- Is the writer's voice interested and authoritative?
- Can I follow the writer's ideas smoothly?
- Does the ending wrap up the essay in a clear way?

Sample Revision

The writer of this essay improved the piece by moving, adding, deleting, and reworking parts.

Playing with Fire

The most exciting moment of any Olympic opening ceremony is the lighting of the flame. A torchbearer sprints into the stadium, flaming torch in hand. Anticipation builds. The runner's torch ignites a roaring fire in a huge cauldron, symbolizing the official opening of the games. ⌐The flame has already traveled a great distance and has been carried by many people to get to its destination.

The Olympic Torch Relay begins with the lighting of the torch. This happens at the site of the first Olympic Games in Olympia, Greece. From there, torchbearers carry the torch

from country to country

until it reaches the site of the host city where that year's games are being held.

Running isn't the only way the flame is moved from place to place. It can be carried by other forms of "transportation". ~~In the past, it has been transported by~~ plane, car, boat, bicycle, horse, even dogsled! In places where open flames are not allowed, the flame is stored in a special enclosed lamp.

The Olympic Games Organizing Committee (OCOG)

is responsible for planning how the torch will travel from

~~determines the route and forms of transportation that will~~

Greece to the host city.

~~convey the flame from Greece to the host location.~~ The torch travels through many places on its way to the games. . . .

A sentence is moved for clarity.

A key detail is added.

An unnecessary detail is cut.

A passage is reworded for appropriate voice.

Checking for Snapshots

One way of improving your writing is to check for places where you can show instead of tell. Writer Barry Lane suggests thinking in terms of "snapshots" to add effective, specific details to your writing.

Creating a Snapshot Moment

1. Choose one important "moment" from your essay or story.

2. Imagine that you are viewing it through a camera lens. Zoom in, and take a picture.

3. Now write about the snapshot.

The writer of "Playing with Fire" (see page **119**) decided to improve her writing by creating a snapshot of the torchbearer. Here is the result.

> The torchbearer sprints toward the platform, flaming torch in hand. The flame struggles in the wind for a split second; then it flares up in defiance. A hush falls over the stadium. The only sound is the torchbearer's footsteps. He stops. Slowly and ceremoniously, he touches the flame to the base of a thick, glass column. It shoots up the column. Whoosh! Fire explodes in a giant, silver cauldron towering over the stadium. The Olympic Games have begun!

Try It!

Write two snapshot moments—first, of a person you know very well, and second, of a place. Remember to focus on just one small part and zoom in on the details. Show the reader what is happening.

Tip

If you get stuck, try asking yourself the 5 W and H questions *(who? what? when? where? why?* and *how?)* about the moment: *Who* is this? *What* is she or he doing? *When* and *how* did this happen? *Why* is the person doing this? *Where* is this person?

Peer Responding

Good friends constantly ask for and provide feedback: "Does this top look good on me?" "I'm not sure that red is really your color." "How did we sound?" "You guys nailed every song." Sharing opinions and considering the opinions of others enhances life. It helps you to see things from different perspectives. You may even decide to change your mind on occasion—a prerogative.

Writing peers also share their opinions, letting each other know what makes sense and what could be clearer in a piece of writing. In this chapter, you will learn how to conduct peer-responding sessions. At first, you may be reluctant to have your classmates respond to your writing; however, once you realize how helpful their feedback can be, you'll come to appreciate the importance of this activity. Your peers' feedback is especially helpful for evaluating a first draft during the early stages of revising.

- **Peer-Responding Guidelines**
- **Using the Traits to Respond**
- **Trying a New Strategy**

"Criticism, like rain, should be gentle enough to nourish a man's growth without destroying his roots."

—Frank A. Clark

Peer-Responding Guidelines

The guidelines below will help you participate in peer response sessions. (If you're just starting out, work in small groups of two or three classmates.)

The Writer's Role

Come to the session with a meaningful piece of your writing—perhaps a recently completed first draft. Make a copy for each member of the group (if this is what the group usually does).

- **Introduce your writing.** Give a brief explanation of what your piece is about without going into too much detail.
- **Read your writing aloud.** However, if you don't feel comfortable reading aloud, ask group members to read your piece silently.
- **Ask for feedback.** Listen carefully and consider all suggestions. Don't be defensive since this will stop some members from commenting honestly.
- **Take notes.** Record your classmates' comments on your copy so you can decide later what to change.
- **Answer questions.** If you're unsure of an answer, it's okay to say, "I don't know" or "I'll look into that."
- **Seek assistance.** If you have trouble with a specific part of your writing, ask for help.

Seeking constructive criticism

To get constructive criticism, you may need to ask the responders some direct questions. Consider your purpose, your intended audience, and the focus of your writing. Knowing these three things will help you form your questions.

Try It!

Choose one piece of writing to review with your peers. Using the 5 W and H questions *(who? what? when? where? why?* and *how?),* form questions that will help the group provide constructive criticism. Sample questions follow:

1. Who will be most interested in my story?
2. What is the strongest or the weakest part of my essay?
3. When do you seem to lose interest?
4. Where do I need more detail?
5. Why will the reader appreciate the beginning?
6. How can I change the ending to make it more effective?

The Responder's Role

You need to be honest in your feedback without hurting the writer's feelings. Your comments should always be polite and constructive.

Giving Constructive Criticism	
Don't make demands . . . "Change the ending so the reader has something to think about."	**Do make suggestions . . .** "The ending could be stronger if you leave the reader with a question to think about."
Don't focus on the writer . . . "Nobody understands what you're trying to say in the middle part."	**Do focus on the writing . . .** "Don't you think your ideas would be easier to follow if you switched paragraphs two and three?"
Don't focus on the problem . . . "The beginning paragraph is boring."	**Do focus on the solution . . .** "Descriptive details might make the beginning more interesting."
Don't give general comments . . . "Your sentences aren't very interesting."	**Do give specific advice . . .** "Changing from passive to active voice in a few places could liven things up."

Responding Tips

- Listen carefully to the writer's reading and questions.
- Take notes in the margins of your copy so you can show the writer where changes need to be made.
- Ask questions. If you are not sure of something, ask for clarification.

Try It!

Read the following paragraph. Write three strong, constructive criticisms about the writing, using the tips above.

Dr. Condoleezza Rice is a native of Birmingham, Alabama. She was born in 1954, one year before Emmett Till was murdered and Rosa Parks refused to give up her seat on the bus. As a child, she was an excellent student and a gifted musician who played the piano. In fact, Dr. Rice started college when she was only 15. Her plan was to become a concert pianist. Along the way, she became interested in politics. She ended up working at the White House as Secretary of State under President George W. Bush. Most people don't know that she didn't give up playing the piano. In 2002, she performed a concert in Washington, D.C., with cellist Yo-Yo Ma.

Process

Using the Traits to Respond

Responders help writers rethink, refocus, and revise their writing. As a responder, you may find it helpful to base your responses on the traits of writing.

Addressing Ideas, Organization, and Voice Early On

Ideas: **Help the author focus on ideas.**

- Can you tell us the main idea of your writing?
- It seems like you're trying to say . . . Is that right?
- Are these points the main ideas in your writing?
- The most convincing details are . . .
- A few details like . . . may make this part more interesting.
- In my opinion, details like . . . may distract from your main idea.
- Your writing left me thinking . . . Is that what you intended?

Organization: **Help the author focus on organization.**

- You got my attention in the beginning by . . .
- This sentence seems to state your focus. Is that correct?
- Are the middle paragraphs organized according to . . . ?
- Why did you place the information about . . . in the fourth paragraph?
- Is the purpose of your ending to . . . ?
- I wonder if a transition is needed between the second and third paragraphs.

Voice: **Help the author focus on voice.**

- The sentences that most clearly show your personality are . . .
- How would you describe your attitude about this topic?
- What audience did you have in mind when you wrote this?
- The third paragraph sounds too formal to me. Do you think it fits in with the rest of your writing?
- The overall feeling I get from your writing is . . .
- The middle part of your essay might be too subjective.

Try It!

Read the following sentence and afterward write two constructive criticisms: one about the quality of the ideas and one about the voice.

The investigative nature of a forensic pathologist's personality provides a foundation for detecting microscopic details to explain a crime.

Addressing Word Choice and Fluency Later On

Word Choice: Help the author focus on the nouns, verbs, and modifiers.

- The most powerful verbs in the writing are . . .
- I found these general nouns: . . . What specific nouns could you use instead?
- Do you think there are too many modifiers in the first paragraph?
- I'm confused by the meaning of . . . Can you define it, please?
- The words . . . feel wrong to me. You could use . . . instead.
- Have you used . . . too often in the first part of your writing?

Sentence Fluency: Help the author focus on the sentences.

- I like the flow of the sentences in the beginning paragraph.
- Check your sentences in the middle part. Do you think too many of them begin the same way?
- It might add interest to vary the sentences in the closing paragraph.
- Could some of the sentences in the second paragraph be combined?
- For the most part, your sentences have a nice rhythm.

Try It!

Read the following paragraph. Then write some constructive criticisms about word choice and sentence fluency.

> At Christmas time, it was Aunt Anne who always brought a bunch of cookies over to our house for the annual tree-trimming party. It was Anne who did most of the tree trimming. It was Anne who would some years disappear with my shopping list entitled "I Have No Idea What to Get for So and So," and she'd come back several hours later with the perfect gift. She asked only that I make her a cup of coffee while she wrapped it for me. We always knew we could crash at Aunt Anne's house. She wouldn't mind if her house got messy; she had all the time in the world to clean it.

Reacting to Criticism

You don't have to incorporate all of your classmates' suggestions. The following tips will help you get the most out of response sessions.

- Trust your own judgment about your writing.
- Determine which issues are most important.
- Pay attention to comments made by more than one responder.
- Get another opinion if you are not sure about something.
- Be patient. Focus on one problem area at a time.

Process

Trying a New Strategy

Here's a simple and effective four-step strategy that you can use in peer response sessions.

Minding Your OAQS

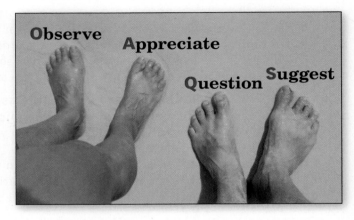

Observe means noticing what another person's writing is designed to do. Then say something about the design or purpose. For example, "Even though you mean to write objectively about the November election, your political opinions come through."

Appreciate means to identify something in the writing that impresses or pleases you. Positive comments are important to a writer. As a responder, it's important to balance your criticism. For example, you could say, "I really like the way you . . ." or "The best part of your essay is . . ."

Question means to ask whatever you want to know after you have read the writing. You can ask for background information, a definition, an interpretation, or an explanation. For example, "Could you tell us more about how you felt when you found the letter?"

Suggest means to give helpful advice about possible changes. Offer advice honestly and courteously. Be specific and positive. For example, "If you add a few details about what happened in the second paragraph, maybe what you heard and felt, I think your essay will be perfect!"

 ## Try It!

Read this excerpt from Mark Twain's *How to Tell a Story and Others.* Write one positive comment and one question about the writing.

The humorous story may be spun out to great length, and may wander around as much as it pleases, and arrive nowhere in particular; but the comic and witty stories must be brief and end with a point. The humorous story bubbles gently along, the others burst. The humorous story is strictly a work of art—high and delicate art—and only an artist can tell it; but no art is necessary in telling the comic and the witty story; anybody can do it.

Editing

Two hundred years ago, Thomas Jefferson gave his daughter this advice: "Take care that you never spell a word wrong. Always before you write a word, consider how it is spelled, and, if you do not remember, turn to a dictionary." Editing was just as important back then as it is now. A good writer is also a skillful editor, fully versed in the conventions of the language.

Editing is the process of checking your revised writing for spelling, punctuation, and grammar errors. Unfortunately, few people know *all* of the rules for conventions. That's why spell-checkers, grammar checkers, dictionaries, thesauruses, and writing handbooks are important editing tools. This chapter, along with the "Proofreader's Guide" on pages **604–763**, will help you improve your editing skills.

- **Checklist for Editing and Proofreading**
- **Editing in Action**
- **Errors to Watch For**
- **Special Editing and Proofreading Strategies**

"Good writers are those who keep the language efficient. That is to say, keep it accurate, keep it clear."

—Ezra Pound

"In writing, punctuation plays the role of body language.
It helps readers hear you the way you want to be heard."
—Russell Baker

Checklist for Editing and Proofreading

Use this checklist as a guide when you edit and proofread your revised writing. Also refer to "Errors to Watch For" on pages 130–131.

Tip

Always have a trusted friend or peer serve as a second editor. You're too close to your work to catch every error.

Conventions

LOOK AT PUNCTUATION . . . (See pages 605–647.)

_____ Do my sentences end with the proper punctuation?

_____ Do I use commas correctly in compound sentences?

_____ Do I use commas correctly in a series and after long introductory phrases or clauses?

_____ Do I use apostrophes correctly?

_____ Do I punctuate dialogue correctly?

LOOK AT MECHANICS . . . (See pages 648–671.)

_____ Do I start my sentences with capital letters?

_____ Do I capitalize proper nouns?

_____ Have I checked for spelling errors (including those the spell-checker may have missed)?

LOOK AT GRAMMAR . . . (See pages 700–737.)

_____ Do the subjects and verbs agree in my sentences?

_____ Do my sentences use correct and consistent verb tenses?

_____ Do my pronouns agree with their antecedents?

_____ Have I avoided any other usage errors?

LOOK AT PRESENTATION . . . (See pages 91–95.)

_____ Does the title effectively lead into the writing?

_____ Are sources of information properly presented and documented?

_____ Does my writing meet the requirements for final presentation?

Editing in Action

Note the editing corrections made in these paragraphs from a student essay. See the inside back cover of this book for an explanation of the editing symbols used.

Gender Equality

Should young women be grateful for their education? Absolutely. According to the united nations (UN), two-thirds of the world's illiterate people are female. Just as shocking is that two-thirds of the world's children who don't go to school are female. In point of fact, females in developing countries are disadvantaged in many aspects of life.

In September 2000, the UN set specific goals for the twenty-first century to address this problem. Eight goals were outlined in a resolution called the "United Nations Millennium Declaration." Two of the goals directly address promoting gender equality and primary education worldwide. The UN believes that placing more emphasis on educating girls in developing countries will have significant economic benefits. The organization's hope is that educated women will participate more fully in public and political life and break the cycle of poverty. A UN 2006 report shows the effort is slowly succeeding, but there is much more to be done.

The UN wants to eliminate gender discrimination in all levels of education no later than 2015. The declaration states that "by 2015 children everywhere, boys and girls alike, will be able to complete a full course of primary schooling and that girls and boys will have equal access to all levels of education."

A proper noun is capitalized.

A comma is placed after a transition.

A title is punctuated.

An apostrophe is added to show singular possession.

A spelling error is corrected.

A usage error is corrected.

Errors to Watch For

These two pages show 10 common errors to check for in your writing.

1. Problem: Missing Comma After Long Introductory Phrases
  Solution: Place a comma after a long introductory phrase.

> Because of the snowstorm ˄, school was canceled for the day.

2. Problem: Confusing Pronoun Reference
  Solution: Be sure the reader knows whom or what your pronoun refers to.

> When Angel talked with Samantha, ~~she~~ *Angel* said she would drive.

3. Problem: Missing Comma in Compound Sentence
  Solution: Use a comma between two independent clauses joined by a coordinating conjunction—*and, but, or, nor, so, for,* or *yet.*

> I tried to call Jake this morning ˄, but his cell phone was turned off.

4. Problem: Missing Comma(s) with Nonrestrictive Phrases or Clauses
  Solution: Use commas to set off a phrase or clause that is not needed to understand the sentence. (See page **612**.)

> I gave five dollars to my little brother ˄, who gave me a big smile.

5. Problem: Comma Splices
  Solution: When only a comma separates two independent clauses, add a conjunction or create two sentences.

> Javon is graduating from college on Sunday, *so* ˄ we're having a family party.

6. Problem: Subject-Verb Agreement Error
  Solution: Verbs must agree in number with their subjects.

> The ballots list~~s~~ four candidates for class president.

7. Problem: **Missing Comma in a Series**
   Solution: Use commas to separate individual words, phrases, or clauses in a series.

> Our van was cluttered with CD's⁁candy wrappers⁁and empty water bottles.

8. Problem: **Pronoun-Antecedent Agreement Errors**
   Solution: A pronoun must agree in number with the word that the pronoun refers to. (See page **756**.)

> Either Rose or Emily brought⁁~~their~~ DVD's to Adrian's house.

(correction: *her*)

9. Problem: **Missing Apostrophe to Show Ownership**
   Solution: Use an apostrophe after a noun to show possession.

> Jorge's dream is to attend a World Series game.

10. Problem: **Misusing *Its* and *It's***
   Solution: *Its* is a possessive pronoun meaning "belonging to it." *It's* is a contraction of "it is" or "it has."

> It's a fact that the distance from earth's surface to its center is about 3,963 miles.

Try It!

Copy the paragraph below on your own paper, exactly as it appears. Then find and correct the eight errors it contains. Use the correction symbols on the inside back cover of this book.

Almost 60,000 teens participated in *USA Weekend Magazine*s recent music survey. The magazine published the results on it's Web page. One of the findings which was a big surprise to everyone showed that teens often borrowed and listened to their parents CD's. In the final analysis it remains clear that teens need their tunes, their favorite types of music include hip-hop, rap pop and punk rock.

Special Editing and Proofreading Strategies

The following three strategies will help you become a more efficient and effective editor and proofreader. Professional editors and proofreaders employ these types of strategies.

1. **Read from the bottom to the top.** Begin at the end of your writing and work back through your paper, word by word and line by line. This will help you focus on spelling errors, repeated words, and so on.
2. **Know your most common errors.** If spelling is your most frequent mistake, always check your writing for that problem first. After that, go back and proofread for other types of errors, one at a time if necessary.

Try It!

Read this passage backward. See if you can find three errors.

The wind meandered though the ancient trees, methodically shakeing loose the the thick armor of ice that encrusted the rigid branches.

Tip

Some editors like to place a ruler under each line of text as they read it. Focusing on a small amount of text at a time results in fewer missed errors.

3. **Use editing and proofreading marks.** Editing and proofreading marks (see the inside back cover of this book) offer a uniform way of marking the errors in your writing.

Try It!

Copy the following passage. Use the editing and proofreading marks to correct the mistakes.

The wind meandered though the ancient trees, methodically shakeing lose the the thick armor of ice that encrusted the rigid branches. Icicles plunged like swords from the sky peircing snowdrifts caught silent and unaware. Oh that it were only rain falling gently through leafs onto the mossy forest floor.

Note: Be careful when using grammar checkers and spell-checkers on your computer. Although these programs are helpful, they aren't foolproof. They can easily misread your intentions and give you bad advice. The best editors are human editors.

Publishing

Writing becomes real when you publish it. Publishing is to a writer what a live performance is to a musician or an exhibit is to an artist. It is why you have worked so hard in the first place—to share a finished piece of writing that expresses your thoughts and feelings. It makes all of your prewriting, drafting, and revising worth the effort.

The most helpful form of publishing is sharing a finished project with one or more of your classmates. As writer Tom Liner states, "You learn ways to improve your writing by seeing its effect on others."

You can also select a piece of writing for your classroom portfolio or submit something to your school newspaper or literary magazine. If you're really adventurous, you may even want to submit your writing outside of school. This chapter will help you with all your publishing needs.

- **Preparing to Publish**
- **Places to Publish**
- **Preparing a Portfolio**
- **Parts of a Portfolio**
- **Creating Your Own Web Site**

"To make your unknown known—that's the important thing."

—Georgia O'Keefe

> "A writer is unfair to himself when he is unable to be hard on himself."
> —Marianne Moore

Preparing to Publish

Publishing is the final step in the writing process, offering that "other audience"—your readers—a chance to enjoy your writing. The following guidelines will help you prepare your writing for publishing.

Publishing Tips

- **Work with your writing** until you feel good about it from start to finish. If any parts still need work, then it isn't ready to publish.

- **Ask for input and advice** during the writing process. Your writing should answer any questions the reader may have about your topic. Confusing parts must be made clear.

- **Save all drafts for each writing project** so you can keep track of the changes you have made. If you are preparing a portfolio, you may be required to include early drafts as well as finished pieces. (See pages **136–138**.)

- **Check for the traits of writing** to be sure that you have effectively addressed ideas, organization, voice, word choice and sentence fluency in your work. (See pages **51–88**.)

- **Carefully edit and proofread for conventions** after you have completed all of your revisions. (See pages 89–90.)

- **Prepare a neat final copy** to share with the reader. Use pen (blue or black ink) and one side of the paper if you are writing by hand. If you are using a computer, avoid fancy, hard-to-read fonts and odd margins. (See pages **91–95**.)

- **Know your publishing options** since there are many ways to publish. (See page **135**.)

- **Follow the requirements** indicated by the publisher. Each publisher has its own set of requirements, which must be followed exactly.

Try It!

Use these guidelines once you decide to publish a piece of writing. Be sure to ask your teacher for help if you have any questions about the publishing process.

Places to Publish

Listed below are four well-respected publications that accept student submissions and three writing contests to enter. You can also look in the *Writer's Market*—available in most libraries—for more places to publish.

Publications

Teen Ink (Grades 6–12)
FORMS: Articles, art, photos, reviews, poems, fiction
SEND TO: P.O. Box 30
          Newton, MA 02461

The High School Writer (Grades 9–12)
FORMS: Fiction, poetry, nonfiction
SEND TO: Writer Publications
          P.O. Box 718
          Grand Rapids, MN 55744

Skipping Stones: A Multicultural Children's Magazine (Ages 8–16)
FORMS: Stories, articles, art (any language)
SEND TO: P.O. Box 3939
          Eugene, OR 97403

Writing Contests

Read Writing Contests (Grades 2–12)
FORMS: Short stories, personal essays
SEND TO: Read Essay Contest
          Weekly Reader Corporation
          200 First Stamford Place
          P.O. Box 120023
          Stamford, CT 06912-0023

The American Library of Poetry: Student Poetry Contest (Grades 8–9 and 10–12)
FORMS: One poem of no more than 20 lines on any subject, and in any form
SEND TO: Review Committee
          The American-Library of Poetry
          P.O. Box 978
          Houlton, ME 04730

Scholastic Writing Awards (Grades 9–12)
FORMS: Short story, essay, dramatic script, poetry, humor, science fiction, fantasy, writing portfolio
SEND TO: The Scholastic Art and Writing
          Awards
          557 Broadway
          New York, NY 10012

Tip

Check with the publication or contest and with your teacher about the submission guidelines. Always include a self-addressed stamped envelope (SASE) when submitting your work to an outside publisher.

Preparing a Portfolio

A writing portfolio is a collection of your work that shows your skill as a writer. It is different from a writing folder that contains writing in various stages of completion. Your teacher will probably ask you to compile a *showcase portfolio*—a collection of your best writing for a quarter or a semester. Compiling a showcase portfolio allows you to participate in the assessment process. You decide which writing samples to include, and you reflect upon your writing progress.

Working Smart

Use the following information as a guide when you compile a showcase portfolio. There are no shortcuts when it comes to putting together an effective portfolio, so don't skip any of these suggestions.

1. Organize and keep track of your writing (including planning notes and drafts). Then, when it comes to compiling your portfolio, you will have all the pieces to work with.

2. Make sure that you understand all of the requirements for your portfolio. If there's something you're unsure of, ask your teacher for help.

3. Keep your work in a safe place. Use a good-quality, expandable folder for your portfolio to avoid dog-eared or ripped pages.

4. Maintain a regular writing/compiling schedule. It will be impossible to create an effective portfolio if you approach it as a last-minute project.

5. Develop a feeling of pride in your portfolio. Make sure that it reflects a positive image of yourself. Look your best! (Remember that your teacher will be reviewing your portfolio for assessment.)

FYI

A showcase portfolio may follow you into the next school year. Your next year's teacher will use the portfolio to assess your competencies and weaknesses as a writer. Of special interest will be your personal reflections on your writing progress.

Try It!

Imagine that you are compiling a showcase portfolio. List at least two or three pieces that you would include. Explain in a brief paragraph why you think these three pieces represent your best work.

Parts of a Portfolio

Check with your teacher about specific requirements for your portfolio. Most showcase portfolios contain the following parts.

- **A table of contents** listing the pieces included in the portfolio.
- **An opening essay or letter** detailing the story behind your portfolio (how you organized it, what it represents to you, and so on).
- **Specific finished pieces** representing your best writing. (Your teacher may ask you to include all of the planning, drafting, and revising for one or more of your writing samples.)
- **A best "other" piece** related to your work in another content area.
- **A cover sheet** attached to each piece of writing, discussing the reason for its selection, the work that went into it, and so on.
- **Evaluation sheets or checklists** charting the basic skills you have mastered as well as the skills you still need to work on. (Your teacher will supply these sheets.)

Writing Your Opening Pages

The first two pages of a showcase portfolio are shown here.

Table of Contents

Showcase Portfolio
Chantele Barnes

Table of Contents

Opening Letter

Dear Mr. _____

    I'm pleased with my writing progress this semester. My goal was to write about topics that were important to me, in hopes that I would enjoy writing more. I think I succeeded. I really felt connected to the topics in my main writing projects. I did some of my best writing this semester because I seemed to care so much about what I was saying. I still have a long way to go, but I now feel much more confident about my writing ability.

    My first piece is a personal narrative about a memorable experience. Picking a topic was easy because my sophomore trip to Italy was the most memorable thing that has ever happened to me. I was part of the All-City Choir that had the privilege of singing in Rome. My challenge was to select only the most important things to say about the experience. At first I just went on and on ("First, I did this . . . Then I did . . .), but then I figured out that I could only focus on the most important details. I enjoyed finding just the right words to capture the feeling of the time.

    I also included a response to *The Great Gatsby*. It was easier to analyze Jay Gatsby than I thought it would be. That may be because I plan to study psychology in college. It was interesting to explore Gatsby's personality.

    My favorite selection is "Seashells, Sparks, and Stars." I liked playing with alliteration in this poem, which is a playful ode to summer. I hope you enjoy reading it as much as I enjoyed writing it.

    This summer my goal is to become a regular reader and a regular writer. I plan to keep a writer's notebook and write some more poems.

Sincerely,
Chantele Barnes

Creating a Cover Sheet

When you create your showcase portfolio, you should attach a cover sheet to each writing project you include. (See the sample below written for a student essay about *The Great Gatsby*.) Your cover sheet should do one or more of the following things:

- Explain why you chose the piece for your portfolio.
- Tell about the process of writing you used, including problems you encountered.
- Describe the strong points and the weak points in the writing.
- Reflect on the writing's importance to you.

Sample Cover Sheet

Our assignment was to write a literary response about *The Great Gatsby*. We had several topic choices, but I chose to analyze the main character, Jay Gatsby.

Because Gatsby is such a complex character, I didn't know where to start. Using the webbing and freewriting techniques we practiced early in the year helped me dig into his character. In addition, what I learned about writing a thesis statement made it easier to put my essay together and organize the different parts.

I think my voice is a strong feature of my analysis. My interest in people and their actions really comes through. Throughout my analysis, I kept my classmates in mind. I wanted them to share my fascination with Gatsby and his flawed character. I think that my analysis would have been more effective if I had included a few more direct quotations from the novel. I also appreciate the importance of asking a trusted peer to edit my work. I can't find all of the errors on my own.

This writing project taught me to look beyond the surface in a novel. The truth is often hidden. I think authors do that on purpose. They want the reader to enjoy the story, but they also want the reader to think about the characters' actions, to look deep into their souls, and to discover their secrets.

Try It!

Write a cover sheet for a piece of writing that you would like to include in your portfolio.

Creating Your Own Web Site

Creating a Web site is one way to showcase your work. Use a social-networking site or check with your Internet service provider to find out how to get started. If you are designing your page at school, ask your teacher for help. The questions and answers below will help you get started.

Q. How do I begin planning my site?

A. Think about the number of pages you want on your site. Do you want just one page to showcase a piece of your work, or do you want multiple pages (a home page, a page of poetry, a short story, a page of favorite links, and so on)? Check out other students' Web pages for ideas. Then sketch out your pages. Note how the pages will be linked by marking the "hot spots" on your sketches.

Q. How do I make the pages?

A. Each page is created as a separate file. Many word-processing programs let you save a file as a Web page. Otherwise, you may have to learn HTML (hypertext markup language). This is a code that allows you to add text and graphics to a page. Your teacher may be able to help you with it. If not, you can find instructions on the Internet. (See the "Web Design" page on our Web site at *www.thewritesource.com* for help.)

Q. How do I know if my pages work?

A. You should always test your pages. Using your browser, open your first page. Then follow the links to make sure they work correctly.

Q. How do I get my pages on the Web?

A. You must upload your finished pages to your Internet provider's computer. Ask your provider how to do this. (If you're working on your home computer, get a parent's approval. If you're using a school computer, work with your teacher.) Your provider will tell you how to access the pages later, in case you want to make changes. After you upload a page, visit your site and make sure it still works.

Try It!

Get the word out about your site. E-mail your friends and ask them to visit your site. Your service provider can provide tips on how to get your site listed on various search sites.

Narrative Writing

Narrative Writing
Writing a Personal Narrative

Everyone makes a bad decision occasionally, and every bad decision usually results in conflict—the key to a good narrative. What makes a narrative interesting is how the writer deals with the conflict.

A personal narrative is a true story told from the writer's point of view. It is more than just an entertaining tale. It is the retelling of an event or experience that has affected the writer's life. The story should be real and natural, allowing readers to experience the event for themselves.

In this chapter, you will write a personal narrative about a difficult—and bad—decision. You will examine why you made the choice and reflect on how you felt about it—then and later. Include action, sensory details, and dialogue to bring the event to life.

Writing Guidelines

   Subject: **A bad decision**
      Form: **Personal narrative**
   Purpose: **To share an important experience**
  Audience: **Classmates**

"Our deeds determine us, as much as we determine our deeds."

—George Eliot

Personal Narrative

In the following personal narrative, Faraz writes about a poor choice and how he dealt with the consequences.

The Wrong Club

Beginning
The writer is faced with a decision and makes a choice.

I stared at the club sign-up sheets on the office bulletin board. The choices swam before me: outdoor club, computer club, photography, astronomy, and a dozen more, all enticing me. Still, because our club period was built into the school week, we were allowed to sign up for only one. But which one should I choose?

The debate club beckoned me. I remembered lifting the forensics trophy that I had won in my old school, but this was a new school, and here debate was considered "geeky." I knew that the photography club was the "cool" club to join, and there was just one more space on that list. I quickly added my name. My pen kept going dry, scratching on the paper, and I had to shake it a few times. It felt like an omen, as though even the pen knew I should have been signing up for debate. I mentally scolded myself for the thought, assuring myself that photography would be fun. It had to be, because I needed it to be. I needed to feel I belonged.

"Aren't you joining debate?" My brother Kavi was suddenly there, looking over my shoulder.

Middle
The writer presents reasons for his choice.

"No, I thought I'd try something different." He shrugged and reached past me, smelling of soap and confidence, to sign up for drama. It was considered another "geek" class, but Kavi had always whistled to his own tune. Still, it was easier for him. Kavi was a freshman, so he was on equal footing with every other freshman seeking to find a niche in the school. It was harder for me, a junior, to become established. I wanted to be cool, to belong, and I thought the photography club might be the way.

The writer explains the disappointment of his choice.

We met for the first time the following week, and I knew immediately I had made the wrong choice. I didn't even own a camera, and there I was, listening to the others excitedly discussing angles and pixels. The sharp stink of chemicals filled my nose. The stark black-and-white photos strung on a line across the back wall stared down at me as if I didn't belong. It was like picking the wrong chocolate from an assortment—bitter and hard instead of sweet and chewy.

I asked to leave to get a drink, but I really slipped down the hall to the room where the debate team was meeting. I stopped outside the door to hear Mrs. Holmes, the advisor, discussing the various issues they would be debating. I was a statue, still, listening to her explanation of the structure of a debate, and words like "rebuttal" and "logical argumentation." This was what I wanted, what I needed, where I belonged. Finally, I could stand it no more. I stepped inside; heads turned, and a sea of faces stared at me.

> An attempt to remedy the situation is shared.

"Excuse me, Mrs. Holmes," I gulped. "I was wondering if I could still join the team."

She shook her head. "I'm afraid we have a full team already." I must have looked pathetic, because she smiled. "If you like, you can be an alternate, taking the place of anyone who can't make it to a meet. You'd have to learn to argue both sides of an issue."

"I can do that," I grinned broadly. "I'll be right back."

I explained my situation to the photography advisor. I was so convincing, he agreed immediately that I should be in debate. Then I practically skipped down the hall to Mrs. Holmes's room.

> **Ending**
> The writer reveals the consequences of his choice and the lesson learned.

No one on our team missed a meet, so I didn't get to debate that season. It was hard going to all the meets and not being able to participate. But at least I realized it was more important to be myself than to be popular. In fact, being myself was the only way to "be cool."

Narrative

Respond to the reading. Answer the following questions.

Ideas (1) What is the bad choice the writer made? (2) What reasons are given for the choice?

Organization (3) How does the writer begin the narrative? (4) How is the narrative organized?

Voice & Word Choice (5) Identify at least two sensory details that help create a specific feeling.

Prewriting Selecting a Topic

To select a topic for his personal narrative, Faraz created a web showing bad decisions he had made at school, at home, and out with friends. He was trying to remember a choice that had brought difficult consequences and taught him an important lesson. After creating the web, he put an asterisk next to the topic he wanted to write about.

Topic Web

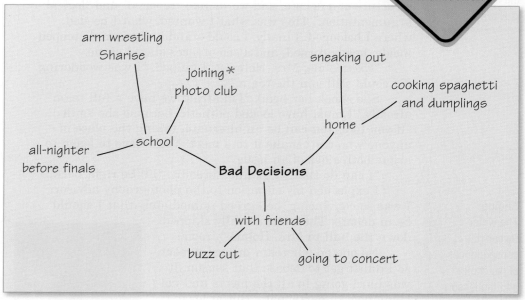

Prewrite

Select a topic. Create a web, first writing "Bad Decisions" in the center, and "school," "home," and "with friends" beyond it. Write down bad decisions you made in each situation. Think of the consequences and the lessons learned for each decision. Put an asterisk (*) next to the topic you want to write about.

Focus on the Traits

Ideas Your personal narrative will focus on the conflict created by the choice you made. Each consequence of the choice builds tension into the narrative. Finally, you face up to your decision and learn from it.

Mapping Your Narrative

Your personal narrative begins with the bad decision you made, tells why you made it, and reveals its consequences. The natural order of such events is *chronological*. That means you write about what happened in the order that it occurred. Faraz used a narrative map to plan his narrative.

Narrative Map

Narrative Map

Decision: __I signed up for photography club instead of debate team.__

Reasons: __I thought photography was "cool" and debate was "geeky."__

Consequences:

  First: __Kavi questioned me, showing how confident he was.__

  Next: __I went to photography club and didn't even have a camera.__

  Then: __I sneaked away to listen to debate team.__

  After: __I asked to join debate team and got an alternate position.__

What I learned: __It's more important to be myself than to be popular.__

Narrative

Prewrite

Map your narrative. Create a narrative map like the one above, listing the bad decision, your reasons for making it, the consequences in chronological order, and what you learned.

Focus on the Traits

Organization Most events in a personal narrative follow chronological order, but in special circumstances, you may decide to move forward or backward in time:

- **Flashbacks** tell about an important event that happened earlier.
  I remembered lifting the forensics trophy I had won in my old school.

- **Foreshadowing** forecasts what is about to happen.
  It felt like an omen, as though even the pen knew I should have been signing up for debate.

Writing Creating a Beginning, a Middle, and an Ending

A personal narrative is basically a true story that relates and reflects on a pivotal moment in the writer's life. All narratives have a beginning, a middle, and an ending.

Beginning Catch the reader's interest. The beginning should introduce the situation and the people involved and convince the reader to continue reading.

- Start with an intriguing question.
- Start with dialogue to pull the reader into the action.
- Start with a statement that piques the reader's curiosity.

Faraz chose the third technique. *I stared at the club sign-up sheets on the office bulletin board.* Immediately, the reader is compelled to wonder why the writer was staring and what was on the board.

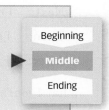

Middle Build suspense through action and details. The middle presents the details that support the narrative's main idea. In the sample essay, Faraz uses his conversation with his brother, his thoughts, and the description of the photography club meeting to illustrate the idea that he had made the wrong choice.

Ending Explain what the writer learned from the situation. The ending wraps up the story and brings the essay to a close. It is the writer's chance to reflect on the situation and on the lesson learned. Faraz's ending reveals how he learned the importance of being true to himself.

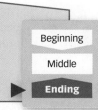

Write

Develop your first draft. Catch your reader's interest, build suspense through action and details, and reveal the lesson you learned.

Focus on the Traits

Voice A personal narrative should sound natural, as though you are talking to the reader. Use dialogue to create interest and achieve a spontaneous voice.

Revising Using Sensory Details to Create Different Effects

Writing about what you see, hear, smell, taste, and touch lets the reader experience the event with you. Remember that each sensory category has a different impact on the reader.

- **Sight:** "Seeing is believing." Sight is connected to truth. Give sensory details such as shape, size, and color to help the reader believe something is true.

   The stark black-and-white photos strung on a line across the back wall stared down at me as if I didn't belong.

- **Sound:** "I heard it through the grapevine." Hearing relates to communication and community. Let the reader hear dialogue to understand how people relate to each other.

   She shook her head. "I'm afraid we have a full team already."

- **Smell:** "I smell a rat." Smell depicts positive or negative feelings. Use pleasant smells to describe good situations and unpleasant smells to describe bad ones.

   He reached past me, smelling of soap and confidence.

   The sharp stink of chemicals filled my nose.

- **Taste:** "It's all a matter of taste." Taste tells the exact quality of something. Use *sweet, sour, tangy, spicy, salty, bitter,* and other taste words to capture quality.

   It was like picking the wrong chocolate from an assortment—bitter and hard instead of sweet and chewy.

- **Touch:** "Your words touched me." Touch is connected to emotion. Use touch words such as *warm, sharp, rough, shivering,* and *prickly* to show how you feel.

   My pen kept going dry, scratching on the paper, and I had to shake it a few times. It felt like an omen . . .

Revise

Check your sensory details. Create a sensory chart, checking how often you include each type of sensory detail. If necessary add more details, considering the information above.

See	Hear	Smell	Taste	Touch
✓	✓	✓	✓	✓

Narrative

Revising Improving Your Writing

Revise

Use a checklist. On your own paper, write the numbers 1 to 12. Put a check next to the number if you can answer "yes" to that question. If not, go back and revise that part of your personal narrative.

Revising Checklist

Ideas

_____ **1.** Do I present a clear choice and consequences?

_____ **2.** Do I include a reason for my decision?

_____ **3.** Do I use sensory details to allow the reader to experience the events?

Organization

_____ **4.** Do I include an interesting beginning that draws in the reader?

_____ **5.** Are my actions and details arranged chronologically?

_____ **6.** Does the ending show what I learned?

Voice

_____ **7.** Does my narrative sound natural, as though I am telling someone about the event?

_____ **8.** Does my voice reflect my feelings about the event?

Word Choice

_____ **9.** Do I use specific nouns and active verbs?

_____ **10.** Do I use descriptive modifiers?

Sentence Fluency

_____ **11.** Do I use a variety of sentence lengths and beginnings?

_____ **12.** Do my sentences read smoothly?

Revise

Make a clean copy. After you've finished your revisions, make a fresh copy of your writing to edit.

Editing Checking Your Writing

Edit

Use a checklist. On your own paper, write the numbers 1 to 12. Put a check by the number if you can answer "yes" to that question. If not, go back and edit your narrative for that convention.

Editing Checklist

Conventions

PUNCTUATION

_____ **1.** Do I use punctuation after all my sentences?

_____ **2.** Do I use commas after long introductory word groups?

_____ **3.** Do I use commas correctly in compound and complex sentences?

_____ **4.** Do I punctuate dialogue correctly?

_____ **5.** Do I use apostrophes correctly?

CAPITALIZATION

_____ **6.** Do I begin all my sentences with capital letters?

_____ **7.** Do I capitalize all proper nouns?

SPELLING

_____ **8.** Have I spelled all my words correctly?

_____ **9.** Have I checked for words my spell-checker might miss?

GRAMMAR

_____ **10.** Do I use correct forms of verbs?

_____ **11.** Do my pronouns agree with their antecedents?

_____ **12.** Do my verbs agree with their subjects?

Narrative

Publishing Sharing Your Writing

Here are several ways to publish your personal narrative.

- Read your narrative out loud to the class.
- Send the narrative to a local newspaper.
- Submit the narrative to your school's creative writing magazine.
- Send your narrative to a student-writing magazine.
- For more ideas, visit the Write Source Web site at <*www.thewritesource.com*> and click the "Publish It!" link.

Rubric for Narrative Writing

Use the following rubric as a guide for assessing your personal narrative. Refer to it whenever you want to improve your writing.

6 Ideas	**5**	**4**
The narrative shares a memorable event. Details bring the essay to life.	The writer shares an interesting experience. Specific details help maintain interest.	The writer tells about an interesting experience. Details should show, not tell.
Organization		
The structure of the narrative makes it enjoyable and easy to read.	The narrative has a clear beginning, middle, and ending. Transitions are helpful.	For the most part, the narrative is organized. Most of the transitions are helpful.
Voice		
The writer's voice captures the experience for the reader.	The writer's voice sounds natural. Dialogue helps hold the reader's interest.	The writer's voice creates interest in the essay, but dialogue should sound more natural.
Word Choice		
The writer's excellent word choice creates a vivid picture of the event.	Specific nouns, verbs, and modifiers create clear images and feelings.	Some stronger nouns, verbs, and/or modifiers would create a clearer picture.
Sentence Fluency		
The sentences are skillfully written to hold the reader's interest.	The sentences show variety and are easy to understand.	The sentences are varied, but some should flow more smoothly.
Conventions		
The narrative has no errors in spelling, grammar, or punctuation.	The narrative has a few minor errors in punctuation, grammar, or spelling.	The narrative has some errors that may distract the reader.

3	2	1
The writer should focus on one event. Some details do not relate to the essay.	The writer should focus on one experience. More details are needed.	The writer should select an experience and provide details.
The order of events must be corrected. More transitions are needed.	The beginning, middle, and ending all run together. The order is unclear.	The narrative must be better organized.
The writer's voice usually can be heard. More dialogue is needed.	The voice is weak. Dialogue is needed.	The writer sounds uninvolved or disinterested in the essay.
More specific nouns, verbs, and modifiers would paint a clearer picture of the event.	Better words are needed. Many are overused or too general to paint a clear picture.	The writer has not considered word choice or has used words incorrectly.
A better variety of sentences is needed. Sentences do not flow smoothly.	Many incomplete or short sentences make the writing choppy.	Few sentences are written well. Help is needed.
The narrative has several errors.	Numerous errors make the narrative hard to read and confusing.	Help is needed to find errors and make corrections.

Evaluating a Personal Narrative

As you read the narrative below, focus on the writer's strengths and weaknesses. **(The essay contains a few errors.)** Then read the self-assessment on page 153.

Driving into Trouble

Ever since I was a kid I wanted to drive. While other girls dressed their dolls I drove mine around in my brother's toy trucks. While other girls spent hours in front of a mirror, styling their hair my favorite hairstyle came from rolling down the window and letting the wind hit my face. After 16 years of waiting I was about to get my license and my freedom!

Flash! The camera caught my grin as I stood in front of the blue screen. The lady at the DMV took my license. From the laminating machine and slid it across the counter toward me. I grabbed at it—still hot—but the lady didn't let go. "You realize this is a graduated license," she said. Peering over her reading glasses. "Until you're eighteen, you can't drive more than one teenaged friend and you can't use a cell phone while driving."

"Yeah, yeah," I said. In the picture my eyes looked round and kind of spooked. "Thanks!"

My dad walked back to work just up a few blocks, so I had the car all to myself. I jumped in, fired the car up, and drove out of the parking lot. Cruising onto the main drag I rolled down the windows. Cranked up the radio and flipped open my cell phone. "Jenna! It's me! I got it! I'm a driver! Yeah, I'm coming to pick you up, like I promised. See ya. Bye."

The light in front of me went red. I slammed on the brakes leaving black skids on the road and making everything smell like burned rubber. Oh well the light let me call Ashley and Jarisse. I was going to pick them all up, and we'd go cruising.

Except that there were lights flashing in my rearview mirror. When I saw the green light I pulled through the intersection, hoping the policeman would turn after some real criminal. He was after me. I pulled over and he did too.

The officer walked up. "May I see your license?"

I nodded and handed it to him.

He glanced at it. "You just got it today? It's still warm!"

"Yes, sir," I said.

"Didn't they tell you about cell phone calls?"

"Yes," I said despondently.

"It's going on your record as a warning. I'm sorry."

"Since the engine's off, can I make another call?" He nodded.

While the officer went back to his car, I called Jenna, Ashley, and Jarisse and told them I didn't feel like celebrating. After I hung up I thought back on all those years I'd wanted to drive. Now I had a mark on my record and my license wasn't even an hour old. I made a change that day. I've been careful to follow the rules and I've not gotten stopped again. I've learned that freedom and responsibility go hand in hand.

Student Self-Assessment

Narrative Rubric Checklist

Title: Driving into Trouble

Writer: Ellen Lightfield

5 **Ideas**
- Is the narrative about a bad choice?
- Does it give a reason for the decision?
- Do sensory details help the reader experience the events?

6 **Organization**
- Does the narrative have an interesting beginning?
- Are events in chronological order?
- Does the ending show what was learned?

5 **Voice**
- Does the narrative sound natural?
- Does the voice reflect the writer's feelings about the event?

5 **Word Choice**
- Does the writing contain specific nouns and active verbs?
- Does it contain descriptive modifiers?

3 **Sentence Fluency**
- Do the sentences have varied lengths and beginnings?
- Do the sentences read smoothly?

4 **Conventions**
- Does the narrative avoid errors in punctuation, spelling, and grammar?
- Is the dialogue punctuated correctly?

OVERALL COMMENTS:

I guess I implied my reasons more than stating them.

Some of my sentences don't read very smoothly, and I use a fragment or two. Also, too many sentences in the last paragraph start the same way.

I'm having trouble with commas.

Review your narrative.
Rate your narrative and write comments that explain why you gave yourself the scores you did.

Narrative

Reflecting on Your Writing

You've worked hard to write a personal narrative that your classmates will enjoy. Now take some time to think about your writing. Finish each of the sentence starters below on your own paper. Thinking about your writing will help you see how you are growing as a writer.

My Narrative

1. The strongest part of my personal narrative is . . .

2. The part that still needs work is . . .

3. The main thing I learned about writing a personal narrative is . . .

4. In my next personal narrative, I would like to . . .

5. One question I still have about writing personal narratives is . . .

Writing a Reflective Narrative

A mirror reflects the person you are on the outside: the color of your eyes, shape of your nose, and clothes you wear. But what reflects the person you are on the inside: your personality, hopes, fears, and experiences?

Writing is a powerful mirror. When you write a reflective narrative, you explore who you are now and who you were "back then." A reflective narrative focuses on a change you have experienced and reflects on how that change makes you unique.

In this chapter, you will read a personal narrative in which the writer recalls his changing relationship with his younger brother. Then you will write a reflective narrative of your own.

Writing Guidelines

    Subject: **A change in your life**
        Form: **Reflective narrative**
    Purpose: **To reflect on the impact of the change**
  Audience: **Classmates**

"They always say time changes things, but you actually have to change them yourself."

—Andy Warhol

Reflective Narrative

A reflective narrative looks back at a change in the writer's life. Linc wrote about his changing relationship with his little brother.

Beginning
The beginning provides background and introduces the topic.

Middle
The middle provides details and events leading up to the change.

The writer comes to a realization.

Not Taken for Granted

I guess I was spoiled. At first, I was an only child, cuddled and cooed over by parents, grandparents, aunts, and uncles. Up until I was eight years old, life was sweet. Then along came Grant, and everything changed.

Grant is my little brother. I don't remember all the details, but he was born a month prematurely, so he needed a lot of extra attention, especially from Mom. My mom and dad didn't ignore me, but I was no longer the center of their universe, and I resented the change in dynamics. And at first, I also resented Grant.

Fortunately, Grant's early birth didn't cause any real problems in his growth, and he crawled, toddled, and talked pretty much on schedule. My parents were still somewhat protective of him, but as he got older, he developed the obnoxious habit of attaching himself to me, following my every move. My parents warned me to be nice to him, but I found him totally annoying. By the time I became a teenager, he was, at five, my shadow, following me around, copying my every move, asking questions, and generally being a pest.

Still, despite my irritation, I began to enjoy him. He was a funny little guy, and I began to find his hero-worship endearing. He copied the way I walked, the way I talked, and even the way I ate.

I remember one time we were eating jelly sandwiches, and he was humming away as he ate.

"Grant, why are you humming?" I asked.

He looked genuinely surprised. "You do it, too."

"Do not," I growled. I took a bite then and realized I had been humming! Apparently, I hummed a lot and never even knew. I looked at Grant and the delighted little smirk on his face and had to laugh. He laughed, too, although I don't think he understood exactly why. Still, from then on, whenever one of us hummed, we both burst into laughter.

The writer reflects on the way the realization affected him.

As we got older, we established boundaries and alliances, becoming more considerate of each other. Grant stopped asking to go along on dates with me, and I set aside time to go fishing with him. He cheered me on at my soccer games, and I volunteered to coach his T-ball team. I taught him to moonwalk, and he taught me to laugh at myself.

I wonder if the transition happened because as he grew older he became less annoying and more of a buddy. Or was it because I had done the growing, becoming more patient, more able to share, more receptive to the unconditional love he offered? Looking back, I have come to the conclusion that maybe it was a combination of both.

Ending
The ending sums up the writer's reflection about the change.

Today, I am happy to say that after a rocky beginning, Grant and I are a team. We've already talked about how he'll come visit me when I am in college. It will be hard to be separated, but I know that we will always be close, if not in age or distance, then in that love shared by brothers.

Narrative

 Respond to the reading. Answer the following questions about the sample reflective narrative.

Ideas (1) What change does the writer reflect on? (2) What details and events does the writer use to show what life was like before the change and afterward?

Organization (3) How do the first and last paragraphs differ? How are they related? (4) What would you consider the turning point in the relationship?

Voice & Word Choice (5) What descriptive words show the changing relationship?

Prewriting Selecting a Topic

One way to find a topic for a reflective narrative is to think of ways that you have changed and explore the reasons for those changes. Linc made a chart of several ways he has changed and put an asterisk by the one he wanted to write about.

Then/Now Chart

Then	Now	Reason for Change
I wanted to be a professional football player when I grew up.	I plan to become a marine biologist.	I wasn't any good at football, but I love sea life.
* My little brother, Grant, was a real pest.	My brother is a lot of fun, and we're friends.	We both grew up.
I really wanted to date Bette.	I'm going out with Lyndsey.	Lyndsey and I have more in common.

Prewrite

Make a then/now chart. List how things used to be and how they are now. Then tell why they changed. Put an asterisk by the topic you would like to write about.

Gathering Details

Once you have your topic, you can collect and arrange your details to create the frame of your essay. Linc made a T-chart, listing events and details about life before and after the change.

T-Chart

Things that annoyed me then	Our relationship now
– He took up all the family's attention.	– I don't mind when he gets attention.
– He tattled on me to Mom and Dad.	– We have some "secrets."
– He asked a lot of annoying questions.	– I like his questions, and he listens to me.
– He copied how I walked, talked, and ate.	– I encourage him to be himself.
– We were kind of adversaries.	– We are friends.

Prewrite

Make a T-chart. List events that happened "then" and "now." Try to include at least five events and details in each list.

Organizing Details

Your reflective narrative may cover quite a long period of time, so you can't include every event or detail. Instead, you should include only events that demonstrate how your life was before, during, and after the change.

Linc used a time line to plot his narrative. First he focused on background (before the change), then on his realization (during the change), and finally reflection (after the change).

Time Line

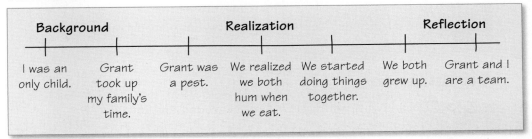

Background | Realization | Reflection

| I was an only child. | Grant took up my family's time. | Grant was a pest. | We realized we both hum when we eat. | We started doing things together. | We both grew up. | Grant and I are a team. |

Narrative

Prewrite

Create a time line for your reflective narrative. Order the points of your story to include your background, realization, and reflection.

Writing Creating Your First Draft

Use your prewriting to write your first draft. If you think of new ideas, go ahead and add them. Write freely, and don't worry about spelling or grammar at this time.

Beginning	Middle	Ending
Provide background details and events that build your narrative and lead up to the change.	Include an anecdote that helps demonstrate the change. Remember to show readers what is happening and use dialogue.	Reflect on events after the change and think about how your life was different.

Write

Write your first draft. Be sure to include a beginning, a middle, and an ending. Use all of your planning notes as a guide, and remain open to new ideas as you write.

Revising Improving Your Writing

Use the following checklist to decide how to improve your writing. Number your paper from 1 to 11. If you can answer "yes" to a question, place a check next to the number. If not, go back and revise your paper for that trait.

Revising Checklist

Ideas

_____ **1.** Is the change that I write about interesting?

_____ **2.** Have I included details and events that demonstrate the change?

Organization

_____ **3.** Does my beginning provide background and introduce the topic?

_____ **4.** Do the middle paragraphs show how I changed?

_____ **5.** Does the ending reflect on how my life was altered by this experience?

Voice

_____ **6.** Do I sound interested in the topic?

_____ **7.** Does my dialogue sound natural?

Word Choice

_____ **8.** Have I used specific nouns and vivid verbs?

_____ **9.** Have I used descriptive modifiers?

Sentence Fluency

_____ **10.** Do my sentences read smoothly?

_____ **11.** Have I varied the lengths and beginnings of my sentences?

Revise

Revise your first draft. Use the checklist above to revise your first draft. When you are finished, make a clean copy to edit.

Editing Checking for Conventions

Once you have revised your reflective narrative, you're ready to edit your writing for conventions. Use the following checklist to review your writing for punctuation, capitalization, spelling, and grammar errors.

Editing Checklist

Conventions

PUNCTUATION

_____ **1.** Have I used end punctuation correctly?

_____ **2.** Have I used apostrophes to show possession *(Grant's smile)*?

_____ **3.** Have I used commas correctly?

CAPITALIZATION

_____ **4.** Have I capitalized all proper nouns?

_____ **5.** Have I capitalized each speaker's first word in dialogue?

SPELLING

_____ **6.** Have I checked my spelling?

GRAMMAR

_____ **7.** Have I used the correct forms of verbs *(I saw,* not *I seen)*?

_____ **8.** Do my subjects and verbs agree in number *(We were going,* not *We was going)*?

_____ **9.** Have I used the right words?

Edit

Edit your narrative. Use the checklist above to find and correct any errors. Then ask someone else to check your work. Create a neat final copy and proofread it.

Publishing Sharing Your Writing

When you publish something, you make it public. By sharing your reflective narrative with an appreciative audience, you can let them know more about who you are.

Publish

Share your reflective narrative. Ask a friend or family member to read your narrative, or read it aloud to the person.

Expository Writing

Expository Writing
Writing an Informative Article

When you pick up a newspaper or magazine, you are entering a world of information. It's almost impossible to read a periodical and not learn something new. Informative articles in newspapers or magazines cover every topic under the sun, from aardvarks to zoology. These articles share common characteristics: They're created to inform and entertain. They contain timely information, even when the topic is historical. And they employ a lively writing style to hook the reader, present information in a logical sequence, and explain a topic clearly.

The best way to learn about article writing is to read articles in your favorite periodicals. Pay careful attention to the topic and focus, the way in which the writer hooks the reader, the development of the middle part, and so on. Then incorporate some of these techniques in your own writing.

In this chapter, you'll learn how to develop a well-organized, entertaining informative article suitable for publication in a newspaper or magazine.

Writing Guidelines

Subject: A timely topic
Form: Informative article
Purpose: To engage and inform
Audience: Local or school newspaper or magazine readers

"All glory comes from daring to begin."
—Eugene F. Ware

Expository Writing Warm-Up Processing Information

As a student, you are an expert at handling information. Every day in class, you hear information, you see it, you write it down, and you discuss it. Here are examples of the many types of information you process every day.

Facts: Things that can be proven

The great American author William Faulkner had a tough time making enough money in his early years.

Statistics: Facts that give precise numerical values

Faulkner wrote his novel *As I Lay Dying* in only six weeks while working the night shift at a local power plant, making less than seventy cents an hour.

Quotations: The exact words of a speaker

"Everything goes by the board: humor, pride, decency . . . to get the book written. If a writer has to rob his mother, he will not hesitate; the *Ode on a Grecian Urn* is worth any number of old ladies."
—William Faulkner

Anecdotes: Little stories that give insight

Faulkner hired himself out to write screenplays but hated living and working in Hollywood. Once when he struggled over a tough screenplay in his office, he asked his boss if he could go home to work on it. The boss agreed, thinking Faulkner was heading back to his Hollywood apartment. Instead, he headed back to Mississippi.

Try It!

Think about the classes you have had so far today. Which was most memorable? Choose one class period and write down a fact, a statistic, a quotation, and an anecdote that came from that class period. You will be using these details as you write an informative paragraph on the next page.

Writing an Informative Paragraph

An informative paragraph focuses on one main idea, supporting it with different types of details. Alex wrote the following informative paragraph about the money troubles of William Faulkner. Remember that a paragraph has three parts.

- The **topic sentence** introduces the main point of the paragraph.
- The **body sentences** use a variety of details to support the main point.
- The **closing sentence** restates the main point in an interesting way.

Topic Sentence

Body Sentences

Closing Sentence

Expository

Writing on a Dime

Though William Faulkner became one of the most famous American writers of the twentieth century, he had to struggle to make enough money. After publishing his classic novel *The Sound and the Fury,* Faulkner wrote the novel *Sanctuary* just to make money, but his publisher rejected it. Desperate, he took a night-shift job at a factory, making less than seventy cents an hour. Over a six-week period, while working at the factory, he spent his days writing the classic *As I Lay Dying.* Later, Faulkner hired himself out to write screenplays, but he hated working in Hollywood. Once he asked his boss if he could go home to work on a screenplay, and the boss agreed—not realizing Faulkner was heading all the way back to Mississippi. Faulkner had a sense of humor about his money troubles: "If a writer has to rob his mother, he will not hesitate; the *Ode on a Grecian Urn* is worth any number of old ladies." Luckily for his mother, Faulkner never stooped so low, and luckily for modern readers, he kept writing, even when he wasn't getting paid.

Write

Write your own informative paragraph. Write about an interesting class period you had today. Create a topic sentence that focuses on a main point about the class and include a variety of details to support your topic sentence.

"I reckon I'll be at the beck and call of folks with money all my life."
—William Faulkner

Understanding Your Goal

Your goal in this chapter is to write a well-organized informative article that engages and informs the reader. The traits listed in the chart below will help you plan and write your article.

Traits of Expository Writing

- **Ideas**
  Choose a topic that will interest the reader, write a clear focus statement, and include details that support the focus.

- **Organization**
  Start with a hook that captures the reader's attention. Expand the main focus in the middle paragraphs. Sum up the topic in the closing paragraph.

- **Voice**
  Use an engaging voice that shows your knowledge of the topic.

- **Word Choice**
  Choose words that explain your topic clearly. Use technical terms accurately.

- **Sentence Fluency**
  Write clear sentences with varied beginnings and lengths.

- **Conventions**
  Be sure that your punctuation, capitalization, spelling, and grammar are correct.

Get the big picture. Look at the rubric on pages 198–199 before you begin to write. You can use the rubric as a guide to develop your essay and as a tool to assess your completed writing.

"There are a thousand ways to write, and each is as good as the other if it fits you."
—Lillian Hellman

Informative Article

An informative article provides information in the form of statistics, anecdotes, quotations from experts, and even the writer's own experiences. In this sample, a student presents information about the high-risk sport of ice climbing.

Beginning
The beginning introduces the topic and presents the thesis statement (underlined).

Middle
The first middle paragraph uses a personal example to explain the sport's popularity.

The second middle paragraph explains how many ice climbers get their start.

Life on Ice

For most people, walking across an icy sidewalk is enough danger for one day. The thought of scaling a frozen waterfall with ropes and an ice ax might seem like a sure shortcut to the intensive-care unit, but for many high school students, the thrill of ice climbing is irresistible. More and more young outdoor enthusiasts are discovering the sport of ice climbing—and living on the edge.

Ice climbing isn't for everyone, but it's attracting a steady stream of newcomers. Danielle Harris is typical of the new breed of ice climbers. She's a high school senior who is tired of "ordinary" recreational pursuits like in-line skating and cycling. So last winter, Harris headed to New Hampshire's White Mountains to give ice climbing a try. "I was terrified at first," Harris says. "It looked just plain crazy." But once she was on the ropes, she discovered that while physically and mentally demanding, the sport was far from impossible. "I was able to do some good climbing on that first day," says Harris. "And from then on, I was hooked." She isn't alone. The number of high school students who have tried ice climbing continues to grow.

Believe it or not, many ice climbers get their start indoors—and for good reason. Indoor rock gyms have become increasingly popular as training grounds for inexperienced climbers ("Ice Geeks"). The gyms consist of vertical walls studded with hundreds of plastic handholds of various sizes and shapes. The handholds simulate the holds a climber might find on a real rock face, from large, chunky handles to tiny nubs of rock. Steve Carstens, a high school junior who has been ice climbing for two years in New York's Adirondack Mountains, got his start at an indoor rock gym. "Ice climbing isn't for everyone," Carstens point out. "And the rock gym is a great way to get a taste of the thrills of ice climbing without so much risk."

Expository

The third middle paragraph provides important safety information.

Because ice climbing is so risky, many first-time climbers find an experienced instructor to guide them. Every year, dozens of deaths and serious injuries happen to careless or unprepared rock and ice climbers (Brown and William 32). Falling, avalanches, and even hypothermia (a dangerously low body temperature caused by overexposure to cold weather) are all dangers of ice climbing. Guides can help beginning climbers follow safety rules and avoid taking unnecessary risks. "We have a saying in this business," says Ellen Gustafson, a veteran ice-climbing guide in Colorado. "There are old climbers. And there are bold climbers. But there are no old, bold climbers" ("Ice Forum").

The fourth middle paragraph gives the reader a feel for the experience of climbing.

If the risks of ice climbing are greater than in other sports, so are the thrills. From a hundred feet up a massive blue-green wall of ice, the view is breathtaking, and getting there means a physical and mental challenge that few have experienced. From the bottom of a wall, it's a constant battle of mind and muscle, as the climber chooses a viable route and uses a combination of poise and power to get to the top. "There's no workout like it," says Danielle Harris, "and there's no gym in the world as beautiful as an ice wall" ("Ice Forum").

Ending
The ending summarizes the article's main ideas and gives the reader something to think about.

Boosted by the enthusiasm of new participants such as Danielle Harris, the sport of ice climbing is growing, drawing climbers to ice walls from Alberta's Jasper National Park to the Bitterroot Mountains of Montana and New Hampshire's White Mountains. Ice climbing's unique combination of challenging workouts and heart-racing thrills is part of the draw. The feeling of accomplishment is no doubt another attraction for participants. After all, few individuals can show up at school on Monday morning and talk about scaling a 100-foot tower of ice over the weekend.

Respond to the reading. Answer the following questions.

Ideas (1) What are some of the characteristics of newcomers to ice climbing? (2) Why do many ice climbers get their start in the rock gym?

Organization (3) What is the purpose of the first sentence of each paragraph? Of the other sentences in each paragraph? (4) How does the ending paragraph help to summarize the main ideas in the essay?

Voice & Word Choice (5) Does the writer's interest in the topic come through in the writing? Explain.

Prewriting

All effective writing begins with prewriting. In the prewriting stage, you'll choose a topic, do some research, gather details, and organize your ideas.

Keys to Effective Prewriting

1. Choose a topic that you know well or would like to know more about. Focus on finding a topic that will interest your reader as well.

2. Identify sources of information and begin your research.

3. Gather a variety of interesting details about your topic.

4. Write a thesis statement and topic sentences.

5. Plan your essay using an outline or an organized list.

Expository

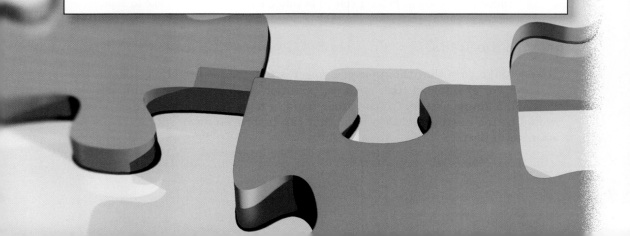

Prewriting Selecting a Topic

To create an interesting and effective informative article, you need to select a topic that interests both you and your reader. One way to begin your search is to look at a "Basics of Life" list, which includes general subject areas. Karla read through the list and selected four subject areas that interested her.

"Basics of Life" List

communication	energy	medicine	sports
computers	environment	politics	travel
economics	food	schools	weather

Gathering Details

Then she created a gathering chart, writing the general subject areas across the top and listing specific topic ideas under each one. She put a star beside the topic that interested her most.

Gathering Chart

Environment	Politics	Energy	Weather
pollution	computer voting	biofuels	hurricanes
hybrid cars	new political	"green" building*	global warming
land conservation	parties	windmills	raindrops
	our new governor		

Prewrite

Create a gathering chart. Select four general subject areas that interest you and list them across the top of a piece of paper. Then, beneath each one, list specific topic ideas. Place a star (*) beside the topic you would like to explore.

Focus on the Traits

Ideas Make sure that the topic you select is neither too broad nor too narrow. For example, a topic such as "pollution" would be too difficult to cover in a single article. On the other hand, a topic such as "raindrops" would be too narrow. Select a topic that can be broken down into a number of parts.

Researching Your Topic

In order to create an informative article that engages and informs an audience, you'll need to do some research. Remember that you'll need the most current information possible. The following strategies can help you to find engaging, informative content for your article.

- **Begin with your own experience.** Think about why this topic interests you. What connection do you have to the ideas? What personal experiences or anecdotes could you share?
- **Search traditional sources.** Visit a library and use the *Readers' Guide* to find recent magazine articles on your topic. Also check out books with recent copyright dates. Surf the Internet, but carefully evaluate each Web page: Is it current? Is it correct? Is it reliable? Is it balanced (not biased)?
- **Do some investigating.** Experts surround you. Think of teachers in your school who are knowledgeable about your topic, or people in your community who are involved with the issue. Arrange an interview with such a person, or go someplace to gather information firsthand.

Listing Your Sources

Karla made a list of sources of information about "green" building practices.

Sources List

Personal Experience:
  Buying a new water heater
  Insulating the basement

Traditional Sources:
  <u>Green Builder</u> magazine
  <u>Nature's Architect</u> by Ronald Stratt
  U.S. Green Building Council Web site

Experts and Special Sites:
  Hal Jefferson, Green City Contractors
  Karen Johnson, Energy Alliance

Expository

Prewrite

List sources and begin your research. Write down the personal experiences, traditional sources, and experts and special sites you can investigate. Then conduct your research.

Prewriting Gathering Different Types of Details

An informative article should be filled with different types of details:

- **Facts** are details that can be proven. Facts provide strong support for the main points of your essay, and they show that you understand the topic.

  The generous use of foam insulation provides protection from summer heat and winter cold, thus reducing both heating and air-conditioning costs.

- **Statistics** present significant numerical information about your topic. Statistics make the information you present precise and quantifiable.

  After Hurricane Katrina in 2005, gas and oil production in the Gulf fell 60 percent, and prices of home heating oil rose to record levels.

- **Quotations** are the exact words of someone involved with your topic. A quotation provides significant opinions or information about your topic.

  Hal Jefferson of Green City Contractors says, "People understand that they'll be paying utility bills on a new home or business for a long time. That's why more and more of them are asking us to make energy efficiency a part of our plans."

- **Examples** are representative items or ideas that illustrate a main point. Examples demonstrate an abstract idea in a concrete way.

  Other designs may include alternative heating technologies, such as furnaces that burn wood pellets, wood chips, or even corn stalks.

- **Anecdotes** are little stories that prove your point. Use anecdotes from your own life or the lives of others, but make sure that each story demonstrates a specific point about your topic.

  Green building can also be expressed in small ways. When the water heater at my home broke down, my dad turned bad luck into good luck by buying a model that was 30 percent more efficient. We now enjoy more hot water for less money.

Prewrite

Gather different types of details. As you research, gather a variety of details that will explain your topic and strengthen your essay.

Focus on the Traits

Organization As you gather the different types of details above, remember to note the source. If your teacher requires you to include parenthetical references and a works-cited page, see pages **425–438** and **392**.

Writing a Thesis Statement

After completing her research, Karla was ready to write her thesis statement. She used the following formula:

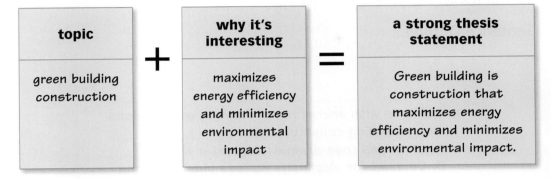

topic		why it's interesting		a strong thesis statement
green building construction	**+**	maximizes energy efficiency and minimizes environmental impact	**=**	Green building is construction that maximizes energy efficiency and minimizes environmental impact.

Prewrite

Write your thesis statement. Use the model above to create a thesis statement for your essay. Try different versions until you are satisfied.

Writing Topic Sentences

Every thesis needs the support of three or more main points. Karla reviewed her research, listed main points, and wrote a topic sentence for each.

Main Points List

1. Energy problems make green building important.

   Topic sentence 1: Problems with energy are changing people's ideas about building construction.

2. Green buildings use energy efficiently.

   Topic sentence 2: Green buildings are designed to use energy efficiently.

3. Some green buildings generate energy.

   Topic sentence 3: Green building practices not only save energy but can also generate it.

4. Location and materials also are important.

   Topic sentence 4: Builders of green structures also pay attention to where they build and what materials they use.

Prewrite

Write topic sentences. List main points that will support your thesis statement. Then, for each main point, write a topic sentence.

Expository

Prewriting Outlining Your Paper

Before writing your informative article, organize your ideas and details in an outline. Include topic sentences and supporting points. Karla wrote a sentence outline, but your teacher may prefer a topic outline.

Sentence Outline

I. Problems with energy are changing people's ideas about building construction.
   A. Oil prices rose dramatically after Katrina.
   B. Demand for electricity causes blackouts and brownouts.
   C. People are growing more aware of the value of energy efficiency and want energy-efficient homes.
II. Green buildings are designed to use energy efficiently.
   A. Building sites make use of natural sunlight.
   B. Efficient materials and appliances are built in.
   C. Designs save water as well as energy.
III. Green building practices not only save energy but can also generate it.
   A. Some designs use solar panels and windmills.
   B. Other designs use furnaces that burn wood chips or other biofuels.
   C. Some designs even use fuel cells.
IV. Builders of green structures also pay attention to where they build and what materials they use.
   A. Green building sites are chosen to minimize dependence on cars.
   B. They recycle building sites and use materials that have low environmental impact.

Prewrite

Create an outline. Use the example above as your guide to create a sentence outline, or create a topic outline if your teacher prefers. (See page 591.)

Writing

You have identified a topic, done some research, and created an outline with main ideas and details. Now you are ready to draft your informative article.

Keys to Effective Writing

1. Use your outline as a writing guide.

2. Write on every other line or double-space if you are using a computer. This will allow room for changes.

3. Introduce the topic and state your thesis in the first paragraph.

4. Include your topic sentences in your first draft.

5. Use specific details to support your topic sentences.

6. Restate your thesis at the end.

Expository

Writing Seeing How the Parts Fit Together

The graphic below shows how the elements of an informative article should fit together. Use this graphic as a guide to help you write your first draft. (The examples are from the student essay on pages **177–180**.)

Beginning

The **beginning** introduces the topic and states the writer's thesis.

Thesis Statement
Green building is construction that maximizes energy efficiency and minimizes environmental impact.

Middle

The **middle** paragraphs support the writer's thesis.

Topic Sentences
Problems with energy are changing people's ideas about building construction.

Green buildings are designed to use energy efficiently.

Green building practices not only save energy but can also generate it.

Builders of green structures also pay attention to where they build and what materials they use.

Ending

The **ending** restates the thesis, sums up the main ideas, and gives the reader something to think about.

Closing Sentence
This powerful combination of monetary savings and environmental benefits is the reason builders and buyers everywhere are going green.

Starting Your Article

The beginning paragraph of your informative article should engage the reader, introduce your topic, and provide a thesis statement. Here are three strategies for engaging the reader:

> Beginning
> Middle
> Ending

- **Make a startling statement.**
  The United States faced serious energy problems long before Hurricane Katrina ravaged Gulf Coast oil refineries.

- **Ask a provocative question.**
  How can consumers fight high energy costs?

- **Begin with a strong quotation.**
  According to Alan Davidson of the Energy Council, "The secret to solving the energy crisis is not to use less energy, but to make better use of the energy."

- **Connect the idea with current events.**
  After the rolling blackouts during the heat wave last summer, many local residents are wondering how they can conserve energy.

Beginning Paragraph

Karla began her essay by connecting with current events. Then she introduced the topic and presented her thesis statement.

The writer engages the reader and states her thesis (underlined).

> With energy costs rising, owners of homes and businesses are taking the heat. They're paying more to heat and cool the buildings they own, and they're spending more to run appliances and office machines, too. But green building, a new trend in the construction industry, is making things easier on homeowners, business owners, and the environment. Green building is construction that maximizes energy efficiency and minimizes environmental impact.

Expository

Write a beginning paragraph. Use the guidelines above to help you begin your informative article. (Also refer to the sample beginning on page 167.)

Writing Developing the Middle

The middle part of your informative article adds ideas and details that expand upon your thesis statement. To write the middle part of your article, begin each paragraph with a topic sentence. Write additional sentences that add a variety of supporting details. Be sure to use your outline (see page 174) as a guide.

Middle Paragraphs

This is the middle part of Karla's informative article on green building practices. Read it carefully and notice how she has used topic sentences, facts, statistics, examples, and quotations to build her paragraphs.

> The topic sentence offers a main point (underlined).

> The body includes facts, statistics, examples, and quotations that expand on the topic sentence.

> Each paragraph explores a new main idea about the topic.

<u>Problems with energy are changing people's ideas about building construction.</u> After Hurricane Katrina, gas and oil production in the Gulf of Mexico fell 60 percent, and prices of home heating oil rose to record levels ("Post Katrina" 6). For that matter, brownouts and blackouts, or partial and total losses of electricity, regularly plague urban areas during the summer. These problems, says Hal Jefferson, president of Green City Contractors, have made people more aware of the importance of energy-efficient building. "People understand that they'll be paying utility bills on a new home or business for a long time," Jefferson says. "That's why more and more of them are asking us to make energy efficiency a part of our plans."

<u>Green buildings are designed to use energy efficiently.</u> Builders start by using materials that maximize efficiency. The generous use of foam insulation provides protection from summer heat and winter cold, thus reducing both heating and air-conditioning costs. In addition, light-colored exterior paints and roofing materials reflect sunlight, cutting cooling costs even more. Carefully placed windows take advantage of free natural lighting, and motion-detecting light switches turn lights on when people enter a room and off when they leave it. Water costs can be reduced, too, by using low-flow water fixtures and high-efficiency water heaters.

<u>Green building practices not only save energy but can also generate it.</u> Some designs for green homes and

businesses incorporate on-site energy generation technologies such as solar panels or windmills. Other designs may include alternative heating technologies such as furnaces that burn wood pellets, wood chips, or even corn stalks. And even more efficient technologies such as fuel cells have also begun to find their way into green designs (Stratt 263). Over the long run, these technologies help building owners cut energy costs and save money.

Builders of green structures also pay attention to where they build and what materials they use. Whenever possible, they recycle building sites instead of carving up untouched land. In addition, builders prefer sites near city centers, thus decreasing the need for residents and workers to use cars. Wherever a structure is placed, green builders study the natural light and shade of the spot so that they can make the best use of the environment. Green builders also prefer recycled building materials. If new materials are used, builders prefer those that have a minimal environmental impact, such as bamboo flooring and low-vapor paint.

The final middle paragraph addresses the last main idea.

Expository

Write

Write your middle paragraphs. Create middle paragraphs that expand upon your thesis statement. Start each paragraph with a topic sentence. Then follow with explanations and details that support the topic sentence.

Focus on the Traits

Organization As you write, remember to connect your ideas. Repeat a key word from one sentence in the next.

Builders start by <u>using</u> materials that maximize efficiency. The generous <u>use</u> of foam insulation provides protection from summer heat and winter cold.

Use transition words and phrases like these:

after	for that matter	thus	in addition	too
some	whenever possible	both	other	also

Writing Ending Your Article

Beginning

Middle

Ending

The ending paragraph needs to effectively wrap up your essay. The following guidelines will help.

- **Restate your thesis.**
  Green building has found new ways to apply the old maxim "Reduce, reuse, and recycle."

- **Summarize the main ideas of your article.**
  Due to increased energy demand, dwindling supply, and higher prices, builders are designing dwellings that use less energy and even generate their own.

- **Make the reader think.**
  By building more efficient homes and using the free energy supplied by the sun and the wind, green builders are constructing the future, one house at a time.

Ending Paragraph

Karla's ending paragraph restates her thesis and supports it with a powerful example and a final insight.

The thesis is powerfully restated.

The essay ends with a final insight.

> With energy prices predicted to rise, it looks like green building is here to stay—and for good reason. According to the U.S. Green Building Council, building green admittedly adds about 2 percent to the initial construction cost of an average home. But, over a 20-year period, the energy savings will replace 20 percent of the construction cost and benefit the environment besides. This powerful combination of monetary savings and environmental benefits is the reason builders and buyers everywhere are going green.

Write

Write the ending paragraph. Restate your thesis in the topic sentence, summarize the supporting ideas, and leave your reader something to think about.

Prepare a copy of your entire article. Double-space on a computer or write on every other line. This gives you room to revise.

Revising

Revision improves your work in many ways. When you revise, you may add or delete details, rearrange parts of your writing, or create a more engaging, informative voice. You also check your word choice and sentence fluency.

Keys to Effective Revising

1. Read your essay aloud to yourself or to a friend.

2. Be sure you have provided engaging, accurate information about your topic.

3. Check your topic sentences to confirm that you have followed your outline.

4. Be sure you have included a variety of details—facts, statistics, quotations, and examples.

5. Check your draft for strong word choice and variety in sentence length and structure.

6. To mark revisions on your first draft, use the editing and proofreading marks found on the inside back cover of this book.

Expository

Revising for Ideas

 6 My essay brims with fascinating details that engage the reader.

5 My essay includes a clear thesis statement and a wide variety of details.

 4 My thesis statement is clear, but I need more variety in my details.

When you revise for *ideas,* you make sure you have written a clear thesis statement and included a variety of details. The rubric strip above will guide you.

Have I included a variety of details?

You have included a variety of details if you have used facts, statistics, quotations, examples, and anecdotes. Use a details grid to check your details.

Details Grid

	Facts	Statistics	Quotations	Examples	Anecdotes
Beginning	✓				
Paragraph 1	✓		✓		
Paragraph 2	✓	✓		✓	✓

 ## Exercise

Create a details grid for the following paragraph. Make a check mark for each kind of detail you find.

1   Scientists have made many recent discoveries that indicate life spans could
2 be lengthened—possibly indefinitely. One study conducted on mice showed that a
3 low-calorie diet caused a "survival gene" to trigger, making the mice superefficient
4 at using energy and repairing damage to their bodies. Another study, performed on
5 fruit flies, indicated that reproduction was the key to longevity. Flies, whose normal
6 life spans were 35 days, were prevented from reproducing until much later. After a
7 few generations, the life spans reached 70 days. Of course, most people faced with
8 the option of eating very little and not reproducing until late in life may wonder if it
9 just seems that you live longer!

Revise

Check the variety of your details. Create a details grid and check the types of details you used in each paragraph.

3 I need a clearer thesis statement and more types of details to support it.

2 I need a thesis statement and many more supporting details.

1 I need help understanding how to write a thesis statement and conduct research.

Have I created a clear thesis statement?

You have created a clear thesis statement if it does the following:

1. Identifies your topic.

2. Provides interesting, engaging information.

Check your thesis statement by underlining the part that identifies the topic and double-underlining the part that provides interesting information.

Scientists who work on aging envision a future in which human beings can outlive 240-year-old Galápagos turtles.

◢ Exercise

Copy each of the following thesis statements. Underline the part that identifies the topic and double-underline the part that provides interesting information. If a thesis statement lacks one or both parts, write a replacement.

1. In the fight against aging, scientists have enlisted the aid of some unlikely helpers: fruit flies and field mice.

2. Scientists are working hard to discover things.

3. In addition to promoting diet, exercise, and medical care, scientists now are devising gene therapies to help all of us live longer.

4. Everybody gets to benefit from science—well, everybody but flies.

Revise

Check your thesis statement. Make sure you name your topic and reveal what is interesting about it.

Ideas
A statistic provides more specific support.

After Hurricane Katrina in 2005, gas and oil production in the Gulf of Mexico fell, ^60 percent^ and prices of home heating oil rose to record levels. For that matter, brownouts and blackouts . . .

Expository

Revising **for** Organization

 6 Each part of my essay does its job perfectly, providing engaging information.

 5 My essay has a clear beginning and ending, and the middle paragraphs are ordered and unified.

 4 My essay has a beginning and ending. The middle paragraphs are in order, but some lack unity.

When you revise for *organization,* you check the structure of your essay. Make sure the paragraphs are in order and have unity. The rubric strip above will guide your revision.

Have I chosen the best order for my paragraphs?

You have chosen the best order for your paragraphs if you begin with basic information and advance toward the more-complicated ideas. Ask yourself these questions:

- What **background information** does my reader need to know?
- What **basic information** should I provide next?
- What **higher-level knowledge** can I supply afterward?
- What **complex ideas** should I present last?

 ## Exercise

The topic sentences below are out of order. Read the thesis statement and then use the questions above to decide how to order the topic sentences.

Thesis statement: A black hole seems to break all the laws of physics, but actually those laws demonstrate that black holes exist.

If the force of gravity is powerful enough to overcome both electron degeneracy and neutron degeneracy, the star shrinks until all its mass takes up no more space than a pinpoint.

The first law of black holes is gravity—the force that forms and feeds a black hole.

As the star shrinks, it reaches the point where the electrons are pressing upon each other—a phase called *electron degeneracy.*

When a massive star runs out of fuel, it may explode, becoming a supernova, or implode, becoming a black hole.

 Revise

Check the order of your paragraphs. Make sure that you have begun with background and basic information and progress to more complex issues.

3 My essay has a beginning and an ending, but the middle paragraphs are out of order and lack unity.

 2 My essay runs together without a clear beginning, middle, or ending, and the paragraphs lack unity.

 1 I need help understanding how to organize an informative essay.

Does each paragraph have unity?

A paragraph has unity if each of its details supports the topic sentence. If a detail does not support the topic sentence, it should be cut.

Exercise

The following paragraph includes details that do not support the topic sentence. Indicate which sentences should be eliminated to create unity.

1　　**Not all salamanders that begin the annual migration finish it. That's because**
2　**they face a number of hazards along the way. At road crossings, automobiles take**
3　**a heavy toll on the tiny amphibians. Birds, which migrate by air, do not face this**
4　**particular hazard. Raccoons are always on the look out for salamanders, which**
5　**make an easy meal. But owls are no threat because they eat rodents instead. And**
6　**even curious humans can harm salamanders by picking them up with dry hands,**
7　**which can transmit diseases.**

Organization
Any detail that does not support the topic sentence is cut, giving the paragraph unity.

Green building practices not only save energy but can also generate it. Some designs for green homes and businesses incorporate on-site energy generation technologies such as solar panels or windmills. ~~Both of these technologies have been around for decades.~~ Other designs may include alternative heating technologies . . .

Expository

Revising for Voice

| 6 | My voice sounds professional and polished from start to finish. | 5 | My voice is knowledgeable. Level of language and tone are appropriate. | 4 | My voice is knowledgeable, but either the level of language or tone needs adjusting. |

When you revise for *voice,* you make sure you have used an appropriate tone and the correct level of language. The rubric strip above can guide you.

How can I create an appropriate tone?

You create an appropriate tone by using language that is courteous and shows your interest in the topic. The chart below includes words that would create an appropriate tone as well as those that would not.

Create a voice that sounds . . . interested	Avoid a voice that sounds . . .		
	sarcastic	flippant	bored
unique	weird	wacky	odd
gigantic	bloated	puffy	fat
microscopic	insignificant	wee	puny

Exercise

Read the following paragraph from an informative article about growing giant pumpkins. The tone should be friendly and interested, but it currently sounds hostile. For each underlined word or phrase, write a replacement that would make the tone more appropriate.

1   It's important, says Smith, to keep your pumpkin patch weed free. To do this,
2   he uses some <u>disgusting-looking</u> composted manure. The compost attracts <u>these</u>
3   <u>nasty little</u> bugs that help to <u>slaughter</u> garden pests like hornworms. If this doesn't
4   work, Smith uses <u>deadly</u> natural pesticides. These chemicals come from plants and
5   so won't <u>kill or maim</u> humans.

Revise

Check your tone. Watch for words and phrases that create an inappropriate tone. Replace them with synonyms that show your interest in the topic in a courteous way.

3 My voice is sometimes uncertain because of inappropriate level of language and tone.

2 I need to make my tone consistent and use the right level of language in my writing.

1 I need help understanding what level of language and tone are.

How can I create the right level of language?

You create the right level of language by making sure your voice does not sound too formal or informal for your audience: your classmates.

- A voice that is **too formal** sounds stuffy and arrogant, uses long, impressive-sounding words, avoids contractions, and seems self-important.
- A voice that is **too informal** uses slang, catchphrases, and jargon and sounds sloppy and slapdash.
- A voice that is **just right** sounds conversational, welcoming, and knowledgeable.

Exercise

Each of the following sentences deals with the same topic, though only one has the right level of language. Identify which sentence is too formal, which is too informal, and which is just right. Explain your choices.

1. Though the labor may prove taxing, the final product—an elephantine gourd—justifies the effort.
2. Though you gotta work yourself near to falling over, you get this big huge punkin pal when all's said and done.
3. Though growing giant pumpkins takes hard work, the hobby offers big rewards.

Revise

Check your level of language. Make sure your article isn't too formal or informal for your audience.

Voice
The writer improves the language level and tone of the essay.

The generous use of foam insulation
~~Builders squirt all this foamy junk in the walls to~~ provide**s**

protection from summer heat and winter cold, ~~so these~~
thus reducing both heating and air-conditioning costs.
~~dudes at the gas company don't wind up with so much cash.~~

Expository

Revising for Word Choice

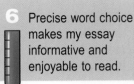

6 Precise word choice makes my essay informative and enjoyable to read.

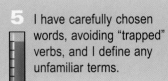

5 I have carefully chosen words, avoiding "trapped" verbs, and I define any unfamiliar terms.

4 My writing does not have many "trapped" verbs, and I usually define unfamiliar terms.

When you revise for *word choice,* you check for "trapped" verbs and define any unfamiliar terms. The rubric strip above will guide you.

How can I check for "trapped" verbs?

You have trapped a verb if you have turned it into a noun by adding an ending such as *ion, tion, ing, ent, ance, ence, ancy, ency, tian,* or *sis.* Sentences that contain trapped verbs tend to be wordy and should be rewritten to free the verbs.

Sentence with Trapped Verbs

The occurrence of global warming is partly due to the production of greenhouse gases by automobiles.

Sentence Rewritten to Free Verbs

Global warming occurs partly because automobiles produce greenhouse gases.

Exercise

Rewrite each sentence below, freeing the trapped verb (in bold).

1. The **tendency** of Americans to drive large vehicles adds to the problem.
2. Scientists performed an **analysis** of the worldwide climate.
3. Their **conclusion** is that the temperature is already changing.
4. Governments cannot seem to offer a **solution** to the problem.
5. Individual drivers, however, can make the **resolution** to buy fuel-efficient cars.

Revise

Free trapped verbs. Read your article, watching for words that end in *ion, tion, ing, ent, ance, ence, ancy, ency, tian,* or *sis.* Look for the verb trapped in the word. Then think of ways to rewrite the sentence using the freed verb.

I have a number of "trapped" verbs in my writing, and I need to define some terms.

 My writing sounds wordy because of "trapped" verbs, and I need to define many technical terms.

 I need help choosing the right words in my writing.

How should I handle unfamiliar terms?

You can handle unfamiliar terms in one of two ways:

Replacing the Term

Extruded polystyrene **provides a high** R-value **for buildings.**
Foam insulation **helps create** fuel-efficient **buildings.**

Defining the Term

Some houses in Iceland use geothermal energy, **which literally means heat from the earth.**

Exercise

Read the paragraph below, noting the words highlighted in blue. Rewrite the paragraph, replacing some of the highlighted terms and defining others. If necessary, use a dictionary.

1   Energy companies have found a unique source of energy—your local landfill.
2   When garbage undergoes decomposition, it produces large amounts of methane.
3   This methane can be used to power turbines that produce electricity. Because the
4   combustion of methane produces little particulate matter, the gas is a relatively
5   clean fuel.

Revise

Check for unfamiliar terms. Read your essay and underline terms the reader may not understand. Replace the terms or define them.

Word Choice
The writer defines unfamiliar terms.

For that matter, brownouts and blackouts, , or partial and total losses of electricity, regularly plague

urban areas during the summer. These problems, . . .

Expository

Revising for Sentence Fluency

 6 My sentences are skillfully written and easy to follow.

 5 My sentences flow well, and I have avoided rambling sentences and fragments.

 4 Most of my sentences flow well, but one or two may ramble a bit.

When you revise for *sentence fluency,* you make sure your sentences have a variety of lengths and beginnings. Break up any rambling sentences and fix sentence fragments. The rubric strip above can help you revise for fluency.

How can I fix rambling sentences?

To fix a rambling sentence, watch for places in which coordinating conjunctions such as *and, or,* or *but* are used to join several clauses. Break any rambling sentences into shorter sentences, rewriting as necessary.

Rambling Sentence

Snowboarders are more likely to visit the slopes during the week and weekends tend to be more popular with downhill skiers but cross-country skiers can be found in equal numbers on weekdays and weekends.

Separate Sentences

Snowboarders are more likely to visit the slopes during the week, while weekends tend to attract more downhill skiers. Cross-country skiers can be found in equal numbers on weekdays and weekends.

 ## Exercise

Rewrite the following paragraph to eliminate rambling sentences.

1   Many people like portable table saws because they are versatile. A portable
2 table saw can cut plywood and such saws can also be used for precision cuts
3 in furniture making and they are perfect for cutting framing timber for home
4 construction. In addition, you can take a portable saw with you wherever you go
5 and maybe that's why sales of such saws have increased 50 percent since 2003.

Revise

Fix rambling sentences. Read your essay carefully. Fix any rambling sentences by creating shorter sentences, rewriting as necessary.

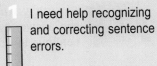
3 Some of my sentences ramble, and I have a few fragments.

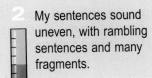
2 My sentences sound uneven, with rambling sentences and many fragments.

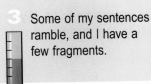
1 I need help recognizing and correcting sentence errors.

How can I fix sentence fragments?

You can fix sentence fragments by making sure that each of your sentences has a subject and a predicate and represents a complete thought.

Sentence Fragments

Hungry bears.	missing verb
Catch salmon with their paws.	missing subject
When they fish.	incomplete thought

Complete Sentence

Hungry bears catch salmon with their paws when they fish.

Exercise

Rewrite the following paragraph to eliminate sentence fragments.

1   Geese migrate to avoid winter weather. When they stop in fields and marshes
2 along the way. Eat grains, grasses, and other plant products. Once they arrive in
3 warmer climates. The geese adapt to life there. They generally spend about six
4 months in the South.

Revise

Eliminate sentence fragments. Correct groups of words that are missing a subject or a predicate or do not express a complete thought.

Sentence Fluency
A sentence fragment is corrected.

In addition, builders prefer sites near city centers. Thus
decreasing the need for residents and workers to use cars.

Expository

Revising Improving Your Writing

Revise

Check your revising. On a piece of paper, write the numbers 1 to 12. If you can answer "yes" to a question, put a check mark next to that number. If not, continue to work on that part of your article.

Revising Checklist

Ideas

_____ **1.** Have I chosen an interesting topic?
_____ **2.** Do I state my thesis clearly?
_____ **3.** Have I included a variety of details to support my thesis?

Organization

_____ **4.** Have I created an effective beginning, middle, and ending?
_____ **5.** Have I chosen the best order for my middle paragraphs?
_____ **6.** Does each paragraph have unity?

Voice

_____ **7.** Do I use an appropriate tone?
_____ **8.** Have I created the right level of language?

Word Choice

_____ **9.** Have I avoided "trapping" any verbs?
_____ **10.** Have I replaced or explained any unfamiliar terms?

Sentence Fluency

_____ **11.** Have I avoided rambling sentences?
_____ **12.** Have I fixed sentence fragments?

Revise

Make a clean copy. When you've finished revising, make a clean copy of your essay for editing.

Editing

Now that you have finished revising your essay, you are ready to edit for conventions: punctuation, capitalization, spelling, and grammar.

Keys to Effective Editing

1. Use a dictionary, a thesaurus, and the "Proofreader's Guide" (see pages 604–763) as editing resources.

2. Check your writing for punctuation, capitalization, spelling, and grammar errors.

3. Edit your essay on a printed copy and enter the corrections on your computer. Otherwise, complete a clean handwritten copy that includes the corrections.

4. Use the editing and proofreading marks on the inside back cover of this book.

Expository

Editing for Conventions

6 My grammar and punctuation are correct, and the copy is free of spelling errors.

5 I have a few minor errors in grammar, spelling, or punctuation, but they won't distract the reader.

4 I must correct some errors in punctuation, spelling, or grammar that may distract the reader.

When you edit for *conventions*, check your punctuation, capitalization, spelling, and grammar. The rubric strip above will guide your editing.

How can I check my subject-verb agreement?

You can check your subject-verb agreement by making sure singular subjects have singular verbs and plural subjects have plural verbs. (Remember that a singular verb often ends in *s,* and a plural verb often does not.)

The planet Mercury orbits **nearest the sun, but** Venus is **the hottest planet.**
The terrestrial planets include **Mercury, Venus, Earth, and Mars.**

Compound Subjects with *and*

Compound subjects connect with *and* require a plural verb.
Mercury, Venus, Earth, and Mars have **solid surfaces.**

Compound Subjects with *or*

If the subjects are joined by *or,* the verb must agree with the subject nearest to it.
Either **Pluto** or **Uranus is** farthest from the sun at any given time, due to Pluto's elliptical orbit.

Exercise

Rewrite each sentence below to correct subject-verb agreement errors.

1. Both Saturn and Jupiter has rings around them.
2. The rings around Saturn is much more spectacular.
3. The Kuiper Belt contain billions of asteroids.
4. Halley's comet or other occasional visitors flies into view every few decades or so.
5. Either Jupiter or Saturn are almost massive enough to become a star.

Edit

Check your subject-verb agreement. Make sure that singular subjects have singular verbs and plural subjects have plural verbs.

3 I need to correct a number of errors that will confuse my reader.

2 I need to fix many errors that make my writing hard to read and understand.

1 I need help finding errors and making corrections.

Are my pronouns clearly linked to their antecedents?

Your pronouns are clearly linked to their antecedents if the pronoun clearly refers to the most recent noun with the same number and gender.

Galileo discovered four moons of Jupiter with his homemade telescope.

If another noun intervenes, the antecedent may be unclear. The pronoun should be replaced or the sentence should be rewritten.

Galileo's discovery showed that not all things revolved around Earth, and it angered many people.

Galileo's discovery showed that not all things revolved around Earth, and this idea angered many people.

Exercise

Rewrite each of the following sentences to clear up the antecedent problems.

1. Most **people** believed the planets and stars circled Earth, and **they** held to their belief.
2. Galileo's **denial** of his belief was reluctant, and **it** made him feel sick.
3. Even after recanting, Galileo murmured about **Earth** and its orbit around the sun, "And yet, **it** moves."

Check your antecedents. Make sure each pronoun refers to the last noun that agrees with it in number and gender.

Expository

Conventions
A sentence is rewritten because of an unclear pronoun.

Green builders also prefer recycled building materials. ~~When~~ If new materials are used, builders prefer ~~they choose new materials, they use~~ those that have a minimal environmental impact, such as bamboo flooring . . .

Editing Checking for Conventions

Edit

Check your editing. On a piece of paper, write the numbers 1 to 10. If you can answer "yes" to a question, put a check mark after that number. If you can't, continue to edit for that convention.

Editing Checklist

Conventions

PUNCTUATION

_____ **1.** Do I use end punctuation after all my sentences?

_____ **2.** Do I use commas after long introductory phrases and clauses?

_____ **3.** Have I cited sources correctly in my essay? (See pages **425–438**.)

CAPITALIZATION

_____ **4.** Do I start all my sentences with capital letters?

_____ **5.** Do I capitalize all proper nouns and adjectives?

SPELLING

_____ **6.** Have I spelled all words correctly?

_____ **7.** Have I double-checked words my spell-checker may have missed?

GRAMMAR

_____ **8.** Do my subjects and verbs agree in number?

_____ **9.** Are my pronouns clearly linked to their antecedents?

_____ **10.** Have I used the right words *(there, their, they're)*?

Creating a Title

After your editing is complete, add a title that engages your reader and sums up your article. Here are a few ways to approach this task.

- Be creative: **Building Green and Saving Green**
- Use a line from the article: **Maximum Efficiency and Minimum Impact**
- Use a saying: **It *Is* Easy Being Green**

Publishing Sharing Your Essay

The purpose of an informative article is to engage and inform your reader. After preparing a final copy of your essay, consider reaching the public with your ideas in one of the ways presented below.

Publish

Format your final copy. To format a handwritten essay, use the guidelines below or follow your teacher's instructions. (If you are using a computer, see pages 91–95.) Make a clean copy and carefully proofread it.

Focusing on Presentation

- Write neatly using blue or black ink.
- Place your name in the upper left corner of page 1.
- Skip a line and center your title; skip another line and start your essay.
- Indent every paragraph and leave a one-inch margin on all four sides.
- Write your last name and the page number in the upper right corner of every page.

Publish Your Article

Use e-mail or the postal service to send your article to a local or school-based magazine or newspaper. Before sending your article, make sure it conforms to the publication's submission guidelines.

Publish It Yourself

With today's desktop publishing software, you can easily format and print copies of your article. Depending upon the topic you've chosen, you may even be able to add your own photographs or illustrations. Once you've printed your article, you can give it to members of your audience or post it on a bulletin board or other prominent site. Be sure to get permission before posting.

Give a Public Reading

Another way to share your article is to give a public reading to classmates, friends, or family. Schedule a time that is convenient for you and your audience. Practice reading your article in advance to ensure a smooth, clear presentation.

Expository

Rubric for Expository Writing

Use the following rubric to guide and assess your expository writing. Refer to it whenever you want to improve your writing using the six traits.

6 Ideas	**5**	**4**
The ideas in the essay are compelling from start to finish.	The essay shows a clear relationship between thesis and supporting evidence.	The essay presents a clear topic and thesis. More support is needed.

Organization

6	5	4
The essay shows thoughtful use of an organizational pattern. Transitions are strong.	The essay uses an effective organizational pattern. Transitions are appropriate.	The essay follows an organizational pattern. Transitions could be stronger.

Voice

6	5	4
The writing voice is lively, engaging, and memorable.	Voice is appropriate for the topic, purpose, and audience and sounds knowledgeable.	Voice fits the audience and sounds knowledgeable in most places.

Word Choice

6	5	4
Word choice is vivid and precise. Special terms are defined or explained.	Word choice is effective. Words are not repeated and special terms are defined.	Word choice is adequate. Some overused words could be replaced.

Sentence Fluency

6	5	4
Sentences are carefully crafted. Sentences flow naturally and vary in type and length.	Sentences flow well and are varied in type and length.	Sentences could use more variety in type and length.

Conventions

6	5	4
Editing shows mastery of conventions. Essay is error free.	Editing is effective, but a few errors in grammar, spelling, or punctuation remain.	A few too many errors remain.

3	2	1
The essay shows some understanding of the topic and thesis. More support is needed.	The topic and thesis should be more focused. The essay needs specific support that relates to the topic.	The topic should be reworked and a new thesis formed.
The essay does not follow an organizational pattern. Key points need separate paragraphs and transitions.	The beginning, middle, and ending parts need to be made clear.	The essay must be rewritten using an organizational plan.
Voice sounds uneven. It should match topic, purpose, and audience.	Voice sounds as if the writer does not have a good understanding of the subject.	Voice does not show confidence.
Word choice needs to be more precise, and overused words need to be replaced.	A thesaurus is needed to find more-expressive words in many places.	The writer needs help choosing stronger words throughout.
Sentences are basic. More variety is needed in sentence type and length.	Too many sentences are simple and begin the same way.	Most sentences need to be rewritten.
Control of conventions is basic. Errors sometimes get in the way of understanding.	Many corrections are needed to make the essay less confusing.	The writer needs help in understanding editing conventions.

Expository

Evaluating an Informative Article

Read the informative article below, focusing on its strengths and weaknesses. **(The article contains some errors.)** Then read the student's self-assessment.

A Good Cold Is Hard to Beat

If you're like most people, you catch a cold 2-4 times each year. Each cold means 1-2 weeks of sneezing, sniffing, and misery, and while you're feeling so lousy, you may be doing some thinking (National 3). Science can put people on the moon—and on the bottom of the ocean. It has discovered new treatments for all sorts of serious diseases, from diabetes to cancer, but why can't doctors find a cure for the one of the most common disease—the cold? The answer is both simple and complex. The fact is that the cold is an extremely difficult bug to beat.

People have been battling colds for thousands of years. In fact, the ancient Egyptians even had a hieroglyphic that represented the illness (Paris 328). Over that long time, people have tried any number of cures—from medicinal herbs to antibiotics—with little success. For the longest time, people didn't know what caused a cold—or even how people got them. That changed in 1914, when scientists learned that colds were caused by viruses. Tiny disease-carrying microbes. Unfortunately, discovering the cause of colds hasn't made thngs easier.

One reason for this is that viruses can reproduce very quickly. Here's how they work to make you sick. A virus come along and grabs one of your cells. It injects the cell with genetic information. The genetic information hijacks the cell and reprograms it to make more viruses. The cell gets so full of viruses that it explodes, sending its deadly cargo out to invade even more cells. In no time, they've invaded your system, and the sneezing, snifflng, and misery begin. But why is this so hard to stop?

Another reason cold viruses are hard to stop is that there are many different kinds of them. Over 200 different viruses can cause a cold ("Cold"). In order to stop people from getting sick, scientists would have to invent a treatment that works on every one of them. That would be a tall order. Even now, medical science has a hard time just keeping up with the flu virus, which only has about half a dozen different varieties.

Another reason the cold virus is hard to stop is because viruses can mutate quickly. Each year, scientists prepare a vaccine to deal with the influenza virus, but that vaccine won't work the following year. That because the virus has mutated. Cold viruses do the same thing, very quickly. So even if scientists found a treatment that would kill most of the cold viruses in your body, it probably wouldn't kill all of them. Some would be resistant to the treatment, and those would survive to quickly multiply. In no time, an individual's body would be full of viruses again.

    The good news is that even if people can't beat a cold, they can try to make cold symptoms less severe. Warm fluids and rest will help. Gargling with salt water or using throat lozengers will ease a sore throat. Antibiotics, however, won't do a thing to help a cold. That's because antibiotics kill bacteria, not viruses. When a person gets a cold, he or she is not alone. All people get them—and they all feel miserable when it happens!

Student Self-Assessment

Expository Rubric Checklist

Title: A Good Cold Is Hard to Beat

Writer: Allison Carter

5 **Ideas**
- Does my article include a clear thesis?
- Do I support my thesis with a variety of details?

5 **Organization**
- Does the beginning introduce the topic?
- Are the middle paragraphs in order?
- Does my ending restate my thesis?

4 **Voice**
- Does my voice have an appropriate tone?
- Do I use the right level of language?

4 **Word Choice**
- Do I use words that are powerful and precise?
- Do I explain technical terms?

4 **Sentence Fluency**
- Do I use different types of sentences?
- Do I vary their lengths and beginnings?
- Do I avoid rambling sentences and fragments?

4 **Conventions**
- Does my essay avoid most errors in punctuation, spelling, and grammar?

OVERALL COMMENTS:

I think my article offers some interesting information about colds. My organization is also quite strong.

My tone is confident, engaging, and informative. I could improve my article by defining some technical terms such as "vaccine."

My article includes a few errors in spelling and punctuation and one sentence fragment. I should check more carefully for errors like these in the future.

Review your essay. Rate your essay and write comments that explain why you gave yourself the scores you did.

Reflecting on Your Writing

Now that you have completed your informative article, take some time to reflect on your writing experience. On a separate sheet of paper, complete each sentence below. This writing will help reinforce what you've learned about writing an informative article.

My Informative Article

1. The strongest part of my article is . . .

2. The part that still needs work is . . .

3. The prewriting activity that worked best for me was . . .

4. The main thing I learned about writing an informative article is . . .

5. In my next informative article, I would like to . . .

6. One question I still have about writing an informative article is . . .

Expository Writing

Writing a Comparison-Contrast Essay

A CD player and an MP3 player have some things in common. Both are digital music technologies, both can be portable, and both are quite popular. But they are different in some ways, too. A CD player does not store digital files; it only plays files stored on a disk. However, an MP3 player can store thousands of songs, offering users the ability to take hours of music with them wherever they go.

In a comparison-contrast essay, a writer takes a close look at two separate ideas—technologies, cultures, people, events, and so on. Then he or she explains the ways in which the two are similar and the ways in which they are different. A well-written comparison-contrast essay provides the reader with fresh insight into two topics by examining how they relate to each other.

In this chapter, you'll read a sample comparison-contrast essay about gasoline-electric hybrid cars and fuel-cell cars. Then you'll write your own comparison-contrast essay that shows the similarities and differences between two other technologies.

Writing Guidelines

Subject: Two technologies

Form: Comparison-contrast essay

Purpose: To show how two topics are the same and different

Audience: Classmates

"Shall I compare thee to a summer's day?
Thou art more lovely and more temperate."
—William Shakespeare

Comparison-Contrast Essay

In the following essay, Ang looks at the similarities and differences between hybrid and fuel-cell cars.

Beginning
The writer clearly identifies the topics and provides a thesis statement (underlined).

Middle
The first middle paragraph presents the major similarities.

The second middle paragraph details one major difference.

Another major difference is explained.

Cars of Today—and Tomorrow

For many years, people have understood the main problem with the internal-combustion gasoline engine. This engine, which powers most American cars, burns gasoline for fuel, a process that releases many pollutants into the air. Today's carmakers have developed two similar—yet ultimately different—solutions to the car pollution problem. Hybrid and fuel-cell cars both battle pollution, but one is the car of today, and the other is the car of the future.

Gasoline-electric hybrids and fuel-cell cars have a number of structural and operational similarities. Both vehicles look and handle like regular cars. They come equipped with the features common to all automobiles—tires, steering wheels, brakes and signals, safety features like air bags and seat belts, and even optional features like air conditioning and CD players. To the people who drive them, both hybrid and fuel-cell vehicles seem like regular cars.

Look under the hood, however, and the differences between the two cars begin to emerge. A hybrid car has two motors. The first is a standard internal-combustion motor that runs on gasoline. It drives the car at high speeds, during acceleration, or with heavy loads that require hauling power. The second motor is electric, powered by a battery, and it drives the car at low speeds, during stops and starts, and with light loads. The battery is charged using a system called regenerative braking—the force that slows the car also runs a generator that charges the battery ("How it Works"). In contrast, a fuel-cell car has an electric motor, too, but this single motor drives the car at all times. The fuel cell is powered by a chemical process that extracts electrons from hydrogen. The only emission from this process is water (Davidson 132).

The differences in the drive systems mean differences in the amount of emissions created by each. Both hybrid and fuel-cell cars pollute less than traditional gasoline engines, but the fuel-cell car is potentially cleaner. The hydrogen needed to run a fuel cell can be extracted from water using solar or wind power ("Fuel"). Fuel produced in this way would make a fuel-cell car pollution free. Hybrid cars, on the other hand, run on gasoline, so they always produce some pollution, no matter what. Still, the hybrids generally produce 30 to 50 percent fewer pollutants than gasoline engines do (Clark 17).

> **The most critical difference is explained.**

Perhaps the most critical difference between the two car types is availability. Ten different hybrid models are on the market today, and buyers have purchased more than 200,000 of them (Clark 23). With current trends, as many as 780,000 may be purchased in 2012 ("Hybrids on the Rise"). Unfortunately, today's fuel-cell cars are mostly experimental and might not be available to consumers for years. One reason for this is that there are very few fueling stations that can dispense hydrogen. In order for fuel-cell cars to become popular, a network of fueling stations must be available (Davidson 135).

> **Ending**
> The ending summarizes the writer's thesis.

Hybrid and fuel-cell cars look alike and operate in similar ways, but the differences between the two are substantial. While the fuel-cell car offers the potential of pollution-free operation, mainstream production is still years away. Hybrids, on the other hand, offer both significant pollution reduction and current availability. These differences make hybrids the high-tech model for today, and fuel-cells the cars of the future.

Expository

Respond to the reading. Answer the following questions.

Ideas (1) What are the main similarities between hybrid and fuel-cell cars? (2) Name two differences between fuel-cell and hybrid cars.

Organization (3) How does the writer organize the presentation of similarities and differences?

Voice & Word Choice (4) What phrases signal comparisons and contrasts?

Prewriting Selecting the Topics

The purpose of your comparison-contrast essay is to take a closer look at two technologies and explain their similarities and differences. To find topics for his essay, Ang made a list of tasks and related technologies.

Tasks and Technologies List

Tasks	One Technology	Another Technology
send messages	e-mail	telephone
travel on land	gas-electric hybrid car *	fuel-cell car *
travel in the air	propeller-driven plane	jet plane
play music	CD player	MP3 player
cook food	microwave oven	gas oven

At first, Ang thought he might write a comparison-contrast essay about microwave and gas ovens. But he thought his audience would be more interested in the similarities and differences between hybrid and fuel-cell automobiles. He chose automobiles as his topics.

Prewrite

Select the topics. Make a three-column chart. In the first column, list tasks that can be performed using technology. In the other columns, list technologies for accomplishing the tasks. Consider your own interests and those of your audience before choosing your topics.

Hybrid engine

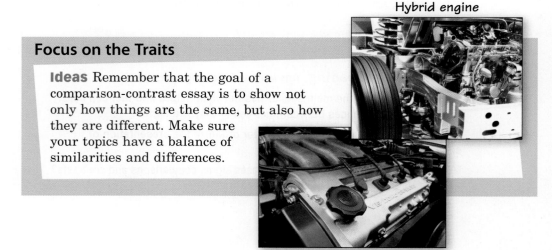

Focus on the Traits

Ideas Remember that the goal of a comparison-contrast essay is to show not only how things are the same, but also how they are different. Make sure your topics have a balance of similarities and differences.

Gasoline engine

Gathering and Organizing Details

After you choose two topics for your comparison-contrast essay, you need to gather and organize details about them. Ang did this with a T-chart.

T-Chart

Hybrid Car	Fuel-Cell Car
– Operates and has features like a regular gas car	– Operates and has features like a regular gas car
– Has two motors; one is gas powered and the other runs on batteries that recharge by braking	– Has one motor powered by an electric fuel cell that uses hydrogen
– 30 to 50 percent cleaner than gas engine	– Potential to be 100 percent pollution free
– Available today; more than 200,000 on the road	– May take years before widely available

Prewrite

Gather your details. Make your own T-chart. On each side, list characteristics of one of the technologies you will write about.

Writing a Thesis Statement

A thesis statement offers the focus of your essay. For a comparison-contrast essay, your thesis statement should name the two topics and sum up the comparison and contrast. Ang used this formula to develop his thesis statement.

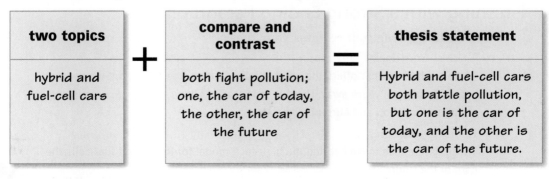

two topics		**compare and contrast**		**thesis statement**
hybrid and fuel-cell cars	**+**	both fight pollution; one, the car of today, the other, the car of the future	**=**	Hybrid and fuel-cell cars both battle pollution, but one is the car of today, and the other is the car of the future.

Prewrite

Write your thesis statement. Name the two technologies and sum up the comparison and contrast between them. Try two or three versions of your thesis statement until you are satisfied with it.

Expository

Writing Creating Your First Draft

The following tips will help you to write your comparison-contrast essay. Use your prewriting as a guide.

Writing Your Beginning Paragraph

The **beginning** paragraph should introduce your two topics and make a clear thesis statement.

- Get your reader's attention and introduce the topic.
  For many years, people have understood the main problem with the internal-combustion gasoline engine.

- End with your thesis statement.
  Hybrid and fuel-cell cars both battle pollution, but one is the car of today, and the other is the car of the future.

Creating Your Middle Paragraphs

The **middle** paragraphs explain how your topics are similar and different.

- Start each paragraph with a topic sentence that indicates the similarity or difference that will be addressed.
  Gasoline-electric hybrids and fuel-cell cars have a number of structural and operational similarities.

- Include examples to support each topic sentence.
  They come equipped with the features common to all automobiles—tires, steering wheels, brakes and signals, safety features like air bags and seat belts, . . .

Finishing with a Strong Ending Paragraph

The **ending** paragraph restates your thesis.

- Take a final look.
  While the fuel-cell car offers the potential of pollution-free operation, mainstream production is still years away. Hybrids, on the other hand, offer both significant pollution reduction and current availability.

- Restate your thesis.
  These differences make hybrids the high-tech model for today, and fuel-cells the cars of the future.

Write

Write your first draft. Use the guidelines above, your prewriting work, and the sample essay to help you write a first draft of your comparison-contrast essay.

Revising Improving Your First Draft

As you revise, use the checklist below to polish your first draft.

Revising Checklist

Ideas

_____ **1.** Do I clearly introduce my topics?
_____ **2.** Do I include a thesis statement that names the topics and sums up the comparison and contrast?
_____ **3.** Do I include both similarities and differences?
_____ **4.** Do I support my topic sentences with examples?

Organization

_____ **5.** Does my essay have a strong beginning, middle, and ending?
_____ **6.** Have I presented my points in a logical order?

Voice

_____ **7.** Is my voice confident and convincing?
_____ **8.** Does my voice show interest in my topics?

Word Choice

_____ **9.** Have I chosen words that make my explanations clear?

Sentence Fluency

_____ **10.** Do my sentences flow and exhibit a variety of lengths?

Revise

Revise your first draft. Read your essay carefully. Then use the checklist above to help you revise your first draft.

Creating a Title

- Draw on your thesis: **Cars of Today—and Tomorrow**
- Ask a question: **Can Hybrids and Fuel Cells Save Earth?**
- Appeal to your reader's interest: **Your Future Car**

Expository

Editing Checking for Conventions

After revising your essay, you can use the following checklist to edit your writing for punctuation, capitalization, spelling, and grammar errors.

Editing Checklist

Conventions

PUNCTUATION

_____ **1.** Have I ended my sentences with the correct punctuation?

_____ **2.** Have I used commas, semicolons, and colons correctly?

_____ **3.** Have I punctuated quotations correctly?

CAPITALIZATION

_____ **4.** Do I capitalize the first word in every sentence?

_____ **5.** Do I capitalize all proper nouns and adjectives?

SPELLING

_____ **6.** Do I spell all my words correctly?

_____ **7.** Have I double-checked for easily confused words that my spell-checker would miss?

GRAMMAR

_____ **8.** Do I use the correct forms of verbs *(they did,* not *they done)?*

_____ **9.** Do my subjects and verbs agree in number?

_____ **10.** Do my pronouns agree with their antecedents?

Edit

Edit your essay. Use the checklist above to edit for conventions. Ask a partner to help you review your essay, too. Then prepare a final copy and proofread it.

Publishing Sharing Your Work

You can share your comparison-contrast essay by reading it aloud in the classroom or by posting it on a bulletin board. If you present your essay, consider taking questions from the audience as a follow-up.

Publish

Publish your essay. Give your writing to classmates or family members to read. Also consider presenting it as a speech, posting it on a bulletin board, or uploading it to a Web site.

Writing for Assessment
Responding to Expository Prompts

In expository writing, you share your knowledge about a topic by explaining or informing your reader about it. Depending upon the topic and approach you've chosen for your essay, you might summarize, illustrate, analyze, classify, or compare. Sometimes, you'll be given days to complete an expository essay. Other times, you'll be given minutes to respond to an expository prompt. In such a situation, you'll need to quickly plan, draft, revise, and proofread your writing.

Many high school exit exams and college entrance exams include timed-writing components. This chapter will show you how to respond to an expository prompt with a well-organized, powerful essay within minutes—your ticket out of high school or into college.

Writing Guidelines

Subject: Expository prompt
Form: Response essay
Purpose: To demonstrate competence
Audience: Instructor

"If you can't explain it simply, you don't understand it well enough."

—Albert Einstein

Prewriting Analyzing an Expository Prompt

In order to respond effectively to an expository prompt, you need to read and analyze the prompt. To analyze a prompt effectively, use the **STRAP questions:**

> **Subject:** What topic should I write about?
>
> **Type:** What form of writing should I create (essay, letter, editorial, article, report)?
>
> **Role:** What role should I assume as the writer (student, son or daughter, friend, employee, citizen)?
>
> **Audience:** Who am I writing to (teacher, parents, classmates, employer, official)?
>
> **Purpose:** What is the goal of my writing (inform, summarize, illustrate, analyze, classify, compare)?

<u>Subject</u>
<u>Type</u>
Role
Audience
Purpose

Holiday celebrations are important in most families. Yet each family has its own traditions that make the celebration of a holiday unique. Choose <u>a holiday</u> that your family celebrates. *As a member of your family,* write an <u>article</u> informing your classmates about the family traditions that make your celebration of that holiday unique.

Try It!

Analyze these prompts by answering the STRAP questions. (Some answers may be implied or left open. Use your best judgment.)

1. The First Amendment to the Constitution guarantees freedom of expression. The framers of the Constitution believed this freedom essential to a strong democracy. Write an essay that explains how freedom of expression contributes to democracy.

2. People travel by many different means, each with advantages and disadvantages. Choose two of the following modes of transportation and write an essay comparing and contrasting them: walking, bicycling, driving a car, taking a train, flying, and sailing by ship.

Planning Your Response

After answering the STRAP questions, you need to begin planning your expository response. Graphic organizers are wonderful tools for planning and organizing an effective response.

Quick List (Any Essay)

1. First Point
   —Detail 1
   —Detail 2
2. Second Point
   —Detail 1
   —Detail 2
3. Third Point
   —Detail 1
   —Detail 2

Time Line (How-To/Process)

First
Next
Then
After
Last

T-Chart (Two-Part Essay)

Topic:

Part A	Part B
*	*
*	*
*	*
*	*

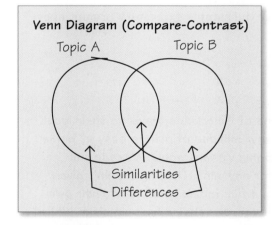

Venn Diagram (Compare-Contrast)

Topic A   Topic B

Similarities
Differences

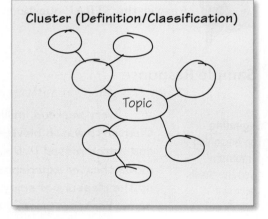

Cluster (Definition/Classification)

Topic

Prewrite

Use a graphic organizer. Reread the expository prompts on page 212. Choose one prompt and then use a graphic organizer to plan and organize your response. Keep the STRAP questions in mind as you work.

Tip

Be sure to manage your time carefully. For example, if you have 45 minutes to respond to a prompt, use the first 5 minutes to analyze the prompt and plan your response, the last 5 minutes to revise and edit your response, and the 35 minutes in between for writing your response.

Expository

Writing Responding to a Prompt

Once you have answered the STRAP questions and planned your response using a graphic organizer, you can begin writing.

Sample Expository Prompt

Millions of Americans enjoy movies. Today's technology offers people the option of viewing movies in the theater or watching them at home on DVD. Both of these viewing choices have advantages and disadvantages. Write a brief essay comparing and contrasting the experience of watching a movie at home on DVD and watching it in a theater.

Try It!

Answer the STRAP questions for the sample expository prompt above.

Sample Response

Beginning
The beginning paragraph gives the thesis statement (underlined).

Every weekend, millions of Americans travel to their local theater to watch movies, and millions of others stay at home and watch rented DVD's. Some viewers wouldn't trade the movie theater experience for anything. Others wouldn't give up the pleasure of enjoying a film in the comfort of their own home. For most people, though, the choice isn't as clear. <u>While the movie and "home theater" experiences are similar, each offers unique advantages and disadvantages.</u>

Movie theaters and home theaters have a lot in common. Both offer the opportunity to watch a range of current films. Both also offer comfortable settings, a range of snacking options, and the chance to share quality time with family members or friends. With advances in video and audio technology, a home theater can deliver both picture and sound that rival those at a movie theater. Yet the differences between the two viewing options are significant.

One major difference between watching a movie in a theater and watching one at home is comfort. While newer movie theaters offer more comfortable seats, many home cinema fans argue that nothing beats the opportunity to curl up on the sofa in one's home. In addition, while the movie theater offers a range of snacks, they are usually limited to sweets, popcorn, and soda. At home, it's possible to watch a movie while enjoying healthful snacks like fruit, or even a full meal.

Middle
Each middle paragraph supports and explains the thesis.

Cost is another major difference between going to a movie theater and watching a movie at home. Movie tickets for a family of four can cost $40 or more, and that's before the expense of concession-stand snacks, which can easily add another $25. In contrast, a current-run DVD can be rented for about $5. And snacking at home is a lot cheaper than eating at the movie theater. So the total cost of the home-theater experience is usually much less—provided, of course, that the viewer returns the video on time, thus avoiding late fees.

So far, it may sound like home theater is a hands-down winner, yet one main difference remains—the opportunity to see a film on the first run. Many movie buffs don't want to wait for the film to come out on DVD—they want to see it as soon as possible. They also want to see the movie with an eager crowd. Theaters make movies into events.

Ending
The ending sums up the comparison and contrast.

The similarities and differences between watching a movie in a theater and watching one at home provide choices for everyone. Most people who prefer the movie-theater experience probably rent DVD's on occasion. And most people who prefer renting movies will occasionally find their way to the movie theater. Diehard film fans, however, continue to flock to the movie theaters.

Expository

Write

Respond to an expository prompt. Review the prompt you chose on page 212. Then use your answers to the STRAP questions and your graphic organizer to write a response within the time limit set by your teacher.

Revising Improving Your Response

Before you begin a writing test, find out whether you will be allowed to make revisions to your response or not. If changes are allowed, make them as neatly as possible. Use the STRAP questions to guide your revisions.

Subject: Have I responded to the topic of the prompt?
Do my main points support my thesis?

Type: Have I responded in the correct form (essay, letter, article)?

Role: Have I assumed the role called for in the prompt?

Audience: Have I used an appropriate level of language for my audience?

Purpose: Does my response accomplish the goal outlined by the prompt?

Revise

Revise your work. Read your response carefully. Use the STRAP questions above as your guide to revise your response within the allotted time period.

Editing Checking Your Response

Be sure to check your expository response and correct any errors in punctuation, capitalization, spelling, and grammar.

Editing Checklist

Conventions

_____ **1.** Have I used end punctuation for every sentence?
_____ **2.** Have I capitalized all proper nouns and the first word of every sentence?
_____ **3.** Have I spelled all words correctly?
_____ **4.** Have I made sure my subjects and verbs agree?
_____ **5.** Have I used the right words (*their, they're, there*)?

Edit

Check your conventions. Review your response for any errors in punctuation, capitalization, spelling, and grammar. Make neat corrections within the allotted time.

Expository Writing on Tests

Use the following tips when you respond to an expository writing prompt.

Before you write . . .

- **Analyze the prompt.**
  Use the STRAP questions. Remember that an expository prompt asks you to explain or inform.
- **Budget your time carefully.**
  Be sure to spend several minutes planning and organizing your response before beginning to write. Use a graphic organizer to gather details and organize your response.

As you write . . .

- **Provide a clear thesis statement in your opening paragraph.**
  Keep your main idea and purpose in mind.
- **Include examples.**
  Choose examples that support and clarify your focus.
- **End by restating your thesis.**
  In the final paragraph, summarize your explanation.

After you've written a first draft . . .

- **Revise and edit.**
  Use the STRAP questions to guide your revision.
- **Check conventions.**
  Check your punctuation, capitalization, spelling, and grammar.

 Try It!

Plan and write a response. Choose one of the prompts below. Analyze it with the STRAP questions and use a graphic organizer to gather details and make a plan. Then write, revise, and edit your response.

- Cell phones provide an incredible amount of convenience, but they cause problems, too. People who use their phones in inappropriate settings can cause tempers to flare—and can even cause auto accidents. Write a set of guidelines for the safe and respectful use of cell phones.
- Cross-country and downhill skiing share certain similarities, yet they offer different experiences. Field hockey and ice hockey also require different skills. Think of two similar sports or activities that you enjoy, and write a brief essay to compare and contrast them.

Persuasive Writing

Persuasive Writing
Defending a Position

Political controversies force people to take sides. For example, you may favor lifting United States sanctions against Cuba, or you may oppose the use of nuclear power plants to generate energy. Whatever position you take, someone else will take the opposite viewpoint. In order to convince others to adopt your position, you'll need to defend it with a solid, well-organized argument.

One way to convince people to accept your side of a controversial issue is to write a position essay. Writing a position essay means more than just airing your opinions. It means organizing your ideas, supporting your position with facts and persuasive arguments, and answering objections that others may have.

In this chapter, you'll write a position essay about a national or international political topic. You'll consider some controversies, choose one, and then decide on your position, gather evidence, and explore opposing viewpoints. Then you'll write an essay to convince others of the worthiness of your position.

Writing Guidelines

Subject: A national or international political controversy

Form: Position essay

Purpose: To convince people to accept your position

Audience: Classmates and community members

"I'm a controversial figure. My friends either dislike me or hate me."

—Toni Morrison

Persuasive Writing Warm-Up Understanding Controversy

The word *controversy* is made up of the prefix *contro* (against) and the root *versy* (turn). A controversy is simply an issue that makes people turn against each other. One way to map a controversy is to use a T-graph.

Elisa wrote a controversial issue at the top of a piece of paper. Then she created a T-graph that listed arguments for and against the idea. At the bottom, she wrote her opinion.

T-Graph

<u>Controversy:</u> The state is considering requiring each senior to take one online class before graduating.

Arguments for . . .	Arguments against . . .
• Students can take specialty classes—like Russian or computer animation—that the school doesn't offer. • Our generation will take more and more classes online and should get used to it. • Online classes let students from our town study beside students from Argentina, India, and other countries.	• Some students don't have home computers with high-speed Internet access. • Some online classes have little value; don't really teach much. • Seniors often are working jobs after school, and online courses would only overload them.

<u>My Opinion:</u> I'm in favor of the state's proposal because I would enjoy getting some of my credits online instead of in the classroom.

Try It!

Create a T-graph. Think about controversies in your school or community—any issue that makes people take sides. Write the controversy at the top of a piece of paper. Then create a T-graph to list arguments for and against the idea. Last, write your own opinion about the issue.

Writing a Position Paragraph

A position paragraph states your opinion about a controversy, argues for your position, and answers an important objection raised against it. A position paragraph has three main parts.

- The **topic sentence** states the position.
- The **body sentences** support the position and respond to an objection.
- The **closing sentence** restates the position.

Elisa wrote the following position paragraph, using the details from her T-graph on page **220**.

Sample Position Paragraph

The **topic sentence** states the position.

The **body sentences** argue for the position and respond to an objection.

The **closing sentence** restates the position.

Being Brave in a New World

The state should require each senior to take at least one online course before graduation. For one thing, this generation will be learning more and more online—in high school, college, on the job, and even after retirement. Also, online classes offer many subjects that the school can't provide—such as computer animation, music composition, paleontology, and Native American languages. Most importantly, though, online courses move students into the larger world. They can take classes with people from Pakistan or Zimbabwe and become citizens not just of our city or state but of the world. Some people worry about whether students have enough after-school time or have access to high-speed Internet at home. If the online courses are offered through the school, however, those difficulties are solved. If the state requires each student to take an online course, a whole new world will open for schools and for students.

Persuasive

Write

Write a position paragraph. Review the T-graph you created on the previous page. Then write a position paragraph with a topic sentence, arguments for your position, an answer to an objection, and a closing sentence.

Understanding Your Goal

Your goal in this chapter is to write a well-organized persuasive essay that effectively states and defends a position. The traits listed in the chart below will help you plan and write your position essay.

Traits of Persuasive Writing

- ### Ideas
  State a clear position about a national or international controversy, support your position with solid reasons, and answer a major objection.

- ### Organization
  Create a beginning that includes your position statement, middle paragraphs arranged by order of importance, and an ending that restates your position.

- ### Voice
  Use language that shows you care about your position and are respectful of opposing viewpoints.

- ### Word Choice
  Use fair and precise words to state and defend your position.

- ### Sentence Fluency
  Create a variety of sentence types and beginnings to convey your ideas smoothly.

- ### Conventions
  Check your writing for errors in punctuation, capitalization, spelling, and grammar.

Get the big picture. Look at the rubric on pages 254–255. You can use that rubric to assess your progress as you write. Your goal is to write a persuasive essay that states a position and convinces your audience to accept it.

Position Essay

A position essay identifies an issue and clearly states and defends a position on it. In this essay, the writer defends her position on economic sanctions.

Beginning
The beginning introduces the topic and states the position (underlined).

Middle
The first middle paragraph provides one reason sanctions do not work.

The second middle paragraph provides another clear reason for the position.

The third middle paragraph provides another reason and supports it with compelling facts.

Sanctions Won't Solve Political Problems

In July of 1941, the United States imposed economic sanctions against Japan, banning exports to the country and freezing any of its assets that were under U.S. control. These sanctions were meant to stop Japanese military aggression in Asia. On December 7, 1941, however, Japan attacked the U.S. naval base at Pearl Harbor. Instead of reducing aggression, the sanctions had helped push both nations into a war. Though economic sanctions appear to be a powerful peacetime weapon, they actually do more harm than good.

To begin with, economic and political sanctions often prolong bad situations rather than end them. They create a stalemate. Political sanctions usually come about when an international dispute cannot be resolved by discussion and compromise. In order to get what it wants, one nation reduces or stops trade with another nation. It may also freeze any assets the "offending" nation has invested in the country. In 1962, for example, Communist leader Fidel Castro took power in Cuba. His government took control of U.S. businesses there. The United States imposed sanctions, cutting trade with Cuba, hoping the action would speed the fall of Castro's government ("United States Sanctions"). More than 40 years later, the sanctions were still in place, and Castro was still in power.

One reason that sanctions are ineffective is that they often reduce dialogue between disputing nations. Instead of searching for common ground, sanctions rely on unilateral force and provoke anger, which only makes matters worse. For the duration of the sanctions, talks are focused almost exclusively on their removal instead of on the common ground the parties may be able to find.

Another reason for the ineffectiveness of sanctions is that they often harm innocent victims while doing little or nothing to affect the lives of those in power. In August of 1990, the United Nations imposed sanctions on Iraq following its invasion of Kuwait. The sanctions shut off the sale of broad categories of goods to Iraq and prohibited Iraq from selling its oil on the international market. In place for more than 10 years, the sanctions led to a near collapse of the Iraqi economy ("Iraq"). Hundreds of thousands of Iraqis died because of malnutrition or because of lack of medical care. Meanwhile, Iraqi president Saddam Hussein and other Iraqi leaders lived in luxury, unaffected by the embargo. There was no reason for Hussein to bend to international will because he and those closest to him were not suffering.

The most important reason a country should think twice before applying sanctions is that they may backfire. For example, when the United States sanctioned Cuba, Cuba simply increased its trade with Mexico, Canada, and the Soviet Union (Smith 238). Thus, the United States lost out. This pattern is especially common when the international community disagrees with the sanctions. The sanctioning nation may find itself isolated from the rest of the world.

Those who support sanctions insist that they represent a useful tool in international diplomacy that is preferable to war. The real truth is that sanctions are ineffective and that they often succeed in hastening war, not preventing it. If the efforts made to impose sanctions were redirected toward finding common ground and dialoguing to solve problems, wars may more often be avoided.

When two friends disagree, they can negotiate, or they can use manipulative games to try to "win" the argument. The latter passive-aggressive behavior doesn't work for friends, and it doesn't work for nations, either. In international disputes, economic sanctions all too often put nations on a "peaceful" path to war.

The fourth middle paragraph presents the writer's most important reason.

The last middle paragraph defends the position against an important objection.

Ending
The ending restates the position and personalizes the argument.

Respond to the reading. Answer the following questions about the sample essay.

Ideas (1) What are three reasons the writer gives for opposing sanctions? (2) What are three examples of failed sanctions?

Organization (3) Where does the writer first state her position?

Voice & Word Choice (4) How do concrete examples help the writer sound authoritative? Explain.

Prewriting

In prewriting, you will select a political controversy of national or international importance. You'll decide on your position, gather reasons and facts to support it, and organize your ideas.

Keys to Effective Prewriting

1. Choose a political controversy that affects people in the United States or in the international community. Form your position on the controversy.

2. Gather the best reasons and details to support your position.

3. Identify an important objection to your position.

4. Create a clear position statement to guide your writing.

5. Use a list or an outline as a planning guide.

Persuasive

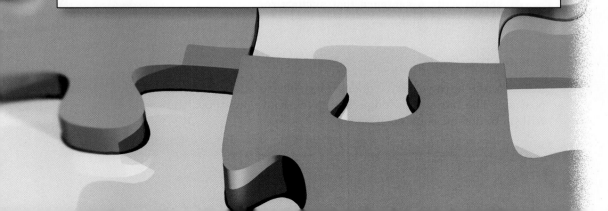

Prewriting Selecting a Political Controversy

A political controversy is a disagreement about a political issue. To find a writing topic, Lee, a student, answered some key questions about national or international political controversies.

List of Political Controversies

In the recent past, what political disagreements have made headlines in national newspapers, on news shows, and on Internet sites?

- political campaign contributions
- electronic voter registration
- the Iraq War
- the rising national debt *

What national or international political controversies have we discussed recently in class?

- controlling international pollution
- providing health care in Africa
- stopping genocide

After Lee chose her controversy, she wrote a sentence that summarized her position.

The rapidly growing national debt is bad for the United States.

Prewrite

List controversies. On your own paper, answer the two key questions above. Try to come up with at least three controversies that answer each question. Then place an asterisk (*) beside a controversy you feel strongly about. Write a sentence that summarizes your position on it.

Focus on the Traits

Ideas Make sure you have enough reasons to adequately defend your position. The more knowledge you have about your topic, the easier it will be to defend your position.

Conducting Research

A position is only as strong as the reasons and details that support it. Here are tips for researching the controversy you have chosen.

- **Search national newspapers and magazines.** Visit a library and scan the opinion and editorial pages of large newspapers such as the *New York Times* or the *Chicago Tribune.* Also use the *Readers' Guide* to find recent magazine articles on your topic.

- **Find timely books.** Make sure that books you use have the latest information on the issue.

- **Search Web sites.** Carefully evaluate each site, making sure the information is current, correct, reliable, and balanced.

- **Ask an expert.** Find a politician who takes part in the debate and interview him or her in person, on the phone, or by e-mail.

- **Gather many types of support.** Write down facts, statistics, examples, quotations, and anecdotes and keep track of where you find the information. (If your teacher requires parenthetical citations or a works-cited page, see page **407**.)

- **Find details that support and oppose your opinion.** Your essay will be stronger if you can answer the main objections against your position.

Lee used note cards to keep track of the information she gathered. At the top of each card, she wrote a question. Then she wrote answers to the question and, at the bottom, noted the source. Here is an example note card.

Note Card

Why can't we just cut the budget?

Budget cuts take away vital programs:

* In 2005, budget cuts took $12.7 billion away from education.

* Child-support enforcement and nursing-home benefits were cut.

Source: The Boston Globe online

Write

Conduct research. Read articles in national newspapers and magazines, find timely books and Web sites, and gather supporting details.

Persuasive

Prewriting Listing Reasons That Support Your Position

After conducting research, think about your position. Do you still have the same opinion? Adjust your position statement as necessary. Then decide on the main reasons that support your position. Lee used a "why" chart to list her main reasons.

"Why" Chart

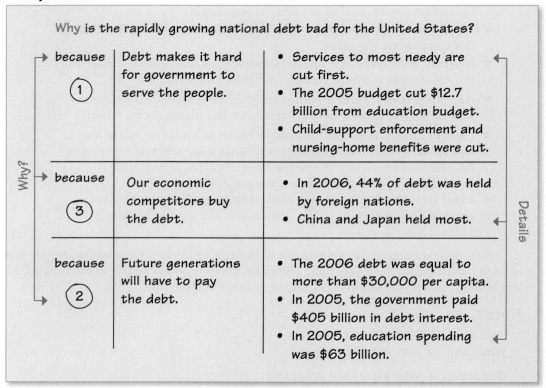

Why is the rapidly growing national debt bad for the United States?

Why?	because ①	Debt makes it hard for government to serve the people.	• Services to most needy are cut first. • The 2005 budget cut $12.7 billion from education budget. • Child-support enforcement and nursing-home benefits were cut.	Details
	because ③	Our economic competitors buy the debt.	• In 2006, 44% of debt was held by foreign nations. • China and Japan held most.	
	because ②	Future generations will have to pay the debt.	• The 2006 debt was equal to more than $30,000 per capita. • In 2005, the government paid $405 billion in debt interest. • In 2005, education spending was $63 billion.	

Prewrite

Create a "why" chart. On top, write your position in the form of a "why" question. In the middle sections, write three reasons that answer the question. Then provide details that support each reason.

Focus on the Traits

Organization Persuasive essays are often organized by order of importance. After you have finished your chart, rank your reasons— 1, 2, 3—from least important to most important.

Identifying Objections

In order for your essay to be effective, you must be able to answer possible objections to your position. If you can do this, your argument will be stronger, and you'll be more likely to convince people to accept your position. Start by identifying objections.

- ■ **Check news sources,** including newspapers, magazines, television news, and Internet news sites. Editorials are a great place to start.
- ■ **Try to recall classroom discussions** or conversations with your peers about your topic. What were the objections to your position?
- ■ **Ask the opinions of your friends,** family, or others you respect. Identify their objections and think about ways to counter them.

After researching opposing arguments, Lee listed the following objections to her position on the federal debt.

> <u>Position:</u> The rapidly growing national debt is bad for the United States.
> <u>Objections:</u>
>   The government can always find the money it needs.
>   The debt is necessary to keep the government running. ✳
>   We have more important problems than the national debt.

Prewrite

Gather objections. Use the strategies above to gather and list three objections to your position. Put an asterisk (*) next to the strongest objection.

Countering an Objection

Countering an objection means simply arguing against it. Lee listed three reasons why she disagreed with the strongest objection to her position.

> The debt is necessary to keep the government running.
>   1. Some debt is necessary, but this debt is too big.
>   2. Borrowing money is a bad way to run a business.
>   3. Cutting wasteful spending is better than more borrowing.

Prewrite

Counter an important objection. Write down the strongest objection to your argument. List several reasons why you disagree with it.

Prewriting Outlining Your Argument

Before writing your position essay, organize your information in an outline. The main points will become the topic sentences in the body paragraphs of your essay. The supporting points will become details in each paragraph. (Lee's outline uses complete sentences, though your teacher may let you write a topic outline, using phrases.)

Sentence Outline

<u>Position Statement:</u> The rapid growth of the national debt is bad for the United States' future.

I. First of all, a high national debt makes it difficult for the government to serve its people effectively.
  A. In late 2006, the national debt topped $8.8 trillion.
  B. Faced with debts, the president decided to cut spending.
  C. Cuts were made to education, child-support collection, and nursing homes.
  D. Those who need government most suffered.

II. In addition, a high national debt passes a burden on to future generations.
  A. The government sells bonds to raise money.
  B. It must pay interest on these bonds.
  C. In 2006, the government paid more than $405 billion in interest on the debt.

III. Perhaps most important, a high debt makes the United States less economically competitive.
  A. Foreign nations hold 44% of our national debt.
  B. China and Japan hold the most.

IV. Some people argue that the federal government needs more money and must take on debt in order to function.
  A. This is true, but only to a point.
  B. Much of the debt is due to wasteful spending.

Prewrite

Create an outline. Using the example above, create an outline for your position essay. Organize your reasons by order of importance. At the end, answer an important objection to your opinion.

Writing

You have researched a political controversy, chosen a position, developed reasons for its support, and considered an objection to your opinion. You have also organized your ideas in an outline. Now you are ready to begin writing.

> ### Keys to Effective Writing
>
> 1. Use your outline as a writing guide.
>
> 2. To allow room for changes, write on every other line, or double-space if you are using a computer.
>
> 3. In the first paragraph, introduce the controversy and state your position.
>
> 4. Write topic sentences that give your supporting reasons. Include a variety of details in each middle paragraph.
>
> 5. In the last middle paragraph, respond to an important objection.
>
> 6. In your closing paragraph, restate your position and leave your reader with something to think about.

Persuasive

Writing Getting the Big Picture

The graphic below shows how the elements of a position essay should fit together. Use it to guide your writing. (The examples are from the student essay on pages 233–236.)

Beginning

The **beginning** introduces the controversial issue and states the writer's position.

Position Statement
The rapid growth of the national debt is bad for the United States' future.

Middle

Each **middle** paragraph supports the writer's position.

Topic Sentences
First of all, a high national debt makes it difficult for the government to serve its people effectively.

In addition, a high national debt passes a burden on to future generations.

Perhaps most important, a high debt makes the United States less economically competitive.

The last middle paragraph answers an important objection.

Some people argue that the federal government needs more money and must take on debt in order to function.

Ending

The **ending** restates the position, sums up the reasons, and offers the reader something to think about.

Closing Sentence
Reducing the national debt will put our nation on a more secure path to the future.

Starting Your Essay

The beginning paragraph of your position essay should capture the reader's attention, introduce the controversy, and state your position clearly.

- **Begin with a dramatic opening sentence.** Captivate the reader by using an active voice, precise verbs, and strong adjectives and adverbs that empower your writing.

  The growth of the national debt threatens the ability of our nation to function and to compete effectively in the international economy.

- **Provide important background information.** Give basic information about the controversy.

  The national debt is the difference over the years between the money the government collects in taxes and the money it spends.

- **Build powerfully toward your position statement.** All sentences in your beginning paragraph should lead the reader toward your position statement (or focus).

  The growth of the debt is reducing the ability of the government to provide necessary services.

Beginning Paragraph

> The writer introduces the controversy.

The growth of the national debt threatens the ability of our nation to function and to compete effectively in the international economy. The national debt is the difference over the years between the money the government collects in taxes and the money it spends. Today, the national debt is skyrocketing. The growth of the debt is reducing the ability of the government to provide necessary services. It's creating a staggering financial burden for future generations, and it's even weakening the economic competitiveness of our nation. The rapid growth of the national debt is bad for the United States' future.

> The writer takes a position (underlined).

Persuasive

Write

Write a beginning paragraph. Create your essay's opening and read it to a friend. Is your friend interested in what you've written? If not, write another version. Keep trying until you have your reader hooked.

Writing **Developing the Middle Part**

Beginning

Middle

Ending

The middle part of your essay uses reasons and details to support your position. Begin each paragraph with a topic sentence. Write additional sentences that include supporting details. Don't forget to address a significant objection in the last middle paragraph. Use your outline (page **230**) as your guide.

Using Transitions

Transitions help your reader move easily from one idea to the next. They also help you arrange your ideas in order of importance. The following chart includes transitions that could connect your middle paragraphs.

Paragraph 1	Paragraph 2	Paragraph 3
First of all, ⟶	Also, ⟶	The best reason . . .
One reason . . . ⟶	In addition, ⟶	Finally,
To begin with, ⟶	Another reason . . . ⟶	Most importantly,

Middle Paragraphs

A topic sentence (underlined) introduces each reason.

> <u>First of all, a high national debt makes it difficult for the government to serve its people effectively.</u> By late 2006, the national debt had risen to almost $9 trillion, or more than $30,000 for every man, woman, and child in the U.S. That was up from $5.6 trillion in 2000. Faced with mounting debts and under pressure to reduce spending, President Bush proposed a budget bill that cut spending. Cuts included education and benefits for nursing homes. Anyone who wants to go to college or has a relative who needs nursing care is affected by these cuts, and the rising debt means more cuts could come soon ("Fight Looms").

The body sentences include compelling details that support each topic sentence.

> <u>In addition, a high national debt passes a burden on to future generations.</u> When the government spends more than it collects in taxes, it makes up the difference by selling bonds. Investors buy these bonds for a certain amount, and the U.S. promises to pay that money back along with interest at a later date. This interest burden only increases the amount of

debt. In fact, in 2006, the government paid more than $405 billion in interest on the federal debt. In comparison, the government spent about $63 billion on education (Spencer 23). With more and more interest, the debt will continue to skyrocket.

The middle paragraphs build to the most important reason.

Perhaps most important, a high debt makes the United States less economically competitive. That's because the buyers of bonds that finance the debt are economic competitors of the United States. As of December 2006, about 44 percent of the national debt was held by foreign nations. Japan and China held the most (Concord Coalition). Being in debt to these nations only increases our dependence on them as well as their power over our economy.

The fourth middle paragraph counters an objection.

Some people argue that the federal government needs more money and must take on debt in order to function. They say this is how government meets its obligations while keeping taxes low. This may be true, but the amount of debt now has reached staggering proportions. At least some of this debt results from government waste.

Write

Write your middle paragraphs. Create middle paragraphs that support your position. Start each paragraph with a topic sentence. Then follow with details that support the topic sentence. Your final middle paragraph should respond to a significant objection.

Tip

- **Build your paragraphs** using your outline as a guide.
- **Use transitions between paragraphs** to show the order of importance.
- **Include clear reasons to support your position;** avoid overly emotional language.
- **Answer a significant objection** with logical, reasonable ideas.

Persuasive

Writing Ending Your Essay

So far, your essay has identified a political controversy, taken a position, defended the position using solid reasons, and responded to a significant objection. Now you are ready to write your ending paragraph. To do the job effectively, use the following guidelines.

| Beginning |
| Middle |
| **Ending** |

- Restate your position clearly and powerfully.
- Summarize the main reasons that support your position.
- Summarize your response to the objection.
- Add a final insight that makes the reader think.

Ending Paragraph

The position is powerfully restated.

The writer sums up support for her position.

The essay ends with a final insight.

<u>The rising national debt threatens the United States' future—and that's a concern for all of us.</u> In order for the federal government to meet the needs of Americans now and in the future, it must practice fiscal responsibility. By balancing taxes and spending, politicians can cut the national debt, thus preserving necessary services, reducing the burden on future generations, and keeping this country competitive. Reducing the national debt will put our nation on a more secure path to the future.

Write

Write your ending paragraph. Write the ending paragraph of your essay. Restate your position and summarize the reasons that support it. Finally, leave your reader something to think about.

Write

Prepare a complete first draft. Write a copy of your entire essay. Double-space if you use a computer, or write on every other line if you write by hand. Double-spacing gives you room to revise.

Revising

When you revise, you add or delete details, rearrange parts of your writing, and create a more powerful, persuasive voice. You also check your word choice and improve sentence structure and variety.

Keys to Effective Revising

1. Read your essay aloud and decide whether it sounds convincing.

2. Make sure you have clearly explained the controversy and your position.

3. Check your topic sentences to make sure they follow your outline.

4. Make sure all of your details support your topic sentences. If necessary, add or delete details.

5. Check your draft for convincing reasons, powerful word choice, and sentence variety.

6. To mark revisions on your draft copy, use the editing and proofreading marks found on the inside back cover of this book.

Persuasive

Revising for Ideas

 6 My position is very well defended and compels the reader to act.

 5 My position is supported with reasons, and each reason is well developed.

4 I have three reasons and answer an objection, but I need more support for my reasons.

When you revise for *ideas,* you make sure your position has solid support and effectively answers an objection. The rubric strip above will guide your revision.

Do I have solid support for my position?

You have solidly supported your position if you have provided at least three main reasons, which are in turn supported by three or more details. This is called the "rule of threes." Use a table like the one below to graph your support.

"Rule of Threes" Table

Thesis		
Tighter environmental regulations would actually save the United States money.		

Reason 1 protect priceless resources	**Reason 2** prevent costly cleanup	**Reason 3** create a level field for competition

Detail 1 Ogalala aquifer vanishing	**Detail 2** Phoenix water costs	**Detail 3** Great Lakes receding	**Detail 1** Lake Erie cleanup stats	**Detail 2** dirty site cleanup costs	**Detail 3** quotation from David Jeffers	**Detail 1** unequal state laws for aquifer	**Detail 2** federal law results	**Detail 3** new company list

Revise

Check your support. Create a "rule of threes" table, charting your reasons and supporting details. If you do not have enough reasons or details, add some to improve your support. (You may not always be able to include three supporting details for each reason.)

3 I need to answer an objection and provide more support for my main reasons.

 2 I need to find three main reasons to support my position, and I need to answer an objection.

 1 I need help understanding how to support a position.

Have I effectively answered a significant objection?

You have answered a significant objection if you have stated the objection and provided facts to refute it. Answer the following questions to evaluate how well you fulfilled this requirement.

1. Does my last middle paragraph answer an objection?
2. What is the main point of the objection?
3. Do I address the main point?
4. Do I use clear facts to refute the objection?

Exercise

Read the following answer to an objection and use the questions above to analyze it. Then make some suggestions for improvement.

1   **Owners of power plants say pollution controls will cost them money. "And**
2 **besides," says Electric Board President William Samuels, "we haven't completed**
3 **testing the equipment." But the plants often have to pay fines for breaking pollution**
4 **laws. And they also spend money to fight off civil pollution suits. Installation of**
5 **pollution-control devices is fast and easy, and it will even provide more jobs.**

 Revise

Check your answer to an objection. Use the questions above to check your own answer to an objection. If necessary, revise to make it more effective.

Persuasive

Ideas
Changes make the main point of an objection clear.

Some people argue that the federal government needs
and must take on debt in order to function.
more money. They say this is how government ~~can keep on~~
meets its obligations while keeping taxes low.
~~going~~ This may be true, but the amount of debt now has . . .

Revising **for** Organization

 6 All of the parts of my essay work together to build a thoughtful, convincing position.

 5 My paragraphs have a logical order, and the ideas in my sentences are clearly connected.

 4 My paragraphs follow a logical order, but sometimes the ideas should be more clearly connected.

When you revise for *organization,* you make sure that the order of your reasons is clear and that the ideas in your sentences are connected. The rubric strip above will guide your revision.

How can I make the order of my reasons clear?

You can make the order of your reasons clear by using transition words and phrases to introduce each reason (and your answer to an objection). Here are transitions to try:

Reason 1	Reason 2	Reason 3	Objection Answer
First of all	In addition	Most importantly	Some people say . . .
To begin	For that matter	The strongest reason	Opponents argue . . .
For starters	Besides	Fundamentally	Though some say . . .

Exercise

Read the following topic sentences for a persuasive essay supporting seat-belt laws. Decide on a logical order for the topic sentences and rewrite them, adding transitions to the beginnings. Explain your choice for the most important reason.

1. Seat-belt laws save 4,000 American lives every year.
2. Seat-belt laws are easy for police to enforce.
3. People should be free to decide whether or not to wear seat belts.
4. Seat-belt laws save drivers and insurance companies millions of dollars per year.

Revise

Check your transitions. Make sure you have ordered your reasons clearly and indicated which is most important. Also introduce your answer to an objection.

3 I need to order my paragraphs logically and make stronger connections between sentences.

2 My paragraphs run together, and my sentences sound disconnected.

1 I need help understanding how to connect and organize my ideas.

How can I connect the ideas in my sentences?

You can connect the ideas in your sentences by repeating a key term from one sentence in the next. The repeated term makes the sentences interlock like puzzle pieces.

In most states, troopers do not pull over a vehicle for a seat-belt **violation** alone.

The **violation** is cited only if the driver is stopped for other **reasons**.

The **reason** for seat-belt laws, obviously, is not to hamper drivers, but to keep them safe.

 ## Exercise

In the following paragraph, find the key words or phrases that are repeated to connect the sentences.

1   A seat belt helps its wearer survive the tremendous forces involved in an
2   accident. The force of a 150-pound body moving at 45 miles an hour cannot be stopped
3   merely by bracing against the dashboard. The unbelted rider will strike the dashboard
4   or go through the windshield. A rider with a belt will stay in the seat and benefit from all
5   the crumple zones designed to absorb the tremendous impact forces.

Revise

Connect your ideas. Read your essay and watch for places where the ideas are disconnected. Rewrite sentences, using key words to connect the ideas.

Organization
Changes introduce and clarify the most important reason.

Perhaps most important,
A high debt makes the United States less economically
competitive. That's because the buyers of bonds that finance the debt are economic
competitors of the United States. As of December . . .

Persuasive

Revising **for** Voice

6 My persuasive voice creates total confidence in my position.

5 I sound like I care about my position, and I treat opposing positions fairly.

4 I usually sound like I care about my position, though I'm not always fair in dealing with other positions.

When you revise a position essay for *voice,* you make sure that you sound like you care about your position but are fair in dealing with other viewpoints. The rubric strip above will guide your revision.

How can I show that I care about my position?

You can show that you care about your position by following these tips.

- **Use serious language.** Avoid sarcasm, overstatement, slang, cliches, and jargon.
- **Use specific details.** Show that you are well informed about the situation.
- **Use a moderate tone.** Avoid the extremes—sounding either flat or overly emotional.

Exercise

In each of the following sentences, the underlined words and phrases create an inappropriate tone. Use the tips above and your imagination to rewrite each sentence so that it sounds serious, specific, and moderate.

1. When it comes to energy consumption, businesses are <u>hogs feeding at an ever-shrinking trough</u>.

2. Though a single business computer uses little energy, a thousand computers displaying a thousand screen savers on a thousand desks <u>send out a pretty glow that dooms the world</u>.

3. In search of <u>dirt-cheap</u> real estate, downtown businesses move to <u>Hicksville</u>.

4. Providing inadequate public transportation, city officials force <u>wage slaves</u> to drive <u>gas-guzzling SUV's</u>.

Revise

Check your voice. Read through your essay, underlining any words or phrases that create an inappropriate tone. Rewrite these parts of your essay to sound serious, thoughtful, respectful, and well informed.

3 I sometimes sound like I don't care about my position, and I'm not fair to opposing viewpoints.

2 My voice sounds like I don't care and am unfair to my opponents.

1 I need help understanding how to create a persuasive voice.

How can I sound fair when I answer an objection?

You can sound fair when answering an objection by following these tips.

- **Focus on the issue.** Do not comment on the people who oppose your position.
- **Keep your voice "cool."** Don't use emotional language when dealing with an opposing viewpoint.
- **Use solid logic.** Avoid misrepresenting the other position, ridiculing it, or using other forms of fuzzy logic.

Exercise

Notice the underlined voice error in each sentence below. Then, using the tips above, rewrite each sentence to correct the problem.

1. Some people think that businesses naturally try to conserve energy, but those people don't know what they're talking about.

2. People who are in favor of big business are just slaves to the establishment.

3. Those who oppose government regulations of energy consumption just want to steal power from homeowners.

Persuasive

Voice
Changes improve the voice, making it serious, specific, and moderate in tone.

In addition, a ~~gianormous~~ high national debt passes a ~~plague~~ burden on to future generations. When the government, ~~run by fat-cat politicians,~~ spends more than it collects in taxes, it makes up the difference by selling bonds. Investors buy these bonds for a certain amount, and the U.S. promises to pay . . .

Revising for Word Choice

 6 My words make a powerful case for my position.

 5 I have used technical terms well and have eliminated wordy intensifiers.

 4 I have used some technical terms well, but I need to get rid of some wordy intensifiers.

When you revise for *word choice*, you make sure you have used technical terms well and eliminated wordy intensifiers. The rubric strip above can guide you.

How should I use technical terms?

You should use technical terms to communicate an exact idea about your topic, but you should always make sure to define technical terms. Otherwise, you may confuse or even offend your reader and lose your opportunity to persuade. You can define a term in one of three ways.

- Give an **outright definition** of complex terms.
  The law of *imminent domain,* **which allows governments to purchase private property for public works,** may force the property owners to sell.

- Use a **synonym** for less-complex terms.
  Even so, the *fens,* or **wetlands,** on the south side of the White River may cause lawmakers to rethink the dam.

- Provide a **contextual definition** for more common terms.
  Not a stone of the new dam's *footings* will be laid until the legal issues are resolved.

Exercise

Read the following sentences, noting the underlined technical term. Look up the word in a dictionary and then rewrite each sentence, adding a definition of the word. Write one sentence with an outright definition, one with a synonym, and one with a contextual definition.

1. The simplest plan for the dam calls for a <u>spillway</u> along one side.
2. A more ambitious plan suggests <u>sluices</u> in the center.
3. Some architects have even suggested a dam fitted with <u>turbines</u> to generate electricity.

Revise

Check your use of technical terms. Read your essay, watching for technical terms. If you find any, make sure you have provided a suitable definition.

3 I need to use and define some technical terms, and I need to get rid of wordy intensifiers.

 2 I should find precise terms and eliminate many wordy intensifiers.

 1 I need to learn how to handle technical terms and how to recognize intensifiers.

How can I eliminate wordy intensifiers?

You can eliminate wordy intensifiers by watching out for adverbs that "shout" about how strongly you believe something. These words do not provide real support for your position.

Wordy Intensifiers

obviously   clearly   certainly   surely   definitely   absolutely

 ## Exercise

In the paragraph below, identify wordy intensifiers that should be removed.

1   A new dam certainly would provide new recreation opportunities. Surely the
2   reservoir would allow for boating, fishing, and even waterskiing. Two miles of riverfront
3   property would certainly become ten miles of lakefront property. Clearly the project
4   would create new opportunities, but it would definitely remove old opportunities
5   as well.

Revise

Eliminate wordy intensifiers. Read your essay to identify any wordy intensifiers. Remove them to make your essay more concise.

Word Choice
An intensifier is deleted, and words are added to strengthen the position.

~~Obviously,~~ In order for the federal government to meet the

needs of Americans now and in the future, it must practice
By balancing taxes and spending,
fiscal responsibility. Politicians can cut the national debt . . .

Persuasive

Revising for Sentence Fluency

 6 My sentences spark the reader's interest in my position.

 5 My sentences have varied beginnings and types, and I use emphasis words effectively.

4 Most of my sentence beginnings and types are varied, but I should use some emphasis words.

When you revise for *sentence fluency,* you check that you have used different types of sentences with a variety of beginnings. The rubric strip above can help you revise for fluency.

How can I create a sentence rhythm?

To create sentence rhythm, vary the beginnings and types of your sentences.

Varying Sentence Beginnings

Start some sentences with a modifying word, phrase, or clause.

Beginning with the Subject	Varied Beginnings
People rarely take time to vote.	Rarely do people take the time to vote.
The polls are open on Saturday morning.	On Saturday morning, the polls are open.
People can vote when they run errands.	When they run errands, people can vote.

Varying Sentence Types

Use four different types of sentences.

Declarative I want to vote in the presidential election.

Interrogative When will people realize how important it is to vote?

Imperative Be sure to vote in this year's election.

Exclamatory Last year, only 40 percent of eligible citizens under 24 voted!

Revise

Create sentence rhythm. Review your essay for sentence variety. Make sure you use a variety of sentence beginnings and types.

3 I need more variety in my sentence beginnings and types, and I should add some emphasis words.

 2 My sentences all sound similar, and I have not made wise use of emphasis words.

 1 I need help creating sentence fluency.

How can I emphasize an important word in a sentence?

You can emphasize an important word by placing it first or last in the sentence. These are the *positions of emphasis*. Note how the following sentence is made more powerful when the most important word is in a position of emphasis.

The recent problems with fraud have discouraged voter turnout.

Fraud in recent elections has discouraged voter turnout.

Voter turnout in recent elections has diminished due to fraud.

Exercise

In each of the following sentences, decide which word you would like to emphasize. Then rewrite the sentence twice, using the word in the first and last positions. What effect does each rewrite produce?

1. In some districts, convenience of polling places is a problem.

2. The requirement that voters preregister also reduces numbers at the polls.

3. Most officials throughout the country consider apathy the main difficulty.

Revise

Use positions of emphasis. Read your essay, underlining words you would like to emphasize. Rewrite some sentences, placing those words first or last.

Persuasive

Sentence Fluency
A sentence is rewritten to emphasize a key word.

This may be true, but the amount of debt now has reached staggering proportions. At least some of this debt is ~~created by wasteful spending on the government's part.~~ results from government waste.

Revising Improve Your Writing

Revise

Check your revising. On a piece of paper, write the numbers 1 to 12. If you answer "yes" to a question, put a check mark next to that number. If not, continue to work on that part of your essay.

Revising Checklist

Ideas

_____ **1.** Do I state my position clearly?

_____ **2.** Have I included reasons that support my position?

_____ **3.** Do I effectively respond to a significant objection?

Organization

_____ **4.** Does the overall structure of my essay work well?

_____ **5.** Have I chosen the best order for my reasons?

_____ **6.** Have I used key words to connect the ideas in my sentences?

Voice

_____ **7.** Do I sound like I care about my position?

_____ **8.** Do I sound fair when I answer an objection?

Word Choice

_____ **9.** Have I defined any technical terms?

_____ **10.** Have I eliminated wordy intensifiers?

Sentence Fluency

_____ **11.** Have I varied the types and beginnings of my sentences?

_____ **12.** Have I placed important words in a position of emphasis—first or last in the sentence?

Revise

Make a clean copy. When you are finished with your revision, make a clean copy of your essay for editing.

Editing

You have finished revising your position essay. Now you are ready to edit for *conventions:* punctuation, capitalization, spelling, and grammar.

Keys to Effective Editing

1. Use a dictionary, a thesaurus, and the "Proofreader's Guide" in the back of this book to check your writing.

2. Mark corrections using the editing and proofreading marks in the back of this book.

3. Edit your essay on a printed copy and enter the corrections on your computer. Otherwise, complete a clean handwritten copy that includes the corrections.

4. Check for commonly misused words to be sure you have made the correct choice.

5. Check your writing for punctuation, capitalization, spelling, and grammar errors.

Editing for Conventions

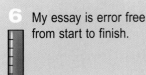 **6** My essay is error free from start to finish.

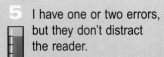 **5** I have one or two errors, but they don't distract the reader.

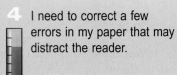 **4** I need to correct a few errors in my paper that may distract the reader.

When you edit for *conventions,* you correct punctuation, capitalization, spelling, and grammar errors. The rubric strip above can guide your editing.

How can I check for commonly misused pairs?

You can check for commonly misused pairs by watching for words that sound the same but are spelled differently. Here are the most commonly misused pairs:

- **it's, its** ▪ *It's* is the contraction of "it is." *Its* is the possessive form of "it."
- **their, there, they're** ▪ *Their* is a possessive personal pronoun. *There* is an adverb used to point out location. *They're* is the contraction for "they are."
- **to, too, two** ▪ *To* is a preposition that can mean "in the direction of." *To* is also used to form an infinitive. *Too* means "also" or "very," and *two* is the number.
- **your, you're** ▪ *Your* is a possessive pronoun. *You're* is the contraction for "you are."

Exercise

Find the commonly misused words in this paragraph. Correct them as you rewrite the paragraph.

1 Many people who don't vote claim its not in there best interest to get involved in
2 politics. But think twice before you surrender you're franchise. A number of elections
3 have been decided by just one vote. Imagine that a candidate you supported lost by
4 only one vote, and you didn't take the time to go two the polls. Fortunately, their is a
5 simple way to avoid this. On election day, make sure you're vote counts, to!

Edit

Watch for commonly misused words. Read your essay, looking for words that have the same sound but different spellings. Make sure each word is used correctly.

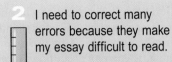

3 I need to correct several errors in my paper because they confuse the reader.

2 I need to correct many errors because they make my essay difficult to read.

1 I need help finding errors and making corrections.

Have I used numbers and numerals correctly?

You have used numbers and numerals correctly if you follow these simple rules:

1. Write out numbers one to nine.

    one   **three**   **five**   **seven**   **nine**

2. Use numerals for 10 and above.

    10   **43**   **695**   **1,432**   **10,000**

3. Use numbers and numerals together for very large amounts.

    35 billion   **3.4 trillion**   **253 million**

4. Use numerals for decimals, percentages, dates, and statistics.

    26.2   **82 percent**   **July 22, 1966**   **a vote of 4 to 6**

Exercise

Identify the number errors in the following paragraph.

1   In the Bush-Kerry presidential race in two thousand four, President Bush
2 received fifty point seven three percent of the popular vote, whereas Senator Kerry
3 received forty-eight point two seven percent. Voters above forty-five years of age
4 had the highest voter turnout, well above sixty percent. Voters below twenty-four
5 years of age had the lowest voter turnout, with fewer than one out of two voting.

Edit

Use numbers correctly. Review your essay to correct your use of numbers. Follow the rules above.

Persuasive

Conventions
Number and numeral errors are corrected.

By late 2006, the national debt had risen to almost ~~nine~~ $9

trillion ~~dollars~~, or about ~~thirty thousand dollars~~ $30,000 for every

man, woman, and child in the U.S. That . . .

Editing Checking for Conventions

Edit

Check your editing. This checklist will help you to thoroughly edit your essay for conventions of punctuation, capitalization, spelling, and grammar. On a piece of paper, write the numbers 1 to 10. If you can answer "yes," put a check mark after that number. If you can't, continue to edit for that convention.

Editing Checklist

Conventions

PUNCTUATION

_____ **1.** Do I use end punctuation after all my sentences?

_____ **2.** Do I use commas after long introductory phrases and clauses?

_____ **3.** Have I used apostrophes correctly?

CAPITALIZATION

_____ **4.** Do I start all my sentences with capital letters?

_____ **5.** Do I capitalize all proper nouns and adjectives?

SPELLING

_____ **6.** Have I spelled all words correctly?

_____ **7.** Have I checked for commonly misused pairs?

GRAMMAR

_____ **8.** Do my subjects and verbs agree in number?

_____ **9.** Do my pronouns agree with their antecedents?

_____ **10.** Have I used numbers and numerals correctly?

Creating a Title

After your editing is complete, add a title that describes your essay and catches your reader's attention. Here are a few ways to approach this task.

- Sum up the position: **The National Debt Means Danger**
- Call the reader to action: **Put a Damper on the Debt**
- Hook the reader: **National Debt: How Much Do You Owe?**

Publishing Sharing Your Essay

After you've finished editing your essay for conventions, it's time to give the essay a public debut—by reading it in a debate, publishing it in a newspaper, or sending it to an official involved in the controversy you've explored.

Publish

Format your final copy. To format a handwritten essay, use the guidelines below or follow your teacher's instructions. (If you are using a computer, see pages 91–95.) Make a clean copy and carefully proofread it.

Focusing on Presentation

- Write neatly using blue or black ink.
- Place your name in the upper left corner of page 1.
- Skip a line and center your title; skip another line and start your essay.
- Indent every paragraph and leave a one-inch margin on all four sides.
- Write your last name and the page number in the upper right corner of every page.

Contact an Official

Identify an official who can play a role in resolving the political controversy. Send your essay to that person along with a cover letter briefly outlining your position and asking for help. Remember to use a respectful tone in your letter and to encourage the official to take action to support your position.

Publish a Letter

Reformat your essay as a letter to the editor of a newspaper, magazine, or news Web site. Be sure your letter conforms to the publication's submission guidelines. Then send your letter.

Stage a Debate

Invite a group of friends or family members to hold a debate on the political controversy you've chosen. Include audience members who have not taken a position. Present and defend your position. Then allow others to present and defend theirs. After the debate, ask the audience to adopt a position based on the debate.

Persuasive

Rubric for Persuasive Writing

Use this rubric to assess your persuasive essay using the six traits.

6   5   4

Ideas		
The position is convincingly presented and supported; it compels the reader to act.	The position is supported with logical reasons; an important objection is countered.	Most of the reasons support the writer's position. An objection is addressed.

Organization		
All parts of the essay work together to build a very thoughtful, convincing position.	The opening states the position, the middle provides clear support, and the ending reinforces the position.	Most parts of the essay are organized adequately except for one part.

Voice		
The writer's voice is completely confident, knowledgeable, and convincing.	The writer's voice is persuasive, knowledgeable, and respectful.	The writer respects the audience but needs to sound more persuasive or knowledgeable.

Word Choice		
The writer's choice of words makes a powerful case.	The writer's word choice helps persuade the reader.	The writer avoids inflammatory (unfair) words but needs to remove some qualifiers.

Sentence Fluency		
The sentences flow smoothly throughout the strong essay.	Variety is seen in both the types of sentences and their beginnings.	Variety is seen in most of the sentences.

Conventions		
The writing is error free.	Grammar and punctuation errors are few. The reader is not distracted by the errors.	Distracting grammar and punctuation errors are seen in a few sentences.

3	**2**	**1**
More supporting reasons and a more convincing response to an objection are needed.	A clearer position statement is needed. Better support for the position must be provided.	A new position statement and reasons are needed.
Some parts of the essay need to be reorganized.	The beginning, middle, and ending run together.	The organization is unclear and incomplete.
The writer's voice needs to be more persuasive and respectful.	The writer's voice sounds too emotional and unconvincing.	The writer needs to learn about voice in persuasive writing.
The writer needs to change some inflammatory words and remove some qualifiers.	The words do not create a clear message. Some inflammatory words are used.	Word choice for persuasive writing has not been considered.
More variety is needed in the beginnings or kinds of sentences used.	Too many sentences are worded in the same way.	Sentence fluency has not been considered.
There are a number of errors that will confuse the reader.	Frequent errors make the essay difficult to read.	Nearly every sentence contains errors.

Evaluating a Persuasive Essay

Read the position essay below and focus on its strengths and its weaknesses. Then read the student's self-assessment on the next page. **(The essay may contain some errors.)**

A Strong Dollar Weakens America

In 2006, the United States economy was the largest in the world. The Gross Domestic Product of $12.98 trillion amounted to $43,500 per person (CIA). But despite the encouraging statistics, the economy faced a number of problems. More and more good jobs were being exported. Many Americans found themselves on the unemployment line or working in low paying jobs. Struggling to survive. At least part of this problem was attributable to strong dollar policies. Simply put, the strong dollar is bad for today's US economy.

Tourism is one industry that can be hit hard by strong dollar policies. When tourists visit the United States, they trade there currency for US dolars. If the dollar is strong, these visitors receive fewer dollars in trade for their own currency. This makes a visit too the US more expensive, and tourists are less likely to visit. That means fewere jobs and less pay for people working in the tourism industry.

Second, a strong dollar makes it hard, for United States firms to compete in foreign markets. That's because products made here are usually priced in US dollars, so when a computer made in the US is sold in another country, it costs more compared to products made in places with weaker currency. That means fewer products sold in foreign markets by US companies. It also means fewer good jobs in the United States, and a weaker economy. That's right!

Perhaps the worst problem with the strong dollar is that it makes it harder for US companies to compete with Foreign Companies here at home. When the dollar is stronger, products made in the US tend to be more expensive when compared to products made in countries with weaker currencies. That means Americans are likely to buy cheaper foreign-made products than products made in the United States. This means more American manufacturing jobs lost.

Some economists argue that a strong dollar is a benefit, because it provides Americans with more buying power. In a sense, this is true. The strong dollar makes the relative cost of imported goods cheaper, but when people in this country buy foreign-made goods, US dollars flow out of our economy and into the economies of the producing nations. In fact, thanks in part to strong dollar policies, the economy of China is growing at a phenomenal rate, and it is challenging the US as the world's economic leader (Allain).

While strong dollar policies can mean some advantages for consumers now, they tend to hurt the US economy in the long run. Fewer exports for American businesses, fewer jobs for Americans, and lower pay for American workers are the result. Support for strong dollar policies is misguided, and should be stopped.

Student Self-Assessment

Persuasive Rubric Checklist

Title: A Strong Dollar Weakens America
Writer: Jesse Ryder

5 **Ideas**
  • Do I have a clear position statement?
  • Do I defend my position with clear, compelling reasons?

5 **Organization**
  • Does the beginning introduce the controversy and my position?
  • Does the middle include reasons for supporting my position?
  • Does my ending sum up my reasons and leave the reader with a final thought?

4 **Voice**
  • Do I sound like I care about my position?
  • Does my voice sound fair?

4 **Word Choice**
  • Do I handle technical terms well?
  • Do I avoid wordy intensifiers?

5 **Sentence Fluency**
  • Do I use different types of sentences?
  • Do I vary my sentence beginnings?

3 **Conventions**
  • Does my essay avoid most errors in punctuation, spelling, and grammar?

OVERALL COMMENTS:

My position essay carefully outlines the controversy about the strong dollar and provides support for my position.

I could have ended by connecting the strong dollar to the reader's life.

My sentence variety was good, but at times, my voice sounded a bit too emotional.

I spell-checked my document but did not proofread carefully enough.

Review your essay. Rate your essay and write comments that explain why you gave yourself the scores you did.

Persuasive

Reflecting on Your Writing

After you finish your position essay, take some time to reflect on your essay and your writing experience. On a separate sheet of paper, complete each sentence below. This activity will reinforce what you've learned and help you to apply it to future assignments.

My Position Essay

1. The strongest part of my essay is . . .

2. The part that still needs work is . . .

3. The prewriting activity that worked best for me was . . .

4. The main thing I learned about writing a position essay is . . .

5. In my next position essay, I would like to . . .

6. One question I still have about writing a position essay is . . .

Persuasive Writing

Writing a Satire

Persuasive writing is a serious business, but that doesn't mean you always need to take a serious approach. In satire, a writer uses humor, exaggeration, and sarcasm to make a point or to express an opinion. Often, the writer adopts the opposing position and defends it in a ridiculous way. For example, imagine that you oppose the creation of a new landfill in your town. You could begin a satirical essay in this way: "If sensible people vote for the landfill, the sweet smell of garbage may soon perfume the air of Centreville." Then you'd go on to point out all the "advantages" of having your town host a new dump.

In this chapter, you'll read a sample piece of satirical writing that supports the creation of a youth recreation center in the town of Harriston. Then you'll write your own satirical persuasive essay to express your opinion about a topic you feel strongly about. Keep in mind that using humor to convey an important opinion is actually serious business. Such an essay must be carefully crafted and well organized to achieve success.

Writing Guidelines

Subject: A school or community issue
Form: Satire
Purpose: To make a point
Audience: Classmates

"You can't make up anything anymore. The world itself is a satire. All you're doing is recording it."

—Art Buchwald

Satire

In the following satirical persuasive essay, Julia shares her opinion that her town needs a recreation center. She does so by mocking the opposing view with humor and sarcasm. (Sarcasm uses praise in an ironic way—saying, usually, the opposite of what is meant.)

Beginning
The beginning introduces the issue. Because this is satire, the position (underlined) is actually the opposite of what the writer believes.

Middle
Each paragraph states and defends an obviously ridiculous position.

A Youth Recreation Center Would Be a Disaster

Recently, a group of teens spoke before the city council in support of a youth recreation center for the city of Harriston. The teens, many of whom were joined by their parents, asked voters to provide $100,000 to convert the old Elm Street Gym into a place where young people could go to play basketball, lift weights, enjoy a game of chess, or just hang out with their friends. While many people spoke in favor of this measure, a youth recreation center would be a disaster for Harriston.

First of all, the recreation center's activities would interfere with many thrilling educational and cultural opportunities kids already enjoy. After school, a typical Harriston youth goes home to a world of adventure, including TV reruns and hours of mind-numbing video games. Roy Hibbard recently scored 40,000 on Spud Stomper during an afternoon of gaming. If he'd had the option of playing chess or working on his jump shot at the recreation center, he might have missed out on such a golden opportunity.

Second, a teen recreation center would cause a deadly epidemic of physical fitness in our city. Today, many of the young people in Harriston couldn't play basketball for ten minutes without collapsing. If a recreation center is created, the city's youth could lose all this unhealthiness they've come to love. It's proven that activities like basketball and weight lifting result in increased physical fitness. And it's clear what a danger physically fit kids represent. In later years, they might even stay healthy, decreasing levels of heart disease and obesity. The hospital might have to close.

Third, the money required to build the recreation center could be better used for more important projects. For example, the town's fire hydrants look terrible, and it's been nearly six months since the mayor was given a pay raise. So why should the city waste $100,000 on the kids who represent the future of our community?

Finally, a recreation center might disrupt the time-honored relationship between teens and adults. The relations between teens and adults in Harriston are strained, and they have been for years. If the city council opens a recreation center for teens, relations between adults and teens may very well improve. Before long, kids and grown-ups will actually get along. That would destroy years of tradition.

People who support the teen center argue that it will give kids a safe, healthful place to go after school. Why is that a concern? Kids have plenty of places to go after school—like the street corners of Harriston, the abandoned steel plant, or even their own ordinary homes.

Ending
The ending restates the writer's "position" and leaves the reader something to think about.

In conclusion, a recreation center would send the wrong message to the youth of Harriston. The center would give the teens of this city a variety of recreational opportunities, and they may even be grateful for it. That could be awkward. If people want to avoid being thanked by a local youth, they should oppose the youth recreation center.

 Respond to the reading. Answer the following questions.

Ideas (1) What is the literal main point of this essay? (2) What is the implied (true) main point of the writing?

Organization (3) What transitions does the writer use to connect her key points?

Voice & Word Choice (4) How does the phrase "deadly epidemic of physical fitness" help the reader to know that the writing is a satire?

Persuasive

Prewriting Selecting a Topic

The purpose of your satire is to express your opinion about a timely issue in your community or school. To find a topic for her satire, Julia checked local newspapers and made a list of issues that were being discussed.

In the Community	At School
lack of support for senior center	unhealthful cafeteria food
cutting trees in city park	restrictions on student parking
teen recreation center *	elimination of gymnastic team

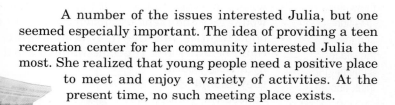

A number of the issues interested Julia, but one seemed especially important. The idea of providing a teen recreation center for her community interested Julia the most. She realized that young people need a positive place to meet and enjoy a variety of activities. At the present time, no such meeting place exists.

Prewrite

Choose your topic. In a chart like the one above, list timely issues in your community and in your school. Then put an asterisk (*) next to the issue you want to write about.

Focus on the Traits

Ideas Remember that the goal of a satire is to use humor and sarcasm to make the opposing idea seem ridiculous. To do this, think of reasons for supporting your position, and ridiculous or illogical reasons for opposing it. (See the next page.)

Gathering and Organizing Details

After you choose an issue, gather your thoughts about it. In a detail chart, Julia first listed serious arguments in favor of a recreation center. Then, for each serious point, she listed a ridiculous opposing argument. These "new arguments" served as the basis for her satire.

Details Chart

Youth Recreation Center in Harriston	
Serious Arguments in Favor	Ridiculous Arguments Against
positive opportunities for kids	TV and computer games
physical fitness	"deadly epidemic" of physical fitness
community investment	better use of money to paint fire hydrants and give the mayor a raise
improve relations between kids and adults	abnormal for kids and adults to get along

Writing a Position Statement

A persuasive satire needs a strong position statement. But remember, your position statement should reflect the opposite of what you truly believe. Here's how Julia created her position statement.

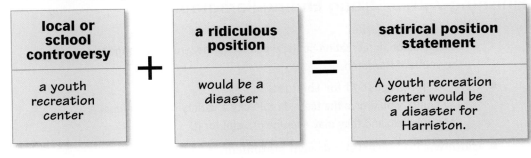

local or school controversy	+	**a ridiculous position**	=	**satirical position statement**
a youth recreation center		would be a disaster		A youth recreation center would be a disaster for Harriston.

Prewrite

Write a satirical position statement. Be sure that your statement exposes a ridiculous position, one that is the opposite of what you really believe. Use the formula above as a guide.

Persuasive

Writing Creating Your First Draft

The following tips will help you to write a satirical persuasive essay. Also refer to the planning you did on the previous page.

Writing Your Beginning Paragraph

The beginning paragraph will introduce the topic and present your "position."
- Open by clearly identifying the topic.

    Recently, a group of teens spoke before the city council in support of a youth recreation center for the city of Harriston.

- Present some details that explain the topic.

    The teens, many of whom were joined by their parents, asked voters to provide $100,000 to convert the old Elm Street Gym . . .

- End with your position statement.

    . . . a youth recreation center would be a disaster for Harriston.

Writing Your Middle Paragraphs

The middle paragraphs support your argument with several ridiculous ideas.
- Start each paragraph with a topic sentence that expresses a main point (one of your arguments).
- Develop each main point in a satirical way.
- Present supporting details with sarcasm and exaggeration, maintaining a serious undertone.

Finishing with a Strong Ending Paragraph

- Restate your position.

    In conclusion, a recreation center would send the wrong message to the youth of Harriston.

- Give your reader food for thought.

    The center would give the teens of this city a variety of recreational opportunities, and they may even be grateful for it.

- Close with a powerful satirical statement.

    If people want to avoid being thanked by a local youth, they should oppose the youth recreation center.

Write

Write your first draft. Use the guidelines above and your prewriting work as you develop your satirical essay.

Revising Improving Your First Draft

After you have completed your first draft, it's time to do some revising. Use the guidelines below to help you revise.

Revising Checklist

Ideas

_____ **1.** Do I clearly introduce the topic?

_____ **2.** Do I approach the topic satirically, from the position statement through the supporting arguments and details?

Organization

_____ **3.** Does my essay have a strong beginning, middle, and ending?

_____ **4.** Have I included topic sentences in all middle paragraphs?

_____ **5.** Have I used transitions to connect my paragraphs?

Voice

_____ **6.** Does my voice sound serious throughout?

_____ **7.** Does my real position come through in the essay?

Word Choice

_____ **8.** Have I used humor, exaggeration, and sarcasm?

Sentence Fluency

_____ **9.** Do my sentences flow smoothly?

Revise

Revise your first draft. Read your essay carefully. Then use the checklist above to help you improve your first draft.

Creating a Title

A good title catches the reader's interest and helps introduce your topic. Here are some examples of satirical titles.

- Ask a question: **Who Needs Fun and Fitness?**
- State your case: **A Youth Recreation Center Would Be a Disaster**
- Call for action: **Keep Teens from Wholesome Fun**

Persuasive

Editing Checking for Conventions

After revising your satire, be sure to edit it for conventions: punctuation, capitalization, spelling, and grammar.

Editing Checklist

Conventions

PUNCTUATION

_____ **1.** Have I ended my sentences with the correct punctuation?

_____ **2.** Have I used commas, semicolons, and colons correctly?

_____ **3.** Have I punctuated quotations correctly?

CAPITALIZATION

_____ **4.** Do I capitalize the first word in every sentence?

_____ **5.** Do I capitalize all proper nouns and adjectives?

SPELLING

_____ **6.** Do I spell all my words correctly?

_____ **7.** Have I double-checked words my spell-checker would miss?

GRAMMAR

_____ **8.** Do I use the correct forms of verbs (*he saw*, not *he seen*)?

_____ **9.** Do my subjects and verbs agree in number?

_____ **10.** Do my pronouns agree with their antecedents?

Edit your essay. Use the checklist above to edit for conventions. You may want to ask a partner to check your work, too. Then prepare a final copy and proofread it.

Publishing Sharing Your Work

It's time to make your ideas public—by publishing them.

Publish your satirical essay. Choose one of the following methods.

■ Read your work aloud to your classmates or family.

■ Submit your essay to a school or local newspaper.

■ Post your essay on a Web site.

Writing for Assessment
Responding to Persuasive Prompts

Sometimes you have the luxury of taking your time to develop a persuasive argument. If you receive a writing assignment with a one-week deadline, for example, you have time to do some research, write a draft, revise it carefully, and even ask a friend to help you test your argument. Other times, you need to organize and present a persuasive argument quickly. For example, if you're trying to convince a friend to let you borrow her tennis racket for the weekend, you need to come up with some good reasons on the spot.

Writing tests may also require you to present a persuasive argument quickly. After reading a prompt, you need to choose a position, structure your argument, and present it in a logical manner. And you need to do all this within a strict time limit. This chapter will show you how to use the writing process to create an effective persuasive response to a prompt.

Writing Guidelines

    Subject: **Persuasive prompt**
       Form: **Response essay**
   Purpose: **To demonstrate competence**
  Audience: **Instructor**

"Opinions cannot survive if one has no chance to fight for them."

—Thomas Mann

Prewriting Analyzing a Persuasive Prompt

The first step in responding to a persuasive prompt is to carefully analyze the prompt. What topic should you write about? What form should your response take? To whom should you address your response? To analyze a prompt effectively, use the **STRAP questions**:

> **Subject:** What topic should I write about?
>
> **Type:** What form of writing should I create (essay, letter, editorial, article, report)?
>
> **Role:** What position should I assume as the writer (student, son or daughter, friend, employee, citizen)?
>
> **Audience:** To whom am I writing (teacher, parents, classmates, employer, official)?
>
> **Purpose:** What is the goal of my writing (persuade, respond, evaluate, tell, describe)?

<u>Subject</u>
<u>Type</u>
Role
Audience
Purpose

Imagine that your class must vote between two <u>choices for a</u> <u>class trip</u>—the Museum of Fine Arts or the Oak Beach Aquarium. *As a student of the junior class,* write a <u>letter</u> to the school newspaper that will <u>persuade</u> your <u>classmates</u> to vote for one of these choices.

Try It!

Analyze these prompts by answering the STRAP questions. (Some answers may be implied or left open. Use your best judgment.)

1. Your school board has announced plans to cut funding for sports teams. As a concerned student, write a letter to the school board airing your opinion about funding cuts.
2. You have recently learned that your town is planning to use 10 acres of the 100-acre town park to build affordable housing for low-income families. Write an editorial supporting or opposing the building plan.

Tip

Some prompts may not include answers for every STRAP question. Use your judgment to answer those questions.

Planning Your Response

After answering the STRAP questions, you can use these graphic organizers to plan your response quickly.

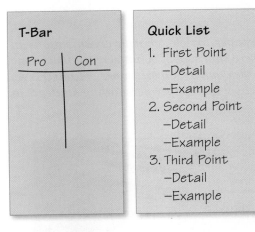

T-Bar	
Pro	Con

Quick List

1. First Point
   —Detail
   —Example
2. Second Point
   —Detail
   —Example
3. Third Point
   —Detail
   —Example

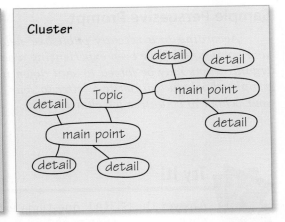

Cluster

Looking at Both Sides

Some prompts ask you to look at two sides of an argument and write persuasively in support of the strongest argument. First you'll need to consider both sides carefully and then choose the side that is most reasonable.

A pro-con chart is a great tool for thoroughly examining both sides of an argument. Placing the "pros" and "cons" side by side will make it easier for you to choose the stronger side.

Looking at both sides of an argument will also prepare you to respond to the weaker side. Explaining an important objection as flawed can strengthen your argument.

Prewrite

Use a graphic organizer. Reread the persuasive prompts on page 268. Use a graphic organizer to plan your response to one of the prompts.

Tip

In a timed writing test, be sure to manage your time carefully. For example, if you have 45 minutes to respond to a prompt, use the first 5 minutes to analyze the prompt and plan your response, the last 5 minutes to revise and edit your response, and the 35 minutes in between for writing.

Persuasive

Writing Responding to a Prompt

Once you have answered the STRAP questions and planned your response using a graphic organizer, you can begin writing.

Sample Persuasive Prompt

According to a recently published newspaper article, charity organizations in your community have been experiencing a severe shortage of volunteers. In fact, some organizations may be forced to shut down if they cannot attract more volunteers. As a high school student, write a letter to your school newspaper persuading students at your school to volunteer for charity work.

Try It!

Answer the STRAP questions for the above prompt. (See page 268.)

Sample Response

> **Beginning**
> The beginning paragraph states the opinion (underlined).

Dear Editor:

Read about the early days of almost any town, and you'll see that volunteers played a critical role in its history. From organizations like the Red Cross to community libraries, from school tutors to people working on local committees, volunteers have made a tremendous impact. Sadly, it appears that the times are changing. Recently, a number of local charity organizations have announced they may no longer be able to carry on their missions. They lack the volunteers they need to get the job done. <u>Students at Harris High should step up and volunteer—not only for the good of the community but also for their own benefit.</u>

One reason to volunteer is to help keep local taxes low. Volunteers provide necessary services that local governments could not afford. Most libraries, for example, could not provide a sufficient level of service without volunteer help. Hiring more workers would increase local taxes. People who volunteer at schools, seniors centers, and food pantries provide free services that help keep taxes low.

Volunteering also benefits the volunteer. When you volunteer to support a community organization, you gain friends and learn new skills, as you enjoy the good feeling of helping people in need. At a time when many people suffer from a lack of physical exercise and personal interaction, volunteering offers a chance to exercise your body and your mind.

Middle
The middle paragraphs express reasons for supporting the position.

The most important reason for becoming a community volunteer is that no matter what skills you have, the need for help is real. From young children who need help with studying and learning to senior citizens who need help with getting to appointments, community volunteers get important jobs done. Spending an hour or two a week as a volunteer, you could make a positive difference in people's lives.

The final middle paragraph addresses an objection.

Those who don't take the time to volunteer may think that someone else will do the job—or even that their skills are not useful. Nothing could be further from the truth. As last week's newspaper article pointed out, some of our vital community organizations are in danger of shutting their doors due to lack of volunteer help. When it comes to volunteering, even something as simple as talking and listening can be life changing.

Ending
The ending restates the writer's position and makes a call to action.

In conclusion, if you've thought about volunteering but put it off, now is the time to step forward. And if you've never considered volunteering, now is the time to try it. You'll benefit the community, you'll benefit yourself, and most of all, you'll benefit the people who need help. Volunteer today, and you'll be glad you did.

Sincerely,

Nick DiCarlo

Persuasive

Write

Respond to a persuasive prompt. Use the prompt you chose on page 268, your answers to the STRAP questions, and your graphic organizer to write a response. Be sure to finish your response in the time allotted.

Revising Improving Your Response

Some writing tests allow you to make changes in your writing; others don't. Before you begin a writing test, find out whether you will be allowed to make changes or not. If changes are allowed, make them as neatly as possible. Use the STRAP questions to guide your revisions.

> **Subject:** Have I responded to the topic of the prompt?
> Do all my main points support my persuasive argument?
>
> **Type:** Have I used the form requested in the prompt (essay, letter, editorial, article, report)?
>
> **Role:** Have I assumed the role called for in the prompt?
>
> **Audience:** Have I addressed the audience named in the prompt?
>
> **Purpose:** Does my response accomplish the goal indicated in the prompt?

Revise

Improve your work. Reread your response, using the STRAP questions above as your guide. Within the time allowed, make neat changes to your response.

Editing Checking Your Response

After revising, you should read through your response one final time. As you read, check for and correct any errors in conventions: punctuation, capitalization, spelling, and grammar.

Editing Checklist

Conventions

_____ **1.** Have I used end punctuation for every sentence?

_____ **2.** Have I capitalized all proper nouns and the first word of every sentence?

_____ **3.** Have I spelled all words correctly?

_____ **4.** Have I made sure my subjects and verbs agree?

_____ **5.** Have I used the right words *(their, there, they're)*?

Edit

Check your conventions. Read through your response one final time. In the time allowed, neatly correct any errors in punctuation, capitalization, spelling, and grammar.

Persuasive Writing on Tests

Use this guide when preparing to respond to a persuasive writing prompt.

Before you write . . .

- **Understand the prompt.**
  Use the STRAP questions, and remember that a persuasive prompt asks you to use facts and logical reasons to persuade or convince.
- **Plan your time wisely.**
  Spend 5 to 10 minutes planning before starting to write.

As you write . . .

- **Decide on a focus for your essay.**
  Keep your main idea or purpose in mind as you write. Be sure all your points clearly support your argument.
- **Be selective.**
  Use examples that directly support your opinion.
- **End in a meaningful way.**
  Remind the reader about the topic and your point of view.

After you've written a first draft . . .

- **Check for completeness and correctness.**
  Use the STRAP questions to revise your work. Then check for errors in punctuation, capitalization, spelling, and grammar.

Try It!

Plan and write a response. Choose one of the prompts below. Analyze it with the STRAP questions; use a graphic organizer to gather details and plan; then write, revise, and edit your response.

- Your school budget will allow for an additional class to be offered in the coming school year, and your principal has asked students to make suggestions. Write a letter to the principal explaining what class you think should be offered and why.
- As a class project, your English teacher wants to view and analyze a current movie. In preparation for this unit, she would like students to recommend a movie to study. In a memo or an e-mail message, convince your teacher to use the movie of your choice.

Response to Literature

Response to Literature
Analyzing a Theme

One thing that's just as enjoyable as reading a good fictional story is reading a good *true* story. As amazing as it may be to read about a character such as Captain Ahab or Harry Potter, it's just as amazing to read about real people.

For centuries, writers have written biographies and autobiographies, true stories about significant people. In the 1960s, writers such as Truman Capote, Tom Wolfe, and Norman Mailer began writing "nonfiction novels." A nonfiction novel is basically the creative retelling of an event or a time period rather than the story of an individual person.

Nonfiction novels, biographies, and autobiographies tell many stories, from the creation of the space program in *The Right Stuff* to the life of dancer Fred Astaire in *Steps in Time*. These books prove that truth can be just as forceful as fiction—and just as enjoyable to read.

Writing Guidelines

Subject: A nonfiction book that tells a story
Form: Literary analysis
Purpose: To analyze a main theme
Audience: Classmates

"Whenever you say 'well that's not convincing' the author tells you that's the bit that wasn't made up. This is because real life is under no obligation to be convincing."

—Neil Gaiman

Writing Warm-Up Thinking About Amazing Lives

As a warm-up, you'll write a paragraph response to a biographical article. Begin by considering the types of interesting people you could write about:

activists	astronauts	explorers	musicians
actors	athletes	inventors	scientists
artists	business people	leaders/rulers	writers

One student chose three categories from the list above and listed people who interested her. Then she chose one person to write about.

Amazing People Chart

Actors	Leaders/Rulers	Writers
Johnny Depp	Margaret Thatcher	Maya Angelou
Oprah Winfrey *	Nelson Mandela	John Neihardt

Prewrite

Create an amazing people chart. Choose three categories of people from the list above and write these categories at the top of a piece of paper. Then, under each category, list famous people. Put an asterisk (*) next to the one you would like to write about.

Finding a Biographical Article

After choosing Oprah Winfrey, the student searched for articles about Oprah. She checked the *Readers' Guide to Periodical Literature* and the Internet. Once she found a well-documented article from a reliable source, she read it and prepared her response.

Prewrite

Search for a biographical article about the person you chose. Be sure the article contains enough interesting information to write about in a response paragraph. Then carefully read the article.

Writing a Paragraph Analysis

You can analyze the article you chose by following these guidelines:

- In the **opening sentence,** name the article, author, and subject.
- In the **body sentences,** briefly summarize the article and provide insight into its main point.
- In the **closing sentence,** restate the main point of article.

Sample Paragraph Analysis

In the following paragraph, a student writer analyzes a biographical article about Oprah Winfrey.

The **opening sentence** names the article, the writer, and the subject.

The **body sentences** summarize the article and its main point.

The **closing sentence** restates the main theme of the article.

An Uncommon Woman

In "The Life and Times of O," Sarah Williams shows how Oprah Winfrey used her "common touch" to become a most uncommon woman. Born in Mississippi, Oprah did most of her growing up in Milwaukee. At age 13, she suffered abuse and went to live in Nashville with her father. He was strict but expected Oprah to make something of herself. At 17, she got a job at a radio station, and at 19, she became a TV news anchor. After college, she landed the position as host of *AM Chicago* and turned it into the number one talk show in the nation—*The Oprah Winfrey Show.* Oprah next appeared in the movie *The Color Purple,* and its success allowed her to set up her own production company, called Harpo (Oprah backward). In time, she became the first female African American billionaire. Oprah may have had a humble start and faced many challenges, but she also learned to believe in herself—and in other people. She used her common touch to build an entertainment empire and inspire millions of people around the world.

Literature

Write an analysis paragraph. Read the biographical article you selected on the previous page. Then write a response paragraph in which you summarize the article and provide insight into its main point.

"My interest is in people—what they do and what they say."

—William Zinsser

Understanding Your Goal

Your goal in this chapter is to write an essay that analyzes the theme in a nonfiction book that tells a story. The chart below lists the key traits of a literary analysis essay, with specific suggestions for this assignment.

Traits of a Response to Literature

■ Ideas

Write a thesis statement that explains one main theme of the book. Then paraphrase and quote passages that summarize the book and demonstrate the theme.

■ Organization

Write clear beginning, middle, and ending parts. Use transitions to effectively connect sentences and paragraphs.

■ Voice

Sound interested in and knowledgeable about the book you analyze.

■ Word Choice

Use literary terms that reveal your understanding of the book. Use words that reflect the author's word choice.

■ Sentence Fluency

Write sentences that read well and have a variety of beginnings and lengths.

■ Conventions

Check your writing for punctuation, capitalization, spelling, and grammar errors.

Get the big picture. Review the rubric on pages 310–311 before you begin writing. This rubric will guide you throughout the revising and editing steps in the writing process.

Response Essay

In the following essay, Tyrell analyzes *Blue Highways* by William Least Heat-Moon, the nonfiction story of the author's travels along the back roads of this country.

A Search for Harmony

Beginning
The beginning names the book and author and states the main theme (underlined).

Blue Highways begins as William Least Heat-Moon's life is falling apart. He loses his job teaching English and finds out that his separation from his wife is leading to a divorce. In response, Least Heat-Moon packs up Ghost Dancing, his van, with a sleeping bag, a cooler, a portable toilet, some food, and $428. Then he heads out to drive the back roads of America (8). At first, even Least Heat-Moon is unsure of his reason for making this trip, but he soon identifies it as a search for harmony, which he finds in amazing places.

Least Heat-Moon begins by driving to escape his own life, but he ends up running into the lives of others. In Shelbyville, Kentucky, he meets men restoring log cabins, and in nearby Brooklyn Bridge, he meets a couple building a boat that will carry them away from the heartland. He also stays with a police-officer-turned-Trappist-monk in Conyers, Georgia. The people Least Heat-Moon meets tell him about their lives, but Least Heat-Moon realizes he is hearing about his own life at the same time. As Father Patrick says, "As a kid, I was always searching for something beyond myself, something to bring harmony and make sense of things . . . but I didn't find harmony until I came here" (85). The Trappist's words echo Least Heat-Moon's own quest—looking for harmony, and finding himself along the way.

Middle
The middle paragraphs discuss the meaning of the events in the book.

In Selma, Alabama, Least Heat-Moon meets two men living in "the project" who have found harmony, even on the mean streets. When a telephone repair truck keeps circling the three men, Least Heat-Moon experiences the prejudice the men deal with every day. The truck is an undercover police vehicle, and the officers inside suspect Least Heat-Moon of being a "dealer." "White dude in the project at night, drivin' a van, Northern license. Yeah, man, you be dealin' all right" (102). This sort of encounter happens over and over: Least Heat-Moon meets people who seem entirely different from him, but quickly discovers that he has more in common with them than he thought.

Literature

Least Heat-Moon realizes early on that his search for harmony relies on what Walt Whitman calls "the profound lesson of reception" (17). Throughout his journey, Least Heat-Moon learns to stop, look, and listen, to hear what people are saying, to see the land around him, to let the present and the past and the future all advise him. As he drives through "nothing" outside Eldorado, Texas, Least Heat-Moon decides to make a "list of nothing in particular" (149–151). The list turns out to have thirty items, including things he sees and hears and thinks. This list of nothing is, in fact, everything. Only by opening his senses and his mind can he learn the lessons of his journey.

In Utah, Least Heat-Moon finds a symbol for his journey, a maze pattern called "the emergence symbol." The Hopi Indians refer to this as the map of the soul's wandering, a journey beyond the materialistic world. Least Heat-Moon learns that "he belongs to two families, his natural clan and that of all things" (186–187). Least Heat-Moon's journey of the soul is a quest that takes him away from smallness and selfishness toward a much bigger world.

Ending
The ending paragraph reflects on the main theme of the book.

In the end, what did Least Heat-Moon finally learn? He admits, "I can't say over the miles that I had learned what I wanted to know because I hadn't known what I wanted to know" (411). But he did learn how a thousand different people in a thousand different places find harmony. He followed the wandering path of the soul and found that harmony doesn't reside in one place alone, but in the attitude a person has toward all places.

Respond to the reading. Answer the following questions about the essay:

Ideas (1) What theme becomes the focus of the analysis? (2) Which key quotation from the book supports this theme?

Organization (3) Where does the writer summarize the main action of the book? (4) Where does the writer focus on analyzing the theme?

Voice & Word Choice (5) Does the writer sound knowledgeable about the book? Explain.

Prewriting

If you've ever had writer's block—the fear of the blank page—prewriting can help. Step-by-step, you'll find the ideas you need to fill that page. Listed below are prewriting guidelines for planning your analysis.

Keys to Effective Prewriting

1. Select an interesting nonfiction book that tells a story.

2. Summarize major events in the book.

3. Review the major events to decide what themes they point to.

4. Write a clear thesis statement stating a main theme.

5. Decide how to organize the information in your middle paragraphs.

6. Write a topic sentence for each middle paragraph.

Literature

Prewriting Selecting a Book

You may already have read a nonfiction book that you would like to analyze. Otherwise, follow the directions on this page. Biographies and autobiographies work well for this assignment, as do the modern nonfiction novels. One way to find a book is to brainstorm a list of people, events, and animals that interest you. Malaya brainstormed the following list.

Topics List

People	Events/Animals
Katharine Hepburn	the fall of the Berlin wall
Spike Lee	Koko the Gorilla
Jane Austen	September 11, 2001
Gloria Steinem	Seabiscuit *

Prewrite

Brainstorm a topics list. Write "People" in one column and "Events/Animals" in another column. Write down topics you'd like to read about. Put an asterisk (*) next to the topic you choose.

Searching the Library Catalog

Once you've chosen a subject, do a subject search in your library's computer catalog to find *nonfiction* books about the subject. Here is the computer catalog entry that Malaya found. The first book was too basic, so Malaya chose to read the second one.

Seabiscuit: The saga of a great champion
Beckwith, Brainerd Kellogg, 1903-
Pages: 69
ISBN: 1594160007
798.4 BEC

Seabiscuit: An American legend
Hillenbrand, Laura.
Pages: 339
ISBN: 0375502912
798.4009 HIL

Prewrite

Search for a book. Perform a subject search and select a nonfiction book that fits your reading level. Take time to read it.

Writing Down Main Events

After reading the book you selected, take some time to think about its main events. A time line can help you focus on the main events. Here is the time line that Malaya created for the book *Seabiscuit:*

Time Line

1903	Charles Howard starts an auto dealership in San Francisco.
1926	Howard loses son to car crash; he and his wife divorce.
1929	Howard meets Marcela, falls in love with horse racing.
1935	Howard meets "old plainsman" Tom Smith.
1936	Howard buys worn-out 3-year-old horse named Seabiscuit.
	Jockey Red Pollard meets Seabiscuit.
1937	Seabiscuit is second at Santa Anita and wins San Juan Capistrano.
1938	Fair Knightess falls, crushing Red Pollard.
	Pollard's leg crushed in accident on Modern Youth.
	Seabiscuit beats War Admiral in match race.
	Seabiscuit pulls up lame.
1939	Pollard and Seabiscuit work together to heal.
	Pollard rides Seabiscuit to win Santa Anita Handicap.

Prewrite

Create a time line. After you finish reading the book, page through it, writing down important events in the order that they occurred.

Focus on the Traits

Ideas Even nonfiction stories follow this classic pattern:

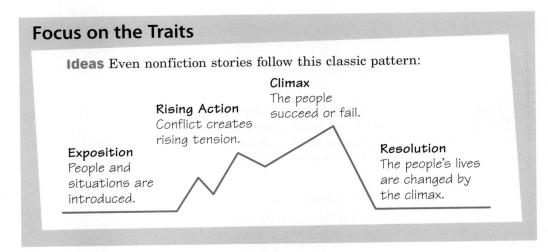

Climax
The people succeed or fail.

Rising Action
Conflict creates rising tension.

Exposition
People and situations are introduced.

Resolution
The people's lives are changed by the climax.

Prewriting Considering Themes

Study your time line of the book's major events to identify a theme, or major lesson about life. Malaya thought about themes by creating a quotation chart. On the left, she listed major events from the story, and on the right, she listed quotations about the importance of these events. (For each quotation, she noted a page number in parentheses.)

Quotation Chart

Major Events	What Laura Hillenbrand Wrote
Howard starts a car dealership.	"Howard had a weakness for lost causes" (6).
Howard meets Smith.	"The two men stood in different halves of the century. Smith was the last of the true frontiersmen; Howard was paving Smith's West under the urgent wheels of his automobiles" (29).
Howard buys Seabiscuit.	"His stubby legs were a study in unsound construction, with squarish, asymmetrical 'baseball glove' knees that didn't quite straighten all the way, leaving him in a permanent semi-crouch" (33).
Seabiscuit loses at Santa Anita.	" . . . at the most critical moment of their careers, Pollard and Seabiscuit faltered. For fifteen strides, more than the length of a football field, Pollard remained virtually motionless" (123).

Prewrite

Create a quotation chart. List the novel's major events. Then gather quotations in which the writer reflects on the meaning of the events. Note in parentheses the page on which each quotation appears. Afterward, write down possible themes. Here are Malaya's ideas.

> Themes: winning and losing
>   finding victory in defeat
>   the way the world changes

Writing a Thesis Statement

Your thesis statement identifies the book or writer and introduces the theme you want to explore. The following formula can help you.

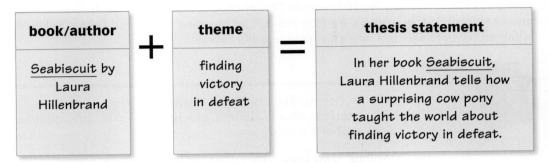

book/author		theme		thesis statement
Seabiscuit by Laura Hillenbrand	**+**	finding victory in defeat	**=**	In her book Seabiscuit, Laura Hillenbrand tells how a surprising cow pony taught the world about finding victory in defeat.

Prewrite

Form a focus. Write a thesis statement for your response essay using the formula above.

Organizing the Middle Paragraphs of Your Essay

The first few middle paragraphs should focus on the main events of the novel. The later paragraphs should focus on the meaning of the events—demonstrating the theme. Malaya wrote the following topic sentences for her middle paragraphs.

Topic Sentence 1 (First middle paragraph)
The book traces the life of Seabiscuit, a broken-down three-year-old racehorse.

Topic Sentence 2 (Second middle paragraph)
Along comes Charles Howard, who "had a weakness for lost causes."

Topic Sentence 3 (Third middle paragraph)
A string of race wins follows, in Detroit, in Cincinnati, and all through the racecourses of California.

Topic Sentence 4 (Fourth middle paragraph)
Seabiscuit is, on the surface, a book about winning, but Hillenbrand also provides much compassionate commentary about losing.

Topic Sentence 5 (Fifth middle paragraph)
The ending of *Seabiscuit* perfectly demonstrates the theme of victory from defeat.

Prewrite

Create topic sentences. Write topic sentences for your middle paragraphs. The first paragraphs should focus on the main events of the book. The later paragraphs should focus on the theme you wish to explore.

Literature

Prewriting Including Paraphrases and Quotations

Most of your responses about the book should be paraphrases—ideas expressed in your own words. However, when the author's exact words are especially concise and powerful, you will want to quote the author. An effective quotation allows you to showcase the author's writing voice. The exercise below will help you learn when to paraphrase and when to include a quotation.

Try It!

Read the passage below. Then write a paragraph that paraphrases *most* of the information. Also include a concise, powerful quotation to demonstrate the author's writing voice.

I was in the thick of my latest project when the phone rang: the blasted phone. Telemarketers were the bane of my existence. Still, this could be my boss.

I lifted the receiver and barked, "What?"

"Turn on the TV," came the voice on the other end—a man's voice, grave and slightly trembling. Even as I staggered to the TV and punched the "on" button, I realized it was the voice of my friend Steve.

The screen brightened, and the scene that appeared was strange—two great glass towers, straight and smooth, with two columns of black smoke pouring and twisting sideways from them.

"Somebody's flown planes into the World Trade Center," Steve explained.

I stood there gaping, unsure of what I was seeing, torn between the deadline that a moment ago had seemed of ultimate significance and this terrible sight, which meant the whole world was changing forever.

"What?" I repeated stupidly.

Before Steve could answer, one of the towers began to fall.

Focus on the Traits

Voice When you use a quotation from the book, you allow the author to speak in your essay. Carefully choose quotations to reveal both the theme you are focusing on and the voice of the author.

Writing

Now that you have finished prewriting, you are ready to write the first draft of your response. At this stage, focus only on getting your ideas on paper. You can make improvements later.

Keys to Effective Writing

1. Write on every other line so that you have room to make changes later.

2. Use your thesis statement and topic sentences to guide your writing.

3. Support your topic sentences with paraphrased information and direct quotations.

4. In your first middle paragraphs, summarize important events from the book; then analyze the main theme in the later paragraphs.

5. Tie your ideas together with transitions.

Literature

Writing Getting the Big Picture

Remember that an essay includes three parts—the beginning, the middle, and the ending. You are ready to begin writing your response if you have . . .

1. written a clear thesis statement that identifies the theme,

2. gathered events and quotations that reveal the theme, and

3. written topic sentences to organize your paragraphs.

The chart below shows how the three parts of a theme analysis fit together. The examples are from the essay on pages **289–292**.

Beginning

The **beginning** names the book and the author, tells what the story is about, and states the thesis.

Thesis Statement
In her book *Seabiscuit,* Laura Hillenbrand tells how a surprising cow pony teaches the world about finding victory in defeat.

Middle

The **middle** paragraphs summarize the important events and analyze the main theme.

Topic Sentences
The book traces the life of Seabiscuit, a broken-down three-year-old racehorse.

Along comes the wealthy Charles Howard, who "had a weakness for lost causes."

A string of race wins follows, in Detroit, in Cincinnati, and all through the racecourses of California.

Seabiscuit is, on the surface, a book about winning, but Hillenbrand also provides much compassionate commentary about losing.

The ending of *Seabiscuit* demonstrates the theme of victory from defeat.

Ending

The **ending** paragraph reemphasizes the main theme.

Closing Sentences
The story of Seabiscuit proves that there are third acts and fourth acts and fifth acts, too. That's a horse that all of us can cheer for.

Starting Your Essay

The opening of your analysis grabs the reader's interest and should include . . .

- **the title and author of the book,**
- **background information about people and events, and**
- **your thesis statement.**

> **Beginning**
> Middle
> Ending

Beginning Paragraph

Malaya places the story of Seabiscuit in its historical context.

> The first part introduces the novel and gives the thesis statement (underlined).

> It is the Great Depression. Unemployment rises to 25 percent, the average family income drops 40 percent, and dictators control Germany, Italy, and Russia. Franklin Delano Roosevelt tries to speak hope into American living rooms, and Hollywood produces thousands of escapist movies. But in 1938, newspaper coverage of Hitler and F.D.R. and Clark Gable slumps. The hottest story is a horse named Seabiscuit (xvii). In her book *Seabiscuit*, Laura Hillenbrand tells how a surprising cow pony teaches the world about finding victory in defeat.

Write

Write your beginning. As you develop your beginning paragraph, include the title and author of the book, background information that introduces the story, and your thesis statement. Write as many versions as it takes to compose a beginning that says what you want it to say.

Tip

If you have trouble getting started, review these tips to trigger your thinking.

- **Talk about your story with a classmate** before you begin to write.
- **Write freely** without worrying about producing the perfect analysis. First drafts are often called *rough drafts* for a reason.
- **Review the book** to find supporting details for your thesis statement.
- **Show your personal interest** in the novel and in your analysis by using natural, sincere, though careful language.
- **Focus on these key traits of writing:** ideas, organization, and voice.

Literature

Writing Developing the Middle Part

Your first job is to summarize the events of the story. Afterward, you'll shift your focus to the main theme. Begin each middle paragraph with one of your topic sentences. Supply support for each topic sentence by paraphrasing and quoting parts of the book.

Middle Paragraphs

In the middle paragraphs, Malaya begins by recounting the important events of Seabiscuit's rise to fame. She then shifts her focus to the main theme.

The first middle paragraphs summarize the main events in the novel.

> The book traces the life of Seabiscuit, a broken-down three-year-old racehorse. Though he is the son of the fast and temperamental racehorse named Hard Tack, Seabiscuit has none of his sire's sleek beauty. Hillenbrand describes Seabiscuit as "blunt, coarse, rectangular, stationary. . . . His stubby legs were a study in unsound construction, with squarish, asymmetrical 'baseball glove' knees that didn't quite straighten all the way, leaving him in a permanent semi-crouch" (33). The horse has had a hard life, running more races in two years than most horses run in a lifetime. By his third year, he seems used up and useless, and many people think him lame.

The writer includes some of the author's creative descriptions.

> Along comes the wealthy Charles Howard, who "had a weakness for lost causes" (6). He sees potential in Seabiscuit and purchases him. Howard gives the horse over to the care of Tom Smith, who is himself a lost cause—an old washed-up horse trainer who rarely speaks and who "had a colorless translucence about him that made him seem as if he were in the earliest stages of progressive invisibility" (20). For a jockey, Howard lines up a luckless firebrand named Red Pollard, who literally wanders penniless up to the stable after having crawled out of a car wreck. As Hillenbrand puts it, "The scattered lives of Red Pollard, Tom Smith, and Charles Howard had come to an intersection" (95). They glimpse greatness in this broken-down horse, and as they nurture Seabiscuit, they begin to discover greatness in themselves.

The middle paragraphs include paraphrased and quoted material.

A string of race wins follows, in Detroit, in Cincinnati, and all through the racecourses of California. During that time, Seabiscuit's star is rising, and the handicap weights he carries become heavier and heavier—often 20 to 30 pounds more than any other horse in the field. In his six years of racing, Seabiscuit "won thirty-three races and set thirteen track records at eight tracks over six distances" (325). He goes on to beat the Triple Crown winner, War Admiral, in a head-to-head race considered the greatest race in the sport's history.

Seabiscuit is, on the surface, a book about winning, but Hillenbrand also provides much compassionate commentary about losing. The reason this horse captures the imagination of Depression-era America is that he looks like a commoner, a "cow pony" that has more heart than the most beautiful thoroughbred. While people in the '30s are reading stories about Horatio Alger and his rise from poverty, they are seeing a real-life Horatio Alger in this "mean, restive, and ragged" horse (31). Hillenbrand carries the theme further, showing how Smith and Pollard and even Howard himself find new life through this amazing animal.

The later middle paragraphs use events and quotations to demonstrate the main theme.

The ending of Seabiscuit perfectly demonstrates the theme of victory from defeat. After pulling up lame in a race in 1939, the six-year-old Seabiscuit is considered finished. So, too, is his longtime rider, Red Pollard, who has suffered such terrible injuries in track accidents that doctors tell him he will never ride a horse again. "We were a couple of old cripples together," said Red (296). But during that year, he and the old horse both recover. They return in 1940 to win the "hundred grander" at Santa Anita, with Seabiscuit carrying 130 pounds—more than 15 pounds over what the second- and third-place horses had to carry, though they were only half the age of Seabiscuit.

Literature

Write

Write your middle paragraphs. Use your topic sentences, time line, and quotations chart to guide your writing. Try to include examples of creative descriptions or figurative language to reveal the author's voice.

Writing Ending Your Essay

The ending of your response reflects on the main theme. Here are some strategies for an effective conclusion:

Beginning
Middle
Ending

- **Use a strong quotation** from the writer.
  A lame Red Pollard and a lame Seabiscuit, who had "four good legs between them," have shocked the racing world by winning the Santa Anita Handicap (312).

- **Refer** to the beginning.
  Out of the depths of the Depression, out of the looming shadow of World War II, a game-legged cow pony has risen up to show the world that victory can be born from defeat.

- **Describe** the historical context for the theme.
  In the same year that Seabiscuit makes his great comeback, the novelist F. Scott Fitzgerald lies on his deathbed and says, "There are no second acts in American lives." He is wrong.

Ending Paragraph

In the final paragraph, Malaya places the theme in its historical context.

The ending applies the theme to life in general.

The main theme of Seabiscuit is that no matter how much you lose, you can always rise again to victory. During the same year that Seabiscuit makes his great comeback, the novelist F. Scott Fitzgerald lies on his deathbed and says, "There are no second acts in American lives." He is wrong. The story of Seabiscuit proves that there are third acts and fourth acts and fifth acts, too. That's a horse that all of us can cheer for.

Write

Write your ending and form a complete first draft. Develop the last paragraph of your essay, using one or more of the suggestions listed above. Make a complete copy of your essay. Double-space or write on every other line so that you have room for revising.

Revising

You've written a first draft, pouring your ideas onto the page. Now it's time to revise, making whatever changes are necessary to improve the content of your essay.

Keys to Effective Revising

1. Read your essay aloud to see whether it holds together from start to finish.

2. Check your beginning to confirm that it names the book and author and expresses the main theme in a thesis statement.

3. Be sure that each middle paragraph supports the thesis statement.

4. Revise your voice to make it engaging.

5. Review your word choice and sentence fluency.

6. Use the editing and proofreading marks inside the back cover of this book.

Revising **for** Ideas

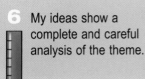
6 My ideas show a complete and careful analysis of the theme.

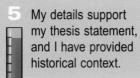
5 My details support my thesis statement, and I have provided historical context.

4 My details support my thesis statement, but I should provide more historical context.

When you revise for *ideas,* be sure that you have included only important details and that you have provided some historical context for the main events of book. Use the rubric strip above to help you revise.

Have I included only important details?

You have included only important details if every one of them does either or both of the following things. The best details accomplish both points.

1. Help the reader understand the book.
2. Support the main theme.

Exercise

Read the thesis statement below. Then read the sample middle paragraph. Identify two details that should be deleted.

Thesis statement: In *Louis Armstrong: In His Own Words,* the great jazzman reflects on a life of glorious music and racial conflict.

1   Armstrong began his career as a boy in New Orleans, saving up his salary of
2 50 cents a week to buy a $5 cornet. Armstrong is famous for playing the trumpet
3 and singing, but he started out playing the cornet. He described it as "All dirty—
4 but was soon pretty to me. After blowing into it a while, I realized that I could play
5 'Home Sweet Home' and then 'Here Comes the Blues'" (1). As a child, Armstrong
6 was steeped in the Delta blues, but he also heard Russian folk songs and lullabies
7 sung by the Jewish family for which he worked. Later, he had a Jewish manager
8 named Joe Glaser. These two influences—black blues and Jewish folk songs—
9 eventually combined to form the new music Armstrong would help to invent: jazz.

Revise

Check your details. Read through your first draft, making sure that each detail either helps the reader understand the book or supports the theme—or does both. Delete any unneeded details.

3 I have some unnecessary details, and I need to provide historical context.

 2 I need a thesis statement and details that support it.

 1 I need to learn more about how to analyze the theme of a nonfiction book.

How can I add historical context?

You can add historical context by relating the events in the book to other important events of the time. Researching the time period and the author will help you to develop an insightful analysis.

 ### Exercise

Read the following paragraph and find two ways that the author uses historical context to explore the theme.

1   Above all else, *Louis Armstrong: In His Own Words* is a book about a musical
2 and social pioneer. Armstrong was born in the age of the minstrel show and Jim
3 Crow laws, but he invented a new type of music that transcended the boundaries
4 of color. When he began performing in the early 1920s, he played his music to all-
5 black audiences. By the end of his career, in the 1970s, he played to every color of
6 person on the planet. Armstrong became not only an ambassador for jazz, but also
7 for integration, racial tolerance, and understanding.

Revise

Add historical details. Research the time period and the author of the book. Consider adding details that show the events in historical context and strengthen the significance of the theme.

Ideas
Context is provided.

It is the Great Depression. Unemployment rises to 25 percent, the average family income drops 40 percent, and Dictators control Germany, Italy, and Russia. Franklin Delano Roosevelt tries to speak hope into American living rooms, and Hollywood produces thousands of escapist movies. But in 1938, . . .

Literature

Revising for Organization

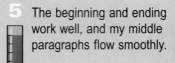

6 All the parts of my essay work together to create an insightful analysis.

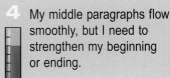

5 The beginning and ending work well, and my middle paragraphs flow smoothly.

4 My middle paragraphs flow smoothly, but I need to strengthen my beginning or ending.

When you revise for *organization,* you make sure your beginning and ending work well and that your ideas flow smoothly in the middle paragraphs. The rubric strip above will help you revise for organization.

Does my beginning work well?

Your beginning works well if it does all of the following things:

1. Grabs the reader's attention.
2. Introduces the subject of the book.
3. Provides the name of the book and the author's name.
4. Gives your thesis statement.

Exercise

Here are four strategies (and examples) for getting your reader's attention. For each one, write a one-sentence example that could work for your essay.

1. **Make a startling claim.**
   The modern masterpiece *In Cold Blood* succeeds in part because it portrays the full personality of a cold-blooded killer.

2. **Ask an intriguing question.**
   What modern masterpiece is hailed as both horrifying and hypnotically beautiful?

3. **Begin with an anecdote.**
   When Truman Capote first laid eyes on Perry Smith, a cold-blooded killer, the writer seemed to fall under a terrible spell.

4. **Use a quotation from the book.**
   "Until one morning in mid-November of 1959, few Americans—in fact, few Kansans—had ever heard of Holcomb" (5).

Revise

Check your beginning. Be sure it grabs the reader's attention, names the book and author, introduces the subject, and provides the thesis statement. Consider using one of your new beginning lines from the exercise above.

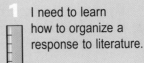

3 I need to strengthen the beginning and the ending of my essay.

2 My essay runs together, and my paragraphs do not flow well.

1 I need to learn how to organize a response to literature.

Does my ending work well?

Your ending works well if it applies the theme of the book to life in general. Because a theme makes a basic statement about life, an effective ending relates the book's ideas to real life.

Exercise

Read the following ending. Then explain how the writer of this paragraph connects the book's theme to the present-day world.

1   By writing *In Cold Blood,* Capote was doing more than introducing the genre of
2 the nonfiction novel. He was showing that in real life, villains and victims are not as
3 separate as they may seem. Clearly, the Clutter family was victimized by a horrible
4 crime, but one of the villains who committed the crime—Perry Smith—was himself
5 the victim of an abusive home. Capote is unflinching in portraying the humanity
6 of criminals as well as that of their victims. Until that humanity is recognized,
7 people can't understand the roots of crime. In this day and age of grand villains
8 such as Osama Bin Laden and Saddam Hussein, people still make the mistake of
9 dehumanizing them. Capote would say that by taking away their humanity, we take
10 away the hope of ever understanding the source of their terrible acts.

Revise

Check your ending. Be sure that you have applied the theme of the book to life in general. Revise as needed.

Organization
The ending is revised to connect the theme to real life.

"There are no second acts in American lives." He is wrong.

The story of Seabiscuit proves that there are third acts and
fourth acts and fifth acts, too. ∧
       That's a horse that all of us can cheer for.

Literature

Revising for Voice

 6 My writing voice sounds distinctive and engaging from start to finish.

 5 My voice sounds engaging, and I show understanding of the author's voice.

 4 My voice sounds engaging most of the time, and I show some understanding of the author's voice.

When you revise for *voice,* make sure you sound engaging and also show an understanding of the author's voice. The rubric strip above will guide you.

Does my writing voice sound engaging?

Your writing voice sounds engaging when your words show strong feeling about the events you are describing. Note the difference between the following two passages.

A Flat Voice

Fred Astaire started out as a tap dancer in vaudeville **before he** appeared in his first movie, ***Flying Down to Rio.***

An Engaging Voice

Fred Astaire tapped his way across thousands of vaudeville stages **before he** got his big break in the film ***Flying Down to Rio.***

Exercise

Rewrite any two of the flat sentences below, replacing the underlined words with new ones that say the same thing *with feeling.*

1. Fred practiced a lot.
2. He asked his directors to film each dance many times.
3. Fred wanted each number filmed from start to finish without breaks.
4. For Fred Astaire, dancing was important.
5. Dancers today still try to learn something from his moves.

Revise

Check your voice. Read through your first draft and underline words and phrases that sound flat. Rewrite them to show your feeling about the subject.

3 Sometimes I need to show more feeling, and I need to show understanding of the writer's voice.

2 My voice sounds flat, and I show no understanding of the writer's voice.

1 I need to learn more about voice.

How can I describe the author's voice?

You can describe the author's voice by using adjectives that show the writer's personality, feeling about the topic, and relationship with the reader.

- **Writer's personality:** Meticulous, lazy, capricious, caustic
- **Feeling about the topic:** Enthusiastic, hopeful, sarcastic, amazed
- **Relationship with the reader:** Welcoming, formal, friendly, gruff

Exercise

Read the following paragraph and write down adjectives that describe the voice of the author.

> Fred Astaire's autobiography, *Steps in Time,* exhibits the same graceful ease as the man himself. Fred writes with a welcoming tone and in a simple, down-to-earth manner. The words he uses are gentle, smiling, reflecting the same light step of Fred's dancing style. His writing, like his moves on the stage, embodies this autobiography's theme: grace.

 Revise

Check your understanding of the author's voice. Brainstorm a list of adjectives that describe the voice of the author and consider using some of them in your essay.

Voice
Adjectives capture the author's voice, and a sentence is changed to be engaging.

~~Seabiscuit~~ is a book about winning, but Hillenbrand , on the surface,

~~also says a whole lot of stuff~~ about losing. The reason this provides much compassionate commentary

captures the imagination of
horse ~~interests~~ Depression-era America is that he looks like

a commoner, a "cow pony" that has more heart than . . .

Revising for Word Choice

6	My word choice demonstrates my careful thinking about the novel.	5	My word choice reflects the author's use of figurative language and specific words.	4	I have included some figurative language and specific terms, but I should add more.

When you revise for *word choice,* you reflect the author's use of figurative language and specific words. Use the rubric strip above to revise for word choice.

How can I understand the use of figurative language?

To understand the author's use of figurative language, watch for these techniques. (The sample sentences come from Laura Hillenbrand's *Seabiscuit.*)

- **Similes:** Compare two things using *like* or *as.*
  "Pent up from trailing the field, Seabiscuit spun through the gap like a bullet rifling down a barrel" (178).

- **Metaphors:** Say one thing *is* another.
  "All his [Smith's] features but that big shovel of a jaw vanished in the shade of his hat brim" (39).

- **Personification:** Give a nonhuman thing human qualities.
  "While being unsaddled, he [Seabiscuit] leveled his wide-set intelligent eyes on Smith again. Smith liked that look, and nodded at the horse. 'Darned if that little rascal didn't nod back at me,' Smith later said, 'kinda like he was paying me an honor to notice me'" (34).

Exercise

Read the following sentences and identify which is a simile, which is a metaphor, and which is personification.

1. When I was twelve, our old VW was a starship.
2. It had a strange little air-cooled engine that sputtered rhythmically like a glorified lawn mower.
3. On hills, our speed would drop dramatically until we kids pushed on the backs of the seats. The VW always thanked us for our efforts.

Revise

Review the figurative language the author uses. Find examples of similes, metaphors, and personification. These techniques reveal the author's true feelings about the subject. Consider quoting one or two in your essay.

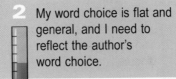

3 I need to reflect the author's figurative language and specific words.

2 My word choice is flat and general, and I need to reflect the author's word choice.

1 I need to learn more about word choice.

How can I reflect the author's word choice?

You can reflect the author's word choice by noticing the special words the author uses. Consider the following words and sentences from *Seabiscuit.*

- **Technical terms:** Words related to the specific subject
  backstretch   thoroughbred   handicap   mudder

- **Colloquialisms:** Words related to a region or subgroup of people
  cowpuncher   dingbustingest   bug boys   the wire

- **Vivid action words:** Verbs and verbals that express strong action
  "Seabiscuit and Ligaroti ripped out of the gate side by side" (243).

  "War Admiral flung himself around, bucking and thrashing and tearing divots out of the Belmont lawn" (203).

Using some of these words in your essay will help energize your writing and reflect the author's word choice. When you use technical terms and colloquialisms, however, make sure that you define their meaning for your audience.

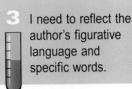
Revise

Revise for precise words. Search your book, looking for technical terms, colloquialisms, and vivid action words. Season your essay with some of the words you find.

Word Choice
A metaphor and vivid verbs are inserted.

For a jockey, Howard ~~gets a rider~~ named Red Pollard, who
                    lines up a luckless firebrand
literally ~~comes~~ penniless up to the stable after having crawled
          wanders
out of a car wreck. As Hillenbrand puts it, "The scattered lives
of Red Pollard, Tom Smith, and Charles Howard had come to
an intersection" (95). They ~~see~~ greatness in this broken-down
                              glimpse
horse, and as they ~~help~~ Seabiscuit, they begin to discover . . .
                    nurture

Revising for Sentence Fluency

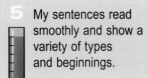

6 The sentences in my analysis make my ideas really stand out.

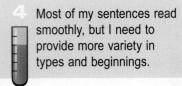

5 My sentences read smoothly and show a variety of types and beginnings.

4 Most of my sentences read smoothly, but I need to provide more variety in types and beginnings.

To revise for *sentence fluency,* check that you have used a variety of sentence types and beginnings. The rubric strip above will help you.

Have I used a variety of sentence types?

You have used a variety of sentence types if your essay contains simple, compound, and complex sentences. (The sample sentences below come from *I Know Why the Caged Bird Sings* by Maya Angelou.)

- **Simple sentences** contain a subject (which may be compound) and a verb (which may be compound).
  "The champion picker of the day before was the hero of the dawn."

- **Compound sentences** consist of two simple sentences joined with a comma and a coordinating conjunction *(and, but, or, nor, for, so, yet).*
  "I had seen the fingers cut by the mean little cotton bolls, and I had witnessed the backs and shoulders and arms and legs resisting any further demands."

- **Complex sentences** consist of an independent clause (a simple sentence) and a dependent clause (a word group with a subject and a verb that can't stand alone as a sentence).
  "No matter how much they had picked, it wasn't enough."

▶ Exercise

Label each sentence below as simple (S), compound (C), or complex (CX).

(1) Angelou's early life is tough, but it is also rich. (2) She remembers a world where wandering troubadours would sing on the old front porch of her grandma's general store. (3) These rich sensations sink into young Angelou's mind, and they teach her a kind of natural poetry. (4) She is learning her craft. (5) Later on, Angelou learns to overcome racism and sexism to transform her world.

Revise

Check your sentence variety. Choose one paragraph in your essay and label each sentence as simple (S), compound (C), or complex (CX). Revise for sentence variety as necessary. Then check your other paragraphs.

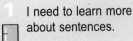

3 Some sentences do not read smoothly, and I need more variety in types and beginnings.

2 My sentences have no variety, and some of them are confusing or incomplete.

1 I need to learn more about sentences.

Do I vary my sentence beginnings?

You vary your sentence beginnings if your sentences start in different ways. Varied sentence beginnings add fluency to your writing. Here are different ways to begin the same sentence.

- **The subject**
  Maya Angelou **does not avoid controversy.**

- **An adverb**
  Rarely **does Maya Angelou avoid controversy.**

- **A phrase (or series of phrases)**
  In spite of her age, **Maya Angelou does not avoid controversy.**

- **A clause**
  Though she is a private person at heart, **Maya Angelou does not avoid controversy.**

Revise

Check for varied beginnings. Read your essay, watching for strings of sentences that begin the same way. Revise to create variety.

Sentence Fluency
Changes improve sentence variety.

Along comes the wealthy Charles Howard, who
⌃ ~~Charles Howard, a wealthy man, comes along.~~ He "had a

weakness for lost causes" (6). He sees potential in Seabiscuit

and purchases him. Howard gives the horse over to the care of

Tom Smith. He is himself a lost cause. He is an old washed-
        who ⌃
up horse trainer. He rarely speaks. He "had a colorless
        ⌃ *who* ⌃   *and who* ⌃
translucence about him that made him seem as if he were in

the earliest stages of progressive invisibility" (20). . . .

Literature

Revising Improving Your Writing

Revise

Check your revising. On a piece of paper, write the numbers 1 to 12. If you can answer "yes" to a question, put a check mark after that number. If not, continue to work with that part of your essay.

Revising Checklist

Ideas

_____ **1.** Is my thesis statement clear and complete?
_____ **2.** Have I included details and quotations that support the theme?
_____ **3.** Have I provided historical context?

Organization

_____ **4.** Does my beginning effectively introduce the book?
_____ **5.** Do my middle paragraphs flow smoothly from one to the next?
_____ **6.** Does my ending connect the theme to real life?

Voice

_____ **7.** Is my voice engaging?
_____ **8.** Do I show understanding of the author's voice?

Word Choice

_____ **9.** Have I used quotations to show the author's word choice?
_____ **10.** Have I used specific terms from the book?

Sentence Fluency

_____ **11.** Do I use simple, compound, and complex sentences effectively?
_____ **12.** Do I vary my sentence beginnings?

Revise

Make a clean copy. When you finish revising your essay, make a clean copy before you begin to edit.

Editing

Now that you have improved the content of your essay, it's time to edit for conventions: punctuation, capitalization, spelling, and grammar.

Keys to Effective Editing

1. Use a dictionary, a thesaurus, and the "Proofreader's Guide" in the back of this book (pages 604–763).

2. Check your use of any comparative and superlative modifiers.

3. Check your writing for punctuation, capitalization, spelling, and grammar errors.

4. If you use a computer, edit on a printed copy and enter your changes on the computer.

5. Use the editing and proofreading marks inside the back cover of this book.

Editing for Conventions

 6 My grammar and punctuation are correct, and the copy is free of spelling errors.

 5 I have one or two errors in grammar, spelling, or punctuation, but they won't distract the reader.

 4 I need to correct a few errors in punctuation, spelling, or grammar, which may distract the reader.

Conventions are the rules you follow for punctuation, capitalization, spelling, and grammar. To edit for conventions, use the rubric above and the information below.

How should I form comparative and superlative adjectives?

Comparative and superlative adjectives are formed using the following rules. (Also see page **728**.)

- For one-syllable adjectives, use *–er* (comparative) or *–est* (superlative).

fast	faster	fastest
high	higher	highest

- For most adjectives of two or more syllables, use *more* or *less* (comparative) or *most* or *least* (superlative).

courageous	more courageous	most courageous
successful	less successful	least successful

- Watch for *irregular* forms, such as the following:

good	better	best
bad	worse	worst

Exercise

Correct the comparative/superlative errors in the following paragraph.

1   In *The Right Stuff,* Tom Wolfe tells the story of the most brave test pilots of
2 the last century. They flew the toughest missions of any Air Force fliers, climbing
3 into the least stablest aircraft. Many of the test pilots suffered serious injuries, and
4 some suffered the most bad fate of all: death. As hard as the lifestyle was for the
5 pilots, it was even more hard for their wives, who waited fearfully to hear the bad
6 news. But the pilots who survived had the "right stuff" to take the controls of an
7 even more risky type of machine: a spacecraft.

Edit

Check comparatives and superlatives. Read your essay and make sure you have correctly formed comparative and superlative adjectives.

3 I need to correct a number of errors that will probably confuse the reader.

2 I need to fix many errors that make my writing hard to read and understand.

1 I need help making corrections.

When should I hyphenate compound adjectives?

Hyphenate compound adjectives that appear before the nouns they modify.

DO hyphenate: Thrilled, wide-eyed spectators watched John Glenn blast off.
DON'T hyphenate: The spectators, thrilled and wide eyed, watched John Glenn blast off.

Exercise

In the following paragraph, indicate where compound adjectives should be hyphenated.

1   During his flight, Glenn saw a swarm of free floating lights around his
2   capsule. He thought they were beautiful, but mission control knew they were
3   friction-generated. Engineers feared a heat shield failure. Upon reentry, these
4   fairy fire sparks could turn into an all encompassing inferno that would burn up
5   the capsule and John Glenn inside it. Mission control told him the news, though
6   there wasn't much he could do about it. John Glenn began his nail biting descent,
7   and the world nervously watched a piloting feat that was awe-inspiring.

Edit for conventions. Read through your essay and watch for compound adjectives. Make sure you have correctly hyphenated them.

Conventions
Hyphens are added, and a superlative form is corrected.

He goes on to beat the Triple Crown winner, War Admiral, in a head-to-head race considered the ~~most great~~ *greatest* race in the sport's history.

Literature

Editing Checking for Conventions

Edit

Check your editing. On a piece of paper, write the numbers 1 to 12. Put a check by the number if you can answer "yes" to that question. If not, continue to edit your essay for that convention.

Editing Checklist

Conventions

PUNCTUATION

_____ 1. Does each sentence have correct end punctuation?

_____ 2. Have I used quotation marks and correctly cited direct quotations?

_____ 3. Have I correctly hyphenated compound adjectives?

_____ 4. Have I used parentheses to set off page numbers?

_____ 5. Do I use apostrophes to show possession *(in Hillenbrand's book)*?

CAPITALIZATION

_____ 6. Do I start all my sentences with capital letters?

_____ 7. Have I capitalized all proper nouns?

SPELLING

_____ 8. Have I spelled all my words correctly?

_____ 9. Have I double-checked the spelling of names and terms from the book?

GRAMMAR

_____ 10. Have I used correct verb tenses throughout?

_____ 11. Have I used the correct comparative and superlative forms?

_____ 12. Have I used the right words *(its, it's)*?

Creating a Title

- Use ideas from the book: **A Game-Legged Pony**
- Refer to the theme: **Victory out of Defeat**
- Be creative: **The Horse That Saved Three Men**

Publishing Sharing Your Essay

After all the work of writing, revising, and editing your essay, you should share it with others. See the suggestions in the boxes below for a variety of ways to present your essay.

Make a final copy. Follow your teacher's instructions or use the guidelines below to format your paper. (If you are using a computer, see pages **91–95**.) Prepare a final copy of your essay and proofread it for errors.

Focusing on Presentation

- Use blue or black ink and write neatly.
- Write your name in the upper left corner of page 1.
- Skip a line and center your title; skip another line and start your essay.
- Indent every paragraph and leave a one-inch margin on all four sides.
- Write your last name and the page number in the upper right-hand corner of every page.

Create a Multimedia Presentation

Convert your report into a speech, scan in photos from the book or from the time period, and gather other visual aids to highlight your work.

Submit to a Newspaper

Check the submission guidelines for your local newspaper, write a cover letter introducing your response essay, and send it in.

Post Your Essay on a Bookseller's Site

Check out bookselling Web sites to determine how to submit your writing. Upload your essay to the site.

Literature

Rubric for a Response to Literature

Use this rubric to guide and assess your writing. Refer to it whenever you want to improve your writing using the six traits.

6 Ideas	**5**	**4**
The ideas show a complete understanding of the reading.	The essay has a clear focus statement and necessary supporting details.	The essay has a clear focus statement. Unnecessary details need to be cut.

Organization		
All the parts work together to create an insightful essay.	The organization pattern fits the topic and purpose. All parts of the essay are well developed.	The organization pattern fits the topic and purpose. A part of the essay needs better development.

Voice		
The voice expresses interest and complete understanding. It engages the reader.	The voice expresses interest in and understanding of the topic.	The voice expresses interest but needs to show more understanding.

Word Choice		
The word choice reflects careful thinking about the reading.	The word choice, including the use of figures of speech, creates a clear message.	The word choice is clear, but more figures of speech would improve the essay.

Sentence Fluency		
The sentences in the essay make the ideas really stand out.	The sentences are skillfully written and keep the reader's interest.	No sentence problems exist. More sentence variety is needed.

Conventions		
Grammar and punctuation are correct, and the copy is free of all errors.	The essay has one or two errors that do not interfere with the reader's understanding.	The essay has a few careless errors in punctuation and grammar.

3	**2**	**1**
The focus statement is too broad. A variety of details are needed.	The focus statement is unclear. More details are needed.	The essay needs a focus statement and details.
The organization fits the essay's purpose. Some parts need more development.	The organization doesn't fit the purpose.	A plan needs to be followed.
The voice needs to be more interesting and express more understanding.	The voice does not show interest in or an understanding of the topic.	The writer needs to understand how to create voice.
The word choice is too general, and more figures of speech are needed.	Little attention is given to word choice.	The writer needs help with word choice.
A few sentence problems need to be corrected.	The essay has many sentence problems.	The writer needs to learn how to construct sentences.
The errors in the essay confuse the reader.	The number of errors make the essay hard to read.	Help is needed to make corrections.

Literature

Evaluating a Response to Literature

Read the following analysis of an autobiography. Then read the student's self-evaluation on the next page. **(There may be errors in the essay below.)**

Playing with Nothing

Anyone who has seen the Marx Brothers has wondered what was going on beneath Harpo's mop of curly red hair and behind his wide staring eyes. In their old movies such as *Duck Soup* and *A Night at the Opera,* Harpo always wears a mischievous smile, but he never speaks. In his autobiography, *Harpo Speaks,* Harpo does speak, telling how he spent his life finding fun in little things.

Adolph "Harpo" Marx grew up poor in New York City. His father was a bad tailor, which meant that the family never had much money—but he was a wonderful cook, which meant they always had excellent food to eat. Harpo's family lived in a Jewish neighborhood, but he attended a Catholic school, where one bully was in the habit of throwing him out the first floor window. One day in second grade, Harpo got thrown out the window and simply walked away, never returning to school again.

As an adolescent, Adolph and his brothers Julius, Leonard, and Milton showed singing talent, and their stage mother Minnie Marx got them into vaudeville. Their act was called the "Four Nightingales." The four boys often didn't have enough money for a room, but Harpo loved the vaudeville lifestyle. "I can't remember ever having a poor night's sleep. . . . I slept on pool tables, dressing-room tables, piano tops, bathhouse benches, in rag baskets and harp cases." During one card game on the road, each of the young men got a nickname that matched his character—Julius became Groucho because of his moods, Leonard became Chico because he chased "chicks," Adolph became Harpo because he'd taught himself to play the harp, and Milton became Gummo due to his chewing habits. The four boy's often ditched the script and broke into ad-libbed comedy.

The words of one critic created the Harpo that the world knows and loves: "Adolph Marx performed beautiful pantomime which was ruined whenever he spoke." From then on, Harpo didn't say a word. This Jewish kid with a second-grade education, a beat-up trench coat, a smashed top-hat, a red wig, and no voice soon became an international sensation. He became friends with Alexander Woollcott, drama critic for *The New Yorker,* and thereby became part of the Algonquin Round Table with authors Dorothy Parker and James Thurber. When asked how he fit in among so many intellectuals, Harpo simply said that he "listened."

All throughout Harpo's life, he found fun in the littlest of things. When he was a child, he had only a single ice skate, and became the best single-skate skater in the world. When he was a young man, he taught himself to play harp and became so good that trained harp players wanted to learn his techniques. He once took his trench coat and a bunch of butter knives to Soviet Russia and did a pantomime act that tore down barriers between east and west.

Harpo Speaks is the story of a playful man creating delight out of vary little. Only the ending is bittersweet. Harpo began to have heart attacks, and his doctor told him he must give up the harp, thinking that playing it was too strenuous. Harpo tried, but eventually drifted back to playing, and suffered another attack. He ended his days torn between wanting to play harp and wanting to live. It was a sad ending for a man who spent his life making joy out of nothing.

Student Self-Assessment

Response Rubric Checklist

Title: "Playing with Nothing"
Writer: Robert Wade

__5__ **Ideas**
  • Do I have a clear thesis statement?
  • Do I use effective details?

__5__ **Organization**
  • Does the beginning name the book and author and give the thesis statement?
  • Does the middle summarize the book and explore the theme?
  • Does the ending effectively revisit the theme?

__5__ **Voice**
  • Does my voice sound knowledgeable?
  • Do my quotations reveal the author's voice?

__4__ **Word Choice**
  • Have I used correct literary terminology?

__5__ **Sentence Fluency**
  • Do my sentences read smoothly?

__4__ **Conventions**
  • Have I avoided usage and agreement errors?

OVERALL COMMENTS:

I think I really captured the main theme of the book.

Most of the essay works well, but the end stops a little short.

My voice is interested and knowledgeable.

I forgot to include page numbers for quotations.

Use the rubric. Rate your essay using the rubric on pages 310–311. Write comments about your scores.

Literature

Reflecting on Your Writing

Reflect on your finished analysis by completing each starter sentence below. These comments will help you monitor your progress as a writer.

My Literature Analysis

1. The strongest part of my analysis is . . .

2. The part that most needs change is . . .

3. The main thing I learned about writing an analysis of a theme is . . .

4. In my next response to literature, I would like to . . .

5. Here is one question I still have about writing an analysis of a theme:

6. Right now I would describe my writing ability as (excellent, good, fair, poor) because . . .

Response to Literature
Analyzing a Poem

Robert Frost once said, "Like a piece of ice on a hot stove, the poem must ride on its own melting." When you analyze a poem, you "melt" it, looking at the parts that make up the whole. By close examination of the elements that make up the poem—theme, structure, and language—you can find more meaning in the poem and develop a deeper appreciation of the author's craft.

In this chapter, you will learn how to analyze a poem: how to break it down into its various elements and see how they fit together. You will read a sample poem and see how a student writer organizes his analysis. Then you will read a second poem and write your own analysis of the poem's content and message.

Writing Guidelines

  Subject: **Poem**
    Form: **Analysis**
  Purpose: **To explore meaning**
  Audience: **Instructor**

"Genuine poetry can communicate before it is understood."

—T. S. Eliot

Sample Poem

Read the poem below and think about its content, theme, organization, and use of poetic techniques. Then read student writer Stefano Giangregorio's analysis on the next two pages. The margin comments point out important elements of that analysis.

I AM THE PEOPLE, THE MOB
By Carl Sandburg

I AM the people—the mob—the crowd—the mass.
Do you know that all the great work of the world is
    done through me?
I am the workingman, the inventor, the maker of the
    world's food and clothes.
I am the audience that witnesses history. The Napoleons
    come from me and the Lincolns. They die. And
    then I send forth more Napoleons and Lincolns.
I am the seed ground. I am a prairie that will stand
    for much plowing. Terrible storms pass over me.
    I forget. The best of me is sucked out and wasted.
    I forget. Everything but Death comes to me and
    makes me work and give up what I have. And I
    forget.
Sometimes I growl, shake myself and spatter a few red
    drops for history to remember. Then—I forget.
When I, the People, learn to remember, when I, the
    People, use the lessons of yesterday and no longer
    forget who robbed me last year, who played me for
    a fool—then there will be no speaker in all the world
    say the name: "The People," with any fleck of a
    sneer in his voice or any far-off smile of derision.
The mob—the crowd—the mass—will arrive then.

Response Essay

As you read the essay on this page and the next, consider how Stefano's ideas compare with your own ideas about "I Am the People, the Mob."

Beginning
The thesis statement (underlined) reveals the theme of the poem.

Middle
The middle supports the thesis statement with specific examples.

Verse quotations of more than one line include slashes to show line breaks.

The writer shows how poetic techniques reveal a poem's theme.

Identifying with the Masses

Carl Sandburg was a poet "of the people," and his working-class background and socialist leanings are reflected in his writing. Sandburg believed that the common people had great potential, but that it was too often wasted. He admired their strength and endurance, but he also grieved over the suffering caused by their ignorance and complacency. The poem "I Am the People, the Mob" illustrates Sandburg's mixed feelings toward the masses.

In organization, the poem opens with positive thoughts about the people, then transitions to negative images, and finally returns to a hopeful conclusion. Sandburg begins with the affirming question, "Do you know that all the great work of the world is / done through me?" (2-3) and supports this idea with specific examples in the next two lines. Then he shifts the mob to a more passive role, as the "audience that witnesses history" (6). Still, he says, it is from this passive soil that heroes (Lincolns) and villains (Napoleons) come forth. This soil is repeatedly plowed, it bears many storms, and it has its best "sucked out and wasted," but each time it forgets the abuse (10-14). Occasionally, like a beast, the mob is briefly roused to anger, to "spatter a few red / drops for history to remember"; then it forgets again (15-16). However, this brief image of uprising allows Sandburg to transition into hope that the people may someday "learn to remember" (17). He says, "The mob—the crowd—the mass—will arrive then," at last attaining its destiny (23).

Besides imagery, Sandburg uses other poetic techniques to make this a powerful poem. He uses repetition and parallelism, repeating the opening words, "I am," five times in all, four times at the beginning of a line. In doing so, he strongly identifies himself with the masses. He also repeats "I forget" four times, twice at the beginning of the line, and once split across two lines, adding even more emphasis to this forgetfulness. However, during the repetition of "I forget," Sandburg also plants the word "remember" (16), then expands it to "learn to remember" one line later (17), bringing the poem into his hope for the future. That this message of hope and challenge is intended for the common people themselves is shown in Sandburg's choice of form—free verse rather than a formal structure—and by his commonplace language.

Clearly, Sandburg believes that the people have a tremendous potential, but that they fall short due to forgetfulness and lack of motivation. Clearly he wishes for a better future in which the people take responsibility for their own welfare instead of blindly following heroes and villains. By identifying with the masses and speaking frankly to them in this poem, Sandburg hopes to inspire the people to the greatness they are capable of achieving.

Ending
The ending restates the thesis and leaves the reader with something to think about.

 Respond to the reading. On your own paper, reflect on the ideas, organization, and voice of the analysis above.

Ideas (1) How do the details Stefano includes compare to the details you noticed in the poem?

Organization (2) Why do you think Stefano pays most attention to the organization of the poem and less on poetic techniques?

Voice (3) What do you believe Stefano's feelings are about the poem? Support your opinion with examples from the analysis.

Prewriting Selecting a Topic

If your instructor does not assign a poem for you to analyze, you need to find one yourself or analyze the brief poem provided here.

Fire and Ice
By Robert Frost

Some say the world will end in fire,
Some say in ice.
From what I've tasted of desire
I hold with those who favor fire.
But if it had to perish twice,
I think I know enough of hate
To say that for destruction ice
Is also great
And would suffice.

Prewrite

Select a poem. Search your library and your literature book, looking for poems that interest you. Select one to analyze—or analyze the poem on this page.

Considering the Elements

The various elements of a poem can give you a clue to its purpose and meaning. Ask yourself the following questions and note the answers.

- Does the poem have a specific shape? What meaning does this organization suggest?
- What images does the poem contain? What is the effect of these images on the reader?
- What poetic techniques (pages **368–369**) does the poet use? How do they affect the reader?
- What is the tone of the poem? Serious? Humorous? Sad? Angry?
- Who is the probable audience for this poem? Why?
- What is the writer's purpose for writing this poem?

Prewrite

Consider the elements. Use the questions above to think deeply about your poem. Write down an answer to each question and keep the answers on hand as you write your analysis.

Writing Your Thesis Statement

Once you have thought deeply about the elements and purpose of the poem, it's time to write a thesis statement. An effective thesis statement names the poem and indicates a strong feeling about it. Here is the pattern Stefano used to write his thesis statement.

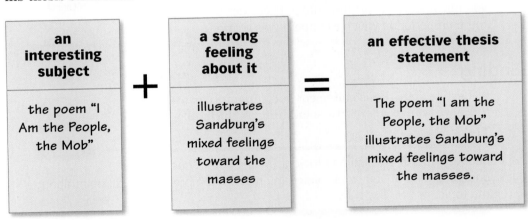

an interesting subject		a strong feeling about it		an effective thesis statement
the poem "I Am the People, the Mob"	**+**	illustrates Sandburg's mixed feelings toward the masses	**=**	The poem "I am the People, the Mob" illustrates Sandburg's mixed feelings toward the masses.

Prewrite

Develop a thesis statement. Follow the example above as you create a thesis statement for your analysis. Try two or three versions until you feel satisfied.

Literature

Writing Getting Your Ideas Down

Your first draft is your chance to get all your ideas on paper. Start by reading through your prewriting and getting your main ideas firmly in your mind. Then start writing. Don't be concerned with spelling or mechanics yet. (You can fix problems when you revise.) If new ideas come to you as you write, go ahead and add them. Below is a brief guide to writing your first draft.

Beginning

- Write your introductory paragraph.
- Include your thesis statement.

Tip

Include the name of the poem and the author's name in your opening paragraph.

> **Beginning**
> Middle
> Ending

Middle

- Use a separate paragraph for each of your main points.
- Support the topic sentence of each paragraph with details from the poem.
- Include quoted words and phrases and specific examples from the poem to support your ideas.

Tip

If the information helps support your thesis, include anything you might know about the author, his or her other works, or the time period in which the poem was written.

> Beginning
> **Middle**
> Ending

Ending

- Restate your thesis statement and sum up your main points.
- Leave your reader with something to think about.

Tip

Because your reader comes to your ending with a deeper understanding of your topic, you can end with a more thoughtful point about the topic.

> Beginning
> Middle
> **Ending**

Write

Develop your first draft. Use your prewriting and the guidelines above as you create the first draft of your analysis.

Revising Improving Your Writing

After you have written a first draft, take some time away from your analysis to get some perspective. Then revise your work for the first five traits.

Revise

Revise your analysis. Use the checklist below to guide your revision. Number a paper from 1 to 12, and when you can answer any of the following questions "yes," check off the number. Keep revising until you can check off all the numbers.

Revising Checklist

Ideas

_____ **1.** Have I clearly stated the theme or purpose of the poem?

_____ **2.** Have I included the main points that support the theme?

_____ **3.** Do my details support those main points?

Organization

_____ **4.** Does my beginning grab the reader's attention and communicate the poem's theme or purpose?

_____ **5.** Does each main point in the middle have its own paragraph with a focused topic sentence?

_____ **6.** Does my ending include a personal insight?

Voice

_____ **7.** Is my thinking reasonable and understandable?

_____ **8.** Do I sound authoritative and interested?

Word Choice

_____ **9.** Do I use words that clearly show my understanding?

_____ **10.** Do I avoid any "loaded" words that make me sound biased in my interpretation?

Sentence Fluency

_____ **11.** Do my sentences move naturally from one thought to the next?

_____ **12.** Do I use logical transitions?

Editing Checking for Conventions

After you have made major improvements to your work by revising, you need to edit your work to make sure the punctuation, capitalization, spelling, and grammar are correct.

Edit

Edit for conventions. Use the following conventions checklist to guide your editing. Write the numbers 1 to 5 on a piece of paper. When you can answer a given question "yes," place a check mark beside the number. Keep editing until you can answer all the questions "yes."

Editing Checklist

Conventions

_____ **1.** Have I used the correct punctuation throughout?

_____ **2.** Have I spelled everything correctly and checked any words I'm not sure of?

_____ **3.** Do my subjects and verbs agree in number?

_____ **4.** Have I placed quotation marks around exact words I quoted from the poem?

_____ **5.** Have I included line numbers in parentheses for these quotations?

Publishing Sharing Your Analysis

An analysis of this kind is a great way to get other people interested in a poem you have enjoyed or in a poet you admire. So let your written analysis have a life beyond the classroom. This sort of writing is perfect for a Web log or Internet message board entry. If you don't have a blog or Web space of your own, you may find sites devoted to the poet, maintained by fans or literary societies. You can also share print copies of your own essay with friends and family members. You may be surprised at the conversation it spawns!

Publish

Publish your analysis. Choose a way to share your work—with family and friends, with your school or community, or with the world—and publish your analysis.

Writing for Assessment
Responding to Prompts About Literature

Your response to a literature prompt on an assessment test will show how well you understand the literature. For responses to fiction, you should focus on *plot, character, theme, setting,* and *style.* For responses to nonfiction, you should focus on the writer's ideas and how he or she conveys them. Responding to such prompts reveals how well you've analyzed the literature, as well as the prompt.

This chapter will help you respond effectively to literature prompts. You will use the writing process in practice test situations to respond to fiction and to nonfiction. Your goal is to produce a focused, clear response that discloses your own insights into the reading.

Writing Guidelines

Subject: **Literature prompt**
Form: **Response essay**
Purpose: **To demonstrate competence**
Audience: **Instructor**

"In a real sense, people who have read good literature have lived more than people who cannot or will not read."

—S. I. Hayakawa

"In the highest civilization, the book is still the highest delight. He who has once known its satisfactions is provided with a resource against calamity."

—Ralph Waldo Emerson

Prewriting Analyzing a Literature Prompt

A prompt about literature asks you to respond to specific characteristics of a story, a poem, a novel, or a nonfiction selection. As you read a prompt, look for key words that tell you exactly what the prompt requires. In the sample prompt below, key words and phrases are underlined. The word *explain* gives the main direction or focus for the response.

Sample Prompt

In Elie Wiesel's memoir Night, *a teenage boy deals with his guilt at having survived the Holocaust. Write an essay in which you explain how his despair leads him first to question his faith and then to make sure that the world never forgets this evil. How do his personal characteristics affect him and the way he resolves his crisis? Support your thesis with evidence from the story.*

Try It!

Copy the following sample prompts on a sheet of paper. Underline key words and phrases in each prompt and make notes about the kinds of supporting information that you would need for a response.

1. Joseph Ratzinger, the subject of Paul Elie's article "Behind the Scenes at the Vatican," became the leader of the Catholic church after the death of Pope John Paul II. In an essay, explain what characteristics contributed to his rise. Include specific examples to support your ideas.

2. "In Late Spring," by Ted Kooser, is a poem that opens with an image of a military jet but evolves into a description of a typical spring day. In an essay, discuss how the author ties the two ideas together and why he might have done so. What does his personification of the season say about his feelings for it?

Planning Your Response

Once you analyze and understand a prompt, you are ready to plan your response. If a reading selection is provided, read it with the prompt in mind, picking out the information you need for your response. Then form your topic sentence and organize the details.

Sample Prompt and Selection

In the following excerpt from Lafcadio Hearn's "Fuji-No-Yama," the author describes Mt. Fuji. In a paragraph, discuss the comparison created by the author. What details create the comparison?

From "Fuji-No-Yama" by Lafacadio Hearn

You can <u>seldom distinguish</u> the snowless base, which remains <u>the same color</u> as the sky: you <u>perceive</u> only the white cone <u>seeming to hang in heaven</u>. . . . Even lighter than a fan <u>the vision appears</u>—rather <u>the ghost or dream</u> of a fan—yet the <u>material reality a hundred miles away</u> is grandiose among the mountains of the globe.

> The underlined words refer to the mountain's ghost-like qualities.

Writing a Topic Sentence

After reading the prompt and selection, one student wrote this topic sentence.

Hearn's description of Mt. Fuji (specific topic) **compares it to an apparition** (particular focus related to the prompt).

Creating a Graphic Organizer

The student also used a graphic organizer to gather details.

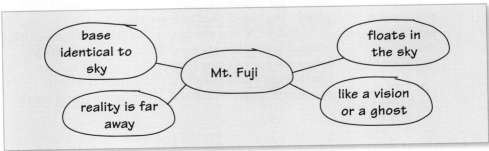

Writing Responding to a Fiction Prompt

The following prompt and fiction selection show how a student underlined key words and phrases and added some notes on a copy of the selection to address the focus of the prompt.

Sample Prompt and Selection

Many science fiction writers have described future scenarios in their stories. In the following excerpt from The Time Machine, *a time traveler describes a future civilization and his thoughts about it. In an essay, explain how the narrator foreshadows disturbing events to come despite the seemingly ideal conditions described in this excerpt. What feeling does the author convey about the culture he encounters?*

From *The Time Machine* by H. G. Wells

At first the narrator describes the future world using words such as "ideal," "triumphs," and "paradise."

The air was free from gnats, the earth from weeds or fungi; everywhere were fruits and sweet and delightful flowers; brilliant butterflies flew hither and thither. The ideal of preventive medicine was attained. Diseases had been stamped out. I saw no evidence of any contagious diseases during all my stay. And I shall have to tell you later that even the processes of putrefaction and decay had been profoundly affected by these changes.

Social triumphs, too, had been effected. I saw mankind housed in splendid shelters, gloriously clothed, and as yet I had found them engaged in no toil. There were no signs of struggle, neither social nor economical struggle. The shop, the advertisement, traffic, all that commerce which constitutes the body of our world, was gone. It was natural on that golden evening that I should jump at the idea of a social paradise. The difficulty of increasing population had been met, I guessed, and population had ceased to increase.

The word "but" signals the narrator's change in focus.

But with this change in condition comes inevitably adaptations to the change. What, unless biological science is a mass of errors, is the cause of human intelligence and vigour? Hardship and freedom: conditions under which the active, strong, and subtle survive and the weaker go to the wall; conditions that put a premium upon the loyal alliance of capable men, upon self-restraint, patience, and decision. And the institution of the family, and the emotions that arise therein, the fierce jealousy, the tenderness for offspring, parental self-devotion, all found their justification and support in the imminent dangers of the young. *Now, where are these imminent dangers?*

Writing a Thesis Statement

After reading the excerpt and making notes, the student wrote the following thesis statement for his response essay.

The narrator's reservations about the future utopian civilization (specific topic) **seem to foreshadow events that will later reveal this civilization's true nature** (particular focus related to the prompt).

Creating a Graphic Organizer

The student also created a T-graph, listing the good aspects of the utopian society and the author's fears for the future.

Good Aspects	Fears for the Future
no bugs or weeds	adaptations not best for species
much natural beauty	hardship needed for intelligence
no social struggle	no "vigour"
no economic struggle	freedom connected to risk
fine clothes and shelter	danger needed for family strength
no overpopulation	emotions not natural
no disease	

Writing Student Response

In this student response to the excerpt from *The Time Machine,* note how the writer uses details from the story to support the thesis statement.

Beginning
The first paragraph leads up to the thesis statement (underlined).

Middle
One paragraph focuses on the "perfect" society.

The next paragraph focuses on the narrator's reservations about the society.

Storm Clouds in Paradise

The excerpt from The Time Machine by H. G. Wells begins with a description of a utopian civilization that the narrator, a time traveler, has encountered. Following his glowing review, however, he expresses misgivings about it. The narrator's reservations about the future utopian civilization seem to foreshadow events that will later reveal this civilization's true nature.

The future world the narrator travels to is, at first glance, a paradise. There are no nasty bugs, only butterflies. There are no weeds, only "sweet and delightful flowers." Disease has been wiped out, and overpopulation is no longer a concern. Despite a lack of commerce or, indeed, any work being done by the inhabitants, they are well clothed and live in "splendid shelters." The narrator observes no apparent competition or strife between people. What could possibly be wrong with such a picture?

The first clue that the narrator is, perhaps, uncomfortable with what he sees is the word but beginning the third paragraph: "But with this change in condition comes inevitably adaptations to the change." It's as if he is warning against feeling too smug about achieving the ideal he previously described. He continues to express his reservations, discussing the lack of "hardship and freedom—

conditions under which the active, strong, and subtle survive." He is implying, of course, that the paradise fosters passive, weak, and unperceptive beings. His sense that there is no danger to the young leads him to believe that the ability to feel emotions—"the fierce jealousy, the tenderness for offspring, parental self-devotion"—has died, as has the concept of family.

Ending
The closing reiterates the thesis.

Although Wells's time traveler does not come right out and say that there is trouble within the society he's witnessed, he certainly conveys a feeling of distrust. His description of the paradise followed by his qualms about it give the reader a sense of foreboding. The last paragraph of the excerpt suggests that the narrator's suspicions will play a role later in the novel.

 Respond to the reading. Answer the following questions about the student response.

Ideas (1) What is the focus of the student writer's thesis statement? (2) Does the thesis statement accurately reflect the prompt? Explain.

Organization (3) How does the writer organize the middle part of the response?

Voice & Word Choice (4) Which words or phrases quoted from the story are the most effective? Name two and explain your choices.

Practice Fiction Prompt

Whenever you respond to a writing prompt, especially in a timed situation, begin by studying the prompt. Find the key word that indicates what you are to do in the response: *compare, explain, describe,* and so on.

After you understand the prompt and the specific points you need to address in your response, read the selection. Of course, it is important to quote examples and specific details from the selection to support your thesis. However, it is equally important to share your own insights about the selection.

Practice Prompt and Selection

The 1906 novel The Jungle *by Upton Sinclair portrays capitalism as thinly disguised exploitation and oppression. In this excerpt, the author explains how the working conditions of Ona, a Lithuanian immigrant who works in a meatpacking plant, affect her. Discuss how Sinclair's attitude about unregulated "frontier" capitalism becomes clear, especially as the passage ends. What comparison does he make?*

From *The Jungle* by Upton Sinclair

For a long time Ona had seen that Miss Henderson, the forelady in her department, did not like her. At first she thought it was the old-time mistake she had made in asking for a holiday to get married. Then she concluded it must be because she did not give the forelady a present occasionally—she was the kind that took presents from the girls, Ona learned, and made all sorts of discriminations in favor of those who gave them. In the end, however, Ona discovered that it was even worse than that. Miss Henderson was a newcomer, and it was some time before rumor made her out; but finally it transpired that she was a kept woman, the former mistress of the superintendent of a department in the same building. . . . Worse than this, the woman lived in a bawdy house downtown, with a coarse, red-faced Irishman named Connor, who was the boss of the loading-gang outside, and would make free with the girls as they went to and from their work. In the slack seasons some of them would go with Miss Henderson to this house downtown—in fact, it would not be too much to say that she managed her department at Brown's in conjunction with it. Sometimes women from the house would be given places alongside of decent girls, and after other decent girls had been turned off to make room for them. When you worked in this woman's department the house downtown was never out of your thoughts all day—there were always whiffs of it to be caught, like the odor of the Packingtown rendering plants at night, when the wind shifted suddenly. There would be stories about it going the rounds; the girls opposite you would be telling them and winking at you. In such a place Ona would not have stayed a day, but for starvation; and, as it was, she was never sure that she could stay the next day. She understood now that the real reason that Miss Henderson hated her was that she was a decent married girl; and she knew that the talebearers and the toadies hated her for the same reason, and were doing their best to make her life miserable.

But there was no place a girl could go in Packingtown, if she was particular about things of this sort; there was no place in it where a prostitute could not get along better than a decent girl. Here was a population, low-class and mostly foreign, hanging always on the verge of starvation, and dependent for its opportunities of life upon the whim of men every bit as brutal and unscrupulous as the old-time slave drivers; under such circumstances immorality was exactly as inevitable, and as prevalent, as it was under the system of chattel slavery. Things that were quite unspeakable went on there in the packing houses all the time, and were taken for granted by everybody; only they did not show, as in the old slavery times, because there was no difference in color between master and slave.

 Respond to a fiction prompt. Read the practice prompt again to make sure that you understand its focus. Then carefully reread the selection by Upton Sinclair. Next, form a thesis statement, quickly arrange your main supporting details in a graphic organizer, and write your essay. Use the revising and editing tips on page 338 to check your response before turning it in.

Literature

Writing Responding to a Nonfiction Prompt

The following prompt and nonfiction selection show how a student underlined key words and phrases related to the prompt's focus and jotted notes in the margin.

Prompt and Selection

This excerpt is from an article originally published in Harper's New Monthly Magazine, *June 1864. In a time when it was highly unusual for women to be published writers, a young Louisa Barker decided she would be one. In an essay, compare your feelings about your future with those of Ms. Barker as she began her last year of school. Despite the passing of more than 140 years, do you see any similarities?*

From "Why I Wrote It" by Louisa W. Barker

Words like "hope," "promise," and "inspiration" signal her excitement.

I shall never forget the feeling of refreshing relief with which I received the announcement that I was to spend a year in a Northern school. There was hope and promise in it. I believed that some opening would present itself by which I could achieve my independence. At the South a woman can not teach or engage in any work without losing caste; but at the North work is acknowledged. There was inspiration in the thought. A few weeks later I was steaming up the turbid Mississippi.

She's also troubled by questions about her future.

In a few days I had entered, in a Northern city, my last school year. My school duties were not heavy, leaving me a fair margin of unappropriated time. This was spent in discussing the ever-present question: What can I do? How can I earn a living? How can I achieve an independence of my uncle?

She gives reasons why she leans away from one option . . .

Two avenues invited me. Of course I thought of teaching, every educated woman seeking employment thinks of it. But this could not be entered upon for a year, and, in the mean time, my dependence must continue. I shrank, too, from applying for a teacher's situation, as such a step would have compelled an explanation, and started troublesome questions and surmises. I was aware that already my schoolmates wondered at the absence of style in my wardrobe—at my old-fashioned dresses; I knew they suspected me of a mean parsimony that I did not return some of their numerous kindnesses forced upon me in the way of suppers, fruits, rides, etc. Ah! those were days of heart-burnings, of impatient longings. It was hard when I was called on for a contribution for some picnic or festival, or for a present to a teacher, to say that I could give nothing. They didn't know that every penny I spent had to be taken from the hand of a man whom I sometimes feared that I hated.

... and leans toward the other.

The other road to independence of which I thought the oftener was the higher and more ambitious way which authors tread. I thought I should like my old friends and acquaintances, my uncle, and Charles to hear of me as famous. It would be pleasant to know that they were reading my articles, thinking and talking about me. I wrote some things which delighted me during the excitement and glow of writing and disgusted me two days after.

Writing a Thesis Statement

After reading the excerpt, the student wrote the following thesis statement.

> A young person's feelings about a potential **career** (specific topic) **can be clouded with doubt—today or 140 years ago** (focus related to the prompt).

Creating a Graphic Organizer

The student used a Venn diagram to plan her response.

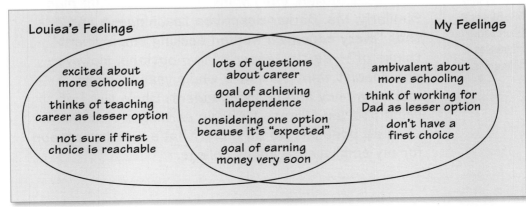

Louisa's Feelings — excited about more schooling; thinks of teaching career as lesser option; not sure if first choice is reachable

(shared) — lots of questions about career; goal of achieving independence; considering one option because it's "expected"; goal of earning money very soon

My Feelings — ambivalent about more schooling; think of working for Dad as lesser option; don't have a first choice

Literature

Student Response

Having completed her planning, the student wrote the following essay in response to the prompt and excerpt from Louisa Barker's article.

Gaining Independence

Beginning
The first paragraph identifies the excerpt's author and introduces the thesis statement (underlined).

In an article written as the Civil War raged, Louisa W. Barker describes her excitement at returning to school and her confusion about a career. In 2006, I am finishing up my high school education and wondering what I should do afterward. A young person's feelings about a potential career can be clouded with doubt—today or 140 years ago.

Ms. Barker is clearly excited about returning to school in the North, where a woman's "work is acknowledged." She feels she can begin a career and gain her independence. While I also want to begin a career and gain my independence, I have mixed feelings about continuing my education. For various reasons—financial, time, my less-than-fantastic grades—I'm just not sure I want to go to college, even though I think it might help me get a good job.

Middle
The middle paragraphs compare the student's feelings with Ms. Barker's. Each paragraph addresses a different issue.

Some people in my family want me to work at my dad's company right after graduation, so I do have that option, but I think of it as a backup plan. Similarly, Ms. Barker describes teaching—a career that "every educated woman seeking employment thinks of"—as the lesser of two options. However, she doesn't want to wait a whole year to begin making money and be independent. She's tired of being poor and wants to begin earning an income as soon as possible. So do I, and that's another reason for my ambivalence about college.

Perhaps if I knew with certainty what I wanted to do with my life, I wouldn't be confused. Louisa knows what she wants to do. She sees a career as a writer as a "higher and more ambitious way" to make a living. She dreams about her family and acquaintances reading her work and talking about her. Although she's not really sure of her ability (she speaks of pieces that "disgusted me two days after" writing them), she seems determined to try. I, too, am unsure of my abilities, but it only leaves me feeling bewildered.

It's overwhelming to think about all the career choices I have, especially compared to the very few that Louisa Barker had. Yet both of us confess to ambiguity about our career choices. The time in which we live doesn't seem to matter; making decisions about the future is tough.

Ending
The closing repeats the assertion made in the thesis statement.

Jobs Careers

Respond to the reading. Answer the following questions about the student response.

Ideas (1) What is the thesis of the student response? (2) What details does the student use to support the thesis? Name two or three.

Organization (3) How does the writer organize her response—point by point or by completely discussing one person and then the other?

Voice & Word Choice (4) Which words and phrases indicate the student's attitude toward the topic? Name two.

Literature

Practice Nonfiction Prompt

Whether you are reading and responding to fiction or nonfiction, remember that the author of the selection carefully chose the words to describe a person, establish a setting, share information, arouse an emotion, and so on. You also need to carefully choose your words when you respond to a literature prompt.

Practice Prompt and Selection

The excerpt that follows is from the autobiography of Samuel Langhorne Clemens, whose pen name was Mark Twain. Words, phrases, and sentences throughout the excerpt hint at Twain's longing for "romance" on the river. In an essay, explain what you think Twain means by this "romance" and why he would desire it. Support your ideas with examples.

From *Life on the Mississippi* by Mark Twain

In the head of every crossing, and in the foot of every crossing, the government has set up a clear-burning lamp. You are never entirely in the dark, now; there is always a beacon in sight, either before you, or behind you, or abreast. One might almost say that lamps have been squandered there. Dozens of crossings are lighted which were not shoal when they were created, and have never been shoal since; crossings so plain, too, and also so straight, that a steamboat can take herself through them without any help, after she has been through once. Lamps in such places are of course not wasted; it is much more convenient and comfortable for a pilot to hold on them than on a spread of formless blackness that won't stay still; and money is saved to the boat, at the same time, for she can of course make more miles with her rudder amidships than she can with it squared across her stern and holding her back.

But this thing has knocked the romance out of piloting, to a large extent. It, and some other things together, have knocked all the romance out of it. For instance, the peril from snags is not now what it once was. The government's snag-boats go patrolling up and down, in these matter-of-fact days, pulling the river's teeth; they have rooted out all the old clusters which made many localities so formidable; and they allow no new ones to collect. Formerly, if your boat got away from you, on a black night, and broke for the woods, it was an anxious time with you; so was it also, when you were groping your way through solidified darkness in a narrow chute; but all that is changed now—you flash out your electric light, transform night into day in the twinkling of an eye, and your perils and anxieties are at an end. Horace Bixby and George Ritchie have charted the crossings and laid out the courses by compass; they have invented a lamp to go with the chart, and have patented the whole. With these helps, one may run in the fog now, with considerable security, and with a confidence unknown in the old days.

With these abundant beacons, the banishment of snags, plenty of daylight in a box and ready to be turned on whenever needed, and a chart and compass to fight the fog with, piloting, at a good stage of water, is now nearly as safe and simple as driving stage, and is hardly more than three times as romantic.

Respond to a nonfiction prompt. Read the practice prompt on the previous page again to be sure that you understand its focus. Then reread the selection. Next, form a thesis statement, briefly list your main ideas in a graphic organizer, and write your response essay. Before turning your response in, check it using the revising and editing tips on the next page.

Literature

Revising Improving Your Response

Always review your response at the end of a writing test. Make any changes and corrections as neatly as possible. Use the following questions to help you revise your response.

- **Ideas** Does my thesis statement address the focus of the prompt? Do the details support the thesis?

- **Organization** Have I included a beginning, a middle, and an ending? Does each paragraph have a focus? Do I conclude with an insight about the literature selection?

- **Voice** Do I sound confident and clear?

- **Word Choice** Do the words that I use reflect my understanding of the literature selection? Have I avoided any unnecessary repetition?

- **Sentence Fluency** Are all of my sentences complete? Do my sentences flow smoothly from one to the next?

Revise

Improve your work. Reread your practice response, asking yourself the questions above. Make any changes neatly.

Editing Checking Your Response

In your final read through, check your punctuation, capitalization, spelling, and grammar.

Editing Checklist

Conventions

_____ **1.** Have I used end punctuation for every sentence?

_____ **2.** Have I capitalized all proper nouns and first words of sentences?

_____ **3.** Have I checked my spelling?

_____ **4.** Have I made sure my subjects and verbs agree?

_____ **5.** Have I put quotation marks around the exact words that I quoted from the selection?

Edit

Check your response. Read over your work, looking for errors in punctuation, capitalization, spelling, and grammar. Make corrections neatly.

Responding to Literature on Tests

Use the following tips as a guide whenever you respond to a prompt about literature. These tips will help you respond to both fiction and nonfiction selections.

Before you write . . .

- **Be clear about the time limit.**
  Plan enough time for prewriting, writing, and revising.
- **Understand the prompt.**
  Be sure that you know what the prompt requires. Pay special attention to the key word that tells you what you need to do.
- **Read the selection with the focus of the prompt in mind.**
  Take notes that will help you form your thesis. If you're working on a copy of the selection, underline important details.
- **Form your thesis statement.**
  The thesis statement should identify the specific topic plus the focus of the prompt.
- **Make a graphic organizer.**
  Jot down main points and possible quotations for your essay.

As you write . . .

- **Maintain the focus of your essay.**
  Keep your thesis in mind as you write.
- **Be selective.** Use examples from your graphic organizer and the selection to support your thesis.
- **End in a meaningful way.**
  Start by revisiting the thesis. Then try to share a final insight about the topic with the reader.

After you've written a first draft . . .

- **Check for completeness and correctness.**
  Use questions like those on page 338 to revise your essay. Then check for errors in punctuation, capitalization, spelling, and grammar.

 Try It!

Plan and write a response. Read a prompt your teacher supplies. Analyze it, read the selection, form a thesis statement, list ideas in a graphic organizer, and write your essay. Then revise and edit your response. Try to complete your work within the time your teacher gives you.

Literature

Creative Writing

Writing Stories

It seems that everybody wants something. That "thing" might be as huge as to be accepted into a prestigious college or as small as wanting to buy a certain pair of shoes. What is true in life is also true in stories. A story becomes interesting only when the main character wants something that is difficult to obtain. That's called conflict, and it's what makes fiction—and life—interesting.

Someone once described a story as getting your main character up in a tree, throwing rocks at him, and then getting him down again. The tree is your conflict; the rocks are complications or rising action. Resolving the conflict gets the character out of the tree. Developing a story means fitting your ideas into this pattern in your own way so the story is yours alone.

In this chapter you will write a story about someone facing a life challenge. You will learn how to build a story using rising action and show how that rising action leads to a change in the main character.

Writing Guidelines

Subject: A life challenge
Form: Short story
Purpose: To engage and entertain
Audience: Classmates

"There have been great societies that did not use the wheel, but there have been no societies that did not tell stories."

—Ursula K. LeGuin

The Shape of Stories

As a child, you probably wrote stories that simply gave one event after another: "And then . . . and then . . . and then . . . " Now you should write stories in which events build upon each other, using the classic plot line.

Plot Line

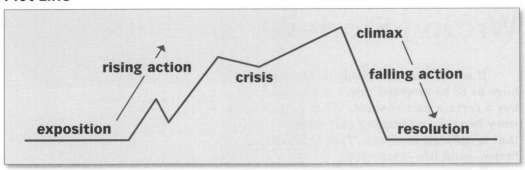

The **exposition** introduces the main character(s), the setting, and the conflict. It gives background information the reader needs to understand the story.

The **rising action** is a series of events, called *complications,* that build suspense. Each event develops the story line. During the rising action, the stakes increase as the character faces complications that block his or her way.

The **crisis** is a moment of realization for the main character, when he or she comes to some decision or does something that will determine the outcome of the story. The crisis is not the climax but will lead to it.

The **climax** is the moment of truth, or the emotional high point of the story, when the main character either triumphs or fails. The climax should also somehow cause a change, either obvious or subtle, in the main character.

The **falling action** shows how the main character adjusts to the change.

The **resolution,** also called the *denouement,* is the ending. The falling action and the resolution should be short, bringing the story to a satisfying close.

Try It!

Think about a short story or novel you have recently read and answer the following questions.

1. Who was the main character, and what was the setting? (exposition)

2. What challenges did the main character face? (rising action)

3. When did the main character make a difficult decision? (crisis)

4. What was the high point of the story? (climax)

5. What happened afterward? (falling action and resolution)

Sample Story

In her story, Chandra examined a conflict between a young woman and her father. Note how the use of a flashback helps establish the main character's motivation for her feelings. (See page **347**.)

The exposition introduces the main character, sets the scene, and provides the conflict.

The rising action elevates the conflict.

A flashback helps the reader understand the conflict.

Small Steps

Hannah sat sullenly, watching the unfamiliar desert landscape glide by the truck window. Her father drove silently, his fingers beating a little pattern on the wheel to the rhythm of the music from the CD player. *His* music. *His* truck. *His* home. It all used to be *us* and *we*. Now it was only *him*.

At the airport, he had tossed her suitcase and backpack into the back of the truck, as carelessly as he had tossed her from his life nearly a year ago. That was when he had left her and her mother to "find himself" in this sagebrush and saguaro wasteland. And now he expected her to forget all the hurt!

"Almost there." He smiled at her.

"Whoopee," Hannah growled, and he looked at her sadly.

"Look, Pooh, I—"

"Don't call me that," Hanna snapped at the pet name her father had given her as a child. He had no right anymore. "This was Mom's idea, not mine. She seems to think I need to spend time with my—dad!" The word was bitter, and she almost spat it out.

"I'm sorry. Hannah, I know I can never make up the lost time, but you've got to believe how sorry I am. I love you, Honey, and I missed you. Couldn't you understand, and maybe forgive me?"

Understand and forgive. Those had been her mother's words when Hannah had asked why her father left.

"He's not running away from us, Hannah," Mom had said sadly. "He's running toward something, and we just can't go with him. I understand, and I can forgive him."

But Hannah didn't understand, and she didn't forgive. As he looked at her hopefully, she felt herself boiling inside.

"You were only thinking of yourself!" Hannah exploded. "I needed you, and you weren't there! Where were you when my cat got run over? Or when I sprained my ankle? Or when I didn't make the volleyball team? I needed you then!"

"I know," her father said softly, miserably. "I wasn't there. But I want to be there for you now."

His voice, which had always been sharp and hurried, was softer somehow, sad and pleading, not at all as she remembered it. Hannah eyed him coldly. "You're too late. I don't need you anymore."

He flinched, and she thought, "Good." Now you know how it feels to be rejected. She turned back to the window, and they finished the ride in silence.

The next morning Hannah followed her nose out of her room toward the smell of fresh coffee. She found her father at the stove, where bacon and fried eggs sizzled in a cast-iron skillet.

"Since when do you cook?" Hannah asked, surprised.

"Since I had to," her father replied simply, setting a glass of orange juice in front of her. The only times she had seen him in the kitchen at home was late at night when he got home from work and sat down to eat some warmed-over dinner.

"Listen, I thought maybe we'd go hiking today," he said. "But I've got to go into the office for a little while first. Want to come?"

The office. She knew he couldn't have changed. It had always been work first, family second. While Hannah's mom rushed to get her fed and off to school, Hannah's dad rushed out the door in suit and tie, affidavits clutched under his arm. "All right, I guess." Hannah grabbed a book out of her backpack, figuring that once he got to work it would be a long time before they got out again.

"Let's go," he called from the door.

"Like that?" she said, surprised that he was still in his T-shirt and jeans.

"They've seen me in worse," he laughed.

"Aren't you still a lawyer?"

"Yeah, but not the same kind of lawyer as I was. People around here don't care if I wear a suit and tie, as long as I help them. And that's what I try to do."

His tiny office was squeezed between a coffee shop and a souvenir shop that boasted "genuine hand-polished native

Margin notes: Hannah notices a difference in her father. | Past information is given to help the reader understand Hannah's feelings. | Another complication occurs as Hannah notices another difference in her father.

stones." He checked the messages on his desk, then sat down to make some calls. Hannah settled down in the small reception area near the desk of a pleasant-looking woman who was going through some papers with a highlighter. She tried to read her book, but couldn't help overhearing some of his conversation.

"Can we meet next week to settle this, Bob? My daughter's visiting—yeah, from St. Louis. Sixteen. Rough, but that's why—Thanks. Sure, Monday's fine. Thanks." He punched in another call. "Mrs. Whitefern? John Kirk. They've accepted our offer. You'll be getting a check later this week. No, thank YOU for the cactus jelly." Hannah was curious.

"Was that payment? The cactus jelly?"

The woman at the desk popped her head up and smiled. "Oh, partially. Most of our clients are pretty poor. They pay what they can, and sometimes they like to throw in a little extra to make up the difference. Your dad's always so gracious about it!" Shaking her head, she chuckled and went back to work.

Hannah had never seen her father so relaxed and happy. Before he left, he had usually been surly or silent. He hung up the phone and smiled at her.

"All done?" she asked, surprised.

"All done and ready to go hiking." He thought a moment. "We do have some big hills to climb, don't we?"

"Yes, we do," she considered this idea. "And they're pretty steep. It'll probably take a long time to reach the top."

Hannah understood exactly how high those hills were—but she also knew that every climb begins with small steps. She saw the hopeful look on his face.

"I'm willing to try," she said, and added, "Dad." She tasted the word on her tongue and found it was not bitter at all.

> A secondary character is used to present new information.

> The **climax** occurs when Hannah decides to try to get along with her father.

> The **resolution** lets us know that Hannah has changed.

Respond to the reading Answer the following questions.

Ideas (1) Who is the main character? (2) What is the conflict?

Organization (3) What method of organization did the writer use?

Voice & Word Choice (4) In whose point of view is the story written? (5) What specific words and terms does the writer use to establish the setting?

Prewriting Planning Your Writing

Stories focus on people (characters) who face a problem (conflict) in a particular place and time (setting). The story shows what the people do (action) and say (dialogue) to resolve the conflict. Plan each of these elements before you begin writing.

Creating Characters

Your main character is called the **protagonist**. He or she should be likable—but not perfect, or there would be nothing to learn or change, and no real story.

Sometimes a minor character can add insight to the story. Chandra used the secretary to tell Hannah something that helped her understand her father better.

Creating Conflict

The protagonist must want something that is blocked by an obstacle—the antagonist. This obstacle creates the **conflict** that the character must overcome.

The antagonist may be a physical barrier, an idea, or another person. Hannah's antagonist was her own hurt and anger, which kept her from forgiving her father.

Establishing a Setting

Where and when does the struggle between the protagonist and antagonist happen? The setting might be relatively unimportant, or it might actually *be* the antagonist, as in a story about someone trying to find a way out of a forest. It might also provide a metaphor. In the sample story, the dry, barren desert symbolizes Hannah's angry feelings for her father.

A short story is easiest to write when there is one setting and the action happens in a brief period of time.

Planning Action and Dialogue

Let readers see what your characters are doing and hear what they are saying. Action and dialogue help you show instead of tell.

Instead of writing that a character is angry, show the person ripping open a bag of chips. Don't tell the reader that a character yelled at his brother; let the reader hear the character shout, "Get out of my room, Henry!"

Prewrite

Plan your story. Create characters, a conflict, and a setting. Plan action and dialogue to move the story along.

Mapping Your Plot

The plot is the series of events that build from exposition to climax and end in resolution. In any plot, the climax occurs when the main character confronts the conflict head-on and learns something or changes. You can map your story by creating a plot graph.

Plot Graph

			She notices he doesn't worry only about money anymore.		
		She observes that he doesn't worry about his outward appearance.		She is touched that he shows that she is more important than his work.	
	She is surprised that he has learned to cook.				
At first, Hannah hates her father because he left.					At the end of the story, she resolves to try to repair their relationship.

Prewrite

Create a plot graph. Write events and discoveries that build toward the climax of your story and end in your resolution.

Using Flashbacks

Writers use flashbacks to show events that occurred before the story. A flashback provides context for the reader, showing how the character got into the situation or contrasting current events with previous events.

In the sample story, Chandra used a flashback to show how Hannah ended up in the truck with her father. Another flashback showed how her father had left Hannah and her mother earlier.

> At the airport, he had tossed her suitcase and backpack into the back of the truck, as carelessly as he had tossed her from his life nearly a year ago. That was when he had left her and her mother to "find himself" in this sagebrush and saguaro wasteland. And now he expected her to forget all the hurt!

Later on, flashbacks help show how Hannah's father has changed.

Prewrite

Plan flashbacks. Review your plot chart, looking for places in which flashbacks can provide context for your story.

Writing Creating Your First Draft

Every story has a beginning, a middle, and an ending. Follow these guidelines as you develop each part of your story.

Starting Strong

Use one of the following strategies to capture your reader's attention and get your story started. (Chandra used strong imagery.)

- **Begin with dialogue.**

  "He's not running away from us, Hannah," Mom had said sadly. "He's running toward something, and we just can't go with him."

- **Begin with action.**

  Hannah's father carelessly tossed her suitcase and backpack into the back of his truck, as carelessly as he had tossed her from his life nearly a year ago.

- **Use strong imagery.**

  Hannah watched the desert glide by the truck window. Her father drove silently, his fingers beating a little pattern on the wheel to the rhythm of the music from the CD player. *His* music. *His* truck. *His* home.

After capturing the reader's attention, get your story underway by introducing the characters, setting, and conflict.

Building the Action

Increase the seriousness of the problem, leading the protagonist toward a direct confrontation with the conflict. Follow these tips:

- Use **action** that shows what the protagonist is experiencing.
- Use **natural-sounding dialogue** so that each character gets to speak.
- Include **sensory details,** allowing the reader to participate in the story.
- Intensify the **conflict** as the character approaches the climax.

Bringing the Story to a Close

Show how the character is changed by the climax. Then, in the falling action and resolution, indicate how life will be different.

Write

Write your first draft. Use your planning from page 346 and the information above as a general guide to your writing.

Revising Improving Your Writing

Revise

Revise your writing. Use the following checklist to guide your revision. Make changes until you can answer every question "yes."

Revising Checklist

Ideas

_____ **1.** Is the story's conflict clear and believable?
_____ **2.** Does my character come across as a real person?

Organization

_____ **3.** Do I give enough information in the beginning?
_____ **4.** Do I present steps that carry my character toward the climax?

Voice

_____ **5.** Does my dialogue sound natural?

Word Choice

_____ **6.** Are all of the words easy to follow?

Sentence Fluency

_____ **7.** Do my sentences flow smoothly?
_____ **8.** Do I use a variety of sentence types and beginnings?

Editing Checking for Conventions

Edit

Edit your writing. When you edit, check your capitalization, punctuation, grammar, and spelling.

Editing Checklist

Conventions

_____ **1.** Have I used commas after introductory word groups and in series?
_____ **2.** Have I correctly punctuated dialogue?

Elements of Fiction

Antagonist The person or force that works against the hero of the story (See *protagonist.*)

Character A person or an animal in a story

Climax The moment of change when the protagonist either succeeds or fails and is somehow changed by the action

Conflict A problem or clash between two forces in a story
- **Person vs. person** A problem between characters
- **Person vs. self** A problem within a character's own mind
- **Person vs. society** A problem between a character and society, the law, or some tradition
- **Person vs. nature** A problem with an element of nature, such as a blizzard or a hurricane
- **Person vs. destiny** A problem or struggle that appears to be beyond a character's control

Narrator The person or character who tells the story, gives background information, and fills in details between dialogue

Plot, Plot Line See page 342.

Point of View The angle from which a story is told
- In **first-person point of view,** one character is telling the story.
- In **third-person point of view,** someone outside the story, a narrator, is telling it.
- In **omniscient point of view,** the narrator tells the thoughts and feelings of all the characters.
- In **limited omniscient point of view,** the narrator tells the thoughts of only one character.
- In **camera view** (objective), the narrator records the action from his or her own point of view, without any of the characters' thoughts.

Protagonist The main character or hero in a story (See *antagonist.*)

Rising Action A series of events that propel the protagonist toward the climax

Setting The place and time period in which a story takes place

Theme The author's message about life or human nature

Tone The writer's attitude toward his or her subject (*angry, humorous,* and so on)

Writing Plays

Most writers work alone, getting help from a peer only during revising or editing. However, playwrights create works that are truly collaborative. In a sense, a play is not a play until actors perform it in front of an audience.

Plays engage sight and sound, creating the illusion that real events are unfolding before the viewers. Through the use of simple sets and props, lighting and sound, playwrights transport their audiences across space and time.

This powerful medium has been used throughout the years to express feelings about social problems such as racism or injustice. In this chapter, you will read a brief play about a student faced with the prospect of cheating to help a friend. Then, following the guidelines, you'll write your own play about a person facing a dilemma.

Writing Guidelines

Subject: **Facing a personal dilemma**
Form: **Brief play**
Purpose: **To entertain and enlighten**
Audience: **Classmates**

"The play's the thing wherein I'll catch the conscience of the king."

—William Shakespeare

Sample Play

In the following play by student writer Jamie Lin, Missy faces the problem of "helping" a friend on the test. The side notes identify key points in the development of the play.

The Test

Characters: **Missy,** a high school student
Cali, Missy's self-absorbed friend
Steve, Missy's friend
James, Cali's friend
Mr. Day, their social studies teacher
Other students in the class

Scene 1

Stage Directions
The opening scene is described.

(The curtain rises on a classroom with desks arranged in rows. A teacher's desk is set at an angle stage left, where Mr. Day is seated grading papers. A bell rings, and students start to file in and take their places, chatting about the day. James, Missy, Cali, and Steve come in and take their places, in that order, in the front row.)

MR. DAY: Okay, everyone, we'll start the test as soon as the bell rings.

CALI: Oh no! Missy, I forgot all about the test!

MISSY: Cali, I reminded you about it yesterday.

Beginning
The characters are introduced and the problem is presented.

CALI: Hey, who listens? I've been *totally* thinking about the pom routine we're doing for homecoming.

MISSY: Well, you are *totally* out of luck now!

CALI: Listen, no problem. You can just kind of slip me your pages as you finish.

MISSY: You want to *copy* mine?

JAMES: What's the dif?

MISSY: Who asked you, James?

Background information is given.

CALI: If I mess up my grade in here, I won't be on the pom squad.

MISSY: Not my problem.

JAMES: Come on, Missy, be a bud.

STEVE: Hang in there, Missy. Don't let them bully you.

JAMES: *(Sneering)* Listen to Mr. Good Guy.

STEVE: Yeah? Well, maybe I'll just let Mr. Day know about your little plan.

Middle
Complications are introduced as rising action.

CALI: Steve, you are such a jer—*(A thought hits her, and she is suddenly very cute.)* Aw, come on,

STEVE: Stevey. Be a good sport. Hey, have you got a date for the homecoming dance yet?

STEVE: *(Taken off guard)* Uh—no, but—*(Looking at Missy)*

CALI: How would you like to go with me? Hmmm?

STEVE: *(Flustered)* Well, I mean, sure, but . . .

CALI: Just keep quiet about this little—um—arrangement, and you can go out with a homecoming queen.

STEVE: Uh—sure.

(Cali flashes him a megawatt smile and then turns and exchanges glances with James. Missy looks at Steve, disgusted. The bell rings.)

MR. DAY: All right, everyone, everything off your desks.

(He hands a pile of papers to a student in the back, who takes a packet and passes it on, moving the papers around the class.)

CALI: *(Whispering to Missy)* So, you in?

MISSY: *(Taking her test papers)* Just shut up.

(The students begin writing, and Mr. Day stands at his desk for a moment, then goes to sit down. The lights go down.)

Scene 2

(The lights come up again. Mr. Day is seated at his desk, working on some papers, and the class is frantically writing. Cali looks up, glances at Mr. Day, and then nudges Missy, who ignores her. Cali nudges her harder, and Missy passes a paper over to her. James notices and grins. Steve glances over at the action and scowls. The lights go down.)

Scene 3

(The lights come up. It is the end of the class. The bell rings.)

MR. DAY: All right, everyone, hand in your papers.

(There are some groans. Students begin filing out, handing in their papers as they go.)

MR. DAY: Oh, Missy and Cali, would you two please stay after class a moment?

(James shakes his head with a laugh, and Steve gives the girls a sympathetic look.)

CALI: Uh-oh. He knows!

MISSY: *(Feigning innocence)* What do you mean?

Different scenes are used to allow for the passing of time.

Creative Writing

MR. DAY: You girls know the school policy about cheating. I'm going to have to report you.

MISSY: For what?

MR. DAY: Missy, I saw you pass that paper to Cali.

MISSY: I did give her a paper, but I didn't pass her any answers.

MR. DAY: Give me that paper, Cali. (*Reading and looking confused.*) For the question, "Whose faces are on Mt. Rushmore?" you wrote, David Crosby, Steven Stills, Graham Nash, and Neil Young."

Climax
The problem is solved.

MISSY: (*Smiles*) I took two tests and answered one just as a joke to ease my nerves. Here's my real test.

(*She hands him the other paper.*)

CALI: A joke?

(*Mr. Day takes it from her and reads it.*)

MR. DAY: I don't think Cali realized it was a joke. Well, Missy, I'm not sure how to handle this one, but it certainly doesn't look like you were trying to help Cali, so I won't turn you in.

MISSY: Thank you.

MR. DAY: And Cali, it looks like your failing grade will be punishment enough!

Falling Action
Results of the action are given.

CALI: (*Turning toward Missy*) You rat!

(*Cali starts to stomp out, but is stopped by Steve.*)

STEVE: So are we still on for homecoming?

Resolution
Two characters set a new course of action.

(*Cali just stares at him, makes a little screech and goes out.*)

STEVE: Guess not.

MISSY: Come on, Steve, let's get to class. Maybe I'll go to homecoming with you if you don't think you'll be cheating on Cali!

(*They go out. The lights go down.*)

Respond to the reading. Answer the following questions about the play.

Ideas (1) What is the problem Missy faces?

Organization (2) What is the purpose of having three separate scenes?

Voice & Word Choice (3) How does the writer make the dialogue sound realistic? Give three examples.

Prewriting Creating a Protagonist

Your first step in writing a play is choosing a main character or protagonist, a word that means literally "first contender." Your protagonist can be very much like you (*a high school student*) or very different (*a nursing-home resident*), very likeable (*a kindly veterinarian*) or very dislikable (*Scrooge*). One way to quickly develop a protagonist is to create a character grid.

Character Grid

Gender	Age	Height	Strength	Weakness	Name
female	6	4' 2"	imagination	afraid of dogs	Amelia
male	73	5' 5"	singing	loneliness	Chester
female	17	5' 7"	"A" student	peer pressure	Missy*

Create a character grid. Write "gender, "age," and so forth across the top. Beneath each heading, list vital statistics for four characters and give each a name. Put an asterisk (*) next to the character you'd like to write about.

Choosing a Conflict

Next, you need to decide on a conflict, something that will test your main character's strengths and weaknesses. There are five basic types of conflict:

- **Person vs. person:** The protagonist has a problem with an antagonist (a person who contends against him or her).
- **Person vs. society:** The protagonist has a problem with some element of society: the school, the law, and so on.
- **Person vs. self:** The protagonist has trouble deciding what to do.
- **Person vs. nature:** The protagonist endures an element of nature.
- **Person vs. destiny:** The protagonist battles an uncontrollable problem or a supernatural force.

In the sample play, Missy clashes with her friend Cali, who pressures her to pass answers on a test.

Choose a conflict. Review the five basic types of conflict and decide which would best test your character. Write down the specific conflict the protagonist will have to overcome. (Tip: Use a character grid to generate an antagonist and other characters for your play.)

Prewriting Deciding on a Tone

The tone of your play reflects your feelings about the character and conflict. Because tone is about feelings, any adjective that describes emotions can also describe tone:

joyful	smug	petulant	serious	paranoid	capricious
angry	hopeful	rollicking	buoyant	patient	resigned

Most often, the tone of a play should express your true feelings about the character and the conflict. However, sometimes playwrights adopt a satirical tone—using an opposite feeling than the one they truly have. For example, if characters break into song about the fun of appendicitis, the playwright is being satirical.

Prewrite

Choose a tone. Ask yourself "How do I feel about this character and conflict?" Write down three adjectives that describe your feeling. Choose one to represent your tone—or choose an opposite feeling for a satirical tone.

Selecting a Setting

The setting is the place and time of the play. You may have two or three locations, each one suggesting a different time in the action, or you could focus the action in one main location. To decide on the setting for her play, Jamie created a T-graph listing places and times. She decided to focus her play in one location at slightly different points in time.

Setting T-Graph

Settings	
Places	Times
the football field	during poms practice
the hallway	before the test *
the history classroom *	during the test *
Missy's locker	after the test *

Prewrite

Select a setting. Make a T-graph, listing places and times where your character could deal with the conflict. Then choose one or more locations and times for your play. Think about ways to suggest the settings with furniture, props, lighting, and so forth.

Mapping Your Plot

A play generally follows the standard plot line, shown below. The beginning introduces the characters and setting and initiates the conflict. The middle builds tension to a climax in which the protagonist faces the conflict head-on. The ending resolves the conflict one way or another. Jamie used a plot chart to map out her play. She also divided the action into scenes.

Plot Chart

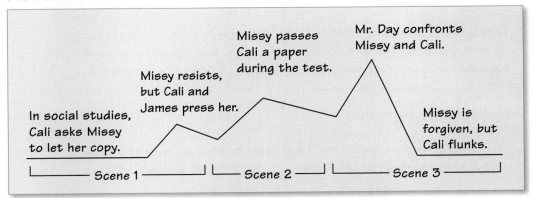

Mr. Day confronts
Missy and Cali.

Missy passes
Cali a paper
during the test.

Missy resists,
but Cali and
James press her.

In social studies,
Cali asks Missy
to let her copy.

Missy is
forgiven, but
Cali flunks.

Scene 1   Scene 2   Scene 3

Prewrite

Map your plot. Create a plot chart like the one above. Introduce the characters and situation, start the conflict, build tension to a climax, and resolve the conflict. If possible, also divide up the action into at least two scenes.

Learning Stage Terminology

As you write stage directions, use stage shorthand to indicate the acting areas.

Stage Diagram

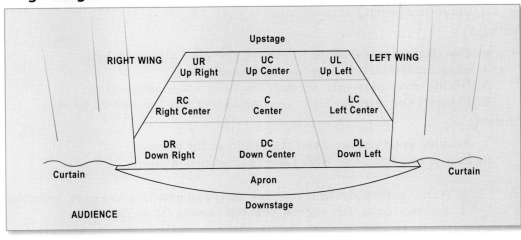

Upstage

RIGHT WING

UR
Up Right

UC
Up Center

UL
Up Left

LEFT WING

RC
Right Center

C
Center

LC
Left Center

DR
Down Right

DC
Down Center

DL
Down Left

Curtain

Curtain

Apron

Downstage

AUDIENCE

Creative Writing

Writing Creating Your First Draft

Follow the guidelines below as you develop your play.

Writing Stage Directions

Some playwrights describe the exact placement of every piece of furniture and prop. Others present general ideas, giving directors complete freedom.

Specific Stage Direction

> *(The scene is the Harris' living room. A green love seat is set stage right at an angle. It has grease stains on the back, and cigarette burns dot the sagging cushions. An orange-plaid wingback chair has torn cushions.)*

General Stage Direction

> *(The general wear of the Harris' living room creates an aura of a stuffed animal that has been handed down generation after generation.)*

Developing the Three Main Parts

Beginning

1. **Give your opening stage directions.** Set the scene with any information that you feel is necessary. (See above.)
2. **Introduce your characters and conflict.** Include any background information necessary for the audience to understand how the characters got to the opening point.
3. **Start in the middle of the action.** The reader should immediately understand what the conflict is.

Middle

4. **Use dialogue and action to move the play along.** Include complications (difficulties) to add suspense.
5. **Divide your play into scenes.** Use scenes to condense time.
6. **Present the climax.** Make the protagonist face the conflict head-on.

Ending

7. **Resolve your action.** Show the results of the climax.
8. **End your play.** Close with a final exchange of dialogue.

Write

Write your play. Write your play, using your prewriting as a guide. Include at least two scenes. Add any new ideas that come to you as you write.

Revising Improving Your Writing

Revise

Revise your writing. Read your play out loud or have someone else read it to you. Change any lines that sound forced or unnatural. Use these questions as a revising guide.

Revising Checklist

Ideas

_____ **1.** Is the conflict believable?

_____ **2.** Have I created tension and suspense?

_____ **3.** Do the characters seem real?

Organization

_____ **4.** Does my play build to a climax?

_____ **5.** Do my stage directions clearly explain the action?

Voice

_____ **6.** Does the dialogue sound natural?

_____ **7.** Does the tone help convey my ideas?

Sentence Fluency

_____ **8.** Do my sentences read smoothly?

Editing Checking for Conventions

Edit

Edit your writing. Use the following checklist as a guide when you check your play for proper formatting and for conventions.

Editing Checklist

Conventions

_____ **1.** Does the play follow correct script form?

_____ **2.** Have I checked for punctuation and capitalization?

_____ **3.** Have I checked for spelling errors?

Sample Advertising Script

Every commercial you see on TV comes from a script. One way to write a commercial is to include columns for both the audio (what you hear) and the video (what you see). The sample below is a brief commercial "spot."

The **beginning** establishes a mood.

The **middle** uses a voice-over to give the message.

The **problem** is established.

The **product** is introduced.

The **ending** suggests the problem is solved by the product.

Video	Audio
1. A boy and a girl are strolling a city street.	1. (Jazzy music)
2. Close-up of boy and girl, obviously in love, smiling, sweet innocence.	2. (Announcer) Ah, love! Time frozen in one sweet instant.
3. Suddenly, slow motion goes to normal time. Close-up of girl's face as she winces.	3. (Music turns sharp and out of tune.) Would you want this perfect moment spoiled because of . . .
4. Girl limps and reaches down to her foot.	4. . . . sore feet?
5. Sparks fly as her shoes become Heelers.	5. Avoid foot pain with new Heelers, the world's most comfortable shoes.
6. Close-up of girl's feet, with animation of clouds floating around the foot.	6. Heelers cushion your feet in comfort with built-in air pockets. You'll be walking on air!
7. Long shot of girl and boy, who start to dance.	7. So enjoy every moment, and never worry about sore feet—with Heelers.

Try It!

Write an ad script. Think of a product or service to promote—or satirize. Create a commercial using images and words to convey your point.

Writing Poetry

Poetry is often considered the language of feelings, from the smiles of a summer morning to the cry of a breaking heart. The compact form and precise use of words is the perfect frame for exploring emotions, expressing beauty, or questioning the unfairness of the world.

The goal of the poet is to share intensely personal emotions that the reader can relate to his or her own life. You have probably read a poem and thought, "Yeah, that's right." It's that ability to read someone else's feelings and recognize them in your own experience that makes poetry universal. Poetry reaches across barriers of age, race, or nationality to touch a shared part of the human soul.

In this chapter, you will write a free-verse poem in which you reflect on a relationship. It could be a family relationship or a connection with a teacher, a classmate, someone you love, or even a pet. You will also explore the use of rhythm and rhyme patterns and learn about two other distinct forms of poetry.

Writing Guidelines

Subject: A relationship
Form: Free-verse poem
Purpose: To entertain
Audience: Friends, family, and classmates

"Poetry is language at its most distilled and most powerful."

—Rita Dove

Sample Free-Verse Poem

Although free-verse poems are not restricted to a specific rhythm or rhyme scheme, they usually have within them their own distinct pattern. Student writer Nina Whitefeather wrote the following poem examining changes in her relationship with her friend Marla. As you read, watch for the subtle rhythm and rhyme within the poem.

Windows and Doors

Wire-bound in the Sisterhood of Braces
    (and of giggles secretly shared),
We gazed through open summer windows,
And dreamed the same dreams,
Of princes who would love us
    (gap-toothed and freckled).
Do you remember the window we broke,
Playing baseball in my neighbor's yard?
We ran, laughing, tumbling, scared,
Two pairs of feet matching step for step
    (Mine, size nine; yours, size seven).

Then our braces were gone,
And with no gated guardians,
Our secrets escaped
    (Couldn't you hear the pain?)
Our feet turned toward different doors,
    (Different faces, different places).
Our smiles stretched to others,
And our friendship lay in brittle shards,
    (Like that long-ago window)
Perfect, empty smiles beneath our feet
    (Mine, size nine; yours, size seven).

Respond to the reading. Use the following questions to guide your reflection on the free-verse poem above.

Ideas (1) Describe the relationship in the above poem.

Organization (2) Where does the relationship change? Explain how it changes.

Voice (3) What is the overall feeling of the poem?

Word Choice (4) Give two examples of alliteration used in the poem.

Prewriting Choosing a Topic and a Focus

Your challenge is to write a poem about a relationship. First you must choose a relationship, and then decide on your focus—the one aspect of the relationship that you want to write about. Nina listed the various relationships she had had in her life.

Topic List

Family members: mother, father, my brother John, Grandpa George, Aunt Lucy
Friends: boyfriend Bobby, former best friend Marla, friend Kristi
Other people: teacher Ms. Friedman, boss Mr. Tortelli, neighbor Mrs. Konjak
Pets: dog Heinz, guinea pig Rags

Nina decided to write about her best childhood friend, Marla, and chose to focus on how their relationship changed as they grew older.

Prewrite

Find a topic and a focus. Make a list of the various relationships you have had in your life. Select one you would like to write about and choose a focus.

Gathering Images

Writing a poem about a relationship is an emotional exercise. You can express your feelings by finding a metaphor to represent them. How do you decide which image, or metaphor, to use? Nina did a little freewriting.

Freewriting

What images would represent my friendship with Marla? We were the best of friends, and we did a lot of fun and stupid stuff together, like the time we broke my neighbor's window and ran away. Boy, did we laugh about that, but we were so scared! We were equal when we both had braces, but things changed when she got hers off first. She thought she was better than me, just because she was tiny and cute. She made different friends and left me to find my own. That really hurt. A sharp hurt, like broken glass. Windows. Glass. Broken glass looks like teeth. I can use the image of windows and broken glass.

Prewrite

Gather images. Ask yourself what metaphors or images represent the relationship you are writing about. Freewrite for 5 to 10 minutes to discover metaphors you can use.

Writing Writing Your First Draft

Begin to write your poem. Let your first draft flow freely, without worrying about what's good and what's not so good. Watch for opportunities to use poetic techniques such as rhythm and line breaks. (See other techniques on pages **368–369**.)

Using Rhythm

While free verse is not locked into a specific meter, rhythm is still important for carrying readers through a poem, and for adding emphasis to particular words and phrases. Compare the rhythm in both versions of the short poem below.

Trains (Version 1)
> Like capillaries, reaching all through a city,
> they deliver people to workplaces every day
> and return them home each night.

In this version, there is no rhythm; the words read more like prose.

Trains (Version 2)
> Vascular system of every metropolis,
> daily delivering workers to workplaces,
> nightly returning them home.

In the second version, a definite sense of rhythm carries the reader along.

Tip

Not every poem needs as strong a rhythm as "Trains (Version 2)," but every poem ought to have *some* sense of rhythm. Choose your words and their order carefully to make the rhythm of your poems flow smoothly.

Using Line Breaks

There are no hard-and-fast rules for using line breaks. There are, however, strategies that poets consider when deciding where to break to a new line.

- **Emphasis:** A word at the end of a line gains extra attention. Poets use this to dramatic effect in free verse, breaking a line just after an especially important or interesting word. (Avoid breaking after a weak word, such as a preposition.)
- **Rhythm:** Long lines have a leisurely feel, while short lines tend to have more punch. This affects the overall rhythm of a poem.
- **Shift in ideas:** A line break can separate ideas, even within a sentence.
- **Appearance:** The line breaks of a poem determine its overall appearance on a page.

Write

Write your first draft. Allow ideas to pour out of you and experiment with poetic images and techniques.

Revising Improving Your Poem

Poetry should also reflect the traits of good writing. As you revise your poem, use the following questions as a guide.

- **Ideas** Have I established a focus about the relationship in the poem? Are my feelings about the relationship clear?
- **Organization** Do my line breaks make sense? Do I establish a sense of rhythm without locking my poem into a specific meter?
- **Voice** Do I establish and maintain a consistent tone throughout?
- **Word Choice** Are my words appropriate? Do I use poetic devices? (See pages **368–369**.)
- **Sentence Fluency** Does the arrangement of lines move the reader smoothly through the poem?

Revise

Revise your poem. Using the questions above, revise your poem until it is the best that it can be.

Editing Checking Your Poem

Punctuation is especially important in a poem, since each mark affects the poem's rhythm, readability, or even its meaning. Notice, on page **362**, how Nina used parentheses to set apart lines that emphasize certain ideas and emotions. Use punctuation to enhance the meaning of your poem.

Edit

Edit your poem. Don't be afraid to break the rules of punctuation in your poem, but be sure that each mark accomplishes the purpose you intend.

Publishing Sharing Your Poem

It's fun to share poems and discuss their ideas. Here are some suggestions for how to do that.

- **Have a class poetry reading.** Sit on cushions in an informal circle on the floor. Ask each person to reads his or her poem out loud.
- **Submit your poem** to a magazine, a Web site, or a contest.
- **Print your poem on a bookmark.** Then make copies and hand them out to friends and family.

Publish

Publish your poem. Share your poem with others and discuss the ideas and feelings it presents. Ask your teacher for other publishing ideas.

Writing Bouts-Rimés Verse

Bouts-rimés (boo ree MAY) means "rhymed ends." The poem is usually created from a set of rhyming words decided on beforehand, which must be used in the order given. Making up bouts-rimés verse was a popular parlor game in the seventeenth and nineteenth centuries. The two examples on the right were created by Cassandra Austen, mother of novelist Jane Austen. Notice how the author takes poetic license with the word *rehearse* in place of *hearse* in the second poem.

I've said it in prose, and I'll say it in verse,
That riches bring comfort and poverty sorrow,
That it's better to ride in a coach than a hearse,
That it's better to fill than to empty your purse,
And to feast well today than to fast till tomorrow.

Why d'you ask me to scribble in verse
When my heart's full of trouble and sorrow?
The cause I will briefly rehearse,
I'm in debt, with a sad empty purse,
And the bailiffs will seize me tomorrow.

Sari Hakala's class decided to write bouts-rimés poems using the words *merry, half, bury, laugh, vary,* and *graph.* These are the poems Sari wrote.

Would you like to be merry? Are you too sad by half? If it's not time to bury you, there is still time to laugh. Fortunes can vary like a parabolic graph.	Hey, Murray! What's that you have? A poison berry? Oh . . . boysenberry. Sure, you can laugh. But you didn't speak very well—like some scratchy old phonograph.

Tip

To write a bouts-rimés poem,

- examine the words for an idea that could link them all,
- make a list of images or phrases that end with the rhymes, and
- write your poem, keeping a consistent tone or mood and pleasing rhythm.

Write a bouts-rimés poem. Brainstorm a group of words with a specific rhyme scheme. Then write as many verses as you can, following that pattern.

Writing Quatrains

Quatrains are poems with four lines and a definite rhyming pattern. There are a variety of acceptable patterns, and four of the most common are modeled here.

- **abcb** The second and fourth lines rhyme.

  As a child, I thought my parents
  Didn't have a clue.
  When I'd grown I was surprised
  By just how much they knew!

- **abab** The first and third lines rhyme, and the second and fourth lines rhyme.

  I love to hear a froggy croak,
  It is a lovely thing.
  It sings of life that's newly woke,
  And of the joy of spring.

- **abba** The first and fourth lines rhyme, as do the second and third.

  Don't look at me and say you'll be my friend,
  When all you really want is to be free.
  If you would rather be a *you* than *we,*
  Say honestly our time is at an end.

- **aabb** The first and second lines rhyme, as do the third and fourth. (This sort of rhyme is often used for humorous subjects.)

  I hear the thud
  And think, Oh, crud!
  My car's been hit
  And bent a bit.

Note: Although quatrains are often written in iambic meter (see page 369), other patterns may also be used.

Write your own quatrain. Pick a subject, select a rhyme scheme and rhythm pattern, and write four lines about your topic.

Using Special Poetry Techniques

Poets use a variety of special techniques in their work. This page and the next define some of the most important ones.

Figures of Speech

- A **simile** *(sĭm´ə-lē)* compares two unlike things with the word *like* or *as.*

  Her smile was warm
  as hot cocoa on a cold day.

- A **metaphor** *(mĕt´ə-fôr)* compares two unlike things without using *like* or *as.*

  The leaf was a dancer
  whirling madly
  to the wind's wild music.

- **Personification** *(pər-sŏn´ə-fĭ-kā´shən)* is a technique that gives human traits to something that is nonhuman.

  Rocks stubbornly bite the plowshares,
  leaving ragged teeth marks in the metal.

- **Hyperbole** *(hī-pûr´bə-lē)* is an exaggerated statement, often humorous.

  He lived so near, across the street,
  a million miles away.

Sounds of Poetry

- **Alliteration** *(ə-lĭt´ə-rā´shən)* is the repetition of consonant sounds at the beginning of words.

  The muck and mire made movement slow.

- **Assonance** *(ăs´ə-nəns)* is the repetition of vowel sounds anywhere in words.

  Blame the day, not the place.

- **Consonance** *(kŏn´sə-nəns)* is the repetition of consonant sounds anywhere in words.

  We drank sparkling water from trickling brooks.

- **Line breaks** help control the rhythm of a poem. The reader naturally pauses at the end of a line. There's also added emphasis on the last word in a line.

  Branches reaching out,
  stretching,
  as though fingers yearning
  to strum the wind.

- **Onomatopoeia** (*ŏn´ə-mät´ə-pē´ə*) is the use of words that sound like what they name.

  The plip-plop of the leaky faucet

- **Repetition** (*rĕp´i-tĭsh´ən*) uses the same word or phrase more than once, for emphasis or for rhythm.

  I wish to fly beyond the world,
  beyond the clouds,
  beyond the sun,
  across the universe.

- **Rhyme** (*rīm*) means using words whose endings sound alike.

  - **End rhyme** happens at the end of lines.

    Through the fog, so thick and pale,
    red lights slice as sirens wail.

  - **Internal rhyme** happens within lines.

    I stop running and turn,
    To see burning embers pepper the sky.

- **Rhythm** (*rĭth´əm*) is the pattern of accented and unaccented syllables in a poem.
  - **Iambic:** an unstressed followed by a stressed syllable (*I am´*)
  - **Trochaic:** a stressed followed by an unstressed syllable (*la´-ter*)
  - **Anapestic:** two unstressed followed by a stressed syllable (*to the moon´*)
  - **Dactylic:** a stressed followed by two unstressed syllables (*stealth´-i-ly*)

The rhythm of free-verse poetry tends to flow naturally, like speaking. Traditional poetry follows a more regular pattern, as in the following example.

  Moón on snów
  Évening glów

Research Writing

Research Writing
Research Skills

"Research" is a strange word. One might think that its meaning is obvious from the prefix *re* ("again") and the root *search* ("to look for"). And in a way, that definition is correct: When you do research, you investigate facts not in just one place but in many. You need to look and look again.

This is why knowing where to find reliable information is so important when writing research papers. You have to discover the facts before you can interpret them. In this chapter, you'll read about finding information on the Internet and in the library. You will also learn that every source needs a critical eye to determine its worth.

- **Primary vs. Secondary Sources**
- **Evaluating Sources of Information**
- **Using the Internet**
- **Using the Library**
- **Using Reference Books**

"Research is formalized curiosity. It is poking and prying with a purpose."

—Zora Neale Hurston

Primary vs. Secondary Sources

Primary sources are original sources. These sources *(diaries, people, events, surveys)* inform you directly, not through a second person's explanation or interpretation. Ideally, when you research a topic, you should find as much primary information as possible. (See below.)

Primary sources include . . .

- **Diaries, journals, and letters:** You can often find these in museums, in libraries, or at historic sites.

- **Presentations:** A speaker at a museum or a historic site can give you firsthand information, but be aware of the presenter's own interpretation of events.

- **Interviews:** Talk to an expert on your research topic. You can do this by phone, e-mail, or letter.

- **Surveys and questionnaires:** These tools help you gather a great deal of data from many people.

- **Observation and participation:** Your own observations of a person, a place, or an event provide excellent firsthand information. Participating in an event can give you insights that cannot be discovered through the reports of others.

Secondary sources are third-person accounts found in research done by other people. Much of the news *(television, radio, Internet, books, magazines)* can be considered a secondary source of information. Keep in mind that, by their very nature, secondary sources represent filtered information that may contain biases or misunderstandings.

Primary Sources

1. Reading the journal of a travel guide
2. Listening to a presentation by a travel guide
3. Interviewing a travel guide

Secondary Sources

1. Exploring a Web site about being a travel guide
2. Reading a magazine article about a travel guide
3. Watching a TV documentary about a travel guide

Try It!

List two primary and two secondary sources you might use to learn about life in the military. Be as specific as you can.

Research

Evaluating Sources of Information

You may find a lot of information about your research topic. However, before you use any of it, decide whether or not the information is dependable. Use the following questions to help you decide about the reliability of your sources.

Is the source a primary source or a secondary source?

You can usually trust any information you've collected yourself, but be careful with secondary sources. Although many of them are reliable, others may contain outdated or incorrect information.

Is the source an expert?

An expert knows more about a subject than other people. Using an expert's thoughts and opinions can make your paper more believable. If you aren't sure about a source's authority, ask a teacher or librarian what he or she thinks.

Is the information accurate?

Sources that people respect are usually very accurate. Big-city newspapers *(New York Times* or *Chicago Tribune)* and well-known Web sites (CNN or ESPN) are reliable sources of information. Little-known sources that do not support their facts or that contain errors may not be reliable.

Tip

Be especially cautious about the accuracy of information on the Internet. While there is an incredible amount of solid information available on the Net, there is also a lot of misinformation.

Is the information fair and complete?

A reliable source should provide information fairly, covering all sides of a subject or an issue. If a source presents only one side of a subject, its information may not be accurate. To make themselves sound better, politicians and advertisers often present just their side of a subject. Avoid sources that are one-sided, and look for those that are balanced.

Is the information current?

Usually, you want to have the most up-to-date information about a subject. Sometimes information changes, and sources can become outdated quickly. Check the copyright page in a book, the issue date of a magazine, and the posting date of online information.

Using the Internet

Because you can access many resources by surfing the Web, the Internet is a valuable research aid. You can find government publications, encyclopedia entries, business reports, and firsthand observations on the Internet. The increasing speed of computers makes the Internet even more inviting. When researching on the Internet, keep in mind the following points.

Internet Guidelines

- **Use the Internet wisely.** Sites that include *.edu, .org,* and *.gov* in the Web address are often reliable. These sites are from educational, nonprofit, or government agencies. If you have questions about the reliability of a site, talk to your teacher. (See also page **373**.) Remember to check the date of the Web site. Abandoned Web sites may contain outdated information.

- **Try several search engines.** When you type a term into a search engine's input box, the search engine scans its database for matching sites. Then the engine returns recommendations for you to explore. Because there is an enormous amount of information on the Web, no one search engine can handle it all. So employ at least two search engines when you surf the Web. Enter keywords to start your research or enter specific questions to zero in on your topic.

- **Take advantage of links.** When you read a page, watch for links to other sites. These may offer different perspectives or points of view on your topic.

- **Experiment with keywords.** Sometimes you must ask a number of different questions or use different keywords to find the information you need.

- **Ignore Web sites that advertise research papers for sale.** Using these sites is dishonest. Teachers and librarians can recognize and verify when a paper is someone else's work.

- **Learn your school's Internet policy.** Using a computer at school or at home is a privilege. To maintain that privilege, follow your school's Internet policy and any guidelines your parents may have set.

Try It!

Select a topic that would be appropriate for a research paper. Come up with at least three keywords to use in a search engine. Which one, in your opinion, provides the best results? Explain in a brief paragraph.

Using the Library

The Internet may be a good place to initiate your research, but a library is often a more valuable place to continue your research. A library offers materials that are more in-depth and reliable than what you find on the Internet. Most libraries contain the following resources.

Books

- **Reference** books include encyclopedias, almanacs, dictionaries, atlases, and directories, plus resources such as consumer information guides and car repair manuals. Reference books provide a quick review or overview of research topics.

- **Nonfiction** texts are a good source of facts that can serve as a foundation for your research. Check the copyright dates to be sure you are reading reasonably up-to-date information. (Some libraries organize nonfiction using the Library of Congress system, but most libraries use the Dewey decimal system as shown on page **377**.)

- **Fiction** can sometimes aid or enhance your research. For example, a historical novel can reveal people's feelings about a particular time in history. (Fiction books are grouped together in alphabetical order by the authors' last names.)

Periodicals

Periodicals (*newspapers* and *magazines*) are grouped together in a library. Use the *Readers' Guide to Periodical Literature* to find articles in periodicals. (See page **382**.) You will have to ask the librarian for older issues.

The Media Section

The media section of your library includes DVD's, CD-ROM's, CD's, cassettes, and videotapes. These resources can immerse you in an event. Keep in mind, however, that directors and screenwriters may present events in a way that accommodates their personal views.

Computers

Computers are available in most libraries, and many are connected to the Internet, although there may be restrictions on their use.

Try It!

Ask a local public librarian whether you may access the library's catalog online. If so, you can check to see if your needed materials are available before you visit the library.

Using the Computer Catalog

Some libraries still use a card catalog located in a cabinet with drawers. Most libraries, however, have put their entire catalog on computer. Each system varies a bit, so ask for help if you're not sure how the system in your library works. A *computer catalog* lists the books held in your library and affiliated systems.

Using a Variety of Search Methods

When you are using a computer catalog, you can find information about a book with any of the following methods:

- If you know it, enter the **title** of the book.
- If you know the **author** of the book, enter the first and last names.
- A general search of your **subject** will also help you find books on your topic. Enter either the subject or a related keyword.

Sample Computer Catalog Screen

In the illustration below, the key to the right identifies the types of information provided for a particular resource, in this case, a book. Once you locate the book you need, make note of the call number. You will use this to find the book on the shelf.

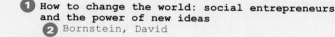

1 How to change the world: social entrepreneurs and the power of new ideas
2 Bornstein, David

3 Publisher: Oxford UP
Publishing date: 2004
Pages: 320p.
ISBN: 0-195-13805-8
Copy information: 1 copy at Racine Main Library

4 Call number:
361.2
B645h

5 Discusses social entrepreneurs as creative people who apply the tactics of business innovation to social problems. Offers case studies of social entrepreneurs around the globe who are shaking up the status quo and developing new solutions to old problems to make the world a better place.

6 Subject: Social action -- case studies
Social service -- case studies

7 Availability: Return date: Reserve:
Checked out May 12, 2009 Yes ___

8 Location: Nonfiction

1 Title heading
2 Author's name
3 Publisher, copyright date, and other book information
4 Call number
5 Descriptive info
6 Subject heading(s)
7 Availability status
8 Location information

Try It!

Use the computer catalog to find audio or video sources on a topic of your choice. Ask the librarian if you need help to do this.

Research

Understanding Call Numbers

All nonfiction books in the library have **call numbers**. The books are arranged on the shelves according to these numbers. Call numbers are usually based on the **Dewey decimal classification** system, which divides nonfiction books into 10 subject categories.

000–099	**General Works**	500–599	**Sciences**
100–199	**Philosophy**	600–699	**Technology**
200–299	**Religion**	700–799	**Arts and Recreation**
300–399	**Social Sciences**	800–899	**Literature**
400–499	**Languages**	900–999	**History and Geography**

A call number often has a decimal in it, followed by the first letter of an author's name. Note how the following call numbers are ordered on the shelf.

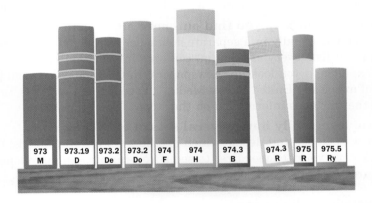

973 M | 973.19 D | 973.2 De | 973.2 Do | 974 F | 974 H | 974.3 B | 974.3 R | 975 R | 975.5 Ry

Try It!

Make up appropriate titles (based on their placement in the Dewey decimal classification system) and authors for three of the books on the shelf above.

Identifying the Parts of a Book

Each part of a book provides valuable information. The **title page** includes the title of the book, the author's name, and the publisher's name and city. The **copyright page** follows with the year the book was published. The **preface, foreword,** or **introduction** comes before the table of contents and tells why the book was written. The **table of contents** lists the names and page numbers of sections and chapters in the book. At the end of the book, you may find at least one **appendix,** containing various maps, tables, and lists. Finally, the **index** is an alphabetical list of important topics and their page numbers in the book.

Using Reference Books

A reference book is a special kind of nonfiction book that contains specific facts or background information. The reference section includes encyclopedias, dictionaries, almanacs, and so on. Usually, reference books cannot be checked out, so you must use them in the library.

Referring to Encyclopedias

An encyclopedia is a set of books (or a CD-ROM) that contains basic information on topics from A to Z. Topics are arranged alphabetically.

Tips for Using Encyclopedias

- **At the end of an article, there is often a list of related articles.**
  You can read these other articles to learn more about your topic.

- **The index can help you find out more about your topic.**
  The index is usually in a separate volume or at the end of the last volume. It lists every article that contains information about a topic. For example, if you look up "newspapers" in the index, you would find a list of articles—"United States Media," "Freedom of the Press," and so on—that includes information on that topic. (See below.)

- **Libraries usually have several sets of encyclopedias.**
  Review each set and decide which one best serves your needs. (Always check with your teacher first to see if you can use an encyclopedia as a source for your research.)

Sample Encyclopedia Index

Encyclopedia volume ———→ **Voting Rights V:** 308 with pictures and illustrations
Democracy **D: 235**
Free Press **F: 213**
Page numbers ———→ Minorities and the vote **V: 310–312**
Women **V: 311**
See also related topics in the Voting Rights *article.*
Related topics ———→ Fraud in elections **V: 312**
Electronic balloting **C: 375**
Paper ballots **C: 375**
Photo ID cards **V: 312**

Consulting Other Reference Books

Most libraries contain several types of reference books in addition to encyclopedias. The most common ones are listed below.

Almanacs

Almanacs are books filled with facts and statistics about many different subjects. *The World Almanac and Book of Facts* contains celebrity profiles; statistics about politics, business, and sports; plus consumer information.

Atlases

Atlases contain detailed maps of the world, continents, countries, and so on. They also contain statistics and related information. Specialized atlases cover topics such as outer space and the oceans.

Dictionaries

Dictionaries contain definitions of words and their origins. Biographical dictionaries focus on famous people. Specialized dictionaries deal with science, history, medicine, and other subjects.

Directories

Directories list information about groups of people, businesses, and organizations. The most widely used directories are telephone books.

Periodical Indexes

Periodical indexes list articles in magazines and newspapers. These indexes are arranged alphabetically by subject.

- The *Readers' Guide to Periodical Literature* lists articles from many publications. (See page **382.**)
- The *New York Times Index* lists articles from the *New York Times* newspaper.

Other Reference Books

Some reference books do not fit into any one category but are recognized by their names:

- *Facts on File* includes thousands of short but informative facts about events, discoveries, people, and places.
- *Facts About the Presidents* presents information about all of the presidents of the United States.
- *Bartlett's Familiar Quotations* lists thousands of quotations from famous people.

Checking a Dictionary

A dictionary gives many types of information:

- **Guide words:** These are the first and last words on the page. Guide words show whether the word you are looking for will be found alphabetically on that page.
- **Entry words:** Each word defined in a dictionary is called an entry word. Entry words are listed alphabetically.
- **Etymology:** Many dictionaries give etymologies (word histories) for certain words. An etymology tells what language an English word came from, how the word entered our language, and when it was first used.
- **Syllable divisions:** A dictionary tells you where you may divide a word.
- **Pronunciation and accent marks:** A dictionary tells you how to pronounce a word and also provides a key to pronunciation symbols, usually at the bottom of each page.
- **Illustrations:** For some entries, an illustration, a photograph, or a drawing is provided.
- **Parts of speech:** A dictionary tells you what part(s) of speech a word is, using these abbreviations:

n.	**noun**		*tr. v.*	**transitive verb**
pron.	**pronoun**		*interj.*	**interjection**
intr. v.	**intransitive verb**		*conj.*	**conjunction**
adj.	**adjective**		*adv.*	**adverb**
prep.	**preposition**			

- **Spelling and capitalization:** The dictionary shows the acceptable spelling, as well as capitalization, for words. (For some words, more than one spelling is given.)
- **Definitions:** Some dictionaries are large enough to list all of the meanings for a word. Most standard-size dictionaries, however, will list only three or four of the most commonly accepted meanings. Take time to read all of the meanings to be sure that you are using the word correctly.

Try It!

Look up the word *set* in the dictionary. Name the parts of speech that are listed for it and tell how many definitions there are for each.

Research

Sample Dictionary Page

Guide words

Entry word

cir·cle (sûr′kəl) *n.* **1.** A plane curve everywhere equidistant from a given fixed point, the center. **2.** A planar region bounded by a circle. **3.** Something, such as a ring, shaped like such a plane curve. **4.** A circular course, circuit, or orbit. **5.** A traffic circle. **6.** A curved section or tier of seats in a theater. **7.** A series or process that finishes at its starting point or repeats itself; a cycle. **8.** A group of people sharing an interest, activity, or achievement. **9.** A territorial or administrative division, esp. of a province, in some European countries. **10.** A sphere of influence or interest; domain. **11.** *Logic* A vicious circle. ❖ *v.* **-cled, -cling, -cles** —*tr.* **1.** To make or form a circle around; enclose. **2.** To move in a circle around. —*intr.* To move in a circle. —*idiom:* **circle the wagons** To take a defensive position. [ME *cercle* < OFr. < Lat. *circulus,* dim. of *circus,* circle < Gk. *kirkos, krikos.*] —**cir′cler** (-klər) *n.*

Etymology

circle graph *n.* See **pie chart.**

Syllable divisions

cir·clet (sûr′klĭt) *n.* A small circle, esp. a circular ornament. [ME *cerclet* < OFr., dim. of *cercle,* circle. See CIRCLE.]

Pronunciation and accent marks

cir·cuit (sûr′kĭt) *n.* **1a.** A closed, usu. circular line that goes around an object or area. **b.** The region enclosed by such a line. **2a.** A path or route that returns to its starting point. **b.** The act of following such a path or route. **c.** A journey made on such a path or route. **3.** *Electronics* **a.** A closed path followed by an electric current. **b.** A configuration of electrically or electromagnetically connected components or devices. **4a.** A regular or accustomed course from place to place; a round: *the lecture circuit.* **b.** The area or district thus covered, esp. a territory under the jurisdiction of a judge in which periodic court sessions are held. **5a.** An association of theaters among which plays, acts, or films move for presentation. **b.** A group of nightclubs, show halls, or resorts at which entertainers appear in turn. **c.** An association of teams or clubs. **d.** A series of competitions held in different places. ❖ *intr. & tr.v.* **-cuit·ed, -cuit·ing, -cuits** To make a circuit or circuit of. [ME, circumference < OFr. < Lat. *circuitus,* a going around < p. part. of *circumīre,* to go around : *circum-,* circum- + *īre,* to go; see ei- in App.]

Illustration

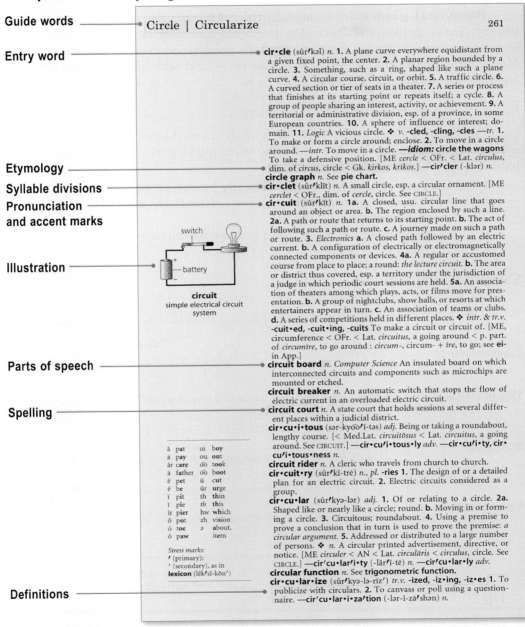

switch

battery

circuit
simple electrical circuit system

Parts of speech

circuit board *n. Computer Science* An insulated board on which interconnected circuits and components such as microchips are mounted or etched.

circuit breaker *n.* An automatic switch that stops the flow of electric current in an overloaded electric circuit.

Spelling

circuit court *n.* A state court that holds sessions at several different places within a judicial district.

cir·cu·i·tous (sər-kyoo′ĭ-təs) *adj.* Being or taking a roundabout, lengthy course. [< Med.Lat. *circuitōsus* < Lat. *circuitus,* a going around. See CIRCUIT.] —**cir·cu′i·tous·ly** *adv.* —**cir·cu′i·ty, cir·cu′i·tous·ness** *n.*

circuit rider *n.* A cleric who travels from church to church.

cir·cuit·ry (sûr′kĭ-trē) *n., pl.* **-ries 1.** The design of or a detailed plan for an electric circuit. **2.** Electric circuits considered as a group.

cir·cu·lar (sûr′kyə-lər) *adj.* **1.** Of or relating to a circle. **2a.** Shaped like or nearly like a circle; round. **b.** Moving in or forming a circle. **3.** Circuitous; roundabout. **4.** Using a premise to prove a conclusion that in turn is used to prove the premise: *a circular argument.* **5.** Addressed or distributed to a large number of persons. ❖ *n.* A circular printed advertisement, directive, or notice. [ME *circuler* < AN < Lat. *circulāris* < *circulus,* circle. See CIRCLE.] —**cir′cu·lar′i·ty** (-lăr′ĭ-tē) *n.* —**cir′cu·lar·ly** *adv.*

circular function *n.* See **trigonometric function.**

Definitions

cir·cu·lar·ize (sûr′kyə-lə-rīz′) *tr.v.* **-ized, -iz·ing, -iz·es 1.** To publicize with circulars. **2.** To canvass or poll using a questionnaire. —**cir′cu·lar·i·za′tion** (-lər-ĭ-zā′shən) *n.*

ă	pat	oi	boy
ā	pay	ou	out
âr	care	ŏŏ	took
ä	father	ōō	boot
ĕ	pet	ŭ	cut
ē	be	ûr	urge
ĭ	pit	th	thin
ī	pie	*th*	this
îr	pier	hw	which
ŏ	pot	zh	vision
ō	toe	ə	about,
ô	paw		item

Stress marks:
′ (primary);
′ (secondary), as in
lexicon (lĕk′sĭ-kŏn′)

Using Periodical Guides

Periodical guides are located in the reference or periodical section of the library. These guides alphabetically list topics and articles found in magazines, newspapers, and journals. Some guides are printed volumes and some are CD's. Many libraries are linking to Web sites for periodical searches. Ask your librarian for the most up-to-date Web site.

Readers' Guide to Periodical Literature

The *Readers' Guide to Periodical Literature* is a well-known periodical reference source and is found in most libraries. The following tips will help you look up your topic in this and other similar resources:

- Articles are always listed alphabetically by author and topic.
- Some topics are subdivided, with each article listed under the appropriate subtopic.
- Cross-references refer to related topic entries where you may find more articles pertinent to your topic.

Sample *Readers' Guide* Format

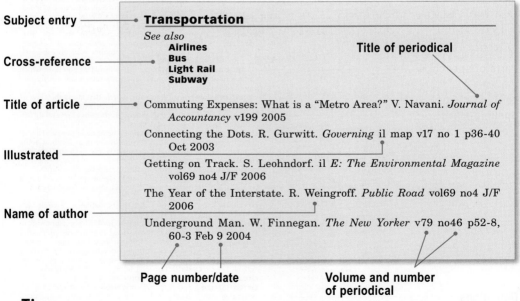

Subject entry — **Transportation**

See also
Cross-reference — **Airlines**
Bus
Light Rail
Subway

Title of periodical

Title of article — Commuting Expenses: What is a "Metro Area?" V. Navani. *Journal of Accountancy* v199 2005

Connecting the Dots. R. Gurwitt. *Governing* il map v17 no 1 p36-40 Oct 2003

Illustrated — Getting on Track. S. Leohndorf. il *E: The Environmental Magazine* vol69 no4 J/F 2006

The Year of the Interstate. R. Weingroff. *Public Road* vol69 no4 J/F 2006

Name of author — Underground Man. W. Finnegan. *The New Yorker* v79 no46 p52-8, 60-3 Feb 9 2004

Page number/date

Volume and number of periodical

Tip

When you find a listing for your topic, write down the name and issue date of the magazine and the title and page numbers of the article. Your librarian may get the periodical for you, or you may need to find it yourself.

Research Writing
MLA Research Paper

Thomas Jefferson once said, "If a nation expects to be ignorant and free, in a state of civilization, it expects what never was and never will be." The point is, maintaining a civilization takes work and requires knowledge. What sort of knowledge? Franklin D. Roosevelt said, "If civilization is to survive, we must cultivate the science of human relationships—the ability of all peoples, of all kinds, to live together, in the same world, at peace." In other words, civilization depends on the social interaction of all sorts of people.

In this chapter, you will learn to write an MLA research paper about an important social issue. In the process, you will study that issue and communicate what you learn to your classmates. In effect, your research paper itself will serve as one small part of the process by which civilization is maintained.

Writing Guidelines

Subject: A solution to a social issue

Form: MLA research paper

Purpose: To research and explain a solution to a social issue

Audience: Classmates

"Civilization is a movement and not a condition, a voyage and not a harbor."
—Arnold Toynbee

Research Paper

Fidel Novielli got excited as he read a magazine article about "social capitalism." He researched the topic further and wrote the following paper. Margin notes point out important features of organization and formatting.

Meeting the Needs of the Future

Fidel Novielli
Ms. Palacek
Language Arts
23 February 2009

Title Page
Center the title one-third of the way down the page. Center author information two-thirds of the way down.

Meeting the Needs of the Future

THESIS STATEMENT: "Social entrepreneurs" have begun to apply business strategies to human problems, with impressive results.

I. The root problem is that social systems are about 300 years behind the times.
   A. The industrial revolution made businesses competitive and innovative.
   B. Government and other social systems remained uncompetitive.
   C. For 300 years, business continued to evolve, while the social systems fell further behind.

II. The industrial revolution brought new challenges.
   A. The Tofflers explained that society had become more urban.
   B. The rural support system, primarily the family, did not carry over to urban life.
   C. Relocation resulted in poverty, crime, and disease.

III. About 25 years ago, this dichotomy began to change dramatically.
   A. Faced with such need and opportunity, social entrepreneurs began to appear.
   B. Bill Drayton founded Ashoka to help foster . . .

Outline
Center the title one inch from the top of the page. Double-space throughout. Include the outline after the title page and before the first page of the report.

Note: If your teacher requires a title page or an outline, follow the guidelines above or any special instructions you are given.

Novielli 1

Fidel Novielli
Ms. Palecek
Language Arts
23 Feb. 2009

Meeting the Needs of the Future

      In a small community, when tragedy strikes, everyone knows it, and everyone can see how best to step in and help. In the global community, tragedy strikes somewhere every day, but knowing how to respond is much more difficult. Even in the wealthiest countries, far too many social needs remain unmet. In the United States alone, 13.8 million American children live with hunger, and nearly 20 million have little or no health care ("Childhood"). Globally, 30,000 children a day die from malnutrition and disease ("Global").

      Faced with numbers like these, an individual might be tempted to despair and cry out, "I'm only one person. What can I do?" Fortunately, a new breed of concerned citizenry has begun to demonstrate that one person can do a lot, given a little imagination and determination. In the business world, these qualities have long been recognized as the features of an entrepreneur. Now "social entrepreneurs"—sometimes called "social capitalists"— have begun to apply business strategies to human problems, with impressive results.

The entire report is double-spaced.

Beginning The opening grabs the reader's attention with a dramatic comparison.

The beginning part leads up to the thesis statement (underlined).

Research

The Problem

According to Bill Drayton, founder of Ashoka, an organization that promotes social entrepreneurship, the root problem is that social systems are about 300 years behind the times. When the industrial revolution started in the early 1700s, the business sector became competitive and innovative. However, government and other social systems remained uncompetitive, supported by taxes or donations and bolstered by tradition. As business continued to evolve over the centuries, social systems fell further and further behind in their cost-effectiveness (Hammonds).

Worse, the Industrial Age brought new challenges that the old social systems were simply not equipped to handle. As futurists Alvin and Heidi Toffler explain, society had become increasingly urban, drawing people away from farms and villages to work in factories. The social support of rural communities, with their multigenerational families, could not carry over into the cities, where many people had relocated, living alone or in a "nuclear family" of father, mother, and a few children (19-24). As any Dickens novel reveals, and every modern metropolitan newspaper repeats, far too often this relocation has resulted in poverty, crime, and disease.

The Solution

Drayton believes that roughly 25 years ago, this situation began to change dramatically. The social sectors

Novielli 3

started applying the lessons of business. In his words, "It was like hearing the ice breaking up at the end of winter in a lake. Creak, creak, groan, crash! The need was so big, the gap so huge, the opportunity to learn was right before people's eyes" (Hammonds). Faced with such need and opportunity, a new breed of entrepreneur began to emerge, this time in the social sector. Drayton created Ashoka as a means of fostering this social entrepreneurship on a global scale. His goal is literally to change the world.

A quotation is integrated into the paper for voice and authority.

If that seems audacious, it is important to understand Drayton's vision and his experience. As one former employer explains, "Everything that Drayton did he focused on the fundamentals." In other words, Drayton believes in attacking the root of a problem. For example, while serving as assistant administrator for the Environmental Protection Agency, he successfully championed a "bubble" method of cheaply and effectively combating pollution. Under this plan, pollution is tackled as a whole, rather than as individual processes. Instead of dictating specific details for reducing emissions, the plan gives each business an emissions target, and that business can determine the most cost-effective way to meet that goal. Businesses can even trade gains at one location against shortfalls at another, to bring the overall level of pollution down. This "bubble and trading" plan quickly became the official policy of the U.S. Since then, it has also been included

The writer provides an example to clarify a point.

Novielli 4

as a central part of the Kyoto Protocol for international emissions, and the European Parliament has adopted it for their global emissions-trading market (Bornstein 53–58).

It is this sort of "fundamental solution" thinking that characterizes social entrepreneurship and that distinguishes it from traditional social work. Traditional social programs tend to be a one-sided, top-down approach to solving a problem. This approach involves the *have's* handing something down to the *have-not's*. More often than not, a response focuses on a crisis. Social capitalism, on the other hand, seeks to change the situation that causes the need. It looks for opportunities by which the needy can better themselves. In the process, society benefits as well.

Consider the example of Erzsébet Szekeres of Hungary, whose son Tibor was born with microcephalus (an abnormally small skull) and severe mental retardation. Under the strain of caring for Tibor during his early years, Szekeres' marriage and career began to suffer. Friends and family urged the woman to put her son in a state institution and go on with her life. Szekeres saw, however, that these institutions were little more than prisons where the severely handicapped were shut away from public view. She dreamed of a group home where people like Tibor could care for themselves, with assistance, and even have meaningful work.

It took years of determined effort on Szekeres' part to make that dream a reality. Often, the government itself

> When a source has page numbers, the appropriate numbers are included in the citation.

> A technical term is defined for the reader.

Novielli 5

opposed her efforts because she was not a member of the health-care profession. Eventually, however, with two loans from disability organizations, she purchased an abandoned farming cooperative and turned it into a community for the disabled. Today, this facility includes dorm-style rooms, a cafeteria, a community room where dances are held and movies are shown, and work facilities where people like her son earn money by assembling curtain clips and other such assembly-line jobs. To date, Szekeres has created 21 institutions across Hungary, where more than 600 multiply-disabled people live and work. Her efforts are even changing the way the state itself deals with the handicapped (Bornstein 98–116).

Perhaps an even clearer example of social capitalism is shown in the food-bank program created by Wojciech Onyszkiewicz in Poland. During the years that Soviet communism ruled Poland, the very existence of poverty was denied. After the fall of the Soviet Union, it was estimated that 20 percent of the population lived below the poverty line, and 31 percent of those in poverty were multi-child families. While rural communities often had a surplus of food, there were no systems in place for getting it to urban populations ("Ashoka"). In addition, rural citizens were not happy about giving charity to people they perceived as "parasites" (Bornstein 201). On the other hand, these same rural people envied the

Each paragraph contains effective supporting details.

An example helps explain "social capitalism."

opportunities for education and culture that were available to urban citizens.

Onyszkiewicz came up with a plan in which rural communities would donate excess food for urban use, and in exchange, rural children would travel to the cities to help distribute that food, visit museums, attend sessions of parliament, and take part in other such activities ("Ashoka"). Under a similar plan, Onyszkiewicz organized computer training for rural children by recruiting physically disabled computer users from the city. In exchange for their expertise, these city dwellers are able to visit the countryside. Villagers prepare wheelchair ramps and arrange outdoor activities that the urbanites could not otherwise experience (Bornstein 201). In both of these cases, "commodities" are exchanged in a very capitalistic manner, and in both cases, important human needs are met.

Ashoka itself is actually another example of social capitalism at work. The organization's goal is to identify promising social entrepreneurs in the earliest stages of their work and to provide support to help that work flourish. While some of this support is monetary—a small stipend to allow the blossoming entrepreneur to work full-time on the project—most of it is less tangible. Ashoka fellows "get support, ideas, and, quite literally, protection," as in the case of a Brazilian Ashoka fellow whose work in drug rehabilitation resulted in attacks by local police. The

The writer provides clear explanation throughout the paper.

Smooth-reading sentences make the paper very "readable."

Novielli 7

organization took the case to the local governor, and the attacks stopped (Hammonds). What makes this support capitalistic is that by applying it early in the work of a social entrepreneur, Ashoka gets the greatest "return" on its investment—the most good from the least assistance.

Conclusion

Ending
The closing paragraphs summarize the main points and leave the reader with a final thought.

These are only a few examples from thousands of programs around the world. (Ashoka alone has more than 1,500 fellows.) Social entrepreneurs are tackling problems at all levels, from helping inner-city children fill out college applications to training health-care workers for the millions of AIDS victims in South Africa. It is no exaggeration to say that their efforts often lift entire communities out of poverty. Since 2004, Fast Company and the Monitor Group have given awards recognizing the 25 best social entrepreneurs each year ("25"). The competition is stiff, and the stories of the finalists are every bit as inspiring as those of the award-winners.

Bill Drayton believes that the next step in this social evolution is a partnering of business and social entrepreneurs, which he sees as only natural. It was the splitting of business and social concerns 300 years ago that was unnatural. Eventually, he believes, everyone will be a change-maker, and as a result, everyone will feel that his or her life has meaning.

Novielli 8

Works Cited

"Ashoka Fellow Profile—Wojciech Onyszkiewicz." <u>Ashoka</u>.
    1996. Ashoka. 23 Feb. 2006 <http://www.ashoka.org/
    fellows/viewprofile3.cfm?reid=97167>.

Bornstein, David. <u>How to Change the World: Social
    Entrepreneurs and the Power of New Ideas</u>. New York:
    Oxford, 2004.

"Childhood Hunger in the United States." <u>Learn About
    Hunger</u>. 2006. America's Second Harvest. 10 Feb. 2006
    <http://www.secondharvest.org/learn_about_hunger/
    child_hunger_facts.html>.

"Global Hunger Facts." <u>Fast</u>. 19 Feb. 2006. Concern
    Worldwide. 10 Feb. 2006 <http://www.concernusa.org/
    fast/GlobalHungerFacts.asp>.

Hammonds, Keith H. "A Lever Long Enough to Move the
    World." <u>Fast Company</u>. Jan. 2005: 61.

Toffler, Alvin, and Heidi Toffler. <u>Creating a New Civilization</u>.
    Atlanta: Turner, 1995.

"25 Entrepreneurs Who Are Changing the World." <u>Fast
    Company</u>. Jan. 2006. 19 Feb. 2006 <http://
    www.fastcompany.com/social/>.

A separate page alphabetically lists sources cited in the paper.

Lines that run over are indented five spaces.

Respond to the reading. Answer the following questions.

Ideas (1) What details make this report convincing? (2) How are the two terms "social entrepreneurship" and "social capitalism" alike and different?

Organization (3) Why is the "Problem" part shorter than the "Solution" part?

Voice (4) Why do you think the author chose to quote Bill Drayton's exact words about the change in society 25 years ago?

Prewriting

Your research paper must start with planning. During this prewriting stage, you will organize your initial thoughts, decide what the type of information you need, and gather that information in preparation for writing your paper.

Keys to Effective Prewriting

1. For your topic, choose a social issue that interests you.

2. Make a list of questions you want to have answered about that subject.

3. Use a gathering grid to organize your research questions and answers. Use note cards to keep track of longer answers. (See page 397.)

4. Be careful to record the sources of any information you summarize or quote.

5. Note the publication details of all your sources, for making a works-cited page later. (See pages 429–438.)

6. Make sure that you find enough to say about your topic, including an explanation of the problem and a discussion of possible solutions.

Prewriting Selecting a Topic

When you brainstorm for a specific topic on a general subject such as "a social issue," you can make a cluster. Fidel made a cluster using stages of life as main categories. Then he listed specific examples of social issues for each age category. You can see part of his cluster below.

Cluster

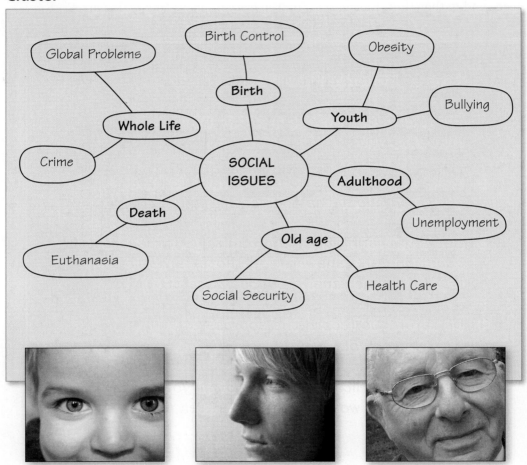

Prewrite

Make a cluster. To find a topic for your research paper, make a cluster. Start by writing the general subject inside a circle. Next, add circles around it with main categories related to social issues. (You may choose to use stages of life, as Fidel did, or something different.) Around those categories, list specific issues. Choose an issue that interests you as the topic for your research paper.

Sizing Up Your Topic

An effective research paper about an important social issue should cover three main areas.

- **The issue:** What is the social issue? Define the problem.
- **The solution:** How can the problem be solved? Explain a likely solution. This might also include a history of solutions that have been tried in the past.
- **The conclusion:** What steps should be taken next? Start with a summary of the issue and the suggested solution. Then include a call to action, or leave the reader with something to think about.

When Fidel prepared his report on social entrepreneurship, he did some quick initial research. He took notes about what he found.

Research Notes

What is the issue?
- The human race is facing global problems of hunger, disease, overpopulation, and poverty.
- Current social systems seem unable to address these problems.

What is the solution?
- Social entrepreneurship looks for new ways to solve old problems.
- Social capitalism makes problem solving cost-effective, not just charity.
- This approach matches needs with opportunities so that everyone benefits.
- It tackles the root of a problem rather than treating the symptoms.

What are the next steps?
- Continue to encourage social entrepreneurs.
- Look for ways that common people can be involved.
- Match business interests with social needs.

Fidel found sufficient information to know that there would be plenty to write about for his topic. He understood that in order to make his points, he would have to describe specific examples of social capitalism. Finding those examples would require further research.

Prewrite

Size up your topic. Look up your topic on the Internet or use another reliable basic resource. List the key details you find. Are there enough details to support a research paper? If not, consider another topic.

Prewriting Using a Gathering Grid

Fidel made a grid to organize the information he found during his research about social capitalism. Down the left-hand side, he listed questions about the topic. Across the top, he listed sources that answered those questions. For answers too long to fit in the grid, Fidel used note cards. (See the next page.) Part of Fidel's grid is shown below.

Gathering Grid

SOCIAL CAPITALISM	How to Change the World (book)	"Childhood Hunger" (Web page)	"A Lever Long Enough . . ." (magazine article)
What is the problem?	See card 2.	13.8 million children in the United States living with hunger	See card 1.
What is a solution?	Apply business entrepreneurship to change the world.		See card 3.
What next steps are needed?	People have to believe the problems can be solved. (282)		Match business needs with public needs.

Prewrite

Create a gathering grid. List questions in the left-hand column of your grid. Across the top, list sources that you will use. Fill in the grid with answers that you find. Use note cards for longer, more detailed answers.

Creating Note Cards

A gathering grid allows you to see your research at a glance, but sometimes you need space for an in-depth answer. In that case, use note cards. Number each new card and write a question at the top. Then answer the question with a list, a quotation, or a paraphrase (see page **398**). At the bottom, identify the source of the information (including a page number if appropriate).

Note Cards

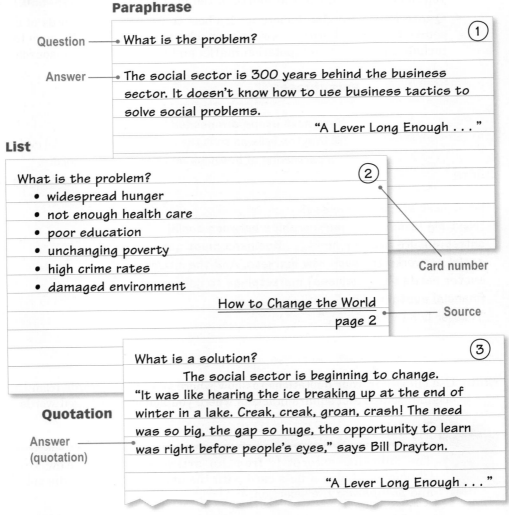

Paraphrase

Question ———• What is the problem?   ①

Answer ———• The social sector is 300 years behind the business
sector. It doesn't know how to use business tactics to
solve social problems.
                                        "A Lever Long Enough . . ."

List

What is the problem?   ②
  • widespread hunger
  • not enough health care
  • poor education
  • unchanging poverty
  • high crime rates   Card number
  • damaged environment
                              How to Change the World
                                        page 2   — Source

What is a solution?   ③
        The social sector is beginning to change.
    "It was like hearing the ice breaking up at the end of
Quotation   winter in a lake. Creak, creak, groan, crash! The need
                was so big, the gap so huge, the opportunity to learn
Answer ———• was right before people's eyes," says Bill Drayton.
(quotation)
                                        "A Lever Long Enough . . ."

Prewrite

Create note cards. Make note cards like the examples above whenever your answers are too long to fit on your gathering grid.

Avoiding Plagiarism

It's always important to give other people credit for their words and ideas. If you don't, that is called **plagiarism,** and it is stealing. As you note facts and ideas during your research, take care to note the source, and to indicate whether your note is a paraphrase or a quotation.

- **Paraphrase:** It's usually best to put ideas you find into your own words, so that your paper sounds like you. This is called paraphrasing. Still, you must give credit to the source of the ideas. (See pages **548–550**.)

- **Quote exact words:** Sometimes it's best to use the exact words of a source to add authority or interesting color to your report. Be sure to include those words in quotation marks and give credit to the source.

Paraphrase

> What next steps are needed?
> Bill Drayton believes that the next step in this social evolution
> is a partnering of business and social entrepreneurs.
>
> "A Lever Long Enough . . ."

Quote

> What next steps are needed?
> "Next big idea: Global partnerships between social
> entrepreneurs and business . . . Business must use
> social networks to reach new markets. And the citizen
> sector needs the [business] marketplace to gain
> financial sustainability."
> "A Lever Long Enough . . ."

Note: Use ellipses in your quotations to show where you left out words from the original source and square brackets where you added or changed words.

Try It!

The following excerpt is from an article entitled "A New Breed of Champion." Label a note card with the question "What is the solution?" and *paraphrase* the selection.

Many people assume that wealth and poverty go hand in hand. That is to say, ever since the invention of money, some people have had a lot and others have had little.

Keeping Track of Your Sources

As you do your research, keep careful track of the sources of information you find so that you can correctly cite them in your final paper. You'll need to record the following information.

- **Book:** Author's name. Title. Publisher and city. Copyright date.
- **Magazine:** Author's name. Article title. Magazine title. Date published. Page numbers.
- **Newspaper:** Author's name. Article title. Newspaper title. City. Date published. Section. Page numbers.
- **Internet:** Author's name (if listed). Page title. Site title. Date posted or copyright date (if listed). Site sponsor. Date accessed. Electronic address.
- **Videocassette or DVD:** Title. Distributor. Release date. Medium.

Source Notes

Book
David Bornstein. How to Change the World: Social Entrepreneurs and the Power of New Ideas. Oxford UP. New York. 2004.

Magazine
Keith H. Hammonds. "A Lever Long Enough to Move the World." Fast Company. January 2005. Page 61.

Newspaper
Andi Atwater. "State Shuts Medicaid Payment System." The Wichita Eagle. February 11, 2006. Section E. Page 2.

Internet
"Childhood Hunger in the United States." Learn About Hunger. Posted in 2006. Accessed February 10, 2006. <http://www.secondharvest.org/learn_about_hunger/child_hunger_facts.html>

Interview
Lu Tribby. E-mail. January 31, 2006.

Television Program
"Delivering the Goods." Rx for Survival: A Global Health Challenge. WNET, New York. February 13, 2006.

Prewrite

List sources. Keep a list of each of your sources with the information shown above. Whenever you find a new source, add it to the list.

Writing Your Thesis Statement

With your research completed, it is time to write a thesis statement. It states the main idea of your paper and guides your writing. The rest of your paper will serve to explain and support this main idea. You can use this formula to help you write your thesis statement.

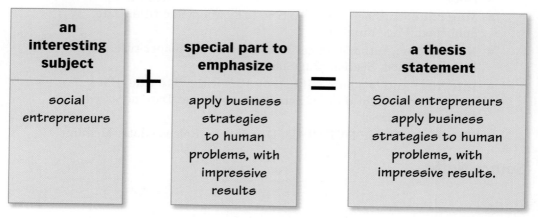

an interesting subject		special part to emphasize		a thesis statement
social entrepreneurs	**+**	apply business strategies to human problems, with impressive results	**=**	Social entrepreneurs apply business strategies to human problems, with impressive results.

Sample Thesis Statements

The globalization of human civilization (an interesting subject) **means that a threat to one part of the world threatens the well-being of the whole world** (a special part to emphasize).

In the Information Age (an interesting subject), **wealth is no longer a limited commodity to be hoarded by some and denied to others** (a special part to emphasize).

Gandhi recognized a new type of ethics (an interesting subject) **based not on rules but on empathy** (a special part to emphasize).

Prewrite

Form your thesis statement. Review your research notes and choose a main point you could make about your topic. Using the formula above, write a thesis statement for that idea.

Research

Outlining Your Ideas

One way to organize and plan your research paper is to make an outline. An outline is like a map of the ideas in your paper. You can list those ideas in either a topic outline that lists ideas as words or phrases or as a sentence outline that lists ideas in full sentences. (Also see page **591**.)

Below is the first part of a sentence outline for the paper on pages **385–392**. Notice that the outline begins with the thesis statement. Next, it lists the topic sentence for each middle paragraph as a major point, with a Roman numeral. Below each topic sentence is a list of supporting points, each identified by a capital letter. Compare this partial outline with the first two paragraphs of the finished paper.

Sentence Outline

Remember, in an outline, if you have a I., you must have at least a II. If you have an A., you must have at least a B.

Thesis statement

THESIS STATEMENT: "Social entrepreneurs" have begun to apply business strategies to human problems, with impressive results.

Major Points (I., II.)

I. The root problem is that social systems are about 300 years behind the times.

Supporting details (A., B., C.)

  A. The industrial revolution made businesses competitive and innovative.

  B. Government and other social systems remained uncompetitive.

  C. For 300 years, business continued to evolve, while the social systems fell further behind.

II. The industrial revolution brought new challenges.

  A. The Tofflers explain that society had become more urban.

  B. The rural support system, primarily the family, did not carry over to urban life.

  C. Relocation resulted in poverty, crime, and disease.

Prewrite

Create your outline. Write a sentence outline for your research paper, using the details from your research. Be sure that each topic sentence (I., II., III., . . .) supports the thesis statement and that each detail (A., B., C., . . .) supports its topic sentence. Use your outline as a guide for writing your first draft.

Writing

Now that you have finished your research and prepared an outline, it's time to begin writing your paper. This is your first attempt at connecting your thoughts and feelings about the topic. Don't worry about getting everything perfect in this first draft; you'll have time to revise your paper later. For now, just get things down on paper in a way that makes sense to you. The following keys will help.

Keys to Effective Writing

1. Use your first paragraph to get your reader's attention, introduce your topic, and present your thesis statement.

2. In the next section, define and explain the social problem.

3. After that, present a solution or solutions, with examples.

4. In the final section, summarize the paper and give the reader a call to action.

5. Remember to cite the sources of any ideas you paraphrase or quote and list those sources alphabetically on a works-cited page.

Writing Starting Your Research Paper

The opening paragraphs of your research paper are critical. They must grab your reader's attention, introduce your topic, and present your thesis statement. Here are several effective ways to begin your opening.

- Start with an interesting fact (or question).

   Hunger and disease are not strangers in the United States. Nearly 14 million children live with hunger, and almost 20 million have little or no health care.

- Start with a quotation.

   "It was like hearing the ice breaking up at the end of the winter . . . " said Drayton.

Beginning Paragraph(s)

The beginning paragraph starts with an interesting observation.

> In a small community, when tragedy strikes, everyone knows it, and everyone can see how best to step in and help. In our global community, tragedy strikes somewhere every day, but knowing how to respond is much more difficult. In the United States alone, 12.4 million children live with hunger ("Childhood"), and nearly nine million have no little or no health care ("Coverage"). Globally, 30,000 children a day die from malnutrition and disease ("Global").
>
> Faced with numbers like these, we might be tempted to despair and cry out, "I'm only one person. What can I do?" Fortunately, a new breed of social champion has begun to demonstrate that one person can do a lot, given a little imagination and determination. In the business world, these qualities have long been recognized as the features of an entrepreneur. Now "social entrepreneurs"—sometimes called "social capitalists"—have begun to apply business strategies to human problems, with impressive results.

The opening ends with the thesis (focus) statement.

Write

Write your beginning paragraph(s). Using one of these approaches, write your opening paragraph(s). Be sure to grab the reader's interest at the beginning, then introduce your topic, and end with a clear thesis statement.

Writing Developing the Middle Part

In the middle part of your research paper, give details that support your thesis statement. Start by defining the social problem, giving examples, if necessary. Then present one or more possible solutions, again giving examples.

Each middle paragraph should cover one main idea. Near the beginning of the paragraph, include a topic sentence. (Usually, the topic sentence is the first sentence in the paragraph. However, some paragraphs may begin with a sentence that provides a transition from the previous paragraph.) After the topic sentence, include sentences with supporting details. Use your sentence outline as a guide to your writing.

Middle Paragraphs

The first middle paragraph(s) define the problem.

All the details in each paragraph support the topic sentence (underlined).

The Problem

According to Bill Drayton, founder of Ashoka, an organization that fosters social entrepreneurship, the root problem is that social systems are about 300 years behind the times. When the industrial revolution started in the early 1700s, the business sector became competitive and innovative. However, government and other social systems remained uncompetitive, supported by taxes or donations and bolstered by tradition. As business continued to evolve in expertise and influence over the centuries, social systems fell further and further behind in their cost-effectiveness (Hammonds).

Worse, the Industrial Age brought new challenges that the old social systems were simply not equipped to handle. As futurists Alvin and Heidi Toffler explain, society had become increasingly urban, drawing people away from farms and villages to work in factories. The social support of rural communities, with their multigenerational families, could not carry over into the cities, where many people had relocated, living alone or in a "nuclear family" of father, mother, and a few children (19-24). As any Dickens novel reveals, and every modern metropolitan newspaper repeats, far too often this relocation has resulted in poverty, crime, and disease.

The Solution

<u>Drayton believes that roughly 25 years ago, this situation began to change dramatically.</u> In his words, "It was like hearing the ice breaking up at the end of winter in a lake. Creak, creak, groan, crash! The need was so big, the gap so huge, the opportunity to learn was right before people's eyes" (Hammonds). Faced with such need and opportunity, a new breed of entrepreneur began to emerge, this time in the citizen sector. Drayton created Ashoka as a means of fostering this social entrepreneurship on a global scale. His goal is literally to change the world.

<u>If that seems audacious, it is important to understand Drayton's vision and his experience.</u> As one former . . .

> The next middle paragraphs present one or more solutions, with examples.

> Sentences are arranged so that the reader can easily follow the ideas.

Write

Write your middle paragraphs. Keep these tips in mind as you write.

1. Use a topic sentence and supporting details in each paragraph.
2. Refer to your outline for direction. (See page 401.)
3. Add parenthetical references to give credit to all sources. (See page 426.)

Writing Ending Your Research Paper

Your ending paragraph should sum up your research and bring your paper to a thoughtful close. To accomplish that, you might . . .

- remind the reader of the thesis of the paper.
- give a "call to action" for the future.
- leave the reader with something to think about.

Ending Paragraph(s)

The conclusion summarizes the thesis.

The writer points out a next step for people to take.

Conclusion

These are only a few examples from thousands of programs around the world. (Ashoka alone has more than 1,500 fellows.) Social entrepreneurs are tackling problems at all levels, from helping inner-city children fill out college applications, to training workers for the millions of AIDS victims in South Africa. It is no exaggeration to say that their efforts often lift entire communities out of poverty. Since 2004, Fast Company and the Monitor Group have given awards recognizing the twenty-five best social entrepreneurs each year ("25"). The competition is stiff, and the stories of the finalists are every bit as inspiring as those of the award-winners.

Bill Drayton believes that the next step in this social evolution is a partnering of business and social entrepreneurs, which he sees as only natural. It was the splitting of . . .

Write

Write your ending paragraph(s). Draft your ending paragraph(s) using the guidelines above.

Note: Review your first draft. Read your draft to make sure it is complete. Check your research notes and outline to make sure you haven't forgotten any important details. In the margins and between the lines, make notes about anything you should change.

Creating Your Works-Cited Page

The purpose of a works-cited page is simply to let your readers find and read the sources you used. Work from the notes you have taken and format the sources you used. Then list those sources in alphabetical order. For additional information about the standard format of common types of sources see pages **429–438**. Also review the works-cited page on **392**.

Book

Bornstein, David. How to Change the World: Social Entrepreneurs and the Power of New Ideas. New York: Oxford UP, 2004.

Magazine

Hammonds, Keith H. "A Lever Long Enough to Move the World." Fast Company Jan. 2005: 61.

Newspaper

Atwater, Andi. "State Shuts Medicaid Payment System." The Wichita Eagle 11 Feb. 2006, sec. E: 2.

Internet

"Childhood Hunger in the United States." Learn About Hunger. 2006. America's Second Harvest. 10 Feb. 2006. <http://www.secondharvest.org/ learn_about_hunger/child_hunger_facts.html>.

Interview

Tribby, Lu. E-mail to the author. 31 Jan. 2006.

Television Program

"Delivering the Goods." Rx for Survival: A Global Health Challenge. WNET, New York. 10 Feb. 2006.

Write

Format your sources. Check your paper and your list of sources (page 399) to see which sources you actually used. Then follow these directions.

1. Write your sources using the guidelines above. You can write them on a sheet of paper or on note cards.

2. List your sources in alphabetical order.

3. Create your works-cited page. (See the example on page 392.)

Revising

In first draft of your research paper, you put your thoughts down in a logical order. Now it's time to revise. During revising, you make changes to ensure that your ideas are clear and interesting, the organization is smooth, the voice sounds knowledgeable, the words are specific, and the sentences are varied.

Keys to Effective Revising

1. Read your entire draft to get an overall sense of your research paper.

2. Review your thesis statement to be sure that it clearly states your main point about the topic.

3. Be certain that your beginning engages the reader and that your ending offers an insightful final thought.

4. Check that the middle part clearly and completely supports the thesis statement.

5. Review and adjust your voice to sound knowledgeable and interested in the topic.

6. Check for effective word choice and sentence fluency.

Revising Improving Your Writing

A first draft is never a finished paper. There is always room for improvement. In the following paragraphs, Fidel makes several revisions. Each improves the *ideas, organization, voice, word choice,* or *sentence fluency* in the writing.

Word choice is varied.

Underlining for italics signifies special use.

A definition is added for clarity.

Wording is changed to improve voice.

A long, confusing sentence is split into two sentences for fluency.

It is this sort of "fundamental solution" thinking that characterizes social entrepreneurship and that distinguishes it from traditional ~~charity~~ [social work]. Traditional ~~charity~~ [social programs] tends to be a one-sided, top-down approach to solving a problem. This approach involves the have's handing something down to the have-not's. And more often than not, it focuses on a crisis. Social capitalism, on the other hand, seeks to change the situation that causes the need. It looks for opportunities by which the needy can better themselves. In the process, society benefits as well.

Consider the example of Erzsébet Szekeres of Hungary, whose son Tibor was born with microcephalus [(an abnormally small skull)] and severe mental retardation. Under the strain of caring for Tibor during his early years, Szekeres' marriage and career ~~started falling apart~~ [began to suffer]. Friends and family urged her to put him in a state institution and go on with her life, ~~but~~ Szekeres saw [, however,] that these institutions were little more than prisons where the severely handicapped were shut away from public view. She dreamed of a group home where people like Tibor could care for themselves, with assistance, and even have meaningful work.

It took years of determined effort on Szekeres' part to make that dream a reality. Often, the government itself opposed her efforts because she was not a member of the health-care profession. **Eventually, however,** With two loans from disability organizations, she purchased an abandoned farming cooperative and turned it into a community for the disabled. To date, Szekeres has created twenty-one such institutions across Hungary, where more than 600 multiply-disabled people live and work. Today, this facility includes dorm-style rooms, a cafeteria, a community room where dances are held and movies are shown, and work facilities where people like her son earn money by assembling curtain clips and other such assembly-line jobs. Her efforts are even changing the way the state itself deals with the handicapped (Bornstein 98-116).

Perhaps an even clearer example of social capitalism is shown in the food-bank program created by Wojciech Onyszkiewicz **in Poland**. During the years that Soviet comunism ruled Poland, the very existence of poverty was denied. After the fall of the Soviet Union, it was estimated that **twenty percent of the population** ~~many~~ lived below the poverty line, and ~~many~~ **thirty-one percent** of those in poverty were multi-child families. While rural communities. . .

A transition is added for organization and sentence fluency.

An idea is moved for better organization.

Details are added.

Write

Revise your writing. Check your first draft for problems with ideas, organization, voice, word choice, and sentence fluency. Make any needed changes.

Revising Using a Checklist

Revise

Revise your writing. On a piece of paper, write the numbers 1 to 14. If you can answer "yes" to a question, put a check mark after that number. Continue to revise until you can answer all of the questions with a "yes."

Revising Checklist

Ideas

_____ 1. Have I chosen an interesting social issue to write about?
_____ 2. Does my thesis statement clearly state the main idea of my paper?
_____ 3. Do I include enough details to support my thesis?
_____ 4. Do I give credit for ideas that I have summarized or quoted from other sources?

Organization

_____ 5. Does my beginning paragraph capture the reader's interest and introduce my topic?
_____ 6. Do my first middle paragraphs explain the problem?
_____ 7. Do my next middle paragraphs detail a solution or solutions, with examples?
_____ 8. Does my ending bring the paper to an interesting closing?

Voice

_____ 9. Does my voice sound knowledgeable and engaging?
_____ 10. Does my voice sound natural, like me?

Word Choice

_____ 11. Have I used specific nouns and active verbs?
_____ 12. Do I avoid unnecessary modifiers?

Sentence Fluency

_____ 13. Do my sentences read smoothly?
_____ 14. Have I used a variety of sentence lengths and constructions?

Editing

When you finish revising your research paper, you edit it by checking for conventions in spelling, punctuation, capitalization, and grammar.

Keys to Effective Editing

1. Read your essay out loud and listen for words or phrases that may be incorrect.

2. Use a dictionary, a thesaurus, your computer's spell-checker, and the "Proofreader's Guide" in the back of this book.

3. Look for errors in punctuation, capitalization, spelling, and grammar.

4. Check your paper for proper formatting. (See pages 384–392.)

5. If you use a computer, edit on a printed copy. Then enter your changes on the computer.

6. Use the editing and proofreading marks inside the back cover of this book. Check all citations for accuracy.

Checking for Conventions

After revising the first draft of his paper, Fidel checked the new version carefully for spelling, usage, and punctuation errors. He also asked a classmate to look it over.

A spelling error is corrected.	Perhaps an even clearer example of social capitalism is shown in the food bank program created by Wojciech Onyszkiewicz in Poland. During the years in which Soviet ~~comunism~~ *communism* ruled that country, the very existence of poverty was denied. After the fall of the Soviet Union, it was
Two number references are corrected.	estimated that ~~twenty~~ *20* percent of the population lived below the poverty line, and ~~thirty-one~~ *31* percent of those in poverty were multi-child families. While rural communities often had
An error in verb agreement is corrected.	surplus food, there ~~was~~ *were* no systems in place for getting it to urban populations ("Ashoka"). Further, rural citizens were not happy at the idea of giving charity to people they perceived as "parasites" (Bornstein 201). On the other
A comma is added after a transitional phrase	hand, these same rural people envied the opportunities for education and culture that were available to urban citizens.
	Onyszkiewicz came up with a plan in which rural communities would donate excess food for urban use, and in exchange, their children would travel to the cities to help distribute that food, and to attend museums, sessions of
A capitalization error is marked.	Parliament, and other such activities ("Ashoka"). Under a similar plan, Onyszkiewicz organized computer training for

rural children by recruiting physically disabled computer users from the city. In exchange for their expertise, these city dwellers are able to visit the countryside. Villagers prepare wheelchair ramps and arrange outdoor activities *(Bornstein 201)* that the urbanites could not otherwise experience. In both of these cases, "commodities" are exchanged in a very capitalistic manner, and in both cases, an important human need is met.

Ashoka itself is actually another example of social capitalism at work. The organization's goal is to identify promising social entrepreneurs in the earliest stages of their work, and to provide support to help that work flourish. While some of the support is monetary—a small *stipend* (stipened) to allow the blossoming *entrepreneur* (entreprenuer) to work full-time on the project—most of it is less tangible. Ashoka fellows "get support, ideas, and, quite literally, protection," as in the case of a Brazilian Ashoka fellow whose work in drug rehabilitation resulted in attacks by local police. The organization took the case to the local governor, and the attacks stopped (Hammonds).

A missing citation is added.

An unnecessary comma is deleted.

Spelling is corrected.

Placement of punctuation is corrected.

Edit

Check your work for conventions. Use your computer spell-checker and grammar checker to search your work. Then print a copy of your report and read it carefully for errors the computer cannot catch. Use the editing and proofreading marks on the inside back cover of this book for your editing. Also ask a classmate to check your work for errors.

Editing Using a Checklist

Edit

Edit your writing. On a piece of paper, write the numbers 1 to 12. If you can answer "yes" to a question, put a check mark after that number. Continue editing until you can answer all of the questions with a "yes."

Editing Checklist

Conventions

PUNCTUATION

_____ **1.** Do I correctly punctuate compound and complex sentences?

_____ **2.** Have I correctly cited sources in my research paper?

_____ **3.** Do I use quotation marks around all quoted words from my sources?

_____ **4.** Do I use underlining for all italicized words?

_____ **5.** Have I correctly formatted a works-cited page?

CAPITALIZATION

_____ **6.** Have I capitalized proper nouns and adjectives?

_____ **7.** Do I begin each sentence with a capital letter?

SPELLING

_____ **8.** Have I spelled all my words correctly?

_____ **9.** Have I double-checked the words my spell-checker may have missed?

GRAMMAR

_____ **10.** Do I use the correct forms of verbs *(he saw*, not *he seen)*?

_____ **11.** Do my subjects and verbs agree in number?

_____ **12.** Have I used the right words *(there, their, they're)*?

Italics and Underlining in MLA Research Papers

In high school, research papers are commonly written in MLA format. (See pages **384–392.**) MLA stands for Modern Language Association. The MLA suggests that writers of research papers use underlining instead of italics for titles and specialized words. However, always follow your teacher's instructions.

Publishing Sharing Your Paper

After you edit and proofread your paper, make a neat final copy to give to your teacher. You may also wish to make extra copies for family and friends.

A research paper can also be presented as a speech, in a multimedia presentation, or on a Web page. (See pages **439–449**.) You worked hard on the report, so find ways to share it with other people.

Publish

Make a final copy. Use the following guidelines to format your paper. (Also see pages **91–95** for instructions about designing on a computer.) Create a clean final copy and share it with your classmates and family.

Focusing on Presentation

- Use blue or black ink and double-space the entire paper.
- Write your name, your teacher's name, the class, and the date in the upper left corner of page 1.
- Skip a line and center your title; skip another line and start your writing.
- Indent every paragraph and leave a one-inch margin on all four sides.
- For a research paper, you should write your last name and the page number in the upper right corner of every page of your paper.
- If your teacher requires a cover page and outline, follow your teacher's requirements. (See page **384**.)

Creating a Title

Take some extra time and thought and give your paper an interesting title. You can try one of the following approaches.

- Be creative: **Social Entrepreneurs, Take a Bow**
- Identify the topic:
  Meeting the Needs of the Future
- Use an idea from your paper:
  Competing to Save the World
- Use compelling words:
  Innovation + Initiative = Impact

Writing Responsibly

A good part of your learning process involves reading and then interpreting or analyzing what you've read. In a research paper, you develop your own ideas while writing knowledgeably about material you've gathered. It's your chance to show that you understand the subject matter. Often, this will entail quoting material as well as paraphrasing—and then identifying the source of the information for your reader.

By citing your sources, you give credit to the authors whose thinking has influenced the ideas you've developed. You also lend integrity to your own ideas by being honest about how you arrived at them.

- **Using Sources**
- **Avoiding Plagiarism**
- **Writing Paraphrases**
- **Using Quoted Material**

"Rules are not necessarily sacred; principles are."
—Franklin D. Roosevelt

Using Sources

What does *research* mean? Research means "searching out answers to questions."

Beginning Your Research

- **Consider your topic.** What do you already know about your topic? If you had to write your paper right now, what would you write?
- **Begin with the basics.** An encyclopedia or Web search will turn up basic information. Use these sources for an overview of the topic.
- **Ask questions.** What do you wonder about your topic? Make a list of questions; then consider what sources you will search to find answers.

Try It!

Choose a research topic that interests you and do the "Ask questions" activity above.

Reflecting on Your Research

- **Think about what you have read.** How has your initial research affected your thinking about the topic? What new questions do you have as a result of your reading?
- **Refine your topic, if necessary.** What new questions and ideas have occurred to you? Should you broaden or narrow your topic?

Doing Further Research

- **Focus your efforts.** Look for answers to your new questions.
- **Use the best sources.** Use trustworthy books, periodicals, and Web sites to find answers to your questions. Also consider conducting surveys and personal interviews and writing letters to experts.

Presenting Your Results

- **Make the topic your own.** Your research paper should not just repeat other people's ideas. First and foremost, it should present your own thoughts and understanding of the topic.
- **Paraphrase or quote appropriately.** To support your ideas, paraphrase or quote credible sources as needed. Remember, however, that references to other sources should be used only to enhance or support your own thinking.
- **Credit your sources.** Let your reader know the source of each idea you summarize or quote.

Avoiding Plagiarism

You owe it to your sources and your reader to give credit for others' ideas in your research paper. If you don't, you may be guilty of *plagiarism*—the act of presenting someone else's ideas as your own. (See the following pages for examples.) Cite every piece of information that you borrow, unless you're sure that the information is common knowledge.

Forms of Plagiarism

- **Submitting another writer's paper:** The most blatant form of plagiarism is to put your name on someone else's work (another student's paper, an essay bought from a "paper mill," the text of an article from the Internet, and so on) and turn it in as your own.
- **Using copy-and-paste:** It is unethical to copy phrases, sentences, or larger sections from a source and paste them into your paper without giving credit for the material.
- **Neglecting necessary quotation marks:** Whether it's just a phrase or a larger section of text, if you use the exact words of a source, they must be put in quotation marks and identified with a citation.
- **Paraphrasing without citing a source:** Paraphrasing (rephrasing ideas in your own words) is an important research skill. However, paraphrased ideas must be credited to the source, even if you reword the material entirely.
- **Confusing borrowed material with your own ideas:** While taking research notes, it is important to identify the source of each idea you record. That way, you won't forget whom to credit as you write your paper.

Other Source Abuses

- **Using sources inaccurately:** Be certain that your quotation or paraphrase accurately reflects the meaning of the original. Do not misrepresent the original author's intent.
- **Overusing source material:** Your paper should be primarily your own words and thoughts, supported by outside sources. If you simply string together quotations and paraphrases, your voice will be lost.
- **"Plunking" source material:** When you write, smoothly incorporate any information from an outside source. Dropping in or "plunking" a quotation or paraphrased idea without comment creates choppy, disconnected writing.
- **Relying too heavily on one source:** If your writing is dominated by one source, the reader may doubt the depth and integrity of your research.

Original Article

The excerpt below about the Ogallala Aquifer is an original-source article. Take note of the examples of plagiarism on the next page.

"Ancient Water for the Future" by James Stator

The Ogallala Aquifer has helped transform the Great Plains states into a great agricultural region. The aquifer is a huge, natural underground reservoir that extends through most of the Plains states. These states experience very little rainfall compared to other parts of the country, and without irrigation, they could not support agriculture. **Thanks to the Ogallala, farmers can make a living in this semiarid region, producing beef and grain in record amounts.** How important is the aquifer to the country? The United States Department of Agriculture estimates that 65 percent of all irrigated land in the country is supplied by that aquifer.

For some time, scientists have worried about the Ogallala Aquifer. This great water system has been tapped beyond its capacity to replenish itself, and as a result, the aquifer has shrunk drastically. According to *Choices,* **a farm magazine, the Ogallala showed significant losses as early as the 1970s, which forced policy makers to figure out how this limited resource can be properly used and conserved.**

The aquifer directly provides water for every aspect of life on the Great Plains. The Docking Institute of Public Affairs in 2001 found that current practices take too much water from the Ogallala. For example, the institute noted that in one year Kansas pumped 2 million more acre-feet from the aquifer than was replaced by rain. The rain and snow that renew the aquifer cannot keep up with the demands of modern irrigation and growing cities.

Farmers are worried. They appreciate how important the aquifer is to life on the Great Plains. Farmers know their livelihood is at risk, so they have found ways to cut back their use of water from the Ogallala. Rotation of crops and new irrigation methods have reduced water loss due to evaporation. The Department of Agriculture has determined that water levels have not dropped as rapidly as was predicted. Unfortunately, conservation is not a simple matter. More and more people are living in the aquifer states, and they need water as well. In addition, demands by other western cities ultimately impact the amount of water available to replenish the Ogallala. A collapse of the . . .

Examples of Plagiarism

Below are the three common types of plagiarism, sometimes committed on purpose and sometimes by accident. The plagiarized text is shown in bold type.

⊘ Using copy-and-paste

- In this sample, the writer pastes in two sentences from the original article without using quotation marks or a citation.

> The Plains states are typically flat and dry, but **the Ogallala Aquifer has helped transform the Great Plains states into a great agricultural region. Thanks to the Ogallala, farmers can make a living in this semiarid region, producing beef and grain in record amounts.** The aquifer allows farmers in the United States to export food to the world. That's one reason why the Great Plains became known as the nation's breadbasket.

⊘ Paraphrasing without citing a source

- Below the writer accurately paraphrases (restates) a passage from the original article, but she includes no citation.

> **Since the 1970s, researchers have been concerned about the alarming depletion of the Ogallala. Agricultural experts have scrambled to see how to save the great aquifer. Too many demands on the Ogallala have overwhelmed the capacity to replenish this magnificent reservoir.**

⊘ Neglecting necessary quotation marks

- In the sample below, the writer cites the source of the exact words that she uses from the original article, but she doesn't enclose those words in quotation marks.

> In the early days of irrigation, crops were bountiful, and everyone was pleased. Today, things are different. In "Ancient Water for the Future," James Stator states that **farmers are worried. They appreciate how important the aquifer is to life on the Great Plains. Farmers know their livelihood is at risk, so they have found ways to cut back their use of water from the Ogallala.** These farmers realize that they cannot afford to lose this life-giving source of water.

Writing Paraphrases

There are two ways to share information from another source: (1) quote the source directly or (2) paraphrase the source. When you quote directly, you include the exact words of the author and put quotation marks around them. When you paraphrase, you use your own words to restate someone else's ideas. In either case, you must cite your source. To paraphrase, follow the steps below.

1. **Skim the selection first** to get the overall meaning.
2. **Read the selection carefully,** paying attention to key words and phrases.
3. **List the main ideas** on a piece of paper.
4. **Review the selection** again.
5. **Write your paraphrase;** restate the author's ideas using your own words.

   - Stick to the essential information. Drop anecdotes and details.
   - Put quotation marks around key words or phrases taken directly from the source.
   - Arrange the ideas into a smooth, logical order.

6. **Check your paraphrase** for accuracy by asking these questions: *Have I kept the author's ideas and viewpoints clear in my paraphrase? Have I quoted only as necessary? Could another person understand the author's main ideas by reading my paraphrase?*

FYI

A *quotation,* a *paraphrase,* and a *summary* reference a source in different ways.

- **Quoting:** A quotation states the words of a source exactly. Quoting should be used sparingly in a research paper so that your writing doesn't sound like a patchwork of other people's statements. Use a quotation only when the exact words of the source are essential.

- **Paraphrasing:** In a paraphrase, you recast an idea from a source into your own words. Paraphrasing demonstrates that you understand the idea, and it maintains your voice within your paper. Paraphrasing is more commonly used than quoting or summarizing.

- **Summarizing:** A summary is a condensed version of an entire source. In a research paper, there is seldom any need to summarize an entire work unless that work is the subject of the paper. For example, you might summarize the plot of *King Lear* in a research paper about that play.

Sample Paraphrases

Following the original passage below (from page 26 of a book by Travis Taylor), you'll find two properly cited paraphrases.

Original Passage

Kyudo, which means "the way of the bow" in Japanese, is the Zen martial art of archery. It was adapted into traditional Buddhist practice from medieval Japanese archers who used seven-foot asymmetrical bows called yumi. Although kyudo lacks the widespread popularity of karate or judo, it is often regarded as one of the most intensive martial arts in existence, taking 30 years to master.

The standard execution of kyudo involves a series of specific actions, including assuming the proper posture, approaching the intended target, nocking the arrow, drawing it, releasing it, and then repeating the process. After the second arrow has been released, the archer approaches the target, withdraws the arrows, and thus completes the exercise.

There is far more to kyudo, however, than simply shooting arrows. For every movement, the archer must maintain a specific posture, inhaling and exhaling at predetermined points throughout the exercise. The repetitive action and deep breathing greatly relaxes the archer—heightening his alertness and lowering his stress.

Basic Paraphrase

Kyudo is the Zen martial art of archery. It was adapted from medieval Japanese archery into a spiritual and physical exercise. Through a series of specific actions, the archer prepares and shoots an arrow into a target and then repeats the action one more time. The archer's control comes from focused breathing and balanced posture, which lessen stress and increase the archer's ability to concentrate (Taylor 26).

Basic Paraphrase with Quotation

Kyudo is the Zen martial art of archery. It was adapted from traditional medieval Japanese archery into a spiritual and physical exercise. "The standard execution of kyudo involves a series of specific actions, including assuming the proper posture, approaching the intended target, nocking the arrow, drawing it, [and] releasing it . . . " (Taylor 26). An archer's control comes from focused breathing and balanced posture, which lessen stress and increase the archer's ability to concentrate (Taylor 26).

Using Quoted Material

A quotation can be a single word or an entire paragraph. Choose quotations carefully, keep them as brief as possible, and use them only when they are necessary. When you do quote material directly, be sure that the capitalization, punctuation, and spelling are the same as that in the original work. Clearly mark changes for your readers: (1) changes within the quotation are enclosed in brackets [like this]; (2) explanations are enclosed in parentheses at the end of the quotation before closing punctuation (like this).

Short Quotations

If a quotation is four typed lines or fewer, work it into the body of your paper and put quotation marks around it.

Long Quotations

Quotations of more than four typed lines should be set off from the rest of the writing by indenting each line 10 spaces and double-spacing the material. When quoting two or more paragraphs, indent the first line of each paragraph three additional spaces. Do not use quotation marks. (See **632.3**.)

Note: Place the parenthetical reference after the final punctuation mark of the quotation. Generally, a colon is used to introduce quotations set off from the text. (See **620.4**.)

Quoting Poetry

When quoting up to three lines of poetry (or lyrics), use quotation marks and work the lines into your writing. Use a diagonal (/) to show where each line of the poem ends. For quotations of four lines or more, indent each line 10 spaces and double-space. Do not use quotation marks.

Note: To show that you have left out a line or more of verse in a longer quotation, make a line of spaced periods the approximate length of a complete line of the poem.

Partial Quotations

If you want to leave out part of the quotation, use an ellipsis to signify the omission. An ellipsis (. . .) is three periods with a space before and after each one. (See page **642**.)

Note: Do not take out something that will change the author's original meaning.

Documenting Research

Most academic disciplines have their own manuals of style for research paper documentation. The style manual of the Modern Language Association *(MLA Handbook for Writers of Research Papers),* for example, is widely used in the humanities (literature, philosophy, history, and so on), making it the most popular manual in high school and college writing courses. (For complete information about MLA style, refer to the latest version of the *MLA Handbook.)* For papers in social sciences and social studies, the documentation style of the American Psychological Association (APA) is often used.

This chapter will provide you with guidelines for citing sources in both the MLA and APA styles. (The MLA works-cited list is very extensive; the APA reference listed is abbreviated.) *Remember:* Always follow your teacher's directions, which may include special requirements or exceptions for the use of either documentation style. Because these styles continue to evolve, the Write Source Web site maintains the most up-to-date information about documenting electronic sources. You will also find a sample APA research paper at www.thewritesource.com/apa.htm.

- **Guidelines for In-Text Citations**
- **MLA Works-Cited List**
- **APA Reference List**

"Research is the process of going up alleys to see if they are blind."

—Marston Bates

Guidelines for In-Text Citations

The simplest way to credit a source is to insert the information in parentheses after the words or ideas taken from that source. These in-text citations (often called "parenthetical references") refer to the "Works Cited" page at the end of an MLA paper or the "References" page at the end of an APA paper.

Points to Remember

- Make sure each in-text citation clearly points to an entry in your reference list or list of works cited. Use the word or words by which the entry is alphabetized.
- Keep citations brief and integrate them into your writing.
- When paraphrasing rather than quoting, make it clear where your borrowing begins and ends. Use stylistic cues to distinguish the source's thoughts ("Kalmbach points out . . . ") from your own ("I believe . . . ").
- Place your parenthetical citation at the end of a sentence, before the end punctuation.
- Do not offer page numbers when citing complete works. If you cite a specific part, give the page number, chapter, or section, using the appropriate abbreviations (p. or pp., chap., or sec.). Do not, however, use p. and pp. in MLA parenthetical citations.

MLA	APA
• Place the **author's last name** (or, if unavailable, the first word or two of the title) and/or **page number** (if available) in parentheses following the cited text, except when these items are included in the text.	• Place the **author** (or title), **date of the source,** and **page number** (if any) in parentheses, separated by commas, following the cited text, unless these items have been included in the text.
• For inclusive **page numbers** larger than 99, give only the two digits of the second number (113–14, not 113–114).	• **Titles** are italicized, but APA style requires that only first words and proper nouns in titles be capitalized.
• For **titles,** use underlining, not italics.	

Model In-Text Citations

MLA	APA

A Work by One Author

Genetic engineering was dubbed "eugenics" by a cousin of Darwin's, Sir Francis Galton, in 1885 (Bullough 5).	Bush's 2002 budget was based on revenue estimates that "now appear to have been far too optimistic" (Lemann, 2003, p. 48).

A Work by Two or Three Authors

Students learned more than a full year's Spanish in ten days using the complete supermemory method (Ostrander and Schroeder 51).	Love changes not just who we are, but who we can become, as well (Lewis, Amini, & Lannon, 2000, p. 25).

Note: For APA, this format also applies to a work by up to five authors. After the first citation, list only the first author followed by "et al." (meaning "and others").

A Work by Many Authors

This format applies to a work by four or more authors in MLA format or six or more authors in APA format. List only the first author followed by "et al."

Communication on the job is more than talking; it is "inseparable from your total behavior" (Culligan et al. 111).	Among children 13 to 14 years old, a direct correlation can be shown between cigarette advertising and smoking (Lopez et al., 2004, p. 75).

An Anonymous Work

When there is no author listed, give the title or a shortened version of the title as it appears on the works-cited or reference page.

Statistics indicate that drinking water can make up 20 percent of a person's total exposure to lead (Information 572).	. . . including a guide to low-impact exercise (*Staying Healthy,* 2004, p. 30).

Personal Communications

For an MLA paper, this parenthetical reference is the same as that for a publication with one author. In an APA paper, cite letters, e-mail messages, phone conversations, and so on as "personal communication" with their full date.

MLA	APA
. . . concern for the wetland frog population (Barzinji).	The management team expects to finish hiring this spring (R. Fouser, personal communication, December 14, 2004).

A Work Referred to in Another Work

In MLA, use the abbreviation *qtd. in* (quoted in) before the source in your reference. For APA, credit the source by adding *as cited in* within the parentheses.

Quoting Prose

In MLA format, when you are quoting any sort of prose that takes more than four typed lines, do not use quotation marks. Instead, indent each line of the quotation one inch (10 spaces), and put the parenthetical citation (the pages and any chapter or other numbers) outside the end punctuation mark of the quotation.

Allende describes the flying machine that Marcos has assembled:

> The contraption lay with its stomach on terra firma, heavy and sluggish and looking more like a wounded duck than like one of those newfangled airplanes they were starting to produce in the United States. There was nothing in its appearance to suggest that it could move, much less take flight. (12; ch. 1)

Note: In APA format, quotations of 40 or more words are handled similarly, although the block of lines is indented only 5 spaces, and the abbreviation p. or pp. is included in the parenthetical reference.

Try It!

Paraphrase the following passage and refer to the source in a parenthetical citation in both MLA and APA styles.

> "He explained that they were all worried and resentful; they could not believe a young girl would come all the way from England just to look at apes, and so the rumor had spread that I was a government spy."

Source: page 16 of *In the Shadow of Man* by Jane Goodall, published 1971

MLA Works-Cited List

The works-cited section of your report lists all of the sources you have referred to in your text. It does not include sources you may have read but did not refer to in your paper. Begin your list on a new page.

List each entry alphabetically by author's last name. If there is no author, use the first word of the title (disregard *A, An, The*). Note that titles are underlined, not italicized. Use a single space after all punctuation in a works-cited entry.

List only the city for the place of publication unless it is outside the United States. In that case, add an abbreviation of the country, if necessary, for clarity. If several cities are listed, give only the first.

Additionally, note that publishers' names should be shortened by omitting articles *(a, an, the)*, business abbreviations *(Co., Inc.),* and descriptive words *(Books, Press).* Cite the surname alone if the publisher's name includes the name of one person. If it includes the names of more than one person, cite only the first of the surnames. Abbreviate "University Press" as UP. Also use standard abbreviations whenever possible.

Books

Basic Format

Author's last name, First name. Book Title. City: Publisher, date.

Opie, John. Ogallala: Water for a Dry Land. Lincoln: U of
    Nebraska P, 1993.

Add page numbers if the citation is to only a part of the work. In the rare instance that a book does not state publication information, use the following abbreviations in place of information you cannot supply:

n.p.	No place of publication given	n.p.	No publisher given
n.d.	No date of publication given	n. pag.	No pagination given

A Work by Two or Three Authors

Haynes, John Earl, and Harvey Klehr. In Denial: Historians, Communism, & Espionage.
    San Francisco: Encounter, 2003.

List the authors in the same order as they appear on the title page. Reverse only the name of the first author.

A Work by Four or More Authors

Schulte-Peevers, Andrea, et al. Germany. Victoria, Austral.: Lonely Planet, 2000.

Two or More Books by the Same Author

List the books alphabetically according to title. After the first entry, substitute three hyphens for the author's name.

Dershowitz, Alan M. Rights from Wrongs. New York: Basic, 2005.

---. Supreme Injustice: How the High Court Hijacked Election 2000. Oxford: Oxford UP, 2001.

An Anonymous Book

Chase's Calendar of Events 2002. Chicago: Contemporary, 2002.

A Single Work from an Anthology

Mitchell, Joseph. "The Bottom of the Harbor." American Sea Writing.
    Ed. Peter Neill. New York: Library of America, 2000. 584–608.

An Article in a Familiar Reference Book

It is not necessary to give full publication information for familiar reference works (encyclopedias, dictionaries). List the edition and publication year. If an article is initialed, check the index of authors for the author's full name.

Lum, P. Andrea. "Computed Tomography." World Book. 2000 ed.

A Government Publication

State the name of the government (country, state, and so on) followed by the name of the agency. Most federal publications are published by the Government Printing Office (GPO).

United States. Dept. of Labor. Bureau of Labor Statistics. Occupational Outlook
    Handbook 2000–2001. Washington: GPO, 2000.

When citing the *Congressional Record,* give only the date and page numbers.

Cong. Rec. 5 Feb. 2002: S311–15.

A Pamphlet, Brochure, Manual, or Other Workplace Document

Treat any such publication as you would a book.

Grayson, George W. The North American Free Trade Agreement. New York: Foreign
    Policy Assn., 1993.

If publication information is missing, list the country of publication [in brackets] if known. Beyond that, use n.p. and n.d. as for a book.

Pedestrian Safety. [United States]: n.p., n.d.

One Volume of a Multivolume Work

Cooke, Jacob Ernest, and Milton M. Klein, eds. North America in Colonial Times.
Vol. 2. New York: Scribner's, 1998.

Note: If you cite two or more volumes in a multivolume work, give the total number
of volumes after each title. Offer specific references to volume and page
numbers in the parenthetical reference in your text, like this: (8:112–14).

Salzman, Jack, David Lionel Smith, and Cornel West. Encyclopedia of African-American
Culture and History. 5 vols. New York: Simon, 1996.

An Introduction, a Preface, a Foreword, or an Afterword

To cite the introduction, preface, foreword, or afterword of a book, list the
author of the part first. Then identify the part by type, with no quotation marks or
underlining, followed by the title of the book. Next, identify the author of the work,
using the word *By*. (If the book author and the part's author are the same person,
give just the last name after *By*.) For a book that gives cover credit to an editor
instead of an author, identify the editor as usual. Finally, list any page numbers
for the part being cited.

Barry, Anne. Afterword. Making Room for Students. By Celia Oyler. New York: Teachers
College, 1996.

Lefebvre, Mark. Foreword. The Journey Home. Vol. 1. Ed. Jim Stephens. Madison: North
Country, 1989. ix.

Second and Subsequent Edition

An edition refers to the particular publication you are citing, as in the third
(3rd) edition.

Joss, Molly W. Looking Good in Presentations. 3rd ed. Scottsdale: Coriolis, 1999.

An Edition with Author and Editor

The term *edition* also refers to the work of one person that is prepared by
another person, an editor.

Shakespeare, William. A Midsummer Night's Dream. Ed. Jane Bachman. Lincolnwood:
NTC, 1994.

Periodicals

Basic Format

Author's last name, First name. "Article Title." Periodical Title
date: page nos.

Stearns, Denise Heffernan. "Testing by Design." Middle Ground
Oct. 2000: 21–25.

An Article in a Weekly or Biweekly Magazine

List the author (if identified), article title (in quotation marks), publication title (underlined), full date of publication, and page numbers for the article. Do not include volume and issue numbers.

Goodell, Jeff. "The Uneasy Assimilation." Rolling Stone 6–13 Dec. 2001: 63–66.

An Article in a Monthly or Bimonthly Magazine

As for a weekly or biweekly magazine, list the author (if identified), article title (in quotation marks), and publication title (underlined). Then identify the month(s) and year of the issue, followed by page numbers for the article. However, do not give volume and issue numbers.

"Patent Pamphleteer." Scientific American Dec. 2001: 33.

An Article in a Scholarly Journal Paginated by Issue

Rather than by month or the full date of publication, scholarly journals are identified by volume number. If each issue is numbered from page 1, your works-cited entry should identify the issue number, as well. List the volume number immediately after the journal title, followed by a period and the issue number, the year of publication (in parentheses), and the page numbers of the article.

Chu, Wujin. "Costs and Benefits of Hard-Sell." Journal of Marketing Research 32.2
(1995): 97–102.

An Article in a Scholarly Journal with Continuous Pagination

For scholarly journals that continue pagination from issue to issue, no issue number is needed in the works-cited entry.

Tebble, Nicola J., David W. Thomas, and Patricia Price. "Anxiety and Self-
Consciousness in Patients with Minor Facial Lacerations." Journal of Advanced
Nursing 47 (2004): 417–26.

Note: For articles that are continued on a nonconsecutive page, whatever the publication type, add a plus sign (+) after the first page number.

A Printed Interview

Begin with the name of the person interviewed.

> Cantwell, Maria. "The New Technocrat." By Erika Rasmusson. <u>Working Woman</u> Apr.
> 2001: 20–21.

If the interview is untitled, use *Interview* (no italics) in place of the title.

A Newspaper Article

> Bleakley, Fred R. "Companies' Profits Grew 48% Despite Economy."
> <u>Wall Street Journal</u> 1 May 1995, Midwest ed.: 1.

If a local paper does not name the city, add it in brackets (not underlined).

To cite an article in a lettered section of the newspaper, list the section and the page number (A4). If the sections are numbered, however, use a comma after the year (or the edition); then indicate sec. 1, 2, 3, and so on, followed by a colon and the page number (sec. 1: 20). An unsigned newspaper article follows the same format:

> "Bombs—Real and Threatened—Keep Northern Ireland Edgy." <u>Chicago Tribune</u> 6 Dec.
> 2001, sec. 1: 20.

A Newspaper Editorial

If an article is an editorial, put *Editorial* (no italics) after the title.

> "Hospital Power." Editorial. <u>Bangor Daily News</u> 14 Sept. 2004: A6.

A Review

Begin with the author (if identified) and title of the review. Use the notation *Rev. of* (no italics) between the title of the review and that of the original work. Identify the author of the original work with the word *by* (no italics). Then follow with publication data for the review.

> Olsen, Jack. "Brains and Industry." Rev. of <u>Land of Opportunity</u>, by Sarah Marr. <u>New</u>
> <u>York Times</u> 23 Apr. 1995, sec. 3: 28.

Note: If you cite a review of a work by an editor or a translator, use *ed.* or *trans.* instead of *by*.

An Article with a Title or Quotation Within Its Title

> Morgenstern, Joe. "Sleeper of the Year: <u>In the Bedroom</u> Is Rich Tale of Tragic Love."
> <u>Wall Street Journal</u> 23 Nov. 2001: W1.

Note: Use single quotation marks around the shorter title if it is a title normally punctuated with quotation marks.

Online Sources

The format for most online sources is the same as for other media, but with the addition of the electronic publication information.

Basic Format

Author's last name, First name. "Title." Site Title. Date of posting or last update. Site sponsor. Date accessed <address>.

Tenenbaum, David. "Dust Never Sleeps." The Why Files. 28 July 1999. U of Wisconsin, Board of Regents. 26 April 2005 <http://whyfiles.org/shorties/air_dust.html>.

Note: If certain details are not available, go on to the next item in the entry.

A Site with a Long URL

If you must include a line break in a URL, do so only after a slash, and do not add a hyphen. For a long and complicated address, give the URL of the site's search page instead.

MacLeod, Donald. "Shake-Up for Academic Publishing." EducationGuardian.co.uk. 10 Nov. 2004 <http://www.guardian.co.uk/Archive/>.

If no search page is available, give the home page URL and path of links to the document.

"Frederica: An 18th-Century Planned Community." National Register of Historic Places. National Parks Service. 27 Feb. 2004 <http://www.cr.nps.gov/nr/>. Path: Education; Hispanic Heritage Month; Frederica.

An Article in an Online Periodical

Begin with the author's name; the article title in quotation marks; and the underlined name of the periodical, its volume or issue number, and date of publication. Include page numbers (or other sections) if numbered. Close with the date of access and URL.

Dickerson, John. "Nailing Jello." Time.com 5 Nov. 2001. 9 Dec. 2001 <http://www.time.com/time/columnist/dickerson/>.

An Article in an Online Reference Work

Unless the author of the entry is identified, begin with the entry name in quotation marks. Follow with the usual online publication information.

"Eakins, Thomas." Britannica Concise Encyclopedia 2004. Encyclopædia Britannica. 26 Sept. 2004 <http://concise.britannica.com/ebc/article?tocId=9363299>.

An Article in an Online Service

When you use a library to access a subscription service, add the name of the database if known (underlined), the service, and the library. Then give the date of access followed by the Internet address for the home page of the service (if known). If no Internet address is given for an entry, add a keyword or path statement in its place, if appropriate.

> Davis, Jerome. "Massacre in Kiev." Washington Post 29 Nov. 1999, final ed.: C12. National Newspapers. ProQuest. Gateway Technical College Elkhorn Campus Library. 30 Nov. 1999 <http://proquest.umi.com/pqdweb>. Path: World Events; Conflict; Kiev.

An Online Governmental Publication

As with a governmental publication in print, begin with the name of the government (country, state, and so on) followed by the name of the agency. After the publication title, add the electronic publication information.

> United States. Dept. of Labor. Office of Disability Employment Policy. Emergency Preparedness for People with Disabilities. Apr. 2004. 12 Sept. 2004 <http://www.dol.gov/odep/ep/eps.pdf>.

When citing the *Congressional Record,* only the date and page numbers are required.

> Cong. Rec. 5 Feb. 2002: S311–15. 22 Jan. 2007 <www.gpoaccess.gov/crecord/index.html>.

An Online Multimedia Resource: Painting, Photograph, Musical Composition, Film or Film Clip, Etc.

After the usual information for the type of work being cited, add the electronic publication information.

> Goya, Francisco de. Saturn Devouring His Children. 1819-1823. Museo del Prado, Madrid. 13 Dec. 2003 <http://www.usc.edu/schools/annenberg/asc/projects/comm544/library/>.

An E-Mail Communication

Identify the author of the e-mail, then list the "Subject" line of the e-mail as a title, in quotation marks. Next, include a description—usually *E-mail to the author* (no italics), meaning the author of the paper. Finally, give the date of the message.

> Barzinji, Atman. "Re: Frog Populations in Wisconsin Wetlands." E-mail to the author. 1 Jan. 2002.

Other Sources: Primary, Personal, and Multimedia

The following examples of works-cited entries illustrate how to cite sources such as television or radio programs, films, live performances, and other miscellaneous nonprint sources.

A Television or Radio Program

"Another Atlantis?" Deep Sea Detectives. The History Channel. 13 June 2005.

A Film

The director, distributor, and year of release follow the title. Other information may be included if pertinent.

The Aviator. Dir. Martin Scorsese. Perf. Leonardo DiCaprio. Miramax Films, 2004.

A Video Recording

Cite a filmstrip, slide program, videocassette, or DVD just as you would a film, but include the medium before the name of the distributor.

Beyond the Da Vinci Code. DVD. A&E Home Video, 2005.

An Audio Recording

If you are not citing a CD, indicate *LP, Audiocassette,* or *Audiotape* (no italics). If you are citing a specific song on a musical recording, place its title in quotation marks before the title of the recording.

Welch, Jack. Winning. Harper Audio, 2005.

An Interview by the Author (Yourself)

Brooks, Sarah. Personal interview. 15 Oct. 2002.

A Cartoon or Comic Strip (in Print)

Luckovich, Mike. "The Drawing Board." Cartoon. Time 17 Sept. 2001: 18.

A Lecture, a Speech, an Address, or a Reading

If there is a title, use it instead of the descriptive label (for example, Lecture).

Annan, Kofi. Lecture. Acceptance of Nobel Peace Prize. Oslo City Hall, Oslo, Norway. 10 Dec. 2001.

APA Reference List

The reference list begins on a separate page and includes all retrievable sources cited in a paper. List the entries alphabetically by author's last name. If no author is given, then list by title (disregarding *A, An,* or *The*).

Leave a single space after all end punctuation marks. Quotation marks are not used for article titles; italicize other titles. Capitalize only the first word (and any proper nouns) of book and article titles; capitalize the names of periodicals in the standard upper- and lowercase manner.

Books

Basic Format

Author's last name, Initials. (year). *Book title.* Location: Publisher.

Guttman, J. (1999). *The gift wrapped in sorrow: A mother's quest for healing.* Palm Springs, CA: JMJ.

Note: Give the city or publication alone if it is well-known. Otherwise, include the state. Include the state or province and the country if outside the United States.

A Book by Two or More Authors

Lynn, J., & Harrold, J. (1999). *Handbook for mortals: Guidance for people facing serious illness.* New York: Oxford.

List up to six authors; abbreviate subsequent authors as "et al." List all authors' names in reverse order. Separate authors' names with commas, and include an ampersand (&) before the last.

An Anonymous Book

If an author is listed as "Anonymous," treat it as the author's name. Otherwise, follow this format:

American Medical Association essential guide to asthma. (2003). New York: American Medical Association.

A Single Work from an Anthology

Nichols, J. (2005). Diversity and stability in language. In B. D. Joseph & R. D. Janda (Eds.), *The handbook of historical linguistics* (pp. 283–310). Malden, MA: Blackwell.

An Article in a Reference Book

Lewer, N. (1999). Non-lethal weapons. In *World encyclopedia of peace* (pp. 279–280). Oxford: Pergamon.

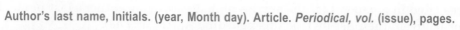

Periodicals

Basic Format

Author's last name, Initials. (year, Month day). Article. *Periodical, vol.* (issue), pages.

Silberman, S. (2001, December). The geek syndrome. *Wired, 9*(12), 174–183.

A Journal Article, Two Authors

Newman, P. A., & Nash, E. R. (2005). The unusual southern hemisphere stratosphere winter of 2002. *Journal of the Atmospheric Sciences, 62*(3), 614–628.

A Journal Article, More Than Six Authors

Watanabe, T., Bihoreau, M-T., McCarthy, L., Kiguwa, S., Hishigaki, H., Tsaji, A., et al. (1999, May 1). A radiation hybrid map of the rat genome containing 5,255 markers. *Nature Genetics, 22,* 27–36.

A Journal Article, Paginated by Issue

When the page numbering of the issue starts with page 1, the issue number (not italicized) is placed in parentheses after the volume number.

Lewer, N. (1999, summer). Nonlethal weapons. *Forum, 14*(2), 39–45.

A Newspaper Article

For newspapers, use "p." or "pp." before the page numbers; if the article is not on continuous pages, give all the page numbers, separated by commas.

Stolberg, S. C. (2002, January 4). Breakthrough in pig cloning could aid organ transplants. *The New York Times,* pp. 1A, 17A.

Online Sources

Basic Format

Author's last name, Initials. (year, Month day). Article. *Periodical, vol.* (issue), pages if available. Retrieved Month day, year, from electronic address

Volz, J. (2000, January). Successful aging: the second 50. *Monitor on Psychology, 31*(1). Retrieved Apr. 26, 2006, from http://www.apa.org/monitor/jan00/cs.html

Note: If you have read an exact duplicate of a print article online, simply use the basic journal reference, but add [Electronic version] after the title of the article.

Making Oral Presentations

A good public speaker is like a good book. When you read the book, you get caught up in the ideas, not in the cover or the page design. In the same way, when you listen to the speaker, you are drawn to the message, not to the presenter.

Delivering a presentation well takes preparation and practice. It means knowing the information so thoroughly that you don't stumble. It means being comfortable enough to engage and capture the audience with your ideas. This chapter will help you do just that. You'll learn how to organize the material, how to bring it to life with visual aids, and how to practice your way to a smooth, effective delivery.

- **Planning Your Presentation**
- **Creating Note Cards**
- **Considering Visual Aids**
- **Practicing Your Speech**
- **Delivering Your Presentation**
- **Evaluating a Presentation**
- **Preparing a Multimedia Report**
- **Multimedia Report Traits Checklist**

"Make sure you have finished speaking before your audience has finished listening."

—Dorothy Sarnoff

Planning Your Presentation

To transform a research paper into an oral presentation, you need to consider your purpose, your audience, and the content of your paper.

Determining Your Purpose

Your purpose is your reason for giving a presentation.

- **Informative** speeches educate by providing valuable information.
- **Persuasive** speeches argue for or against something.
- **Demonstration** speeches show how to do or make something.

Considering Your Audience

As you think about your audience, keep the following points in mind.

- **Be clear.** Listeners should understand your main points immediately.
- **Anticipate questions** the audience might have and answer them. This helps keep the audience connected.
- **Engage your listeners** through thought-provoking questions, revealing anecdotes, interesting details, and effective visuals.

Reviewing Your Report

During an oral report, obviously your audience cannot go back and listen again to earlier statements, so you must be sure to share your ideas clearly from beginning to end. Review your paper to see how the different parts will work in an oral presentation. Use the following questions as a review guide.

- Will my opening grab the listeners' attention?
- What are the main points that listeners need to know?
- How many supporting details should I include for each main point?
- What visual aids can I use to create interest in my topic? (See page **444**.)
- Will the ending have the proper impact on the listeners?

Try It!

Identify your purpose. If you were to orally present your most recent research paper, what would your purpose be (to inform, to persuade, or to demonstrate)? List some of your ideas for accomplishing that goal. Also consider visual aids that would enhance your presentation.

Adapting Your Paper

To create a more effective oral presentation, you may need to rewrite certain parts of your paper. The new beginning below grabs the listeners' attention by using short, punchy phrases. The new ending makes a more immediate connection with the beginning.

Written Introduction (page 385)

In a small community, when tragedy strikes, everyone knows it, and everyone can see how best to step in and help. In the global community, tragedy strikes somewhere every day, but knowing how to respond is much more difficult. . . . Faced with numbers like these, an individual might be tempted to despair and cry out, "I'm only one person. What can I do?" . . .

Oral Introduction

Do you remember when the Baptist church in town burned down last year? Everyone knew it, and many people stepped in to help. It's a different story with tragedies like hunger, malnutrition, and disease, especially when they're far from home. As individuals, we feel . . .

Written Conclusion (page 391)

. . . It is no exaggeration to say that their efforts often lift entire communities out of poverty. . . . Bill Drayton believes that the next step in this social evolution is a partnering of business and social entrepreneurs, which he sees as only natural. It was the splitting of business and social concerns 300 years ago . . .

Oral Conclusion

We see that the efforts of individuals are able to lift entire communities out of poverty. We see that tragedies can be overcome. Businesses will begin to see that they, too, have something to gain by partnering with social entrepreneurs. Everyone benefits, and the world becomes a better place.

"It usually takes more than three weeks to prepare a good impromptu speech."

—Mark Twain

Creating Note Cards

If you are giving a prepared speech rather than an oral reading of your paper, you should use note cards to remind you of your main ideas. The guidelines below will help you make effective cards.

Note Card Guidelines

Write out your entire introduction and conclusion on separate note cards. For the body of your speech, write one point per card, along with specific details. Clearly number your cards.

- Place each main point at the top of a separate note card.
- Write supporting ideas on the lines below the main idea, using key words and phrases to help you remember specific details.
- Number each card.
- Highlight any ideas you want to emphasize.
- Mark the places that call for visual aids.

Three Main Parts to Consider

As you prepare your note cards, keep the following points in mind about the three parts of your oral presentation: the introduction, body, and conclusion.

- **The introduction** should grab the listeners' attention, identify the topic and the focus of your presentation, and provide any essential background information about the topic. (See pages **440–441**.)
- **The body** should contain the main points from your paper and present details that will hold your listeners' attention. Remember to note the visual aids that you plan to use. (See the bold notes on the sample cards on page **443**.)
- **The conclusion** should restate your focus and leave the listeners with a final thought about your topic. (See pages **440–441**.)

Try It!

Using one of your recent research papers, adapt the introduction and conclusion for an oral report. Write your complete beginning and ending on separate note cards.

Sample Note Cards

Below are the note cards Fidel used for his oral presentation about social entrepreneurs.

Introduction   1
photo: burned church

    Do you remember when the Baptist church in town burned down last year? Everyone knew it, and lots of people stepped in to help. It's a different story with tragedies like hunger, malnutrition, and disease, especially when they're far

---

The Problem   2

- early 1700s—business sector is competitive and innovative
- government, other social support systems uncompetitive
- result is slow response to problems

The Solution   3
photo: Bill Drayton, founder Ashoka

- Ashoka: organization that fosters entrepreneurs
- offers monetary support as well as ideas
- citizen entrepreneurs seek to change situations that cause need
- the needy better themselves, and society benefits as well

Example 1   4
- Erzsébet Szekeres of Hungary—son severely mentally retarded
- instead of institution, she made a group home (assisted living)
- so far she has created 21 group homes
- state's way is changing as a result

Example 2   5
Chart

- Wojciech Onyszkiewicz, Poland—food-bank program
- rural communities: surplus food that urban people need
- exchanged for education and culture
- disabled urbanites teach computer skills to rural children

Conclusion   6

    We see that the efforts of individuals are able to lift entire communities out of poverty. We see that tragedies can be overcome. Businesses will begin to see that they, too, have something to gain by partnering with social entrepreneurs. Everyone benefits, and the world becomes a better place.

Considering Visual Aids

Consider using visual aids during your speech. They can make your presentation clearer and more meaningful. Here are some examples.

Posters	can include words, pictures, or both.
Photographs	illustrate what you are talking about.
Charts	explain points, compare facts, or give statistics.
Maps	identify or locate specific places being discussed.
Objects	show important items related to your topic.
Computer slides	project your photographs, charts, and maps onto a screen and turn your speech into a multimedia presentation. (See pages 448–449.)

Indicating When to Present Visuals

Write notes on your note cards to indicate where a visual aid would be helpful. Fidel considered the following visuals for his presentation about social entrepreneurs.

- **photo of the local church that burned**
- **photo of Bill Drayton, founder of Ashoka**
- **a chart showing the exchange of goods for services in Poland**

Try It!

Identify two or three visual aids you could use in your presentation. Explain when and how you would use each one.

Tip

When creating visual aids, keep these points in mind.

- **Make them big.** Your visuals should be large enough for everyone in the audience to see.
- **Keep them simple.** Use labels and short phrases rather than full sentences.
- **Make them eye-catching.** Use color, bold lines, and simple shapes to make the contents clear and interesting.

Practicing Your Speech

Practice is the key to giving an effective oral presentation. Knowing what to say and how to say it will help eliminate those butterflies speakers often feel. Here are some hints for an effective practice session.

- **Arrange your note cards in the proper order.** This will eliminate any confusion as you practice.
- **Practice in front of a mirror.** Check your posture and eye contact and be sure your visual aids are easy to see.
- **Practice in front of others.** Friends and family can help you identify parts that need work.
- **Record or videotape a practice presentation.** Do you sound interested in your topic? Are your voice and message clear?
- **Time yourself.** If your teacher has set a time limit, practice staying within it.
- **Speak clearly.** Do not rush your words, especially later when you are in front of your audience.
- **Speak up.** Your voice will sound louder to you than it will to the audience. If you sound too loud to yourself, you are probably sounding just right to your audience.
- **Work on eye contact.** Look down only to glance at a card.
- **Look interested and confident.** This will help engage your listeners.

Practice Checklist

To review each practice session, ask yourself the following questions.

_____ **1.** Did I appear at ease?
_____ **2.** Could my voice be heard and my words understood?
_____ **3.** Did I sound like I enjoyed and understood my topic?
_____ **4.** Were my visual aids interesting and used effectively?
_____ **5.** Did I avoid rushing through my speech?
_____ **6.** Did I include everything I wanted to say?

 Try It!

Practice your presentation. Give your speech to family or friends. Also consider videotaping your speech.

Delivering Your Presentation

When you deliver a speech, concentrate on your voice quality and body language. They communicate as much as your words do.

Controlling Your Voice

Volume, tone, and *pace* are three aspects of your formal speaking voice. If you can control these, your listeners will be able to follow your ideas.

- **Volume** is the loudness of your voice. Imagine that you are speaking to someone in the back of the room and adjust your volume accordingly.
- **Tone** expresses your feelings. Be enthusiastic about your topic and let your voice show that.
- **Pace** is the speed at which you speak. For the most part, speak at a relaxed pace.

Tip

You can make an important point by slowing down, by pausing, by increasing your volume, or by emphasizing individual words.

Considering Your Body Language

Your body language *(posture, gestures,* and *facial expressions)* plays an important role during a speech. Follow the suggestions given below in order to communicate effectively.

- **Assume a straight but relaxed posture.** This tells the audience that you are confident and prepared. If you are using a podium, let your hands rest lightly on the surface.
- **Pause before you begin.** Take a deep breath and relax.
- **Look at your audience.** Try to look toward every section of the room at least once during your speech.
- **Think about what you are saying** and let your facial expressions reflect your true feelings.
- **Point to your visual aids** or use natural gestures to make a point.

Try It!

Deliver your presentation. As you do, be sure to control your voice and exhibit the proper body language.

Research

Evaluating a Presentation

You can use an evaluation sheet to rate a classmate's speech. Circle the best description for each trait. Then offer at least one positive comment and one helpful suggestion.

Peer Evaluation Sheet

Speaker _____   Evaluator _____

1. Vocal Presentation

Volume:
Clear and loud   Loud enough   A little soft   Mumbled

Pace:
Relaxed   A little rushed or slow   Rushed or slow   Hard to follow

Comments:

a. _____

b. _____

2. Physical Presentation

Posture:
Relaxed, straight   A bit stiff   Fidgeted a lot   Slumped

Eye contact:
Excellent contact   Some contact   Quick glances   None

Comments:

a. _____

b. _____

3. Information

Thought provoking   Interesting   A few points   Not informative

Comments:

a. _____

b. _____

4. Visual Aids

Well used   Easy to follow   Not clear   None

Comments:

a. _____

b. _____

Preparing a Multimedia Report

You can enhance an oral report by using electronic aids such as slides and sound. In order to use these effectively, you must plan exactly how each will fit into your speech.

Here is a planning script for a multimedia report on social entrepreneurship. What will be seen appears in the "Video" column, and what will be heard appears in the "Audio" column. (Note that the speaker's directions are general, not the actual script.)

Planning Script

Video	Audio
1. Title Screen: "Meeting the Needs of the Future"	Sound: Music
2. Slide 2: Photo of burned church	Speaker: Introduction Sound: Music continues in background.
3. Slide 3: "The Problem: Social systems are about 300 years behind the times."	Speaker: Explain the problem.
4. Slide 4: "The Solution: Social Entrepreneurship"; photo of Bill Drayton	Speaker: Explain Bill Drayton's organization. Sound: Upbeat background music
5. Slide 5: "One Example: Erzsébet Szekeres"; photos of scenes inside group homes	Speaker: Describe Szekeres' achievement. Sound: Music continues.
6. Slide 6: "Another Example: Wojciech Onyszkiewicz"; chart showing exchange process	Speaker: Describe Onyszkiewicz' achievement. Sound: Music continues.
7. Slide 7: Photos of other social entrepreneur examples	Speaker: Conclusion Sound: Music up and out

Multimedia Report Traits Checklist

Revise

Revise your writing. Use the following checklist to help you improve your multimedia report. When you can answer "yes" to all of the questions, your report is ready.

Revising Checklist

Ideas

_____ 1. Have I included the main ideas of my research paper in my multimedia report?

_____ 2. Have I effectively supported my main ideas?

_____ 3. Does each slide or sound bite suit the audience and the purpose of the paper?

Organization

_____ 4. Do I state the topic in my introduction?

_____ 5. Do I include the important main points in the body?

_____ 6. Do I restate my focus in the conclusion?

Voice

_____ 7. Do I sound interested and enthusiastic?

_____ 8. Is my voice clear, relaxed, and expressive?

Multimedia and Word Choices

_____ 9. Are the words and pictures on each slide easy to see and read?

_____ 10. Have I chosen the best audio and video clips?

Presentation Fluency

_____ 11. Does my oral report flow smoothly from point to point?

Conventions

_____ 12. Is each slide free of errors in grammar, spelling, capitalization, and punctuation?

Writing Across the Curriculum

Writing in Science

Writing is central to science. It allows scientists to express their hypotheses, to record observations, and to communicate their conclusions. Writing gives structure to the scientific method.

In science classes—chemistry, physics, geology, astronomy, and life sciences—you can make discoveries about the natural world and learn ways to explore it further. Writing about the practical applications of science in your everyday life requires thoughtful research skills, accurate observations, and clear explanations.

This chapter covers types of writing that you will encounter in your science classes and in projects that require scientific knowledge. In research papers and responses to prompts, you share what you learn with your teacher and others. Practical writing allows you to apply what you've learned about science to jobs, hobbies, or day-to-day situations.

- **Taking Classroom Notes**
- **Taking Reading Notes**
- **Keeping a Learning Log**
- **Writing Guidelines: Cause-Effect Essay**
- **Writing Guidelines: Procedure Document**
- **Response to an Expository Prompt**

"Science is the desire to know causes."
—William Hazlitt

Taking Classroom Notes

Taking good notes helps you remember key lecture points, understand new material, and prepare for tests and writing assignments. Follow these tips to take good notes in your classes.

Before you take notes . . .

- **Set up your notes** in a three-ring binder so that you can insert handouts. A spiral notebook with a folder in the back is another option.
- **Date each entry** in your notebook and write down the topic.
- **Organize each page.** A two-column format with lecture information on the left and questions on the right works well.

As you take notes . . .

- **Listen for key words.** Pay attention to information that comes after phrases like *for example, as a result,* or *most importantly.*
- **Use your own words** as much as possible.
- **Write down questions** as they occur to you.
- **Draw pictures** or quick sketches to capture complex ideas.

After you've taken notes . . .

- **Reread your notes** after class and add any information needed to make them clearer.
- **Study your notes** to prepare for tests and exams.

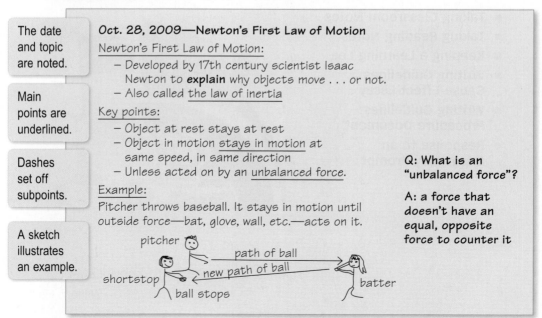

The date and topic are noted.

Main points are underlined.

Dashes set off subpoints.

A sketch illustrates an example.

Oct. 28, 2009—Newton's First Law of Motion

Newton's First Law of Motion:
- Developed by 17th century scientist Isaac Newton to **explain** why objects move . . . or not.
- Also called the law of inertia

Key points:
- Object at rest stays at rest
- Object in motion stays in motion at same speed, in same direction
- Unless acted on by an unbalanced force.

Example:
Pitcher throws baseball. It stays in motion until outside force—bat, glove, wall, etc.—acts on it.

Q: What is an "unbalanced force"?

A: a force that doesn't have an equal, opposite force to counter it

pitcher
path of ball
new path of ball
shortstop
ball stops
batter

Taking Reading Notes

Note taking can increase your understanding of reading assignments. Here are some tips on taking reading notes.

Before you take notes . . .

- **Write the date, chapter, book title, and topic** before each entry.
- **Organize each page.** For a two-column format, put your notes on the left and your thoughts and questions on the right.
- **Quickly skim the assigned text.** Read the title, introduction, headings, and chapter summaries. Examine any graphics, charts, and examples.

As you take notes . . .

- **Write down headings or subtopics** and the most important details under each.
- **Use your own words** to help you understand the material better.
- **Summarize graphics.** Write down or sketch out main ideas.
- **List vocabulary words** and look up definitions later.

After you've taken notes . . .

- **Review your notes.** When you're done reading, write down any other questions you have. Research the answers and add them to your notes.

Nov. 10, 2009—Today's Physics: Chap. 4, Sec. 5
Centrifugal and Centripetal Force

1. Centripetal means force that causes objects to follow a circular path.

2. This force is perpendicular to the line of travel.

3. Centrifugal force is the apparent outward force of circular motion.

4. This force is an effect of rotation inertia and is not a true force.

Q: How does this fit into the laws of motion?

Example: Whirling a can on a string—the string is the force.

Q: What's the difference between centripetal and centrifugal?

A: Centrifugal means "center fleeing." Centripetal means "center seeking."

Questions and thoughts are listed in the second column.

Try It!

Use the information above as a guide the next time you take notes for a reading assignment. For the best results, be sure to follow all of the tips.

Keeping a Learning Log

A learning log is a specialized journal you use to reflect on things you are learning. In a learning log, you write about new concepts by connecting them to previous learning or personal experiences. Here are some tips for keeping a learning log.

Before you make an entry . . .

- **Set up your learning log** in a binder or notebook.
- **Write the topic and date of each entry** so that you can find it easily.
- **Leave wide margins** so you have room for your own thoughts and questions.

As you make an entry . . .

- **Summarize key concepts** and develop meaningful comparisons.
- **Apply new ideas** to things you already know.
- **Think about questions** you may have about the subject.
- **Predict how the new ideas** may prove helpful in the future.
- **Make personal connections** by explaining what the ideas mean to you.

After you've made an entry . . .

- **Review your entries** periodically to see how your thoughts have been developing.
- **Research any questions** you have and write down the answers.
- **Continue your reflections** by writing new observations in the margins.

Tip

You can use an approach called "stop and write" for your learning log. Stop in the middle of your reading or at the end of your classroom discussion and immediately write down your thoughts about what you've just learned. This can show how well you understand the topics in your science class. Your learning-log entries can also help you prepare for exams by revealing which concepts were the most difficult for you.

Try It!

Follow the guidelines above to set up your own learning log. When you have a few minutes during class, stop and write, reflecting on what you are learning. Make personal observations about the ideas.

Learning-Log Entries

Here are some sample learning-log entries from a student in an earth science class focusing on geology. The student thinks about the ideas discussed in class, analyzes them, and applies the theories to current news events.

The date and topic are given, and ideas from the class are reviewed.

Questions are listed, and answers from the teacher and from additional reading are added.

Another entry shows growing understanding.

March 12, 2009 – Plate Tectonics

Today we discussed plate tectonics, a theory that has changed the way geologists view the earth. Alfred Wegener proposed the theory in 1912, but it wasn't widely accepted until the mid-20th century.

Plate tectonics theory says the earth is made up of large plates, which move and change over time. Where plates meet, volcanoes and earthquakes occur and mountains are likely to form.

Plate tectonics suggests that continents are drifting, and new oceanic crust is being created at mid-ocean ridges, then moving out from there. This is called sea floor spreading.

March 13, 2009 – Earth's Layers

We saw a presentation on plate tectonics. The earth has three layers — the core, the mantle, and the crust. The crust and upper mantle, called the lithosphere, are rigid plates. The softer, lower mantle is called the asthenosphere. Convection from radioactive heat in the earth's core occurs here, causing plates to move.

Plates move away from each other, toward each other, and over each other. There are 7 major plates and 20 smaller ones.

Q: Why didn't scientists accept Wegener's theories at first?

A: Scientists couldn't understand what force would be strong enough to move continents.

Q: What evidence supports plate tectonics?

A: New, more precise tools help scientists measure activity at plate boundaries and explore deeper in the earth.

Q: Why is this important?

A: Scientists can more accurately predict earthquakes and tsunamis.

Writing Guidelines Cause-Effect Essay

In your science classes, you might be called on to research the causes and effects of scientific phenomena. Your focus might be on one cause and one main effect, multiple causes and effects, one effect and its many causes, or so on. Follow these guidelines.

Prewriting

- **Select a topic.** If your teacher doesn't assign a specific topic, review your class notes, learning log, and textbook for ideas. Think about topics you have discussed in class. Choose a topic with a number of causes and/or effects.
- **Gather details.** Research your topic so that you understand it thoroughly. List the topic's cause and effects, or the central effect and its causes. (Consider using a graphic organizer. See page **586**.)
- **Outline your essay.** Write a thesis statement that names your topic. Then write down the causes and effects, in order of importance. Include any important details explaining the cause and its effects (or the effect and its causes).

Writing

- **Connect your ideas.** Create a beginning that introduces the topic and leads to your thesis statement. Write a middle that outlines the causes and effects in order of importance. Include the details you gathered in your research. Conclude by explaining what was learned.

Revising

- **Review your writing.** Review your first draft for *ideas, organization, and voice.* Ask yourself the following questions: *Does my essay focus on the causes and effects? Does it include plenty of scientific details? Does my voice sound knowledgeable and appropriate?*
- **Improve your style.** Check your *word choice* and *sentence fluency,* asking yourself these questions: *Have I correctly used and defined scientific terms? Do my ideas flow smoothly?*

Editing

- **Check for conventions.** Use the rubric on pages **198–199** as a final revising and editing guide. Then, proofread your essay for errors.
- **Prepare a final copy.** Make a neat final copy of your cause-effect essay and check it for errors.

Cause-Effect Essay

In this essay, Chan discusses the effects of natural events and human actions on lakes, rivers, streams, and aquifers.

Balancing Nature: How Drought, Floods, and Irrigation Impact Watersheds

The **beginning** introduces the topic and leads to the thesis statement (underlined).

Increasingly, water supplies depend on well-managed watersheds, areas that receive precipitation and then hold it as groundwater or as a form of surface water (freshwater lakes and marshes). Extensive woodlands absorb and hold water that would otherwise simply run off into streams and rivers and be lost for local water needs. Various types of vegetation and ground cover, artificial reservoirs, as well as natural lakes and marshes, also serve as vital watersheds. A number of natural conditions and human activities cause the consistent supply of clean, fresh water to be put at risk in this country and around the world.

Drought, an extended period of dramatically below-normal precipitation, directly affects lakes, rivers, and streams. Insufficient rain and snow mean that river flow will decrease and groundwater levels will fall. Such conditions often produce stagnant pools that are breeding grounds for algae, mosquitoes, and other harmful organisms. In addition, wells may not provide enough water or may dry up altogether.

The **middle** first discusses two major natural causes that affect a watershed. Examples of unwanted effects are identified.

Of course, too much moisture can also cause serious problems. Ground cover can be ripped away, increasing the chances that water will flow violently across the land. Flooding will not only destroy crops and homes, but it can also wash pollutants into lakes and rivers, raising bacteria levels. As a result, authorities have been forced to close beaches and use more chemicals to treat drinking water. Fertilizer, a benefit to crops, becomes a menace when washed into the watershed because it feeds algae. The nutrients in the fertilizer cause this small plant to bloom wildly and cloud the water. If conditions are right, algae blooms can sufficiently deplete the oxygen supply in the water to kill fish. In such extreme cases, recreational use of lakes and streams sharply declines, impacting local communities dependent on tourist trade.

Two major actions that affect watersheds are described, and their effects are listed.

In the western part of the country, irrigation and the rapid growth of cities are more likely to be a problem. Even though farmers are guaranteed consistent yields and cities can increase in size, irrigation and the demand for water in cities draw down the levels of the lakes, rivers, and aquifers (underground water sources). Cities enter into legal battles with farmers to keep irrigation from harming the water supply. In some areas, irrigation increases the likelihood of saline seep, a condition in which salts accumulate in the topsoil, destroying its crop potential. Since the average moisture levels in the West are low, these two phenomena result in watershed levels drastically reduced and rivers almost drained of water.

As towns and cities grow and more people build in rural areas, natural drainage and water collection are changed or destroyed. Trees and other plants are removed during construction. Buildings and roads quickly shed water. This means an important source for replenishing local aquifers is lost. Also, oil, battery acid, and antifreeze (from cars, buses, and trucks) are quickly washed into the water system. Trash thoughtlessly discarded adds to the trouble. These unfortunate by-products of development affect the water quality for other communities downstream.

The **ending** summarizes the importance of the topic.

Many causes have negative effects on watersheds. Scientists, officials, and the public have a growing awareness of how vital watersheds are to clean, clear water for refreshment, agriculture, industry, and recreation. Well-maintained watersheds can minimize the problems created by drought. Protection of expanses of wetlands produces a natural overflow area to trap water and offsets the damage done by floodwaters. Keeping a "big picture" view of irrigation can reduce draining vital groundwater and avoid inefficient uses of water that rob watersheds. Development must take watershed issues into account by protecting existent watersheds and creating new ones.

Try It!

Write a cause-effect essay. Select a topic that interests you and follow the writing guidelines on page 456.

Writing Guidelines **Procedure Document**

Sometimes you have the opportunity to write about science outside of school. For example, you may be asked to write technical directions for others, based on scientific concepts you've learned in class. While this type of writing is more informal than academic writing, it still requires careful attention to details. The following writing tips will help.

Prewriting

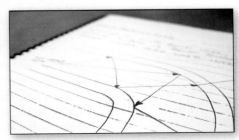

- **Focus on the purpose** of your writing assignment.
- **Jot down key points** you want to make. If you are describing a process, list the key steps.

Writing

- **Keep your purpose in mind** as you write.
- **Provide details** that support that purposé. Include all the key points you listed during your prewriting.
- **Use examples** where needed to make your key points clear.
- **Define any technical terms** to make sure that your reader understands the entire message.
- **Sum up** in your conclusion, restating the thesis of your writing.

Revising

- **Improve your writing.** Review your first draft for *ideas, organization,* and *voice.* Ask these questions: *Have I clearly stated my purpose? Have I included all necessary details? Have I given examples where needed?*
- **Improve your style.** Check your *word choice* and *sentence fluency* by asking these questions: *Have I used the best words for my purpose? Have I defined all technical terms I used? Do my sentences flow smoothly from one to the next?*

Editing

- **Check for conventions.** Proofread your writing for errors in punctuation, capitalization, spelling, and grammar. Remember, even a few errors in your writing may decrease the reader's trust in your information.
- **Prepare a final copy.** Make a neat final copy for your readers.

Procedure Document

Lena, a junior in high school, has been hired for a summer job supervising new lifeguards at her community swimming pool. One of her jobs is to train the lifeguards how to test the pool water and add needed chemicals. Lena knows from her chemistry class how dangerous chemicals can be if used in the wrong way. She prepared the following written guidelines for new workers.

<table>
<tr>
<td>

The **beginning** introduces the topic and leads to the thesis statement.

</td>
<td>

Safety Precautions for Pool Cleaning

Test the pool water regularly to measure the chlorine pH (alkalinity/acid) and calcium (hardness and softness) levels. Follow the testing schedule posted on the locked shed where pool chemicals are kept. Before using any of the chemicals for the first time, be sure to view the safety video. Mixing the wrong chemicals together or using them the wrong way can cause dangerous reactions, including the formation of toxic gas and even explosions. It is important to follow all safety precautions.

Observe the following safety precautions for handling pool chemicals:

</td>
</tr>
<tr>
<td>

The **middle** provides clear details.

</td>
<td>

- Read and follow all directions on the package.
- Observe any precautions on the package. This includes wearing goggles and gloves when handling certain chemicals.
- Store the chemicals only in proper containers.
- Add the chemicals to water. Do not add water to the chemicals.
- Use separate measuring cups for each chemical.
- Wear goggles and gloves when handling the chlorine.
- Wash your hands thoroughly after handling the chemicals.
- Don't touch your eyes, nose, or mouth when using chemicals.
- Keep the pool chemicals in the locked storage shed when not in use.

</td>
</tr>
<tr>
<td>

The **ending** summarizes the information and reinforces the thesis.

</td>
<td>

Being sure the pool water is clean is one of the most important regular maintenance procedures. Following these safety precautions will ensure protection while handling pool chemicals.

</td>
</tr>
</table>

Response to an Expository Prompt

On a science test, you may be asked to write a response to an expository prompt. This sort of test question is a great way to evaluate your knowledge and understanding of a scientific concept. You may have limited time to answer the question, so prepare using a writing strategy. Make the best of your time.

Before you write . . .

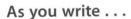

- **Understand the prompt.** Review the STRAP questions listed on page **212**. Remember that an expository prompt asks you to explain something or to share information.
- **Plan your time wisely.** Start by making notes and planning before you write. Save a few minutes at the end of the timed writing to read over what you have written. Then spend the main part of your time writing.
- **Make a graphic organizer.** Jot down main points and details for your essay.

As you write . . .

- **Decide on a focus or thesis for your essay.** Keep this main idea or purpose in mind during your writing.
- **Be selective.** Working from your notes, use examples and explanations that directly support your focus.
- **End in a meaningful way.** Close your essay by restating your main idea in a new way.

After you've written a first draft . . .

- **Check for completeness.** Use the STRAP questions on page **212** as a guide to revision.
- **Check for correctness.** Correct any errors in punctuation, capitalization, spelling, and grammar.

Tip

Many students feel nervous when taking a test, and that is only natural. However, by taking time to plan your response before you begin writing, you can increase your feeling of confidence about the subject.

Response to an Expository Prompt

The writer uses scientific knowledge to answer the following prompt. Notice how he responds to each aspect of the prompt.

Prompt

> *An outbreak of salmonellosis has occurred in your neighborhood. The victims had all eaten at Rob's Delicatessen, a neighborhood restaurant. Explain what salmonellosis is, why health officials might suspect the delicatessen as the source, and how to avoid future outbreaks.*

The first part of the prompt is addressed.

The second part of the prompt is discussed.

The final part of the prompt is answered.

Salmonellosis

Salmonellosis is the most common food-borne infection in the United States. Common symptoms of the disease are nausea, vomiting, fever, headache, abdominal cramps, and diarrhea. The condition is caused by salmonella bacteria, which usually enters the human intestines through food, especially undercooked poultry and raw eggs. Unrefrigerated foods containing cooked meat or eggs can also be a source of salmonellosis.

Because the infection is a result of improper food care, health officials are often able to track down the source. The fact that victims had eaten at Rob's Delicatessen makes that a likely source for this outbreak. By observing restaurant practices and testing foods served at the restaurant, health officials may be able to determine exactly what food caused the disease.

Meats and eggs must be fully cooked and properly refrigerated. Raw meats and eggs should always be kept separate from prepared foods. By following these health rules, the staff of Rob's Delicatessen can help avoid another salmonellosis outbreak.

Try It!

Use this before-and-after strategy the next time you respond to an expository prompt in a science class. (See pages **211–217** for more information about responding to a prompt.)

Writing in Social Studies

Social studies involves taking a close look at people and their cultures. In order to get a clear picture of a social studies topic, you will often use information from a variety of sources (texts, charts, graphs, maps, photos, and so on). Besides gathering the information, you'll need to analyze, summarize, organize, and present it in a compelling fashion.

In social studies, you may be asked to respond to a topic in a number of different ways, including writing a biographical essay, responding to an editorial cartoon, or responding to a series of documents. This chapter contains information about how to accomplish all of these writing tasks. In addition, you'll find helpful tips for taking notes and for organizing data.

- **Taking Classroom Notes**
- **Keeping a Learning Log**
- **Writing Guidelines: Biographical Essay**
- **Writing Guidelines: Response to an Editorial Cartoon**
- **Writing Guidelines: Document-Based Essay**

"The power to question is the basis of all human progress."

—Indira Gandhi

Taking Classroom Notes

Effective class notes can help you to prepare for tests and do better on writing assignments. Here are some tips for taking effective notes in class.

Before you take notes . . .

- **Write the topic and date** at the top of each notebook page.
- **Read any class assignments thoroughly** before you come to class. This makes it easier to follow the classroom discussion.

As you take notes . . .

- **Listen carefully** to the discussion **and write down** the main ideas.
- **Copy what the teacher writes** on the board or on an overhead.
- **Condense information.** Write your notes in phrases and lists rather than in complete sentences.
- In general, **use your own words** to explain ideas and concepts.
- **Note new or unfamiliar terms** and add a definition later.

After you've taken notes . . .

- **Review your notes** as soon as possible.
- **Do reading or other research to answer questions** you still have.

Classroom Notes

The date and topic are noted.	September 15, 2009 **American Women's Campaign for Suffrage** <u>Early Years</u>

Main points are underlined.	– Started in the mid 1800s. **Many women**
	– 1848 women's rights convention in **involved also**
	  Seneca Falls, N. Y. **worked in**
	– Key figures: Lucretia Mott, Elizabeth Cady **the abolition**
	  Stanton, Susan B. Anthony, Clarina Nichols **movement.**

Dashes set off subpoints.	<u>A Long Battle</u> – Women fought for decades for the right to vote. – Efforts included public speeches, rallies, newspaper articles, handbills, and appeals to political leaders.

Try It!

The next time you take notes in class, use the sample and tips above as your guide.

Keeping a Learning Log

A learning log is a specialized notebook in which you can reflect on the ideas and facts you learn in class. Writing in a learning log can clarify your understanding of a topic and help you connect it to other ideas.

Before you make an entry . . .

- **Write the date and topic** on the page each time you make an entry.

As you make an entry . . .

- **Summarize key concepts** and compare them to more familiar ideas.
- **Explain in your own words** what the facts and ideas mean to you.

After you've made an entry . . .

- **Review your entries** to see how well you understand the class material. Also research any questions that occur to you.

Learning Log

Questions and thoughts are listed in the second column.

September 15, 2009
American Women and the Fight for Suffrage

Today we learned about American women's long battle to win the right to vote. It took decades of hard work and lobbying.

It's hard to imagine that at one time women did not have the same right to vote as men did. That meant that men made every political decision, from passing laws to declaring war. And women had to live under those laws, even though their ideas were not used to create them. I think many good ideas must have been wasted because women thought of them.

One woman who worked hard for suffrage was Elizabeth Cady Stanton. She was a national women's leader from 1848 to 1902. I am interested in her and plan to choose her as the subject of my biographical essay.

How would history be different if women had demanded the vote sooner?

Try It!

Keep a learning log for one of your classes. Concentrate on understanding topics and making a personal connection to what you learn.

Writing Guidelines Biographical Essay

In a biographical essay, you try to discover as much as possible about an individual through interviewing, reading, researching, and reflecting. Your goal is to present the individual's story in an interesting, engaging way.

Prewriting

- **Select a topic.** If a topic has not already been assigned by your teacher, choose a person who interests you and who is related to a social studies topic you are studying.
- **Gather details.** Learn all you can about your subject. Read books and Web site articles. Study the person's own writings, if any are available. Remember to focus on the most important events in your subject's life.

- **Outline your essay.** Organize your notes in a logical way. In a biographical essay, events in the subject's life are usually presented in chronological order.

Writing

- **Connect your ideas.** Introduce your topic with an interesting detail that will capture the reader's attention. In the middle paragraphs, include details about significant events in your subject's life. Write an ending that sums up your subject and his or her significance.

Revising

- **Improve your writing.** Review your first draft for *ideas, organization,* and *voice.* Make sure that you have included facts and ideas that bring your subject to life.
- **Improve your style.** Check for *word choice* and *sentence fluency.* Make sure that your sentences flow smoothly and that you have clearly defined any unfamiliar terms.

Editing

- **Check for conventions.** Proofread your essay and correct any errors in punctuation, capitalization, spelling, and grammar.
- **Prepare a final copy.** Make a neat final copy of your biographical essay. Proofread this copy and make any necessary changes before sharing it.

Biographical Essay

In this essay, a student writes about the life and political career of women's rights activist Elizabeth Cady Stanton, using class notes as a source.

Elizabeth Cady Stanton, Political Pioneer

Today, American women enjoy the right to vote in elections, from local offices all the way up to the presidency, but this was not always the case. Women fought a long, hard battle to win suffrage. No one fought harder—or longer—than Elizabeth Cady Stanton.

Elizabeth Cady's early life prepared her for a career as an activist. She was born on November 12, 1815, in Johnstown, New York, to a powerful and well-educated family. She attended school at the Troy Female Seminary in Troy, New York, where she got a good education. Later, she studied law in the office of her father, Daniel Cady, who also served as a U.S. congressman.

In 1840, Elizabeth Cady married Henry Stanton, and her political career began. Henry Stanton, an abolitionist, was working to put an end to slavery. Elizabeth Cady Stanton joined the fight. At the World Antislavery Congress in 1840, she met Lucretia Mott, another abolitionist. Angry that women were not allowed to speak at the convention, the two began to discuss a campaign for women's rights.

In 1848, Cady Stanton helped organize the first-ever women's rights convention, held in Seneca Falls, New York. There, she presented the Declaration of Sentiments. Modeled on the Declaration of Independence, Stanton's document told of the unfair treatment women received and demanded that they be given equal rights.

Just three years later, Cady Stanton met Susan B. Anthony, another activist. The two became friends, beginning a political partnership that lasted more than 50 years. They worked hardest on a single issue—trying to earn women the right to vote. During much of this time, Cady Stanton was also raising a family, and she was unwilling to travel to give speeches and attend conventions. So she wrote powerful speeches for Anthony, who delivered them at gatherings all over America.

Elizabeth Cady Stanton died in 1902, and she never got to see women win the right to vote. That moment came in 1920, with the passage of the Nineteenth Amendment to the Constitution. This victory might never have happened without the work of Elizabeth Cady Stanton, who fought for women's rights for more than 50 years.

Writing Guidelines Response to an Editorial Cartoon

Editorial cartoons use words, images, and a sense of humor to make a serious point. To do this, they rely on exaggerated representations called caricatures. Editorial cartoons also employ symbols, labels, and brief captions to help relay their message. The following guidelines can help you respond to an editorial cartoon.

Prewriting

- **Analyze the cartoon.** Carefully consider both the visual and text elements in the cartoon. Ask for help if you are not sure what a particular element means.
- **Gather details.** List the different elements of the cartoon on a piece of paper. Write a brief description next to each element. (The two examples below relate to the cartoon on the next page.)

> **Polar bear:** The bear balances precariously on a tiny ice floe.
> **Talk show host:** The host is labeled "Skeptic."

- **Plan your response.** Identify the main point of the cartoon, and write a topic sentence that focuses on the main point. Then arrange the elements of the cartoon and their meanings to support your topic sentence.

Writing

- **Connect your ideas.** Begin with your topic sentence, which states the main idea. Then present your supporting details. End with a sentence that restates the main point of the cartoon.

Revising

- **Improve your writing.** Review your writing to make sure you have clearly and completely explained the editorial cartoon. If necessary, revise.
- **Improve your style.** Check your word choice and sentence fluency.

Editing

- **Check for conventions.** Proofread your response for punctuation, capitalization, spelling, and grammar. Correct any errors.
- **Prepare a final copy.** Make a clean final copy of your response.

Editorial Cartoon

"Are you sure global warming is real?"

ON AIR

SKEPTIC

RADIO

shrinking Arctic ice

Response to an Editorial Cartoon

Student writer Melba Fitzgerald wrote the following paragraph after taking some time to analyze the editorial cartoon above.

Ignoring the Call of the Wild

This editorial cartoon points out that despite the evidence in the natural world, many skeptics refuse to believe the reality of global warming. In the cartoon, a polar bear balances on a tiny ice floe, which is a polar bear's habitat. The floe is labeled "shrinking Arctic ice." The bear is connected by phone to a talk show host labeled "Skeptic," who challenges the bear's evidence about global warming. The cartoon expresses a powerful point: that nature is being changed by global warming, and that skeptics are refusing to believe the obvious evidence.

Try It!

Choose an editorial cartoon in a newspaper or magazine. Write a paragraph in response to the cartoon using the guidelines on page **468** and the sample above to help you.

Writing Guidelines Document-Based Essay

Your social studies teacher may ask you to respond to a prompt based on a series of documents. Text-based documents may include excerpts from books, newspapers, Web pages, diaries, or other text sources. Visual documents may include maps, charts, tables, graphs, time lines, editorial cartoons, or photographs.

Often, you will be asked to write an essay based on the documents; you may also be asked to translate information from the documents into a new form, such as placing data into a graph or a table. To complete such an assignment, you need to carefully analyze the documents and prepare your response. These guidelines can help.

Prewriting

- **Review the prompt to be sure you understand it.** Focus on key words such as *compare, explain, define,* and so on, which indicate the type of thinking and writing required.
- **Read all the information thoroughly.** Reread, if necessary, to understand the introduction to the topic as well as the meaning of the documents themselves before you begin to write.
- **Analyze each document.** Consider how the documents work together to present a picture of the topic. Be aware of documents that present opposing views.
- **Organize your facts.** Use an outline or other graphic organizer to plan your essay. Pull together information from all the documents and from your own prior knowledge.

Writing

- **Write a beginning paragraph.** Include a thesis statement based on the prompt.
- **Write the middle of the essay.** Follow your outline, beginning each paragraph with a topic sentence that explains part of your thesis.
- **Write an ending paragraph.** Briefly restate your position.

Revising

- **Improve your writing.** Be sure to review your essay for *ideas, organization,* and *voice.* Check *word choice* and *sentence fluency.*

Editing

- **Check for conventions.** Correct any errors in punctuation, capitalization, spelling, and grammar.
- **Prepare a final copy.** Make a neat final copy of your essay.

Sample Documents

Introduction: The increasing cost of health care has made staying healthy more and more difficult for many people in the United States. In the past decade, health-care costs have risen dramatically, putting both insurance and treatment out of reach for many people.

Document One
The High Cost of Health Care

Ask many people in this country today what worries them most, and sooner or later you'll get to the subject of health care. While today's advanced health-care technologies and procedures offer an unprecedented ability to keep people healthy, the cost of these technologies and procedures is skyrocketing. And with employers increasingly unwilling to shoulder the burden of health insurance coverage, many people who might benefit from modern health care are unable to afford it.

In the not too distant past, most employers offered their workers health insurance packages that allowed people and their families to maintain their health. But in an effort to cut costs and increase profits, many businesses have asked their employees to pick up a greater portion of the health insurance tab—or have cut health-care benefits altogether. Workers have few options—pay high premiums on their own, apply for limited benefits issued by the government, or simply live insurance free and hope to stay healthy.

Source: Hill, Ennis. *A System in Crisis.* Health Solutions Press, 2003.

Task: Summarize the relationship between businesses and the health-care crisis.

Many businesses used to pay for health insurance for their employees. But insurance is expensive, and many businesses are cutting or eliminating health benefits. That makes it harder for workers to get the health care they need.

> Only the most important information is included in the summary.

Document Two

Varied Views on the Health-Care Crisis

"We are proud to offer a broad range of medical treatment to our customers, and we are constantly working to expand coverage while keeping premium costs as low as possible."

Alan Singer, Health Insurance Council

"While I understand the needs of my patients, my costs are going up as well. Last year I paid $60,000 in malpractice insurance premiums."

Dr. Joanna Voss, orthopedic surgeon

"I pay $1,200 per month for health insurance for me, my wife, and my son. And I only bring home about $400 per week from my full-time job. Do the math."

Will Cartwright, security guard

"We'd like to offer our employees better health insurance, but the cost of premiums is going up. If I offer everyone health insurance, I may well have to go out of business."

Susan Chin, bookstore owner

"We feel that technology offers us promise. Using computers to manage and distribute medical records effectively, we can dramatically cut health-care costs."

Anna Lopez, health insurance claims adjuster

"The bottom line is that treatment comes first. I cannot and will not turn a patient away because he or she does not have insurance."

Dr. Bill Craig, general practitioner

Source: Comments from the Norfolk Regional Health Care Symposium, July 2005

Task: Make a chart showing the perspectives of consumers, doctors, and insurance companies on the health-care crisis.

A word or two is all that is needed to list answers in a chart.

Consumers	Doctors	Insurance Companies
– forced to choose between health care and other expenses	– pinched by costs of their own insurance – dedicated to patient care	– working to cut the cost of insurance – proud of helping people stay healthy

Document Three

People Without Health Insurance, United States, 2000-2004

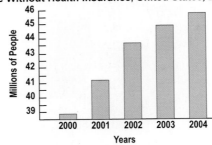

Millions of People

46 — 45 — 44 — 43 — 42 — 41 — 40 — 39

2000 2001 2002 2003 2004

Years

Task: Express the total increase in uninsured people from 2000 to 2004 as a simple number and as a percentage increase.

Graph information is changed to text form.

The total number of people in the United States who did not have health insurance increased by 7 million from 2000–2004. Reflected as a percentage, the growth of uninsured Americans was 18.04 percent.

Document Four

Task: State how the cartoonist feels about the health-care industry.

There. Does that feel better?

Health-Care Industry

An inference is used to interpret the cartoon.

The cartoonist is saying that the health-care industry cares more about money than making people healthy.

Document Five

Average Percentage without Health Insurance, 2002-2004

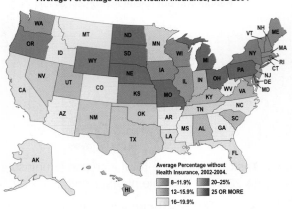

Average Percentage without
Health Insurance, 2002-2004.

- 8–11.9%
- 12–15.9%
- 16–19.9%
- 20–25%
- 25 OR MORE

Task: based on this map, identify state or regional trends in health insurance coverage.

> Statistics are used to make some generalizations.

     Overall, states in the Northeast and Midwest seem to be doing the best job of providing their residents with health insurance. In the South and the West, rates of uninsured tend to be higher. The state with the lowest percentage of uninsured is Minnesota. The state with the highest percentage of uninsured is Texas.

Document Six

     The quest to reform the health insurance industry could take years—maybe even decades. But meanwhile, there is plenty that United States citizens can do to lower the cost of health care. As a nation, U.S. citizens are remarkably unhealthy. By quitting smoking, losing weight, exercising more, and eating balanced diets, they can become dramatically healthier. This improved fitness would lead to a reduction of health-care costs not just for individuals, but for the nation as a whole.

Task: How does the writer propose to reduce health-care costs?

By encouraging Americans to improve their fitness levels.

Document-Based Essay

In this sample, a student writes an essay that draws on information presented in the six original documents.

Task: Extended Essay

Using all six documents and your own knowledge about this topic, write an essay about the health-care crisis in the United States.

Documents 1, 2, 3, 5, and 6
The opening defines the health-care problem and outlines the thesis.

The High Cost of Health Care

More and more United States citizens are asking themselves if they can afford to get sick. Faced with rising health-care costs and deprived of the solid insurance packages once offered by employers, many cannot afford health care. Even those who can are struggling under expensive premiums and prescription drugs. Will Cartwright, who told his story at the recent Norfolk Health Care Symposium, is a typical example of those burdened by a health-care system in crisis. He earns $400 a week as a security guard, and his health insurance costs $1,200 per month. Cartwright's plight is common, and a solution to the health-care crisis remains elusive.

Today, more and more U.S. citizens are unable to afford health care. From 2000 to 2006, federal, state, and local governments all worked to address the health-care crisis. Meanwhile, the number of uninsured people rose from 38.8 million to 46.6 million—a 20% increase. The hardest hit areas include the South and West; people in the Northeast and Midwest are more likely to be insured. But even in Minnesota, where the percentage of insured is highest, over 8% of people are not insured.

Health-care consumers aren't the only ones feeling pressured by health-care costs. Physicians have seen dramatic rises in malpractice insurance, and many have been forced to pass these increases on to their patients. Employers are feeling the pinch as well. While some employers cut their contribution to employee health insurance to increase their

Document 2
The problem is viewed from all angles.

profits, many employers still want to provide their workers with good coverage. It's just becoming harder to do. As premium costs rise, business owners are often forced to cut their health-care expenses or risk losing their businesses. Even insurance companies, often portrayed negatively, are struggling. They are proud to offer quality care but have trouble getting that care to the people who need it.

As the health-care crisis worsens, consumers, legislators, health-care practitioners, and health-care insurance representatives are desperately looking for a solution. The range of solutions is varied, from dramatic reforms to small, incremental ones. Among the former, the idea of a single national health insurance program, like that in Canada and many European countries, has been one of the most often proposed. Its proponents argue that cutting down the number of insurance providers will dramatically reduce paperwork and streamline operations, saving billions in costs.

Documents 2, 4, 6, and prior knowledge
Solutions are examined.

At the other end of the spectrum is a simple solution that many say could have dramatic results—making people in this country healthier. Proponents of this solution argue that by forcefully addressing public health issues such as smoking, obesity, nutrition, and physical fitness, the U.S. could dramatically reduce its dependence on the health-care system.

A powerful ending paragraph summarizes the situation and leaves the reader with something to think about.

As people search for a solution to the health-care crisis, the goal is clear—a system that offers quality care to more of our citizens. For those struggling with or locked out of the health-care system, the solution may come too late.

Essay Checklist

_____ **1.** Do all the ideas in my essay support my thesis statement?
_____ **2.** Do I fulfill the requirements outlined in the task?
_____ **3.** Do I summarize my main points in conclusion?
_____ **4.** Do I refer to information from all my documents?
_____ **5.** Do I include some of my own knowledge about this topic?
_____ **6.** Have I checked my punctuation, grammar, and spelling?

Writing in Math

As you move through high school, you may choose to take accelerated math courses, or not. No matter what you decide, you will find that it is important to understand mathematics. This is true whether you go to college, enroll in a technical program, or enter directly into the workplace.

Mathematics surrounds us in our daily lives. Balancing a checkbook, understanding loan interest, completing tax forms, and interpreting sports statistics all require knowledge of math. In this chapter, you will learn how writing can enhance your understanding of mathematics, both inside and outside the classroom.

- **Taking Classroom Notes**
- **Keeping a Learning Log**
- **Writing Guidelines:**
  Analysis of a Comparison Problem
- **Writing Guidelines:**
  Persuasive Essay
- **Response to a Math Prompt**
- **Other Forms of**
  Writing in Math

"The essence of mathematics is not to make simple things complicated, but to make complicated things simple."

—S. Gudder

Taking Classroom Notes

Using your own words to write down math steps and formulas can help you understand and remember them. Here are some note-taking tips.

Before you take notes . . .

- **Use a three-ring binder to store your notes** so that you can add handouts, worksheets, tests, and so on.
- **Write the date, textbook pages, and topic** at the beginning of each entry.

As you take notes . . .

- **Write down what your teacher puts on the board or overhead.** This information often contains math concepts, definitions, math terms, formulas, and important examples.
- **Put concepts in your own words.** Also write down questions you have about the material.
- **Draw pictures.** Use diagrams to help you visualize the problem.

After you've taken notes . . .

- **Find the answers** to your questions.
- **Study your notes** before the next class and again before exams.

Notes

Nov. 3, 2009, pages 344–345
Trigonometric Function Applications

Recall: Pythagorean Theorem is used to find the missing side of a right triangle if we know two side lengths. If we know one side of a right triangle, we can use the trigonometric functions to help us find another side.

$$\sin \theta = \frac{opposite}{hypotenuse}$$

$$\cos \theta = \frac{adjacent}{hypotenuse}$$

$$\tan \theta = \frac{opposite}{adjacent}$$

Problem: Find the missing side of the right triangle given.

We can use the cosine formula to find the hypotenuse, x.

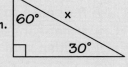

$$\cos \theta = \frac{adjacent}{hypotenuse}$$

We know that cos 60° = 0.5, so:

$$0.5 = \frac{5}{x}$$

Solving for x:

$$0.5(x) = \frac{5}{x}(x)$$

$$0.5x = 5$$

$$x = \frac{5}{0.5} = 10 \quad \text{So the length of the hypotenuse is 10 inches.}$$

Keeping a Learning Log

A learning log allows you to write about what you are learning, think through new concepts, ask questions, and find answers.

Before you write . . .

- **Set up the log.** Use a section of your three-ring binder so you have your learning log together with your notes.
- **Write the date and topic** at the beginning of each entry.
- **Leave wide margins** for writing questions and answers.

As you write . . .

- **Reflect on what you learn** by writing about what you understand and what is still confusing to you.
- **Summarize key concepts** and think about how they connect to your own experiences and to other ideas you have learned in math.

After you've written . . .

- **Answer any questions** you may still have about the topic.
- **Review your log** before a test or when you study a new topic.

Learning Log

Nov. 3, 2009 – Trig Apps

The sine and cosine functions can help us to find missing sides of right triangles.

We can use the definitions of the functions and patterns for right triangles with angles of "certain" degrees:

    30-60-90 degree triangles have sides of lengths x and $x \cdot \sqrt{3}$ and $2 \cdot x$

    45-45-90 degree triangles have sides of lengths x and x and $x \cdot \sqrt{2}$

The side opposite the 30° angle is x (5).

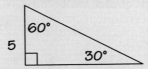

Using the pattern, the side opposite 60° is $5\sqrt{3}$ and the side opposite 90° is $2 \cdot 5 = 10$.

The size of the angles corresponds to the side length. (The shortest side is always across from the smallest angle.)

We could use the definition of cosine to find the other sides (see notes).

Try It!

Write a learning-log entry about a concept from a recent math class.

Writing Guidelines Analysis of a Comparison Problem

You may be asked to analyze a math problem, compare information, and then decide which of two options is better. To do this, you must understand these math concepts.

- **Assumptions** are statements believed to be true.
- **Evaluations** are step-by-step calculations and manipulations.
- **Explanations** clarify any confusing part of the estimate.

Prewriting

- **Select a topic.** If your teacher does not assign a specific mathematical comparison problem, review your learning log or textbook for ideas.
- **Review the assumptions.** Be sure you understand the assignment. Write down any assumptions and write down what you are comparing.
- **Plan the steps.** Break down the process into steps and write each step in the correct order.

Writing

- **Write your first draft.** First, introduce the problem and explain it step-by-step. Identify what it is you are comparing.
- **Perform the calculations** using the information provided about the comparisons.
- **Take into account that your answer involves choosing the better option.** Explain why it is better, using mathematics to support your conclusion.

Revising

- **Improve your writing.** Review your *ideas, organization,* and *voice.* Ask yourself the following: *Do I identify the assumptions and explain the process clearly? Do I sound knowledgeable?*
- **Improve your style.** Check your *word choice* and *sentence fluency.* Ask yourself the following: *Have I correctly used and defined any math terms? Do my ideas flow smoothly? Is the process clear?*

Editing

- **Check for conventions.** Mark all errors for correction.
- **Prepare a final copy.** Make a neat final copy of your work.

Analysis of a Comparison Problem

When a problem requires you to compare options, it's important to explain what you are comparing and to clearly show the reasons for your choice.

You are charged $20 per month for your cellular phone's calling plan. The first 30 minutes of local calls are free, but then you are charged $1 for each additional minute. You are also charged a roaming fee of $3 for each call that is placed outside of your local calling area, and $2 for each minute the call lasts (when outside of the area).

Last month you placed 32 minutes of local calls and made one three-minute call outside your calling area. Assume that all taxes are included in the prices given. Determine the answers to the following questions.

1. You heard about another calling plan. It would charge you $1 for each minute, local or long distance. Would this have been a better deal for you last month?

> The original plan cost $20 for the first 30 min. and $2 for min. over 30. The long-distance charge was $3 + $2(3 min.) = $9 for a total of 20 + 2 + 9 = $31.
>
> The new plan would cost $32 for the local calls ($1 per min.). The long-distance call would be $3 ($1 per min.). The new plan would cost 32 + 3 = $35. The new plan would not have been a better deal.

2. If you made the one long-distance call described above, how many minutes of local calls would you need to make the new plan a better deal?

> Original plan: New plan:
> $20 for 30 min. $30 for 30 min.
> + $9 long distance = $29   + $3 long distance = $33
>
> You would need to make fewer than 26 minutes of local calls since the plans are equal at 26 minutes.
>
> Original plan: New plan:
> $20 for 26 min. $26 for 26 min.
> + $9 long distance = $29   + $3 long distance = $29
>
> As can be seen, the two plans cost the same at 26 minutes. Therefore, the new plan is only a better deal for less than 26 minutes of local calls since the cost will fall below $29 while the original plan's cost will remain the same ($29).

Writing Guidelines Persuasive Essay

Mathematics is the study of numbers and symbols, and the methods of study can spark controversy. One controversial issue is the use of calculators in the classroom. Should students be forced to make calculations in the traditional way, or should they be allowed to use calculators for daily homework, and even on tests? At some point, you may be asked to decide on such an issue and defend your position. Use the guidelines below to help you develop persuasive essays about mathematics.

Prewriting

- **Select a topic that interests you.** Think about problems or issues related to mathematics in your school or your community.
- **Gather information.** Gather your own thoughts about the topic; then refer to other sources of information. Form your opinion. In your notes, label supporting points "pro" and opposing points "con."
- **Consider your reader.** Determine what your reader needs to know to appreciate your opinion.

Writing

- **Identify your position.** In your opening paragraph, introduce your topic and state your opinion about it.
- **Support your position.** Present the main supporting points and details that advance your argument. Be sure to present your main points in the best possible order.
- **Restate your position.** In the closing paragraph, restate your opinion and leave the reader with a final key idea.

Revising

- **Improve your writing.** Review your *ideas, organization,* and *voice.* Ask yourself the following questions: *Have I presented a reasonable argument? Do I sound logical and convincing? Is my essay easy to follow?*
- **Check your style.** Review your *word choice* and *sentence fluency.* Ask yourself the following questions: *Have I defined or explained any specialized words? Do my sentences read smoothly?*

Editing

- **Check for conventions.** Correct any punctuation, capitalization, spelling, and grammar errors.
- **Prepare a final copy.** Proofread this copy before sharing it.

Persuasive Essay

The following persuasive essay explains why one student thinks calculators should be allowed in high school math classes.

It All Adds Up to Yes

Students should be allowed to use calculators in math class. Because of the number-crunching speed of calculators, students can deal quickly with ordinary tasks such as long division, multiplication, and addition. Then they can focus on advanced math problems and the process of solving those problems. In addition, students can use calculators to see how different values can dramatically change the solution of a problem. For example, they can easily find the solution to the number of feet per second a car travels at 70 miles per hour versus 60 miles per hour. Of course, math teachers are worried that calculators may negatively affect math learning. It's possible that students could simply calculate answers without understanding the math process behind the solutions, but a simple test can show which students have mastered basic math skills. Only those students would be allowed to use calculators in class. To keep students' skills sharp, other tests could be given once every three months, or students could be required to do class work every Friday without using a calculator. Calculators could actually help to improve math understanding; therefore, students should be able to use calculators in math class.

Try It!

Think of another issue involving mathematics at your school. Gather information and write a persuasive essay that supports your position on the issue. Follow the guidelines on page **482**.

Writing Guidelines **Response to a Math Prompt**

Math prompts propose word problems. You are asked to respond in writing in addition to showing your mathematical calculations and your answers. First you must analyze the prompt and decide what you are supposed to do. Then you respond one step at a time. Follow these guidelines.

Before you write . . .

- **Read the prompt.** Read carefully and watch for key words such as *find, solve, justify, demonstrate,* or *compare.* Then carry out the requested actions only. Be aware that some prompts have more than one part.
- **Gather details and data.** Write down any values, assumptions, or variables provided in the prompt.

As you write . . .

- **Build your solution.** Respond to each part of the prompt. Jot down formulas or equations and sketch brief diagrams if they will help solve the problem. Make the necessary calculations to get an answer. Be sure to show all of your work.

After you've written a first draft . . .

- **Improve your response.** Reread the prompt after you do your calculations. If the problem has more than one part, be sure you have answered every part. Work the problem in another way to check that your solution is correct.
- **Check for conventions.** Check your solution for errors in punctuation, capitalization, spelling, and grammar.
- **Prepare a final copy.** Make a neat copy of your solution.

Response to a Math Prompt

The following math prompt contains more than one part. The writer answers each part using words, numbers, and diagrams.

Compare and contrast the graphs of the sine and cosine functions.

The sine and cosine functions have graphs that are similar in that they both have a period of 360°. This means they will repeat their pattern every 360°. They also have values that range between -1 and 1.

The graphs are different because the cosine function is really a shifted sine function. The graphs are the same (as explained above), but just shifted 90°.

The similarities and differences described above can be seen in the graphs of each.

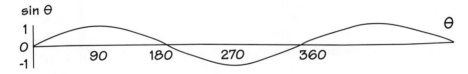

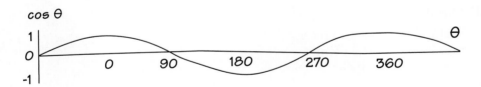

Try It!

Find a math prompt and write a response. Choose a practice prompt from your textbook or one recommended by your teacher. Follow the guidelines on page **484**.

Other Forms of Writing in Math

Descriptive Writing

Geometry or Trigonometry—Write a description of the water at a beach using geometry and/or trigonometry.

Definition

Trigonometry—Write a detailed expository paragraph on the definition of the word "trigonometry."

Classification

Geometry—Write an essay comparing and contrasting types of triangles.

Narrative

Any Math—Write a narrative essay about how you may be using math in your daily life three years after your high school graduation.

Process

Algebra—Write a process paragraph about the details needed to solve a linear equation.

Research

Any Math—Write a report on a famous mathematician. In your report, explain the historical context of this individual as well as his or her mathematical contribution.

Writing in the Applied Sciences

You take notes and write essays in school, of course, but writing is also an important part of the world outside of school. As an adult, you may need to write directions for someone, leave a note with instructions for the babysitter, write a letter of complaint for poor service or a faulty product, or compose a letter requesting funds for a PTA project. On your job, you may be asked to write reports, letters, summaries, and e-mail messages. Writing will always be a part of your life, and knowing how to write will allow you to effectively interact with the world around you.

In this chapter you will learn about taking classroom notes and keeping a learning log. You will also learn how to write a classification essay, a restaurant review, and a response to a test prompt.

- **Taking Classroom Notes**
- **Keeping a Learning Log**
- **Writing Guidelines: Classification Essay**
- **Writing Guidelines: Restaurant Review**
- **Writing Guidelines: Response to a Prompt**
- **Other Forms of Practical Writing**

"I learned from watching and I learned from doing."

—Claire Bloom

Taking Classroom Notes

Note taking can help you keep your projects organized and on track.

Before you take notes . . .

- **Keep a separate notebook for each class,** or use a three-ring binder with tabbed dividers for separate sections.
- **Divide your paper into two columns.** Use one for notes, and the other for questions or drawings.

As you take notes . . .

- **Date each entry** and keep the pages in order.
- **Briefly jot down teacher instructions** as they are given in class.
- **Draw diagrams** and use graphics to organize details.

After you've taken notes . . .

- **Review your notes** with a partner and highlight main ideas.
- **Study your notes** before beginning a project or before a test.

April 8, 2010

New food-group pyramid from U.S. Dept. of Agriculture:

- different pyramids for different age groups
- encourages exercise to balance nutrition
- calls for more nutrient-dense foods (more nutrients than calories)
- need to increase potassium and decrease sodium
- need to increase fiber, vitamins E and C, and calcium and magnesium

New teen food-group pyramid

- Whole Grains — 6–7 oz
- Vegetables — 2 ½–3 c.
- Fruits — 1 ½–2 c.
- Milk — 3 c.
- Meat and beans — 5–6 oz.
- Fats and oils — 5–6 tsp. max.

Try It!

Prepare a notebook to take notes in your next applied-sciences class.

Keeping a Learning Log

A learning log is a journal for recording what you learn in a class. The log lets you reflect on ideas, make drawings, and comment on projects.

Before you write . . .

- **Use a separate section in your notes** or a separate notebook.
- **Leave space** for writing questions and answers later on.

As you write . . .

- **Date each entry** and keep the pages in order.
- **Write about what you experienced,** what you learned, what worked, and what didn't. Also write any questions you still have.
- **Consider your next steps.** Write about how the material connects with other things you have learned and where it might lead.

After you've written . . .

- **Use your log as a supplement** to your notes to review for a test.
- **Write the answers to questions** you had in class or during a project.

May 4, 2010—Home Maintenance

    To replace a faucet, you just have to remember to shut off the water valve and to think ahead.

    After shutting off the water, I opened the faucet to drain the pipes, and then removed the water supply lines from the faucet. I made the mistake of twisting one of the lines when I turned it out, and it kinked so badly I had to get a new line.

    I had to crawl under the sink on my back to remove the nuts holding everything in place.

    When I fitted the new faucet into place, I forgot to put putty around the base to make a tight seal, so I had to take it up and redo it. Then all I had to do was reverse the steps.

What if the nuts are corroded and won't come loose?

Spray a little lubricant like WD-40 on the nut and let it work down to the threads. Wrap the wrench teeth with masking tape to keep from etching into the nut casing.

Try It!

Set up a learning log in a notebook or in a section of a three-ring binder. Be sure to date your entries and review them regularly.

Writing Guidelines Classification Essay

A classification essay divides a subject into different parts and proceeds to explain each part in turn. The goal is to completely explain each part.

Prewriting

- **Select a topic.** If your teacher does not assign a specific topic, review your notes, manual, or textbook for ideas. For example, in a metals class you might categorize different tools into groups. In a class on textiles, you could explain different kinds of needlework.
- **Gather details.** Use a graphic organizer to help you arrange your categories and details. Include work techniques, tools, and other materials used for each part.
- **Plan and organize.** Decide in which order to present your categories. How are they related? Decide on a pattern for moving smoothly from one category or item to the next.

Writing

- **Connect your ideas.** Introduce your points and their connection in the beginning paragraph. Then present each point, covering one completely before moving on to the next.

Revising

- **Improve your writing.** Examine your work for *ideas, organization,* and *voice.* Rework any ideas that are unclear or incomplete.
- **Improve your style.** Look at your *word choice* and *sentence fluency* and make any changes necessary to improve clarity and flow.

Editing

- **Check for conventions.** Look for errors in spelling, punctuation, and grammar.
- **Make a neat final copy.**

Classification Essay

For his building construction class, Carlo examined and wrote about the different types of windows.

The **beginning** introduces the topic and presents the thesis statement (underlined).

The **middle** examines each type in a separate paragraph.

The **ending** wraps up the essay and gives a final statement.

Windows on the World

One of the most important parts of new home construction is the type of window used. <u>There are three main types, each with its own advantages and disadvantages.</u>

One type is the double- or single-hung window. This type has two separate sashes that slide up and down on side tracks. In the double-hung window, both sashes move independently. In a single-hung window, only one of the sashes moves while the other is fixed. In both, a screen and/or storm window is usually attached to the outside. Some newer windows are designed to pull out for easy cleaning of both sides.

A second type of window is the casement window, which cranks out. An "awning" window has the hinge at the top. Sky windows—skylights that open—are usually of this type. A casement window can be adjusted to catch a breeze. These windows usually have the screen on the inside, and are cost efficient because of the tight seal they create when closed. However, because they open out, it is more difficult to clean the outside glass.

Sliding windows, or sliders, move sideways and comprise a third type of window. Because of their structure, sliding windows might have a screen either on the inside or outside. Cleaning these windows might be a little difficult, especially if they are located on upper floors.

All three types of windows have advantages and disadvantages. When considering which type of window to install in their homes, homeowners should consider the look desired along with efficiency and ease of care. The right window can certainly improve a home, as well as the homeowner's outlook on the world.

Try It!

Write a classification essay about something you are studying. Select a topic that you can break down into several categories.

Writing Guidelines Restaurant Review

A restaurant review is a specific type of writing. The review should cover all aspects of a restaurant, not just the food.

Prewriting

- **Pinpoint your purpose.** Explain why you are writing the review. Consider your audience. What will they want to know about the restaurant?
- **Gather details.** A restaurant review should include details about the menu, service, prices, and physical environment of the establishment. Include anything that makes the restaurant stand out or fall short.
- **Plan and organize.** Decide how to present your information. Reviews often use chronological order, as though the writer were taking the reader through the dining experience.

Writing

- **Include a clear beginning.** Present your first impressions or reason for visiting the restaurant.
- **Write the middle.** Describe the experience, noting both positive and negative points.
- **End with a final comment.** Wrap up by suggesting the reader either try or avoid the restaurant.

Revising

- **Improve your writing.** Check your *ideas, organization,* and *voice.* Add sensory details to describe the restaurant and your experience as completely as possible.
- **Improve your style.** Be certain your sentences vary in type and length and read smoothly. Avoid angry or inflammatory language, and keep your tone cool and neutral.

Editing

- **Check for conventions.** Look for any errors in spelling, punctuation, and grammar.
- **Make a clean final copy.**

Restaurant Review

Leona's Foods Service class focuses on running a cafeteria or restaurant. She used what she had learned to write the following restaurant review.

The **beginning** gives the purpose for the review.

The **middle** covers the atmosphere and service but focuses on the food.

A negative aspect is presented in a nonjudgmental manner.

The **ending** offers a wrap-up and a final thought.

Feed Mill Offers Old-Time Flavor

A new restaurant, The Feed Mill, recently opened in the Uptown District, an area greatly in need of new businesses. This restaurant should become an important part of this district for years to come.

Housed in the old Clayton Feed building, the restaurant draws its theme from its historic home. Huge sepia-colored photos of farms line the walls, while rusted farm equipment hangs from the ceiling. Old-time touches such as potbellied stoves and water pumps dot the dining area, which is enhanced by warm wood trim and red leather chairs and booths.

The menu continues the down-on-the-farm feel, with such home-style fare as "Mom's Meatloaf," but each dish boasts a distinctive twist. For example, the meatloaf is spiraled around a sweet potato filling. Even the restaurant's signature dessert, "Apple Brown Delia," is set apart by a hint of fresh ginger.

A nice touch is the huge list of country side dishes available, from "mulled applesauce" to "cheesy broccoli." Warm, crusty sourdough bread accompanies every meal. Prices run in the moderate range, and the a la carte option allows for affordable family meals. This is truly old-school cooking, and patrons will not find much in the way of heart-healthy or low-carb options.

Service is well paced, with attentive waitstaff dressed in butcher aprons, arm garters, and straw hats. The restaurant boasts a completely smoke-free environment.

The Feed Mill provides good, hearty food and is a bridge between cheap fast food and high-priced elegant dining. As such, it is a welcome addition to Clayton.

Try It!

Visit a local restaurant and write a review. Include details about the physical environment, service, menu, and overall quality.

Writing Guidelines Response to a Prompt

Before you write . . .

- **Know your time limit.** Plan your time to accomplish prewriting, writing, and revising.
- **Examine the prompt.** Look for key words that will help you determine the following elements:
  - **Subject** What is the topic of your writing?
  - **Purpose** Will you explain, inform, analyze, or persuade?
  - **Focus** What aspect of the subject should you examine?
- **Plan your response.** Write your thesis or opinion statement and organize details in a brief outline or graphic organizer.

As you write . . .

- **Write an effective opening paragraph.** Grab your reader's attention, provide necessary background information, and include your thesis statement.
- **Develop the middle.** Develop a clear topic sentence for each paragraph. Support each main point with details, including examples and paraphrases. If you are allowed to look at class notes or texts, include quotations and statistics.
- **Write a strong closing paragraph.** Restate your thesis statement and offer a final thought. If you are writing a persuasive piece, include a call to action.

After you've written a first draft . . .

- **Read through your work.** Add, cut, or move your details to make your work stronger. Make the most important changes, keeping your time limit in mind.
- **Check for conventions.** Correct any errors you find.

Response to a Prompt

Mai Li wrote a response to the following prompt.

> *Convince the school board to improve one of your classes.*

The **beginning** supplies background information and presents the thesis statement (underlined).

The **middle** paragraphs cover the main supporting ideas.

An objection is dealt with.

The **ending** restates the thesis and offers a final statement.

Real Baby Care

Our parenting class tries to teach students what it's like to care for an infant. We have used eggs and sacks of flour to represent babies, but we need a more accurate feel for taking care of a real baby. <u>The school board should purchase Baby Do All dolls.</u>

The Baby Do All doll is physically realistic and offers sounds, from a contented sigh to an ear-piercing shriek. A student must feed, change, burp, or cuddle the doll. The baby can also be programmed to cry no matter what, just like a real baby, to help students understand that having a baby can be frustrating.

While students can easily ignore an egg or a flour sack, the Baby Do All doll cannot be ignored. The doll interacts with its "parent" through an electronic wristband. Wireless control units transmit data to the control board, so teachers can monitor care conveniently and accurately grade students on their baby care.

Although the Baby Do All doll is somewhat expensive, it can present students with the reality of caring for a baby. This may lower the number of teen pregnancies. Statistics support this idea, showing that a realistic doll has much more impact on students than an egg or a sack of flour. The entire experience of child care becomes more intense, more exhausting, and more real.

The school board should consider purchasing these dolls for the parenting class. If our students have a real taste of parenting short term, they may think twice before becoming parents for real and always.

Try It!

Choose a writing prompt from those given you by your teacher. Write your response in the time limit your teacher sets.

Other Forms of Practical Writing

Process Essay

Auto Mechanics Class— Explain the steps necessary for changing a tire. Use imperative sentences with verbs that give commands.

Letter of Complaint

*Living On Your Own Class—*Write a letter of complaint to your landlord, who has put off fixing a leaky faucet in your apartment. Include specific details about why you need it fixed soon. State your case in a cool, neutral tone, and include a call to action.

Essay of Analysis

Food and Nutrition Class— Analyze a popular weight-loss plan, giving both the positives and negatives of the plan. Give specific possible short-term and long-range effects on the body.

Persuasive Essay

Home Construction Class— Persuade a client building a new home to include central air-conditioning. Include details about cost, efficiency, comfort, and value.

Essay of Explanation

Sewing for the Home Class— Explain what fabrics you would use to create a sofa slipcover, a lamp shade, formal draperies, and throw pillows. Give your reasons for choosing each fabric.

Problem-Solution Essay

*Advanced Metals Fabrication Class—*You are suddenly faced with a contaminated electrode while working on a project. Give possible causes of the problem and explain your solution.

Personal Narrative Essay

*Child Care Class—*Remember a time you received a punishment you thought was unfair. Describe how you felt about it then, and explain whether you still feel the same way. Suggest a different punishment that may have been more effective.

Writing in the Arts

Works of art or music stimulate your mind and trigger questions. Why did a painter use a particular medium? Why does an architect use certain materials? What are the roots of a particular style of music? How do different types of music and styles of art affect people's feelings? How are computer synthesizers and digital cameras changing music and art today?

As you explore the arts, through writing, you can deepen your understanding and enjoyment of these creative expressions. This chapter will help you write learning-log entries, essays, and reports about the arts. You may even want to try writing reviews of performances to share with others on your blog, on a Web site, or in the school newspaper.

- **Taking Classroom Notes**
- **Keeping a Learning Log**
- **Writing Guidelines:**
  Research Report
- **Writing Guidelines:**
  Performance Review
- **Writing Guidelines:**
  Response to an Art Prompt

"Music was my refuge. I could crawl into the space between the notes and curl my back to loneliness."

—Maya Angelou

Taking Classroom Notes

In art and music classes you usually work with a variety of art materials or practice for vocal or instrumental performances. However, it may occasionally be necessary to take notes in class. (See pages **528–530** for more information.)

Take notes when . . .

- **your teacher writes information on the board or overhead.**
  Taking notes helps make important information part of your own thinking. Be sure to write down new vocabulary words as well as names, dates, and key phrases.

- **you have a demonstration in class.**
  Your class may view slides of art pieces or listen to recordings of various musical styles. Taking notes will help you organize and remember the various works.

- **you have a guest speaker or performer.**
  Professional artists may visit your class and demonstrate or discuss their work. Your notes can help you think about the presentation. You may want to jot down questions you'd like to ask after the presentation.

Tip

- Date each entry and give it a topic heading so you can find it quickly when reviewing.

- List new vocabulary words. Leave room for adding definitions or examples later.

- Write down hints or examples to help jog your memory about a name, a term, or a concept.

- Draw sketches that may help you remember artworks.

- Mark a spot in your notes with a question mark if something confuses you and ask about it later.

- Divide note pages into two columns with one side wider than the other, so you can put notes on one side and questions on the other.

- Work with a "study buddy." You can compare notes, go over questions, and review for tests together.

Keeping a Learning Log

In project-based classes such as theater, art, and music, a learning log can help you keep track of, and reflect on, your progress. Latoya wrote the following entries in her learning log for an improvisational acting class. On the left side she made notes about what the teacher said, and on the right side she added comments about how the exercise worked for her.

Learning-Log Entry

Learning to improvise Understand improvisation.	Nov. 5, 2009 Improvisation means creating a character or scene that's not written out in a script.
Improvisation helps develop skills, ideas, and dialogue for sketches or longer works.	I think it would be easier to improvise comedy since there are so many improv comedy groups around today on TV and on the stage.
Tips from experts 1. Listen to the other actors . . . give and take. 2. Don't negate. 3. Avoid questions. 4. Use "yes, and" technique. 5. Be active—show as well as tell.	My group and I tried an improv comedy exercise. It was really hard the first time—it looks so easy on TV. I see why it's important to listen to what the other characters are saying, and not stop the scene by dismissing what they say—"negating." Asking a question also stopped the skit in its tracks. The "yes, and" technique keeps a scene or skit moving because you respond positively to what the other characters are saying and then add something new of your own.
Use your body . . . be the character.	This is easy for me since I like to watch people. In the exercise on character development, I thought about my aunt Yvette who always wears big flowery hats, sings off-key, and loves to dance – even when she's walking.
Exercise your acting muscles.	I found some books and lots of Web sites with improv exercises to try alone or with my group.
Keep energetic.	I haven't played a bear since kindergarten . . . that was fun!

Try It!

Set up a learning log for your drama, art, or music class. Keep one side for notes or instructions and the other side for your own comments.

Writing Guidelines Research Report

You may be asked to write a research report in your art or music class. You may decide to write about a famous painter or analyze a trend in music. The following guidelines will help you create a research report.

Prewriting

- **Choose a subject.** If your teacher doesn't provide a specific subject, list artworks, artists, musical trends, or other ideas that interest you.
- **List what you already know** about the subject, jotting down questions that you have.
- **Conduct research** about the subject. Check school or public library catalogs for books, look through magazines, and explore Web sites.
- **Write a thesis statement.** Review your research notes. Then write a thesis statement that clearly identifies the specific topic and focus for your research paper.
- **Plan and organize.** Outline your paper, putting details in the most appropriate order—for example, you may put key points in spatial order, chronological order, or order of importance.

Writing

- **Connect your ideas.** Introduce your topic, give background information, and state your thesis.
- **In the middle paragraphs,** support the thesis statement with specific details. Finally, summarize what you have learned or what you have to say about the topic.

Revising

- **Improve your writing.** Check your *ideas, organization,* and *voice.* Ask these questions: *Have I created a clear thesis? Have I supported it with a variety of details? Are my details in the best order? Do I sound knowledgeable?*
- **Improve your style.** Check your *word choice* and *sentence fluency.* Ask these questions: *Have I explained any technical terms? Do my sentences flow smoothly?*

Editing

- **Check for conventions.** Look for errors in spelling, punctuation, and grammar.
- **Prepare your final copy.** Proofread your research paper before turning it in.

Research Report

Artists reflect their own culture and background when they create works of art. Kerrie Shiver saw a painting by artist Frida Kahlo in a museum and became interested in her work. After researching this famous Mexican artist, she wrote the following report.

The introduction presents the thesis statement of the report (underlined).

Frida Kahlo: Pioneering Mexican Artist

Frida Kahlo was born in Mexico in 1907. Her father was a German immigrant and photographer while her mother was of Mexican and Indian background. Her dual heritage and her early work helping her father touch up photographs with delicate brushstrokes both influenced her art. The strong colors in her paintings reflect the simple, vivid tones popular in Mexican clothing and decoration. Kahlo incorporates her country's folk art and her painful personal struggles into her art.

When she was 18, Kahlo, then a medical student, was seriously injured in a bus accident. Her injuries resulted in long hospitalizations, multiple surgeries, and a lifetime filled with pain. As she recuperated over many months, Kahlo began painting. Her parents had fitted a mirror on her bed, so she became her own first subject, leading to many future self-portraits. "I paint myself because I am so often alone and because I am the subject I know best," she once said (Hubbard).

The body of the report links Kahlo's art to her heritage.

A turbulent marriage to fellow artist Diego Rivera contributed to the pain and unhappiness that fueled Kahlo's art, according to biographer Hayden Herrera (Herrera, 1983). For much of her life, Kahlo's art was overshadowed by her husband's work. In fact, when she died in 1954, the *New York Times* described her as the wife of the great Mexican muralist Diego Rivera and only mentioned that "she also was a painter" in the second paragraph of the story (Gates).

Kahlo's work was provocative, revolutionary, and sometimes disturbing. She painted herself as she was—with thick, straight eyebrows and a shadow of a mustache. Often, her pain and physical ailments were symbolized in her paintings—a broken column in place of her spine, for example. "They thought I was a surrealist," Kahlo said, "but I wasn't. I never painted dreams. I painted my own reality" (Lee).

The artist identified strongly with Mexico's indigenous people and was influenced by a surge of nationalism that developed in the early twentieth century. She often wore traditional Mexican clothing and braided and decorated her hair with flowers, ribbons, and bows in her self-portraits. Her black hair and strongly marked eyebrows contributed to the vivid impact of the self-portraits.

Kahlo frequently adapted folk forms and religious symbols and devices in her work. For example, in one famous self-portrait, she used the form of a *retablo*. The retablo was a traditional Mexican folk style that showed saints and miracles. Kahlo put her own portrait in the space usually filled by a saint.

Although her artistic accomplishments weren't recognized until shortly before her death (at age 47) in 1954, Kahlo's talent has made her art extremely popular in recent years. She was a key figure in the development of avant-garde art, pouring personal pain and her country's beautiful folk heritage onto canvases splashed with bright color (Garza).

Today Kahlo's Casa Azul, or Blue House, in Mexico City is a major tourist attraction and a source of Mexican national pride. "Mexicans don't lead what you would call an easy life, so in a certain way we see that tragedy reflected in her paintings," says one Mexico City resident, Roberto Munoz in an interview with the *New York Times*. "Although we don't suffer the same exact problems, we can see that she was able to overcome hers . . . and it gives us pride that people in other countries know her and identify with her" (Gates).

> The essay concludes with a summary of the impact of Kathlo's artwork.

Note: Kerrie also included a works-cited page to list the sources she cites in her report. (See pages **392** and **407**).

Writing Guidelines Performance Review

You may be asked to write about the arts by reviewing a specific performance. On the other hand, you may enjoy a performance so much that you want to share your thoughts with others through a blog, on your own Web site, or in a letter to someone.

While this type of writing is more informal, or personal, than most academic writing, you should follow basic writing guidelines. Readers will respect your evaluation if your writing shows clarity and insight, so be sure to maintain your focus throughout the review.

Prewriting

- **Focus on what you want to say.**
- **Make notes** on your impressions of a painting, show, or concert.
- **Write a thesis statement.** Review your notes and state your focus.
- **Plan and organize.** Outline key points you want to make in your review.

Writing

- **Write freely,** always keeping your main idea in mind. Use your outline as a basic writing guide.
- **Use examples to support your points.** Whether readers agree with you or not, they will appreciate what you've written if you support your point of view with solid evidence.
- **Keep your audience in mind** in terms of what you need to explain.
- **Write a strong ending.** Sum up why the topic was important enough for you to write about.

Revising

- **Improve your writing.** Check your *ideas, organization,* and *voice.* Ask these questions: *Have I created a clear thesis? Have I supported it with a variety of details? Are my details in the best order? Do I sound knowledgeable?*
- **Improve your style.** Check your *word choice* and *sentence fluency.* Ask these questions: *Have I explained any technical terms? Do my sentences flow smoothly?*

Editing

- **Check for conventions.** Look for errors in spelling, punctuation, and grammar.
- **Prepare your final copy.** Proofread your research paper before turning it in.

Performance Review

The Lima Beans, the nationally known Lima High School of the Arts jazz ensemble, performed at Antonio's high school. He wrote the following review to post on a jazz fan Web site.

Lima Beans Jazz It Up!

On the cold, rainy evening of March 21, people who attended the Lima Beans in concert at South High School found themselves immersed in a jazzy blast of spring. The Lima Beans dazzled with cool, crisp rhythms and passionate improvisations that lit up the gym. The Ohio-based ensemble from the Lima High School of the Arts proved that young musicians can master the challenges of jazz when they combine creativity and hard work.

The group showcased their knowledge of the fundamentals as they led off with the classic "Satin Doll." Then the Lima Beans explored complex and enchanting improvisations of some jazz standards. Igor Liban on the tenor sax did breathtaking displays of that instrument's range. Keyboardist Johnny Black brought power and a satin-smooth touch to his rendition of "Cry Me a River." Later, Juniper Green drummed up a furious compelling beat in "It Don't Mean a Thing (If It Ain't Got that Swing)." Bass player Aldar Winski led the way through some playful improvisations of "April in Paris" and "The Way You Look Tonight." All the musicians exhibit talent and intense energy as they perform, and it's evident they are having fun.

Because of the demands of their academic studies, the Lima Beans don't have a tour schedule. If given the chance, any jazz enthusiast should hear these gifted young musicians on the road to jazz fame.

Writing Guidelines Response to an Art Prompt

You may be asked to write a short essay in response to a prompt about art or music as a class assignment or as part of a test. Responding to a prompt allows you to express what you have learned about a specific work of art or style of music. Here are guidelines for responding to an art prompt.

Before you write . . .

- **Understand the prompt.** Read the prompt and focus on what you are asked to do. Should you explain, compare, describe, or persuade?

- **Gather your details.** If permitted, review your notes and research materials. Highlight or jot down important details. Note sources for quotations or facts. If you aren't permitted to use notes or research materials, jot down key facts that you remember about the topic.

- **Organize your details.** Check the prompt for clues that will help you organize your response. For example, if the prompt asks you to describe the jazz classic "Take Five" and discuss how improvisation reshapes the music, you might begin with a general description of the piece and then discuss specific musical themes that serve as springboards for improvisation. You could mention how specific instruments and performers develop the basic themes in creative variations.

As you write . . .

- **Write freely.** Use your notes as a guide and try to include all your main ideas. Many short responses are just one paragraph long. If your prompt calls for an essay, use a new paragraph for each main point.

After you've written a first draft . . .

- **Improve your writing.** Read your draft and cut any details that don't fit the prompt. Add information that will clarify your ideas or help answer the prompt. Make your response as complete as possible.

- **Improve your style.** Check your *word choice* and *sentence fluency* so that your response reads smoothly.

- **Check for conventions.** Look for errors in spelling, punctuation, and grammar.

Response to an Art Prompt

In the following two-part response, Juan discusses the way theme music is used in movies and television.

> *Answer the following questions in one or more paragraphs: (1) How does the music in the movie* Jaws *contribute to the mood and story? and (2) How does the signature theme help develop the "character" of the shark?*

First, the writer explains how the movie's sound track contributed to the film's success.

Response #1

Composer John Williams created the music for the 1975 movie <u>Jaws</u> at the request of young director Steven Spielberg. The movie's sound track was such an integral part of the story that people who weren't even born in 1975 hear that ominous theme and know a shark is about to attack.

Then the writer gives specific examples.

Director Spielberg's first response when Williams picked out the two-note theme on a piano was, "Is that all?" But, then the notes were put into a bass line that started at slow intervals, then built into a frenzy of suspense. Other sections of the Williams' sound track for <u>Jaws</u> set a happy mood as tourists pour into town to enjoy the fun of a holiday by the sea. This warm, flowing, nostalgic sound provides a sharp contrast to the tense notes that symbolize the danger lurking below the surface.

Response #2

Next, the writer addresses the importance of the theme music.

In 1975, computer animation graphics were primitive, so Spielberg relied on a mechanical shark, which, unfortunately, didn't always work. So the director used the music to replace the mechanical shark in many scenes. The shark theme established the Great White's presence and power — even when the shark wasn't visible. The two notes mimic the shark's pulse, speeding up as the monster sights a tempting victim.

Try It!

Respond to a short-essay prompt your teacher will supply about a topic you are studying. Write a one- or two-paragraph answer.

Writing in the Workplace

Whatever career you're planning—police officer, customer-service representative, nurse, lawyer, executive assistant, video game designer—chances are writing will be part of your job. Although the forms of writing may be changing—a customer-service representative often writes an e-mail message to a customer rather than a formal, typed letter—the essentials remain the same. A written message becomes a record of important details for both the writer and the recipient in the workplace.

As a student, you will write business letters and e-mail messages to seek information, apply for internships, and deal with problems. You may also use other forms of workplace communication—memos, proposals, and brochures—at school, in a summer or part-time job, or as part of your work with an organization or a club. This chapter shows you some of the tools and techniques that will help you with your workplace writing.

- **Business Letters**
- **Writing Guidelines: Short Report**
- **Writing Guidelines: Proposal**
- **Writing Guidelines: Memo**
- **Writing Guidelines: E-Mail Message**
- **Writing Guidelines: Brochure**

"Put it before them briefly so they will read it, clearly so they will appreciate it, picturesquely so they will remember it, and above all, accurately so they will be guided by its light."

—Joseph Pulitzer

Parts of a Business Letter

Writers use business letters to request information, apply for a job, or file a complaint. The basic format of an effective letter is similar whether it is sent through the regular mail or delivered via e-mail.

- The **heading** includes the writer's complete address, either on company stationery, in a computer template, or typed out manually. The heading also includes the day, month, and year. If the address is part of the letterhead, place only the date in the upper left-hand corner.

- The **inside address** includes the recipient's name and complete address. If you're not sure who should receive the letter or how to correctly spell someone's name, you can call the company to ask. If a person's title is a single word or very short, include it on the same line as the name, preceded by a comma. If the title is longer, put it on a separate line under the name.

- The **salutation** is the greeting. For business letters, use a colon following the recipient's name, not a comma. Use Mr. or Ms. followed by the person's last name, unless you happen to be well acquainted with the person. Do not guess at whether a woman prefers *Miss* or *Mrs.* If the person's gender is not obvious from the name, one acceptable solution is to use the full name in the salutation. For example, *Dear Pat Johnson.* If you don't know the name of the person who will read your letter, use a salutation such as one of these:

  - Dear Manager:
  - Dear Sir or Madam:
  - Attention: Human Resources Department
  - Attention: Personnel Director

- The **body** is the main part of the letter. It is organized in three parts. The beginning states why you are writing, the middle provides the needed details, and the ending focuses on what should happen next. In a business letter, double-space between the paragraphs; do not indent. If the letter is longer than one page, on subsequent pages put the reader's name at the top left, the page number in the center, and the date at the right margin.

- The **complimentary closing** ends the message. Use *Sincerely* or *Yours truly*—followed by a comma. Capitalize only the first word.

- The **signature** makes the letter official. Leave four blank lines between the complimentary closing and your typed name. Write your signature in that space.

- The **notes** tell who authored the letter (uppercase initials and a colon), who typed the letter (lowercase initials), who received a copy (after *cc:*), and what enclosures are included (after *Enclosure* or *Encl.:*).

Workplace

Letter of Inquiry or Request

The management of a local mall has expressed concern about the number of teenagers gathering there after school. The Irving High School Student Council president, Lucas Haynes, wrote a letter to the mall's manager. A list of recommendations is enclosed, and the school's vice principal is copied.

Heading

Irving High School Student Council
512 E. Lincolnview Ave.
Springfield, NY 10081-4310
November 10, 2009

Four to Seven Spaces

Inside Address

Ms. Alicia Guerrero, Manager
Lincoln Mall
598 E. Lincolnview Ave.
Springfield, NY 10081-4310

Double Space

Salutation

Dear Ms. Guerrero:

Double Space

I am writing on behalf of the student council of Irving High School. We are aware of your concerns about student behavior after school in the Lincoln Mall. In addition, some students have complained to school administrators and student council members about their treatment by the mall security staff.

The writer explains who he is and why he is writing, provides needed details, and suggests a next step.

Many students enjoy gathering at the mall after school to visit with friends. During the winter, weather makes it difficult to spend much time outside on the school grounds. Of course, many students also enjoy shopping at Lincoln Mall.

We would like to invite you to meet with the student council officers and Mr. Washington, Irving's vice principal, to discuss the situation and work to resolve any problems.

I have enclosed a list of recommendations the student council developed to help solve the problem. If you are willing to meet with us, please contact Ms. Joyce Brown in the school office at 555-4200 ext. 10 to arrange a date and time.

Double Space

Complimentary Closing

Sincerely,

Signature

Lucas Haynes   Four Spaces

Lucas Haynes,
Student Council President

Double Space

**Initials
Copies
Enclosure**

LH:jb
cc: Mr. Isaac Washington
Encl: Student Council recommendations

Letter of Application

Keisha Bingham wrote the following letter to apply for a summer job at a church camp.

Keisha Bingham
148 Helmer St.
Ft. Wayne, IN 46802-1704
April 28, 2009

Clara Taylor, Camp Director
Missionary Baptist Church
433 Lehner Ave.
Ft. Wayne, IN 46802-1803

Dear Ms. Taylor:

My name is Keisha Bingham. I'm completing my junior year in high school. My friend, Kayla Warner, who is a member of your church, mentioned that Camp Wawasee always needs summer help. I am interested in applying for a job as a counselor this summer.

For the past two summers, I have worked as a full-time babysitter for Mr. and Mrs. Joseph Adams, a couple with four children now ages 5, 7, 8, and 11. I have also volunteered in the Sunday School at Grace Baptist Church, helping with crafts.

In my paid and volunteer positions, I was responsible for caring for and supervising young children. My future goal is to become a school psychologist, so working at the camp would fit with my interests and career plans. I have taken courses in child care and child development.

I can supply letters of recommendation from Mr. and Mrs. Adams and from Grace Sanderson, my supervisor at the Sunday School. You may contact me at the address above, by e-mail at Keishabingham@localmail.com, or by phone at 555-1239. Thank you for considering my application.

Sincerely,

Keisha Bingham

Keisha Bingham

The opening introduces the writer as well as the purpose of the letter.

The middle paragraphs discuss background and qualifications.

The closing adds information and thanks the reader.

Signature

Preparing the Letter for Mailing

Letters sent through the mail will get to their destinations faster if they are properly addressed and stamped. Always include a ZIP code.

Addressing the Envelope

Place the return address in the upper left corner, the destination address in the center, and the correct postage in the upper right corner. Some word processing programs will automatically format the return and destination address.

KEISHA BINGHAM
148 HELMER ST
FT WAYNE IN 46802-1704

MS CLARA TAYLOR
MISSIONARY BAPTIST CHURCH
433 LEHNER AVE
FT WAYNE IN 46802-1803

There are two acceptable forms for addressing the envelope: the traditional form and the new form preferred by the postal service.

Traditional Form	**Postal Service Form**
Liam O'Donnell	LIAM O'DONNELL
Macalester College	MACALESTER COLLEGE
Admissions Office	ADMISSIONS OFFICE
1600 N. Grand Ave.	1600 N GRAND AVE
St. Paul, MN 55105-1801	ST PAUL MN 55105-1801

Following U.S. Postal Service Guidelines

The official United States Postal Service guidelines are available at any post office or online at www.usps.org.

- Capitalize everything in the address and leave out commas and periods.
- Use the list of common state and street abbreviations found in the *National ZIP Code Directory* or on page **660** of this book.
- Use numbers rather than words for numbered streets (for example, 42ND AVE or 9TH AVE NW).
- If you know the ZIP + 4 code, use it.

Writing Guidelines Short Report

Reports are important workplace tools. Business managers write reports to summarize department activities. Nurses write reports to summarize home visits to patients. Salespeople give their supervisors monthly summaries. Police officers make official accident reports. Most workplace business reports record, organize, analyze, and interpret information.

Prewriting

- **Consider your audience** by thinking about who will receive your report. Do they expect just the facts, or will they want you to analyze information and make recommendations?
- **Gather details** through interviews or research based on what your reader needs to know.

Writing

- **Use the organization's specific report format** or follow these general guidelines.

Date:	The month, day, and year
To:	The reader's name
From:	Your first and last name
Subject:	The report's topic in a clear, simple statement

- **Organize the body** into three parts:

Beginning:	State why you are writing the report.
Middle:	Provide all the necessary details. Use bulleted points and lists to summarize information.
Ending:	List recommendations, or next steps. What do you want the reader to do or to know?

Revising

- **Improve your writing.** Ask yourself these questions about *ideas, organization, voice, word choice,* and *sentence fluency: Is my topic clear? Do I have an effective beginning, middle, and ending? Have I organized the information with headings, bulleted points, and visuals—tables, graphs, or illustrations that may help the reader understand? Have I used a concise, conversational, though professional tone? (It is acceptable to use personal pronouns such as* I *or* you *in most reports. Some official reports may use the third person.) Have I explained unfamiliar terms? Is my writing straightforward and factual? Does my report read smoothly?*

Editing

- **Check for conventions.** Be sure your report is free from punctuation, capitalization, spelling, and grammar errors.
- **Prepare a final copy.** Proofread the final copy of your report.

Short Report

Writing a report may involve communicating complex business details or simple factual information. In this example, Detective James Harris writes a report after interviewing a high school student who believes someone has used her social security number to acquire a cell phone. As the investigation proceeds, the officer may make additional reports with conclusions based on evidence found during his investigation.

This report uses an official police department format.

The introduction identifies the officer and the citizen reporting the incident.

The body states information given by the citizen.

The conclusion summarizes the current situation.

The officer gives his name and number.

Supplemental Narrative: Incident # 03-032135

On Tuesday, December 1, 2009, I, Detective Harris, took a walk-in complaint from Baywood resident Sarah Groves, f/w, 03/06/1989 of 2134 Lakeshore Drive, Village of Baywood. She said an unknown person had used her social security number to acquire a cell phone through City Cell. Ms. Groves was accompanied by her mother, Catherine Groves of the same address.

Ms. Groves stated she had received a letter indicating she had defaulted on a $257 cell phone bill to City Cell. Ms. Groves said that although her social security number had been used to open the cell phone account four months previously, she had not opened the account and did not live at the address given on the bill forwarded to her correct address. She said she could provide proof that she had lived at her parent's home address in Baywood for the past 10 years. She said she had never lived at the 4100 N. Gregg Ave. address that was listed on the cell phone bill and knows no one at that address.

According to Ms. Groves, she is very careful with her social security number and does not recall carrying it with her or giving it out via phone or Internet in recent months.

Ms. Groves was given identity-theft information. She and her mother were directed to contact the fraud unit at the cell phone company. The mother stated she had already contacted both credit reporting agencies and the cell phone company's fraud unit. The City Cell fraud unit is investigating.

Detective James Harris #143

Writing Guidelines Proposal

People write proposals to fix problems, address specific needs, or make improvements. A proposal may be a simple letter suggesting the addition of a new microwave to the lunchroom or a complex report recommending establishment of a company day-care center.

Prewriting

- **Consider your audience** by thinking about who will receive your proposal and what you want that person to understand.
- **Determine your purpose** and jot down what you want your proposal to accomplish. What action are you proposing?
- **Gather details** based on what your reader needs to know in order to make a decision. Gather necessary supporting information.

Writing

- **Prepare a heading** that includes the following information:

  Date: The month, day, and year
  To: The reader's name
  From: Your first and last name
  Subject: A concise summary of the proposal

- **Organize the body** into three parts:

  Beginning: State what you are proposing and why.
  Middle: Provide details such as financial costs and other required resources. Write out key points and information supporting them. Show how the action will benefit the organization.
  Ending: Summarize what actions need to be taken next or what recommendations you are making.

Revising

- **Improve your writing.** Ask yourself these questions related to *ideas, organization, voice, word choice, and sentence fluency: Is my proposal clear and logical? Is my purpose obvious? Have I provided sufficient information and detail to convince the reader that action is needed? Do I have an effective beginning, middle, and ending? Do I provide information to support my recommendations? Have I used a positive, persuasive tone? Have I explained any unfamiliar terms? Does my proposal read smoothly?*

Editing

- **Check for conventions.** Be sure punctuation, grammar, and mechanics are correct.
- **Prepare a final copy.** Proofread the final copy of your proposal.

Proposal

Kim Melchor did a summer internship at Daley Insurance Company. Her boss asked her to research the possibility of opening a day-care center at the company and to draft a proposal for review.

Date: May 5, 2009

To: Pat Stevenson

From: Kim Melchor, summer assistant

Subject: On-Site Day Care

Beginning
The proposal is summarized.

Employees are interested in having a day-care center at Daley Insurance Company. My research and employee-survey results indicate there is room for a center, and employees would use it.

Middle
The problem is stated and a plan to solve it is proposed.

Daley Insurance is located in an area with few day-care facilities. The employee survey shows that approximately 58 percent of Daley employees have children under the age of five, and 72 percent live within five miles of the work site. Fewer than 10 percent of these employees with children have family in the area to help out with child care. A survey of all employees with children showed that 81 percent preferred on-site day care.

Benefits to the organization are listed.

Providing quality, affordable day care at work would help the company attract and retain employees with young children. Having children nearby would allow parents to visit them at noon. It would also improve employee morale and absenteeism and lost productivity caused by child-care issues.

Ideas for putting the plan into action are discussed.

The old employee activity center, which has been empty since the new center was built, meets state codes. The remodeling costs would be minimal (see attached estimate from the chief financial officer).

A quality day-care center could be self-supporting once the initial costs of establishing it are covered. Tax credits may be available to help pay the start-up costs (see attached projections by the CFO).

Ending
Recommendations are stated.

Based on my research, I recommend that we complete this proposal for a day-care center and present it to management.

Writing Guidelines Memo

Memos are short messages in which you ask and answer questions, describe procedures, give short reports, and remind others about deadlines and meetings. Memos are important to the flow of information within any organization. Many routine memos in schools and workplaces are distributed electronically, with hard copies posted on bulletin boards or sent by interoffice mail.

Prewriting

- **Consider your audience** by thinking about who will receive your memo and why.
- **Determine your purpose** and jot down your reason for writing the memo.
- **Gather necessary details** based on what your reader needs to know.

Writing

- **Prepare the heading** by typing "Memo" and centering it. Use a preprinted memo form or include a heading that contains the following information:

  Date: The month, day, and year
  To: The reader's name
  From: Your first and last name (You may initial it before sending.)
  Subject: The memo's topic in a clear, simple statement

- **Organize the body** into three parts:

  Beginning: State why you are writing the memo.
  Middle: Provide all the necessary details. Consider listing the most important points rather than writing them out.
  Ending: Focus on what happens next—the action or response you would like from the reader or readers.

Revising

- **Improve your writing** by asking yourself these questions related to *ideas, organization, voice, word choice, and sentence fluency: Is my topic clear? Is my purpose obvious? Do I have an effective beginning, middle, and ending? Have I used a positive, friendly tone? Have I explained any unfamiliar terms? Does my memo read smoothly?*

Editing

- **Check for conventions.** Correct any errors in punctuation, grammar, and mechanics.
- **Prepare a final copy** of your memo before distributing it.

Memo

In this memo, Shannon Li, a part-time manager at Hipp Music store, communicates with co-workers about the store's dress code.

The **heading** identifies the recipients, sender, date, and subject.

The **beginning** introduces the subject.

The **middle** shares necessary details and lists.

The **ending** invites questions.

Memo

Date: April 2, 2009

To: All employees of Hipp Music—Glenview Mall

From: Shannon Li, assistant manager

Subject: Workplace Dress Code

The area manager has asked me to remind all employees about the Hipp Music dress code. We are free to dress like our customers, who are generally young and who dress casually. However, there have been a few complaints from parents and mall management at other Hipp Music locations about inappropriate clothing.

Here are guidelines about what to wear when working at the store:

- Wear clothes that are clean and not ripped.
- Choose T-shirts without graphics or words that may be offensive to customers.
- Do not wear sheer blouses or shirts unless you also wear a T-shirt or tank top underneath.
- Wear shoes (no flip-flops or beach shoes).
- Cover tattoos that have any offensive words or images.

We are fortunate to work for a store with a fun, casual dress policy. Please follow the basic guidelines. If you have any questions, check with me or any of the other assistant managers.

Try It!

Draft a memo to a group of which you are a member. Follow the guidelines on the previous page and in the model above.

Writing Guidelines E-Mail Message

Electronic mail is a fast, convenient way to communicate in the workplace. It saves paper and allows many people to share information simultaneously. Increasingly, e-mail is used not only within the office, but also to communicate with customers and business partners as well.

Prewriting

- **Consider your audience** and your purpose for sending the message.
- **Gather details** based on what the reader needs to know.

Writing

- **Organize the body** in three parts:

  Beginning: Complete your e-mail header, making sure your subject line is clear. Expand on the subject in the first sentences of your message. Get right to the point.

  Middle: Supply all the details of your message while keeping your paragraphs short. Double-space between paragraphs. Try to limit your message to one or two screens and use numbers, lists, and headings to organize your thoughts.

  Ending: Let your reader know what follow-up action is needed and when; then end politely.

Revising

- **Improve your writing** by asking yourself these questions concerning *ideas, organization, and voice: Is my message accurate, complete, and clear? Do I have an effective beginning, middle, and ending? Is my tone appropriate for the topic and the reader?*
- **Improve your style.** Ask yourself these questions related to *word choice and sentence fluency: Have I used clear, everyday language? Does my message read smoothly?*

Editing

- **Check for conventions.** Correct any errors in grammar, punctuation, and mechanics before sending your e-mail.

Tip

- Never use all capital letters in an e-mail message. People feel you are shouting at them.
- Follow grammar conventions.
- Proofread. Because e-mail is so fast, it's easy to dash off a message and overlook a typo.

E-Mail Message

Linda Schmid, a high school student working on a research paper about the early days of the civil rights movement, discovered information about a documentary done by students at another school. She wrote this e-mail message to ask for more information.

The **heading** includes an address and a subject.

The **beginning** greets the reader and introduces the topic.

The **middle** states what the writer needs and provides additional detail.

The **ending** thanks the reader and offers follow-up information.

New Message

To: office@mail.riversidehigh.k12.mn.us

Cc:

Subject: Query About Civil Rights Documentary

Dear Sir or Madam:

I read the May 2, 2008, story in the *Minneapolis Star-Tribune* about the documentary Riverside High School students did on little-known heroes of the civil rights movement. I am currently working on a paper for my American History class on the subject, and I would like to view the film as part of my research.

Would it be possible for me to borrow or buy a copy of the documentary? Is it available commercially?

I am willing to buy a copy, or pay a rental fee, if necessary. I would gladly pay postage if you are willing to lend me a copy of the documentary.

Thank you for your help. You can respond via e-mail, or phone me at the number listed below.

Sincerely,
Linda Schmid
Valley Community School
5956 N. Santa Monica Blvd.
Evergreen, CA 90290
213-555-1234
lindas5956@aol.com

Tip

Most e-mail programs support formatting for titles (bold, italics, and underscore). Or you can emphasize titles with ALL CAPS.

Writing Guidelines Brochure

Organizations and business use brochures to share information about their goals or products. Brochures can be set up in a variety of ways:

- a piece of standard 8½- by 11-inch paper or card stock folded in two,
- the same size material folded into thirds, or
- an 8½- by 14-inch paper folded into thirds or fourths.

Desktop publishing programs let you design and create brochures, and some word-processing programs feature brochure templates. Special paper with pre-printed designs can be purchased from office supply stores or Web sites.

Prewriting

- **Select your topic** by thinking about the service or organization you want to promote, or the product you want to sell.
- **Consider your audience** and the style that will work best.
- **Gather details** based on what your audience needs to know about this product or service. What will convince them of its value? Pull together facts, testimonials, and other details you want to include.

Writing

- **Organize the body** of your brochure into three parts:
  Beginning: State the most important point in large, bold type.
  Middle: State your message concisely. Use bulleted lists to add facts, figures, and testimonials that describe your product or service.
  Ending: Include reader-response instructions and lists of necessary names, addresses, phone numbers, and Web site locations.
- **Design your brochure** with easy-to-read headlines, attention-grabbing visuals, interesting graphics, and adequate "white space," or open areas.

Revising

- **Improve your writing** by asking yourself the following questions about *ideas, organization, and voice: Is my message clear? Do I answer the reader's questions? Do I place the information in the right order? Do I use headings, lists, and graphics effectively? Is my writing persuasive?*
- **Improve your style.** Ask yourself these questions concerning *word choice and sentence fluency: Have I chosen precise words to convey my message? Does my brochure read smoothly?*

Editing

- **Check for conventions.** Correct any errors in grammar, punctuation, and mechanics.
- **Prepare a final copy.** Proofread the final draft of your brochure.

Brochure

Christina works in her family's business, Rossi's Italian Bakery. Because she has taken a computer-design course, her dad asks her to help create brochures to hand out and mail to potential customers.

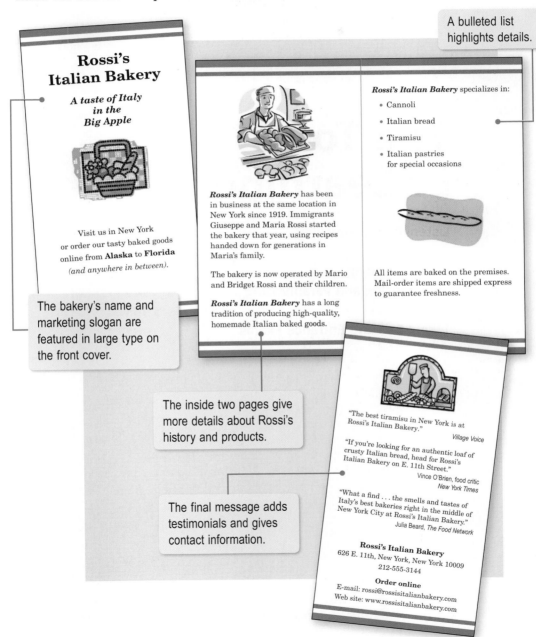

A bulleted list highlights details.

Rossi's Italian Bakery

A taste of Italy in the Big Apple

Visit us in New York
or order our tasty baked goods
online from **Alaska** to **Florida**
(and anywhere in between).

Rossi's Italian Bakery has been in business at the same location in New York since 1919. Immigrants Giuseppe and Maria Rossi started the bakery that year, using recipes handed down for generations in Maria's family.

The bakery is now operated by Mario and Bridget Rossi and their children.

Rossi's Italian Bakery has a long tradition of producing high-quality, homemade Italian baked goods.

Rossi's Italian Bakery specializes in:

- Cannoli
- Italian bread
- Tiramisu
- Italian pastries for special occasions

All items are baked on the premises. Mail-order items are shipped express to guarantee freshness.

"The best tiramisu in New York is at Rossi's Italian Bakery."
Village Voice

"If you're looking for an authentic loaf of crusty Italian bread, head for Rossi's Italian Bakery on E. 11th Street."
Vince O'Brien, food critic
New York Times

"What a find . . . the smells and tastes of Italy's best bakeries right in the middle of New York City at Rossi's Italian Bakery."
Julia Beard, The Food Network

Rossi's Italian Bakery
626 E. 11th, New York, New York 10009
212-555-3144

Order online
E-mail: rossi@rossisitalianbakery.com
Web site: www.rossisitalianbakery.com

The bakery's name and marketing slogan are featured in large type on the front cover.

The inside two pages give more details about Rossi's history and products.

The final message adds testimonials and gives contact information.

The Tools of Learning

Listening and Speaking

Strong listening and speaking skills are important to your future. You will use them to interview for colleges and jobs and to communicate effectively with bosses, co-workers, teachers, and classmates. Listening is the groundwork for all learning. It enables you not only to understand the speaker's main ideas, but also to evaluate and organize information. Speaking is just as important. It allows you to explain, argue, persuade, inform, and even entertain.

During a typical day, you spend 70 percent of your time communicating. Three-fourths of that time is spent listening and speaking. In this chapter, you will find tips and strategies to help you become a better listener and speaker. As you practice and master these skills, you will strengthen the foundation of your future.

- **Listening in Class**
- **Speaking in Class**
- **A Closer Look at Listening and Speaking**

"To listen well is as powerful a means of influence as to talk well and is as essential to all true conversation."
—Chinese proverb

Listening in Class

Listening takes practice and effort. The following tips will help you become a better listener.

- **Know why you're listening.** What is the speaker trying to tell you? Will there be a test? Are you being given an assignment?
- **Listen for the facts.** The 5 W and H questions—*Who? What? When? Where? Why?* and *How?*—will help you identify the most important information.
- **Take notes.** When you hear important information, write it down in your notebook. Add questions and comments in the margins. Review and complete your notes as soon after class as possible.
- **Put the speaker's ideas into your own words.** Paraphrase the speaker's key points as you take notes. Add your own comments.

Try It!

Practice taking notes in class or while listening to a documentary on television. Put the speaker's ideas into your own words. Use the margins to add your questions and comments.

The Ring of Fire

- zone of frequent earthquakes and volcanic eruptions
- holds 75% of the world's active and dormant volcanoes
- located at the borders of the Pacific Plate and other major tectonic plates
- forms an arc: New Zealand, around eastern edge of Asia, north across Aleutian Islands, south along coast of N. and S. America (map in textbook)

Subduction
The Pacific Plate is crashing into and sliding under other plates.

Margin notes:

Which volcano has been most active in the Ring of Fire and why?

What do trenches and mountain ranges have to do with plate tectonics?

Subduction: The pushing edge of one plate goes below the edge of another.

Speaking in Class

Speaking in a group discussion is an important skill to master. A good discussion depends on cooperation. These basic strategies will help you and your classmates become better speakers.

Before you speak . . .

- **Listen** carefully and take notes.
- **Think** about what others are saying.
- **Wait** until it's your turn to speak.
- **Plan** how you can add something positive to the discussion.

As you speak . . .

- **Use a loud, clear voice.**
- **Stick to the topic.**
- **Avoid repeating** what's already been said.
- **Support your ideas** with examples, facts, or anecdotes.
- **Make eye contact** with others in the group or class.

Tips

- Focus your comments on ideas, not on personalities.
- Ask meaningful questions.
- Summarize specific ideas brought up in the discussion.
- Mention another person's comments and expand on them constructively.

Try It!

Warm up your impromptu speaking skills by interacting in the following talk-show activity.

1. Watch excerpts from several talk shows. Notice when and how the host listens. What questions does the host ask to direct the guest to speak in detail about a topic?

2. Pair up with a classmate for a talk-show interview. One of you will assume the role of host, the other of guest.

3. Together, decide on a theme for the interview based on a specific real-life topic from the "guest's" life: a hobby, talent, or sport that the guest participates in, or an interesting event from the guest's life.

4. Present a 5-minute interview in front of the class. Keep the interview on topic and flowing smoothly by using the tips on this page.

A Closer Look at Listening and Speaking

Improving your listening and speaking skills will help you increase your confidence and effectiveness as a communicator. Follow these basic guidelines to carry on productive conversations and discussions.

Good Listeners	Good Speakers
■ think about what the speaker is saying. ■ stay focused so that they are prepared to respond thoughtfully. ■ pay attention to the speaker's tone of voice, gestures, and facial expressions. ■ interrupt only when necessary to ask questions.	■ speak loudly and clearly. ■ make eye contact with their listeners. ■ emphasize their main ideas by changing the tone and volume of their voice. ■ respect their audience by explaining and clarifying information that may be confusing. ■ use gestures and body language effectively to enhance their message.

Try It!

Use the following activity to practice your listening and speaking skills. As a class, view a video of Dr. Martin Luther King, Jr., delivering his famous "I Have a Dream" speech.

1. Following the speech, participate in a class discussion, using these questions as a guide.
- What are the main ideas of the speech?
- What questions would you have wanted to ask Dr. King immediately following the speech?

2. Rate the delivery of the speech using the "Good Speakers" guidelines on this page. Which of the guidelines did you observe while watching and listening to Dr. King's speech?

3. Tell a friend about the speech. Summarize Dr. King's main ideas and describe your reaction to his delivery. Use the speaking tips in this chapter to communicate your thoughts effectively.

Taking Notes

Henry David Thoreau once said, "The writer who postpones the recording of his thoughts uses an iron which has cooled to burn a hole with." Think of it this way: You're listening to a lecture in class. You're certain that you will remember what the teacher says, so you decide not to take notes. Later, you discover that your mind has filled with other things, and you can't remember a word of the lecture.

Active listening and purposeful note taking are critical skills for students to master. Taking good notes can help you process and organize information, prepare for exams, and—ultimately—save time. In this chapter you will sharpen your skills for taking lecture notes, reading notes, and meeting minutes.

- **Taking Classroom Notes**
- **Taking Reading Notes**
- **Taking Meeting Minutes**

"My aim is to put down on paper what I see and what I feel in the best and simplest way."

—Ernest Hemingway

Taking Classroom Notes

Your teacher may give a lecture to explain an important subject, introduce a new topic, or review for a test. The following tips will help you take clear, organized lecture notes.

Guidelines for Class Notes

1. **Write the topic and date at the top of each page.** Number your pages so that you can reorder them if they get mixed up.

2. **Listen carefully.** This is the key to taking good notes. If you are too busy writing, you may miss important clues. For example, when a teacher says, "There are six steps in this process," listen for the six steps. Also listen for key words such as *first, second, next,* or *most importantly.*

3. **Use your own words.** You can't write down everything your teacher says. Instead, try to put the main points into your own words. You can fill in the details later.

4. **Begin taking notes right away** or you may miss something important. It's hard to catch up while taking notes.

5. **Write quickly, but neatly.** Your notes won't be helpful if you can't read them.

6. **Condense information.**
   - Use lists, phrases, and abbreviations *(p=page, ex=for example).*
   - Skip the small, unnecessary words, such as articles *(a, an, the).*
   - Shorten some words *(intro* for *introduction, chap* for *chapter).*
   - Use numbers and symbols *(1st, 2nd,* ↑, ↓, +, =).
   - Develop a personal shorthand *(w=with, w/o=without).*

7. **Draw sketches and diagrams** to explain a concept quickly.

8. **Copy important information** your teacher writes on the board.

9. **Ask your teacher** to explain something you don't understand, to repeat something, or to please slow down.

Try It!

Review some of your recent class notes with the guidelines above in mind. How could you improve your note-taking skills? Explain.

Setting Up Your Notes

Keep your notes in a notebook, preferably one for each subject. You can also take notes on loose-leaf paper kept in a three-ring binder, which lets you add and remove pages as needed. Write on one side of the paper. This makes your notes easier to read and find.

Biology—Cellular Respiration   March 1

Use bullets or numbered lists.

Two requirements for life to continue:
1. Energy must be supplied constantly.
2. Matter must be recycled constantly.

Skip a line between main ideas.

Cellular respration needs O released by photosynthesis (PS).

PS uses CO_2 and H_2O released by cellular resp.

Bodies of living organisms release atoms and molecules into the environment. Reused by decomposers (worms, etc.)

Equations:

PS:

$$C_6H_{12}O_6 + 6H_2O + \text{energy from light} \longrightarrow$$
$$C_6H_2O_6 + 6H_2O + 6O_2$$

Include details such as diagrams and equations.

Cell. Resp.:

$$C_6H_{12}O_6 + 6O_2 \longrightarrow 6CO_2 + 6H_2O + \text{energy (36 ATP)}$$

FYI

Note taking helps you listen better in class, organize your ideas more effectively, and remember more of what you hear.

Reviewing Your Notes

As you read over your notes, do the following:

1. **Circle and correct spelling errors.**
2. **Underline unfamiliar terms.** Look them up in a dictionary or glossary and write the words and their meanings in the margin.
3. **Write questions you have in the margin.** Look for the answers on your own first. Ask a teacher or classmate for help next. Write your answers near the questions.
4. **Use a highlighter to mark the most important notes,** or you can use a different-colored pen to circle or underline key ideas.
5. **Rewrite your notes.** This gives you another chance to learn the material.
6. **Review your notes.** Look over your notes before the next class, especially if you are having a test or class discussion.

Biology—Cellular Respiration ←   March 1

Includes all chemical
reactions that provide
energy for life

Two requirements for life to continue:

1. Energy must be supplied constantly.
2. Matter must be recycled constantly.

respiration

Cellular (respration) needs O released
by photosynthesis (PS).

PS uses CO_2 and H_2O released by cellular resp.

Bodies of living organisms release atoms and molecules into
the environment. Reused by decomposers (worms, etc.)

Equations:

PS:

$$C_6H_{12}O_6 + 6H_2O + \text{energy from light} \longrightarrow$$
$$C_6H_2O_6 + 6H_2O + 6O_2$$

Is this equation right?

Cell. Resp.:

$$C_6H_{12}O_6 + 6O_2 \longrightarrow 6CO_2 + 6H_2O + \text{energy (36 ATP)}$$

Taking Reading Notes

Taking notes while you read an assignment is easier than taking notes during a lecture. You can stop to write at any time, without rushing or feeling lost. Here are some tips for taking notes when reading a class text.

Guidelines for Reading Notes

1. **Preview the assignment.** Page through your reading assignment to see what it is about. Look at the title, introduction, headings, and chapter summary. Also look at any pictures, maps, or graphics. (See page **95**.)

2. **Quickly read the entire assignment** once before taking notes. This gives you an overview of the material and allows you to pick out the main ideas.

3. **Take notes while reading a second time.** Start taking notes as you read your assignment again. Read the material slowly and stop at new ideas or words.

   - **Write down the important information.**
   - **Put notes in your own words.** Don't just copy passages from the book. You learn more when you rewrite ideas in your words. (See pages **543–550** for more information on summarizing and paraphrasing.)
   - **Use headings or subtitles.** Headings and subtitles help to organize your notes. Write down the important information under each heading or subtitle.
   - **Study any pictures, charts, or illustrations,** and write notes about them. Make quick sketches of these visual elements if you choose.
   - **Use graphic organizers.** (See pages **62–63**.)
   - **List and define any new words.** After recording the number of the page on which the word is located, look up each word in the glossary or a dictionary. Write down the appropriate meaning in your notes.

4. **Learn more.** See "Critical Reading" on pages **533–542** for more information on taking reading notes.

Try It!

For your next reading assignment, take notes using the tips above.

Learning

Taking Meeting Minutes

Recording the minutes of a meeting is another form of note taking. Minutes must be well organized and include everything from who is present to what is discussed and decided. Always report minutes in an objective (impersonal) voice. To record minutes during a meeting, you must listen carefully and write down information accurately. The following guidelines will help.

Guidelines for Taking Minutes

- Begin with the organization's name and the date, location, and topic of the meeting.

- Record what time the meeting begins.

- List those present (or absent). Indicate who led the meeting and who recorded the minutes.

- Note "old business" (from a previous meeting) that is discussed or resolved.

- Note "new business" (plans or decisions to be handled in the current meeting).

- Record any votes taken and their results.

- Record when the meeting is adjourned.

Mahone High School Student Senate Minutes
   Date: November 9, 2009
   Location: School Cafeteria (Ms. Wilke, Faculty Advisor)
   Topic: Security

Attending
(Seniors) Pat Gerber, Sharron Johnson (chair), Walt Wilson, Stan DeRusha, Hannah Giles, Bo Chavez; (Juniors) Brett Stein, Heather Hart, Tori Ramirez; (Sophmores) Natalie Manasian (recording), Sheila Beck.

Absent
Dylan Baker

Old Business
A student assembly was held on Friday, November 3, about the recent break-ins to cars in the senior parking lot.

Schmitt Security has agreed to help patrol the lot during school hours.

Principal Layne asked the student senate for additional ideas for improving security.

New Business
The following security ideas will be proposed to Principal Layne.

ID badges:	Student drivers will each be issued an ID badge to hang on the rearview mirror of his or her car. Only cars with badges will be allowed to park in the senior lot.
Locks:	All cars must be locked while in the senior lot. Failure to do so will result in lost privileges to use the lot.
Escorts:	A faculty or security escort will be available after dark to escort students to their cars if they must stay late.

Vote 11-0 for Bo Chavez to present these ideas to Principal Layne on behalf of the senate.

Meeting Time: 2:15 PM –3:00 PM

Tip

When you take minutes to tell what was discussed and decided upon by a group, record only the main points, not all the details. Be sure to accurately record any votes or official action taken.

Critical Reading

Poet and essayist Joseph Addison once said, "Reading is to the mind what exercise is to the body." This is especially true of critical reading. When you read critically, you are forced to stretch your mind. You examine, question, and test what you read as you try to clearly understand the writer's message.

Critical reading involves several important steps. These include *surveying* an assigned reading, *questioning* what you read, *taking notes* about the text, and so on. In this chapter, you will learn to read critically to gain a clearer understanding of your reading assignments as well as any reading tests you take.

- **Critical Reading: SQ3R**
- **Before You Read**
- **As You Read**
- **After You Read**
- **Reading Fiction**
- **Reading Poetry**

"I am not a speed reader. I am a speed understander."

—Isaac Asimov

Critical Reading: SQ3R

An effective reading technique for all types of nonfiction is the SQ3R method. SQ3R stands for the five steps in this reading process: *survey, question, read, recite,* and *review.* The steps in this technique are explained below and on the following pages.

Before you read . . .

- **Survey** Preview the reading assignment for its general content. Read titles, subtitles, headings, and subheadings to see what is being covered. Take note of illustrations and of terms in bold or italic type. Also read the first and last paragraphs.

- **Question** Ask yourself what you already know about the topic of the reading. Write down questions you still want answered. To get started, you could turn the text's titles, subtitles, headings, and subheadings into questions. Asking questions keeps you actively involved while reading.

As you read . . .

- **Read** Read slowly and carefully. Look for the main idea in each paragraph, section, or chapter. Try to answer questions you have already identified. At different points, also ask these questions: *What does this mean? How does it connect with previous material? What will come next?* Take notes as you go along. Take the time to read difficult parts slowly. (Reread them if necessary.)

- **Recite** Test your comprehension of the material by summarizing the main points out loud. Reciting is one of the most valuable parts of SQ3R. After you read a page, section, or chapter, try to answer the 5 W and H questions *(Who? What? Where? When? Why?* and *How?).* Reread any parts as needed.

After you read . . .

- **Review** Assess your knowledge by reviewing your notes. See how well you understand the entire reading assignment. Ask these questions: *Has the text answered all my questions? Can I summarize each main section? Can I summarize or outline the whole assignment?* Consider outlining the material (or using another type of graphic organizer) to help you remember what you have read.

Note: Critical reading means looking beyond surface details and thinking carefully about the information that is presented.

Before You Read

Try to get the big picture of each assignment as you begin to read. The tips that follow will help you get started.

Surveying the Reading

To begin, survey the text to get a general understanding of the main points.

- **Scan** chapter titles, subtitles, headings, and boldfaced type.
- **Identify the purpose** of the text: to inform, to persuade, to entertain.
- **Read** the first and last paragraphs.
- **List** the topic and the main points you identify.

Below, Gabriela surveys the beginning part of an article assigned by her teacher. She writes her notes on a copy of the article.

Sample Survey Notes

Visiting a College Campus

Take Hold of Your Future

Brochures are helpful in selecting a college, but a better way to decide if a specific college is right for you may be to arrange a campus visit. A visit provides an opportunity for you to ask questions you might not be able to ask in a group setting. It also allows you to decide if you will fit into the campus environment.

Seek Out Faculty and Staff for Help

During a campus visit, you should sit down with faculty and staff members to learn about the classes and the programs you are most interested in. Faculty can answer questions about courses you will need to complete to earn the degree you want. You can also ask about class sizes and whether teaching assistants will be available to provide help if you need it. You might even be able to sit in on a class. It is also important to ask how to prepare for your college education while you are still in high school.

Staff can answer questions about financial aid, housing, registration procedures and deadlines, and even the social climate of the campus. They can take you on a campus tour and possibly introduce you to a student advisor who can answer your personal questions about student life.

Purpose:
To inform

Topic:
Making the most of a campus visit

Key Points:
Meet with
1. Faculty:
Ask about classes and programs.
2. Staff:
Ask about financial aid, registration, campus life.

Learning

Questioning the Material

After you have surveyed the entire text, ask questions about the reading. Use the following guidelines.

- **Consider what you already know about the topic.**
- **List questions that you still want answered.** Also, ask the 5 W and H questions.
- **Turn headings and main points into questions.** For example, if a chapter title is "Defining and Pursuing a Liberal Education," your questions might be *What is a liberal education? Do I want to pursue a liberal education?*

Below, Gabriela turned a main heading into a question and formed other questions that occurred to her.

How can faculty and staff help?

1. How do I set up a campus visit?
2. When is the best time to go?
3. Will the college pay for my trip there?
4. Should I bring my parent with me?
5. Will they want to see samples of my work?
6. What if I don't know what kind of degree I want?
7. What kind of staff member should I contact to answer my questions about financial aid and living in the dorms?

Try It!

Ask questions. Write down questions you have about any reading material you have surveyed.

As You Read

Once you have surveyed the assignment and formed questions about it, you are ready to read carefully. Try to turn your reading into a conversation with the text. Respect what the writer has to say even as you question certain parts, and stay open to the unexpected.

Reading (and Taking Notes)

Always have a goal in mind when you read. Follow these guidelines as you read the material and answer the questions you listed.

- **Read slowly** so that you don't miss anything.
- **Reread parts** that seem challenging.
- **Write down key concepts.** (These are often in bold.)
- **Define key concepts** using context or a dictionary.
- **Record any additional questions** you may have.
- **Keep the following questions in mind** as you read:
  - What does this mean?
  - How does it connect with what I already know about the topic?
  - What will probably come next?

 Try It!

Read your chosen assignment critically. Take careful notes as you go along, using the guidelines above.

Reciting Material Out Loud

After you complete the entire reading, it's time to reinforce what you have learned. Repeating information out loud is an effective way to evaluate how well you understand it. Use the following guidelines:

- **Recite the key points** without looking at your notes.
- **Answer the 5 W and H questions** (*Who? What? Where? When? Why?* and *How?*) about the material.
- **Ask (and answer) your other questions** about the topic.
- **Identify any new questions** that occur to you.

 **Try It!**

Recite what you have learned from your reading assignment. Use the guidelines above to help you complete this step.

After You Read

Having completed the first four steps in the SQ3R method, you should review the reading. Reviewing will help you see how well you understand the material.

Reviewing the Material

A final review of your reading will make the information part of your own thinking. Use the following guidelines.

- **Go over your notes** one section at a time.
- **Keep searching for answers** if you have any unanswered questions.
- **Ask for help** if you cannot figure something out on your own.
- **Add illustrations or graphic organizers** to your notes to make complex ideas clearer.
- **Summarize the reading** at the end of your notes.

In the example below, Gabriela wrote a paragraph that summarized the article about campus visits.

Sample Summary

"Visiting a College Campus"—Summary

This article provides helpful information for high school students trying to decide which college is right for them. It explains how to make the most of a visit to a college or university and the importance of a campus visit. It also gives specific examples of how meeting with faculty and staff members can be a valuable tool for students in the decision-making process.

Try It!

Review your reading assignment. Go over your notes and summarize the assignment. Be sure to include the main ideas.

Reading Fiction

Fiction uses imagined characters and events to reveal what is authentic or true about life. This makes fiction a notable way to learn. Here are some tips for reading fiction.

Before you read . . .

- **Learn something about the author** and his or her other works.
- **React thoughtfully** to the title and opening pages.

As you read . . .

- **Identify** the following story elements: *setting, tone, main characters, central conflict,* and *theme.*
- **Predict** what will happen next.
- **Write** your reactions to the short story or novel in a reading journal as you go along.
- **Think** about the characters and what they do.
  - What motivates the characters?
  - Have you encountered people similar to these characters?
  - Have you faced situations similar to the ones faced by the main characters?
  - Would you have reacted in the same way?
- **Consider** how the author's life may have influenced the story.
- **Notice** the author's style and word choice.
  - How effectively has the author used literary devices?
  - Why do you think the author used a particular word or phrase?
- **Discuss** the story with others who are reading it.

After you read . . .

- **Consider** how the main character changes during the course of the story. Often, this is the key to understanding a work of fiction.
- **Determine** the story's main message or theme; then decide how effectively this message is communicated.

Try It!

Use the information above as a guide to help you better understand and enjoy the next short story or novel you read.

Learning

Reacting to Fiction

The excerpt below is from Edith Wharton's classic novel *Ethan Frome*. The margin notes reveal one student's reactions, which she wrote on a photocopy of the story. She makes observations, asks questions, and attempts to define a confusing term.

Ethan Frome
By Edith Wharton

I like Wharton's descriptive style.

I'm not sure what a peristyle is. I looked it up, but I can't picture how it works with the steeple. A peristyle is a series of columns around a building or courtyard.

What is an "exhausted receiver"?

I wonder what misfortunes followed his father's death.

Young Ethan Frome walked at a quick pace along the deserted street, past the bank and Michael Eady's new brick store and Lawyer Varnum's house with the two black Norway spruces at the gate. Opposite the Varnum gate, where the road fell away toward the Corbury valley, the church reared its slim white steeple and narrow peristyle. As the young man walked toward it the upper windows drew a black arcade along the side wall of the building, but from the lower openings, on the side where the ground sloped steeply down to the Corbury road, the light shot its long bars, illuminating many fresh furrows in the track leading to the basement door, and showing, under an adjoining shed, a line of sleighs with heavily blanketed horses.

The night was perfectly still, and the air so dry and pure that it gave little sensation of cold. The effect produced on Frome was rather of a complete absence of atmosphere, as though nothing less tenuous than ether intervened between the white earth under his feet and the metallic dome overhead. "It's like being in an exhausted receiver," he thought. Four or five years earlier he had taken a year's course at a technological college at Worcester, and dabbled in the laboratory with a friendly professor of physics; and the images supplied by that experience still cropped up, at unexpected moments, through the totally different associations of thought in which he had since been living. His father's death, and the misfortunes following it, had put a premature end to Ethan's studies; but though they had not gone far enough to be of much practical use they had fed his fancy and made him aware of huge cloudy meanings behind the daily face of things.

"Poetry is a search for the inexplicable."
—Wallace Stevens

Reading Poetry

You may not understand a poem completely in one reading, especially if it is lengthy or complex. In fact, each time you read a poem, you will probably discover something new about it. Reacting to poetry in a reading journal will also help you appreciate it more. Here are some strategies for reading poetry.

First Reading

- **Read the poem** at your normal reading speed to gain an overall first impression.
- **Jot down brief notes** about your immediate reaction to the poem.

Second Reading

- **Read the poem again**—out loud, if possible. Pay attention to the sound of the poem.
- **Note examples of sound devices** in the poem—alliteration, assonance, rhyme (see pages **368–369**). Finding a poem's phrasing and rhythm can help you discover its meaning.
- **Observe** the punctuation, spacing, and special treatment of words and lines.
- **Think** about the theme of the poem.

Third Reading

- **Identify** the type of poem you're reading. Does this poem follow the usual pattern of that particular type? If not, why not?
- **Determine** the literal sense or meaning of the poem. What is the poem about? What does it seem to say about its topic?
- **Look** for figurative language in the poem. How does this language—metaphors, similes, personification, symbols—support or add to the meaning of the poem? (See pages **600–601** or **368–369**.)

Try It!

Use the strategies above as a guide the next time you read a poem.

Learning

Reacting to Poetry

"The Gift Outright" is a poem by Robert Frost. The notes on the copy of the poem below show one student's reaction. She makes observations, asks questions, reacts to word choice, and so forth. Whenever you read a challenging poem, try to react to it in several different ways.

The Gift Outright
by Robert Frost

Contrast: The first part shows weakness and being possessed. The poem then shifts to a tone representing newfound strength.

The land was ours before we were the land's.
She was our land more than a hundred years
Before we were her people. She was ours
In Massachusetts, in Virginia,
But we were England's, still colonials,
Possessing what we still were unpossessed by,
Possessed by what we now no more possessed.
Something we were withholding made us weak
Until we found out that it was ourselves
We were withholding from our land of living,
And forthwith found salvation in surrender.
Such as we were we gave ourselves outright
(The deed of gift was many deeds of war)
To the land vaguely <u>realizing</u> westward,
But still unstoried, artless, unenhanced,
Such as she was, such as she would become.

Frost uses synecdoche, a kind of metaphor where the part stands for the whole. I think the gift stands for U.S. history.

What does "realizing" mean in this context? "Growing"

Try It!

Write freely for 5 to 10 minutes when you finish reading a poem. Include any thoughts or feelings you have about the poem. Relate it to other poems you have read.

Summarizing and Paraphrasing

Summarizing and paraphrasing are two equally effective learning tools. By putting a writer's message into your own words, you gain a better understanding of it. The information becomes part of your own thinking. As you apply the skills of paraphrasing and summarizing, you will discover that you can understand even the most challenging reading material.

Summarizing means extracting only the main ideas, reasons, and arguments from a piece of writing, while paraphrasing means interpreting and expressing the main ideas in your own words. In this chapter, you will read examples of both kinds of writing and write your own summaries and paraphrases.

- **Sample Article and Summary**
- **Guidelines for Summarizing**
- **Strategies for Paraphrasing**
- **Sample Paragraphs and Paraphrases**

"Good things, when short, are twice as good."

—Baltasar Gracian

Sample Article and Summary

The following article is about one of the most important events in civil rights history in the United States.

The March on Washington for Jobs and Freedom

The early 1960s were tumultuous times for black Americans. Civil rights activists around the country were being met with police brutality, and black people were discriminated against in almost all areas of their lives, most blatantly in the employment arena. Black Americans were habitually turned away from job opportunities. By 1963, the black unemployment rate had escalated until it was more than double that of white Americans.

In this atmosphere of civil unrest, plans were made for a protest march on Washington, D.C. The march was organized by civil rights leaders Philip Randolph, Bayard Rustin, Whitney Young, John Lewis, Martin Luther King, Jr., Roy Wilkins, and James Farmer. Their intent was to march in support of freedom, employment, and civil rights legislation that was being considered by Congress. The March on Washington for Jobs and Freedom was scheduled for August 28, 1963. It was to be a peaceful protest that included carefully planned speeches.

Leaders in the nation's capital anticipated that the march might turn violent. No one knew how many people would participate, and security was tight. Three thousand law enforcement officers from Washington, D.C., were on duty as well as one thousand police officers from neighboring cities. The atmosphere was tense when the march began at eight o'clock. When only about 50 people showed up, leaders thought that the march would not be as great as anticipated. By ten o'clock, a huge crowd had gathered. Before long, it grew to 250,000. Soon the event captured the attention of the nation. Network television covered it all day long as blacks, whites, actors, and even congressional representatives joined in the march. There were songs and speeches by famous Americans, including Dr King's historic "I Have a Dream" speech. The march was nonviolent and considered a huge success.

Because of the march, the Civil Rights Act of 1964 was passed. It made racial discrimination illegal in all public places, government, and employment.

Summary

The following is a student summary of the article on page **544**. The three main parts of the summary—topic sentence, body, and closing sentence—are explained in the side notes.

The topic sentence expresses the main idea.

The body sentences summarize the main ideas from the article.

The closing sentence shares the article's concluding thoughts.

The March on Washington for Jobs and Freedom

On August 28, 1963, 250,000 American civil rights supporters participated in a peaceful march on Washington, D.C. Their goal was to support legislation before Congress concerning jobs, freedom, and civil rights. At that time, black Americans across the nation were suffering discrimination in many ways, especially in employment. Worried that the march might become violent, the city's leaders had thousands of police officers standing guard. However, this much police security proved unnecessary. The event, which got national attention, was very peaceful. It led to the passing of the Civil Rights Act of 1964, which made racial discrimination illegal in public places.

 Respond to the reading. Answer the following questions.

Ideas (1) What details from the original article are included in the summary? (2) What kinds of details are not included?

Organization (3) How is the summary paragraph organized?

Voice & Word Choice (4) Compare the first sentence of the summary with the first paragraph of the original. Which is simpler? Which offers more detail?

Tip

For an effective summary, focus on main ideas and important details like names, dates, times, and locations. For the most part, omit examples and description.

Guidelines for Summarizing

Follow the guidelines below whenever you are asked to write a summary.

Prewriting

- **Select an article on a topic that interests you** or relates to a subject you are currently studying. Make a photocopy of the article if possible.
- **Read the article once,** quickly. Then read it again, underlining passages (if working from a photocopy) or taking notes on the key details.
- **Think about the article.** Identify and write down the main idea. For example, here is the main idea of the sample article: **In 1963, civil rights activists led a peaceful march on Washington, D.C., to support fairness for black Americans.**

Writing

Write a summary paragraph.

- **Write a topic sentence** that states the main idea of the article.
- **Write body sentences** that communicate the most important supporting details in your own words.
- **Conclude** by reminding your reader of the main point of the article. (Remember: A summary should not contain your personal opinions.)

Revising and Editing

Read and revise your summary, making the necessary changes. Also edit for conventions. Ask yourself the following questions.

Ideas	*Do I correctly identify the article's main idea in my topic sentence? Do my body sentences contain only the most important details from the article?*
Organization	*Do I arrange the ideas in a sensible way?*
Voice	*Does my voice sound informed and interested?*
Word Choice	*Have I used my own words for the most part? Are there terms that need to be defined?*
Sentence Fluency	*Have I varied sentence structure and length?*
Conventions	*Have I eliminated all errors in punctuation, spelling, and grammar?*

Summarizing an Article

The following informative article is about the popular beverage cappuccino.

Cappuccino

Today, cappuccino is one of the most popular coffee drinks in the United States. Where did this frothy treat come from? The answer is that no one really knows who made the first cup of cappuccino or where it was served. The word "cappuccino," however, has been with us for centuries.

The word can be traced back to 1525 to a Capuchin order of friars—members of a religious order. They wore hooded cowls, a kind of cloak, which Italians called "cappuccinos." As time went on, the Italians began to call strong, espresso coffee mixed with steamed milk or cream "cappuccino." It was named so because the creamy brown color of the milky coffee reminded them of the color of the friars' "cappuccinos," or hoods. It wasn't until 1948 that the term worked its way from Europe into the English language.

Until the mid-1990s, espresso and its cousin, cappuccino, were most popular in European countries and in a few of this country's most cosmopolitan cities. Slowly, a trend developed throughout the U.S. that brought upscale, European-style coffeehouses to many urban neighborhoods. Before long, cappuccinos, espressos, and flavored coffee drinks were being served all over the country. Today, even fast-food restaurants and convenience stores offer their versions of these popular drinks.

Cappuccino is made by combining one-third espresso (a strong Italian coffee), one-third steamed milk, and one-third frothed milk (whipped to a foamy consistency). The result is a creamy cup of coffee with a velvety texture and sweet taste. No wonder it has become one of the favorite drinks in this country.

Try It!

Summarize the article above. Write a paragraph using the guidelines provided on page **546**. Also refer to the sample on page **545**.

Strategies for Paraphrasing

A paraphrase is a type of summary. It is very effective for clarifying or explaining the meaning of an important passage that you would like to use in your research. While a summary is shorter than the original text and expresses the text's main ideas, a paraphrase can be longer than the original material and *interprets* its key points. Use the following strategies as a guide when you paraphrase.

Follow a plan: In order to complete an effective paraphrase, you must follow a series of important steps. There are no shortcuts.

- **Review the entire passage.** This will help you identify the main ideas and purpose of the material.
- **Carefully read the passage.** If necessary, reread parts that seem especially important or challenging.
- **Write your paraphrase.** Be sure your interpretation is clear and complete. For the most part, use your own words. (See below.)
- **Check your paraphrase.** Make sure that you have captured the tone and meaning of the passage.

Use your own words: Avoid the original writer's words as much as possible. Exceptions include key words *(tribe, repertory theater)* or proper nouns *(Iroquois, Lake Erie, New York)*.

- **Consult a dictionary.** Refer to a dictionary to help you think of new ways to express certain terms or ideas.
- **Refer to a thesaurus.** Find synonyms to use in place of words in the original text. For example, if the writer is describing an empire, a thesaurus will suggest synonyms such as *domain, realm,* and *kingdom.* Pick the synonym that fits the context of the passage.

Capture the original voice: Remember to infuse your paraphrase with the original writer's opinions and feelings. Read the examples that follow.

Original News Report

"Scientists use improved technologies for gathering data about fish populations."

- **Paraphrase lacking voice:** Scientists use technology to collect facts about fish.
- **Paraphrase with the proper voice:** Scientists use the very latest methods to study the fish populations, collecting valuable information with greater ease.

Sample Paragraphs and Paraphrases

The following expository paragraph discusses the subconscious.

In psychology, the concept of subconscious is defined as the deepest level of consciousness. It involves thoughts buried inside the mind of which we are not directly aware. Sigmund Freud, a well-known Austrian neurologist, did extensive studies on the mind. He found three distinct levels of consciousness: waking consciousness, in which we are aware of our thoughts; preconsciousness, when we recall, but with effort; and the unconscious, or subconscious, in which our thoughts are beyond voluntary recall. Surprisingly, subconscious thoughts often affect our conscious behavior.

A student shows her understanding in this paraphrase of the paragraph:

Subconscious thoughts are buried inside our minds and beyond our ability to remember. Sigmund Freud found three levels of consciousness: waking, in which we are aware of our thoughts; preconsciousness, in which we can recall our thoughts with effort; and the subconscious, which is beyond our voluntary remembering. Even though we aren't aware of our subconscious thoughts, they can still affect our behavior.

The following text is part of a published review of a high school football game.

The first half of last Friday's game against the Coyotes was filled with sloppy plays and penalties, including the ejection of defensive back Zeke Thomas, who made contact with an official. Aurora High trailed 17-10 at halftime, which was not surprising since Coyote quarterback Ben Cantwell picked the All-Stars apart, and rookie player Syrus Paine ran through the defense. In the second half, the All-Stars played more like the team that brought Aurora High to the play-offs last year. Mike Mendenhall broke out in the fourth quarter with three forced turnovers, including the final touchdown on a 29-yard interception return by Lonnie Greene. Final score, 20-17 All-Stars.

A student reflects the writer's enthusiasm in his paraphrase of the review:

After a tough first half against the Coyotes, the Aurora All-Stars came back to win last Friday's game 20–17. During the first half, the All-Stars made careless plays and racked up penalties. The half-time score was 17–10 Coyotes. In the second half, Aurora controlled the field with several forced turnovers and a final touchdown that was scored on a 29-yard interception. The All-Stars ended the game looking more like the team that made it all the way to last year's play-offs.

Learning

Paraphrasing a Paragraph

Each sample paragraph below has a main idea and a distinct voice.

There are more than 200,000 words in the recent editions of large dictionaries, but roughly 2,000 should suffice for all your communication needs. Of course, you may disagree. You may be unhappy to call things by their common names; you may be ambitious to show superiority over others with your pretentious, pedantic vocabulary. For instance, you may not want to call a spade a spade. You may prefer to call it a spatulate device for abrading the surface of the soil. Better, however, to stick to the old familiar name that your grandfather used. Yes, call a spade a spade. Simple words have stood the test of time, and old friends are good friends.

In 2009, the Indianapolis Speedway will celebrate its 100th anniversary. The first track, a 2 1/2 mile rectangle, was built in 1909 and paved with 32 million bricks, earning it the nickname the Brickyard. The first race was held on August 19, 1909, and a driver named Louis Schwitzer took the checkered flag that day. During the race, the track broke up, killing two drivers, two mechanics, and two spectators. It has since been rebuilt, and the bricks are all but gone. For the sake of maintaining the Brickyard's history, a few still remain on the start/finish line.

Lightning storms moved over Southern California Monday evening and Tuesday morning, and lightning struck repeatedly throughout the region. Citizens reported smoldering palm trees in several areas of Orange County. In the suburban city of Irvine, darkness came early as heavy clouds blotted out the twilight. Flashes of lightning lit up the sky as often as every 15 seconds. Southern California rarely sees lightning; a thunderstorm rolls through once every few years, typically due to bad weather to the south.

Try It!

Paraphrase one of the paragraphs above. Communicate all important details and the author's point of view in your own words. Use the strategies on page **548** to guide you.

Taking Tests

Taking a test is like performing in a play. A veteran actor may be well prepared yet still feel a little nervous before going on stage. Feeling apprehensive before a test is normal, but if you're prepared, focused, and organized, you'll do fine. That's why it's important to keep up with your assignments and study effectively.

Preparing for a test takes careful planning. You need to arrange the test material, review it, remember it, and finally apply it to the test itself. If you follow this plan, your ability to do well on tests will improve. Studying the guidelines and samples in this chapter will help you improve your test-taking skills.

- **Preparing for a Test**
- **Test-Taking Tips**
- **Taking Objective Tests**
- **Taking Essay Tests**
- **Taking Standardized Tests**

"Always bear in mind that your own resolution to succeed is more important than any other one thing."

—Abraham Lincoln

Preparing for a Test

In order to prepare for a test, you must know what to expect. Usually, you can expect a test to cover whatever you've learned in class. Every day in class, take good notes—and review them often. Keep your graded assignments so you can look them over later. Follow the cycle below to do your best on every test.

Test-Prep Cycle

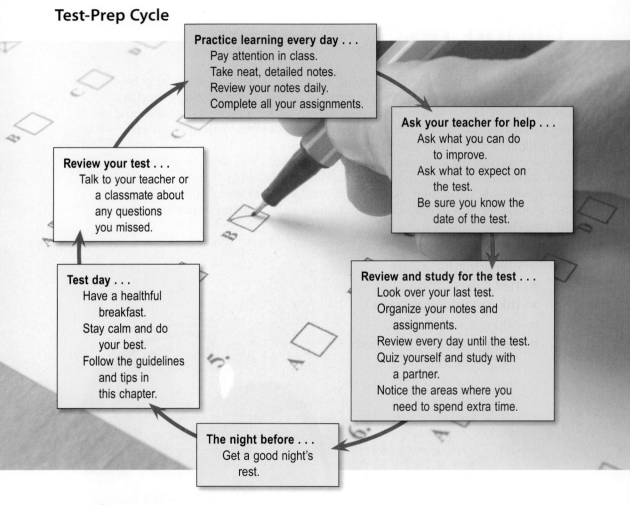

Practice learning every day . . .
Pay attention in class.
Take neat, detailed notes.
Review your notes daily.
Complete all your assignments.

Ask your teacher for help . . .
Ask what you can do
to improve.
Ask what to expect on
the test.
Be sure you know the
date of the test.

Review your test . . .
Talk to your teacher or
a classmate about
any questions
you missed.

Test day . . .
Have a healthful
breakfast.
Stay calm and do
your best.
Follow the guidelines
and tips in
this chapter.

Review and study for the test . . .
Look over your last test.
Organize your notes and
assignments.
Review every day until the test.
Quiz yourself and study with
a partner.
Notice the areas where you
need to spend extra time.

The night before . . .
Get a good night's
rest.

Try It!

Think of the ways you prepared for your last test. Did you leave out any of the above steps? See if you can improve your test scores by following this test-prep cycle.

Test-Taking Tips

- **Listen carefully** as your teacher gives directions, makes any corrections, or provides other information. And don't try to get a head start while your teacher is talking. You may miss important comments such as these:

"Make this change in number three."

"You have 30 minutes to finish the test."

"Write your answer to the final question on the back of the test sheet."

- **Put your name on the test right away.**
- **Take a quick look at the entire test.** This will help you decide how much time to spend on each section or question.
- **Begin the test.** Read the instructions before answering each set of questions. Do exactly what they tell you to do.
- **Read each question carefully.** Be sure you understand the question before answering it.
- **Answer all of the questions you are sure of first.** Then go back to the other questions and do your best to answer each one. Watch the time as you work on the more difficult questions.
- **Check over your answers when you finish the test.** If you skipped any hard questions, try to answer them now.

Try It!

Review these tips right before your next test and put them into practice. Upon completion of the test, ask yourself how closely you followed this advice.

Taking Objective Tests

Tests often have four different types of objective questions: true/false, matching, multiple-choice, and fill-in-the-blank.

True/False

In a true/false test, you decide if a statement is correct or incorrect. Most true/false questions focus on the details, so read each statement carefully.

- **Look for absolutes and qualifiers.** Statements with absolutes such as *always, never, all,* and *none* are often false. Statements that use qualifiers such as *often, rarely,* and *seldom* are more likely to be true.

  False   Republican and Democratic Congressional members follow similar patterns of voting behavior, to the point where the two parties are never obvious. (Republican and Democratic Congressional members follow dissimilar voting behavior.)

  True   When a party system is instituted, the controlling party often attempts to pass laws that make it difficult for other parties to get on the ballot.

- **Test each part.** If even a single word or phrase in a statement is false, then the entire statement is false.

  False   The Republican Party was formed in the early 1850s by pro-slavery activists. (The Republican Party was formed by *anti-slavery* activists.)

- **Watch for negatives.** Words such as *don't, can't, doesn't,* and *wasn't* can confuse, so be sure you know what the statement means.

  False   George Washington wasn't concerned about the development of "responsible party government."
  (Washington *was* concerned and warned against it.)

Matching

In matching tests, you match items in one column to those in another column.

- **Read both columns before answering any questions.** This helps you find the best match for each item.
- **Find grammar clues.** For example, plural subjects need plural verbs.
- **Match the items you know first.** If each answer is used only once, cross out the letter or number after you've used it.

_C_	1. aurora	~~A.~~	the direct opposite
_A_	2. antithesis	B.	passive acceptance
___	3. acquiescence	~~C.~~	a luminous event

Multiple-Choice

For multiple-choice questions, you choose the right answer from several possibilities.

- **Read each question carefully.** Usually, you will be asked to choose the best answer. Sometimes your choices may include "all of the above" or "none of the above."

    1. In The *Crucible,* on what charges is Giles Corey arrested?
        - A. slander
        - B. murder
        - C. contempt of court
        - D. all of the above

- **Anticipate the answer.** Before reading the choices, try to answer the question or complete the sentence.
- **Read all the choices before you answer.** It's tempting to choose the first answer that seems close, but there may be another choice that is better.
- **Consider "all of the above" and "none of the above" answers carefully.** If there is even one choice that you know to be incorrect, do not choose "all of the above." If there is one choice you know to be correct, do not choose "none of the above."
- **Eliminate the wrong or unlikely choices first.**

    2. The Sherman Antitrust Act was passed in
        - A. 1865 *(too early)*
        - B. 1957 *(too late)*
        - C. 1890
        - D. 1914 *(Clayton Antitrust Act)*

Fill-in-the-Blank

Fill-in-the-blank questions require you to supply a missing part of a statement.

- **Check the number of blanks.** Often, there is one for each word.

    1. The jugular vein carries blood from the __head__ to the __heart__.

- **Check for grammar clues.** If there is an *a* before the blank, the answer should begin with a consonant. If there is an *an* before the blank, the answer should begin with a vowel.

    2. A __platelet__ is a blood cell essential to the clotting process.

Try It!

Which types of objective questions are difficult for you? Use one or more of the tips to help you on your next test.

Learning

Taking Essay Tests

Many students feel that essay questions are the hardest parts of a test because, unlike other questions, possible answers are not given. Essay-test prompts require you to show how facts and supporting details are connected. The next few pages offer tips for taking an essay test.

Understanding and Restating the Prompt

- **Read the question carefully.**
- **Underline the key words** that explain what you are being asked to do. Here are some key words and their explanations.

Compare . . . . . Tell how things are alike.

Contrast . . . . . Tell how things are different.

Cause . . . . Describe how one thing has affected another.

Define . . . . Give a clear, specific meaning for a word or an idea.

Describe . . . . . Use sensory details to explain how something looks, sounds, and so on.

Evaluate . . . . . Make a value judgment supported by facts or examples.

Explain . . . . . . Use details and facts to tell what something means or how it works, or give reasons that tell why.

Identify . . . . . . Answer the question using one or more of the 5 W 's.

Illustrate . . . . . Use examples to show how something works or why it's important.

Prove . . . . Use facts and details to tell why something is true.

Review . . . . . . Create an overall picture of the topic.

Summarize . . . Tell the main idea and key points about the topic.

- **Rephrase the prompt into a thesis statement.** It often works well to drop the key word from your thesis statement.

Prompt: Explain how the human body defends itself from an infectious disease.

Thesis Statement: The human body defends itself from an infectious disease in three ways: prevention, attack, and inactivation.

 Try It!

Turn each essay-test prompt below into a thesis statement. (Refer to your textbook or a Web site for information on these topics.)

1. Explain why the United States Federal Reserve System was established.

2. Describe how the Interstate Commerce Act of 1887 affected railroads in the United States.

Planning a One-Paragraph Response

Tests may include one or more prompts that call for a paragraph response rather than a full-length essay. The following guidelines will help you write an effective one-paragraph response to a prompt.

- **Read the prompt carefully.** Underline the key words and phrases.
- **Identify what you are asked to do** (explain, compare, prove, define).
- **Plan your response.**
  1. Turn the prompt into a topic sentence.
  2. Include at least three supporting details. Keep your topic sentences in mind when you select these details.

Prompt

Define and give an example of a limited monarchy.

Planning Notes

Topic sentence: In a limited monarchy, the royal family has no authority to rule the people or make laws.

Supporting details:
  1. The royal family has only ceremonial powers.
  2. Great Britain is an example.
  3. Queen Elizabeth is the queen of England, but Parliament (House of Commons) rules the people.
  4. The queen sustains the family's traditions and ceremonies.

Response

Limited Monarchy

In a limited monarchy, the royal family has no authority to rule the people or make laws; the royals have only ceremonial power. Great Britain is an example of a limited monarchy. Queen Elizabeth is the leader of the British monarchy, but Parliament, more specifically the House of Commons, rules the people. The queen is responsible only for maintaining the traditions and ceremonies associated with the royal family.

Planning an Essay Response

Some essay prompts require you to respond with a full-length essay. The following tips will help you write a clear, well-organized response essay.

- **Read the prompt** and restate it as a thesis statement.
- **Plan your response** by outlining details that support your thesis.
- **Write your essay answer.** Include your thesis statement in your first paragraph. Each main point of your outline becomes the topic sentence for a body paragraph. In the final paragraph, write a meaningful conclusion that shows you truly understand the topic.

Prompt

Agree or disagree with the following quotation, using two examples from history, literature, current events, or personal experience.

"A man's dreams are an index to his greatness."

—Zadok Rabinwitz

Planning Notes

Thesis Statement: When I think about my own dreams, I agree with this quotation: "A man's dreams are an index to his greatness."

I. I've compiled a list of everything that I want to accomplish in my life.
   A. I want to finish college, go to med. school, practice medicine in Africa, climb Mount Everest, and have a family.
   B. It's important that I believe in my dreams without getting sidetracked.
   C. The index to my life won't be finished until I'm gone.

II. When I think of dreams and greatness, I think of *The Great Gatsby.*
   A. He was a dreamer.
   B. He rose from humble beginnings.
   C. He realized many of the dreams on his life list.
   D. His life illustrates that it takes a great person to use what he has.

Essay Response

The following essay response follows the outline on the previous page. The thesis statement appears in the beginning paragraph. The final paragraph is a meaningful conclusion showing that the writer clearly understands the topic.

Dreams and Greatness

When I think about my own dreams, I strongly agree with this quotation: "A man's dreams are an index to his greatness." As I try to decide what to do after high school, I'm dreaming, and I'm dreaming big. I believe that someday my dreams will be the index to my greatness.

I've compiled a list of everything that I want to accomplish in my life. My list includes finishing college and then going on to medical school, practicing medicine in the most remote parts of Africa, going to Nepal and climbing Mount Everest, and eventually getting married and having kids. That's just the beginning of my list. It's ambitious, I know, but I'm a dreamer, and I believe that dreams lead to greatness. "Believe" is the key word. The trick is believing in your dreams without getting sidetracked. When I come to the end of my life and people review my "index," I hope they will say, "It was his dreams that made him great."

When I think of dreams and greatness, I think of The Great Gatsby. Some people look at Gatsby's greed and dishonesty and say that he wasn't great. I see his character differently: Gatsby was a dreamer. He came from an ordinary background, and he built himself up. He realized many of the dreams on his life list, and he completely believed in them. In the end, his "index" was anything but that of an ordinary man. His life illustrates the idea that it takes a great person to use what he has to get to where he dreams to be.

I hope that someday my life, like Gatsby's life, will be an illustration of the quote "A man's dreams are an index to his greatness." My goal is to dream big and to follow my dreams. Check back in about 60 years, and take a look at my index.

Try It!

Plan and respond to the following prompt: "It takes failure to accomplish success." Do you agree or disagree? Support your opinion with two examples from literature, history, or your own observations.

Taking Standardized Tests

At certain times throughout your school life, you will be required to take standardized tests. The guidelines below will help you do well on these tests.

Before the test . . .

- **Know what to expect.** Ask your teacher what subjects will be covered on the standardized test, what format will be used, and what day the test will be given.
- **Get a good night's rest.** Also be sure to eat breakfast before any test.
- **Be prepared.** Bring extra pens, pencils, and erasers. Be sure to have enough blank paper for notes, outlines, or numerical calculations.

During the test . . .

- **Listen to the instructions and carefully follow directions.** Standardized tests follow strict guidelines. You will be given exact instructions on how to fill in information and supply answers.
- **Pace yourself.** In general, don't spend more than one minute on an objective question; move on and come back to it later.
- **Keep your eyes on your own work.** Don't worry if others finish before you.
- **Match question numbers** to answer numbers. If you skip a question in the question booklet, be sure to skip the corresponding number on your answer sheet. Every few questions, double-check the question number against your answer sheet.
- **Answer every question.** As long as there is no penalty for incorrect answers, you should always answer every question. First eliminate all the choices that are obviously incorrect, and then use logic to make your best educated guess.
- **Review your answers.** If you have time left, make sure that you've answered all the questions and haven't made any accidental mistakes. In general, don't change an answer unless you are sure that it's wrong. If you need to change an answer, be sure to erase the original answer completely.

After the test . . .

- **Make sure you have filled in all information correctly.**
- **Erase any unnecessary marks before turning in your test.**

Taking Exit and Entrance Exams

Exit and entrance exams are designed to give teachers and administrators a good idea of a student's level of academic achievement. Many school districts use exit exams to determine if students are qualified to graduate from high school. College admissions departments use entrance exams such as the SAT and ACT to help them determine whether a student will be chosen for admission.

These exams often include objective questions that test revising and editing skills. In the following pages, you'll find numerous sample questions to help you prepare. You'll also find sample writing prompts like those used in "on-demand" writing tests. With the strategies and practice prompts in this chapter, you can prepare for any high-stakes writing exam.

For more practice with specific types of writing prompts, see the following chapters: "Responding to Expository Prompts," "Responding to Persuasive Prompts," and "Responding to Prompts About Literature."

- **Questions About Conventions**
- **Sentence-Revision Questions**
- **Paragraph-Revision Questions**
- **Editing Questions**
- **Responding to Writing Prompts**
- **Budgeting Time for On-Demand Writing**

"Gentlemen, I had hoped you might emulate your Saxon forefathers, who thought it not creditable to be unprepared for anything."
—Woodrow Wilson

Questions About Conventions

Some questions check your understanding of punctuation, capitalization, spelling, and grammar. You may be asked to identify an error and correct it.

Exercise

Read the sample text in *italics* and follow the directions in **bold**. (Answers appear on the bottom of page **563**.)

1. *Brazil is a vast <u>country, it</u> is almost as big as the United States.*
   The best choice for the underlined section is

   A. NO CHANGE
   B. country: it
   C. country; it
   D. country it

2. *A hush <u>past</u> over the crowd as Kurt, our best gymnast, fell from the high bar. Coach Bryant and I ran over and tried to determine <u>whether</u> he was injured, but we wouldn't <u>know</u> if his ankle was <u>all right</u> until the next day when X-rays were taken.*
   Which one of the underlined words is not the right word?

   A. past
   B. whether
   C. know
   D. all right

3. *<u>"It's over they're,"</u> the salesperson said, pointing out the sale item.*
   The best choice for the underlined section is

   A. "It's over their,"
   B. "Its over there,"
   C. "Its over they're,"
   D. "It's over there,"

4. *According to our <u>science</u> teacher, the <u>Mesozoic</u> Era came after the Permian <u>Period</u>.*
   Which one of the underlined words has a capitalization error?

   A. science
   B. Mesozoic
   C. Period
   D. NONE

5. *According to the most reliable calculations, the Leaning Tower of Pisa* <u>*have existed*</u> *for at least 650 years.*

Which of the following is the correct change for the underlined words?

  A. NO CHANGE
  B. will have existed
  C. exists
  D. has existed

6. <u>*He*</u> *and the other players sat in* <u>*silence*</u>*; they* <u>*were*</u> *stunned by* <u>*thier*</u> *sudden defeat.*

Which of the underlined items should be corrected?

  A. He
  B. silence
  C. thier
  D. Both B and C

Tip

When you answer multiple-choice questions, keep these points in mind:

- **Read the question carefully.** *Remember:* You will be asked to analyze a brief passage to determine if it contains an error and, possibly, to correct the error.

- **Watch for negatives.** When directions contain words such as *not, none, never,* and *except,* make sure you understand what is being asked.

- **Read each answer carefully.** Watch for answers such as "Both A and B," "All of the above," or "None of the above."

- **Eliminate some answers.** Cross out choices you know are not correct before you make a choice.

Answer Key

  1. The focus is punctuation, and the answer is **C**.
  2. The focus is words that sound the same and are often confused—*passed/past, weather/whether,* and *know/no.* The answer is **A**.
  3. The focus is words that sound the same and are often confused—*it's/its* and *their/there/they're.* The answer is **D**.
  4. The focus is capitalization, and the answer is **D**.
  5. The focus is verb tenses and subject-verb agreement, and the answer is **D**.
  6. The focus is spelling, and the answer is **C**.

Sentence-Revision Questions

Other multiple-choice questions test your ability to revise, combine, and correct sentences. (See the "Proofreader's Guide" and the Tip on page **563**.)

Exercise

Read the following sentences and choose the *best* revision (or NO CHANGE). (Answers appear on the bottom of page **565**.)

1. *The weather which consisted of seven straight days of rain. It ruined our vacation.*

   A. The weather, which consisted of seven straight days of rain, ruined our vacation.

   B. The weather consisted of seven straight days of rain. And it ruined our vacation.

   C. The weather that consisted of seven straight days of rain. It ruined our vacation.

   D. NO CHANGE

2. *Whipping the willow's branches back and forth, we huddled at the screen door to watch the wind.*

   A. To watch the wind, we huddled at the screen door, whipping the willow's branches back and forth.

   B. We huddled at the screen door to watch the wind whipping the willow's branches back and forth.

   C. Watching the wind whipping the willow's branches back and forth at the screen door, we huddled.

   D. NO CHANGE

3. *Emiko went to the restaurant and ate a sub sandwich and drank a diet cola and then she went back to work.*

   A. Emiko went to the restaurant and ate a sub sandwich and drank a diet cola. Then she went back to work.

   B. Emiko went to the restaurant, and ate a sub sandwich, and drank a diet cola. Then she went back to work.

   C. Emiko went to the restaurant, where she had a sub sandwich and a diet cola before going back to work.

   D. NO CHANGE

4. *I like sushi better than my brother.*

   A. I like sushi more better than my brother.

   B. I like sushi better than my brother does.

   C. I like sushi even better than my brother.

   D. NO CHANGE

5. *No one saw Saul's boat sink after the lightning hit it, which Saul thought was just one more example of his bad luck.*

    A. Saul thought it was just one more example of his bad luck that no one saw his boat sink after the lightning hit it.

    B. No one saw Saul's boat sink after the lightning hit it. Saul thought it was just one more example of his bad luck.

    C. After the lightning hit Saul's boat, no one saw it sink. Saul thought it was just one more example of his bad luck.

    D. NO CHANGE

6. *The car raced down the highway. The highway had ice on it. The car leaned into a sharp curve. It spun out of control and slid over the embankment.*

    A. The car raced down the highway, and the highway had ice on it. The car leaned into a sharp curve and spun out of control and slid over the embankment.

    B. The car raced down the icy highway. The car leaned into a sharp curve and spun out of control. It slid over the embankment.

    C. The car raced down the icy highway, leaned into a sharp curve, spun out of control, and slid over the embankment.

    D. NO CHANGE

7. *The basketball player, with one black sock and one yellow one, scored the most points.*

    A. The basketball player, with one black sock and one yellow one scored the most points.

    B. The basketball player with one black sock and one yellow one, scored the most points.

    C. The basketball player with one black sock and one yellow one scored the most points.

    D. NO CHANGE

Answer Key

    1. The focus is fragments and combining, and the answer is **A**.

    2. The focus is misplaced modifiers, and the answer is **B**.

    3. The focus is rambling or awkward sentences, and the answer is **C**.

    4. The focus is incomplete comparisons, and the answer is **B**.

    5. The focus is ambiguous wording, and the answer is **A**.

    6. The focus is sentence combining, and the answer is **C**.

    7. The focus is restrictive and nonrestrictive phrases and clauses. The answer is **C**.

Learning

Paragraph-Revision Questions

Some questions test paragraph-revising skills. The key to success is to carefully read and reread the sample paragraphs. (See the Tip on page 563.)

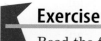

Exercise

Read the following text and answer the questions on page 567.

(1) A dog has a wet nose. *(2)* Whether you think of that nose as annoying or not, it is much more complex than it seems. *(3)* A dog's nose is part of a highly developed system that is good for the dog but even better for mankind.

(4) The dog's acute sense of smell serves humans in many ways. *(5)* Tracker dogs have a long history of tracing escaped criminals and missing children. *(6)* Some dogs focus on finding people trapped alive in avalanches and collapsed buildings. *(7)* Patrol dogs sniff around border checkpoints for things like explosives and illegal drugs. *(8)* But the most amazing benefits are those emerging in medicine. *(9)* Medical companion dogs can detect oncoming epileptic seizures, high blood pressure, heart attacks, migraines, and low blood sugar. *(10)* The most recent medical "miracle" is that dogs seem to be able to smell certain kinds of cancer before they are measurable by lab tests.

(11) The anatomy or structure of a dog's nose helps explain its sophisticated sense of smell. *(12)* The wetness itself is important. *(13)* It allows the dog to smell better by making odors stronger. *(14)* Then behind the nose itself, there are two other important olfactory organs—the receptors and the brain. *(15)* Inside the dog's nose is a very large number of smell receptors—25 times more than in humans. *(16)* These receptors are not active in the dog's normal breathing but come into play during sniffing. *(17)* The sensations from the receptors go to a part of the dog's brain that is four times larger than the corresponding part in a human brain. *(18)* These organs together give the dog the ability to sense odor in concentrations 100 million times lower than humans can. *(19)* Although dogs smell much more than humans do, they are not overwhelmed; they can sort out many layers of odor at the same time.

(20) Dogs have been thought of as man's best friend for a long time. *(21)* They wag their tails and seem to enjoy human company. *(22)* Their personalities are only part of the story, though. *(23)* Sometimes dogs need obedience lessons. *(24)* Scientists are probably only beginning to understand how important the family dog can be.

1. *Which of the following would be better than sentence 1?*

   A. On a sleepy Saturday morning, you suddenly wake up because you feel your dog's cold, wet nose on your hand—then you hear the smoke alarm.
   B. I'd like to talk about a dog's nose.
   C. A dog's wet nose is an extraordinarily perceptive device.
   D. NO CHANGE

2. *Which of the following sentences should be deleted?*

   A. Sentence 8
   B. Sentence 13
   C. Sentence 23
   D. NONE

3. *Which of the following would be the best addition to the beginning of sentence 12?*

   A. On the other hand,
   B. First of all,
   C. Likewise,
   D. In other words,

4. *Which sentence best paraphrases the focus of the essay?*

   A. Medical science is learning more and more about how dogs can help humans.
   B. Humans cannot get along without a dog's help.
   C. Dogs should be given greater respect.
   D. A dog's keen sense of smell has many benefits to humans.

5. *If you were to add a sentence to the end of the essay, which of the following would best reflect the way the writer feels about the topic?*

   A. Dogs can be pretty goofy, but sometimes they're a big help.
   B. The preponderance of evidence says that dogs are beneficial.
   C. All I can say about dogs is, "Cool!"
   D. The animals that have long been considered faithful companions may also be able to help people live better lives.

Learning

Answer Key

1. The focus is openings and closings, and the answer is **C**.
2. The focus is paragraph unity, and the answer is **C**.
3. The focus is transitions, and the answer is **B**.
4. The focus is the main idea or thesis, and the answer is **D**.
5. The focus is tone, and the answer is **D**.

Editing Questions

Some tests assess your editing skills by asking you to spot problems in writing. (See the Tip on page **563**.)

Exercise

Choose the underlined word or words that should be edited (or choose LEAVE AS IS). (Answers appear at the bottom of this page.)

1. *Inez <u>heard the phone ringing</u>, <u>answered it</u>, and <u>has taken the message</u>.*
            A   **B**   **C**

    D. LEAVE AS IS

2. *We <u>recommend</u> that new rules <u>be considered</u> <u>at this point in time</u>.*
           A   **B**   **C**

    D. LEAVE AS IS

3. *She <u>had</u> a habit of speaking <u>too</u> softly <u>when she was saying something</u>.*
           A   **B**   **C**

    D. LEAVE AS IS

4. *Sam, an apprentice, <u>he</u> was afraid he would lose <u>his</u> job, but the boss*
                    A   **B**

   <u>thought</u> Sam was doing good work.
         C

    D. LEAVE AS IS

5. *As she <u>swung</u> her bat at the ball, <u>it</u> whistled <u>through</u> the air.*
             A   **B**   **C**

    D. LEAVE AS IS

6. *One of my <u>friend's</u> favorite books <u>are</u> To Kill <u>a</u> Mockingbird.*
              A   **B**   **C**

    D. LEAVE AS IS

Answer Key

1. The focus is parallel structure, and the answer is **C**.
2. The focus is ineffective writing, and the answer is **C**.
3. The focus is wordiness or redundancy, and the answer is **C**.
4. The focus is double subjects, and the answer is **A**.
5. The focus is indefinite references, and the answer is **B**.
6. The focus is subject-verb agreement, and the answer is **B**.

Responding to Writing Prompts

Some state and district exit exams require you to respond to a writing prompt in the form of an essay, a narrative, or a letter. You may be prompted to write from your own experience, or you may be asked to read one or two short passages and respond to them. These exams are usually timed, but some states and districts give students as much time as they need.

College entrance tests such as the ACT and SAT also include a timed writing section. The prompts on these tests ask you to support your point of view on a topic. The essays are evaluated on clarity, consistency, level of detail, and appropriateness. While correctness is important, evaluators understand that you are working within a limited time frame.

When you respond to a prompt, start by analyzing the prompt so that you know exactly what the test requires you to write. One way to analyze a prompt is to answer the following **STRAP questions** about it.

Subject: What topic (education, friendship, laws) should I write about?

Type: What form (essay, letter, editorial, article, report) of writing should I create?

Role: What position (student, son or daughter, friend, employee) should I assume as the writer?

Audience: Who (teacher, principal, parents, classmates, employer) is the intended reader?

Purpose: What is the goal (persuade, respond, evaluate, explain, tell, describe) of my writing?

Exercise

Analyze the following prompts by answering each STRAP question. (Note: If a prompt does not answer a question specifically, use your best judgment to answer.)

1. Imagine that you could take your senior year online instead of attending classes. Which education option would you prefer? In a letter to your principal, indicate the option you choose and convince your principal that you will succeed.

2. Human beings are social creatures, so friends are an important part of anyone's life. What qualities and behaviors make a person a good friend? Write an essay explaining three or four traits that make a true friend. Use specific details and anecdotes.

Reviewing a Prompt and Response

Before trying to respond to a writing prompt, review the following persuasive prompt and student response.

Sample Prompt

Some parents and educators feel that students need specific rules to guide them. Others maintain that students should be allowed to make their own decisions. What is your opinion about rules? Write an essay that states and defends your position.

STRAP Answers and Quick List

The student writer analyzed the prompt using the STRAP questions, wrote his position, and created a quick list. Other graphic organizers can help plan a response as well.

<u>S</u>ubject: Rules
<u>T</u>ype: Essay of opinion
<u>R</u>ole: Student/son
<u>A</u>udience: Testers
<u>P</u>urpose: Defend my position

Position: The best rules help students now and in the future.
– Rules with short-term value
– Rules that focus on the future
– Case study: Bad grades
– Respond to rule makers

Response

Next, the student developed his response. He paid as much attention to each part—the beginning, the middle, and the ending—as time permitted.

A Ruling on Rules

An opening question leads up to the opinion statement (underlined).

Do kids need rules, or is it more important for them to find out on their own what works and what doesn't work? It all depends on what the rules are supposed to accomplish. <u>The most effective rules are the ones that will help students now and in the future.</u>

<u>Some of the most frustrating rules are the ones that don't seem necessary in the long term.</u> For example,

Each middle paragraph develops one main point.

unreasonable dress and grooming codes are particularly annoying. What lasting benefit do they have? What is gained by regulating hairstyles? Appropriate grooming is something that students can safely learn on their own. After all, everyone looks back at a yearbook picture in 10 years and laughs at the hairstyles.

On the other hand, most students respect rules and requirements that help them stay focused on the future. Every day the world gets more confused about what's important, so it's useful to have guidelines for staying on track. Students may complain about having to take required courses, doing community service, and reading books during summer vacation, but at least they can see that there are clear reasons for these requirements. The future depends more on what a person has learned and how he or she relates to others than on the clothes the person wears in high school.

The writer uses a personal anecdote to support a main idea.

My own lesson in rules happened when I was in eighth grade. Because I got all C's on my first-quarter report card, Dad said that I was limited to one hour of TV on school nights. Of course, I was upset. Dad stood firm, and my grades improved dramatically. More importantly, I got out of the habit of wasting time. I know I wouldn't have come up with the TV rule on my own, and I know it changed my life in a positive way.

The closing concedes an opposing viewpoint.

People who come up with rules usually mean well. However, some rules are more about individual preference than about learning lessons for the future. Good intentions don't always make good rules.

Exercise

Use the STRAP questions to analyze the following prompt. Then create a position statement and quick list and begin your response. Finish writing, revising, and editing in the time your teacher provides.

Teenagers often have different sleep habits than adults. Would you support or oppose moving the start and finish time of school back one hour? As a concerned student, write a letter to the school board convincing them of your position. Include reasons, facts, and examples.

Responding to Prompts About Literature

Prompts may be based on literature that you have read prior to the exam or on selections that you read during the test. Here are some tips on writing responses to literature.

- **Write a thesis (focus) statement.** Reword the prompt so that it applies to the literature you're writing about.
- **Briefly outline your main points.** Support your thesis statement with convincing details.
- **Avoid summarizing the literature.** Follow the plan in your outline; don't simply retell a story or paraphrase a poem.
- **Include comments on the author's techniques.** Point out literary devices (symbols, repetition, ambiguity, word choice) that reveal the author's purpose.
- **Make direct references to the text.** Quote or paraphrase important excerpts to support your analysis.

Sample Prompt and Reading Selections

Many poets have written about the role leaders play in history. The two poems that follow are examples. In "Ozymandias," Percy Bysshe Shelley reflects on the legacy of Egyptian King Rameses II (Ozymandias in Greek texts), who lived from 1304–1237 B.C.E. In "O Captain! My Captain!" Walt Whitman writes about the legacy of U.S. President Abraham Lincoln, assassinated in 1865. Write an essay that explains what these two poems have to say about the role of a leader.

Ozymandias

I met a traveller from an antique land
Who said: Two vast and trunkless legs of stone
Stand in the desert. Near them, on the sand,
Half sunk, a shattered visage lies, whose frown,
And wrinkled lip, and sneer of cold command,
Tell that its sculptor well those passions read
Which yet survive, stamped on these lifeless things,
The hand that mocked them and the heart that fed;
And on the pedestal these words appear:
"My name is Ozymandias, king of kings:
Look on my works ye mighty, and despair!"
Nothing beside remains. Round the decay
Of that colossal wreck, boundless and bare
The lone and level sands stretch far away.

—Percy Bysshe Shelley (1792–1822)

O Captain! My Captain!

O Captain! my Captain! our fearful trip is done,
The ship has weather'd every rack, the prize we sought is won,
The port is near, the bells I hear, the people all exulting,
While follow eyes the steady keel, the vessel grim and daring;
       But O heart! heart! heart!
          O the bleeding drops of red,
              Where on the deck my Captain lies,
                Fallen cold and dead.

O Captain! my Captain! rise up and hear the bells;
Rise up—for you the flag is flung—for you the bugle trills,
For you bouquets and ribbon'd wreaths—for you the shores a-crowding,
For you they call, the swaying mass, their eager faces turning;
       Here Captain! dear father!
         This arm beneath your head!
           It is some dream that on the deck,
             You've fallen cold and dead.

My Captain does not answer, his lips are pale and still,
My father does not feel my arm, he has no pulse nor will,
The ship is anchor'd safe and sound, its voyage closed and done,
From fearful trip the victor ship comes in with object won;
       Exult O shores, and ring O bells!
        But I with mournful tread,
          Walk the deck my Captain lies,
            Fallen cold and dead.

                        —Walt Whitman (1819–1892)

Learning

Sample STRAP Answers and Quick List

Subject: Leaders in "Ozymandias" and "O Captain! My Captain!"
Type: Essay
Role: Reader
Audience: Testers
Purpose: Analyze

Position: These two poems show that leadership isn't about power but about inspiring people.
1. Ozymandias turns to dust.
   – Wreckage, "lifeless things"
   – Ironic inscription
2. Captain lives on in the poet.
   – "Ship" survives
   – People hail and follow

Response

Following his quick list, the student wrote a response that quoted and paraphrased passages from the two poems.

The beginning asks a question that the essay will answer. It ends with a thesis statement (underlined).

History is filled with tales of leaders—some great, and some terrible. What does it take to be a great leader? In the poems "Ozymandias" and "O Captain! My Captain!" Percy Bysshe Shelley and Walt Whitman describe two very different types of leaders and their effects on the world. Taken together, the poems suggest that effective leadership is not about power and authority, but instead about the ability to inspire people.

The first middle paragraph discusses one poem.

"Ozymandias" describes an authority figure with the power to have an enormous stone statue raised in his honor. This ruler declared himself the "king of kings" and flaunted his strength in the face of other rulers, telling them to "look on my works ye mighty, and despair!" Shelley uses images of fear and domination to describe Ozymandias. His "sneer of cold command" keeps people in line during his life, but in death, his greatness fades. Ironically, all that now remains of his monument are a few ruined blocks of stone in the emptiness of a vast desert. The word "despair" now reflects the fleetingness of the king's power.

The next middle paragraph discusses the other poem.

By contrast, the "Captain" has devoted himself to guiding the ship of state through troubled times to safety. "The prize we sought is won," the poet says, and the people cheer the return of their "dear father!" They crowd the shore with "bugle trills," with "bouquets and ribbon'd wreaths." The Captain has inspired his people, and they love him because of it. Unfortunately, the Captain has given his very life in service. Despite the victory of the state, the poet weeps for the loss of the leader—a very different reaction than the tribute to Ozymandias. The Captain's legacy will live on. In fact, the poem itself becomes a memorial to this great leader.

The ending revisits the thesis statement.

As long as the United States survives, Lincoln's sacrifice will be remembered by its people. He held the country together through a great crisis and became a national hero. On the other hand, Rameses II is remembered only for the ruins he left behind. He is mocked by his own inscription. The lesson would seem to be that the best leader is one who sacrifices for others, not one who commands others and demands his own glory.

Budgeting Time for On-Demand Writing

Responding to a prompt in an "on-demand" writing environment requires a special set of skills. The following tips can help you create your best response.

Before you write . . .

- **Know how much time you have.** Structure your response according to the clock. Use an accelerated approach for a 25-minute response, but take more time with prewriting and revising if you have 60 or 75 minutes.
- **Analyze the prompt.** Answer the STRAP questions so that you know exactly how to respond. Here is a sample prompt and student analysis:

> *Authority is more than just a title and a uniform. What is authority, who has it, and who should have it? Write an essay defining what authority is and how it relates to the life of a student.*

Subject: Authority
Type: Essay of definition
Role: Student
Audience: Tester
Purpose: To define

- **Plan your response.** Write your thesis or opinion statement and use a brief outline or graphic organizer to plan your writing.

During your writing . . .

- **Write an effective opening paragraph.** Capture your reader's attention, introduce the topic, and state your thesis.
- **Develop the middle part.** Begin each paragraph with a topic sentence (main point) that supports your thesis. Each topic sentence should answer "why" your thesis is valid. Use a variety of details, including quotations, paraphrases, and analyses. For persuasive writing, answer any major objections to your opinion.
- **Write a strong closing paragraph.** Complete your writing by providing a final thought or by restating your thesis. For persuasive writing, consider a call to action.

After you've written a first draft . . .

- **Read your work.** Watch for places where adding, cutting, or moving details will make your work stronger.
- **Check for conventions.** Correct any errors you find.

Basic Elements of Writing

Basic Paragraph Skills

A paragraph is a concise unit of thinking and writing. It is typically organized around a controlling idea stated in a topic sentence. The main part of a paragraph consists of sentences that support the controlling idea. The final sentence usually summarizes the content of the paragraph and, if the paragraph is part of an essay, prepares the reader for the next main point.

Paragraphs are often called "mini-essays" because they can describe, narrate, explain, or defend an opinion. The form will depend upon your topic and the types of details you have gathered. Whatever form it takes, a paragraph must contain enough information—enough supporting details— to give the reader a clear picture of the topic. Being able to write effective paragraphs can certainly help you gain control of all of your academic writing—essays, reports, analyses, research papers, and so on.

- **The Parts of a Paragraph**
- **Types of Paragraphs: Narrative, Descriptive, Expository, and Persuasive**
- **Patterns of Organization: Classification, Comparison-Contrast, Cause-and-Effect, Process, and Logical Order**

"Good writing is clear thinking made visible."

—Bill Wheeler

The Parts of a Paragraph

A basic paragraph contains three parts: a topic sentence, body sentences, and a closing sentence. The following expository paragraph provides information about an annual rodeo called the Calgary Stampede. Each detail in the body supports the topic sentence.

Topic Sentence

Body

Closing Sentence

The Calgary Stampede

The Calgary Stampede in Alberta, Canada, has grown to become the largest and most exciting rodeo in the world. It began in 1912, when Guy Weadick thought of celebrating the Old West with a show modeled after those he had seen in the United States. The stampede included six days of cowboy competitions and shows and was a huge success, drawing thousands of visitors. Eventually, the stampede merged with Calgary's annual Industrial Exhibition, and by 1968, the 10-day event was being billed as "The Greatest Outdoor Show on Earth." New buildings sprang up. Tourist numbers skyrocketed. Today, purses offer more than a million dollars in prize money for bareback riding, bull riding, barrel racing, roping, steer wrestling, and so on. Each July, the Stampede begins with a two-hour parade followed by rodeo events, grandstand shows, and many other special features. One of the most popular features is the daily Rangeland Derby Chuckwagon Race, called "The Chucks" in which four-horse teams pull chuckwagons on a figure-eight track. The Chucks is followed by more entertainment and a fireworks display. The Stampede also includes a midway, free shows, and agricultural exhibits, as well as a First Nations village offering native foods and exhibits. More than a million people visit the stampede annually to enjoy a brief trip back in time to the Canadian Old West.

Respond to the reading. What is the main idea of this paragraph? What specific details in the body support this idea? Name two or three of them.

A Closer Look at the Parts

Every paragraph, whether written to stand alone or to be part of a longer piece of writing, has three parts.

The Topic Sentence

Every topic sentence should do two things: **(1)** give the specific topic of the paragraph and **(2)** present a specific feature or feeling about the topic. When writing your topic sentence, use the following formula as a guide.

a specific topic

\+ a particular feature or feeling about the topic

= **an effective topic sentence**

the Calgary Stampede in Alberta, Canada

\+ has grown to become the largest and most exciting rodeo in the world

= **The Calgary Stampede in Alberta, Canada, has grown to become the largest and most exciting rodeo in the world.**

Tip

The topic sentence is usually the first sentence in a paragraph. However, it can also be located elsewhere. For example, you can present details that build up to an important summary topic sentence at the end of a paragraph.

The Body

Each sentence in the body of the paragraph should support the topic sentence. These sentences should add new details about the topic.

- Use specific details to make your paragraph interesting.
  Eventually, the stampede merged with Calgary's annual Industrial Exhibition, and by 1968, the 10-day event was being billed as "The Greatest Outdoor Show on Earth."

- Use the method of organization that best suits your topic: classification, order of importance, chronological order, and so on.

The Closing Sentence

The closing sentence ends the paragraph and may restate the topic, summarize the paragraph, or provide a link to the next paragraph.

More than a million people visit the stampede annually to enjoy a brief trip back in time to the Canadian Old West.

Types of Paragraphs

There are four basic types of paragraphs: *narrative, descriptive, expository,* and *persuasive.*

Narrative Paragraph

A **narrative paragraph** tells a story. It may draw from the writer's personal experience or from other sources of information. A narrative paragraph is almost always organized chronologically, or according to time.

Topic Sentence

Body

Closing Sentence

A Leap of Faith

When I applied to work on a mail boat last summer, I went through an unusual application process. Surprisingly, there was no interview for this job. Instead, I had to show that I could leap from boat to pier and back again. On "audition" day, all of the job hopefuls were loaded onto the huge, flat mail boat, which motored away from the dock to start its circle around the large lake. At the first pier, the driver shouted a name. A girl with a long ponytail stepped up, and was handed a fake packet of mail and instructed to make the delivery. She mistimed her jump and hit the water with a loud splash. We pulled her in, laughing and sputtering, and the boat continued to the next pier. One by one, we each had to make the jump from boat to pier. Some of us made it, and some of us didn't. I didn't time my return jump quite right and fell into the cold water. Those in the group who made the leap both ways became mail deliverers. I ended up working for a boat rental business, instead. That wasn't too bad, but it wasn't as exciting as working on the mail boat. So next year I will again leap at the chance to deliver mail.

Respond to the reading. What is the tone of the story (sad, humorous, angry)? What details help make the story interesting?

Write a narrative paragraph. Write a narrative paragraph in which you share your first job interview or your first tryout for an activity.

Basic Elements

Descriptive Paragraph

A **descriptive paragraph** gives the reader a detailed picture of a person, a place, an object, or an event. This type of paragraph should contain a variety of sensory details—specific sights, sounds, smells, tastes, and textures.

Topic Sentence

Body

Closing Sentence

Queen of the Bus

The new passenger made herself known. She stomped up each stair onto the bus, one hand gripping the steel side bar, the other hand firmly pressed on her cane, a thick walking stick with a worn silver duck's head for a handle. She nodded regally to the driver as her coins clattered into the fare box, then surveyed the bus for the likeliest seat. She started slowly down the center aisle, her wizened hand flitting from the back of one seat to the next. The scent of stale lilacs mingled with a trace of fried onions followed her down the aisle. Finally, she stopped in front of a young girl whose ear was dotted with piercings. The old woman tapped her cane against the girl's booted foot, nudging it aside. The girl wordlessly moved over to the window seat. Leaning on her cane, the old woman sat down gingerly, swinging her legs in after her. She smoothed the front of her coat, made of an expensive fabric that had seen better days. Wrapping the coat tightly about her thin frame, she wiggled over slightly as her seat partner pulled closer to the window. Head erect, cloudy black eyes bright with defiant victory, the old woman stared straight ahead, her left hand, adorned with only a worn gold band, gently caressing the silver duck head. Her highness had claimed her kingdom.

Respond to the reading. Is there a clear picture of the woman being described? Which two or three details are particularly effective?

Write a descriptive paragraph. Write a paragraph that describes someone you know or have observed. Use sensory details to let the reader know your exact feeling about that person, but do not be overly critical or negative.

Expository Paragraph

An **expository paragraph** shares information about a specific topic. Expository writing is informative. It might present facts, give directions, define terms, explain a process, and so on. Some ways to organize expository writing include logical order, classification, comparison-contrast, cause-effect, problem/solution, and time order.

Topic Sentence

Body

Closing Sentence

Roundabout Cartoonist

The name Rube Goldberg has become synonymous with convoluted cartoon inventions, yet the artist gave much more to the world. After being awarded his degree in engineering from the University of California, Berkeley, Goldberg followed his love of cartooning to work for several newspapers, first in California and later in New York. In New York, he developed a character known as Professor Lucius Gorgonzola Butts, whose crazy inventions included such gems as the self-operating napkin. But Goldberg's drawings went beyond the merely amusing because in 1948 he was awarded a Pulitzer Prize for his political cartoons. Goldberg was also awarded the Gold T-Square Award by the National Cartoonist Society. After retiring from cartooning in 1964, he created bronze sculptures, presenting them in several one-man shows, including one at the National Museum of American History. In 1970, Rube Goldberg was inducted posthumously into the cartoonist Hall of Fame. The intellectual descendants of his absurd inventions can be seen today in many films, from the *Back to the Future* series to animated features such as *Wallace and Gromit*. Goldberg's talent was obvious and his contributions many, yet he is best known—and best loved—for his crazy cartoon inventions.

Respond to the reading. What is the focus of this paragraph? Name three details that support this focus.

Write an expository paragraph. Write a paragraph that shares information about a topic that truly interests you. Include plenty of details.

Persuasive Paragraph

A **persuasive paragraph** expresses an opinion and tries to convince the reader that the opinion is valid. To be persuasive, a writer must include effective supporting reasons and facts.

Violence Begets Violence

Topic Sentence

Capital punishment should be abolished for three major reasons. First of all, common sense says that two wrongs don't make a right. To kill someone convicted of murder contradicts the reasoning behind the law that taking another's life is wrong. The state, however, is committing the same violent, dehumanizing act it is condemning. In addition, the death penalty is not an effective deterrent. Numerous studies show that murder is usually the result of complex psychological and sociological problems and that most murderers

Body

do not contemplate the consequences of their acts; or, if they do, any penalty is seen as a far-off possibility. The offense, on the other hand, supposedly solves an immediate problem or crisis. Most importantly, death is final and cannot be altered. Errors in deciding guilt or innocence will always be present in a system of trial by jury. There is too great a risk that innocent people will be put to death. Official records show that it has

Closing Sentence

happened in the past. For these reasons, capital punishment should be replaced with a system that puts all doubt on the side of life—not death.

Respond to the reading. What are the three main points that support the writer's opinion? Which of these points is the most important?

Write a persuasive paragraph. Write a paragraph presenting your opinion. Include at least three strong reasons to support your opinion.

Patterns of Organization

On the following pages, sample paragraphs demonstrate a variety of basic patterns of organization.

Classification Order

You organize by classification when you need to break a topic down into categories. The following paragraph classifies the different types of automobile passengers. The writer used a line diagram to help plan his writing.

Line Diagram

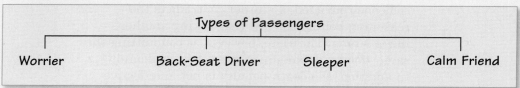

Types of Passengers

| Worrier | Back-Seat Driver | Sleeper | Calm Friend |

Topic Sentence

Body

Closing Sentence

Along for the Ride

The quality of a road trip really depends on the type of passenger riding along. Perhaps the worst passenger is the worrier who is certain that nothing is more dangerous than riding with you in a car. Ironically, the worrier's gasps and shrieks could be enough to startle you into an accident. Another troublesome passenger is the back-seat driver. This person constantly points out all of the things that the driver does wrong, from driving too fast to not checking your mirrors enough. Just as annoying is the sleeper. The minute the car is started, this person passes out, totally oblivious to anything until the destination is reached. So much for stimulating conversation! If a driver is lucky, he or she will share the trip with the best type of passenger, the calm friend. This person talks, keeping the driver alert and entertained throughout the entire trip. In the end, a passenger can make or break a road trip. A successful road trip begins and ends with a good traveling companion.

 Respond to the reading. Which details did you find most amusing or interesting in the above paragraph? Name three you found particularly engaging.

Comparison-Contrast Order

You organize by comparison when you want to show the similarities or differences between two subjects. To compare two styles of Japanese theaters, one student used a Venn diagram to organize her details. In her paragraph, the writer focused most of her attention on the differences between the two styles.

Venn Diagram

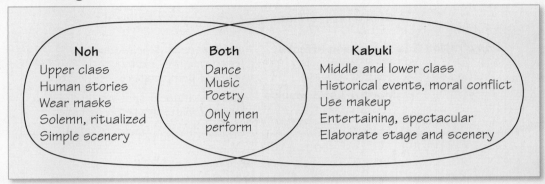

Noh
Upper class
Human stories
Wear masks
Solemn, ritualized
Simple scenery

Both
Dance
Music
Poetry

Only men
perform

Kabuki
Middle and lower class
Historical events, moral conflict
Use makeup
Entertaining, spectacular
Elaborate stage and scenery

Noh and Kabuki

Topic Sentence

Japan's two main styles of theater, Noh and Kabuki, are quite different. Both styles incorporate dance, music, poetry, and drama and are performed only by men. Performances in both theaters can last five hours or longer. The similarities end there. Noh is the older of the two, having begun in the 14th century as entertainment for royalty and the upper class. Kabuki started in the 17th

Body

century, and its style, more entertaining than enlightening, became popular with the common class. Noh plays deal with human failings and dilemmas performed on a simple platform with little scenery or props. Kabuki concentrates on spectacularly produced plays about historical events or dramatic moral conflicts. Noh uses masks to portray women and other characters, but Kabuki actors use makeup to

Closing Sentence

make the transformation. Despite their differences, the two traditional forms of Japanese theater offer theatergoers a choice between two excellent forms of entertainment.

 Respond to the reading. How is the above paragraph organized? What different way might it have been arranged?

Cause-and-Effect Order

You organize by cause and effect when you want to discuss one cause followed by its specific effects or an effect followed by its specific causes. The paragraph below discusses one cause (dehydration) and its effects.

Cause-Effect Organizer

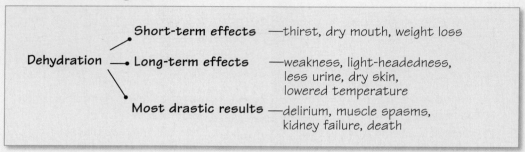

Dehydration

Short-term effects —thirst, dry mouth, weight loss

Long-term effects —weakness, light-headedness, less urine, dry skin, lowered temperature

Most drastic results —delirium, muscle spasms, kidney failure, death

Topic Sentence

Body

Closing Sentence

Dangerous Effects of Dehydration

An individual who does not get enough fluid each day runs the risk of dehydration. In the short term, dehydration creates general thirst—an easy reminder to drink some water. Surprisingly, it may also lead to a rapid drop in weight. In the long term (more than several days), the sufferer may begin to feel weak and light-headed. With the lack of water, the skin loses its elasticity and becomes dry and crinkly. Continued dehydration can lead to a drop in body temperature, causing the sufferer to feel cold. At this point, dehydration could also affect mental functioning and lead to a feeling of general apathy. If the dehydration continues, an individual could experience muscle spasms and delirium. The kidneys could also shut down, and if the condition continues, the entire body could shut down. While the consequences of dehydration are severe, the solution is simple: Be sure to drink enough water, a minimum of 32 ounces every day.

 Respond to the reading. What are the three levels of dehydration? Give one supporting detail for each?

Process Organization

You organize step-by-step when you want to explain a process. The following paragraph explains the process of eutrophication, which essentially kills a freshwater lake.

Process Diagram

> ### The Process of Eutrophication
>
> **phase 1:** oligotrophic
> ↓
> **phase 2:** mesotrophic
> ↓
> **phase 3:** eutrophic
> ↓
> **phase 4:** hypereutrophic
> ↓
> **phase 5:** dystrophic

Topic Sentence

Body

Closing Sentence

Eutrophication

Perhaps the biggest threat to the nation's freshwater lakes is the process of eutrophication, caused by an excess of nutrients. The process begins at the **oligotrophic** phase, when water is clear with little aerobic activity. In the second phase, the **mesotrophic** phase, fertilizers are washed into the water through rain runoff. Rich with nitrates and phosphates, the fertilizers stimulate the growth of algae and other water plants, creating an algal "bloom." By phase three, the **eutrophic** phase, the bloom has grown to affect the oxygen level in the water in two ways. First, it prevents the water from absorbing light needed for oxygen generation. Second, the algae is broken down by aerobic bacteria that further deplete the oxygen in the water. Left unchecked, the process moves to the **hypereutrophic** phase, when algae chokes and kills living organisms. The final stage is the **dystrophic** phase, where water becomes hypoxic, or lacking in enough oxygen to sustain life, and the body of water becomes officially "dead." People in this country must find a way to counteract this process or face losing the nation's clean freshwater supply.

Logical Order

You organize by logical order when your main points are of equal importance and can be placed in any order in your paragraph. Move logically from one point to the next so your writing flows well and is not confusing. In the paragraph below, transitional words and phrases help the writer move from point to point.

Logical Order List (partial)

Braille

- developed by Louis Braille
- alphabetic code of raised dots
- read by running fingers across the page
- basic unit of code is the "cell"
- books in Braille longer than regular books

Braille

Topic Sentence

Braille is a system of communication used by the blind. It was developed by Louis Braille, a blind French student, in 1824. The code consists of an alphabet using combinations of small raised dots. The dots are imprinted on paper and can be felt, and thus read, by running the fingers across the page. The basic unit of the code is called a "cell," which is two dots wide and three dots high. Each letter is formed by different combinations of these dots. Numbers, punctuation marks, and even a system for writing music

Body

are also expressed by using different arrangements. Books written in Braille require many more pages than a print book, and one novel might require many different volumes. The Braille system is used for different languages all over the world and is used for many things other than books. Braille is commonly used in elevators to indicate floors, and some restaurants even provide menus in Braille. There are also Braille codes that are used to read math symbols and music! Special Braille equipment includes typewriters and even a Braille embosser that can be attached to a computer.

Closing Sentence

The small Braille dots, which may seem insignificant to the sighted, have opened up the entire world of books and reading for the blind.

Respond to the reading. This paragraph provides many key details. Which ones do you find the most revealing? Name two.

Basic Essay Skills

At this point in your life, most of your academic writing is essay writing. You take essay tests; you write procedure (how-to) papers; you respond to the books that you read. All of these are essays—writing in which you explain, argue, or describe your thinking on a particular topic. The way you develop an essay depends on the guidelines established by your instructor and on your own good judgment about a particular writing idea. For some essays, a straightforward, traditional approach might be best; for others, a more creative approach might be more effective.

No matter what approach you take, keep in mind that developing an essay can be challenging. You must have a good understanding of your topic, have confidence in your position, and then develop it so that your readers can clearly share in your thinking. The information in this chapter serves as a basic guide to essay writing. (Also see the specific essay-writing chapters earlier in the book.)

- **Understanding the Basic Parts**
- **Outlining Your Ideas**
- **Writing Thesis Statements**
- **Creating Great Beginnings**
- **Developing the Middle Part**
- **Using Transitions**
- **Shaping Great Endings**
- **Key Terms, Techniques, and Forms**

"Essays are how we speak to one another in print."

—Edward Hoagland

Understanding the Basic Parts

Each part of an essay—the beginning, middle, and ending—plays an important role. To develop your writing, refer to the suggestions below and to the sample essays earlier in this book.

Beginning **Your opening paragraph should capture the reader's attention and state your thesis.** Here are some ways to capture your reader's attention:

- Tell a dramatic or exciting story (anecdote) about the topic.
- Ask an intriguing question or two.
- Provide a few surprising facts or statistics.
- Provide an interesting quotation.
- Explain your personal experience or involvement with the topic.

Middle **The middle paragraphs should support your thesis statement.** They provide information that fully explains the thesis statement. For example, in an essay about safety measures in Grand Prix racing, each middle paragraph could focus on one main aspect of improved safety. Follow your own outline while writing this section.

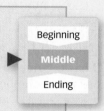

Ending **Your closing paragraph should summarize your thesis and leave the reader with something to think about.** Here are some strategies for creating a strong closing:

- Review your main points.
- Emphasize the special importance of one main point.
- Answer any questions the reader may still have.
- Draw a conclusion and put the information in perspective.
- Provide a significant final thought for the reader.

Outlining Your Ideas

Once you've established a general pattern of development, you're ready to organize the information (main points, supporting details, etc.) that you will cover in your essay. It may work to jot down a brief list of ideas to follow. Then again, you may find it helpful to organize your ideas in a topic or sentence outline.

Topic Outline

An outline is an orderly listing of related ideas. In a **topic outline**, each new idea is stated as a word or phrase rather than in complete sentences. Before you start, write your working thesis statement at the top of your paper to keep you focused on the subject of your essay. Do not attempt to outline your opening and closing paragraphs unless specifically asked to do so.

Introduction
  I. The technology of genetic engineering
      A. Gene manipulation
      B. Gene copying and transferring
      C. Gene recombining and cloning
 II. The uses of genetic engineering
      A. Unpredictable in past
      B. More predictable now
      C. More potential in future
III. The fears about genetic engineering
      A. Release of dangerous organisms
      B. Lack of trust in scientists
Conclusion

Sentence Outline

A **sentence outline** naturally contains more detail than a topic outline because each new idea is expressed as a complete sentence. It is often required for longer essays or a research paper.

Introduction
  I. Genetic engineering is a form of biotechnology.
      A. Scientists can manipulate genes.
      B. Genes can be copied and moved to cells in other species.
      C. Scientists can recombine genes and clone entire organisms.
 II. Genetic engineering affects animal and plant breeding.
      A. Past species improvement efforts proved unpredictable.
      B. Now development time is cut dramatically with better results.
      C. Animals are potential chemical factories, and new animals can be created and patented.
III. Genetic engineering is feared by some.
      A. Dangerous organisms could be released.
      B. Public confidence in scientists has been undermined.
Conclusion

Basic Elements

Writing Thesis Statements

In most cases, a thesis statement takes a stand or expresses a specific feeling about, or feature of, your topic. An effective thesis statement gives you the necessary direction to develop your essay.

Using a Formula

a specific topic *(the Harlem Renaissance)*

+ **a particular feature or feeling about the topic** *(helped the African American intellectual community gain acceptance in mainstream America)*

= **an effective topic sentence** *(The Harlem Renaissance helped the African American intellectual community gain acceptance in mainstream America.)*

Sample Thesis Statements

Writing Assignment: Examine a political theme in a novel.
Specific Topic: *All Quiet on the Western Front*
Thesis Statement: In *All Quiet on the Western Front,* by Erich Maria Remarque, **(topic)** idealistic views of nationalism are brought into question **(particular feeling)**.

Writing Assignment: Explore a current water resource in the area.
Specific Topic: Recreational fishing on Lake Michigan
Thesis Statement: Recreational fishing on Lake Michigan **(topic)** needs more oversight **(particular stand)**.

Writing Assignment: Research on human growth and development.
Specific Topic: Personality traits
Thesis Statement: An individual's peer group **(particular feature)** shapes certain personality traits **(topic)**.

Thesis Checklist

Be sure that your thesis statement . . .

_____ identifies a limited, specific topic,

_____ focuses on a particular feature or feeling about the topic,

_____ can be supported with convincing facts and details, and

_____ meets the requirements of the assignment.

Creating Great Beginnings

The opening paragraph of an essay should grab the reader's attention, introduce your topic, and present your thesis. Try one of these approaches to start an opening paragraph.

- **Start with an interesting fact.**
  In the period between world wars, the Harlem Renaissance thrust African American culture into the United States mainstream.

- **Ask an interesting question.**
  Did you know that the civil rights movement really began with the Harlem Renaissance in the 1920s?

- **Start with a quotation.**
  "As one who loves literature, art, music, and history, I've been deeply rooted in the Harlem Renaissance for many years." So states Debbie Allen, a well-known actress of film and television fame.

Beginning Strategies

If you have trouble coming up with a good opening paragraph, follow the step-by-step example below.

First sentence—Grab the reader's attention.

Start with a sentence that catches your reader's attention (see above).

In the period between world wars, the Harlem Renaissance thrust African American culture into the United States mainstream.

Second sentence—Give some background information.

Provide some information about the topic.

It became a precursor to the civil rights movement, creating an environment of awareness of the black culture.

Third sentence—Introduce the specific topic of the essay.

Introduce the topic in a way that builds up to the thesis statement.

The period was a time of growth in African American literature and art.

Fourth sentence—Give the thesis statement.

Write the thesis statement of the paper (see page 592).

As such, the Harlem Renaissance helped the African American intellectual community gain acceptance in mainstream America.

Basic Elements

Developing the Middle Part

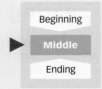

The middle part of an essay is where you do most of the work. In this part, you develop the main points that support your thesis statement.

Use your outline or other planning notes as a guide when you write this section. However, new ideas may pop into your head as you go along. Make note of these ideas in case you may want to explore them further later on.

Advancing Your Thesis

Keep these points in mind as you explain and develop your thesis statement.

- **Cover your main points.** Develop each main point in a paragraph or series of paragraphs.
- **Give background information.** If necessary, provide some history of your topic to help you put it in context.
- **Define terms.** Clarify any terms that your reader is not likely to know.
- **Sort out the main points.** Present the main ideas in a logical order (according to your outline).

Testing Your Ideas

When you write the middle part of an essay, you're testing your first thoughts about your topic. Here are some ways to test your line of thinking as you write.

- **Raise questions**. Anticipate what questions the reader may have about your topic.
- **Consider alternative ideas.** Take inventory of your thesis as you go along: Do you need to strengthen or rethink it? Also look at your main points from different angles.
- **Answer objections.** Address different points of view about your topic.

Building a Coherent Structure

Each middle paragraph should include main points and details that logically develop your thesis.

- **Develop one paragraph at a time.** Start a new paragraph whenever a shift or change in the essay takes place.
- **Connect your main points.** Use transitional phrases to link each new paragraph with the preceding one. (See page **595**.)

Using Transitions

Transitions can be used to connect one sentence to another sentence within a paragraph, or to connect one paragraph to another within a longer essay or report. The lists below show a number of transitions and how they are used. Each colored list is a group of transitions that could work well together in a piece of writing.

Words used to show location

above	around	between	inside	outside
across	behind	by	into	over
against	below	down	near	throughout
along	beneath	in back of	next to	to the right
among	beside	in front of	on top of	under

Above	In front of	On top of
Below	Beside	Next to
To the left	In back of	Beneath
To the right		

Words used to show time

about	during	yesterday	until	finally
after	first	meanwhile	next	then
at	second	today	soon	as soon as
before	to begin	tomorrow	later	in the end

First	To begin	Now	First	Before
Second	To continue	Soon	Then	During
Third	To conclude	Eventually	Next	After
Finally			In the end	

Words used to compare things

likewise	as	in the same way		one way
like	also	similarly		both

In the same way		One way
Also		Another way
Similarly		Both

Basic Elements

Words used to contrast (show differences)

but	still	although	on the other hand
however	yet	otherwise	even though

On the other hand   Although
Even though   Yet
Still   Nevertheless

Words used to emphasize a point

again	truly	especially	for this reason
to repeat	in fact	to emphasize	

For this reason   Truly   In fact
Especially   To emphasize   To repeat

Words used to conclude or summarize

finally	as a result	to sum it up	in conclusion
lastly	therefore	all in all	because

Because   As a result   To sum it up   Therefore
In conclusion   All in all   Because   Finally

Words used to add information

again	another	for instance	for example
also	and	moreover	additionally
as well	besides	along with	other
next	finally	in addition	

For example   For instance   Next   Another
Additionally   Besides   Moreover   Along with
Finally   Next   Also   As well

Words used to clarify

in other words	for instance	that is	for example

For instance   For example
In other words   Equally important

Shaping Great Endings

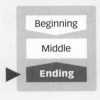

The closing paragraph of a paper should summarize your thesis and leave the reader with something to think about. When writing your closing paragraph, use two or more of the following approaches:

- Review your main points.
- Emphasize the special importance of one main point.
- Answer any questions the reader may still have.
- Draw a conclusion and put the information in perspective.
- Provide a significant final thought for the reader.

Ending Strategies

If you have trouble coming up with an effective closing paragraph, follow the step-by-step example below.

First sentence—Reflect on the topic.

Start by reflecting on the material presented previously about the topic.

> **Although the Harlem Renaissance lasted a brief time, its influence is still felt.**

Second sentence—Add another point.

Include a final point of interest that you didn't mention before.

> **Some argue that the movement failed in its goal of equality, stating the ongoing existence of racism as proof.**

Third sentence—Emphasize the most important point.

Stress the importance of one or more key points that support the thesis.

> **While that may be true, the fact remains that the black voice is strong throughout the creative world. African American writers, artists, and philosophers are heard and their ideas respected.**

Fourth sentence—Wrap up the topic or draw a conclusion.

Add one final thought about the topic, or draw a conclusion from the points you've presented in the writing.

> **Philosopher Alaine Hock says that the Harlem Renaissance gave African Americans their first chance for "group expression and self-determination," and the writers and artists clearly made the most of their opportunities.**

Basic Elements

Learning Key Writing Terms

The next two pages include important terms related to writing. Refer to these pages whenever you have a question about the vocabulary associated with any part of the writing process.

Balance	Arranging words or phrases in a way to give them equal importance
Body	The main part of a piece of writing, containing details that support or develop the thesis statement
Brainstorming	Collecting ideas by thinking freely about all the possibilities; used most often with groups
Central idea	The main point of a piece of writing, often stated in a thesis statement or a topic sentence
Closing sentence	The summary or final part in a piece of writing
Coherence	The logical arranging of ideas so they are clear and easy to follow
Dialogue	Written conversation between two or more people
Emphasis	Giving great importance to a specific idea in a piece of writing
Exposition	Writing that explains and informs
Figurative language	Language that goes beyond the normal meaning of the words used, often called "figures of speech"
Focus (thesis)	The specific part of a topic that is written about in an essay
Generalization	A general statement that gives an overall view, rather than focusing on specific details
Grammar	The rules that govern the standard structure and features of a language
Idiom	A phrase or an expression that means something different from what the words actually say

The answer was really out in left field. (This means the answer was not even close to being correct.)

Next year you'll sing a different tune. (This means you'll think differently.) |
| **Jargon** | The special language of a certain group or occupation

The weaver pointed out the fabric's unique warp **and** woof.

Computer jargon: byte   icon   server   virus |

Limiting the subject	Narrowing a general subject to a more specific one
Literal	The actual dictionary meaning of a word; a language that means exactly what it appears to mean
Loaded words	Words slanted for or against the subject **The new tax bill** helps the rich **and** hurts the poor.
Logic	Correctly using facts, examples, and reasons to support a point
Modifiers	Words, phrases, or clauses that limit or describe another word or group of words
Objective	Writing that gives factual information without adding feelings or opinions (See *subjective*.)
Poetic license	A writer's freedom to bend the rules of writing to achieve a certain effect
Point of view	The position or angle from which a story is told (See page **350**.)
Prose	Writing in standard sentence form
Purpose	The specific goal of the writing
Style	The author's unique choice of words and sentences
Subjective	Writing that includes the writer's feelings, attitudes, and opinions (See *objective*.)
Supporting details	Facts or ideas used to sustain the main point
Syntax	The order and relationship of words in a sentence
Theme	The main point or unifying idea of a piece of writing
Thesis statement	A statement of the purpose, or main idea, of an essay
Tone	The writer's attitude toward the subject
Topic	The specific subject of a piece of writing
Topic sentence	The sentence that carries the main idea of a paragraph
Transitions	Words or phrases that connect or tie ideas together
Unity	A sense of oneness in writing in which each sentence helps to develop the main idea
Usage	The way in which people use language (*Standard language* follows the rules; *nonstandard language* does not.)
Voice	A writer's unique personal tone or feeling that comes across in a piece of writing

Basic Elements

Using Writing Techniques

Experiment with some of these techniques in your own essays and stories.

Allusion	A reference to a familiar person, place, thing, or event **Mario threw me my mitt.** "Hey, Babe Ruth, you forgot this!"
Analogy	A comparison of similar ideas or objects to help clarify one of them **There is no frigate like a book, to take us lands away.** —Emily Dickinson
Anecdote	A brief story used to illustrate or make a point **It is said that the last words John Adams uttered were "Thomas Jefferson survives." Ironically, Jefferson had died just a few hours earlier. Both deaths occurred on July 4, 1826—the 50th anniversary of the Declaration of Independence shepherded by the two great men.** (This ironic anecdote intensifies the importance of both men in our nation's history.)
Colloquialism	A common word or phrase suitable for everyday conversation but not for formal speech or writing **"Cool"** and **"rad"** are colloquialisms suggesting approval.
Exaggeration	An overstatement or a stretching of the truth to emphasize a point (See *hyperbole* and *overstatement.*) **We opened up the boat's engine and sped along at a** million miles an hour.
Flashback	A technique in which a writer interrupts a story to go back and relive an earlier time or event **I stopped at the gate, panting.** Suddenly I was seven years old again, and my brother was there, calling me "chicken" from the edge of the stone well. **Then I opened my eyes and heard only the crickets chirping. The years, the well, and my brother were gone. I turned back to the road, determined to get home before nightfall.**
Foreshadowing	Hints about what will happen next in a story **As Mai explained why she had to break their date, she noticed Luke looking past her.** Turning, she saw Meg smiling—at Luke.
Hyperbole	(*hi-púr-bə-lē*) Exaggeration used to emphasize a point **The music was** loud enough to make your ears bleed.
Irony	An expression in which the author says one thing but means just the opposite **As we all know,** there's nothing students love more than homework.

Juxtaposition	Putting two words or ideas close together to create a contrasting of ideas or an ironic meaning **Ah, the sweet smell of fuel emissions!**
Local color	The use of details that are common in a certain place
Metaphor	A figure of speech that compares two things without using the words *like* or *as* **The sheep were dense, dancing clouds scuttling across the road.**
Overstatement	An exaggeration or a stretching of the truth (See *exaggeration* and *hyperbole.*) **If I eat one more piece of turkey, I will burst!**
Oxymoron	Connecting two words with opposite meanings **small fortune cruel kindness original copy**
Paradox	A true statement that says two opposite things **As I crossed the finish line dead last, I felt a surge of triumph.**
Parallelism	Repeating similar grammatical structures (words, phrases, or sentences) to give writing rhythm **We cannot undo, we will not forget, and we should not ignore the pain of the past.**
Personification	A figure of speech in which a nonhuman thing is given human characteristics **The computer spit out my disk.**
Pun	A phrase that uses words that sound the same in a way that gives them a funny effect **I call my dog Trousers because he pants so much.**
Simile	A figure of speech that compares two things using *like* or *as* **Her silent anger was like a rock wall, hard and impenetrable.**
Slang	Informal words or phrases used by a particular group of people **cool it hang out shoot the curl**
Symbol	A concrete object used to represent an idea
Understatement	The opposite of exaggeration; using very calm language to call attention to an object or an idea **" . . . except for an interruption caused by my wife falling out of the car, the journey went very well."** **—E. B. White**

Basic Elements

Knowing the Different Forms

Finding the right form for your writing is just as important as finding the right topic. When you are selecting a form, be sure to ask yourself who you're writing for (your *audience*) and why you're writing (your *purpose*).

Anecdote	A brief story that helps to make a point
Autobiography	A writer's story of his or her own life
Biography	A writer's story of someone else's life
Book review	An essay offering an opinion about a book, not to be confused with *literary analysis*
Cause and effect	A paper examining an event, the forces leading up to that event, and the effects following the event
Character sketch	A brief description of a specific character showing some aspect of that character's personality
Descriptive writing	Writing that uses sensory details that allow the reader to clearly visualize a person, a place, a thing, or an idea
Editorial	A letter or an article offering an opinion, an idea, or a solution
Essay	A thoughtful piece of writing in which ideas are explained, analyzed, or evaluated
Expository writing	Writing that explains something by presenting its steps, causes, or kinds
Eyewitness account	A report giving specific details of an event or a person
Fable	A short story that teaches a lesson or moral, often using talking animals as the main characters
Fantasy	A story set in an imaginary world in which the characters usually have supernatural powers or abilities
Freewriting	Spontaneous, rapid writing to explore your thoughts about a topic of interest
Historical fiction	An invented story based on an actual historical event
Interview	Writing based on facts and details obtained through speaking with another person
Journal writing	Writing regularly to record personal observations, thoughts, and ideas

Literary analysis	A careful examination or interpretation of some aspect of a piece of literature
Myth	A traditional story intended to explain a mystery of nature, religion, or culture
Novel	A book-length story with several characters and a well-developed plot, usually with one or more subplots
Personal narrative	Writing that shares an event or experience from the writer's personal life
Persuasive writing	Writing intended to persuade the reader to follow the writer's way of thinking about something
Play	A form that uses dialogue to tell a story, usually meant to be performed in front of an audience
Poem	A creative expression that may use rhyme, rhythm, and imagery
Problem-solution	Writing that presents a problem followed by a proposed solution
Process paper	Writing that explains how a process works, or how to do or make something
Profile	An essay that reveals an individual or re-creates a time period
Proposal	Writing that includes specific information about an idea or a project that is being considered for approval
Research report	An essay that shares information about a topic that has been thoroughly researched
Response to literature	Writing that is a reaction to something the writer has read
Science fiction	Writing based on real or imaginary science and often set in the future
Short story	A short fictional piece with only a few characters and one conflict or problem
Summary	Writing that presents the most important ideas from a longer piece of writing
Tall tale	A humorous, exaggerated story about a character or an animal that does impossible things
Tragedy	Literature in which the hero fails or is destroyed because of a serious character flaw

Proofreader's Guide

Marking Punctuation

Period

605.1 At the End of a Sentence

Use a **period** at the end of a sentence that makes a statement, requests something, or gives a mild command.

> (Statement) **The man who does not read good books has no advantage over the man who can't read them.**
>
> —Mark Twain

> (Request) **Please bring your folders and notebooks to class.**
>
> (Mild command) **Listen carefully so that you understand these instructions.**

Note: It is not necessary to place a period after a statement that has parentheses around it and is part of another sentence.

> **My dog Bobot** (I don't quite remember how he acquired this name) **is a Chesapeake Bay retriever—a hunting dog—who is afraid of loud noises.**

605.2 After an Initial or an Abbreviation

Place a period after an initial or an abbreviation (in American English).

> **Ms.   Sen.   D.D.S.   M.F.A.   M.D.   Jr.   U.S.   p.m.   a.m.**
> **Edna St. Vincent Millay   Booker T. Washington   D. H. Lawrence**

Note: When an abbreviation is the last word in a sentence, use only one period at the end of the sentence.

> **Jaleesa eyed each door until she found the name Fletcher B. Gale, M.D.**

605.3 As a Decimal Point

A period is used as a decimal point.

> **New York City has a budget of $46.9 billion to serve its 8.1 million people.**

Exclamation Point

605.4 To Express Strong Feeling

Use the **exclamation point** (sparingly) to express strong feeling. You may place it after a word, a phrase, or a sentence.

> **"That's not the point," said Wangero. "These are all pieces of dresses Grandma used to wear. She did all this stitching by hand. Imagine!"**
>
> —Alice Walker, "Everyday Use"

Question Mark

606.1 Direct Question

Place a **question mark** at the end of a direct question.

> Now what? I wondered. Do I go out and buy a jar of honey and stand around waving it? How in the world am I supposed to catch a bear?
>> —Ken Taylor, "The Case of the Grizzly on the Greens"
>
> Where did my body end and the crystal and white world begin?
>> —Ralph Ellison, *Invisible Man*

When a question ends with a quotation that is also a question, use only one question mark, and place it within the quotation marks.

> On road trips, do you remember driving your parents crazy by asking, "Are we there yet?"

Note: Do not use a question mark after an indirect question.

> Out on the street, I picked out a friendly looking old man and asked him where the depot was.
>> —Wilson Rawls, *Where the Red Fern Grows*
>
> Marta asked me if I finished my calculus homework yet.

606.2 To Show Uncertainty

Use a question mark within parentheses to show uncertainty.

> This summer marks the 20th season (?) of the American Players Theatre.

606.3 Short Question Within a Sentence

Use a question mark for a short question within parentheses.

> We crept so quietly (had they heard us?) past the kitchen door and back to our room.

Use a question mark for a short question within dashes.

> Maybe somewhere in the pasts of these humbled people, there were cases of bad mothering or absent fathering or emotional neglect—what family surviving the '50s was exempt?—but I couldn't believe these human errors brought the physical changes in Frank.
>> —Mary Kay Blakely, *Wake Me When It's Over*

Grammar Practice

Periods, Exclamation Points, and Question Marks

For each line in the paragraphs below, write where periods, exclamation points, or question marks are needed. Write the word preceding or containing each mark, as well. (Write "none" if no marks are needed.)

1   Joaquin had an appointment with his podiatrist, Dr Marston, because

2   of chronic foot pain When he got to the office, he was surprised to see a

3   different name on the door instead—K R Green, M D. He went in, thinking

4   he had the wrong office, and asked the receptionist about the name on the

5   door Then he understood—she had recently gotten married and changed her

6   name. Dr. Marston *was* Dr. Green

7   Joaquin's exam revealed that misalignment of his bones was causing

8   his pain. Dr Green suggested surgery to move the bone a fraction of an

9   inch (125 inch) to relieve the pressure on the nerve Joaquin requested

10   information about other options (wasn't surgery supposed to be a last

11   resort) and considered them.

12   Dr Green asked, "Do you have any further questions" Joaquin asked

13   if he could take a little time to make a decision. The doctor emphatically

14   replied, "Please do"

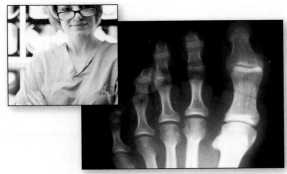

Model

Model the following sentence to practice using question marks for short questions within parentheses.

Todd knew he had seen her before (hadn't he?), but he simply could not recall the woman's name.

—C. Marie, "Skins"

Comma

608.1 Between Two Independent Clauses

Use a **comma** between two independent clauses that are joined by a coordinating conjunction *(and, but, or, nor, for, yet, so)*.

I wanted to knock on the glass to attract attention, but I couldn't move.

— Ralph Ellison, *Invisible Man*

Note: Do not confuse a sentence containing a compound verb for a compound sentence.

I had to burn her trash and then sweep up her porches and halls.

— Anne Moody, *Coming of Age in Mississippi*

608.2 To Separate Adjectives

Use commas to separate two or more adjectives that *equally* modify the same noun. (Note: Do not use a comma between the last adjective and the noun.)

Bao's eyes met the hard, bright lights hanging directly above her.

— Julie Ament, student writer

A Closer Look

To determine whether adjectives modify equally—and should, therefore, be separated by commas—use these two tests:

1. Shift the order of the adjectives; if the sentence is clear, the adjectives modify equally. (In the example below, *hot* and *smelly* can be shifted and the sentence is still clear; *usual* and *morning* cannot.)

2. Insert *and* between the adjectives; if the sentence reads well, use a comma when the *and* is omitted. (The word *and* can be inserted between *hot* and *smelly*, but *and* does not make sense between *usual* and *morning*.)

Matty was tired of working in the hot, smelly kitchen and decided to take her usual morning walk.

608.3 To Separate Contrasted Elements

Use commas to separate contrasted elements within a sentence. Often the word or phrase that is set off is preceded by *not*.

Since the stereotypes were about Asians, and not African Americans, no such reaction occurred.

— Emmeline Chen, "Eliminating the Lighter Shades of Stereotyping"

Grammar Practice

Commas 1

- Between Two Independent Clauses
- To Separate Adjectives
- To Separate Contrasted Elements

 Indicate where commas are needed in the following lines by writing the commas along with the words that surround them. (If no commas are needed, write "none" next to the line.)

1   You see a big hairy spider and your first inclination is to step back.

2   The fact is that a common spider should be afraid of you not the other way

3   around. Of the world's 40,000 spider species, less than 0.1 percent (that's one

4   species out of a thousand) have venom that's harmful to humans. A spider

5   bite may be painful but it's almost always harmless.

6   The only time a spider would bite a human is in self-defense not for

7   blood. Spiders do not feed on the blood of mammals. A spider's prey consists

8   mainly of smaller weaker insects, whose soft tissues are broken down by

9   digestive juices that the spider injects into their bodies. Then the spiders

10   suck everything up for a tasty satisfying meal.

11   So the next time you come upon an eight-legged four-eyed creature

12   from a web, remember the good that spiders do: They eat lots of pests

13   such as mosquitoes and their webs are truly beautiful objects. In addition,

14   researchers have actually found in venom chemicals that may be helpful to

15   humans. Go ahead and step back but don't step on a spider.

Model

Model the following sentences to practice using commas to separate contrasted elements.

I must govern the clock, not be governed by it.

—Golda Meir

It is our responsibilities, not ourselves, that we should take seriously.

—Peter Ustinov

Punctuation

Comma *(continued)*

610.1 To Set Off Appositives

A specific kind of explanatory word or phrase called an **appositive** identifies or renames a preceding noun or pronoun.

> **Benson,** our uninhibited and enthusiastic Yorkshire terrier, **joined our family on my sister's fifteenth birthday.**
>
> —Chad Hockerman, student writer

Note: Do not use commas with *restrictive appositives*. A restrictive appositive is essential to the basic meaning of the sentence.

> **Sixteen-year-old student** Ray Perez **was awarded an athletic scholarship.**

610.2 Between Items in a Series

Use commas to separate individual words, phrases, or clauses in a series. (A series contains at least three items.)

> **Dad likes** meat, vegetables, and a salad **for dinner.** (words)
> **I** took her for walks, read her stories, and made up games **for her to play.** (phrases)
>
> —Anne Moody, *Coming of Age in Mississippi*

Note: Do not use commas when all the words in a series are connected with *or, nor,* or *and.*

> **Her fingernails are pointed** and **manicured** and **painted a shiny red.**
>
> —Carson McCullers, "Sucker"

610.3 After Introductory Phrases and Clauses

Use a comma after an introductory participial phrase.

> Determined to finish the sweater by Friday, **my grandmother knit night and day.**

Use a comma after a long introductory prepositional phrase or after two or more short ones.

> In the oddest places and at the strangest times, **my grandmother can be found knitting madly away.**

Note: You may omit the comma if the introductory phrase is short.

> Before breakfast **my grandmother knits.**

Use a comma after an introductory adverb (subordinate) clause.

> After the practice was over, **Tina walked home.**

Note: A comma is not used if an adverb clause *follows* the main clause and is needed to complete the meaning of the sentence.

> **Tina practiced hard** because she feared losing.

However, a comma is used if the adverb clause following the main clause begins with *although, even though, while,* or another conjunction expressing a contrast.

> **Tina walked home,** even though it was raining very hard.

Grammar Practice

Commas 2

- **To Set Off Appositives**
- **Between Items in a Series**
- **After Introductory Phrases and Clauses**

 Indicate where commas are needed in the following lines by writing the commas along with the words that surround them. (If no commas are needed, write "none" next to the line.)

1   Health officials have recently become concerned about avian flu a viral

2   infection in birds. Avian flu can affect virtually every kind of bird, including

3   ducks geese turkeys and chickens. No one is certain where flu viruses

4   originate, but most doctors realize that people living close to barnyard

5   animals are at risk as well. In some parts of the world people live so close

6   to their farm animals that sometimes the flu makes the jump to humans.

7   Although scientists have studied the problem for many years they are still

8   trying to figure out how the virus mutates to affect humans. Once an avian

9   flu virus is able to infect humans trouble begins. The flu can become a

10   pandemic an epidemic that spans the globe when people transmit the disease

11   to other people.

Model

Model the following sentence to practice using commas between items in a series.

> **The country is the real thing, the substantial thing, the eternal thing; it is the thing to watch over and care for and be loyal to . . .**
> —Mark Twain, *A Connecticut Yankee in King Arthur's Court*

Punctuation

Comma *(continued)*

612.1 To Enclose Parenthetical Elements

Use commas to separate parenthetical elements, such as an explanatory word or phrase, within a sentence.

> **They stood together,** away from the pile of stones in the corner, **and their jokes were quiet, and they smiled rather than laughed.**
>
> —Shirley Jackson, "The Lottery"
>
> **Allison meandered into class,** late as usual, **and sat down.**

612.2 To Set Off Nonrestrictive Phrases and Clauses

Use commas to set off **nonrestrictive** (unnecessary) clauses and participial phrases. A nonrestrictive clause or participial phrase adds information that is not necessary to the basic meaning of the sentence. For example, if the clause or phrase (in red) were left out in the two examples below, the meaning of the sentences would remain clear. Therefore, commas are used to set them off.

> **The Altena Fitness Center and Visker Gymnasium,** which were built last year, **are busy every day.** (nonrestrictive clause)
>
> **Students and faculty,** improving their health through exercise, **use both facilities throughout the week.** (nonrestrictive phrase)

Do not use commas to set off a **restrictive** (necessary) clause or participial phrase, which helps to define a noun or pronoun. It adds information that the reader needs to know in order to understand the sentence. For example, if the clause and phrase (in red) were dropped from the examples below, the meaning wouldn't be the same. Therefore, commas are *not* used.

> **The handball court** that has a sign-up sheet by the door **must be reserved.**
> The clause identifies which handball court must be reserved.
> (restrictive clause)
>
> **Individuals** wanting to use this court **must sign up a day in advance.**
> (restrictive phrase)

A Closer Look

Use *that* to introduce restrictive (necessary) clauses; use *which* to introduce nonrestrictive (unnecessary) clauses. When the two words are used in this way, the reader can quickly distinguish necessary and unnecessary information.

> **The treadmill** that monitors heart rate **is the one you must use.**
> (The reader needs the information to find the right treadmill.)
>
> **This treadmill,** which we got last year, **is required for your program.** (The main clause tells the reader which treadmill to use; the other clause gives additional, unnecessary information.)

Grammar Practice

Commas 3

- To Enclose Parenthetical Elements
- To Set Off Nonrestrictive Phrases and Clauses

 Indicate where commas are needed in the following sentences by writing the commas along with the words that surround them. (Write "none" if no commas are needed.)

1. This lipliner which I sometimes apply as eyeliner is my favorite makeup.

2. Dave Grohl who is the lead singer and guitarist for the Foo Fighters previously played drums for Nirvana.

3. We saw the teacher who subbed for Mr. Planey at the store yesterday.

4. Dakota's handwriting normally illegible was quite neat for last week's poetry assignment.

5. *Harmonia axyridis* also known as Asian lady beetles were first seen in the United States in 1988.

6. They are despite their bothersome nature beneficial as aphids eaters.

7. My friend Judi who has multiple sclerosis asks me to join her in the MS Walk every year.

8. She wept with regret realizing the ring that her husband had given her had slipped down the drain.

9. The radio station's morning DJ's whom we love to listen to as we get ready for school are now syndicated to other stations as well.

10. The driver of the car that hit mine as I turned left was not hurt.

Model

Model the following sentences to practice using commas to enclose parenthetical elements and to set off nonrestrictive clauses.

All adventures, especially into new territory, are scary.
—Sally Ride

Human beings, who are almost unique in having the ability to learn from the experience of others, are also remarkable for their apparent disinclination to do so.
—Douglas Adams, *Last Chance to See*

Punctuation

Comma *(continued)*

614.1 To Set Off Dates

Use commas to set off items in a date.

On September 30, 1997, my little sister entered our lives.

He began working out on December 1, 2005, but quit by May 1, 2006.

However, when only the month and year are given, no commas are needed.

He began working out in December 2005 but quit by May 2006.

When a full date appears in the middle of a sentence, a comma follows the year.

On June 7, 1924, my great-grandfather met his future wife.

614.2 To Set Off Items in Addresses

Use commas to set off items in an address. (No comma is placed between the state and ZIP code.)

Mail the box to Friends of Wildlife, Box 402, Spokane, Washington 20077.

When a city and state (or country) appear in the middle of a sentence, a comma follows the last item in the address.

Several charitable organizations in Juneau, Alaska, pool their funds.

614.3 In Numbers

Use commas to separate numerals in large numbers in order to distinguish hundreds, thousands, millions, and so forth.

1,101   25,000   7,642,020

614.4 To Enclose Titles or Initials

Use commas to enclose a title or initials and names that follow a surname (a last name).

Letitia O'Reilly, M.D., is our family physician.

Hickok, J. B., and Cody, William F., are two popular Western heroes.

614.5 Before Tags

Use a comma before a tag, which is a short statement or question at the end of a sentence.

He's the candidate who lost the election, isn't he?

You're not going to like this casserole, I know.

614.6 Following Conjunctive Adverbs and Transitional Phrases

Use a comma following conjunctive adverbs such as *however, instead,* and *nevertheless,* and transitional phrases such as *for example, in fact,* and *as a result.* (Also see **618.2.**)

Jaleel is bright and studies hard; however, he suffers from test anxiety.

Pablo was born in the Andes; as a result, he loves mountains.

Grammar Practice

Commas 4

- To Set Off Dates
- To Set Off Items in Addresses
- In Numbers
- To Enclose Titles or Initials

 Indicate where commas are needed in the following sentences by writing the commas along with the words or numbers that surround them.

1. According to the *Guinness Book of World Records,* the oldest human footprints were discovered 60 miles north of Cape Town South Africa.

2. The geologist who found them estimates they are 117000 years old.

3. An American woman who was born on August 15 1890 lived until December 11 2006—she was 116 years old!

4. The first heart transplant was performed on December 3 1967 by Christiaan Barnard M.D.

5. ABIOMED, Inc., maker of an artificial heart, is located at 22 Cherry Hill Drive Danvers Massachusetts.

6. Its 11 floors cover an area of 198500 square meters (2.15 million square feet).

7. In July 1999, a participant in an auction in London England paid $3001294 for a Louis XVI clock.

8. Richard Mascola D.D.S. is the president of the American Dental Association, the world's largest with 155400 members.

 ## Model

Model the following sentence to practice using commas to set off items in addresses.

> **Born in Chicago Heights, Illinois, Jacobs attended St. Kieran School for his first four years of formal education.**

Punctuation

Comma *(continued)*

616.1 To Set Off Dialogue

Use commas to set off the speaker's exact words from the rest of the sentence. (It may be helpful to remember that the comma is always to the left of the quotation mark.)

"It's like we have our own government," **adds Tanya, a 17-year-old squatter.**

—Kyung Sun Yu and Nell Bernstein, "Street Teens Forge a Home"

616.2 To Set Off Interjections

Use a comma to separate an interjection or a weak exclamation from the rest of the sentence.

Hey, **how am I to know that a minute's passed?**

—Nathan Slaughter and Jim Schweitzer, *When Time Dies*

616.3 To Set Off Interruptions

Use commas to set off a word, a phrase, or a clause that interrupts the movement of a sentence. Such expressions usually can be identified through the following tests: (1) They may be omitted without changing the meaning of a sentence. (2) They may be placed nearly anywhere in the sentence without changing its meaning.

For me, well, **it's just a good job gone!**

—Langston Hughes

The safest way to cross this street, as a general rule, **is with the light.**

616.4 In Direct Address

Use commas to separate a noun of direct address from the rest of the sentence. A *noun of direct address* is the noun that names the person(s) spoken to.

"You wouldn't understand yet, son, but your daddy's gonna make
a transaction. . . . "

—Lorraine Hansberry, *A Raisin in the Sun*

616.5 For Clarity or Emphasis

You may use a comma for clarity or for emphasis. There will be times when none of the traditional rules call for a comma, but one will be needed to prevent confusion or to emphasize an important idea.

It may be that those who **do most, dream most.** (emphasis)

—Stephen Leacock

What the crew **does, does affect our voyage.** (clarity)

Grammar Practice

Commas 5

- To Set Off Interjections
- To Set Off Interruptions
- In Direct Address
- For Clarity or Emphasis

 Indicate where commas are needed in the following sentences by writing the commas along with the words that surround them.

1. Darn it I can't get these wires untangled!

2. Hey where did this mess come from?

3. Don't ask me because if you must know I just got here.

4. You just got here here in the cafeteria or here to this planet?

5. That's uh very funny Mr. Clean.

6. The song that this band plays plays too much on the radio.

7. Do you know which one I'm talking about Will?

8. Yeah I know the one—it's on at least once an hour.

9. It seems like we hear new music only once a day if that.

10. Will why don't you call the radio station?

11. I hmm never thought of that.

Model

Model the following sentences to practice using commas to set off interruptions and for emphasis.

> I loved to spend time at Thimbleberry's, listening to his rhythmic, even if somewhat nasal, intonations.
>
> —Robert Fox, "The Year of the Dog"

> She felt angry enough to scream, angry enough to say that the dog had grown up in the apartment and had the right to walk around.
>
> —Ann Beattie, "Distant Music"

Semicolon

618.1 To Join Two Independent Clauses

Use a **semicolon** to join two or more closely related independent clauses that are not connected with a coordinating conjunction. (Independent clauses can stand alone as separate sentences.)

> **I did not call myself a poet; I told people I wrote poems.**
> —Terry McMillan, "Breaking Ice"

> **Silence coated the room like a layer of tar; not even the breathing of the 11 Gehad made any sound.**
> —Gann Bierner, "The Leap"

Note: When independent clauses are especially long or contain commas, a semicolon may punctuate the sentence, even though a coordinating conjunction connects the clauses.

> **We waited all day in that wide line, tired travelers pressing in from all sides; and when we needed drinks or sandwiches, I would squeeze my way to the cafeteria and back.**

618.2 With Conjunctive Adverbs and Transitional Phrases

A semicolon is used *before* a conjunctive adverb or transitional phrase (with a comma after it) when the word connects two independent clauses in a compound sentence.

> **"I am faced with my imminent demise; therefore, life becomes a very precious thing."**
> —Amy Taylor, "AIDS Can Happen Here!"

Common conjunctive adverbs

also, besides, finally, however, indeed, instead, meanwhile, moreover, nevertheless, next, still, then, therefore, thus

Common transitional phrases

after all, as a matter of fact, as a result, at any rate, at the same time, even so, for example, for instance, in addition, in conclusion, in fact, in other words, in the first place, on the contrary, on the other hand

618.3 To Separate Groups That Contain Commas

A semicolon is used to separate groups of words that already contain commas.

> **Every Saturday night my little brother gathers up his things—goggles, shower cap, and snorkel; bubble bath, soap, and shampoo; tapes, stereo, and rubber duck—and heads for the tub.**

Grammar Practice

Semicolons

- ■ **To Join Two Independent Clauses**
- ■ **With Conjunctive Adverbs**
- ■ **To Separate Groups That Contain Commas**

 Indicate where a semicolon is needed in the following sentences by writing the semicolon along with the words that surround it.

1. When Jean-Paul was young, he lived in the countryside of southern France his current residence is a tiny apartment in Detroit.

2. Jean-Paul likes space-saving items such as pot racks, under-cabinet appliances, and recessed shelves for canned foods a Murphy bed and an over-the-door ironing board and a wall-mounted TV, a pocket shoe organizer, and under-bed storage boxes.

3. His apartment is nothing like his childhood home nevertheless, he makes the best of it.

4. My older brother uses a wheelchair he is partially paralyzed.

5. He does not feel limited by it indeed, he feels it gives him some freedom.

6. On our backyard deck we have a table, benches, and chairs potted plants, torches, and solar lights and a portable outdoor fire pit.

7. Mom and Dad enjoy the deck a great deal it's like an extra room in the house to them.

8. I like the deck, too however, my friends and I usually hang out in the basement.

◀ Model

Model the following sentences to practice using a semicolon with a conjunctive adverb and to join independent clauses.

> **It is forbidden to kill; therefore, all murderers are punished unless they kill in large numbers and to the sound of trumpets.**
> —Voltaire

> **I believe in getting into hot water; it keeps you clean.**
> —G. K. Chesterton

Punctuation

Colon

620.1 After a Salutation

Use a **colon** after the salutation of a business letter.

Dear Judge Parker: **Dear Governor Whitman:**

620.2 Between Numerals Indicating Time

Use a colon between the hours, minutes, and seconds of a number indicating time.

8:30 p.m.   **9:45 a.m.**   **10:24:55**

620.3 For Emphasis

Use a colon to emphasize a word, a phrase, a clause, or a sentence that explains or adds impact to the main clause (also see **650.3**).

His guest lecturers are local chefs who learn a lesson themselves: Homeless people are worth employing.

—Beth Brophy, "Feeding Those Who Are Hungry"

620.4 To Introduce a Quotation

Use a colon to formally introduce a quotation, a sentence, or a question.

Directly a voice in the corner rang out wild and clear: "I've got him! I've got him!"

—Mark Twain, *Roughing It*

620.5 To Introduce a List

A colon is used to introduce a list.

I got all the proper equipment: scissors, a bucket of water to keep things clean, some cotton for the stuffing, and needle and thread to sew it up.

—Joan Baez, *Daybreak*

A Closer Look

Do not use a colon between a verb and its object or complement, or between a preposition and its object.

Incorrect: Min has: a snowmobile, an ATV, and a canoe.
Correct: Min has plenty of toys: a snowmobile, an ATV, and a canoe.
Incorrect: I watch a TV show about: cooking wild game.
Correct: I watch a TV show about a new subject: cooking wild game.

620.6 Between a Title and a Subtitle

Use a colon to distinguish between a title and a subtitle, volume and page, and chapter and verse in literature.

Encyclopedia Americana IV: 211   Psalm 23:1–6

Grammar Practice

Colons

- ■ After a Salutation
- ■ Between Numerals Indicating Time
- ■ To Introduce a Quotation
- ■ Between a Title and a Subtitle

 Indicate where a colon is needed in the following letter by writing the line number, the colon, and the word that precedes it.

1   Dear Ms. Grey

2   I am excited that you have decided to teach history this year. I

3   believe in the words of Robert Heinlein "A generation that ignores history

4   has no past and no future." Educating young people about history is an

5   important job.

6   As for my reading recommendations for your history class, my first

7   suggestion is *Warriors Portraits from the Battlefield* by Max Hastings. I

8   think your students will find it appealing. Another title you might look into

9   is *A Different Mirror A History of Multicultural America* by Ronald Takaki.

10   If you would like to meet for discussion, I am free between 200 and

11   400 p.m. this coming Tuesday. Please feel free to call.

12   Sincerely,

13   Cameron Neitler

Model

Model the following sentences to practice using a colon for emphasis.

I'm not fond of fish, let alone seaweed, but I like them together: sushi!

—Rob King

Appreciate your mistakes for what they are: precious life lessons that can only be learned the hard way.

—Al Franken

Punctuation

Test Prep!

Read the following paragraphs. Write the letter of the correct way to punctuate each underlined part from the choices given on the next page. If the part is already correct, choose "D."

In the <u>United States politicians</u> representing the public discuss and pass laws
(1)
in the Senate and House of Representatives. <u>However many</u> of these lawmakers
(2)
are also influenced by a group of people known as lobbyists. A lobbyist's job is to
influence <u>legislation and, in some cases</u> public opinion.
(3)
   A lobbyist develops his or her primary <u>skill, packaging and communicating</u>
(4)
<u>information</u> with the aim of persuading <u>lawmakers (The</u> lobbyist would probably
(5)
call this "educating" those people.) In a personal meeting with a <u>senator or</u>
<u>representative,</u> a lobbyist tries to sway the legislator to agree with the views of
(6)
those whom the lobbyist represents. <u>For instance say a</u> lobbyist works for the health
(7)
insurance <u>industry he</u> or she might give a presentation highlighting the risks of a
(8)
national health-care plan. The presentation may include charts, graphs, poll <u>results</u>
<u>and reports,</u> but it must be a <u>confident charming production,</u> as well.
(9)   **(10)**
   Private companies, industrial <u>organizations, labor unions, and political</u> action
(11)
committees hire lobbyists—and pay them well. Lobbying <u>Washington, DC.,</u> costs
(12)
these organizations more than <u>$2,54 billion</u> per year, with some of that going to pay
(13)
former members of <u>Congress who are</u> now lobbyists. Whether or not you agree with
(14)
the <u>concept?</u> Lobbying remains a valid career option for <u>the person, who loves</u> the
(15)   **(16)**
art of persuasion.

1
(A) United States: politicians
(B) United States, politicians
(C) United States; politicians
(D) correct as is

2
(A) However, many
(B) However; many
(C) However many,
(D) correct as is

3
(A) legislation, and in some cases,
(B) legislation and, in some cases,
(C) legislation, and in some cases
(D) correct as is

4
(A) skill packaging and
communicating information
(B) skill packaging and
communicating information,
(C) skill, packaging and
communicating information,
(D) correct as is

5
(A) lawmakers. (The
(B) lawmakers; (The
(C) lawmakers: (The
(D) correct as is

6
(A) senator, or representative,
(B) senator or representative
(C) senator, or representative
(D) correct as is

7
(A) For instance, say, a
(B) For instance say, a
(C) For instance, say a
(D) correct as is

8
(A) industry, he
(B) industry; he
(C) industry he,
(D) correct as is

9
(A) results, and reports,
(B) results, and reports
(C) results and reports
(D) correct as is

10
(A) confident charming,
production,
(B) confident, charming
production,
(C) confident charming production
(D) correct as is

11
(A) organizations, labor unions
and political
(B) organizations labor unions
and political
(C) organizations labor unions,
and political
(D) correct as is

12
(A) Washington D.C.
(B) Washington, D.C.
(C) Washington, D.C.,
(D) correct as is

13
(A) $2.54 billion
(B) $2:54 billion
(C) $1 point 5 billion
(D) correct as is

14
(A) Congress, who are
(B) Congress who, are
(C) Congress: who are
(D) correct as is

15
(A) concept lobbying
(B) concept, lobbying
(C) concept. Lobbying
(D) correct as is

16
(A) the person who loves
(B) the person who, loves
(C) the person: who loves
(D) correct as is

Hyphen

624.1 In Compound Words

Use the **hyphen** to make some compound words.

great-great-grandfather   **maid-in-waiting**   **three-year-old**

624.2 To Create New Words

Use a hyphen to form new words beginning with the prefixes *self-, ex-, all-,* and *half-*. Also use a hyphen to join any prefix to a proper noun, a proper adjective, or the official name of an office. Use a hyphen before the suffix *-elect*.

self-contained   **ex-governor**   **all-inclusive**   **half-painted**
pre-Cambrian   **mid-December**   **president-elect**

Use a hyphen to join the prefix *great-* only to the names of relatives.

great-aunt, great-grandfather (correct)   **great-hall** (incorrect)

624.3 To Form an Adjective

Use a hyphen to join two or more words that serve as a single adjective (a single-thought adjective) before a noun.

In real life I am a large, big-boned woman with rough, man-working hands.
 —Alice Walker, "Everyday Use"

Use common sense to determine whether a compound adjective might be misread if it is not hyphenated. Generally, hyphenate a compound adjective that is composed of . . .

- a phrase   **heat-and-serve meal**   **off-and-on relationship**
- a noun + adjective   **oven-safe handles**   **book-smart student**
- a noun + participle (*ing* or *ed* form of a verb)   **bone-chilling story**

624.4 To Join Letters and Words

Use a hyphen to join a capital letter or lowercase letter to a noun or participle. (Check your dictionary if you're not sure of the hyphenation.)

T-shirt   **Y-turn**   **G-rated**   **x-axis**

A Closer Look

When words forming the adjective come after the noun, do not hyphenate them.

In real life I am large and big boned.

When the first of these words is an adverb ending in *-ly*, do not use a hyphen.

delicately prepared pastry

Also, do not use a hyphen when a number or a letter is the final element in a single-thought adjective.

class B movie

Grammar Practice

Hyphens 1

- To Create New Words
- To Form an Adjective
- To Join Letters and Words

 For each sentence below, write the words that should be hyphenated. Some sentences contain more than one hyphenated word.

1. My friend's mom is still friends with her exhusband.

2. Many financial advisors are promoting the value of T bills for investment.

3. Dane was getting frustrated with the slow moving traffic.

4. The governor elect held a reception for an elite group of supporters.

5. Please email the file right away; it is a very time sensitive document.

6. The neighbors are vacationing at an all inclusive resort in Mexico.

7. Most television sets purchased today have V chip technology.

8. Macy claims she had an out of body experience during her surgery.

9. Such mass produced items are quite easy to acquire.

10. The general population finds a gforce greater than that experienced on a roller coaster extremely uncomfortable.

Model

Model the following sentences to practice using hyphens to create new words and to form an adjective.

> It has always been the prerogative of children and half-wits to point out that the emperor has no clothes.
> —Neil Gaiman, *Sandman*

> It is only possible to live happily ever after on a day-to-day basis.
> —Margaret Bonnano

Hyphen *(continued)*

626.1 | Between Numbers and Fractions

Use a hyphen to join the words in compound numbers from *twenty-one* to *ninety-nine* when it is necessary to write them out (see **658.3**).

Use a hyphen between the numerator and denominator of a fraction, but not when one or both of those elements are already hyphenated.

> **four-tenths   five-sixteenths   (7/32) seven thirty-seconds**

626.2 | In a Special Series

Use hyphens when two or more words have a common element that is omitted in all but the last term.

> **The ship has lovely two-, four-, or six-person cabins.**

626.3 | To Join Numbers

Use a hyphen to join numbers indicating the life span of a person or the score in a contest or a vote.

> **We can thank Louis Pasteur (1822–1895) for pasteurized milk.**
>
> **In the 2007 Rose Bowl, USC defeated Michigan 32–18.**

626.4 | To Prevent Confusion

Use a hyphen with prefixes or suffixes to avoid confusion or awkward spelling.

> **re-create (not *recreate*) the image   re-cover (not *recover*) the sofa**

626.5 | To Divide a Word

Use a hyphen to divide a word, only between its syllables, at the end of a line of print. Always place the hyphen after the syllable at the end of the line—never before a syllable at the beginning of the following line.

Guidelines for Dividing with Hyphens

1. Always divide a compound word between its basic units: **sister-in-law,** not **sis-ter-in-law.**

2. Avoid dividing a word of five or fewer letters: **paper, study, July.**

3. Avoid dividing the last word in a paragraph.

4. Never divide a one-syllable word: **rained, skills, through.**

5. Never divide a one-letter syllable from the rest of the word: **omit-ted,** not **o-mitted.**

6. When a vowel is a syllable by itself, divide the word after the vowel: **epi-sode,** not **ep-isode.**

7. Never divide abbreviations or contractions: **shouldn't,** not **should-n't.**

8. Never divide the last word in more than two lines in a row.

Grammar Practice

Hyphens 2

- In a Special Series
- To Prevent Confusion

In the paragraphs below, find the words that should be hyphenated and write them, along with the line number, correctly on your paper.

1 It was the first time I had enrolled in a multiinstructor course. We'd

2 have different teachers for lectures and labs. To further complicate my

3 schedule, the labs would be either one or two hour sessions, depending on

4 the particular experiment.

5 The first lab was a bit strange. The teacher, a balding man with a

6 thin, pencillike mustache perched on his lip, entered the room. He arranged

7 a bunch of equipment: test tubes, Bunsen burners, 50 and 250 ml beakers,

8 petri dishes, and so on. After he talked about all of them, he resorted them

9 before putting them away.

10 Then he donned latex gloves and a surgical

11 mask and said, "You'll want to wear these to prevent

12 infection from any labborne pathogens." The class

13 was dumbstruck. Some jaws actually dropped . . .

14 but then he said, "Just kidding."

Model

Model the following sentences to practice using hyphens to prevent confusion and in a special series.

The sow bug cannot manage [to curl into a ball], but it does have two tail-like appendages the pill bug lacks. —William Olkowski and Sheila Daar, *The Gardener's Guide to Common-Sense Pest Control*

The hardware includes two one-eighth- and two three-quarter-inch Phillips head screws.

Apostrophe

628.1 | In Contractions

Use an **apostrophe** to show that one or more letters have been left out of a word group to form a contraction.

> hadn't – **o is left out**   they'd – **woul is left out**   it's – **i is left out**

Note: Use an apostrophe to show that one or more numerals or letters have been left out of numbers or words in order to show special pronunciation.

> class of '09 – **20 is left out**   g'day – **ood is left out**

628.2 | To Form Singular Possessives

Add an apostrophe and *s* to form the possessive of most singular nouns.

> Spock's **ears**   Captain Kirk's **singing**   the ship's **escape plan**

Note: When a singular noun ends with an *s* or a *z* sound, you may form the possessive by adding just an apostrophe. When the singular noun is a one-syllable word, however, you usually add both an apostrophe and an *s* to form the possessive.

> San Carlos' **government** (or) San Carlos's **government** (two-syllable word)
>
> Ross's **essay** (one-syllable word)   The class's **field trip** (one-syllable word)

628.3 | To Form Plural Possessives

The possessive form of plural nouns ending in *s* is usually made by adding just an apostrophe.

> students' **homework**   bosses' **orders**

For plural nouns not ending in *s*, an apostrophe and *s* must be added.

> children's **book**   men's **department**

A Closer Look

> It will help you punctuate correctly if you remember that the word immediately before the apostrophe is the owner.
>
> girl's **guitar** (*girl* is the owner)   boss's **order** (*boss* is the owner)
>
> girls' **guitars** (*girls* are the owners)   bosses' **order** (*bosses* are the owners)

628.4 | To Show Shared Possession

When possession is shared by more than one noun, use the possessive form for the last noun in the series.

> Hoshi, Linda, and Nakiva's **water skis** (All three own the same skis.)
>
> Hoshi's, Linda's, and Nakiva's **water skis** (Each owns her own skis.)

Grammar Practice

Apostrophes 1

- To Form Singular Possessives
- To Form Plural Possessives
- To Show Shared Possession

 For each sentence, write the possessive form of the word or words in parentheses.

1. "Is that *(Joaquin and Juan)* car over there?" asked Marinda.

2. Fire was coming from the *(car)* exhaust pipe.

3. Their *(parents)* insurance company might not cover the cost to fix it.

4. I will be pet-sitting for *(Ms. Gedraitis)* cats this weekend.

5. She said I will find the *(cats)* food in the cabinet by the telephone.

6. The sound of the *(mice)* feet skittering over our heads was getting annoying.

7. *(Junji and Padma)* overdue library books are going to cost them $8.00 each.

8. My *(shoes)* laces just won't stay tied!

9. You would not believe the size of the *(women)* room here—it's huge!

10. The newscaster continued, "The full measure of *(agribusiness)* effect on the economy is at stake."

11. The *(actresses)* agents were politely notified that their talents would not be required for this movie.

12. Grandma marveled at the ancient *(dish)* patina.

 ## Model

Model the following sentences to practice using apostrophes to form singular and plural possessives.

> **You can tell a lot about a fellow's character by his way of eating jellybeans.**
> —Ronald Reagan

> **I think that if parents would spend less time worrying about what their kids watch on TV and more time worrying about what's going on in their kids' lives, this world would be a much better place.**
> —Trey Parker and Matt Stone

Apostrophe *(continued)*

630.1 To Show Possession with Indefinite Pronouns

Form the possessive of an indefinite pronoun by placing an apostrophe and an *s* on the last word (see **704.1** and **706.3**).

> everyone's   anyone's   somebody's
>
> **It is** everybody's **responsibility to keep his or her locker orderly.**

In expressions using *else,* add the apostrophe and *s* after the last word.

> **This is** somebody else's **mess, not mine.**

630.2 To Show Possession in Compound Nouns

Form the possessive of a compound noun by placing the possessive ending after the last word.

> **the** secretary of the interior's (singular) **agenda**
>
> **her** lady-in-waiting's (singular) **day off**

If forming a possessive of a plural compound noun creates an awkward construction, you may replace the possessive with an *of* phrase. (All four forms below are correct.)

> **their** fathers-in-law's (plural) **birthdays**
> or **the birthdays of their fathers-in-law** (plural)
>
> **the** ambassadors-at-large's (plural) **plans**
> or **the plans of the ambassadors-at-large** (plural)

630.3 To Express Time or Amount

Use an apostrophe and an *s* with an adjective that is part of an expression indicating time or amount.

> a penny's worth   two cents' worth   this morning's meeting
>
> yesterday's news   a day's wage   six months' pay

630.4 To Form Certain Plurals

Use an apostrophe and *s* to form the plural of a letter, a number, a sign, or a word discussed as a word.

> B – B's   C – C's   8 – 8's   + – +'s   *and* – *and*'s
>
> **Ms. D'Aquisto says our conversations contain too many** *like's* **and** *no way's*.

Note: If two apostrophes are called for in the same word, omit the second one.

> **Follow closely the** *do's* **and** *don'ts* **(not** *don't's***) on the checklist.**

Grammar Practice

Apostrophes 2

- To Show Possession with Indefinite Pronouns
- To Show Possession in Compound Nouns
- To Express Time or Amount
- To Form Certain Plurals

 Write the underlined words from the following paragraphs, correctly placing the apostrophe in each.

I had about three **(1)** <u>weeks</u> laundry with me when I finally made it to the crowded laundromat. After sorting it into piles, I checked for open machines. Although **(2)** <u>someone elses</u> clothes filled most of the other washers, I was able to load two of my piles. I poured a **(3)** <u>dollars</u> worth of detergent (from the vending machine) into each, and then I got out my quarters from **(4)** <u>yesterdays</u> trip to the bank. All of the **(5)** <u>1s</u> and **(6)** <u>$s</u> had been scratched off the **(7)** <u>washing machines</u> slots long ago; each washer now wanted six quarters or more.

When I took out my first load, a "little" surprise was waiting for me: My favorite wool blazer had shrunk! I forgot about this **(8)** <u>dry-clean-onlys</u> need for special treatment—and it was **(9)** <u>nobodys</u> fault but mine. That trip to the laundromat ended up costing me a **(10)** <u>months</u> pay from my part-time job!

 ## Model

Model the following sentence to practice using apostrophes to express time or amount.

> **Space isn't remote at all. It's only an hour's drive away if your car could go straight up.**
> —Fred Hoyle

Quotation Marks

632.1 To Set Off Direct Quotations

Place **quotation marks** before and after the words in direct quotations.

> **"Just come to a game,"** he pleads. **"You'll change your mind."**
>
> —Sandra Lampe, "Batter UP!"

In a quoted passage, put brackets around any word or punctuation mark that is not part of the original quotation. (See **644.1**.)

If you quote only part of the original passage, be sure to construct a sentence that is both accurate and grammatically correct.

> **Much of the restructuring of the Postal Service has involved** "turning over large parts of its work to the private sector."

632.2 Placement of Punctuation

Always place periods and commas inside quotation marks.

> **"Dr. Slaughter wants you to have liquids, Will,"** Mama said anxiously. **"He said not to give you any solid food** tonight."
>
> —Olive Ann Burns, *Cold Sassy Tree*

Place an exclamation point or a question mark *inside* quotation marks when it punctuates the quotation and *outside* when it punctuates the main sentence.

> **"Am I** dreaming?"   Had she heard him say, **"Here's the key to your new** car"?

Always place semicolons or colons outside quotation marks.

> **I wrote about James Joyce's "The** Dead"; I found it thought provoking.

632.3 For Long Quotations

If you quote more than one paragraph, place quotation marks before each paragraph and at the end of the last paragraph (Example A). If a quotation has more than four lines on a page, you may set it off from the text by indenting 10 spaces from the left margin (block form). Do not use quotation marks either before or after the quoted material, unless they appear in the original (Example B).

Example A

> "_____
> _____
> _____.
> "_____
> _____
> _____.
> "_____." "

Example B

> _____.
> _____
> _____
> _____
> _____
> _____
> _____

Grammar Practice

Quotation Marks 1

- **To Set Off Direct Quotations**
- **Placement of Punctuation**
- **For Long Quotations**

 Indicate where quotation marks are needed in the following paragraphs by writing the line number and the quotation marks, along with the words and other punctuation after or before them. (Use an ellipsis to show omitted words in your answers.)

1   Hey, Gerardo, I said. Take a look at this.

2   At what? he asked as he headed my way.

3   I was reading an article that I found particularly interesting. I showed
4   him the following text, hoping he'd get a kick out of it.

5   Do dreams have anything to do with reality? Many online dream
6   interpreters think so and are only too willing to take your money
7   to show you how. A Web site called DreamOn.com charges $25 for
8   an initial consultation and offers a money-back guarantee if their
9   interpretations can be proved wrong.

10   Uh-huh . . . proving a dream interpretation wrong can be pretty sticky
11   business, Gerardo said. But here are some ways.

12   Let's say my dream was about a brown dog
13   that kept following me everywhere I went, and the
14   interpreter said that it obviously means that I am
15   thinking of some social activity. Actually, the brown
16   dog is Hunter, my dog, and I'm dreaming about him
17   because he is staring at me while I sleep.

18   Or how about this: You dream about a mansion
19   with the numbers 377 on it. This is interpreted as
20   wealth gained via a trilogy (the three) of music and
21   art (the sevens). You, however, know that it is your
22   great-great-uncle's old family home in Nagelschmidt,
23   Germany, that you dream of returning to someday.

24   Yeah—I want my money back! I laughed.

Model

Model the following sentence to practice correct placement of punctuation with quotation marks.

> **Inevitably anyone with an independent mind must become "one who resists or opposes authority or established conventions": a rebel.**
> —Aleister Crowley

Quotation Marks *(continued)*

634.1 Quotation Marks Within Quotations

Use single quotation marks to punctuate a quotation within a quotation. Use double quotation marks if you need to distinguish a quotation within a quotation within a quotation.

> **"For tomorrow," said Mr. Botts, "read 'Unlighted Lamps.'"**
> **Sue asked, "Did you hear Mr. Botts say, 'Read "Unlighted Lamps"'?"**

634.2 For Special Words

You may use quotation marks (1) to distinguish a word that is being discussed, (2) to indicate that a word is unfamiliar slang, or (3) to point out that a word is being used in a special way.

> **(1) A commentary on the times is that the word "honesty" is now preceded by "old-fashioned."**
>
> —Larry Wolters
>
> **(2) I . . . asked the bartender where I could hear "chanky-chank," as Cajuns called their music.**
>
> —William Least Heat-Moon, *Blue Highways*
>
> **(3) Tom pushed the wheelchair across the street, showed the lady his "honest" smile . . . and stole her purse.**

Note: You may use italics (underlining) in place of quotation marks in each of these three situations. (See **636.3**.)

634.3 To Punctuate Titles

Use **quotation marks** to punctuate titles of songs, poems, short stories, one-act plays, lectures, episodes of radio or television programs, chapters of books, unpublished works, electronic files, and articles found in magazines, newspapers, encyclopedias, or online sources. (For punctuation of other titles, see **636.2**.)

> "Santa Lucia" (song)
> "The Chameleon" (short story)
> "Twentieth-Century Memories" (lecture)
> "Affordable Adventures" (magazine article)
> "Dire Prophecy of the Howling Dog" (chapter in a book)
> "Dancing with Debra" (television episode)
> "Miss Julie" (one-act play)

Note: Punctuate one title within another title as follows:

> **"Clarkson's 'Breakaway' Hits the Waves"**
> (title of a song in title of an article)

Grammar Practice

Quotation Marks 2

- Quotation Marks Within Quotations
- For Special Words
- To Punctuate Titles

 Write the word or words that should be enclosed in quotation marks in the following sentences.

1. Dr. Polk called his lecture on hybrid engines Green Machines.

2. Martin asked, Did you hear the part when he read directly from the *Times* article Hybrid Sales Rise with Gas Prices?

3. He was upset that many women perceived him as just handsome when he had so much more to offer than just his good looks.

4. In some English-speaking countries, words such as color, theater, and license have different spellings.

5. Reading the book's fifth chapter, New World, New Name, reminded me of my great-grandparents' experience coming into this country.

6. People often use the term whatsername to identify someone whose name's been forgotten.

7. Mr. Cornwall is a repo man, hired by a financial institution to take back cars when people default on their car payments.

8. Corinna said, Poe's Annabelle Lee is one of my favorite poems.

 ## Model

Model the following sentence to practice using quotation marks within quotations.

> In a *Rolling Stone* review, Rob Sheffield wrote, "Even the Swedish guys who wrote 'Since U Been Gone' admit they were just trying to copy the Strokes."

Italics (Underlining)

636.1 Handwritten and Printed Material

Italics is a printer's term for a style of type that is slightly slanted. In this sentence, the word *happiness* is printed in italics. In material that is handwritten or typed on a machine that cannot print in italics, underline each word or letter that should be in italics.

> *My Ántonia* is the story of a strong and determined pioneer woman.
>
> (printed)
>
> Willa Cather's <u>My Ántonia</u> describes pioneer life in America.
>
> (typed or handwritten)

636.2 In Titles

Use italics to indicate the titles of magazines, newspapers, pamphlets, books, full-length plays, films, videos, radio and television programs, book-length poems, ballets, operas, paintings, lengthy musical compositions, sculptures, cassettes, CD's, legal cases, and the names of ships and aircraft. (For punctuation of other titles, see **634.3**.)

> *Newsweek* (magazine) *Cold Sassy Tree* (book)
>
> *Shakespeare in Love* (film) *Law & Order* (television program)
>
> *Caring for Your Kitten* (pamphlet) *Hedda Gabler* (full-length play)
>
> *Chicago Tribune* (newspaper) *The Thinker* (sculpture)

636.3 For Special Uses

Use italics for a number, letter, or word that is being discussed or used in a special way. (Sometimes quotation marks are used for this reason. See **634.2**.)

> I hope that this letter *I* on my report card stands for *incredible* and not *incomplete*.

636.4 For Foreign Words

Use italics for foreign words that have not been adopted into the English language; also use italics for scientific names.

> The voyageurs—tough men with natural *bonhomie*—discovered the shy *Castor canadensis*, or North American beaver.

636.5 For Emphasis

Use italics for words that require particular emphasis.

> I guess it really *was* worth it to put in extra study time.

Grammar Practice

Italics (Underlining)

- In Titles
- For Special Uses
- For Foreign Words

 Write and underline the word or words that should be italicized in the following sentences. If there aren't any, write "none."

1. The letter e is the most common in the English language.

2. We recently saw an off-Broadway production of Phantom of the Opera.

3. The sans serif typeface Verdana is recommended for Web pages.

4. If a coffee has a foreign flavor, it denotes imperfect flavor due to some kind of contamination.

5. Helena was embarrassed at her faux pas and vowed she would know better next time.

6. Napoleon Dynamite was a surprise hit for the film's producers.

7. The Olympic hopeful was elated to see a big 10 on one of her scorecards.

8. Florentina began writing for the Bingham Bugle, her small city's newspaper, when she was in high school.

9. The first article she had published was "Storm Damages Concession Stand."

10. Noah said he'd have to go mano a mano with Cheung over the cheating incident.

Model

Model the following sentences to practice using italics (underlining) for emphasis.

"Oh, not *now*," said Buffie, scandalized. "We can't do that . . . "
—Frederik Pohl, "Punch"

And I had imagined my sisters now being ten or eleven, jumping up and down, holding hands, their pigtails bouncing, excited that their mother—*their* mother—was coming, whereas my mother was dead.
—Amy Tan, *The Joy Luck Club*

Punctuation

Parentheses

638.1 To Set Off Explanatory Material

You may use **parentheses** to set off explanatory or added material that interrupts the normal sentence structure.

> **Benson (our dog) sits in on our piano lessons (on the piano bench), much to the teacher's surprise and amusement.**
> —Chad Hockerman, student writer

Note: Place question marks and exclamation points within the parentheses when they mark the added material.

> **Ivan at once concluded (the rascal!) that I had a passion for dances, and . . . wanted to drag me off to a dancing class.**
> —Fyodor Dostoyevsky, "A Novel in Nine Letters"

638.2 With Full Sentences

When using a full sentence within another sentence, do not capitalize it or use a period inside the parentheses.

> **And, since your friend won't have the assignment (he was just thinking about calling you), you'll have to make a couple more calls to actually get it.**
> —Ken Taylor, "The Art and Practice of Avoiding Homework"

When the parenthetical sentence comes after the period of the main sentence, capitalize and punctuate it the same way you would any other complete sentence.

> **They kiss and hug when they say "hello," and I love this. (In Korea, people are much more formal; they just shake hands and bow to each other.)**
> —Sue Chong, "He Said I Was Too American"

Note: For unavoidable parentheses within parentheses (. . . [. . .] . . .), use brackets. Avoid overuse of parentheses by using commas instead.

Diagonal

638.3 To Show a Choice

Use a **diagonal** (also called a *slash* or forward *slash*) between two words, as in *and/or,* to indicate that either is acceptable.

> **Press the load/eject button.**
> **Don't worry; this is indoor/outdoor carpet.**

638.4 When Quoting Poetry

When quoting more than one line of poetry, use a diagonal to show where each line of poetry ends. (Insert a space on each side of the diagonal.)

> **I have learned not to worry about love; / but to honor its coming / with all my heart.**
> —Alice Walker, "New Face"

Grammar Practice

Parentheses and Diagonals

Write the word or words that should be enclosed in parentheses or divided by a diagonal. Use the correct punctuation.

1. Nona slurped her *tom yum* hot and sour soup at the Thai restaurant.

2. Kirsten Dunst she was in the Spider-Man movies is one of my favorite actresses.

3. Don't forget to change the cable antenna switch on the remote when you want to watch regular TV.

4. Marion Morrison was the given name of John Wayne star of many old Western movies.

5. For Spirit Day, we're supposed to wear red and or blue our school colors.

6. Dave our blue parakeet was always very noisy whenever the phone rang.

7. Larry Bird he was a rookie at the same time Magic Johnson was played for only one team during his 13-year professional career: the Boston Celtics.

8. Catina said she learned all about the fastest search engine from Donnell the walking encyclopedia.

Model

Model the following sentence to practice using parentheses with full sentences.

> From the time we landed, Zeus 7 (I'll never understand why they didn't call the project *Mars*) was considered a success, but we didn't hit the headlines until the third day.
>
> —Paul Bond, "The Mars Stone"

Write the lyrics to a favorite song to practice using diagonals when quoting poetry.

> Worried about my mental state / Don't know if I'll recuperate / Think it's serious, gone from bad to worse / And I'm in trouble . . .
>
> —Gwen Stefani, "Serious"

Dash

640.1 To Indicate a Sudden Break

Use a **dash** to indicate a sudden break or change in the sentence.

> **Near the semester's end**—and this is not always due to poor planning—**some students may find themselves in a real crunch.**

Note: Dashes are often used in place of commas. Use dashes when you want to give special emphasis; use commas when there is no need for emphasis.

640.2 To Set Off an Introductory Series

Use a dash to set off an introductory series from the clause that explains the series.

> A good book, a cup of tea, a comfortable chair—**these things always saved my mother's sanity.**

640.3 To Set Off Parenthetical Material

You may use a dash to set off parenthetical material—material that explains or clarifies a word or a phrase.

> **A single incident**—a tornado that came without warning—**changed the face of the small town forever.**

640.4 To Indicate Interrupted Speech

Use a dash to show interrupted or faltering speech in dialogue.

> **Sojourner: Mama, why are you—**
> **Mama: Isabelle, do as I say!**
> —Sandy Asher, *A Woman Called Truth*

640.5 For Emphasis

Use a dash to emphasize a word, a series, a phrase, or a clause.

> **After years of trial and error, Belther made history with his invention**—the unicycle.

> **After several hours of hearing the high-pitched yipping, Petra finally realized what it was**—coyote pups.

Grammar Practice

Dashes

- To Indicate a Sudden Break
- To Set Off an Introductory Series
- To Set Off Parenthetical Material
- To Indicate Interrupted Speech
- For Emphasis

 A word, a phrase, or a clause follows each sentence below. Write the sentences to include those words, set off by one or two dashes.

1. The words she used made her appear intelligent, even if she was not. *(infinitesimal, querulous)*

2. Until recently, not many people knew that this man was plagued by depression. *(Abraham Lincoln)*

3. At that moment, he finally came to accept something he'd been hiding from for years. *(the truth)*

4. All of these are necessary for a winter day spent outdoors in northern Minnesota. *(long underwear, a hat, gloves, and a heavy coat)*

5. Nearby, the lead singer of the band made his way to the stage. *(but not as near as I wished)*

6. Macintosh High School senior Taneka Reeves has been accepted at Princeton. *(winner of this year's corporate scholarship)*

7. Yasin wanted that car stereo for his own wheels. *(the one he first heard in Grady's car)*

8. These were some of the most popular progressive rock bands of the seventies. *(Genesis, Yes, and Pink Floyd)*

Model

Model the following sentences to practice using a dash to indicate interrupted speech.

> "I—uh—Mrs. Ferman? I got your name from a friend, Bill Seavers? I understand you—" his voice dropped low, "—rent rooms."
>
> —Ray Russell, "The Room"

> Before she realized her mom was right behind her, Nastasia shouted, "Mom, tele—"
>
> —Alicia Kimball, "The Nightstand"

Ellipsis

642.1 To Show Omitted Words

Use an **ellipsis** (three periods with one space before and after each period) to show that one or more words have been omitted in a quotation.

(Original)

We the people of the United States, in order to form a more perfect Union, establish justice, insure domestic tranquility, provide for the common defense, promote the general welfare, and secure the blessings of liberty to ourselves and our posterity, do ordain and establish this Constitution for the United States of America.

—Preamble, U.S. Constitution

(Quotation)

"We the people . . . in order to form a more perfect Union . . . establish this Constitution for the United States of America."

642.2 At the End of a Sentence

If words from a quotation are omitted at the end of a sentence, place the ellipsis after the period that marks the conclusion of the sentence.

"Five score years ago, a great American, in whose symbolic shadow we stand, signed the Emancipation Proclamation. . . . But one hundred years later, we must face the tragic fact that the Negro is still not free."

—Martin Luther King, Jr., "I Have a Dream"

Note: If the quoted material is a complete sentence (even if it was not complete in the original), use a period, then an ellipsis.

(Original)

I am tired; my heart is sick and sad. From where the sun now stands I will fight no more forever.

—Chief Joseph of the Nez Percé

(Quotation)

"I am tired. . . . From where the sun now stands I will fight no more forever."

or

"I am tired. . . . I will fight no more. . . . "

642.3 To Show a Pause

Use an ellipsis to indicate a pause.

I brought my trembling hand to my focusing eyes. It was oozing, it was red, it was . . . it was . . . a tomato!

—Laura Baginski, student writer

Grammar Practice

Ellipses

- To Show Omitted Words
- At the End of a Sentence
- To Show a Pause

 For the following paragraph, select the least important information to replace with ellipses. Write the shortened paragraph on your own paper.

1 Globe artichokes are delicious as an appetizer or as part of a nutritious
2 dinner. Prepare each artichoke for cooking by removing most of the stem.
3 Then cut off about a quarter of each leaf, removing the thorns that make
4 eating the leaves difficult. Now boil the artichokes for 15–45 minutes,
5 depending on their sizes and how many you're cooking. You may also steam
6 them until tender. After cooking, let them cool off a bit. Use your hands to
7 pull off a leaf, and use your teeth to pull off the soft bottom part. You may
8 want to try dipping it first into a sauce or some mayonnaise. (You don't eat
9 the rest of the leaf; put it aside to discard later.) Continue eating the leaves
10 until you get to the really small ones, which you cut off. You'll see a layer
11 of feathery thistle; cut that off, too. You've reached the heart of the
12 artichoke—the best part! Remove it from the stem with a knife and
13 savor its unique flavor.

Exercise

Respond to each of the following situations by writing a sentence or two in which you use an ellipsis to show a pause.

1. Aunt Daphne is wondering where you buy such stylish clothes.
2. You are surprised when something turns out other than how you thought it would.

Brackets

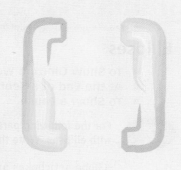

644.1 To Set Off Clarifying Information

Use **brackets** before and after words that are added to clarify what another person has said or written.

> "They'd [the sweat bees] get into your mouth, ears, eyes, nose. You'd feel them all over you."
> —Marilyn Johnson and Sasha Nyary,
> "Roosevelts in the Amazon"

Note: The brackets indicate that the words *the sweat bees* are not part of the quotation but were added for clarification.

644.2 Around an Editorial Correction

Place brackets around an editorial correction inserted within quoted material.

> "Brooklyn alone has 8 percent of lead poisoning [victims] nationwide," said Marjorie Moore.
> —Donna Actie, student writer

Note: The brackets indicate that the word *victims* replaced the author's original word.

Place brackets around the letters *sic* (Latin for "as such"); the letters indicate that an error appearing in the material being quoted was made by the original speaker or writer.

> "'When I'm queen,' mused Lucy, 'I'll show these blockheads whose [*sic*] got beauty and brains'."

644.3 To Set Off Added Words

Place brackets around comments that have been added to a quotation.

> "Congratulations to the astronomy club's softball team, which put in, shall we say, a 'stellar' performance." [groans]

Punctuation Marks

´	Accent, acute	,	Comma	( )	Parentheses
`	Accent, grave	†	Dagger	.	Period
'	Apostrophe	—	Dash	?	Question mark
*	Asterisk	/	Diagonal/Slash	" "	Quotation marks
{ }	Brace	¨ (ü)	Dieresis	§	Section
[ ]	Brackets	. . .	Ellipsis	;	Semicolon
^	Caret	!	Exclamation point	~	Tilde
(ç)	Cedilla	-	Hyphen	___	Underscore
^	Circumflex	...	Leaders		
:	Colon	¶	Paragraph		

Grammar Practice

Brackets

- **To Set Off Clarifying Information**
- **Around an Editorial Correction**

 Follow the directions for each activity below.

1. In the following quotation, the speaker is talking about *tsunamis*. Rewrite the quotation, using the word in brackets to clarify the quotation.

> **"The term 'tidal wave' is incorrect," explained Dr. Crabo, "since they are not related to tides at all. They are caused by earthquakes, volcanic eruptions, and the like."**

2. Quote the following statement and show that the error was made by Carl Braun, the original writer of a letter to the editor.

> **Isn't the separation of church and state part of our great country's constitution?**

3. In the following quotation, replace the speaker's words *Mach 1* with *the speed of sound*. Place brackets around your editorial correction.

> **According to David Scott and Alexei Leonov, "Until Yeager beat it, Mach 1 was regarded as an insuperable barrier, which no human being could cross and emerge alive."**

4. In the following quotation from *Big-Leaf Mahogany,* the speaker is talking about mahogany. Clarify the quotation using brackets.

> **"The natural range is vast, and although the species is not on the verge of extinction, genetic erosion has been alleged," Mr. Colon explains.**

Model

Model the following sentence to practice using brackets to set off clarifying information.

> **It [security] does not exist in nature, nor do the children of men as a whole experience it.**
> —Helen Keller, *Let Us Have Faith*

Punctuation

Test Prep!

From the choices given on the next page, write the letter of the correct way to punctuate each underlined part. If it is already correct, write "D."

"In less than two years, you'll be done with high <u>school." "That's</u> a giant step
(1)

on your way to adulthood," your guidance counselor says. "You have some major

decisions ahead of <u>you . . . it</u> wouldn't hurt to start thinking about them <u>now"</u>
                (2)   **(3)**

Well, your counselor is right. Here are a few pointers that may make it a <u>litt-</u>
                (4)

<u>le</u> easier. Concentrate first on career choice: What do you want to do once your

formal education is complete? Consider things you enjoy doing and what you're good

at. Read a book such as <u>"What Color Is Your Parachute?".</u> If you're still struggling,
                  (5)

you can take one of many online tests to help you come up with some career options.

An alternative is to interview working <u>people—friends, relatives, even strangers,</u> to
                          (6)

discover details about their careers.

Next, do some research about the kind of training <u>and/or</u> education required
                          (7)

for the career you've selected. With this step, you'll find out whether you will need to

continue your education in college or <u>'technical' school,</u> or whether you can enter the
                        (8)

workforce directly. You can also determine whether you'll be staying in your <u>mom</u>

<u>and dads home</u> for a while or moving out (in which case you should make sure you
   (9)

know something about <u>day to day</u> living skills, including managing <u>a budget.</u>
         (10)   **(11)**

If you decide to go on to college, start getting information from those you're

interested <u>in. (At</u> the appropriate time, complete applications for your <u>first- and</u>
     (12)   **(13)**

<u>second choice</u> institutions.) If you decide on a career that entails completing an

apprenticeship, labor unions can direct you to the technical education you'll need.

And if you decide to get a job immediately after high school, there are still a few <u>thi-</u>
                                                  (14)

<u>ngs</u> you need to learn: how to create an effective résumé, search for employment,

and ace an interview.

Your future holds so many choices that it may seem overwhelming at the moment. <u>Don't</u> let that prevent you from taking small steps, one at a time. Remember,
15
if you don't make your future happen, it's <u>anyones'</u> guess what it will bring.
16

1
- (A) school. "That's
- (B) school. Thats'
- (C) school. That's
- (D) correct as is

2
- (A) you. . . it
- (B) you . . it
- (C) you...it
- (D) correct as is

3
- (A) now".
- (B) now."
- (C) now.'
- (D) correct as is

4
- (A) lit-tle
- (B) li-ttle
- (C) little (do not hyphenate)
- (D) correct as is

5
- (A) *What Color Is Your Parachute?*
- (B) *What Color Is Your Parachute?*.
- (C) "What Color Is Your Parachute?"
- (D) correct as is

6
- (A) people, friends, relatives, even strangers—
- (B) people—friends, relatives, even strangers—
- (C) people friends, relatives, even strangers—
- (D) correct as is

7
- (A) and-or
- (B) and, or
- (C) and [or]
- (D) correct as is

8
- (A) "technical" school
- (B) 'technical school'
- (C) technical school
- (D) correct as is

9
- (A) mom's and dad's home
- (B) mom and dad's home
- (C) mom and dads' home
- (D) correct as is

10
- (A) day-to-day
- (B) day- to day
- (C) day to-day
- (D) correct as is

11
- (A) a budget.)
- (B) a budget).
- (C) a budget)
- (D) correct as is

12
- (A) in. (at
- (B) in (At
- (C) in (at
- (D) correct as is

13
- (A) first- and second-choice
- (B) first and second-choice
- (C) first-and-second-choice
- (D) correct as is

14
- (A) thin-gs
- (B) th-ings
- (C) things (do not hyphenate)
- (D) correct as is

15
- (A) Do'nt
- (B) Do'n't
- (C) Dont'
- (D) correct as is

16
- (A) anyones
- (B) anyones's
- (C) anyone's
- (D) correct as is

Punctuation

Checking Mechanics

Capitalization

648.1 Proper Nouns and Adjectives

Capitalize proper nouns and proper adjectives (those derived from proper nouns). The chart below provides a quick overview of capitalization rules. The pages following explain some specific rules of capitalization.

Capitalization at a Glance

Names of people . . . . **Alice Walker, Matilda, Jim, Mr. Roker**

Days of the week, months . . . . **Sunday, Tuesday, June, August**

Holidays, holy days . . . . **Thanksgiving, Easter, Hanukkah**

Periods, events in history. . . . . **Middle Ages, the Battle of Bunker Hill**

Official documents . . . . **Declaration of Independence**

Special events . . . . **Elgin Community Spring Gala**

Languages, nationalities, religions . . . . **French, Canadian, Islam**

Political parties . . . . **Republican Party, Socialist Party**

Trade names . . . . **Oscar Mayer hot dogs, Pontiac Sunbird**

Official titles used with names . . . . **Mayor John Spitzer, Senator Feinstein**

Formal epithets . . . . **Alexander the Great**

Geographical names

    Planets, heavenly bodies . . . . **Earth, Jupiter, the Milky Way**

    Continents. . . . . **Australia, South America**

    Countries. . . . . **Ireland, Grenada, Sri Lanka**

    States, provinces. . . . . **Ohio, Utah, Nova Scotia**

    Cities, towns, villages . . . . **El Paso, Burlington, Wonewoc**

    Streets, roads, highways . . . . **Park Avenue, Route 66, Interstate 90**

    Landforms. . . . . **the Rocky Mountains, the Sahara Desert**

    Bodies of water. . . . . **Yellowstone Lake, Pumpkin Creek**

    Buildings, monuments . . . . **Elkhorn High School, Gateway Arch**

    Public areas . . . . **Times Square, Sequoia National Park**

Grammar Practice

Capitalization 1

■ **Proper Nouns and Adjectives**

For each sentence below, write the word or words that should be capitalized.

1. Hattie Wyatt Caraway of Arkansas was the first woman elected to the united states senate.

2. A giant red spot on jupiter is thrice the diameter of planet earth.

3. Mayor j. b. mcDonald opened this year's winter carnival in colby county.

4. The aswan dam provides egypt with hydroelectric power.

5. About two-thirds of the korean peninsula is composed of pre-cambrian metamorphic and granitic rocks.

6. Anne's roommate at college uses a dell xps notebook computer.

7. The petronas twin towers, the world's tallest office buildings, are located in kuala lumpur, malaysia.

8. The main artery of transportation through the salt lake city metropolitan area is interstate 15.

9. David cobb and patricia LaMarche represented the green party in the 2004 u.s. presidential election.

10. The chang jiang, china's longest river, is also known as the yangtze.

Model

Model this sentence to practice capitalizing proper nouns and adjectives.

> **Clearly, the Arabs served as a conduit, but the math laid on the doorstep of Renaissance Europe cannot be attributed solely to ancient Greece.**
> —Dick Teresi, *Lost Discoveries: The Ancient Roots of Modern Science*

Mechanics

Capitalization (continued)

650.1 First Words

Capitalize the first word of every sentence, including the first word of a full-sentence direct quotation.

> **The crowd was quiet. A girl whispered, "I hope it's not Nancy," and the sound of her whisper reached the edges of the crowd.**
>
> —Shirley Jackson, "The Lottery"

650.2 Sentences in Parentheses

Capitalize the first word in a sentence enclosed in parentheses, but do not capitalize the first word if the parenthetical appears within another sentence.

> **Shamelessly she winked at me and grinned again. (That grin! She could have taken it off her face and put it on the table.)**
>
> —Jean Stafford, "Bad Characters"
>
> **Damien's aunt (she's a wild woman) plays bingo every Saturday night.**

650.3 Sentences Following Colons

Capitalize the first word in a complete sentence that follows a colon when (1) you want to emphasize the sentence or (2) the sentence is a quotation.

> **When we quarreled and made horrible faces at one another, Mother knew what to say: "Your faces will stay that way, and no one will marry you."**

650.4 Sections of the Country

Capitalize words that indicate particular sections of the country; do not capitalize words that simply indicate direction.

> **Mr. Johnson is from the Southwest.** (section of the country)
>
> **After moving north to Montana, he had to buy winter clothes.** (direction)

650.5 Certain Religious Words

Capitalize nouns that refer to the Supreme Being, the word *Bible,* the books of the Bible, and the names for other holy books.

> **God   Jehovah   the Lord   the Savior   Allah   Bible   Genesis**

650.6 Titles

Capitalize the first word of a title, the last word, and every word in between except articles *(a, an, the),* short prepositions, and coordinating conjunctions. Follow this rule for titles of books, newspapers, magazines, poems, plays, songs, articles, films, works of art, photographs, and stories.

> ***Washington Post*   "The Diary of a Madman"   *Nights of Rain and Stars***

Grammar Practice

Capitalization 2

- First Words
- Sentences in Parentheses
- Sentences Following Colons
- Titles

 For each of the following sentences, correctly write any word or word groups that are incorrectly capitalized.

1. Mr. Vance had an announcement: our next play would be *steel magnolias*.

2. Robert Harling authored that play as well as the screenplay for *sister act* (this is a film starring Whoopi Goldberg).

3. *Steel magnolias* opened off-Broadway in 1987 (It ran for 1,126 performances) before it finally opened on Broadway in 2005.

4. in the film version, Shirley MacLaine plays Ouiser. (she is a woman you love to hate.)

5. Ouiser is well-to-do and mean spirited: she annoys everyone in the small Louisiana town where she lives.

6. this production should be even better than our last one, *You can't take it with you.*

7. That play was about a crazy family during the Depression: it affirms that money isn't everything.

8. Our plays always get great reviews in the *mortontown centennial times*.

Model

Model the following sentence to practice capitalizing a sentence following a colon.

[M]y mother had held him up to us as a sort of ogre with which to frighten us into obedience: Don't stray on the mountain, don't play by the river, or Iida will get you!

—Lian Hearn, *Across the Nightingale Floor: Tales of the Otori*

Capitalization (continued)

652.1 Words Used as Names

Capitalize words like *father, mother, uncle,* and *senator* when they are used as titles with a personal name or when they are substituted for proper nouns (especially in direct address).

> **We've missed you, Aunt Lucinda!** (*Aunt* is part of the name.)
>
> **I hope Mayor Bates arrives soon.** (*Mayor* is part of the name.)

A Closer Look

To test whether a word is being substituted for a proper noun, simply read the sentence with a proper noun in place of the word. If the proper noun fits in the sentence, the word being tested should be capitalized; otherwise, the word should not be capitalized.

> **Did Mom (Sue) say we could go?** (*Sue* works in this sentence.)
>
> **Did your mom (Sue) say you could go?** (*Sue* does not work here.)

Note: Usually the word is not capitalized if it follows a possessive—*my, his, your*—as it does in the second sentence above.

652.2 Letters

Capitalize the letters used to indicate form or shape.

> **U-turn   I-beam   S-curve   T-shirt   V-shaped**

652.3 Organizations

Capitalize the name of an organization, an association, or a team.

> **Lake Ontario Sailors   American Indian Movement   Democratic Party**

652.4 Abbreviations

Capitalize abbreviations of titles and organizations. (Some other abbreviations are also capitalized. See pages **660–662**.)

> **AAA   CEO   NAACP   M.D.   Ph.D.**

652.5 Titles of Courses

Capitalize words like *sociology* and *history* when they are used as titles of specific courses; do not capitalize these words when they name a field of study.

> **Who teaches History 202?** (title of a specific course)
>
> **It's the same professor who teaches my sociology course.** (a field of study)

Note: The words *freshman, sophomore, junior,* and *senior* are not capitalized unless they are part of an official title.

> **Rosa is a senior this year and is in charge of the Senior Class Banquet.**

Grammar Practice

Capitalization 3

- ■ **Words Used as Names**
- ■ **Letters**
- ■ **Organizations**
- ■ **Abbreviations**
- ■ **Titles of Courses**

 Write the line number along with the words that should be capitalized.

1	**Date:**	September 15, 2006
2	**To:**	principal Sosa
3	**From:**	Darcella White, president of the junior class
4	**Subject:**	Fundraiser for Danville children's hospital

5   Here is the latest update from the valley high student volunteer committee

6   regarding the dance to benefit Danville children's hospital.

7   • Mr. Baden, who teaches english 101, will serve as our faculty advisor.

8   • The valley high art club has agreed to be in charge of decorations.

9   • Richard Dole, sr., an instructor in electrical engineering at Valley View Tech,

10   will supervise installation of specialty lighting in the gym.

11   • Tomas Rosero, ceo of citywide catering, will donate food and beverages.

12   • Money donations will be handled by superintendent Hayek.

13   • The volunteer committee has ordered 250 t-shirts to sell at the dance.

14   • Next Wednesday, we will meet with members of the Danville children's

15   hospital auxiliary (dcha) to finalize our plans.

16   Please inform me of any questions or comments you may have. Thank you!

 ## Model

Model the following sentence to practice capitalizing abbreviations and the names of organizations.

The National Football League (NFL) estimated that in 2001 43 percent of its total fan base was female.

—Teena Spencer, *The Girlfriend's Guide to Football*

Mechanics

Plurals

654.1 Most Nouns

Form the **plurals** of most nouns by adding *s* to the singular.

cheerleader – cheerleaders
sign – signs   crate – crates

654.2 Nouns Ending in *sh, ch, x, s,* and *z*

Form the plurals of nouns ending in *sh, ch, x, s,* and *z* by adding *es* to the singular.

lunch – lunches   dish – dishes   mess – messes   fox – foxes

Exception: When the final *ch* sounds like *k,* add an *s* (*monarchs*).

654.3 Nouns Ending in *y*

The plurals of common nouns that end in *y* (preceded by a consonant) are formed by changing the *y* to *i* and adding *es.*

fly – flies   jalopy – jalopies

Form the plurals of nouns that end in *y* (preceded by a vowel) by adding only an *s.*

donkey – donkeys   monkey – monkeys

Note: Form the plurals of all proper nouns ending in *y* by adding *s* (*Kathys*).

654.4 Nouns Ending in *o*

The plurals of nouns ending in *o* (preceded by a vowel) are formed by adding an *s.*

radio – radios   rodeo – rodeos   studio – studios   duo – duos

The plurals of most nouns ending in *o* (preceded by a consonant) are formed by adding *es.*

echo – echoes   hero – heroes   tomato – tomatoes

Exception: Musical terms always form plurals by adding *s.*

alto – altos   banjo – banjos   solo – solos   piano – pianos

654.5 Nouns Ending in *ful*

Form the plurals of nouns that end in *ful* by adding an *s* at the end of the word.

two tankfuls   three pailfuls   four mouthfuls

Note: Do not confuse these examples with *three pails full* (when you are referring to three separate pails full of something) or *two tanks full.*

654.6 Compound Nouns

Form the plurals of most compound nouns by adding *s* or *es* to the important word in the compound.

brothers-in-law   maids of honor   secretaries of state

Grammar Practice

Plurals 1

- Most Nouns
- Nouns Ending in *sh, ch, x, s,* and *z*
- Nouns Ending in *y*
- Nouns Ending in *o*
- Nouns Ending in *ful*
- Compound Nouns

 Write the correct plural of the underlined words or phrases in each sentence.

1. Some chemical <u>mix</u> will react violently, generate a lot of heat, or produce toxic <u>gas.</u>

2. Band members heard <u>buzz</u> and <u>echo</u> from Manny's electric guitar, especially during his <u>solo.</u>

3. Erosion is one of the most alarming <u>threat</u> to regional, national, and international <u>beach.</u>

4. Salt <u>marsh</u> are found on the edges of <u>estuary</u> where rivers flow into the ocean.

5. Take two <u>spoonful</u> every four to six <u>hour.</u>

6. Several <u>travel agency</u> are offering low-cost winter <u>getaway.</u>

7. The American Association of <u>Physics Teacher</u> was established in 1930.

8. Rosh Hashana and Yom Kippur are Jewish <u>holiday.</u>

9. There are two <u>McCarthy</u> in my afternoon class.

10. Zack downed two <u>glassful</u> of water after the race.

11. Phan's <u>brother-in-law</u> drive beat-up <u>auto</u> in the demolition derby.

12. The pond near the park is swarming with <u>mosquito.</u>

 ## Exercise

Write the plurals of the following words or phrases. Then use as many of them as you can in one sentence.

hobby, sister-in-law, radio, search, antique shop, dress, latchkey

Plurals *(continued)*

656.1 Nouns Ending in *f* or *fe*

Form the plurals of nouns that end in *f* or *fe* in one of two ways: If the final *f* sound is still heard in the plural form of the word, simply add *s;* but if the final *f* sound becomes a *v* sound, change the *f* to *ve* and add *s*.

> **Plural ends with *f* sound:** roof – roofs; chief – chiefs
> **Plural ends with *v* sound:** wife – wives; loaf – loaves

Note: Several words are correct with either ending.

> **Plural ends with either sound:** hoof – hooves/hoofs

656.2 Irregular Spelling

A number of words form a plural by taking on an irregular spelling.

crisis – crises	child – children	radius – radii
criterion – criteria	goose – geese	die – dice

Note: Some of these words are acceptable with the commonly used *s* or *es* ending.

> index – indices/indexes   cactus – cacti/cactuses

Some nouns remain unchanged when used as plurals.

> deer   sheep   salmon   aircraft   series

656.3 Words Discussed as Words

The plurals of symbols, letters, numbers, and words being discussed as words are formed by adding an apostrophe and an *s*.

> **Dad yelled a lot of *wow's* and *yippee's* when he saw my A's and B's.**

Note: You may omit the apostrophe if it does not cause any confusion.

> **the three R's or Rs   YMCA's or YMCAs**

656.4 Collective Nouns

A collective noun may be singular or plural depending upon how it's used. A collective noun is singular when it refers to a group considered as one unit; it is plural when it refers to the individuals in the group.

> **The class was on its best behavior.** (group as a unit)
> **The class are preparing for their final exams.** (individuals in the group)

If it seems awkward to use a plural verb with a collective noun, add a clearly plural noun such as *members* to the sentence, or change the collective noun into a possessive followed by a plural noun that describes the individuals in the group.

> **The class members are preparing for their final exams.**
> **The class's students are preparing for their final exams.**

Grammar Practice

Plurals 2

- Nouns Ending in *f* or *fe*
- Irregular Spellings
- Words Discussed as Words
- Collective Nouns

 For each sentence below, write the plural form of the words or letters in parentheses.

1. The *(thief)* did not know they were stealing equipment containing radioactive material.

2. The book chronicles the everyday *(life)* of colonial *(person)*.

3. Male baboons somehow recognize their own genetic *(offspring)*.

4. The sample experiment contained four different *(stimulus)*.

5. Jack thought the password had two *(7)* and a couple of *(F)*.

6. While sailing on the ocean last summer, we saw *(tuna)* and *(shark)*.

7. There were lots of *(hurray)* when the class saw their new *(PC)*.

8. There is a strange theory that the Great Pyramids of Giza are actually huge *(antenna)*.

 For each sentence below, choose the correct word in parentheses.

9. The football team has *(its, their)* own bus for away games.

10. After a long day in school, the class finished *(its, their)* essays at home.

 ## Exercise

Write sentences using plurals of these words.

vertebra, alumnus, self, belief, moose

Numbers

658.1 Numerals or Words

Numbers from one to nine are usually written as words; numbers 10 and over are usually written as numerals. However, numbers being compared or contrasted should be kept in the same style.

8 to 11 years old   eight to eleven years old

You may use a combination of numerals and words for very large numbers.

1.5 million   3 billion to 3.2 billion   6 trillion

If numbers are used infrequently in a piece of writing, you may spell out those that can be written in no more than two words.

ten   twenty-five   two hundred   ten thousand

658.2 Numerals Only

Use numerals for the following forms: decimals, percentages, chapters, pages, addresses, phone numbers, identification numbers, and statistics.

26.2	**8 percent**	**Highway 36**	**chapter 7**
pages 287–89	**July 6, 1945**	**44 B.C.E.**	**a vote of 23 to 4**

Always use numerals with abbreviations and symbols.

8%   10 mm   3 cc   8 oz   90° C   24 mph   6' 3"

658.3 Words Only

Use words to express numbers that begin a sentence.

Fourteen students "forgot" their assignments.

Note: Change the sentence structure if this rule creates a clumsy construction.

Clumsy: *Six hundred thirty-nine* teachers were laid off this year.

Better: This year, 639 teachers were laid off.

Use words for numbers that come before a compound modifier if that modifier includes a numeral.

They made twelve 10-foot sub sandwiches for the picnic.

658.4 Time and Money

If time is expressed with an abbreviation, use numerals; if it is expressed in words, spell out the number.

4:00 a.m. (or) four o'clock

If an amount of money is spelled out, so is the currency; use a numeral if a symbol is used.

twenty dollars (or) $20

Grammar Practice

Numbers

- Numerals or Words
- Numerals Only
- Words Only
- Time and Money

For each sentence below, write the underlined numbers the correct way. If a number is already correctly presented, write "correct."

1. In <u>two thousand five</u>, Hurricane Katrina caused <u>$one hundred twenty-five billion</u> worth of damage.

2. <u>20</u> basketball teams make it to the playoffs every year.

3. An <u>Fthree</u> tornado packs winds up to <u>206</u> mph.

4. James Michener's book *Hawaii* has more than a <u>thousand</u> pages.

5. Neptune's moon, Larissa, orbits <u>73,550</u> km from the center of Neptune and measures about <u>one hundred four</u> by <u>eighty-nine</u> km.

6. Many students get up around <u>five</u> A.M.

7. Voters age <u>eighteen</u> to <u>twenty-nine</u> made up <u>17</u> percent of all November <u>two</u>, 2004, voters.

8. My brother's new desktop computer cost <u>$879</u>.

9. The Airbus <u>Athree-eighty</u> is capable of carrying <u>8 hundred</u> passengers.

10. The library's main number is <u>626- five-five-three-zero</u>.

11. CNN was the first news agency to air the special report at <u>two o'clock</u>.

12. Aristotle (<u>three hundred eighty-four</u> – <u>322</u> B.C.E.) was a Greek philosopher.

Model

Complete this sentence using your own numbers.

The girl's varsity basketball team won _____ percent of their games, but ended the season with a _____ – _____ loss.

Abbreviations

660.1 Formal and Informal Abbreviations

An **abbreviation** is the shortened form of a word or phrase. Some abbreviations are always acceptable in both formal and informal writing:

Mr.   Mrs.   Jr.   Ms.   Dr.   a.m. (A.M.)   p.m. (P.M.)

Note: In most of your writing, you do not abbreviate the names of states, countries, months, days, or units of measure. However, you may use the abbreviation *U.S.* after it has been spelled out once. Do not abbreviate the words *Street, Company,* and similar words, especially when they are part of a proper name. Also, do not use signs or symbols (%, &, #, @) in place of words. The dollar sign, however, is appropriate with numerals ($325).

660.2 Correspondence Abbreviations

United States

	Standard	Postal
Alabama	Ala.	AL
Alaska	Alaska	AK
Arizona	Ariz.	AZ
Arkansas	Ark.	AR
California	Calif.	CA
Colorado	Colo.	CO
Connecticut	Conn.	CT
Delaware	Del.	DE
District of Columbia	D.C.	DC
Florida	Fla.	FL
Georgia	Ga.	GA
Guam	Guam	GU
Hawaii	Hawaii	HI
Idaho	Idaho	ID
Illinois	Ill.	IL
Indiana	Ind.	IN
Iowa	Iowa	IA
Kansas	Kan.	KS
Kentucky	Ky.	KY
Louisiana	La.	LA
Maine	Maine	ME
Maryland	Md.	MD
Massachusetts	Mass.	MA
Michigan	Mich.	MI
Minnesota	Minn.	MN
Mississippi	Miss.	MS
Missouri	Mo.	MO
Montana	Mont.	MT
Nebraska	Neb.	NE
Nevada	Nev.	NV
New Hampshire	N.H.	NH
New Jersey	N.J.	NJ
New Mexico	N.M.	NM
New York	N.Y.	NY
North Carolina	N.C.	NC
North Dakota	N.D.	ND
Ohio	Ohio	OH
Oklahoma	Okla.	OK
Oregon	Ore.	OR
Pennsylvania	Pa.	PA
Puerto Rico	P.R.	PR
Rhode Island	R.I.	RI
South Carolina	S.C.	SC
South Dakota	S.D.	SD
Tennessee	Tenn.	TN
Texas	Texas	TX
Utah	Utah	UT
Vermont	Vt.	VT
Virginia	Va.	VA
Virgin Islands	V.I.	VI
Washington	Wash.	WA
West Virginia	W.Va.	WV
Wisconsin	Wis.	WI
Wyoming	Wyo.	WY

Canadian Provinces

	Standard	Postal
Alberta	Alta.	AB
British Columbia	B.C.	BC
Labrador	Lab.	NL
Manitoba	Man.	MB
New Brunswick	N.B.	NB
Newfoundland	N.F.	NL
Northwest Territories	N.W.T.	NT
Nova Scotia	N.S.	NS
Nunavut		NU
Ontario	Ont.	ON
Prince Edward Island	P.E.I.	PE
Quebec	Que.	QC
Saskatchewan	Sask.	SK
Yukon Territory	Y.T.	YT

Addresses

	Standard	Postal
Apartment	Apt.	APT
Avenue	Ave.	AVE
Boulevard	Blvd.	BLVD
Circle	Cir.	CIR
Court	Ct.	CT
Drive	Dr.	DR
East	E.	E
Expressway	Expy.	EXPY
Freeway	Fwy.	FWY
Heights	Hts.	HTS
Highway	Hwy.	HWY
Hospital	Hosp.	HOSP
Junction	Junc.	JCT
Lake	L.	LK
Lakes	Ls.	LKS
Lane	Ln.	LN
Meadows	Mdws.	MDWS
North	N.	N
Palms	Palms	PLMS
Park	Pk.	PK
Parkway	Pky.	PKY
Place	Pl.	PL
Plaza	Plaza	PLZ
Post Office Box	P.O. Box	PO BOX
Ridge	Rdg.	RDG
River	R.	RV
Road	Rd.	RD
Room	Rm.	RM
Rural	R.	R
Rural Route	R.R.	RR
Shore	Sh.	SH
South	S.	S
Square	Sq.	SQ
Station	Sta.	STA
Street	St.	ST
Suite	Ste.	STE
Terrace	Ter.	TER
Turnpike	Tpke.	TPKE
Union	Un.	UN
View	View	VW
Village	Vil.	VLG
West	W.	W

661.1 Other Common Abbreviations

abr. abridged; abridgment
AC, ac alternating current
ack. acknowledge; acknowledgment
acv actual cash value
A.D. in the year of the Lord (Latin *anno Domini*)
AM amplitude modulation
A.M., a.m. before noon (Latin *ante meridiem*)
ASAP as soon as possible
avg., av. average
BBB Better Business Bureau
B.C. before Christ
B.C.E. before the Common Era
bibliog. bibliographer; bibliography
biog. biographer; biographical; biography
C 1. Celsius 2. centigrade 3. coulomb
c. 1. circa (about) 2. cup
cc 1. cubic centimeter 2. carbon copy
CDT, C.D.T. central daylight time
C.E. of the Common Era
chap. chapter
cm centimeter
c.o., c/o care of
COD, C.O.D. 1. cash on delivery 2. collect on delivery
co-op. cooperative
CST, C.S.T. central standard time
cu., c cubic
D.A. district attorney
d.b.a. doing business as
DC, dc direct current
dec. deceased
dept. department
DST, D.S.T. daylight saving time
dup. duplicate
DVD digital video disc
ea. each
ed. edition; editor
EDT, E.D.T. eastern daylight time
e.g. for example (Latin *exempli gratia*)
EST, E.S.T. eastern standard time
etc. and so forth (Latin *et cetera*)
ex. example
F Fahrenheit
FM frequency modulation
F.O.B., f.o.b. free on board
ft foot
g 1. gram 2. gravity
gal. gallon
gloss. glossary
GNP gross national product
hdqrs, HQ headquarters
HIV human immunodeficiency virus

Hon. Honorable (title)
hp horsepower
HTML hypertext markup language
Hz hertz
ibid. in the same place (Latin *ibidem*)
id. the same (Latin *idem*)
i.e. that is (Latin *id est*)
illus. illustration
inc. incorporated
IQ, I.Q. intelligence quotient
IRS Internal Revenue Service
ISBN International Standard Book Number
Jr., jr. junior
K 1. kelvin (temperature unit) 2. Kelvin (temperature scale)
kc kilocycle
kg kilogram
km kilometer
kn knot
kW kilowatt
l liter
lat. latitude
lb, lb. pound (Latin *libra*)
l.c. lowercase
lit. literary; literature
log logarithm
long. longitude
Ltd., ltd. limited
m meter
M.A. master of arts (Latin *Magister Artium*)
Mc, mc megacycle
M.C., m.c. master of ceremonies
M.D. doctor of medicine (Latin *medicinae doctor*)
mdse. merchandise
mfg. manufacturing
mg milligram
mi. 1. mile 2. mill (monetary unit)
misc. miscellaneous
ml milliliter
mm millimeter
mpg, m.p.g. miles per gallon
mph, m.p.h. miles per hour
MS 1. manuscript 2. Mississippi 3. multiple sclerosis
Ms., Ms title of courtesy for a woman
MST, M.S.T. mountain standard time
neg. negative
N.S.F., n.s.f. not sufficient funds
oz, oz. ounce
PA 1. public-address system 2. Pennsylvania
pct. percent
pd. paid

PDT, P.D.T. Pacific daylight time
PFC, Pfc. private first class
pg., p. page
P.M., p.m. after noon (Latin *post meridiem*)
P.O. 1. personnel officer 2. purchase order 3. postal order; post office 4. (also **p.o.**) petty officer
pop. population
POW, P.O.W. prisoner of war
pp. pages
ppd. 1. postpaid 2. prepaid
PR, P.R. 1. public relations 2. Puerto Rico
P.S. post script
psi, p.s.i. pounds per square inch
PST, P.S.T. Pacific standard time
PTA, P.T.A. Parent-Teacher Association
qt. quart
RF radio frequency
RN registered nurse
R.P.M., rpm revolutions per minute
R.S.V.P., r.s.v.p. please reply (French *répondez s'il vous plaît*)
SASE self-addressed stamped envelope
SCSI small computer system interface
SOS 1. international distress signal 2. any call for help
Sr. 1. senior (after surname) 2. sister (religious)
ST standard time
St. 1. saint 2. strait 3. street
std. standard
syn. synonymous; synonym
TBA to be announced
tbs, tbsp tablespoon
TM trademark
tsp teaspoon
UHF, uhf ultra high frequency
UPC universal product code
UV ultraviolet
V 1. *Physics:* velocity 2. *Electricity:* volt 3. volume
V.A., VA Veterans Administration
VHF, vhf very high frequency
VIP *Informal:* very important person
vol. 1. volume 2. volunteer
vs. versus
W 1. *Electricity:* watt 2. *Physics:* (also **w**) work 3. west
whse., whs. warehouse
wkly. weekly
w/o without
wt. weight
yd yard (measurement)

Mechanics

Acronyms and Initialisms

662.1 Acronyms

An **acronym** is a word formed from the first (or first few) letters of words in a phrase. Even though acronyms are abbreviations, they require no periods.

> radar radio detecting and ranging
> CARE Cooperative for American Relief Everywhere
> NASA National Aeronautics and Space Administration
> VISTA Volunteers in Service to America
> LAN local area network

662.2 Initialisms

An **initialism** is similar to an acronym except that the initials used to form this abbreviation are pronounced individually.

> CIA Central Intelligence Agency
> FBI Federal Bureau of Investigation
> FHA Federal Housing Administration

662.3 Common Acronyms and Initialisms

ADD	attention deficit disorder		**LLC**	limited liability company
AIDS	acquired immunodeficiency syndrome		**MADD**	Mothers Against Drunk Driving
AKA	also known as		**MRI**	magnetic resonance imaging
ATM	automatic teller machine		**NASA**	National Aeronautics and Space Administration
BMI	body mass index		**NATO**	North Atlantic Treaty Organization
CD	compact disc; certificate of deposit		**OPEC**	Organization of Petroleum-Exporting Countries
DMV	Department of Motor Vehicles		**OSHA**	Occupational Safety and Health Administration
ETA	estimated time of arrival		**PAC**	political action committee
FAA	Federal Aviation Administration		**PDF**	portable document format
FCC	Federal Communications Commission		**PETA**	People for the Ethical Treatment of Animals
FDA	Food and Drug Administration		**PIN**	personal identification number
FDIC	Federal Deposit Insurance Corporation		**PSA**	public service announcement
FEMA	Federal Emergency Management Agency		**ROTC**	Reserve Officers' Training Corps
FTC	Federal Trade Commission		**SADD**	Students Against Destructive Decisions
FYI	for your information		**SUV**	sport utility vehicle
GPS	global positioning system		**SWAT**	special weapons and tactics
HDTV	high-definition television		**TDD**	telecommunications device for the deaf
IRS	Internal Revenue Service			
IT	information technology			
JPEG	Joint Photographic Experts Group			
LCD	liquid crystal display			

Grammar Practice

Abbreviations, Acronyms, and Initialisms

 For each of the following sentences, write the correct abbreviation for the underlined word or words.

1. Several students from <u>Mister</u> Chang's class participated in a mock trial at the <u>district attorney's</u> office.

2. Satellite radio is quickly becoming as popular as <u>frequency modulation</u> radio.

3. Dred Scott <u>versus</u> John Sandford was a famous pre-Civil War Supreme Court case.

4. Chuck enjoys reading technical books (<u>that is</u>, books about repairing cars and electronics).

5. The <u>gross national product</u> might be the most important indicator of the status of an economy.

6. The senator's flight arrives in New York at 4:38 <u>post meridiem</u>.

7. Several of Dominick's family members work for True-Line <u>Manufacturing</u>.

8. My cousin's wedding invitation said to <u>please reply</u> by March 20.

9. Winter vacation packages include snow sports: skiing, snowboarding, snowshoeing, <u>and so forth</u>.

10. Euripides (485–408 <u>before the Common Era</u>) was the first modern dramatist.

11. My dad is Raul K. Martinez, <u>Junior</u>.

12. Use a meat thermometer to make sure a burger's internal temperature reaches 160 degrees <u>Fahrenheit</u>.

 ## Model

Model the following acronyms and initialisms to come up with your own abbreviations. (Write at least one acronym and one initialism.)

CHAC – Canan High Astronomy Club
WYSIWYG – what you see is what you get
IV – intravenous
BLT – bacon, lettuce, tomato

Spelling Rules

664.1 Write *i* before *e*

Write *i* before *e* except after *c*, or when sounded like *a* as in *neighbor* and *weigh*.

> relief   receive   perceive   reign   freight   beige

Exceptions: There are a number of exceptions to this rule, including these: *neither, leisure, seize, weird, species, science.*

664.2 Words with Consonant Endings

When a one-syllable word *(bat)* ends in a consonant *(t)* preceded by one vowel *(a)*, double the final consonant before adding a suffix that begins with a vowel *(batting)*.

> sum—summary   god—goddess

Note: When a multisyllabic word *(control)* ends in a consonant *(l)* preceded by one vowel *(o)*, the accent is on the last syllable *(con trol ')*, and the suffix begins with a vowel *(ing)*—the same rule holds true: Double the final consonant *(controlling)*.

> prefer—preferred   begin—beginning
> forget—forgettable   admit—admittance

664.3 Words with a Silent *e*

If a word ends with a silent *e*, drop the *e* before adding a suffix that begins with a vowel. Do not drop the *e* when the suffix begins with a consonant.

> state—stating—statement   like—liking—likeness
> use—using—useful   nine—ninety—nineteen

Exceptions: *judgment, truly, argument, ninth*

664.4 Words Ending in *y*

When *y* is the last letter in a word and the *y* is preceded by a consonant, change the *y* to *i* before adding any suffix except those beginning with *i*.

> fry—fries—frying   hurry—hurried—hurrying   lady—ladies
> ply—pliable   happy—happiness   beauty—beautiful

When *y* is the last letter in a word and the *y* is preceded by a vowel, do not change the *y* to *i* before adding a suffix.

> play—plays—playful   stay—stays—staying
> employ—employed

Important reminder: Never trust your spelling even to the best spell-checker. Use a dictionary for words your spell-checker does not cover.

Grammar Practice

Spelling 1

Find the 10 words that are misspelled in the following paragraph and write them correctly. (Each misspelled word is in the "Commonly Misspelled Words" list on pages 666–667.)

1   A summer job can be an excellent oportunity to learn how a business
2   works from the inside out. If you work in a fast-food restaurant, for example,
3   gather knowlege as you work. Talk to the manager and the owner, if
4   possible, and ask questions about things like hygeine requirements, cash
5   flow, staffing, and health department standards. Pondar how the business
6   meets the needs of the cunsumer. Find out what it takes to buy a franchise,
7   and learn what skills a qualifyed owner should possess. Finally, look around
8   you and investagate the responsibilty of each employe. You can learn an
9   incredable amount about business and human nature while working in a
10   fast-food restaurant.

Exercise

Write the words that result by combining the following base words and suffixes. Then write sentences that include them.

lucky + er   excite + ing   love + able   beauty + ful

Commonly Misspelled Words

A

abbreviate
abrupt
absence
absolute (ly)
absurd
abundance
academic
accelerate
accept (ance)
accessible
accessory
accidentally
accommodate
accompany
accomplish
accumulate
accurate
accustom (ed)
ache
achieve (ment)
acknowledge
acquaintance
acquired
across
address
adequate
adjustment
admissible
admittance
adolescent
advantageous
advertisement
advisable
aggravate
aggression
alcohol
alleviate
almost
alternative
although
aluminum
amateur
analysis
analyze
anarchy
ancient
anecdote
anesthetic

annihilate
announce
annual
anonymous
answer
anxious
apologize
apparatus
apparent (ly)
appearance
appetite
applies
appreciate
appropriate
approximately
architect
arctic
argument
arithmetic
arrangement
artificial
ascend
assistance
association
athlete
attendance
attire
attitude
audience
authority
available

B

balance
balloon
bargain
basically
beautiful
beginning
believe
benefit (ed)
biscuit
bought
boycott
brevity
brilliant
Britain
bureau
business

C

cafeteria
caffeine
calculator
calendar
campaign
canceled
candidate
catastrophe
category
caught
cavalry
celebration
cemetery
certificate
changeable
chief
chocolate
circuit
circumstance
civilization
colonel
colossal
column
commercial
commitment
committed
committee
comparative
comparison
competitively
conceivable
condemn
condescend
conference
conferred
confidential
congratulate
conscience
conscientious
conscious
consequence
consumer
contaminate
convenience
cooperate
correspondence
cough
coupon

courageous
courteous
creditor
criticism
criticize
curiosity
curious
cylinder

D

dealt
deceitful
deceive
decision
defense
deferred
definite (ly)
definition
delicious
descend
describe
description
despair
desperate
destruction
development
diameter
diaphragm
diarrhea
dictionary
dining
disagreeable
disappear
disappoint
disastrous
discipline
discrimination
discuss
dismissal
dissatisfied
dissect
distinctly
dormitory
doubt
drought
duplicate
dyeing
dying

E

earliest
efficiency
eighth
elaborate
eligible
eliminate
ellipse
embarrass
emphasize
employee
enclosure
encourage
endeavor
English
enormous
enough
enrichment
enthusiastic
entirely
entrance
environment
equipment
equipped
equivalent
especially
essential
eventually
exaggerate
examination
exceed
excellent
excessive
excite
executive
exercise
exhaust (ed)
exhibition
exhilaration
existence
expensive
experience
explanation
exquisite
extinguish
extraordinary
extremely

FG

facilities
familiar
fascinate
fashion
fatigue (d)
feature
February
fiery
financially
flourish
forcible
foreign
forfeit
fortunate
forty
fourth
freight
friend
fulfill
gauge
generally
generous
genuine
glimpse
gnarled
gnaw
government
gradual
grammar
gratitude
grievous
grocery
guard
guidance

H

happiness
harass
harmonize
height
hemorrhage
hereditary
hindrance
hoping
hopping
hospitable
humorous

hygiene
hymn
hypocrisy

ignorance
illiterate
illustrate
imaginary
immediately
immense
incidentally
inconvenience
incredible
indefinitely
independence
indispensable
industrial
industrious
inevitable
infinite
inflation
innocence
inoculation
inquiry
installation
instrumental
intelligence
interesting
interfere
interrupt
investigate
irregular
irresistible
issuing
itinerary
jealous (y)
jewelry
journal
judgment

knowledge
laboratory
laugh
lawyer
league
legacy
legalize
legitimate
leisure

liaison
license
lightning
likable
liquid
literature
loneliness

MN

maintenance
maneuver
manufacture
marriage
mathematics
medieval
memento
menagerie
merchandise
merely
mileage
miniature
miscellaneous
mischievous
misspell
moat
mobile
mortgage
multiplied
muscle
musician
mustache
mutual
mysterious
naive
nauseous
necessary
neither
neurotic
nevertheless
ninety
nighttime
noticeable
nuclear
nuisance

obstacle
obvious
occasion
occupant
occupation

occurred
occurrence
official
often
omitted
opinion
opponent
opportunity
opposite
optimism
ordinarily
organization
original
outrageous
pamphlet
parallel
paralyze
partial
particularly
pastime
patience
peculiar
pedestal
performance
permanent
permissible
perseverance
personal (ly)
personality
perspiration
persuade
petition
phenomenon
physical
physician
picnicking
planned
playwright
plead
pneumonia
politician
ponder
positively
possession
practically
precede
precious
preference
prejudice
preparation
presence
prevalent
primitive

privilege
probably
proceed
professional
professor
prominent
pronounce
pronunciation
protein
psychology
puny
purchase
pursuing

QR

qualified
quality
quantity
questionnaire
quiet
quite
quizzes
recede
receipt
receive
recipe
recognize
recommend
reference
referred
regard
regimen
religious
repel
repetition
residue
responsibility
restaurant
rheumatism
rhythm
ridiculous
robot
roommate

S

sacrifice
salary
sandwich
satisfactory
scarcely
scenic

schedule
scholar
science
secretary
seize
separate
sergeant
several
severely
sheriff
shrubbery
siege
signature
signify
silhouette
similar
simultaneous
sincerely
skiing
skunk
society
solar
sophomore
souvenir
spaghetti
specific
specimen
statue
stomach
stopped
strength
strictly
submission
substitute
subtle
succeed
success
sufficient
supersede
suppose
surprise
suspicious
symbolism
sympathy
synthetic

TU

tariff
technique
temperature
temporary
tendency

thermostat
thorough (ly)
though
throughout
tongue
tornado
tortoise
tragedy
transferred
tremendous
tried
trite
truly
unanimous
undoubtedly
unfortunately
unique
unnecessary
until
urgent
usable
usher
usually

vacuum
vague
valuable
variety
vengeance
versatile
vicinity
villain
visibility
visual

waif
Wednesday
weird
wholly
width
women
wrath
wreckage

yesterday
yield
yolk

Mechanics

Steps to Becoming a Better Speller

1. **Be patient.**
   Becoming a good speller takes time.

2. **Check the correct pronunciation of each word you are attempting to spell.**
   Knowing the correct pronunciation of a word can help you remember its spelling.

3. **Note the meaning and history of each word as you are checking the dictionary for pronunciation.**
   Knowing the meaning and history of a word provides you with a better notion of how the word is properly used, and this can help you remember its spelling.

4. **Before you close the dictionary, practice spelling the word.**
   Look away from the page and try to "see" the word in your mind. Then write it on a piece of paper. Check your spelling in the dictionary; repeat the process until you are able to spell the word correctly.

5. **Learn some spelling rules.**
   For four of the most useful rules, see page **664**.

6. **Make a list of the words that you often misspell.**
   Select the first 10 and practice spelling them.

   STEP A: Read each word carefully; then write it on a piece of paper. Check to see that you've spelled it correctly. Repeat this step for the words that you misspelled.

   STEP B: When you have finished your first 10 words, ask someone to read them to you as you write them again. Then check for misspellings. If you find none, congratulations! (Repeat both steps with your next 10 words, and so on.)

7. **Write often.**

"There is little point in learning to spell if you have little intention of writing."
—Frank Smith

Grammar Practice

Spelling 2

For each sentence below, fill in the blank with the correct word from the list of "Commonly Misspelled Words" (pages 666–667).

1. There is no s_____u__e for experience.

2. A graphing c_____r can help a student be more effective while taking the SAT test.

3. Planes were unable to land at LaGuardia due to poor v_____.

4. The best s_____v_____ I ever got was a postcard from the Taj Mahal.

5. Seth watched the hot-air balloon slowly d_____d upon the wheat field.

6. The rates listed include all taxes and s_____rs_____ all previous rates.

7. Lightning is a p_____v_____t weather event in the Upper Klamath Basin.

8. Mr. Penski consulted a l_____ about preparing his will.

9. The c_____y is a good place to gather information about a particular family's genealogy.

10. Malik's name was a_____d_____y omitted from the list.

Exercise

Write the words that result by combining the following base words and suffixes. Then write sentences that include them.

occur + ed   stub + ing   permit + ed

Test Prep!

Write the letter of the correct way to express each underlined part from the choices given on the next page. If it is already correct, choose "D."

The death of an <u>african american</u> teenager in 1955 contributed to one of the
(1)
most famous civil rights protests in history. On <u>August thirty-one</u> of that year, the
(2)
body of Emmett Till was found in the <u>tallahatchie river</u> near Money, Mississippi. He
(3)
had been murdered after <u>jokeingly whistling</u> at a white woman at a market.
(4)
The brutal death had a profound effect on Franklin McCain and three
other students at North Carolina A&T State University (<u>Established in 1891</u> as
(5)
Agricultural and Mechanical College for the Colored Race). On February 1, 1960,
they launched a peaceful protest against segregation in <u>the south</u>. They made small
(6)
purchases at a <u>Woolworth's store in greensboro, NC</u>, and then sat down at the store's
(7)
"whites-only" lunch counter. Police were unable to arrest the <u>four students</u> due to
(8)
a lack of provocation, but Woolworth's closed early that day to end the protest. The
men, known as the Greensboro Four, vowed to return.

For the next several days, the students returned, some wearing United States
Army <u>reserve officer training corps (ROTC)</u> uniforms, others wearing coats and ties.
(9)
Time after time, they were denied service, yet they sat peacefully until the store
closed. Soon national news <u>agencies</u> were covering the protest. <u>300</u> students were
(10) **(11)**
protesting at Woolworth's by February 5, <u>paralysing</u> the store's business and other
(12)
businesses nearby.

Similar sit-down demonstrations had spread <u>South to almost 40</u> other cities,
(13)
ultimately leading to desegregation at Woolworth's and other leading chains. This
series of protests, along with subsequent nonviolent demonstrations led by <u>heros</u>
(14)
such as <u>dr. Martin Luther King, jr.</u>, and others, inspired similar movements across
(15)
the country. Segregation as a way of life was <u>finally dieing</u>.
(16)

1
(A) african American
(B) African american
(C) African American
(D) correct as is

2
(A) Aug. thirty-one
(B) August 31
(C) Aug. 31
(D) correct as is

3
(A) Tallahatchie River
(B) Tallahatchie river
(C) tallahatchie River
(D) correct as is

4
(A) jokingly whistleing
(B) jokeingly whistleing
(C) jokingly whistling
(D) correct as is

5
(A) (established in 1891
(B) (Established in eighteen-ninety-one
(C) (established in eighteen ninety-one
(D) correct as is

6
(A) The south
(B) the South
(C) The South
(D) correct as is

7
(A) Woolworth's store in Greensboro, NC
(B) woolworth's store in Greensboro, NC
(C) Woolworth's store in Greensboro, North Carolina
(D) correct as is

8
(A) four studentes
(B) 4 studentes
(C) 4 students
(D) correct as is

9
(A) Reserve Officer training corps (ROtc)
(B) Reserve officer training corps (Rotc)
(C) Reserve Officer Training Corps (ROTC)
(D) correct as is

10
(A) agency's
(B) agencys
(C) agences
(D) correct as is

11
(A) Three Hundred
(B) Three hundred
(C) 3 hundred
(D) correct as is

12
(A) paralyzing
(B) paralizing
(C) paralyzeing
(D) correct as is

13
(A) South to almost forty
(B) S. to almost forty
(C) south to almost 40
(D) correct as is

14
(A) heroes
(B) hero's
(C) herose
(D) correct as is

15
(A) doctor Martin Luther King, Jr.
(B) Dr. Martin Luther King, junior
(C) Dr. Martin Luther King, Jr.
(D) correct as is

16
(A) finaly dying
(B) finally dying
(C) finaly dieing
(D) correct as is

Mechanics

Understanding Idioms

Idioms are phrases that are used in a special way. You can't understand an idiom just by knowing the meaning of each word in the phrase. You must learn it as a whole. For example, the idiom *bury the hatchet* means "to settle an argument," even though the individual words in the phrase mean something much different. This section will help you learn some of the common idioms in American English.

apple of his eye	**Eagle Lake is the** apple of his eye. (something he likes very much)
as plain as day	**The mistake in the ad was** as plain as day. (very clear)
as the crow flies	**New London is 200 miles from here** as the crow flies. (in a straight line)
at a snail's pace	**My last hour at work passes** at a snail's pace. (very, very slowly)
axe to grind	**The manager has an** axe to grind **with that umpire.** (disagreement to settle)
bad apple	**There are no** bad apples **in this class.** (bad influences)
beat around the bush	**Don't** beat around the bush; **answer the question.** (avoid getting to the point)
benefit of the doubt	**Everyone has been given the** benefit of the doubt **at least once.** (another chance)
beyond the shadow of a doubt	Beyond the shadow of a doubt, **this is my best science project.** (for certain)
blew my top	**When I saw the broken statue, I** blew my top. (showed great anger)
bone to pick	**Alison had a** bone to pick **with the student who copied her paper.** (problem to settle)
brain drain	Brain drain **is a serious problem in some states.** (the best students moving elsewhere)
break the ice	**The nervous ninth graders were afraid to** break the ice. (start a conversation)
burn the midnight oil	**Devon had to** burn the midnight oil **to finish his report.** (work late into the night)

bury the hatchet	**My sisters were told to** bury the hatchet **immediately.** (settle an argument)
by the skin of her teeth	**Sumey avoided an accident** by the skin of her teeth. (just barely)
champing at the bit	**The skiers were** champing at the bit **to get on the slopes.** (eager, excited)
chicken feed	**The prize was** chicken feed **to some people.** (not worth much money)
chip off the old block	**Frank's just like his father. He's a** chip off the old block. (just like someone else)
clean as a whistle	**My boss told me to make sure the place was as** clean as a whistle **before I left.** (very clean)
cold shoulder	**I wanted to fit in with that group, but they gave me the** cold shoulder. (ignored me)
crack of dawn	**Ali delivers his papers at the** crack of dawn. (first light of day, early morning)
cry wolf	**If you** cry wolf **too often, no one will believe you.** (say you are in trouble when you aren't)
dead of night	**Hearing a loud noise in the** dead of night **frightened Bill.** (middle of the night)
dirt cheap	**A lot of clothes at that store are** dirt cheap. (inexpensive, costing very little money)
doesn't hold a candle to	**That award** doesn't hold a candle to **a gold medal.** (is not as good as)
drop in the bucket	**The contributions were a** drop in the bucket. (a small amount compared to what's needed)
everything from A to Z	**That catalog lists** everything from A to Z. (a lot of different things)
face the music	**Todd had to** face the music **when he broke the window.** (deal with the punishment)
fish out of water	**He felt like a** fish out of water **in the new math class.** (someone in an unfamiliar place)
fit for a king	**The food at the athletic banquet was** fit for a king. (very special)

Idioms

flew off the handle	**Bill** flew off the handle **when he saw a reckless driver near the school.** (became very angry)
floating on air	**Celine was** floating on air **at the prom.** (feeling very happy)
food for thought	**The boys' foolish and dangerous prank gave us** food for thought. (something to think about)
get down to business	**After sharing several jokes, Mr. Sell said we should** get down to business. (start working)
get the upper hand	**The wrestler moved quickly on his opponent in order to** get the upper hand. (gain the advantage)
give their all	**Student volunteers** give their all **to help others.** (work as hard as they can)
go fly a kite	**Charlene stared at her nosy brother and said, "**Go fly a kite.**"** (go away)
has a green thumb	**Talk to Mrs. Smith about your sick plant. She** has a green thumb. (is good at growing plants)
has a heart of gold	**Joe** has a heart of gold. (is very kind and generous)
hit a home run	**Rhonda** hit a home run **with her speech.** (succeeded, or did well)
hit the ceiling	**When my parents saw my grades, they** hit the ceiling. (were very angry)
hit the hay	**Exhausted from the hike, Jamal** hit the hay **without eating supper.** (went to bed)
in a nutshell	**Can you,** in a nutshell, **tell us your goals for this year?** (in summary)
in one ear and out the other	**Sharl, concerned about her pet, let the lecture go** in one ear and out the other. (without really listening)
in the black	**My aunt's gift shop is finally** in the black. (making money)
in the nick of time	**Janelle caught the falling vase** in the nick of time. (just in time)
in the red	**Many businesses start out** in the red. (in debt)
in the same boat	**The new tax bill meant everyone would be** in the same boat. (in a similar situation)

iron out	**Joe will meet with the work crew to** iron out **their complaints.** (solve, work out)
it goes without saying	It goes without saying **that saving money is a good idea.** (it is clear)
it stands to reason	It stands to reason **that your stamina will increase if you run every day.** (it makes sense)
keep a stiff upper lip	Keep a stiff upper lip **when you visit the doctor.** (be brave)
keep it under your hat	Keep it under your hat **about the pop quiz.** (don't tell anyone)
knock on wood	**My uncle** knocked on wood **after he said he had never had the flu.** (did something for good luck)
knuckle down	**After wasting half the day, we were told to** knuckle down. (work hard)
learn the ropes	**It takes every new employee a few months to** learn the ropes. (get to know how things are done)
leave no stone unturned	**The police plan to** leave no stone unturned **at the crime scene.** (check everything)
lend someone a hand	**You will feel good if you** lend someone a hand. (help someone)
let the cat out of the bag	**Tom** let the cat out of the bag **during lunch.** (told a secret)
let's face it	Let's face it. **You don't like rap.** (let's admit it)
look high and low	**We** looked high and low **for Jan's dog.** (looked everywhere)
lose face	**In some cultures, it is very bad to** lose face. (be embarrassed)
needle in a haystack	**Trying to find a person in New York is like trying to find a** needle in a haystack. (something impossible to find)
nose to the grindstone	**With all of these assignments, I have to keep my** nose to the grindstone. (work hard)
on cloud nine	**After talking to my girlfriend, I was** on cloud nine. (feeling very happy)
on pins and needles	**Emiko was** on pins and needles **during the championship game.** (feeling nervous)

Idioms

out the window	**Once the rain started, our plans were** out the window. (ruined)
over and above	Over and above **the required work, Will cleaned up the lab.** (in addition to)
pain in the neck	**Franklin knew the report would be a** pain in the neck. (very annoying)
pull your leg	**Cary was only** pulling your leg. (telling you a little lie as a joke)
put his foot in his mouth	**Lane** put his foot in his mouth **when he answered the question.** (said something embarrassing)
put the cart before the horse	**Tonya** put the cart before the horse **when she sealed the envelope before inserting the letter.** (did something in the wrong order)
put your best foot forward	**When applying for a job, you should** put your best foot forward. (do the best that you can do)
red-letter day	**Sovann had a** red-letter day **because she did so well on her math test.** (very good day)
rock the boat	**I was told not to** rock the boat. (cause trouble)
rude awakening	**Jake will have a** rude awakening **when he sees the bill for his computer.** (sudden, unpleasant surprise)
save face	**His gift was clearly an attempt to** save face. (fix an embarrassing situation)
see eye to eye	**We** see eye to eye **about the need for a new school.** (are in agreement)
shake a leg	**I told Mako to** shake a leg **so that we wouldn't be late.** (hurry)
shift into high gear	**Greg had to** shift into high gear **to finish the test in time.** (speed up, hurry)
sight for sore eyes	**My grandmother's smiling face was a** sight for sore eyes. (good to see)
sight unseen	**Liz bought the coat** sight unseen. (without seeing it first)
sink or swim	**Whether you** sink or swim **in school depends on your study habits.** (fail or succeed)

spilled the beans	Suddenly, Kesia realized that she had spilled the beans. (revealed a secret)
spring chicken	Although Mr. Gordon isn't a spring chicken, he sure knows how to talk to kids. (young person)
stick to your guns	Know what you believe, and stick to your guns. (don't change your mind)
sweet tooth	Chocolate is often the candy of choice for those with a sweet tooth. (a love for sweets, like candy and cake)
take a dim view	My sister will take a dim view of that movie. (disapprove)
take it with a grain of salt	When you read that advertisement, take it with a grain of salt. (don't believe everything)
take the bull by the horns	It's time to take the bull by the horns so the project gets done on time. (take control)
through thick and thin	Those two girls have remained friends through thick and thin. (in good times and in bad times)
time flies	Time flies as you grow older. (time passes quickly)
time to kill	Grace had time to kill, so she read a book. (extra time)
to go overboard	The class was told not to go overboard. A $50.00 donation was fine. (to do too much)
toe the line	The new teacher made everyone toe the line. (follow the rules)
tongue-tied	He can talk easily with friends, but in class he is usually tongue-tied. (not knowing what to say)
turn over a new leaf	He decided to turn over a new leaf in school. (make a new start)
two peas in a pod	Ever since kindergarten, Lil and Eve have been like two peas in a pod. (very much alike)
under the weather	Guy was feeling under the weather this morning. (sick)
wallflower	Cho knew the other girls thought she was a wallflower. (a shy person)
word of mouth	Joseph learns a lot about his favorite team by word of mouth. (talking with other people)

Idioms

Using the Right Word

a lot ■ *A lot* (always two words) is a vague descriptive phrase that should be used sparingly.

"You can observe a lot just by watching."

—Yogi Berra

accept, except ■ The verb *accept* means "to receive" or "to believe"; the preposition *except* means "other than."

The principal accepted the boy's story about the broken window, but she asked why no one except him saw the ball accidentally slip from his hand.

adapt, adopt ■ *Adapt* means "to adjust or change to fit"; *adopt* means "to choose and treat as your own" (a child, an idea).

After a lengthy period of study, Malcolm X adopted the Islamic faith and adapted to its lifestyle.

affect, effect ■ The verb *affect* means "to influence"; the verb *effect* means "to produce, accomplish, complete."

Ming's hard work effected an A on the test, which positively affected her semester grade.

The noun *effect* means the "result."

Good grades have a calming effect on parents.

aisle, isle ■ An *aisle* is a passage between seats; an *isle* is a small island.

Many airline passengers on their way to the Isle of Capri prefer an aisle seat.

all right ■ *All right* is always two words (not *alright*).

allusion, illusion ■ *Allusion* is an indirect reference to someone or something; *illusion* is a false picture or idea.

My little sister, under the illusion that she's movie-star material, makes frequent allusions to her future fans.

already, all ready ■ *Already* is an adverb meaning "before this time" or "by this time." *All ready* is an adjective meaning "fully prepared."

Note: Use *all ready* if you can substitute *ready* alone in the sentence.

Although I've already had some dessert, I am all ready for some ice cream from the street vendor.

Grammar Practice

Using the Right Word 1

accept, except; adapt, adopt; **affect, effect;** allusion, illusion

 If an underlined word in the following paragraphs is used incorrectly, write the correct word. If it's correct as is, write "OK."

As my thirteenth birthday approached, my parents asked me what I'd like. "I don't want anything **(1)** accept a dog," I replied. I knew it was pointless to say, for I'd been saying it since I was five years old and had never gotten one. Although I *could* **(2)** except that I would never have a dog, I persisted in bringing it up.

Well, my efforts to wear them down must finally have had an **(3)** affect. The morning of December 19, Mom told me to get my coat on; they had a surprise for me. When we pulled into the lot of the animal shelter, I thought it was some kind of **(4)** allusion. I was in utter disbelief that, after so many years of badgering, we were really going to **(5)** adopt a dog!

The handlers at the shelter warned us that it might take several weeks for our chosen dog to **(6)** adopt to her new surroundings. Though she was a fairly young dog, this period of adjustment might **(7)** affect her training somewhat. At this point, Mom and Dad made a thinly veiled **(8)** illusion to books at the library about training dogs. The new dog was going to be *my* responsibility, and they were showing me that they now trusted me enough to indulge my longing for my very own dog. It was the best birthday gift in the world.

Model

Model the following sentences to practice using the words *accept* and *except* correctly.

If you don't accept responsibility for your own actions, then you are forever chained to a position of defense.
—Holly Lisle, *Fire in the Mist*

Use what talents you possess: The woods would be very silent if no birds sang there except those that sang best.
—Henry Van Dyke

Right Word

altogether, all together ■ *Altogether* means "entirely." The phrase *all together* means "in a group" or "all at once."

> "There is altogether too much gridlock," complained the Democrats. All together, the Republicans yelled, "No way!"

among, between ■ *Among* is typically used when speaking of more than two persons or things. *Between* is used when speaking of only two.

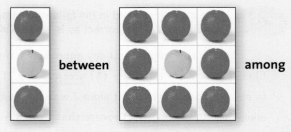

between   among

> The three of us talked among ourselves to decide between going out or eating in.

amount, number ■ *Amount* is used for bulk measurement. *Number* is used to count separate units. (See also *fewer, less.*)

> A substantial amount of honey spilled all over a number of my CD's.

annual, biannual, semiannual, biennial, perennial ■ An *annual* event happens once every year. A *biannual* or *semiannual* event happens twice a year. A *biennial* event happens every two years. A *perennial* event is one that is persistent or constant.

> Dad's annual family reunion gets bigger every year.
> We're going shopping at the department store's semiannual white sale.
> Due to dwindling attendance, the county fair is now a biennial celebration.
> A perennial plant persists for several years.

anyway ■ Do not add an *s* to *anyway.*

ascent, assent ■ *Ascent* is the act of rising or climbing; *assent* is "to agree to something after some consideration" (or such an agreement).

> We completed our ascent of the butte with the assent of the landowner.

bad, badly ■ *Bad* is an adjective. *Badly* is an adverb.

> This apple is bad, but one bad apple doesn't always ruin the whole bushel.
> In today's game, Sumey passed badly.

base, bass ■ *Base* is the foundation or the lower part of something. *Bass* (pronounced like *base*) is a deep sound. *Bass* (pronounced like *class*) is a fish.

> A car's wheel base is the distance between the centers of the front and rear wheels.
> Luther is the bass player in his bluegrass band.

beside, besides ■ *Beside* means "by the side of." *Besides* means "in addition to."

> Mother always grew roses beside the trash bin. Besides looking nice, they also gave off a sweet smell that masked odors.

Grammar Practice

Using the Right Word 2

among, between; amount, number; **ascent, assent;** bad, badly; **base, bass**

 Write the correct word from each choice given in parentheses.

1. The choir director placed Dario, a *(base, bass)*, *(among, between)* two altos.

2. "I will give my *(ascent, assent)* to your sneaky little plan," snorted the troll, "provided that my share is the greatest *(amount, number)* of your haul."

3. Maya wanted to reach the summit so *(bad, badly)* that her *(ascent, assent)* did not seem difficult at all.

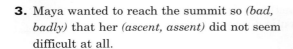

ascent

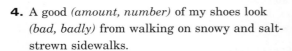

assent

4. A good *(amount, number)* of my shoes look *(bad, badly)* from walking on snowy and salt-strewn sidewalks.

5. Ms. Sawyer selected the trophy with the heaviest *(base, bass)* from *(among, between)* the half-dozen in the display case.

6. I don't think I did too *(bad, badly)* on today's test, but my grade will depend on the *(amount, number)* of others who did well.

7. Several largemouth *(base, bass)* were swimming in the aquarium *(among, between)* catfish, bream, and bluegill.

8. Grandmother Hughes would never *(ascent, assent)* to selling her property— for any *(amount, number)* of money.

Model

Model the following sentences to practice using the words *bad* and *badly* correctly.

Life is a moderately good play with a badly written third act.

—Truman Capote

One of the keys to happiness is a bad memory.

—Rita Mae Brown

Right Word

board, bored ■ *Board* is a piece of wood. *Board* is also an administrative group or council.

> The school board approved the purchase of fifty 1- by 6-inch pine boards.

Bored is the past tense of the verb "bore," which may mean "to make a hole by drilling" or "to become weary out of dullness."

> Watching television bored Joe, so he took his drill and bored a hole in the wall where he could hang his new clock.

bored

brake, break ■ *Brake* is a device used to stop a vehicle. *Break* means "to separate or to destroy."

> I hope the brakes on my car never break.

board

bring, take ■ *Bring* suggests the action is directed toward the speaker; *take* suggests the action is directed away from the speaker.

> Bring home some garbage bags so I can take the trash outside.

can, may ■ *Can* suggests ability while *may* suggests permission.

> "Can I go to the mall?" means "Am I physically able to go to the mall?"
>
> "May I go to the mall?" asks permission to go.

capital, capitol ■ The noun *capital* refers to a city or to money. The adjective *capital* means "major or important." *Capitol* refers to a building.

> The state capital is home to the capitol building for a capital reason. The state government contributed capital for its construction.

cent, sent, scent ■ *Cent* is a coin; *sent* is the past tense of the verb "send"; *scent* is an odor or a smell.

> For forty-one cents, I sent my girlfriend a mushy love poem in a perfumed envelope. She adored the scent but hated the poem.

cereal, serial ■ *Cereal* is a grain, often made into breakfast food. *Serial* relates to something in a series.

> Mohammed enjoys reading serial novels while he eats a bowl of cereal.

chord, cord ■ *Chord* may mean "an emotion" or "a combination of musical tones sounded at the same time." A *cord* is a string or a rope.

> The guitar player strummed the opening chord to the group's hit song, which struck a responsive chord with the audience.

chose, choose ■ *Chose (choz)* is the past tense of the verb *choose (chooz)*.

> Last quarter I chose to read Chitra Divakaruni's *The Unknown Errors of Our Lives*—a fascinating book about Indian immigrants.

Grammar Practice

Using the Right Word 3

bring, take; capital, capitol; cereal, serial; chose, choose

 Select the correct word from the list above to complete each sentence.

1. Veterinarians recommend pet foods without a lot of _____ fillers.

2. "Regina, dear, will you please _____ me an aspirin?" Grandpa asked.

3. Ignacio _____ an electric blue tuxedo for prom.

4. Amber wanted to _____ my black rain umbrella to the beach.

5. A _____ cause of traffic backups in this town is the preponderance of one-way streets.

6. You must have your product's _____ number on hand before talking to the service department personnel.

7. Between 1926 and 1929, Cuba's _____ was built by 8,000 specialized workers.

8. In the near future, you may have to _____ between fingerprint and iris identification rather than a government-issued ID.

Model

Model the following sentences to practice using the words *can* and *may* correctly.

> My spoon is poised over my just-poured-the-milk-in bowl of cereal as she asks if I can go over a few revisions.
> —Peter Bowerman, *The Well-Fed Writer*

> I can start working on my research paper tomorrow if I may borrow your in-line skates to get to the library.

Right Word

coarse, course ■ *Coarse* means "rough or crude"; *course* means "a path or direction taken." *Course* also means "a class or a series of studies."

> Fletcher, known for using coarse language, was barred from the golf course until he took an etiquette course.

complement, compliment ■ *Complement* refers to that which completes or fulfills. *Compliment* is an expression of admiration or praise.

> Kimberly smiled, thinking she had received a compliment when Carlos said that her new Chihuahua complemented her personality.

continual, continuous ■ *Continual* refers to something that happens again and again with some breaks or pauses; *continuous* refers to something that keeps happening, uninterrupted.

> Sunlight hits Iowa on a continual basis; sunlight hits Earth continuously.

counsel, council ■ When used as a noun, *counsel* means "advice"; when used as a verb, it means "to advise." *Council* refers to a group that advises.

> The student council counseled all freshmen to join a school club. That's good counsel.

desert, dessert ■ The noun *desert (dĕz´ərt)* refers to barren wilderness. *Dessert (dĭ zûrt´)* is food served at the end of a meal.

> The scorpion tiptoed through the moonlit desert, searching for dessert.

The verb *desert (dĭ zûrt´)* means "to abandon"; the noun *desert (dĭ zûrt´)* means "deserved reward or punishment."

> The burglar's hiding place deserted him when the spotlight swung his way; his subsequent arrest was his just desert.

die, dye ■ *Die* (dying) means "to stop living." *Dye* (dyeing) is used to change the color of something.

different from, different than ■ Use *different from* in a comparison of two things. *Different than* should be used only when followed by a clause.

> Yassine is quite different from his brother.
> Life is different than it used to be.

farther, further ■ *Farther* refers to a physical distance; *further* refers to additional time, quantity, or degree.

> Alaska extends farther north than Iceland does. Further information can be obtained in an atlas.

fewer, less ■ *Fewer* refers to the number of separate units; *less* refers to bulk quantity.

> Because we have fewer orders for cakes, we'll buy less sugar and flour.

Grammar Practice

Using the Right Word 4

coarse, course; complement, compliment; continual, continuous;
different from, different than; farther, further

 If an underlined word is used incorrectly, write the correct word. If it's correct as is, write "OK."

1. Studies show that a woman accepts a <u>compliment</u> with more ease than a man does.

2. Kure Island, Hawaii, and Elliot Key, Florida, are <u>further</u> from each other than any other United States locations.

3. "You will be punished for the use of any <u>course</u> language in this classroom," the new teacher warned.

4. "At this factory, we use a secret process <u>different from</u> anyone else uses," the line manager boasted.

5. The <u>continual</u> revisions that software undergoes makes it hard to keep up with the latest versions.

6. Upon <u>further</u> investigation, the detectives discovered that Mr. Dall was not the man they thought he was.

7. I think au gratin potatoes are the perfect <u>compliment</u> to roast pork.

8. Have you ever run an obstacle <u>coarse</u> (besides the one in your room)?

9. The <u>continual</u> tinkling of the chimes was an indicator of the wind's staying power that stormy afternoon.

10. Though they appear similar, this pen is quite <u>different than</u> that one.

Model

Model the following sentences to practice using the words *continual* and *continuous* correctly.

Continual improvement is an unending journey.
    —Lloyd Dobens and Clare Crawford-Mason, *Thinking About Quality*

The self is not something ready-made but something in continuous formation through choice of action.
                                                                —John Dewey

flair, flare ■ *Flair* refers to style or natural talent; *flare* means "to light up quickly" or "burst out" (or an object that does so).

> Ronni was thrilled with Jorge's flair for decorating—until one of his strategically placed candles flared, marring the wall.

good, well ■ *Good* is an adjective; *well* is nearly always an adverb. (When *well* is used to describe a state of health, it is an adjective: He was happy to be *well* again.)

> The CD player works well.

> Our team looks good this season.

heal, heel ■ *Heal* means "to mend or restore to health." A *heel* is the back part of a foot.

> Achilles died because a poison arrow pierced his heel and caused a wound that would not heal.

healthful, healthy ■ *Healthful* means "causing or improving health"; *healthy* means "possessing health."

> Healthful foods build healthy bodies.

hear, here ■ You *hear* with your ears. *Here* means "the area close by."

heard, herd ■ *Heard* is the past tense of the verb "hear"; *herd* is a large group of animals.

hole, whole ■ A *hole* is a cavity or hollow place. *Whole* means "complete."

idle, idol ■ *Idle* means "not working." An *idol* is someone or something that is worshipped.

> The once-popular actress, who had been idle lately, wistfully recalled her days as an idol.

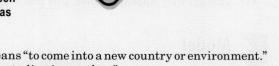

hear

PLACE SHOPPING CARTS HERE

immigrate, emigrate ■ *Immigrate* means "to come into a new country or environment." *Emigrate* means "to go out of one country to live in another."

> Martin Ulferts immigrated to this country in 1882. He was only three years old when he emigrated from Germany.

imply, infer ■ *Imply* means "to suggest or express indirectly"; *infer* means "to draw a conclusion from facts." (A writer or speaker implies; a reader or listener infers.)

> Dad implied by his comment that I should drive more carefully, and I inferred that he was concerned for both me and his new car.

Grammar Practice

Using the Right Word 5

flair, flare; good, well; **healthful, healthy;** immigrate, emigrate; **imply, infer**

 Write the correct choice from those given in parentheses.

One of my neighbors, Mr. Blagovitch, **(1)** *(immigrated, emigrated)* from his native Ukraine when he was only three years old, so he doesn't remember it at all. His parents worked hard to provide a good life for their family in Chicago. His mother had a **(2)** *(flair, flare)* for cooking **(3)** *(healthful, healthy)*, stick-to-the-ribs food and found work in a local ethnic restaurant. His father was **(4)** *(good, well)* at making things grow and began his own landscaping company.

At one point, Mr. Blagovitch was not doing **(5)** *(good, well)* in school. His mother admonished, "We did not **(6)** *(emigrate, immigrate)* to this country to see you fail!" His father's temper **(7)** *(flaired, flared)*. In terse sentences, he **(8)** *(implied, inferred)* that his son had better shape up . . . or else.

Mr. Blagovitch did not even attempt to **(9)** *(imply, infer)* what his father meant by "or else"; he knew from experience it would not be **(10)** *(good, well)*. It took just that one vague threat from his **(11)** *(healthful, healthy)*, muscled father to get Mr. Blagovitch back on track. He improved his grades and even discovered his **(12)** *(flair, flare)* for music, which ultimately led him to make a career of it.

Model

Model the following sentences to practice using the words *flair* and *flare* correctly.

> I have long thought that her flair for melodrama has been wasted on her usual audience, a family that has more often called for the hook than begged for an encore.
> —Jan Burke, *Liar*

> The sailor dropped the flare to the deck, and almost instantly it began to shine with a tremendous light, the heat radiating out to unbearable levels, and toxic fumes spewing forth.
> —Gregory A. Freeman, *Sailors to the End*

Right Word

insure, ensure ■ *Insure* means "to secure from financial harm or loss." *Ensure* means "to make certain of something."

> To ensure that you can legally drive that new car, you'll have to insure it.

it's, its ■ *It's* is the contraction of "it is." *Its* is the possessive form of "it."

> It's hard to believe, but the movie *Shrek* still holds its appeal for many kids.

later, latter ■ *Later* means "after a period of time." *Latter* refers to the second of two things mentioned.

> Later that year we had our second baby and adopted a stray kitten. The latter
> was far more welcomed by our toddler.

lay, lie ■ *Lay* means "to place." *Lay* is a transitive verb. (See **716.1**.)

> Lay your books on the big table.

Lie means "to recline," and *lay* is the past tense of *lie*. *Lie* is an intransitive verb. (See **716.1**.)

> In this heat, the children must lie down for a nap. Yesterday they lay down without one
> complaint. Sometimes they have lain in the hammocks to rest.

lead, led ■ *Lead (lēd)* is the present tense of the verb meaning "to guide." The past tense of the verb is *led (lĕd)*. The noun *lead (lĕd)* is a metal.

> We were led along the path that leads to an abandoned lead mine.

learn, teach ■ *Learn* means "to acquire information." *Teach* means "to give information."

> I learn better when people teach with real-world examples.

leave, let ■ *Leave* means "to allow something to remain behind." *Let* means "to permit."

> Would you let me leave my bike at your house?

lend, borrow ■ *Lend* means "to give for temporary use." *Borrow* means "to receive for temporary use."

> I told Mom I needed to borrow $18 for a CD, but she
> said she could lend only money for school supplies.

She lends.

He borrows.

like, as ■ When *like* is used as a preposition meaning "similar to," it can be followed only by a noun, pronoun, or noun phrase; when *as* is used as a subordinating conjunction, it introduces a subordinate clause.

> You could become a gymnast like her, as you work and practice hard.

medal, meddle ■ *Medal* is an award. *Meddle* means "to interfere."

> Some parents meddle in the awards process to be sure that their kids get medals.

Grammar Practice

Using the Right Word 6

insure, ensure; it's, its; **lay, lie;** leave, let; **like, as;** medal, meddle

 Write the correct choice from those given in each set of numbered parentheses.

Last weekend I got in a little fender-bender accident on my way home. My great-grandmother, an ancient religious woman, told me, "**(1)** *(It's, Its)* not just luck that it wasn't worse. The St. Christopher **(2)** *(medal, meddle)* that I gave you **(3)** *(insured, ensured)* your safety."

"Oh," I replied. "I was going to ask you why you would **(4)** *(leave, let)* something **(5)** *(like, as)* that in my car. Well, thanks, Grandma. I'm exhausted. I'm going to go **(6)** *(lay, lie)* down now."

Then my dad said, "You better start praying that you find another company to **(7)** *(insure, ensure)* your car. We're not going to keep somebody who drives **(8)** *(like, as)* you do on our policy anymore."

"The accident wasn't my fault, Dad! The car's not damaged badly; there's just a dent in **(9)** *(it's, its)* rear panel," I said. "I won't even file a claim."

My mom entered the fray. "That sounds reasonable, Tom. **(10)** *(Leave, Let)* her drive around in a dented car."

"I'd rather you didn't **(11)** *(medal, meddle)* in this conversation, Dee," he fumed. "We need to **(12)** *(lay, lie)* down some rules now!" And, just like that, I'm in the market for my own insurance. Got any advice?

Model

Model the following sentences to practice using the words *lay* and *lie* correctly.

> [People] who get sleepy at night should have a simple, decent place to lay their heads, on terms they can afford to pay.
> —Millard Fuller, founder of Habitat for Humanity

> A man with ambition and love for his blessings here on earth is ever so alive. Having been alive, it won't be so hard in the end to lie down and rest.
> —Pearl Bailey

Right Word

metal, mettle ■ *Metal* is a chemical element like iron or gold. *Mettle* is "strength of spirit."

> **Grandad's mettle during battle left him with some metal in his shoulder.**

miner, minor ■ A *miner* digs for valuable ore. A *minor* is a person who is not legally an adult. A *minor* problem is one of no great importance.

moral, morale ■ A *moral* is a lesson drawn from a story; as an adjective, it relates to the principles of right and wrong. *Morale* refers to someone's attitude.

> **Ms. Ladue considers it her moral obligation to go to church every day.**
> **The students' morale sank after their defeat in the forensics competition.**

passed, past ■ *Passed* is a verb. *Past* can be used as a noun, an adjective, or a preposition.

> **That old pickup truck passed my sports car! (verb)**
> **Many senior citizens hold dearly to the past. (noun)**
> **Tilly's past life as a circus worker must have been . . . interesting. (adjective)**
> **Who can walk past a bakery without looking in the window? (preposition)**

peace, piece ■ *Peace* means "tranquility or freedom from war." *Piece* is a part or fragment.

> **Grandma sits in the peace and quiet of the parlor, enjoying a piece of pie.**

peak, peek, pique ■ A *peak* is a high point. *Peek* means "brief look" (or "look briefly"). *Pique,* as a verb, means "to excite by challenging"; as a noun, it is a feeling of resentment.

> **The peak of Dr. Fedder's professional life was his ability to pique children's interest in his work. "Peek at this slide," he said to the eager students.**

pedal, peddle, petal ■ A *pedal* is a foot lever; as a verb, it means "to ride a bike." *Peddle* means "to go from place to place selling something." A *petal* is part of a flower.

> **Don Miller paints beautiful petals on his homemade birdhouses. Then he pedals through the flea market every weekend to peddle them.**

personal, personnel ■ *Personal* means "private." *Personnel* are people working at a particular job.

plain, plane ■ *Plain* means "an area of land that is flat or level"; it also means "clearly seen or clearly understood."

> **It's plain to see why settlers of the Great Plains had trouble moving west.**

Plane means "flat, level"; it is also a tool used to smooth the surface of wood.

> **I used a plane to make the board plane and smooth.**

Grammar Practice

Using the Right Word 7

metal, mettle; *moral, morale;* **peace, piece;** *peak, peek, pique;* **plain, plane**

 Select the correct word from the list above to complete each sentence. (One word is used twice.)

1. The _____ and quiet of the isolated meadow made her worries dissolve.

2. Each _____ on an electrocardiogram shows a specific electrical activity of the heart.

3. I could see that Jay's _____ was low by his slow gait and sagging shoulders.

4. "Ferrous" means "containing iron"; please give an example of a nonferrous _____ .

5. The group of kids near his new school seemed unfriendly, so Jerry was careful not to _____ them.

6. The choir director told us to wear _____ white shirts for the concert.

7. The dog proved its _____ as it chased the burglar from the house.

8. I hate it when the doctor says, "Let's take a _____ in your ear."

9. Is the study of medical ethics a purely _____ issue?

10. Funding has been cut, and every agency wants its _____ of the pie.

11. In the story of the prodigal son, did the son who had remained at home show any _____ at the father's lavish treatment of the other?

12. By definition, a pebble-textured tabletop does not have a _____ surface.

◤ Model

Model these sentences to practice using *moral* and *morale* correctly.

> It is curious that physical courage should be so common in the world and moral courage so rare.
> —Mark Twain

> Eating well gives a spectacular joy to life and contributes immensely to goodwill and happy companionship. It is of great importance to the morale.
> —Elsa Schiaparelli, *Shocking Life*

Right Word

poor, pour, pore ■ *Poor* means "needy or pitiable." *Pour* means "to cause to flow in a stream." A *pore* is an opening in the skin.

Tough exams on late spring days make my poor pores pour sweat.

principal, principle ■ As an adjective, *principal* means "primary." As a noun, it can mean "a school administrator" or "a sum of money." *Principle* means "idea or doctrine."

His principal concern is fitness. (adjective) The principal retired. (noun)
During the first year of a loan, you pay more interest than principal. (noun)
The principle of *caveat emptor* is "Let the buyer beware."

quiet, quit, quite ■ *Quiet* is the opposite of "noisy." *Quit* means "to stop." *Quite* means "completely or entirely."

quote, quotation ■ *Quote* is a verb; *quotation* is a noun.

The quotation I used was from Woody Allen. You may quote me on that.

real, really, very ■ Do not use *real* in place of the adverbs *very* or *really*.

Mother's cake is usually very (not *real*) tasty, but this one is really stale!

right, write, wright, rite ■ *Right* means "correct or proper"; it also refers to that which a person has a legal claim to, as in copyright. *Write* means "to inscribe or record." A *wright* is a person who makes or builds something. *Rite* refers to a ritual or ceremonial act.

Write this down: It is the right of the shipwright to perform the rite of christening—breaking a bottle of champagne on the stern of the ship.

ring, wring ■ *Ring* means "encircle" or "to sound by striking." *Wring* means "to squeeze or twist."

At the beach, Grandma would ring her head with a large scarf. Once, it blew into the sea, so she had me wring it out.

scene, seen ■ *Scene* refers to the setting or location where something happens; it also may mean "sight or spectacle." *Seen* is a form of the verb "see."

Serena had seen her boyfriend making a scene; she cringed.

seam, seem ■ *Seam* (noun) is a line formed by connecting two pieces. *Seem* (verb) means "to appear to exist."

The ragged seams in his old coat seem to match the creases in his face.

set, sit ■ *Set* means "to place." *Sit* means "to put the body in a seated position." *Set* is transitive; *sit* is intransitive. (See **716.1.**)

How can you just sit there and watch as I set all these chairs in place?

Grammar Practice

Using the Right Word 8

quote, quotation; real, really, very; **right, write, rite;** set, sit

 If an underlined word is used incorrectly, write the correct word. If it's correct as is, write "OK."

1. If I <u>sit</u> the monitor on this shelf, there's no room for the tower.

2. My dad is fond of this Yogi Berra <u>quote</u>: "You can observe a lot just by watching."

3. The bristlecone pines of California's White Mountains are <u>really</u> ancient trees.

4. Lissa is definitely <u>rite</u> when she says she needs a vacation.

5. If you <u>quote</u> a source in a research paper, you must include a reference to that source.

6. Dwayne tried to tell his little sister that the "monster" under her bed was not <u>real</u>.

7. Some college students see a trip to some place that's warm as an annual <u>right</u> of spring.

8. Dr. Levine had a <u>real</u> rough night in the emergency room.

9. When you receive unsatisfactory service from a company, often the best tactic is to <u>write</u> a letter of complaint.

10. "Please have a seat in the waiting room" loosely translates to "<u>Set</u> and wait for a long time."

 ## Model

Model the following sentences to practice using the words *set* and *sit* correctly.

Givers have to set limits because takers rarely do.
                                                        —Irma Kurtz

Even if you're on the right track, you'll get run over if you just sit there.
                                                        —Will Rogers

Right Word

sight, cite, site ■ *Sight* means "the act of seeing"; a *sight* is what is seen. *Cite* means "to quote" or "to summon," as before a court. *Site* means "location."

> In her report, the general contractor cited several problems at the downtown job site. For one, the loading area was a chaotic sight.

sole, soul ■ *Sole* means "single, only one"; *sole* also refers to the bottom surface of the foot. *Soul* refers to the spiritual part of a person.

> As the sole inhabitant of the island, he put his heart and soul into his farming.

stationary, stationery ■ *Stationary* means "not movable"; *stationery* refers to the paper and envelopes used to write letters.

steal, steel ■ *Steal* means "to take something without permission"; *steel* is a type of metal.

> It takes nerves of steel to brazenly steal another's possessions in broad daylight.

than, then ■ *Than* is used in a comparison; *then* tells when.

> Abigail shouted that her big brother was bigger than my big brother. Then she ran away.

their, there, they're ■ *Their* is a possessive personal pronoun. *There* is an adverb used to point out location. *They're* is the contraction for "they are."

> They're a well-dressed couple. Do you see them there, with their matching jackets?

threw, through ■ *Threw* is the past tense of "throw." *Through* means "from beginning to end."

> Through seven innings, Daisha threw just seven strikes.

to, too, two ■ *To* is a preposition that can mean "in the direction of." *To* is also used to form an infinitive. (See **726.2**) *Too* means "also" or "very." *Two* is a number.

vain, vane, vein ■ *Vain* means "valueless or fruitless"; it may also mean "holding a high regard for oneself." *Vane* is a flat piece of material set up to show which way the wind blows. *Vein* refers to a blood vessel or a mineral deposit.

> The vain prospector, boasting about the vein of silver he'd uncovered, paused to look up at the turning weather vane.

vary, very ■ *Vary* means "to change." *Very* means "to a high degree."

> Though the weather may vary from day to day, generally, it is very pleasant.

Grammar Practice

Using the Right Word 9

sight, cite, site; sole, soul; than, then; vain, vane, vein; vary, very

 Write the correct choice from those given in parentheses.

1. Kris has a *(vain, vein)* in her temple that begins to throb when she is angry.

2. A neighbor was *(sighted, cited)* for disturbing the peace after a loud party.

3. The air is *(vary, very)* cold, but the ice on the lake hasn't frozen solid yet.

4. Some people who've had near-death experiences report seeing their *(soles, souls)* as balls of bright light.

5. Turn left and *(than, then)* take an immediate right onto Hayes Road.

6. Decorative weather *(vanes, veins)* sell well at county fairs.

7. The ship's captain was alerted by the lookout who had *(sighted, sited)* land.

8. Anyone who thinks all fashion models are *(vain, vane)* hasn't met Kat Stevens.

9. On a long car trip, I would rather listen to a book on CD *(than, then) to* music or talk radio.

10. Jacinda's nervousness at being the *(sole, soul)* presenter at the awards ceremony was evident.

11. Although your mileage may *(vary, very)*, this model typically gets about 30 mpg on the highway.

12. Pete and his friends chose a grassy, level *(sight, site)* to pitch their tent.

Model

Model the following sentences to practice using the words *sole* and *soul* correctly.

> The keenest sorrow is to recognize ourselves as the sole cause of all our adversities.
>
> —Sophocles

> Nothing contributes so much to tranquilizing the mind as a steady purpose—a point on which the soul may fix its intellectual eye.
>
> —Mary Wollstonecraft Shelley

Right Word

vial, vile ■ A *vial* is a small container for liquid. *Vile* is an adjective meaning "foul, despicable."

It's a vile job, but someone has to clean these lab vials.

waste

waist, waste ■ *Waist* is the part of the body just above the hips. The verb *waste* means "to spend or use carelessly" or "to wear away or decay"; the noun *waste* refers to material that is unused or useless.

Her waist is small because she wastes no opportunity to exercise.

waist

wait, weight ■ *Wait* means "to stay somewhere expecting something." *Weight* refers to a degree or unit of heaviness.

ware, wear, where ■ *Ware* refers to a product that is sold; *wear* means "to have on or to carry on one's body"; *where* asks "in what place?" or "in what situation?"

The designer boasted, "Where can anybody wear my ware? Anywhere."

way, weigh ■ *Way* means "path or route." *Weigh* means "to measure weight" or "to have a certain heaviness."

My dogs weigh too much. The best way to reduce is a daily run in the park.

weather, whether ■ *Weather* refers to the condition of the atmosphere. *Whether* refers to a possibility.

Due to the weather, the coach wondered whether he should cancel the meet.

which, that ■ Use *which* to refer to objects or animals in a nonrestrictive clause (set off with commas). Use *that* to refer to objects or animals in a restrictive clause. (For more information about these types of clauses, see **612.2**.)

The birds, which stay in the area all winter, know where the feeders are located.
The food that attracts the most birds is sunflower seed.

who, whom ■ Use *who* to refer to people. *Who* is used as the subject of a verb in an independent clause or in a relative clause. *Whom* is used as the object of a preposition or as a direct object.

To whom do we owe our thanks for these pizzas? And who ordered anchovies?

who's, whose ■ *Who's* is the contraction for "who is." *Whose* is a pronoun that can show possession or ownership.

Cody, whose car is new, will drive. Who's going to read the map?

your, you're ■ *Your* is a possessive pronoun. *You're* is the contraction for "you are."

Take your boots if you're going out in that snow.

Grammar Practice

Using the Right Word 10

vial, vile; weather, whether; **which, that;** who, whom; **your, you're**

 First decide which pair of words from above belongs in each sentence. Then write them in the correct order to fill in the blanks.

1. Alonzo had to go to Class China Replacements, _____ was about a hundred miles away, to get a replacement for the valuable teacup _____ he had broken last week.

2. The small _____ in Dr. Brown's lab, despite its size, gave off a _____ odor that wafted into the hall.

3. My mom's sister and brother-in-law, _____ live in New Jersey, are the family members _____ we enjoy the most.

4. "I don't care _____ it's raining now or not," Bailee's stern mother said. "The _____ report predicts rain, so you are taking a raincoat."

5. Since _____ going to the store anyway, you can get _____ own hair gel.

Model

Model the following sentences to practice using the words *which* and *that* correctly.

Learn to value yourself, which means to fight for your happiness.

—Ayn Rand

It is difficult to produce a television documentary that is both incisive and probing when every twelve minutes one is interrupted by twelve dancing rabbits singing about toilet paper.

—Rod Serling

Right Word

Test Prep!

Write the letter of the line in which an underlined word is used incorrectly. If all the words are correct, choose "D."

1 Ⓐ There is a difference <u>between</u> the levels of coverage in the two plans.
　Ⓑ Excessive smoking had given her a <u>course</u>, low-pitched voice.
　Ⓒ A pewter <u>medal</u> hung from the blue ribbon.
　Ⓓ All are used correctly.

2 Ⓐ Gloomy, overcast days do not have the same <u>affect</u> on everyone.
　Ⓑ "<u>You're</u> the grand prize winner!" shouted the judge.
　Ⓒ I had nothing to do but <u>sit</u> on a lounge chair by the pool.
　Ⓓ All are used correctly.

3 Ⓐ The orderly carried several <u>vials</u> of blood down the hall.
　Ⓑ The results look promising, but <u>farther</u> study is needed.
　Ⓒ The Kenarbes family, for <u>whom</u> we work, are generous people.
　Ⓓ All are used correctly.

4 Ⓐ Several companies will <u>insure</u> apartment dwellers' belongings.
　Ⓑ The truck lost <u>its</u> mud flap as it hit the large pothole.
　Ⓒ You look <u>very</u> tired today.
　Ⓓ All are used correctly.

5 Ⓐ Ms. Hansen was the <u>sole</u> candidate for the school board position.
　Ⓑ The door alarm will emit a <u>continuous</u> high-pitched noise.
　Ⓒ I was wrong; please <u>except</u> my apology.
　Ⓓ All are used correctly.

6 Ⓐ Children <u>adapt</u> more readily to adverse circumstances than adults do.
　Ⓑ Keisha <u>peaked</u> through a hole in the fence at the neighbors' party.
　Ⓒ The Hellers <u>leave</u> their dogs in the back yard all day.
　Ⓓ All are used correctly.

7 Ⓐ Go ahead and <u>lay</u> down; I'll get something for your headache.
　Ⓑ <u>Weather</u> in this region is notoriously unpredictable.
　Ⓒ The undercover detectives drive a <u>plain</u> gray sedan.
　Ⓓ All are used correctly.

8 Ⓐ Terrence's <u>ascent</u> to his current position was quick but difficult.
　Ⓑ The Constitution guarantees the military's <u>right</u> to bear arms.
　Ⓒ Restrictions limit the number of people who may <u>immigrate</u> into a country.
　Ⓓ All are used correctly.

9 (A) Am I to <u>infer</u> from your silence that you disagree?
(B) Marta recommends eating <u>cereal</u> with lots of fiber.
(C) The <u>moral</u> of the candidate's supporters was slowly sinking.
(D) All are used correctly.

10 (A) All six pups look <u>healthy</u> and adorable!
(B) Do you know what a <u>bass</u> viola looks like?
(C) The weather <u>vane</u> indicates the direction of the wind.
(D) All are used correctly.

11 (A) Quentin <u>sited</u> Mahendra Patel, M.D., as his authority.
(B) You wouldn't think that green <u>complements</u> pink, but sometimes it does.
(C) Stocks performed <u>badly</u> in yesterday's market.
(D) All are used correctly.

12 (A) A career as a firefighter requires a great deal of <u>mettle</u>.
(B) Your <u>illusion</u> to the Crusades doesn't work in this context.
(C) He dreaded having to <u>choose</u> only one winner from all the worthy entries.
(D) All are used correctly.

13 (A) Is high-definition TV really any better <u>then</u> a regular broadcast?
(B) This car looks <u>like</u> some kind of tank.
(C) Jeff placed one <u>flare</u> after another on the road leading to his disabled truck.
(D) All are used correctly.

14 (A) A balanced budget requires <u>capital</u> expenditures to match income.
(B) I'd sure like to give that guy a <u>peace</u> of my mind.
(C) A <u>number</u> of houseplants are poisonous to pets.
(D) All are used correctly.

15 (A) We need to <u>take</u> our old clothes to the charity resale shop.
(B) Rosie, you cook so <u>well</u>!
(C) Each issue of the newsletter features a <u>quote</u> from a literary figure.
(D) All are used correctly.

16 (A) Su is a <u>real</u> believer of astrology.
(B) Plants <u>which</u> conserve moisture are known as *succulents*.
(C) The color of Joseph's hair is slightly <u>different from</u> his brother's.
(D) All are used correctly.

Parts of Speech

Words in the English language are used in eight different ways. For this reason, there are eight parts of speech.

700.1 Noun

A word that names a person, a place, a thing, or an idea

Governor Smith-Jones   Oregon   hospital   religion

700.2 Pronoun

A word used in place of a noun

**I   you   she   him   who   everyone   these   neither
theirs   themselves   which**

700.3 Verb

A word that expresses action or state of being

float   sniff   discover   seem   were   was

700.4 Adjective

A word that describes a noun or a pronoun

young   big   grim   Canadian   longer

700.5 Adverb

A word that describes a verb, an adjective, or another adverb

briefly   forward   regally   slowly   better

700.6 Preposition

The first word or words in a prepositional phrase (which functions as an adjective or an adverb)

away from   under   before   with   for   out of

700.7 Conjunction

A word that connects other words or groups of words

and   but   although   because   either, or   so

700.8 Interjection

A word that shows strong emotion or surprise

Oh no!   Yipes!   Good grief!   Well, . . .

Noun

A **noun** is a word that names something: a person, a place, a thing, or an idea.

governor   Oregon   hospital   Buddhism   love

Classes of Nouns

The five classes of nouns are *proper, common, concrete, abstract,* and *collective.*

701.1 Proper Noun

A **proper noun** names a particular person, place, thing, or idea. Proper nouns are always capitalized.

Jackie Robinson	Brooklyn	World Series
Christianity	Ebbets Field	Hinduism

701.2 Common Noun

A **common noun** does not name a particular person, place, thing, or idea. Common nouns are not capitalized.

person   woman   president   park   baseball   government

701.3 Concrete Noun

A **concrete noun** names a thing that is tangible (can be seen, touched, heard, smelled, or tasted). Concrete nouns are either proper or common.

child	Grand Canyon	music
aroma	fireworks	Becky

701.4 Abstract Noun

An **abstract noun** names an idea, a condition, or a feeling—in other words, something that cannot be touched, smelled, tasted, seen, or heard.

New Deal   greed   poverty   progress   freedom   awe

701.5 Collective Noun

A **collective noun** names a group or a unit.

United States   Portland Cementers   team   crowd   community

Forms of Nouns

Nouns are grouped according to their *number, gender,* and *case.*

702.1 Number of a Noun

Number indicates whether the noun is singular or plural.

A **singular noun** refers to one person, place, thing, or idea.

actor   stadium   Canadian   bully   truth   child   person

A **plural noun** refers to more than one person, place, thing, or idea.

actors   stadiums   Canadians   bullies   truths   children   people

702.2 Gender of a Noun

Gender indicates whether a noun is masculine, feminine, neuter, or indefinite.

Masculine:
uncle   brother   men   bull   rooster   stallion

Feminine:
aunt   sister   women   cow   hen   filly

Neuter (without gender):
tree   cobweb   flying fish   closet

Indefinite (masculine or feminine):
president   plumber   doctor   parent

702.3 Case of a Noun

Case tells how nouns are related to other words used with them. There are three cases: *nominative, possessive,* and *objective.*

■ A **nominative case** noun can be the subject of a clause.

> **Patsy's heart was beating very wildly beneath his jacket. . . . That black horse there owed something to the orphan he had made.**
> —Paul Dunbar, "The Finish of Patsy Barnes"

A nominative noun can also be a predicate noun (or predicate nominative), which follows a "be" verb *(am, is, are, was, were, be, being, been)* and renames the subject. In the sentence below, *type* renames *Mr. Cattanzara.*

> **Mr. Cattanzara was a different type than those in the neighborhood.**
> —Bernard Malamud, "A Summer's Reading"

■ A **possessive case** noun shows possession or ownership.

> **Like the spider's claw, a part of him touches a world he will never enter.**
> —Loren Eiseley, "The Hidden Teacher"

■ An **objective case** noun can be a direct object, an indirect object, or an object of the preposition.

> **Marna always gives Mylo science fiction books for his birthday.**

> (*Mylo* is the indirect object and *books* is the direct object of the verb "gives." *Birthday* is the object of the preposition "for.")

Grammar Practice

Nouns

- Classes
- Number
- Case

For each numbered noun, classify it as *proper or common* and *concrete or abstract*. Also indicate whether it is a *collective* noun. Then write whether it is *singular* or *plural* and identify its case as *nominative, possessive*, or *objective*.

My extended **(1)** family is having a reunion in **(2)** July. **(3)** Invitations went out almost a year in advance. Before the last **(4)** time we tried to get together, a hurricane forced us to cancel.

This time, we've reserved the **(5)** Cantwell Grove Picnic Area in our county park. Even if it rains, we will have **(6)** shelter. We are using my brother **(7)** Dean's stereo system. My nieces and **(8)** nephews from **(9)** Alaska will attend. My **(10)** aunt's husband, a chef, will be whipping up some incredible **(11)** food for us. I'm looking forward to this **(12)** party!

Model

Model the following sentences to practice using an abstract noun in the objective case.

For a list of all the ways technology has failed to improve the quality of life, please press three.

—Alice Kahn

Education is a progressive discovery of our own ignorance.

—Will Durant

Pronoun

A **pronoun** is a word used in place of a noun.

>I, you, she, it, which, that, themselves, whoever, me, he, they, mine, ours

The three types of pronouns are *simple, compound,* and *phrasal.*

>Simple: I, you, he, she, it, we, they, who, what
>Compound: myself, someone, anybody, everything, itself, whoever
>Phrasal: one another, each other

All pronouns have **antecedents**. An antecedent is the noun that the pronoun refers to or replaces.

>Ambrosch **was considered the important person in the family. Mrs. Shimerda and** Ántonia **always deferred to** him, **though** he **was often surly with them and contemptuous toward** his **father.**
>
> —Willa Cather, My Ántonia

>*(Ambrosch is the antecedent of him, he, and his.)*

Note: Each pronoun must agree with its antecedent. (See page **756**.)

704.1 | Classes of Pronouns

The six classes of pronouns are *personal, reflexive and intensive, relative, indefinite, interrogative,* and *demonstrative.*

Personal

I, me, my, mine / we, us, our, ours
you, your, yours / they, them, their, theirs
he, him, his, she, her, hers, it, its

Reflexive and Intensive

myself, yourself, himself, herself, itself, ourselves, yourselves, themselves

Relative

what, who, whose, whom, which, that

Indefinite

all	both	everything	nobody	several
another	each	few	none	some
any	each one	many	no one	somebody
anybody	either	most	nothing	someone
anyone	everybody	much	one	something
anything	everyone	neither	other	such

Interrogative

who, whose, whom, which, what

Demonstrative

this, that, these, those

Grammar Practice

Pronouns 1

■ **Antecedents**

For the sentences below, write each pronoun followed by its antecedent.

1. Two friends have their own cars.

2. Louis Braille, inventor of the Braille reading and writing system, died when he was only 35 years old.

3. The gray squirrel that always tries to get the birdseed is getting rather round.

4. The chorus members sang an anthem as they entered the auditorium.

5. Bryce was upset with Tomás when he fumbled the football.

6. The planning committee granted its permission to build an ice rink on the vacant lot.

7. Yasin insists the MP3 player is his.

8. Julian and Terry blame themselves for the team's loss.

9. The dilapidated log shed, which was built during the Depression, should be dismantled carefully.

10. Grandma Moses based much of her painting on childhood memories.

Model

Model the following sentences to practice using phrasal pronouns.

Let us make one point, that we meet each other with a smile when it is difficult to smile.
—Mother Teresa

Talent hits a target no one else can hit; genius hits a target no one else can see.
—Arthur Schopenhauer

Pronoun *(continued)*

706.1 Personal Pronouns

A **personal pronoun** can take the place of any noun.

> Our coach made her point loud and clear when she raised her voice.

- A **reflexive pronoun** is formed by adding -*self* or -*selves* to a personal pronoun. A reflexive pronoun can be a direct object, an indirect object, an object of the preposition, or a predicate nominative.

  > Miss Sally Sunshine loves herself. (direct object of *loves*)
  >
  > Tomisha does not seem herself today. (predicate nominative)

- An **intensive pronoun** is a reflexive pronoun that intensifies, or emphasizes, the noun or pronoun it refers to.

  > Leo himself taught his children to invest their lives in others.

706.2 Relative Pronouns

A **relative pronoun** relates or connects an adjective clause to the noun or pronoun it modifies.

> Students who study regularly get the best grades. Surprise!
>
> The dance, which we had looked forward to for weeks, was canceled.

(The relative pronoun *who* relates the adjective clause to *students; which* relates the adjective clause to *dance.*)

706.3 Indefinite Pronouns

An **indefinite pronoun** refers to unnamed or unknown people or things.

> I don't know if you've known anybody from that far back; if you've loved anybody that long, first as an infant, then as a child, then as a man. . . . (The antecedent of *anybody* is unknown.)
> > —James Baldwin, "My Dungeon Shook: Letter to My Nephew"

706.4 Interrogative Pronouns

An **interrogative pronoun** asks a question.

> "Then, who are you? Who could you be? What do you want from my husband?"
> > —Elie Wiesel, "The Scrolls, Too, Are Mortal"

706.5 Demonstrative Pronouns

A **demonstrative pronoun** points out people, places, or things without naming them.

> This shouldn't be too hard   That looks about right.
>
> These are the best ones.   Those ought to be thrown out.

Note: When one of these words precedes a noun, it functions as an adjective, not a pronoun. (See **728.1**.)

> That movie bothers me. (*That* is an adjective.)

Grammar Practice

Pronouns 2

- Indefinite Pronouns
- Interrogative Pronouns
- Demonstrative Pronouns

 In the sentences below, identify each underlined pronoun as *indefinite*, *interrogative*, or *demonstrative*.

1. Quan wants to buy <u>those</u> from you.

2. <u>All</u> of the people were asked to leave the stadium aisles.

3. <u>What</u> is <u>that</u>, over there behind the desk?

4. <u>This</u> has been a very positive semester for our junior class.

5. <u>Who</u> thought that <u>anyone</u> in our school would participate in the Olympics?

6. Each season <u>another</u> of the teams tries to break our long-standing record.

7. <u>Neither</u> of us believed a word Claire said.

8. <u>Whose</u> computer just crashed?

9. <u>These</u> look a lot better than the ones you showed me yesterday.

10. A <u>few</u> of the students asked to be excused early.

11. <u>Which</u> is your brother's car?

12. <u>Whom</u> did Denyce choose to travel with her to Washington?

Model

Model the following sentences to practice using indefinite, interrogative, and demonstrative pronouns.

> **Everybody knows that if you are too careful, you are so occupied in being careful that you are sure to stumble over something.**
> —Gertrude Stein

> **Well, if crime fighters fight crime and firefighters fight fire, what do freedom fighters fight?**
> —George Carlin

> **That which is not good for the beehive cannot be good for the bees.**
> —Marcus Aurelius

Forms of Personal Pronouns

The form of a personal pronoun indicates its *number* (singular or plural), its *person* (first, second, third), its *case* (nominative, possessive, or objective), and its *gender* (masculine, feminine, or neuter).

708.1 | Number of a Pronoun

Personal pronouns are singular or plural. The singular personal pronouns include *my, him, he, she, it.* The plural personal pronouns include *we, you, them, our.* (*You* can be singular or plural.) Notice in the caption below that the first *you* is singular and the second *you* is plural.

"Larry, you need to keep all four tires on the road when turning.
Are you still with us back there?"

708.2 | Person of a Pronoun

The **person** of a pronoun indicates whether the person, place, thing, or idea represented by the pronoun is speaking, is spoken to, or is spoken about.

- **First person** is used in place of the name of the speaker or speakers.

  "We don't do things like that," says Pa; "we're just and honest people.
  . . . I don't skip debts."
  —Jesse Stuart, "Split Cherry Tree"

- **Second-person** pronouns name the person or persons spoken to.

  "If you hit your duck, you want me to go in after it?" Eugie said.
  —Gina Berriault, "The Stone Boy"

- **Third-person** pronouns name the person or thing spoken about.

  She had hardly realized the news, further than to understand that she had been brought . . . face to face with something unexpected and final. It did not even occur to her to ask for any explanation.
  —Joseph Conrad, "The Idiots"

Grammar Practice

Pronouns 3

- Number of a Pronoun
- Person of a Pronoun

 Identify the person and number of each underlined pronoun.

1. "You better get up!" Tia Rose said when she noticed that I had hit the "snooze" button one more time.

2. We don't know how long it will take to get to Utah.

3. She ran down the hallway shouting, "Help! Fire!"

4. Whistles and exclamations arose when they saw the motorcycle that Jack bought.

5. I am ordering pizzas to celebrate the end of exams.

6. "Where are you taking them?" Mom asked the boys.

7. It never occurred to him to ask where she had been.

8. I can't understand why Gina won't talk to them.

9. I lost my biology homework.

10. "Will you please try to visit us more often?" Grandpa asked Rob.

 Model

Model the following sentences to practice using first-person pronouns.

> **Call me Ishmael. Some years ago—never mind how long precisely—having little or no money in my purse, and nothing particular to interest me on shore, I thought I would sail about a little and see the watery part of the world.**
> —Herman Melville, *Moby Dick*

710.1 Case of a Pronoun

The **case** of each pronoun tells how it is related to the other words used with it. There are three cases: *nominative, possessive,* and *objective.*

■ A **nominative case** pronoun can be the subject of a clause. The following are nominative forms: *I, you, he, she, it, we, they.*

> **I** like life when things go well. **You** must live life in order to love life.

A nominative pronoun is a *predicate nominative* if it follows a "be" verb (*am, is, are, was, were, be, being, been*) or another linking verb (*appear, become, feel,* etc.) and renames the subject.

> **"Oh, it's only she who scared me just now," said Mama to Papa, glancing over her shoulder.**
> **"Yes, it is I," said Mai in a superior tone.**

■ **Possessive case** pronouns show possession or ownership. Apostrophes, however, are not used with personal pronouns. (Pronouns in the possessive case can also be classified as adjectives.)

> **But as I placed my hand upon his shoulder, there came a strong shudder over his whole person.**
>
> —Edgar Allan Poe, "The Fall of the House of Usher"

■ An **objective case** pronoun can be a direct object, an indirect object, or an object of the preposition.

> **The kids loved it! We lit a campfire for them and told them old ghost stories.** (*It* is the direct object of the verb *loved. Them* is the object of the preposition *for* and the indirect object of the verb *told.*)

Number, Person, and Case of Personal Pronouns

	Nominative	Possessive	Objective
First Person Singular	I	my, mine	me
Second Person Singular	you	your, yours	you
Third Person Singular	he	his	him
	she	her, hers	her
	it	its	it
	Nominative	Possessive	Objective
First Person Plural	we	our, ours	us
Second Person Plural	you	your, yours	you
Third Person Plural	they	their, theirs	them

710.2 Gender of a Pronoun

Gender indicates whether a pronoun is masculine, feminine, or neuter.

Masculine: **he him his**   Feminine: **she her hers**

Neuter (without gender): **it its**

Grammar Practice

Pronouns 4

- Case of a Pronoun
- Gender of a Pronoun

 Identify each underlined pronoun as *nominative, possessive,* or *objective.* If the pronoun is gender specific, write its gender.

Maddie, **(1)** <u>my</u> best friend, and I were sitting in **(2)** <u>our</u> school's cafeteria and talking about **(3)** <u>her</u> recent visit to Texas A&M University. **(4)** <u>She</u> wants to go there after graduation.

(5) "<u>We</u> went to Aggieland on Saturday," Maddie told me. **(6)** "<u>It</u> was so cool! A student guide took **(7)** <u>us</u> on a tour of the campus. **(8)** <u>He</u> showed us **(9)** <u>their</u> classrooms, the library, and other campus buildings. Then, one of the girls took **(10)** <u>me</u> to see the dorms."

"What were **(11)** <u>they</u> like?" I asked.

"The only room I saw was **(12)** <u>hers</u>," Maddie answered. "It was about as big as **(13)** <u>your</u> bedroom at home, and it had **(14)** <u>its</u> own bathroom. I wanted it to be **(15)** <u>mine</u>!"

"I wish I could have gone with **(16)** <u>you</u>," I said.

(17) "<u>I</u> do, too," Maddie replied. "All of **(18)** <u>you</u> can visit me there someday."

◀ Model

Model the following sentences to practice using objective case pronouns.

Dreams are illustrations . . . from the book your soul is writing about you.
—Marsha Norman

There are two ways of spreading light: to be the candle or the mirror that reflects it.
—Edith Wharton

Test Prep!

For each underlined part, write the letter of its specific part of speech from the choices given on the next page.

<u>Dwight and Reba</u> were driving and saw billboards advertising a store selling
(1)
exotic pets. Curious, <u>they</u> found the strip mall and went into the shop. Sure enough,
(2)
among the cages full of puppies and kittens, gerbils and ferrets, and fish and <u>parrots</u>,
(3)
there were cages containing baby tigers, leopards, and cougars. Dwight was smitten

with a cuddly Asian tiger and thought it would be cool to have such an unusual pet.

<u>He</u> also considered what a status symbol it would be. Reba, however, informed him
(4)
of several reasons why wild animals should not be kept as pets.

"First of all," she said, "<u>this</u> is one of 19 states where it's against the law to
(5)
own a big cat." (Sixteen <u>others</u> have partial bans or require permits.) Reba went on
(6)
to describe how demanding the animal would be, in terms of feeding, housing, and

behavior. "If you decided then that <u>you</u> didn't want the tiger, Dwight," she finished,
(7)
"you'd have a really hard time finding a new home for <u>it</u>."
(8)
Despite laws against owning wild animals, the <u>Humane Society of the United</u>
(9)
<u>States</u> estimates that only 10 percent of the 5,000–7,000 captive tigers in this

country reside in well-run zoos or sanctuaries. Further, perhaps 90 percent of all

wild <u>animals</u> kept as pets die within <u>their</u> first year, according to a number of
(10) **(11)**
animal welfare organizations.

In January 2006, the U.S. Fish and Wildlife Service proposed the Captive Wildlife

Safety Act, <u>which</u> would make it illegal to import, export, buy, sell, transport, receive, or
(12)
acquire certain <u>species</u> of exotic big cats. This federal <u>statute</u> may help stem the illegal
(13) **(14)**
trade of exotic animals, often portrayed as one of the international black <u>market's</u>
(15)
biggest moneymakers. Unfortunately, until the demand for privately owned wild

animals disappears, it's the animals <u>themselves</u> that are more likely to disappear.
(16)

1
(A) proper nouns, indefinite
(B) proper singular nouns
(C) abstract nouns, masculine
(D) common plural nouns

2
(A) first-person reflexive pronoun
(B) plural possessive pronoun
(C) indefinite pronoun
(D) third-person nominative pronoun

3
(A) concrete objective noun
(B) common noun, feminine
(C) collective nominative noun
(D) plural nominative noun

4
(A) indefinite nominative pronoun
(B) plural personal pronoun
(C) singular masculine pronoun
(D) plural nominative pronoun

5
(A) singular interrogative pronoun
(B) plural personal pronoun
(C) demonstrative nominative pronoun
(D) demonstrative objective pronoun

6
(A) plural indefinite pronoun
(B) plural intensive pronoun
(C) demonstrative nominative pronoun
(D) demonstrative objective pronoun

7
(A) third-person personal pronoun
(B) second-person personal pronoun
(C) plural intensive pronoun
(D) relative pronoun

8
(A) third-person nominative pronoun
(B) second-person personal pronoun
(C) plural indefinite pronoun
(D) neuter objective pronoun

9
(A) proper nominative noun
(B) collective noun, neuter
(C) common plural noun
(D) abstract possessive noun

10
(A) common noun, indefinite
(B) collective noun, neuter
(C) proper plural noun
(D) abstract noun, neuter

11
(A) neuter objective pronoun
(B) second-person personal pronoun
(C) third-person possessive pronoun
(D) demonstrative nominative pronoun

12
(A) interrogative pronoun
(B) personal pronoun
(C) possessive pronoun
(D) relative pronoun

13
(A) plural nominative noun
(B) singular objective noun
(C) plural objective noun
(D) common collective noun

14
(A) concrete nominative noun
(B) abstract nominative noun
(C) singular objective noun
(D) common noun, indefinite

15
(A) abstract nominative noun
(B) proper feminine noun
(C) plural objective noun
(D) abstract possessive noun

16
(A) plural intensive pronoun
(B) plural reflexive pronoun
(C) singular objective pronoun
(D) third-person feminine pronoun

Verb

A **verb** is a word that expresses action *(run, carried, declared)* or state of being *(is, are, seemed).*

Classes of Verbs

714.1 Linking Verbs

A **linking verb** links the subject to a noun or an adjective in the predicate.

In the outfield, the boy felt confident.
He was the best fielder around.

Common Linking Verbs

| is | are | was | were | be | been | am |

Additional Linking Verbs

| smell | seem | grow | become | appear | sound |
| taste | feel | get | remain | stay | look | turn |

Note: The verbs listed as "additional linking verbs" function as linking verbs when they do not show actual action. An adjective usually follows these linking verbs. (When they do show action, an adverb or a direct object may follow them. In this case, they are action verbs.)

LINKING: This fruit smells rotten.
ACTION: Maya always smells fruit carefully before eating it.

714.2 Auxiliary Verbs

Auxiliary verbs, or helping verbs, are used to form some of the **tenses** (718.3), the **mood** (724.1), and the **voice** (722.2) of the main verb. (In the example below, the auxiliary verbs are in red; the main verbs are in blue.)

The long procession was led by white-robed priests, their faces streaked with red and yellow and white ash. By this time the flames had stopped spurting, and the pit consisted of a red-hot mass of burning wood, which attendants were leveling with long branches.
—Leonard Feinberg, "Fire Walking in Ceylon"

Common Auxiliary Verbs

is	was	being	did	have	would	shall	might
am	were	been	does	had	could	can	must
are	be	do	has	should	will	may	

Grammar Practice

Verbs 1

- Linking Verbs
- Auxiliary Verbs

 Write whether each underlined word is a linking verb or an auxiliary verb.

Some "truths" **(1)** are not worth taking too seriously. For example, perhaps you have **(2)** been told that chewing gum stays in your digestive system for seven years. In reality, your body processes it at the same rate as it does other food. **(3)** Do you believe that you use only 10 percent of your brain? That's another tall tale. Electronic images of the human brain **(4)** appear so colorful because of all the activity going on (even when its host **(5)** is sleeping!).

On the other hand, you **(6)** can learn something from other "legends" that are actually true. One **(7)** is the unfortunate death of a certain cowboy who hawked cigarettes—he died of lung cancer. Perhaps you've **(8)** become smart as a result of eating fish—a "brain food" that contains nutrients very important for brain function. And if you **(9)** are watching your weight, eating celery really does burn more calories than you consume. In general, it would **(10)** be smart for people to verify stories they hear.

Model

Model the following sentences to practice using linking and auxiliary verbs.

> **Then, suddenly, the teacher was a motionless, bent figure standing behind a wooden podium.**
>
> —Mildred Downey Broxon, "Source Material"

> **Every boosterspice plant in the Thousand Worlds could die overnight, leaving you to grow old and gray and wrinkled and arthritic.**
>
> —Larry Niven, "Safe at Any Speed"

716.1 Action Verbs: Transitive and Intransitive

An **intransitive verb** communicates an action that is complete in itself. It does not need an object to receive the action.

> The boy flew on his skateboard. He jumped and flipped and twisted.

A **transitive verb** (red) is an action verb that needs an object (blue) to complete its meaning.

> The city council passed a strict noise ordinance.
>
> Raul takes pictures for the student paper.

While some action verbs are only transitive *or* intransitive, some can be either, depending on how they are used.

> He finally stopped to rest. (intransitive)
>
> He finally stopped the show. (transitive)

716.2 Objects with Transitive Verbs

- A **direct object** receives the action of a transitive verb directly from the subject. Without it, the transitive verb's meaning is incomplete.

  > The boy kicked his skateboard forward. (*Skateboard* is the direct object.)
  >
  > Then he put one foot on it and rode like a pro.

- An **indirect object** also receives the action of a transitive verb, but indirectly. An indirect object names the person *to whom* or *for whom* something is done. (An indirect object can also name the thing *to what* or *for what* something is done.)

  > Ms. Oakfield showed us pictures of the solar system.
  > (*Us* is the indirect object.)
  >
  > She gave Tony an A on his project.

Note: When the word naming the indirect receiver of the action is in a prepositional phrase, it is no longer considered an indirect object.

> Ms. Oakfield showed pictures of the solar system to us.
> (*Us* is the object of the preposition *to*.)

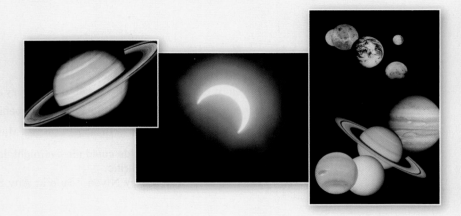

Grammar Practice

Verbs 2

- Transitive and Intransitive Verbs
- Direct and Indirect Objects

Write whether each underlined verb is transitive or intransitive. For a transitive verb, also write its direct object. If there is an indirect object, write it and label it "IO."

Health insurance companies **(1)** <u>exist</u> to pay the medical costs of the people they insure. An insurer **(2)** <u>charges</u> customers a monthly fee—say $200—for coverage. Some members of a group **(3)** <u>will</u> not <u>use</u> $2,400 for medical services in a particular year, and others will use more. In this way, the costs of medical care are spread out among a certain population, and no one who gets sick **(4)** <u>will have</u> unmanageable expenses.

A problem **(5)** <u>arises</u>, however, when an insurance company **(6)** <u>deems</u> its corporate profits more important than the welfare of the people who **(7)** <u>apply</u> for coverage. In cases where an insurance company knows that it **(8)** <u>will pay</u> considerable benefits (for instance, for a person with a chronic disease such as diabetes), the company **(9)** <u>can deny</u> coverage in the first place. Therefore, the people who **(10)** <u>need</u> insurance the most have the hardest time getting it. It's a controversial issue that demands more attention.

Model

Model the following sentences to practice writing sentences with direct and indirect objects.

Those two won't even give you the time of day unless you have something to trade.

—Sue Grafton, *M Is for Malice*

Show me a sane man and I will cure him for you.

—C. G. Jung

Forms of Verbs

A verb has different forms depending on its *number, person, tense, voice,* and *mood.*

718.1 Number of a Verb

Number indicates whether a verb is singular or plural. In a clause, the verb (in **blue** below) and its subject (in **red**) must both be singular or both be plural.

- **Singular**

    One large island floats off Italy's "toe."

    Italy's northern countryside includes the truly spectacular Alps.

- **Plural**

    Five small islands float inside Michigan's "thumb."

    The Porcupine Mountains rise above the shores of Lake Superior.

718.2 Person of a Verb

Person indicates whether the subject of the verb is first, second, or third person (is speaking, is spoken to, or is spoken about). The form of the verb usually changes only when a present-tense verb is used with a third-person singular subject.

	Singular	Plural
First Person	**I sniff**	**we sniff**
Second Person	**you sniff**	**you sniff**
Third Person	**he/she/it sniffs**	**they sniff**

718.3 Tense of a Verb

Tense indicates time. Each verb has three principal parts: the *present, past,* and *past participle.* All six tenses are formed from these principal parts. The past and past participle of regular verbs are formed by adding *ed* to the present form. For irregular verbs, the past and past participle are usually different words; however, a few have the same form in all three principal parts (see **720.2**).

718.4 Simple Tenses

- **Present tense** expresses action that is happening at the present time, or action that happens continually, regularly.

    In September, sophomores smirk and joke about the "little freshies."

- **Past tense** expresses action that was completed at a particular time in the past.

    They forgot that just ninety days separated them from freshman status.

- **Future tense** expresses action that will take place in the future.

    They will recall this in three years when they will be freshmen again.

Grammar Practice

Verbs 3

- Number of a Verb
- Person of a Verb
- Simple Tenses

 Write the person and number of each underlined verb. Also write its tense.

1. Tahi <u>will start</u> college next fall.

2. We <u>listen</u> to books on CD whenever Dad <u>drives</u> us to Michigan.

3. Peter Gabriel <u>played</u> in the band Genesis in the 1970s.

4. Darnell, please <u>vacuum</u> the stairs before you leave.

5. A garbled message <u>popped</u> onto the computer screen; then the computer crashed.

6. Bachelor's buttons <u>are</u> not true perennial flowers, but they <u>will return</u> year after year.

7. Turning onto Cuba Road, I <u>reached</u> for the map in the glove box.

8. The moon <u>has</u> an orange halo tonight.

9. Giraffes <u>have</u> the same number of vertebrae as humans do.

10. Keisha's dog <u>wore</u> spotted pajamas in the animal shelter parade.

Model

Model the following sentences to practice using the correct present-tense verb form with third-person singular subjects.

> **Asking a working writer what he thinks about critics is like asking a lamppost how it feels about dogs.**
> —Christopher Hampton

> **The time to stop talking is when the other person nods his head affirmatively but says nothing.**
> —Henry S. Haskins

Forms of Verbs (continued)

720.1 Perfect Tenses

- **Present perfect tense** expresses action that began in the past but continues in the present or is completed in the present.

  Our boat has weathered **worse storms than this one.**

- **Past perfect tense** expresses an action in the past that occurred before another past action.

  They reported, wrongly, that the hurricane had missed **the island.**

- **Future perfect tense** expresses action that will begin in the future and be completed by a specific time in the future.

  By this time tomorrow, the hurricane will have smashed **into the coast.**

720.2 Irregular Verbs

Common Irregular Verbs and Their Principal Parts

Present Tense	Past Tense	Past Participle	Present Tense	Past Tense	Past Participle	Present Tense	Past Tense	Past Participle
am, be	was, were	been	go	went	gone	shrink	shrank	shrunk
begin	began	begun	grow	grew	grown	sing	sang, sung	sung
bite	bit	bitten	hang (execute)	hanged	hanged	sink	sank, sunk	sunk
blow	blew	blown				sit	sat	sat
break	broke	broken	hang (suspend)	hung	hung	slay	slew	slain
bring	brought	brought				speak	spoke	spoken
buy	bought	bought	hide	hid	hidden, hid	spring	sprang, sprung	sprung
catch	caught	caught	know	knew	known			
choose	chose	chosen	lay	laid	laid	steal	stole	stolen
come	came	come	lead	led	led	strive	strove	striven
dive	dove	dived	leave	left	left	swear	swore	sworn
do	did	done	lie (recline)	lay	lain	swim	swam	swum
draw	drew	drawn				swing	swung	swung
drink	drank	drunk	lie (deceive)	lied	lied	take	took	taken
drive	drove	driven				teach	taught	taught
eat	ate	eaten	lose	lost	lost	tear	tore	torn
fall	fell	fallen	make	made	made	throw	threw	thrown
fight	fought	fought	ride	rode	ridden	wake	waked, woke	waked, woken
flee	fled	fled	ring	rang	rung			
fly	flew	flown	rise	rose	risen	wear	wore	worn
forsake	forsook	forsaken	run	ran	run	weave	weaved, wove	weaved, woven
freeze	froze	frozen	see	saw	seen			
get	got	gotten	shake	shook	shaken	wring	wrung	wrung
give	gave	given	show	showed	shown	write	wrote	written

These verbs are the same in all principal parts: *burst, cost, cut, hurt, let, put, set,* and *spread.*

Grammar Practice

Verbs 4

- **Perfect Tenses**
- **Irregular Verbs**

Parts of Speech

 For each sentence, copy the verb phrase in parentheses, using the past participle of the irregular verb that appears in italics. Then label the tense of each verb (present perfect, past perfect, or future perfect).

1. After Ahmed worked on the car, it was really no surprise to see that the oil pan (had *spring*) a leak.

2. You (will have *spread*) the lawn fertilizer by this weekend, right?

3. I thought I (had *lay*) the blanket over the back of the couch, but it's gone now.

4. The refugees (have *flee*) their country for political reasons.

5. Rebels (had *slay*) family members in a nearby town.

6. Ladonna (has *come*) to my house after school since we were in fifth grade.

7. I hope the pond (will have *freeze*) by the time we return next month.

8. Either your sweaters (have *shrink*) lately, or you are growing really fast.

9. I would (have *go*) to the mall with you if you had asked.

10. My dog never (has *bite*) anyone, but I think she would if she were provoked.

11. In Inez's opinion, a pass to the local pool shouldn't (have *cost*) that much.

12. As soon as he (had *lie*) on the sofa, he started snoring.

Model

Model the following sentences to practice using past and present perfect-tense verbs.

> **When I took office, only high energy physicists had ever heard of what is called the World Wide Web . . . now even my cat has its own page.**
>
> —Bill Clinton

> **My passport photo is one of the most remarkable photographs I have ever seen—no retouching, no shadows, no flattery—just stark me.**
>
> —Anne Morrow Lindbergh

722.1 Continuous Tenses

- A **present continuous tense** verb expresses action that is not completed at the time of stating it. The present continuous tense is formed by adding *am, is,* or *are* to the *-ing* form of the main verb.

  Scientists are learning **a great deal from their study of the sky.**

- A **past continuous tense** verb expresses action that was happening at a certain time in the past. This tense is formed by adding *was* or *were* to the *-ing* form of the main verb.

  Astronomers were beginning **their quest for knowledge hundreds of years ago.**

- A **future continuous tense** verb expresses action that will take place at a certain time in the future. This tense is formed by adding *will be* to the *-ing* form of the main verb.

  Someday astronauts will be going **to Mars.**

  This tense can also be formed by adding a phrase noting the future *(are going to)* plus *be* to the *-ing* form of the main verb.

  They are going to be performing **many experiments.**

722.2 Voice of a Verb

Voice indicates whether the subject is acting or being acted upon.

- **Active voice** indicates that the subject of the verb is, has been, or will be doing something.

  For many years Lou Brock held **the base-stealing record.**

Active voice makes your writing more direct and lively.

- **Passive voice** indicates that the subject of the verb is being, has been, or will be acted upon.

  For many years the base-stealing record was held **by Lou Brock.**

Note: With a passive verb, the person or thing creating the action is not always stated.

The ordinance was overturned. (Who did the overturning?)

Tense	Active Voice		Passive Voice	
	Singular	Plural	Singular	Plural
Present	I see you see he/she/it sees	we see you see they see	I am seen you are seen he/she/it is seen	we are seen you are seen they are seen
Past	I/he saw you saw	we/they saw you saw	I/it was seen you were seen	we/they were seen you were seen
Future	I/you/he will see	we/you/they will see	I/you/it will be seen	we/you/they will be seen

Grammar Practice

Verbs 5

- **Active and Passive Verbs**

In the following paragraphs, if any sentence or part of a sentence is in the passive voice, rewrite it in the active voice. Write "active" if it is already in the active voice.

(1) Few realize the importance that knots and cordage have played in the world's history. **(2)** If it had not been for these simple and everyday things, which as a rule are given far too little consideration, the human race could never have developed beyond savages. **(3)** Indeed, I am not sure, but it would be safe to state that the real difference between civilized and savage man consists largely in the knowledge of knots and rope work. **(4)** No cloth could be woven, no net or seine knitted, no bow strung, and no craft sailed on lake or sea without numerous knots and proper lines or ropes. **(5)** Columbus himself would have been far more handicapped without knots than without a compass.

(6) History abounds with mention of knots, and in the eighth book of *The Odyssey,* Ulysses is represented as securing various articles of raiment by a rope fastened in a "knot closed with Circean art." **(7)** As further proof of the prominence the ancients gave to knots, the famous Gordian Knot may be mentioned. **(8)** Probably no one will ever learn just how this fabulous knot was tied. **(9)** Like many modern knots, it was doubtless far easier for Alexander to cut it than to untie it.

From *Knots, Splices, and Rope Work,* by A. Hyatt Verrill

Model

Use of the passive voice is common in technical and scientific writing or when the "doer" is unknown. Model the following sentence to practice using the passive voice in such instances.

In a time of inflation or recession, the medicine—raising or lowering rates—must be administered in such strong doses that dangerous side effects are almost inevitable.

—Richard J. Barnet, "The Disorders of Peace"

724.1 Mood of a Verb

The **mood** of a verb indicates the tone or attitude with which a statement is made.

■ **Indicative mood** is used to state a fact or to ask a question.

> Sometimes I'd yell questions at the rocks and trees, and across gorges, or yodel, "What is the meaning of the void?" The answer was perfect silence, so I knew.
>
> —Jack Kerouac, "Alone on a Mountain Top"

■ **Imperative mood** is used to give a command.

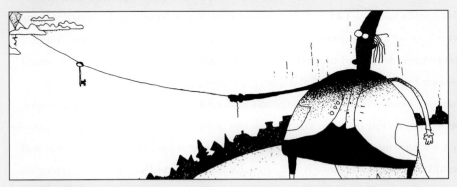

"Whatever you do, don't fly your kite during a storm."

—Mrs. Abiah Franklin

■ **Subjunctive mood** is no longer commonly used; however, careful writers may choose to use it to express the exact manner in which their statements are meant.

Use the subjunctive *were* to express a condition that is contrary to fact.

> If I were finished with my report, I could go to the movie.

Use the subjunctive *were* after *as though* or *as if* to express an unreal condition.

> Mrs. Young acted as if she were sixteen again.

Use the subjunctive *be* in "that" clauses to express necessity, legal decisions, or parliamentary motions.

> "It is moved and supported that no more than 6 million quad be used to explore the planet Earth."

> "Ridiculous! Knowing earthlings is bound to help us understand ourselves! Therefore, I move that the sum be amended to 12 million quad."

> "Stupidity! I move that all missions be postponed until we have living proof of life on Earth."

Grammar Practice

Verbs 6

■ Mood of a Verb

 Write whether each statement shows indicative, imperative, or subjunctive mood.

1. He talks about Yale as if he were already a student there.

2. The first show starts at 6:45 this Friday night.

3. Take a seat in the front section of the auditorium.

4. Do research to find out what happened on the day you were born.

5. What's the name of that new CD you bought?

6. Read chapter 8 before the test on Friday.

7. I move that the meeting be postponed until next month.

8. The answer to the last question was perfectly clear.

9. That game was the best one we've played all year!

10. Notice how my grades have improved this semester.

11. It looked as though she were floating in midair.

12. My parents love music by the Grateful Dead.

Model

Model the following sentences to practice using the imperative mood.

Always behave like a duck—keep calm and unruffled on the surface but paddle like the devil underneath.

—Jacob Braude

Have the courage to act instead of react.

—Earlene Larson Jenks

Verbals

A **verbal** is a word that is derived from a verb but does not function as a verb in a sentence. Instead, a verbal acts as another part of speech—noun, adjective, or adverb. There are three types of verbals: *gerunds, infinitives,* and *participles.* Each is often part of a verbal phrase.

726.1 Gerunds

A **gerund** is a verb form that ends in *ing* and is used as a noun.

> Swimming **is my favorite pastime.** (subject)
>
> I began swimming **at the age of six months.**
> (direct object)
>
> The hardest part of swimming **is the resulting sore muscles.**
> (object of the preposition *of*)
>
> Swimming in chlorinated pools **makes my eyes red.**
> (gerund phrase used as a subject)

726.2 Infinitives

An **infinitive** is a verb form that is usually introduced by *to;* the infinitive may be used as a noun, an adjective, or an adverb.

> Most people find it easy to swim. (adverb modifying an adjective)
>
> To swim the English Channel **must be a thrill.** (infinitive phrase as noun)
>
> The urge to swim in tropical waters **is more common.** (infinitive phrase as adjective)

726.3 Participles

A **participle** is a verb form ending in *ing* or *ed* that acts as an adjective.

> The workers raking leaves **are tired and hungry.**
> (participial phrase modifies *workers*)
>
> The bags full of raked **leaves are evidence of their hard work.**
> (participle modifies *leaves*)
>
> Smiling **faces greeted my father when he returned from a business trip.**
> (participle modifying *faces*)

Note: The past participle of an irregular verb can also act as an adjective:

> That rake is obviously broken.

Grammar Practice

Verbals

■ Verbals

 Find and write the verbal in each sentence below. Identify it as a *gerund,* a *participle,* or an *infinitive.*

1. Falling temperatures will result in icy roads this afternoon.

2. Tyrell likes to experiment with the color of his hair.

3. Avoid watering the plants too much during the winter months.

4. It's a known fact that Leah has been accepted at Princeton.

5. Dan dreams of making money with his photography.

6. Feeling defeated, Jacinda dragged herself to the locker room.

7. To succeed in sales, knowledge of and belief in the product are essential.

8. You must cross the bridge over the Des Plaines River to get there.

9. Going to the mall is Shawn's therapy when she feels down.

10. I was driving Mom's car when, rounding the curve, I saw an accident that had just happened.

Model

Model the following sentences to practice using participles.

> Paula came downstairs wearing clothes so wrinkled you could hardly tell what they were.
> —Ellen Cooney, "A Nurse"

> Do you know anything on earth which has not a dangerous side if it is mishandled and exaggerated?
> —Arthur Conan Doyle, *The Land of Mist*

Adjective

An **adjective** describes or modifies a noun or a pronoun. The articles *a, an,* and *the* are also adjectives.

> The young **driver peeked through** the big **steering wheel.**
>
> (*The* and *young* modify *driver; the* and *big* modify *steering wheel.*)

Types of Adjectives

A **proper adjective** is created from a proper noun and is capitalized.

> In Canada (proper noun), **you will find many cultures and climates.**
>
> Canadian (proper adjective) **winters can be harsh.**

A **predicate adjective** follows a form of the "be" verb (or other linking verb) and describes the subject.

> **Late autumn seems** grim **to those who love summer.** (*Grim* modifies *autumn.*)

Note: Some words can be either adjectives or pronouns (*that, these, all, each, both, many, some,* and so on). These words are adjectives when they come before the nouns they modify; they are pronouns when they stand alone.

> **Jiao made** both **goals.** (*Both* modifies *goals;* it is an adjective.)
>
> Both **were scored in the final period.** (*Both* stands alone; it is a pronoun.)

728.2 **Forms of Adjectives**

Adjectives have three forms: *positive, comparative,* and *superlative.*

- The **positive form** describes a noun or a pronoun without comparing it to anyone or anything else.

  > **The first game was** long and tiresome.

- The **comparative form** (*-er, more,* or *less*) compares two persons, places, things, or ideas.

  > **The second game was** longer and more tiresome **than the first.**

- The **superlative form** (*-est, most,* or *least*) compares three or more persons, places, things, or ideas.

  > **The third game was the** longest and most tiresome **of all.**

  Note: Use *more* and *most* (or *less* and *least*)—instead of adding a suffix—with many adjectives of two or more syllables.

Positive	Comparative	Superlative
big	bigger	biggest
helpful	more helpful	most helpful
painful	less painful	least painful

Grammar Practice

Adjectives

- Types of Adjectives
- Forms of Adjectives

 Write the adjectives (not including articles) in each of the following sentences. Label predicate adjectives, comparative adjectives, and superlative adjectives.

1. This Seattle market offers some of the freshest fish I've ever had.

2. They sell two types of sole from Africa: the slender Agulhas sole and the round West Coast sole.

3. You will also find snoek there, an oily fish that is popular with South African people.

4. Norwegian sardines are young herrings that are smaller than full-grown ones.

5. Along with other varieties caught along the North American West Coast, salmon is a favorite treat for Seattlites.

6. Thomas Beecham said, "Movie music is noise . . . even more painful than my sciatica."

7. Upgrading the ancient computers is the most problematic issue on the agenda.

8. In the dead of gray winter, frequent dreams of cloudless blue skies and lush green grass keep me sane.

Model

Model the following sentences to practice using adjectives well.

> **Small and slightly plump, she had the perfect skin and apple cheeks of a picture poster.**
> —Maeve Binchy, *Firefly Summer*

> **Life, for all its raw talent, has little sense of structure. It creates amazing textures, but it can't be counted on for snappy beginnings or good endings either.**
> —Larry McMurtry

Adverb

An **adverb** describes or modifies a verb, an adjective, or another adverb.

She sneezed loudly. (*Loudly* modifies the verb *sneezed.*)

Her sneezes are really **dramatic.** (*Really* modifies the adjective *dramatic.*)

The sneeze exploded very **noisily.** (*Very* modifies the adverb *noisily.*)

An adverb usually tells *when, where, how,* or *how much.*

730.1 Types of Adverbs

Adverbs can be cataloged in four basic ways: *time, place, manner,* and *degree.*

Time (These adverbs tell *when, how often,* and *how long.*)

today, yesterday   daily, weekly   briefly, eternally

Place (These adverbs tell *where, to where,* and *from where.*)

here, there   nearby, beyond   backward, forward

Manner (These adverbs often end in *ly* and tell *how* something is done.)

precisely   effectively   regally   smoothly   well

Degree (These adverbs tell *how much* or *how little.*)

substantially   greatly   entirely   partly   too

Note: Some adverbs can be written with or without the *ly* ending. When in doubt, use the *ly* form.

slow, slowly   loud, loudly   fair, fairly   tight, tightly   quick, quickly

730.2 Forms of Adverbs

Adverbs of manner have three forms: *positive, comparative,* and *superlative.*

- The **positive form** describes a verb, an adjective, or another adverb without comparing it to anyone or anything else.

  Model X vacuum cleans well **and runs** quietly.

- The **comparative form** *(-er, more,* or *less)* compares how two things are done.

  Model Y vacuum cleans better **and runs** more quietly **than model X does.**

- The **superlative form** *(-est, most,* or *least)* compares how three or more things are done.

  Model Z vacuum cleans best **and runs** most quietly **of all.**

Irregular Forms

Positive	Comparative	Superlative
well	better	best
fast	faster	fastest
remorsefully	more remorsefully	most remorsefully

Grammar Practice

Adverbs

- Types of Adverbs
- Forms of Adverbs

 Write the 18 adverbs you'll find in the following paragraphs. Identify each as an adverb of time, place, manner, or degree. For an adverb of manner, also identify it as positive, comparative, or superlative.

Direction on food safety is badly needed in underdeveloped countries. There, diarrhea caused by contaminated food and water is a leading cause of death. With that in mind, the World Health Organization (WHO) recently revised a poster, available in 32 languages, to more clearly show some simple rules for safe food handling and preparation.

The cardinal rule, of course, involves cleanliness. Dangerous germs (widely found in soil, water, animals, and people) can be transmitted quite easily to food via unwashed hands. In addition, dishrags, utensils, and cutting boards need frequent washing. WHO also pushes for the use of safe water and raw materials.

Temperature is the next concern. Proper cooking kills dangerous microorganisms the best—but it's also important to keep cooked and raw food at a safe temperature. Never leave cooked food unrefrigerated for longer than two hours, and do not thaw frozen food at room temperature.

Finally, do not handle raw food and cooked food together. Meat, poultry, and seafood can be especially dangerous; they should always be separated from other foods during their preparation. These simple steps can dramatically reduce food- and water-borne illness here and around the world.

Model

Model these sentences to practice using comparative and superlative adverbs.

It was one of those perfect English autumnal days that occur more frequently in memory than in life.

—P. D. James

Those who are urged to feel afraid, very afraid, have both the greatest sense of independence and the most finely honed skepticism about government.

—Ellen Goodman

Preposition

A **preposition** is the first word (or group of words) in a prepositional phrase. It shows the relationship between its object (a noun or a pronoun that follows the preposition) and another word in the sentence. The first noun or pronoun following a preposition is its object.

> **To make a mustache, Natasha placed the hairy caterpillar** under **her nose.**
> (*Under* shows the relationship between the verb, *placed*, and the object of the preposition, *nose.*)
> **The drowsy insect clung obediently** to **the girl's upper** lip.
> (The first noun following the preposition *to* is *lip; lip* is the object of the preposition.)

732.1 Prepositional Phrases

A **prepositional phrase** includes the preposition, the object of the preposition, and the modifiers of the object. A prepositional phrase functions as an adverb or as an adjective.

> **Some people** run away from caterpillars.
> (The phrase functions as an adverb and modifies the verb *run.*)
> **However, little** kids with inquisitive minds **enjoy their company.**
> (The phrase functions as an adjective and modifies the noun *kids.*)

Note: A preposition is always followed by an object; if there is no object, the word is an adverb, not a preposition.

> **Natasha never** played **with caterpillars** before. (The word *before* is not followed by an object; therefore, it functions as an adverb that modifies *played,* a verb.)

Common Prepositions

aboard	before	from	of	save
about	behind	from among	off	since
above	below	from between	on	subsequent to
according to	beneath	from under	on account of	through
across	beside	in	on behalf of	throughout
across from	besides	in addition to	onto	till
after	between	in back of	on top of	to
against	beyond	in behalf of	opposite	together with
along	by	in front of	out	toward
alongside	by means of	in place of	out of	under
along with	concerning	in regard to	outside of	underneath
amid	considering	inside	over	until
among	despite	inside of	over to	unto
apart from	down	in spite of	owing to	up
around	down from	instead of	past	upon
aside from	during	into	prior to	up to
at	except	like	regarding	with
away from	except for	near	round	within
because of	for	near to	round about	without

Grammar Practice

Prepositions

■ Prepositional Phrases

For each underlined prepositional phrase, indicate whether it functions as an adjective or an adverb.

1. The sleeping dog's legs twitched as he dreamed <u>of the bothersome squirrel</u> <u>at the bird feeder</u>.

2. All the animals at the zoo <u>except for the polar bears</u> stayed huddled <u>inside their enclosures</u>.

3. <u>In spite of the frigid temperatures</u>, the white bears seemed comfortable.

4. Create a memo <u>regarding the dress code</u> <u>for all employees</u>.

5. Coach Walters had us run <u>around the block</u> ten times.

6. The child standing <u>beside her mother</u> looked quite forlorn.

7. Bonita dances <u>in an uninhibited way</u> when she hears her favorite music.

8. The spiderweb <u>between the ceiling and wall</u> looks like a bit <u>of fuzz</u>.

▶ Model

Model the following sentences to practice using prepositional phrases as adverbs.

> To confine our attention to terrestrial matters would be to limit the human spirit.
> —Stephen Hawking

> To stay ahead, you must have your next idea waiting in the wings.
> —Rosabeth Moss Kanter

Conjunction

A **conjunction** connects individual words or groups of words. There are three kinds of conjunctions: *coordinating, correlative,* and *subordinating.*

734.1 Coordinating Conjunctions

Coordinating conjunctions usually connect a word to a word, a phrase to a phrase, or a clause to a clause. The words, phrases, or clauses joined by a coordinating conjunction are equal in importance or are of the same type.

> I could tell by my old man's eyes that he *was nervous* and *wanted to smooth things over*, but Syl didn't give him a chance.
> —Albert Halper, "Prelude"

(*And* connects the two parts of a compound predicate; *but* connects two independent clauses that could stand on their own.)

734.2 Correlative Conjunctions

Correlative conjunctions are conjunctions used in pairs.

> They were not only exhausted by the day's journey but also sunburned.

734.3 Subordinating Conjunctions

Subordinating conjunctions connect two clauses that are *not* equally important, thereby showing the relationship between them. A subordinating conjunction connects a dependent clause to an independent clause in order to complete the meaning of the dependent clause.

> A brown trout will study the bait before he eats it. (The clause *before he eats it* is dependent. It depends on the rest of the sentence to complete its meaning.)

Kinds of Conjunctions

Coordinating: **and, but, or, nor, for, yet, so**

Correlative: **either, or; neither, nor; not only, but also; both, and; whether, or**

Subordinating: **after, although, as, as if, as long as, as though, because, before, if, in order that, provided that, since, so that, that, though, till, unless, until, when, where, whereas, while**

Note: Relative pronouns (see **706.2**) and conjunctive adverbs (see **618.2**) can also connect clauses.

Interjection

An **interjection** communicates strong emotion or surprise. Punctuation—a comma or an exclamation point—sets off an interjection from the rest of the sentence.

> Oh no! The TV broke. Good grief! I have nothing to do! Yipes, I'll go mad!

Grammar Practice

Conjunctions

Number your paper from 1 to 7. Write the conjunctions you find in the following paragraph and label them coordinating, subordinating, or correlative. (Write both correlative conjunctions as one answer.)

1 Most people know Georgia O'Keeffe as a celebrated artist, but few
2 people know that she almost gave up on her talent. In the early twentieth
3 century, O'Keeffe studied at the Art Institute of Chicago, where she learned
4 imitative realism. Although she had won awards for paintings she had
5 done in this style, she felt the technique did not suit her. Discouraged, she
6 quit making art until she took a course at the University of Virginia in
7 Charlottesville, four years later. There she found the freedom to incorporate
8 her own personal ideas into her art. O'Keeffe not only experimented with
9 new techniques in line, color, and light, but she also discovered her own
10 personal style. She created abstract charcoal drawings that were among
11 the most innovative of the time. She is probably best known for her large-
12 scale paintings of flowers. Before she died in 1986, Georgia O'Keeffe
13 was awarded the Medal of
14 Freedom and the National
15 Medal of Arts.

Model

Model the following sentences to practice using interjections effectively.

> **An apology? Bah! Disgusting! Cowardly! It is beneath the dignity of any gentleman, however wrong he might be.**
> —Baroness Orczy Emmuska

> **The most exciting phrase to hear in science, the one that heralds new discoveries, is not "Eureka!" (I found it!) but "That's funny . . . "**
> —Isaac Asimov

Test Prep!

For each underlined word or group of words, write the letter of the answer that best describes it from the choices given on the next page.

Multiple sclerosis (MS) is a progressive disease <u>of the nervous system</u> that,
(1)
despite affecting 2.5 million people, <u>is</u> not completely understood. The cause of the
(2)
disease is <u>unknown</u>, and there is no cure. Researchers <u>believe</u> that an environmental
(3) **(4)**
factor plays a part in <u>causing the disease</u>, and they theorize that viruses may trigger
(5)
relapses.

Something goes wrong with the immune system in a person with MS. Instead

of fighting a foreign infection, the immune system <u>attacks the protective coating</u>
(6)
(called myelin) of the nerves in the brain and spinal cord. Scar tissue, or sclerosis,

builds up where the myelin <u>is destroyed</u>. The scar tissue disrupts the electrical
(7)
signals <u>transmitted along the nerves</u>, <u>so</u> the brain has trouble relaying messages.
(8) **(9)**
Depending on the area of the brain or spinal cord affected by the sclerosis, different

symptoms <u>result</u>. Tingling, numbness, and weakness in the limbs <u>are</u> common early
(10) **(11)**
symptoms, as are loss of balance and vision problems. <u>Later</u> symptoms include
(12)
muscle spasms and loss of muscle control, heat sensitivity, fatigue, and changes in

the thinking processes.

<u>Fortunately</u>, a number of drugs <u>have proved</u> to slow the progression of MS.
(13) **(14)**
<u>Before</u> these drugs were developed, the progression of the disease often resulted
(15)
<u>in disability</u>. The drugs suppress or somehow change immune system processes,
(16)
and although the drugs do not provide a cure, they reduce the frequency of attacks

and severity of symptoms. The drugs <u>give people</u> with MS the ability <u>to function</u>
(17) **(18)**
<u>normally</u> most of the time.

1
- (A) prepositional phrase functioning as an adverb
- (B) prepositional phrase functioning as an adjective
- (C) participial phrase
- (D) gerund phrase

2
- (A) linking verb
- (B) transitive verb
- (C) verbal
- (D) present perfect verb

3
- (A) predicate adjective
- (B) passive voice verb
- (C) adverb of manner
- (D) participle

4
- (A) singular third-person verb
- (B) plural third-person verb
- (C) plural first-person verb
- (D) linking verb

5
- (A) passive voice verb
- (B) present perfect verb
- (C) gerund phrase
- (D) participial phrase

6
- (A) linking verb and predicate noun
- (B) linking verb and predicate adjective
- (C) transitive verb and indirect object
- (D) transitive verb and direct object

7
- (A) passive voice verb
- (B) present perfect verb
- (C) gerund phrase
- (D) participial phrase

8
- (A) passive voice verb
- (B) present perfect verb
- (C) gerund phrase
- (D) participial phrase

9
- (A) subordinating conjunction
- (B) coordinating conjunction
- (C) correlative conjunction
- (D) adverb of manner

10
- (A) auxiliary verb
- (B) transitive verb
- (C) intransitive verb
- (D) linking verb

11
- (A) auxiliary verb
- (B) transitive verb
- (C) intransitive verb
- (D) linking verb

12
- (A) positive adjective
- (B) comparative adjective
- (C) superlative adjective
- (D) adverb of time

13
- (A) adverb of time
- (B) adverb of place
- (C) adverb of degree
- (D) adverb of manner

14
- (A) passive voice verb
- (B) present perfect verb
- (C) past perfect verb
- (D) participial phrase

15
- (A) subordinating conjunction
- (B) coordinating conjunction
- (C) correlative conjunction
- (D) adverb of time

16
- (A) prepositional phrase functioning as an adverb
- (B) prepositional phrase functioning as an adjective
- (C) participial phrase
- (D) gerund phrase

17
- (A) transitive verb with direct object
- (B) transitive verb with indirect object
- (C) intransitive verb with indirect object
- (D) participial phrase

18
- (A) passive voice verb
- (B) present perfect verb
- (C) infinitive phrase
- (D) participial phrase

Understanding Sentences

Constructing Sentences

A **sentence** is made up of one or more words that express a complete thought. Sentences begin with a capital letter; they end with a period, a question mark, or an exclamation point.

What should we do this afternoon? We could have a picnic. No, I hate the ants!

Using Subjects and Predicates

A sentence usually has a subject and a predicate. The subject is the part of the sentence about which something is said. The predicate, which contains the verb, is the part of the sentence that says something about the subject.

We write **from aspiration and antagonism, as well as from experience.**

—Ralph Waldo Emerson

738.1 The Subject

The **subject** is the part of the sentence about which something is said. The subject is always a noun; a pronoun; or a word, clause, or phrase that functions as a noun (such as a gerund or a gerund phrase or an infinitive).

Wolves **howl.** (noun)
They **howl for a variety of reasons.** (pronoun)
To establish their turf **may be one reason.** (infinitive phrase)
Searching for "lost" pack members **may be another.** (gerund phrase)
That wolves and dogs are similar animals **seems obvious.** (noun clause)

- A **simple subject** is the subject without its modifiers.

  Most wildlife biologists **disapprove of crossbreeding wolves and dogs.**

- A **complete subject** is the subject with all of its modifiers.

  Most wildlife biologists **disapprove of crossbreeding wolves and dogs.**

- A **compound subject** is composed of two or more simple subjects.

  Wise breeders and owners **know that wolf-dog puppies can display unexpected, destructive behaviors.**

738.2 Delayed Subject

In sentences that begin with *there* or *it* followed by a form of the "be" verb, the subject comes after the verb. The subject is also delayed in questions.

There was nothing **in the refrigerator.** (The subject is *nothing;* the verb is *was.*)
Where is my sandwich? (The subject is *sandwich;* the verb is *is.*)

Grammar Practice

Constructing Sentences 1

- **Simple, Complete, and Compound Subjects**
- **Delayed Subjects**

 Write the complete subject of each sentence (and of each dependent clause in a complex sentence). Circle the simple subject or subjects.

(1) One summer long ago, some people took a boat from the northern tip of Wisconsin to Madeline Island in Lake Superior. **(2)** Those hardy souls liked it so much that they decided to build homes and businesses there. **(3)** And then winter came. **(4)** Chequamegon Bay, the body of water between the island and the mainland, froze. **(5)** The islanders were in for a long winter.

(6) There were those who had sleds and dogs to get back to Wisconsin. **(7)** But the time came when another question begged an answer: **(8)** Would the ice hold something heavier, like a car? **(9)** (And who wanted to be the one to find out?)

(10) Fortunately, ice roads are no longer a questionable possibility but a scientific reality. **(11)** Numerous companies and government agencies in frozen climates build and maintain these winter roads to deliver goods to remote locations. **(12)** They use sophisticated equipment to measure the ice thickness and mark the route. **(13)** The dedicated workers keep it solid and plow it as needed. **(14)** Now areas that cannot be reached by road in the summer can be reached in the winter.

◀ Model

Model the following sentences to practice using a compound subject.

Chattering jays and loud wood-pigeons flap thickly overhead, while . . . the measured tapping of Nature's carpenter, the great green woodpecker, sounds from each wayside grove. —Arthur Conan Doyle, *The White Company*

Today, mechanics and technicians need to master a half million manual pages to fix every car on the road. —Chet Williamson, "Mushrooms"

Sentences

740.1 Predicates

The **predicate** is the part of the sentence that shows action or says something about the subject.

> Giant squid do exist.

- A **simple predicate** is the verb without its modifiers.
  > One giant squid measured nearly 60 feet long.

- A **complete predicate** is the simple predicate with all its modifiers.
  > One giant squid measured nearly 60 feet long.
  > (*Measured* is the simple predicate; *nearly 60 feet long* modifies *measured.*)

- Compound and complex sentences have more than one predicate.
  > The sperm whale has an enormous head that is approximately a third of its entire length.
  > A whale is a mammal, but a squid is a mollusk.

- A **compound predicate** is composed of two or more simple predicates.
  > A squid grasps its prey with tentacles and bites it with its beak.

Note: A sentence can have a **compound subject** and a **compound predicate**.

> Both sperm whales and giant squid live and occasionally clash in the deep waters off New Zealand's South Island.

- A **direct object** is part of the predicate and receives the action of the verb. (See **716.2**.)
  > Sperm whales sometimes eat giant squid.
  > (The direct object *giant squid* receives the action of the verb *eat* by answering the question *whales eat what?*)

Note: The **direct object** may be compound.

> In the past, whalers harvested oil, spermaceti, and ambergris from slain sperm whales.

740.2 Understood Subjects and Predicates

Either the subject or the predicate may be "missing" from a sentence, but both must be clearly **understood**.

> Who is in the hot-air balloon?
> (*Who* is the subject; *is in the hot-air balloon* is the predicate.)

> No one.
> (*No one* is the subject; the predicate *is in the hot-air balloon* is understood.)

> Get out of the way!
> (The subject *you* is understood; *get out of the way* is the predicate.)

Grammar Practice

Constructing Sentences 2

■ **Simple, Complete, and Compound Predicates**

Write the complete predicate of each sentence (and of each dependent clause in a complex sentence). Circle the simple predicate or predicates. Underline any direct objects.

1. Cole and his sister Marlene survived the hurricane by going to a public shelter.

2. Julio gave his customized car another coat of wax.

3. Julio and his brothers have been working on the car for almost two years.

4. Service club members who packed boxes to send to troops in Iraq also loaded them into the truck.

5. My cousin chose mint green, lavender, and mauve for her wedding bouquet.

6. Either Alando or Tucker will come by and take me to work.

7. The students who had arrived at the prom relaxed and enjoyed the music and dancing.

8. Who is taking Alisha to the dance?

9. The new telephone system at work has several cool features.

10. A bonobo is a kind of chimpanzee that lives mostly in the Democratic Republic of Congo.

Model

Model the following sentences to practice using a compound predicate.

A person travels the world over in search of what he needs and returns home to find it.

—George Moore

He stepped behind a thick-boled pine tree and peered out at the man in the tree stand seventy yards away.

—Chet Williamson, "First Kill"

Sentences

Using Phrases

A **phrase** is a group of related words that function as a single part of speech. The sentence below contains a number of phrases.

> Finishing the race will require biking up some steep slopes.

finishing the race (This gerund phrase functions as a subject noun.)

will require (This phrase functions as a verb.)

biking up some steep slopes (This gerund phrase acts as an object noun.)

742.1 Types of Phrases

- An **appositive phrase,** which follows a noun or a pronoun and renames it, consists of a noun and its modifiers. An appositive adds new information about the noun or pronoun it follows.

  > The Trans-Siberian Railroad, the world's longest railway, stretches from Moscow to Vladivostok. (The appositive phrase renames *Trans-Siberian Railroad* and provides new information.)

- A **verbal phrase** is a phrase based on one of the three types of verbals: *gerund, infinitive,* or *participle.* (See **726.1, 726.2,** and **726.3.**)

  - A **gerund phrase** consists of a gerund and its modifiers. The whole phrase functions as a noun.

    > Spotting the tiny mouse was easy for the hawk.
    > (The gerund phrase is used as the subject of the sentence.)
    > Dinner escaped by ducking under a rock.
    > (The gerund phrase is the object of the preposition *by.*)

  - An **infinitive phrase** consists of an infinitive and its modifiers. The whole phrase functions either as a noun, an adjective, or an adverb.

    > To shake every voter's hand was the candidate's goal.
    > (The infinitive phrase functions as a noun used as the subject.)
    > Your efforts to clean the chalkboard are appreciated.
    > (The infinitive phrase is used as an adjective modifying *efforts.*)
    > Please watch carefully to see the difference.
    > (The infinitive phrase is used as an adverb modifying *watch.*)

  - A **participial phrase** consists of a past or present participle and its modifiers. The whole phrase functions as an adjective.

    > Following his nose, the beagle took off like a jackrabbit.
    > (The participial phrase modifies the noun *beagle.*)
    > The raccoons, warned by the rustling, took cover.
    > (The participial phrase modifies the noun *raccoons.*)

Grammar Practice

Constructing Sentences 3

- Appositive Phrases
- Verbal Phrases

 Identify each underlined group of words as an *appositive, gerund, infinitive,* or *participial phrase*.

1. Rance decided that <u>rappelling over the side of the cliff</u> was unsafe.

2. The stars <u>arriving at the red-carpet event</u> smiled and waved for the cameras.

3. Most teachers believe their students' parents are willing <u>to vote in favor of the referendum</u>.

4. My grandfather, <u>an avid reader and U.S. historian</u>, will review the article before it is published.

5. <u>Distracted by the shouts</u>, Linc was unable to sink the putt.

6. <u>Surfing in the ocean</u> when the waves are so high seems a little risky.

7. Dyann must decide whether she wants <u>to be part of the debate team</u>.

8. Steve Fossett, <u>a bold adventurer</u>, is known for his long-distance flights.

9. Mr. Geissman pursued his campaign to prevent the city from <u>limiting free parking</u>.

10. <u>Rising before dawn</u>, Jen hit the road early to avoid the crowds at the beach.

Model

Model the following sentences to practice using gerund phrases.

> **Besides the noble art of getting things done, there is a nobler art of leaving things undone.**
> —Lin Yutang

> **He always enjoyed showing people the ropes, fascinating them with his abilities, and teaching them to do the same kind of thing.**
> —Chet Williamson, "Mushrooms"

Sentences

Using Phrases *(continued)*

- A **verb phrase** consists of a main verb preceded by one or more helping verbs.

  Snow has been falling **for days.** (*Has been falling* is a verb phrase.)

- A **prepositional phrase** is a group of words beginning with a preposition and ending with a noun or a pronoun. Prepositional phrases function mainly as adjectives and adverbs.

  Reach for that catnip ball behind the couch. (The prepositional phrase *behind the couch* is used as an adjective modifying *catnip ball*.)

  Zach won the wheelchair race in record time. (*In record time* is used as an adverb modifying the verb *won*.)

- An **absolute phrase** consists of a noun and a participle (plus the participle's object, if there is one, and any modifiers). An absolute phrase functions as a modifier that adds information to the entire sentence. Absolute phrases are always set off with commas.

  Its wheels clattering rhythmically over the rails, **the train rolled into town.** (The noun *wheels* is modified by the present participle *clattering*. The entire phrase modifies the rest of the sentence.)

Using Clauses

A **clause** is a group of related words that has both a subject and a predicate.

744.1 Independent and Dependent Clauses

An **independent clause** presents a complete thought and can stand alone as a sentence; a **dependent clause** (also called a *subordinate clause*) does not present a complete thought and cannot stand alone as a sentence.

Sparrows make nests in cattle barns (independent clause) **so that they can stay warm during the winter** (dependent clause).

744.2 Types of Dependent Clauses

There are three basic types of dependent clauses: *adverb, noun,* and *adjective.*

- An **adverb clause** is used like an adverb to modify a verb, an adjective, or an adverb. Adverb clauses begin with a subordinating conjunction. (See **734.3.**)

  If I study hard, **I will pass this test.** (The adverb clause modifies the verb *will pass*.)

- A **noun clause** is used in place of a noun.

  However, the teacher said that the essay questions are based only on the last two chapters. (The noun clause functions as a direct object.)

- An **adjective clause** modifies a noun or a pronoun.

  Tomorrow's test, which covers the entire book, **is half essay and half short answers.** (The adjective clause modifies the noun *test*.)

Grammar Practice

Constructing Sentences 4

- Absolute Phrases
- Independent Clauses
- Dependent Clauses

 Identify each underlined group of words as an *absolute phrase,* an *independent clause,* or a *dependent clause.* For dependent clauses, also identify their type.

1. Did I tell you about the Olympic skier <u>who spoke at the conference</u>?

2. If everyone cooperates, <u>we can make up the time</u> that we lost yesterday.

3. Adam wanted to leave the party <u>because none of his friends were there</u>.

4. <u>His heart pounding and his legs trembling</u>, he crossed the finish line.

5. Many writers agree <u>that the story contains enough truth to sway even the most skeptical reader</u>.

6. This is the stadium <u>where the Steelers and the Seahawks played in the Super Bowl</u>.

7. The game was over for almost an hour <u>before all the fans left the stadium</u>.

8. Brian climbed the ladder to the burning roof, <u>the fire hose held firmly under his arm</u>.

9. At the beginning of the ceremony, <u>line up at the doors</u> while the principal makes her opening remarks.

10. It is important to ask <u>which chapters will be covered on the exam</u>.

 ## Model

Model the following sentence to practice using adverb and adjective clauses.

> **On the way, Lída and Petra had talked about their discoveries while I observed the countryside, which was still covered with trackless, uninhabited forests.**
> —Ivan Klima, "Archeology"

Using Sentence Variety

A **sentence** may be classified according to the type of statement it makes, the way it is constructed, and its arrangement of words.

746.1 Kinds of Sentences

The five basic kinds of sentences are *declarative, interrogative, imperative, exclamatory,* and *conditional.*

- **Declarative sentences** make statements. They tell us something about a person, a place, a thing, or an idea. Although declarative sentences make up the bulk of most academic writing, there are overwhelmingly diverse ways in which to express them.

  > The Statue of Liberty stands in New York Harbor.
  >
  > For over a century, it has greeted immigrants and visitors to America.

- **Interrogative sentences** ask questions.

  > Did you know that the Statue of Liberty is made of copper and stands more than 150 feet tall?
  >
  > Are we allowed to climb all the way to the top?

- **Imperative sentences** make commands.

  > You must purchase a ticket.

  They often contain an understood subject *(you)* as in the examples below.

  > Go see the Statue of Liberty.
  >
  > After a few weeks of physical conditioning, climb its 168 stairs.

- **Exclamatory sentences** communicate strong emotion or surprise.

  > Climbing 168 stairs is not a dumb idea!
  >
  > Just muster some of that old pioneering spirit, that desire to try something new, that never-say-die attitude that made America great!

- **Conditional sentences** express wishes ("if . . . then" statements) or conditions contrary to fact.

  > If I could design a country's flag, I would use six colors behind a sun, a star, and a moon.
  >
  > I would feel as if I were representing many cultures in my design.

Grammar Practice

Kinds of Sentences

 Write the kind of each sentence below: *declarative, interrogative, imperative, exclamatory,* **or** *conditional.*

1. Do you know where Burkina Faso is?

2. It is a small, landlocked country in West Africa.

3. Try to find it on a globe.

4. The whole country is only slightly larger than Colorado!

5. Burkina Faso's official language is French, but 90 percent of the population speak native African languages.

6. Less than 3 percent of the population is older than 65.

7. If AIDS didn't have such a major impact on its people, the average life expectancy would probably be greater than the present 48 years.

8. About three-quarters of Burkina Faso's people are illiterate, and 45 percent live below the poverty line.

9. It is almost as if the country has been forgotten by the rest of the world.

10. What can be done?

Model

Model the following conditional statements.

> **Youth would be an ideal state if it came a little later in life.**
> —Herbert Henry Asquith

> **She did not talk to people as if they were strange hard shells she had to crack open to get inside.**
> —Marita Bonner

Sentences

748.1 Types of Sentence Constructions

A sentence may be *simple, compound, complex,* or *compound-complex.* It all depends on the relationship between independent and dependent clauses.

- A **simple sentence** can have a single subject or a compound subject. It can have a single predicate or a compound predicate. However, a simple sentence has only one independent clause, and it has no dependent clauses.

  My back aches.
  (single subject; single predicate)

  My teeth **and my** eyes hurt.
  (compound subject; single predicate)

  My throat **and** nose feel **sore and** look **red.**
  (compound subject; compound predicate)

  I must have caught the flu from the sick kids in class.
  (independent clause with two phrases: *from the sick kids* and *in class*)

- A **compound sentence** consists of two independent clauses. The clauses must be joined by a comma and a coordinating conjunction or by a semicolon.

  I usually don't mind missing school, but **this is not fun.**

  I feel too sick to watch TV; **I feel too sick to eat.**

Note: The comma can be omitted when the clauses are very short.

  I wept and **I wept.**

- A **complex sentence** contains one independent clause (in black) and one or more dependent clauses (in red).

  When I get back to school, **I'm actually going to appreciate it.**
  (dependent clause; independent clause)

  I won't even complain about math class, although I might be talking out of my head because I'm feverish.
  (independent clause; two dependent clauses)

- A **compound-complex sentence** contains two or more independent clauses (in black) and one or more dependent clauses (in red).

  Yes, I have a bad flu, and because I need to get well soon, **I won't think about school just yet.**
  (two independent clauses; one dependent clause)

  The best remedy for those who suffer with flu symptoms **is plenty of rest and fluids, but the chicken soup** that Grandma makes for me **always helps, too.**
  (two independent clauses; two dependent clauses)

Grammar Practice

Types of Sentence Constructions

Identify each of the following sentences as *simple, compound, complex,* or *compound-complex.*

1. If you are like the average high school junior, you are eager to register to vote and to enjoy the privilege of voting in local, state, and national elections.

2. You must be 18 years old to vote, and you must be a United States citizen.

3. States have varying registration requirements, so you should check to see what your state requires.

4. It is important to register, and because you are almost of voting age, you should find out about the registration process.

5. In most states, you register by going to the county clerk's office.

6. You may be able to register using a mail-in form.

7. Once you are registered, you will be notified of the location of your polling place.

8. Voting allows you to participate in the political process, and it gives you a voice in issues of great importance.

Model

Model the following sentence to practice forming a compound-complex sentence.

> **They gave me frequent warning to start applying myself—especially around mid-terms, when my parents came up for a conference with old Thurmer—but I didn't do it.**
>
> —J. D. Salinger, *The Catcher in the Rye*

750.1 Arrangements of Sentences

Depending on the arrangement of the words and the placement of emphasis, a sentence may also be classified as *loose, balanced, periodic,* or *cumulative.*

- A **loose sentence** expresses the main thought near the beginning and adds explanatory material as needed.

  We hauled out the boxes of food and set up the camp stove, **all the time battling the hot wind that would not stop, even when we screamed into the sky.**

  Memory performs the impossible for man**—holds together past and present, gives continuity and dignity to human life.**
  —Mark Van Doren, *Liberal Education*

- A **balanced sentence** is constructed so that it emphasizes a similarity or a contrast between two or more of its parts (words, phrases, or clauses).

  The wind in our ears drove us crazy **and** pushed us on.
  (The similar wording emphasizes the main idea in this sentence.)

  Experience is not what happens to you; **it is what you do with** what happens to you.
  —Aldous Huxley

- A **periodic sentence** is one that postpones the crucial or most surprising idea until the end.

  Following my mother's repeated threats to ground me for life, I decided it was time to propose a compromise.

  There is only one way to achieve happiness on this terrestrial ball—and that is to have either a clear conscience or no conscience at all.
  —Ogden Nash, *I'm a Stranger Here Myself*

- A **cumulative sentence** places the general idea in the middle of the sentence with modifying clauses and phrases coming before and after.

  With careful thought and extra attention to detail, I wrote out my plan for being a model teenager, **a teen who cared about neatness and reliability.**

  Not too long ago, architects who planned college classrooms and dormitories were advised against making the furnishings too pleasant or comfortable **lest the students become distracted or fall asleep.**
  —Robert Sommer, "Hard Architecture"

Grammar Practice

Arrangements of Sentences

Classify each of the following sentences as *loose, balanced, periodic,* or *cumulative*.

(1) Despite going through training and tryouts each year, Jamaal had never made the team. **(2)** Last fall, however, he finally aced his tryout. **(3)** He had changed over the summer; he'd grown several inches and put on a few pounds of muscle.

(4) With more than a little envy, the other guys watched him kick the ball over the goalpost from the opposing 47-yard line, something none of them had ever done. **(5)** Jamaal was ecstatic; his teammates weren't sure what to think. **(6)** By now, with two seasons behind them, they were used to playing with Antoine as their kicker. **(7)** They worried that Jamaal was about to bump Antoine out of that role.

(8) In spite of that rocky start with his teammates, Jamaal was soon accepted as one of the guys. **(9)** He and Antoine played together in most of the games, as it turned out, leading the team to an 8–2 winning season. **(10)** They had high hopes for the following season.

Model

Model the following balanced sentences.

> The lamps are going out all over Europe: we shall not see them lit again in our lifetime.
> —Viscount Grey of Fallodon

> It doesn't matter who my father was; it matters who I remember he was.
> —Anne Sexton

Sentences

Getting Sentence Parts to Agree

Agreement of Subject and Verb

A verb must agree in number (singular or plural) with its subject.

> The student was proud of her quarter grades.

Note: Do not be confused by words that come between the subject and verb.

> The manager, as well as the players, is required to display good sportsmanship. (*Manager,* not *players,* is the subject.)

752.1 Compound Subjects

Compound subjects joined by *or* or *nor* take a singular verb.

> Neither Bev nor Kendra goes to the street dances.

Note: When one of the subjects joined by *or* or *nor* is singular and one is plural, the verb must agree with the subject nearer the verb.

> Neither Yoshi nor his friends sing in the band anymore. (The plural subject *friends* is nearer the verb, so the plural verb *sing* is correct.)

Compound subjects connected with *and* require a plural verb.

> Strength and balance are necessary for gymnastics.

752.2 Delayed Subjects

Delayed subjects occur when the verb comes before the subject in a sentence. In these inverted sentences, the delayed subject must agree with the verb.

> There are many hardworking students in our schools.
> There is present among many young people today a will to succeed.

(*Students* and *will* are the true subjects of these sentences, not *there.*)

752.3 "Be" Verbs

When a sentence contains a form of the "be" verb—and a noun comes before and after that verb—the verb must agree with the subject, not the *complement* (the noun coming after the verb).

> The cause of his problem was the bad brakes.
> The bad brakes were the cause of his problem.

752.4 Special Cases

Some nouns that are **plural in form but singular in meaning** take a singular verb: *mumps, measles, news, mathematics, economics, gallows, shambles.*

> Measles is still considered a serious disease in many parts of the world.

Some nouns that are plural in form but singular in meaning take a plural verb: *scissors, trousers, tidings.*

> The scissors disappear whenever I need them.

Grammar Practice

Agreement of Subject and Verb 1

 For each sentence, write the correct verb from the choice given in parentheses.

1. Neither his brothers nor Todd *(have, has)* a driver's license.

2. On the wall *(was, were)* several of Karyn's paintings.

3. Artisans from Indonesia *(was, were)* making decorative drums.

4. *(Is, Are)* you in Kendra's physics class?

5. There *(go, goes)* Malik's stepsister, Melissa.

6. There *(is, are)* a mynah bird at the pet store.

7. There *(is, are)* many qualified applicants for the summer internship.

8. *(Were, Was)* Emily embarrassed when the waiters sang to her?

9. The police *(is, are)* sponsoring this weekend's safety seminar.

10. Arnie, Josh, or Ted *(have, has)* the best chance of winning.

11. I can't believe that those statistics *(are, is)* correct.

12. Current band members, as well as a recent graduate, *(was, were)* invited to play in the winter concert.

Model

Model the following sentences to practice subject-verb agreement.

The surest way to make a monkey out of a man is to quote him.
—Robert Benchley

People with bad consciences always fear the judgement of children.
—Mary McCarthy

Agreement of Subject and Verb *(continued)*

754.1 Collective Nouns

Collective nouns *(faculty, committee, team, congress, species, crowd, army, pair, squad)* take a singular verb when they refer to a group as a unit; collective nouns take a plural verb when they refer to the individuals within the group.

> **The favored team is losing, and the crowd is getting ugly.** (Both *team* and *crowd* are considered units in this sentence, requiring the singular verb *is.*)
>
> **The pair reunite after 20 years apart.**
> (Here, *pair* refers to two individuals, so the plural verb *reunite* is required.)

754.2 Indefinite Pronouns

Some **indefinite pronouns** are singular: *each, either, neither, one, everybody, another, anybody, everyone, nobody, everything, somebody,* and *someone.* They require a singular verb.

> **Everybody is invited to the cafeteria for refreshments.**

Some **indefinite pronouns** are plural: *both, few, many,* and *several.*

> **Several like trail-mix bars. Many ask for frozen yogurt, too.**

Some **indefinite pronouns** are singular or plural: *all, any, most, none* and *some.*

Note: Do not be confused by words or phrases that come between the indefinite pronoun and the verb.

> **One of the participants is** (not *are*) **going to have to stay late to clean up.**

A Closer Look

> Some **indefinite pronouns** can be either singular or plural: *all, any, most, none,* and *some.* These pronouns are singular if the number of the noun in the prepositional phrase is singular; they are plural if the noun is plural.
>
> > **Most of the food complaints are coming from the seniors.**
> > (*Complaints* is plural, so *most* is plural.)
> >
> > **Most of the tabletop is sticky.**
> > (*Tabletop* is singular, so *most* is singular.)

754.3 Relative Pronouns

When a **relative pronoun** *(who, which, that)* is used as the subject of a clause, the number of the verb is determined by the antecedent of the pronoun. (The antecedent is the word to which the pronoun refers.)

> **This is one of the books that are required for geography class.** (The relative pronoun *that* requires the plural verb *are* because its antecedent, *books,* is plural.)

Note: To test this type of sentence for agreement, read the "of" phrase first.

> **Of the books that are required for geography class, this is one.**

Grammar Practice

Agreement of Subject and Verb 2

For each numbered sentence, write the correct verb from the choice given in parentheses.

(1) One of the important themes in Arthur Miller's play *Death of a Salesman (is, are)* abandonment. **(2)** It's a matter that *(arise, arises)* from a traumatic time in the life of the main character, Willy Loman. **(3)** As young boys, he and his brother, Ben, *(were, was)* left with nothing when their father abandoned them.

(4) Willy's fear of abandonment and loss *(cause, causes)* him to set high standards for himself and his family. **(5)** He believes that he can attain the American Dream, which *(lead, leads)* to his inflated sense of self-importance.

(6) He talks as if he were a success, but his family *(is, are)* aware that he is a failure. **(7)** This is one of the character traits that *(lead, leads)* Willy to estrangement with his sons, Biff and Happy.

The theme of abandonment continues. Ben has recently died. He was a wealthy man, a fact that intensifies Willy's underlying sense of failure. **(8)** He feels that none of his accomplishments *(is, are)* enough. **(9)** The day when Willy loses his job as a traveling salesman *(make, makes)* him face reality and, ultimately, his own death.

Model

Model the following sentences to practice subject-verb agreement with indefinite pronouns.

Why is it that nobody understands me and everybody likes me?

—Albert Einstein

I tend to live in the past because most of my life is there.

—Herb Caen

Agreement of Pronoun and Antecedent

A pronoun must agree in number, person, and gender with its *antecedent*. (The *antecedent* is the word to which the pronoun refers.)

> Cal **brought** his **gerbil to school.** (The antecedent of *his* is *Cal*. Both the pronoun and its antecedent are singular, third person, and masculine; therefore, the pronoun is said to "agree" with its antecedent.)

756.1 Agreement in Number

Use a **singular pronoun** to refer to such antecedents as *each, either, neither, one, anyone, anybody, everyone, everybody, somebody, another, nobody,* and *a person*.

> Neither **of the brothers likes** his (not their) **room.**

Two or more singular antecedents joined by *or* or *nor* are also referred to by a **singular pronoun.**

> Either Connie **or** Sue **left** her **headset in the library.**

If one of the antecedents joined by *or* or *nor* is singular and one is plural, the pronoun should agree with the nearer antecedent.

> Neither the manager **nor the** players **were crazy about** their **new uniforms.**

Use a **plural pronoun** to refer to plural antecedents as well as compound subjects joined by *and*.

> Jared **and** Carlos **are finishing** their **assignments.**

756.2 Agreement in Gender

Use a **masculine** or **feminine pronoun** depending upon the gender of the antecedent.

> Tristan **would like to bring** his **dog along on the trip.**
>
> Claire **is always complaining that** her **feet are cold.**

Use a **neuter** pronoun when the antecedent has no gender.

> The ancient weeping willow **is losing many of** its **branches.**

When *a person* or *everyone* is used to refer to both sexes or either sex, you will have to choose whether to offer optional pronouns or rewrite the sentence.

> A person **should be allowed to choose** her **or** his **own footwear.**
> (optional pronouns)
>
> People **should be allowed to choose** their **own footwear.**
> (rewritten in plural form)

Grammar Practice

Agreement of Pronoun and Antecedent

 For each sentence, write the correct pronoun from the choice given in parentheses.

1. J. W. and Marcus hung out and played *(his, their)* video games.

2. Latisha and Corinne submitted *(her, their)* editorials to the local newspaper.

3. Each of the students sent *(his or her, their)* essay with an application.

4. Emily or Trisha works at *(their, her)* parents' restaurant.

5. Monique's scissors were missing, and nobody knew where *(they, it)* were.

6. Most of the cars in the lot had small dents in *(its, their)* hoods from last night's hailstorm.

7. Most of the cake had little Tommy's fingerprints on *(it, them)*.

8. Devon or his brothers are rebuilding *(his, their)* grandfather's '68 Mustang.

9. I told everyone to bring *(his or her, their)* favorite CD's to my party.

10. One of these plants is rapidly losing *(its, their)* leaves.

Model

Model the following sentences to practice making a pronoun and its antecedent agree.

> People can no more be judged by their looks than the sea can be measured in bushels.
> —Chinese proverb

> Just as the sweetest words in the language to a given person are his or her own name, so too are his or her opinions.
> —Gary O. Bosley, *Campaigning to Win*

Sentences

Test Prep!

Write the letter of the best answer for each underlined part from the choices given on the next page.

Imagine that you are seated in the famed Globe Theatre, <u>the home of</u>
(1)
<u>Shakespeare's plays</u>. You <u>are waiting for his play *Julius Caesar* to begin</u>. <u>The year</u>
(2)
<u>is 1599, and the theater is brand new</u>. <u>You and many others</u> are seeing it for the first
(3)   **(4)**
time. It is a large, circular building, three stories high. There is a small, thatched
roof <u>that partially covers the structure</u>. You pay to sit in one of three galleries
(5)
<u>wrapped around the circular interior</u>. It costs you two cents more, but your decision
(6)
<u>to spend the money</u> allows you to sit through the long play under the thatched-roof
(7)
covering. <u>Patrons</u> in the central courtyard, <u>which is uncovered</u>, pay just one penny
(8)   **(9)**
(about 10 percent of their daily wages). Even though they <u>have</u> an excellent view of
(10)
the stage, <u>they must stand for the entire three-hour performance</u>, rain or shine.
(11)

As you sit in the gallery, <u>your eyes darting around the room</u>, you notice the
(12)
center stage. The stage, <u>measuring 44 feet wide by 26 feet long</u>, stands 5 feet off the
(13)
ground. <u>Look up</u>, and you'll see a balcony. If you return to the Globe, you can see
(14)
Juliet speaking to Romeo from this balcony.

The Globe Theatre burned to the ground in 1613. <u>Although it was rebuilt</u>,
(15)
in 1644 the Puritans destroyed it again. In 1997, a working replica of the theater
opened in London. The dream of <u>seeing a Shakespeare play</u> as it was performed
(16)
hundreds of years ago is again a reality.

1
- (A) independent clause
- (B) dependent clause
- (C) verbal phrase
- (D) appositive phrase

2
- (A) complete predicate
- (B) simple predicate
- (C) simple subject
- (D) complete subject

3
- (A) simple sentence
- (B) compound sentence
- (C) complex sentence
- (D) dependent clause

4
- (A) complete predicate
- (B) simple predicate
- (C) simple subject
- (D) complete subject

5
- (A) appositive phrase
- (B) verbal phrase
- (C) independent clause
- (D) dependent clause

6
- (A) gerund phrase
- (B) infinitive phrase
- (C) participial phrase
- (D) appositive phrase

7
- (A) gerund phrase
- (B) infinitive phrase
- (C) participial phrase
- (D) appositive phrase

8
- (A) complete predicate
- (B) simple predicate
- (C) simple subject
- (D) complete subject

9
- (A) appositive phrase
- (B) verbal phrase
- (C) independent clause
- (D) dependent clause

10
- (A) complete predicate
- (B) simple predicate
- (C) simple subject
- (D) complete subject

11
- (A) independent clause
- (B) dependent clause
- (C) verbal phrase
- (D) appositive phrase

12
- (A) gerund phrase
- (B) infinitive phrase
- (C) participial phrase
- (D) absolute phrase

13
- (A) gerund phrase
- (B) infinitive phrase
- (C) participial phrase
- (D) absolute phrase

14
- (A) independent clause
- (B) dependent clause
- (C) verbal phrase
- (D) appositive phrase

15
- (A) independent clause
- (B) dependent clause
- (C) verbal phrase
- (D) appositive phrase

16
- (A) gerund phrase
- (B) infinitive phrase
- (C) participial phrase
- (D) absolute phrase

Sentences

Diagramming Sentences

A **graphic diagram** of a sentence is a picture of how the words in that sentence are related and how they fit together to form a complete thought.

760.1 Simple Sentence with One Subject and One Verb

Chris fishes.

| Chris | fishes | | subject | verb |

760.2 Simple Sentence with a Predicate Adjective

Fish are delicious.

| Fish | are \ delicious | | subject | verb \ predicate adjective |

760.3 Simple Sentence with a Predicate Noun and Adjectives

Fishing is my favorite hobby.

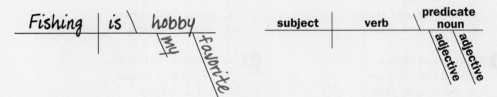

Note: When possessive pronouns (*my, his, their,* and so on) are used as adjectives, they are placed on a diagonal line under the word they modify.

760.4 Simple Sentence with an Indirect and Direct Object

My grandpa gave us a trout.

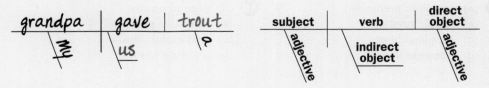

Note: Articles (*a, an, the*) are adjectives and are placed on a diagonal line under the word they modify.

Grammar Practice

Sentence Diagramming 1

 Diagram the following sentences.

1. Danae reads many magazines.

2. The old brick house is a day care center.

3. This fudge torte tastes incredible!

4. Mom showed her nephew a card trick.

5. Martha Washington was the true First Lady.

6. The yellow tulips are gorgeous.

7. Isaiah vacuumed the carpeted stairs.

8. Darcy's dad made us some cookies.

9. David typed.

10. That restaurant serves some tasty food.

 ## Model

Model the following sentences to practice writing simple sentences with direct objects.

The flowers learn their colored shapes.

—Maria Konopnicka

A teacher affects eternity.

—Henry Brooks Adams

Diagramming Sentences *(continued)*

762.1 Simple Sentence with a Prepositional Phrase

I like fishing by myself.

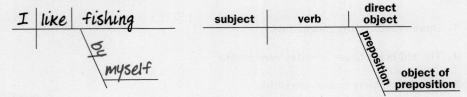

762.2 Simple Sentence with a Compound Subject and Verb

The team and fans clapped and cheered.

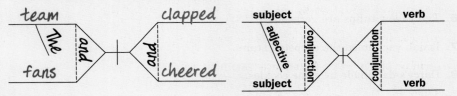

762.3 Compound Sentence

The team scored, and the crowd cheered wildly.

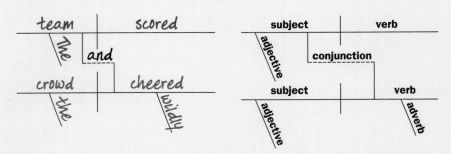

762.4 Complex Sentence with a Subordinate Clause

Before Erin scored, the crowd sat quietly.

Grammar Practice

Sentence Diagramming 2

Diagram the following sentences.

1. Marette enjoyed her first trip to Paris.

2. She stayed near the Louvre and ate at sidewalk cafes.

3. In our neighborhood, the Kellmans have the biggest yard.

4. The postal worker who delivers our mail always wears shorts.

5. A truck driver can earn a good living, but it is hard work.

6. I will be happy when I graduate from high school.

7. Robin and Darita went to the library and got some DVD's.

8. Many radio stations are not independent, so they do not have control over their playlists.

9. The fire that destroyed the Berg's house started in their basement.

10. Jeron and I saw the movie yesterday and bought the sound track today.

◤ Model

Diagram the following model complex sentences.

All men are prepared to accomplish the incredible if their ideals are threatened.

—Hermann Hesse

Success is often achieved by those who don't know that failure is inevitable.

—Coco Chanel

Sentences

Credits

Text:

Page 381: Copyright © 2007 by Houghton Mifflin Company. Adapted and reproduced by permission from *The American Heritage College Dictionary,* Fourth Edition.

Photos:

Artville: p. 298; © **Corbis**: p. 531

Getty Images: p. 3 Don Farrall, p. 114 Todd Davidson, p. 639 Image Source, p. 680 Steve Dunning, p. 750 Digital Vision

GlowImages: p. 735; **Image Source**: p. 335; **ImageState**: p. 14

© **2006 Jupiterimages Corporation**: pages 32, 37, 42, 45, 68, 101, 102, 118, 120, 157, 177, 180, 197, 253, 261, 316, 324, 331, 367 (girl), 416, 526, 528, 553, 607 (doctor), 617, 716, 718, 720, 722, 746, 751, 757

National Security Archive: p. 19

Shutterstock: pages v, 2, 15, 54, 58, 65, 70, 84, 106, 110, 124, 126, 135, 143, 144, 171, 179, 206, 214, 221, 235, 236, 262, 270, 273, 276, 282, 286, 292, 309, 329, 362, 367 (bumper), 368, 369, 378, 394, 426, 429, 432, 434, 436, 438, 448, 456, 459, 461, 466, 471, 483, 484, 486, 492, 494, 496, 498, 504, 536, 538, 545, 547, 552, 558, 570, 572, 579, 587, 588, 607 (X-ray), 611, 615, 619, 621, 622, 625, 627, 631, 633, 635, 640, 643, 645, 649, 654, 656, 657, 658, 662, 664, 665, 669, 681, 682, 686, 694, 696, 700, 702, 703, 705, 709, 714, 715, 717, 719, 725, 726, 727, 728, 729, 733, 740–744, 747, 749, 753, 756, 763

Stockbyte: p. 396; © **Superstock, Inc.**: pages 226, 318

Icon images: various pages; Prewrite icon Electrique/ImageState; Write icon © Corbis; Revise icon/Photodisc/Getty Images

Acknowledgements

We're grateful to many people who helped bring *Write Source* to life. First, we must thank all the teachers and their students from across the country who contributed writing models and ideas.

In addition, we want to thank our Write Source/Great Source team for all their help:

Steven J. Augustyn, Laura Bachman, Ron Bachman, April Barrons, Heather Bazata, Colleen Belmont, Susan Boehm, Linne Bruskewitz, Evelyn Curley, Joanna Dupuis, Chris Erickson, Mark Fairweather, Jean Fischer, Hillary Gammons, Mariellen Hanrahan, Tammy Hintz, Kelly Kaiser, Judy Kerkhoff, Rob King, Lois Krenzke, Mark Lalumondier, Joyce Becker Lee, Ellen Leitheusser, Michele Order Litant, Dian Lynch, Colleen McCarthy, Gary Miller, Pat Moore, Kevin Nelson, Sue Paro, Linda Presto, Kathy Quirk, Mike Ramczyk, Betsy Rasmussen, Pat Reigel, Jason C. Reynolds, Christine Rieker, Susan Rogalski, Steve Schend, Janae Sebranek, Lester Smith, Richard Spencer, Stephen D. Sullivan, Jean Varley, and Claire Ziffer.

Index

The index will help you find specific information in this textbook. Entries in italics are words from the "Using the Right Word" section. The colored boxes contain information you will use often.

D